The Expansion of Metaphysics

The Expansion of Metaphysics

Miklós Vető

Translated by
William C. Hackett

With a foreword by
David Carr

CASCADE *Books* • Eugene, Oregon

THE EXPANSION OF METAPHYSICS

Copyright © 2018 Miklós Vetö. All rights reserved. Except for brief quotations in critical publications or reviews, no part of this book may be reproduced in any manner without prior written permission from the publisher. Write: Permissions, Wipf and Stock Publishers, 199 W. 8th Ave., Suite 3, Eugene, OR 97401.

Cascade Books
An Imprint of Wipf and Stock Publishers
199 W. 8th Ave., Suite 3
Eugene, OR 97401

www.wipfandstock.com

PAPERBACK ISBN: 978-1-4982-3125-1
HARDCOVER ISBN: 978-1-4982-3127-5
EBOOK ISBN: 978-1-4982-3126-8

Cataloguing-in-Publication data:

Names: Vetö, Miklós, author. | Hackett, William C., translator. | Carr, David, foreword.

Title: The expansion of metaphysics / Miklos Vetö ; translated by William C. Hackett ; foreword by David Carr.

Description: Eugene, OR : Cascade Books, 2018 | Includes bibliographical references.

Identifiers: ISBN 978-1-4982-3125-1 (paperback) | ISBN 978-1-4982-3127-5 (hardcover) | ISBN 978-1-4982-3126-8 (ebook)

Subjects: LCSH: subject | subject | subject | subject

Classification: CALL NUMBER 2018 (paperback) | CALL NUMBER (ebook)

Manufactured in the U.S.A.   05/23/18

Contents

Foreword by David Carr | ix
Introduction to Metaphysics | xiii
Introduction | 1

Book One—First Philosophy

I The Image | 11
The Nothing of Subjectivity | 11
Distantiation of the Ectype | 16
The Autonomy of the Image | 20
The Artistic Image | 24
From Dissimilarity to Auto-figuration | 28

II Newness: Premises and Regressions | 32
Renewing Newness | 32
Becoming Less than Perfect: The Withdrawal of God and the Descent of the Son | 35
Thinking the New: The Power of Synthesis | 41
The Thorns of Analysis | 45
Nature: Variations on Immanence | 48
Limits and Pitfalls of Justice | 52
Reciprocity | 56

III Newness: Figures and Paths | 63
The Horizons of Potentiality | 63
From Superabundance to Tearing Away | 64
Self-Exit and Self-Surpassing | 70
Freedom | 73
Meaning | 78
Love | 81
Sacrifice | 85
Double Asymmetry | 87
Faithfulness | 91
Towards the Third | 93

IV The Singular | 95
The Third | 95
Distinction and Differentiation | 98
Intrinsic Differentiation | 102
Syntheses of Singularity | 105
From the Singular to the Unique | 111
Things | 113
The Work of Art | 116
Works of Art | 121

V The Unique | 123
Asymmetrical Love | 123
The Child | 126
Paternity: Creation and Procreation | 128
Monads | 132
Ectypes and Copies | 134
The Shadow and the Double | 136
The Image-Child | 141
The Unique Ones | 144

Book Two—Eidetics

VI Space: From Homogeneity to War | 153
Material Essences and Synthetic A Priori Eidē | 153
The Forms of Dispersion | 155
Extension and Exteriority | 157
From Indifference to Hostility | 160
War | 163

VII Spatial Eidē | 168
Beyond Homogeneity | 168
Space and Color | 169
Figure and Place | 171
Extension and Expansion | 177
Curves | 178
Center: Symmetry and Asymmetry | 182
Dimensions and Directions | 184
Magnitude and Distance | 187
From Breadth to Remoteness | 189
Depth | 193
Height | 196

VIII Time | 201

Change and Corruption | 201
Power and Powerlessness of the Now | 203
The Infinite Divisibility: Work and Money | 207
The Unfolding of the Given | 211
Repetition and Rhythm | 213
The Irreversibility of Death | 217

IX Times | 221

Towards an Eidetic of Chronos | 221
Duration | 222
Synthesis and Schema | 224
Past, Future, Present | 230
The Present: Duration and Differentiation | 233
The Moving Image of Eternity | 235
Pleasure | 238
Peace | 242
The Form of the Past and Retention | 244
Memory and History | 249
Protention and the Future | 252
Hope | 255

X The Will | 261

The Human Self | 261
Desire | 262
Intention | 264
The Indivisibility and Immediacy of the Will | 266
Will, Causality, Temporality | 271
Time and Will | 273
The Renewal of Desire: The Request for Forgiveness | 275

XI The Dual Will and Practical Knowledge | 279

Enlarged Homogeneity | 279
The Wills | 280
How to Want More? | 283
Philosophy of the Will and Moral Formalism | 287
Sincerity and Rigorism | 289
Will and Practical Knowledge | 292
Practical Feeling | 296
The Knowledge of Good and Evil | 300

XII   The Reality and Scope of Evil | 305
Evil as Metaphysical Category | 305
The Positivity of Evil | 306
The Spirituality of Evil | 312
The Impossibility of Evil | 315
Radical Evil | 319
Evil for Evil's Sake | 324
From Evil to the Good | 328

XIII   The Good | 335
Beyond Being, Beyond Essence | 335
From Newness to Goodness | 337
Kenosis as Will | 343
The Good's Self-Diffusion | 344

Bibliography | 350

Foreword

Miklós Vető's *Élargissement de la métaphysique*, published here in English translation, is an original work of metaphysics, very broadly conceived. (A companion volume, called *Explorations métaphysiques,* was published in the same year as the French version.) Vető is a distinguished French philosopher of Hungarian origin who studied in Oxford and Paris and taught in the US (Yale) and Africa (Abidjan) before taking up positions in France at Rennes and then Poitiers. His interests and publications have been as diverse as his background. An early book was on Simone Weil (English translation, *The Religious Metaphysics of Simone Weil,* 1994); another was devoted to the thought of the American theologian Jonathan Edwards (English translation in press); and another concerns the work of Pierre de Bérulle. But the primary focus of Vető's scholarly work has been German Idealism, with a book on Schelling, a collection of articles on Fichte, and a two-volume study entitled *De Kant à Schelling,* which takes on the whole tradition. He is one of the world's most esteemed scholars in this area. After his long labors interpreting the metaphysics of others, this philosopher has decided now to speak in his own voice.

To be sure, the distinction between "systematic" philosophy and scholarly interpretation is somewhat artificial, and there are several reasons for questioning it in connection with the volume at hand. Every work of scholarly interpretation expresses the author's philosophical point of view. In his new work of metaphysics, one can feel the presence of the German philosophical tradition in the background. Moreover, this is not the first "systematic" work for Vető. He has also published on the problem of evil, and on the concept of will.

But there is another reason for avoiding the word "systematic" in describing this work. Invoking Laplace as a cautionary example, the author tells us in the Introduction that "philosophy should abandon the dream of an integral system, of a complete explanation of every nook and cranny and all the structures of reality." Rather than seeking a single founding principle, it should be content if it can find a "plurality of particular principles." Its purpose is not to produce a reflection or "photocopy" of some original state of affairs. Metaphysics is not a technique for doubling the world but "discourse for elaborating and offering images that, all the while being related with relevance and fidelity to sensible or intelligible "things," is able to claim a *sui generis* originality."

To reject the idea of a definitive system is not to say that the great philosophical theories are mere hypotheses or culturally limited expressions of a given historical period. Instead, Vető says we can best understand them by comparing them to Kant's phenomena in relation to noumena. The phenomena indeed necessarily refer to things in themselves, even correspond to them, but "this correspondence has nothing to do with similarity." This relation is in a way more like a causal dependence, but in the case of philosophical theories Vető likens it to a kind of "irradiation" or emanation, in which we are dazzled by the light of the real. This is in keeping, then, with his idea that metaphysics offers "images" with their own *sui generis* originality. Rather than copying reality, these images are produced by it and add to it.

One of the things revealed in this early passage, and borne out in the pages to come, is that the German Idealist to whom Vető is actually closest is Kant. His work can be read as an exercise in Kantian Metaphysics. For him, Kant was the fist philosopher to "expand" metaphysics since Plato and Aristotle. But Vető's relation to Kant's philosophy is a highly original one, an appropriation and transformation that the author of the Critiques might not have recognized. Already the use of the terms "image," "expression," "illumination," and the like, tip us off to this author's highly esthetic and evocative, indeed, creative and original way of doing metaphysics.

The overall structure of the work derives from the distinction between existence and essence, which for Vető is the fundamental distinction (coming from Aquinas) grounding all metaphysics. Thus the first half of the book is devoted to ontology, the second half to "eidetics" or the theory of essences. Part of the novelty of Vető's approach to metaphysics lies in his treatment of this distinction, and in particular to his approach to ontology. It is here that his departure from Aristotelian and Scholastic approaches to metaphysics, and the inspiration he derives from German Idealism, are perhaps the most obvious. For one thing, he entitles the first half of his book "First Philosophy," a term which since Aristotle is synonymous with metaphysics as a whole. Yet Aristotle's treatise is also called Theology, the science of the highest being. For Vető, it is important that the "that-ness" of being, as opposed to the "what-ness" of essence, not be reduced to brute facticity and ineffability, much less necessity or fatality. Like the moderns, from Descartes to Sartre, Vető begins his ontology with subjectivity, which has its own form of facticity and negativity. The focus here is not on necessity but on creativity and novelty. Here Vető relies on Kant's distinction between sterile analyticity and the synthetic a priori which creates new meaning. Kant's synthetic a priori, suitably expanded, is indeed the central concept of Vető's metaphysics. If human subjectivity leads us to images and artistic expression, we can see these as the images, in turn, of the divine act of creation. And if human creativity and pro-creativity lead to the novelty and the uniqueness of the child, these can be seen as parallels to God's creation, incarnation and love. For Vető the religious and theological are not

Foreword

separate topics within metaphysics; rather every aspect of existence is infused—directly or indirectly—with religious meaning.

The second half of this book, in which the attention turns from existence to essence, begins with a discussion of space and time. Departing from a distinctly Kantian approach to space and time as the forms of intuition, Vető moves on to a more phenomenological discourse where space is treated not as a homogeneous medium but as the oriented framework of practical and bodily dimensions. In this section, and even more in the discussion of time, the influence of Husserl, Heidegger, Merleau-Ponty, and Sartre is evident. Past, present, and future open us to memory and history, on the one hand, and desire and hope on the other. This practical and human approach to space and time lead the way, in turn, to the final sections of the book, which are devoted to the practical in the Kantian sense (i.e., to the moral and ethical: the will, evil, and good).

The work ends by returning to the parallel between human action and the divine. The act of creation, the cabalistic notion of *tzimtzum,* and above all the Christian notion of kenosis represent for Vető the ultimate enlargement of metaphysics in which the ontological and the eidetic are united in the idea of the will. Philosophers have often seen the task of metaphysics as the elimination of the paradoxes and mysteries of faith and existence, just as they have tried to deny the reality of evil. Vető will have none of this; he has a wider and more inclusive view of metaphysics. This is a book of broad vision, profound erudition, and inspiring originality.

David Carr

Introduction to Metaphysics

1

Historians debate the circumstances surrounding the birth of philosophy. For some, it appeared first in the cities of Ephesus and Miletus or in Magna Graecia; for others, in the India of the Upanishads. In either case it could be dated *grosso modo* to the first half of the first millennium before the birth of Christ. It cannot, or rather should not, be formulated in geographic or historical terms. Philosophy occurs when the millenary, traditional wisdom of peoples is transposed into a normative discourse, when the particular sciences are subsumed under a global vision, when the pluriform mythological stories about origins cede their place to a conceptual explication. There is philosophy when the image, the particular, the contingent are recapitulated and decanted into the universal and the necessary—in short, into the *intelligible*. There is philosophy as soon as a systematic discourse on the intelligible exists, in other words, *metaphysics*.

Metaphysics means beyond the physical, beyond the given cosmos coordinated by space and time. Yet metaphysics denotes less a place than the condition or status of the intentional object spoken about. Metaphysics is born with the Idea-Forms, ideal realities that ground and explain the beings of our world. Whether the Ideas are entities that exist *in themselves* as Plato taught, or only subsist *in* the material composites that they actualize and determine as Aristotle thought, they are pure, permanent and universal realities. At the heart of an unlimited, unarticulated matter without distinction or difference, the Forms institute difference. The things of the world only exist thanks to the Forms that are united to Matter; they are what they are by virtue of their Forms. Things constitute a contingent multiplicity; they are born and they die. Only their form is permanent within them and they can be understood and explained only by their form. The individuals of a given species are like so many instances of a universal. They are limited and short-lived. They display infinite variations of a common form, of which they are only partial and imperfect actualizations.

For classical philosophy—from its origins to Kant—the individual is only a subrational instance of this universal that is its form; only the universal enjoys a true intelligibility. The intelligibles are simply the Forms diffracted in a multitude of individuals; this intelligibility itself expands on the laws and principles that allow us to conceive the forms in matter. However, if metaphysics can bracket the *multitude* of contingent things, it is not capable of a straightforward reflection on the plurality of forms. Since Plato this plurality has been put in contact with the true Form of Forms, the Good, and with Plotinus will be tied down to an origin, an apophatic foundation in the One. This concern with the foundation of the Forms still essentially falls within the jurisdiction of the order of essences: if the Good is beyond, and the One, so to say, does not reach the forms, it is above all to mark a radical equivocity, though always on the formal plane. The quest for the principle will lead to a division: research into the principle of Essence involves an interrogation of the source of Existence. In Aristotle the question of the origin of existence is posed in a limited and incomplete way. The Prime Mover is not principle of the world according to all the dimensions of causality: it is only the End of the cosmos, neither Creator of the world nor Essence of essences and, correspondingly, its concept does not yet imply a true modification of metaphysics in accordance with its acceptance of the doctrine of the intelligibility of essence. This modification will occur only with Patristic and Scholastic philosophy, which, positing God as the source of the created and uncreated, as the common principle of the contingent and necessary, the temporal and eternal, presents intelligibility both according to essence and existence. This Metaphysics of Essence and Existence remains the *prima philosophia* until the Critique.

This metaphysics is a magnificent system, sufficient in itself, harmonious, a vast edifice in which the stages and degrees are related to one another with perfect regularity, without any deviation, and in which the connections and relations are made as functions of immutable laws and the degrees of existence and the instances of essence constitute a sublime order. But if the order is effectively sublime, if it underlies a universe in which everything has its meaning and participates to diverse degrees in intelligibility, this order concerns only a part of the real because the intelligibility that it recommends and that it recognizes has its limits. Most likely, nothing in the world is completely isolated from the system, nothing is irredeemably excluded from intelligibility but there are immense and essential areas that enjoy only a borrowed intelligibility. The contingent, finite and individual exists only by virtue of the necessary, infinite and universal, which is situated beyond them. Reason and the will cease to meet individual beings living *in* time and space, but time and space are only privations, they are marked only by dispersion and incoherence. Space is synonymous with exteriority, time that of a never-ending flux deprived of any proper structure. The beings that subsist in time and space are individuals, but for classical Metaphysics the individual as individual is deprived of intelligibility, being only an ephemeral instance, an extremely rudimentary and partial realization of form. Nothing appears any more real or significant than an individual and yet the individual has no meaning or value in itself.

At best, the individual is an ectype of its archetype. It reflects and displays some of its traits but this partial presentation contains some shortcomings and difficulties. It can be inaccurate, deficient in relation to its archetype, even flatly opposed to it. Ectypes are images of their archetypes but the metaphysical status of the image is problematic. The image reflects the original, but to be a reflection of a superior, transcendent other in no way amounts to being true to it. The original archetype, the Form, practically concentrates all intelligibility in itself and what is granted to the ectype suffices to make it only a confused and evanescent reality. Undoubtedly, the weakness of being and the poverty of essence pertaining to singular beings do not release them from the laws governing the cosmos. As physical entities they share in permanent structures, yet the contingency that marks their entire being still does not liberate them from obedience to the necessary structures that organize them and cause them to act. Yet there is a being on earth that evidences autonomy in relation to *ananké*, sovereign master of the *physis*. Man is taken from the dust and destined to return to it like every other creature, but he enjoys a special status inasmuch as he is rational and free. But if Classical Metaphysics acknowledges the specificity of man, it does not possess the means of doing him justice. For it, *anthropos*—like every other being—is submitted to necessity. Freedom is in the end only acknowledged necessity. Just as the truth of the singular is the universal, the truth of freedom is necessity.

Freedom has always been understood as the power to choose. But choosing signifies the possibility of deciding and acting otherwise than what is prescribed by the natural order. And it is this oddity, this inconceivable possibility which ought to be the origin of evil. Evil is the result of a choice, but how can one make a bad one? To choose is the activity of a rational being. It presumes knowledge. Is it possible to opt for evil when one knows the good? Since Socrates the escape from this dilemma has involved the declaration that no one freely chooses evil. But this "solution" is ultimately a paradox and it is the doorway to a host of other paradoxes that result in, not so much understanding, but the dissolution of evil. On the moral plane one cannot choose evil with free will and on the ontological plane one cannot attribute to it existence. Things are only insofar as they are good—achieving their nature, their perfection—and the imperfect, lacking its end, straying from its essence, is less of a being. Evil as imperfection is then, in itself, as such, only a face of non-existence. Ignoring the singular, degrading the truth of the image, denaturing the meaning of freedom, Classical Metaphysics is forced into announcing loudly and clearly that the Evil that the world and men suffer does not exist!

2

The absurdities and faults in this magnificent construction arise from its conception of intelligibility. Consequently, this intelligibility must be rethought, expanded. Certainly, the expansion should occur only on a properly philosophical plane, but it can be inspired and assisted by another universe, that of religion—as it happens, biblical religion. Patristic and medieval metaphysics was constructed as a natural theology: philosophy conserved its foundational Hellenic axioms in exercising its task of rendering reason to the central themes of religion. But it is precisely this fidelity to the Hellenic origin that makes metaphysics only halfway capable of a repetition of religion at the level of the concept and, above all, prohibits it from conceptualizing entire sections of reality. Scholasticism tried its best to explicate the dogmas but it never stopped proclaiming the limits of "natural reason" which prohibited it from penetrating the great mysteries of the Trinity, incarnation, creation, and original sin. Nevertheless, these mysteries can be repeated in concept once one realizes that they harbor a load of native intelligibility. Even more, they can play a more important role in *philosophia prima*! The Judeo-Christian dogmas can serve as fecund paradigms for the expansion of intelligibility, permitting a true re-founding of metaphysics. This is an essential moment of their noetic impact.

Hellenic metaphysics is a philosophy of necessity and eternity. It must be, as it were, *unlocked* in order to be made capable of embracing the world of freedom, singularity, and existence in time. This philosophy that was, consciously or unconsciously only a "footnote to Plato" should subsume under the sphere of intelligibility everything that has up to now escaped it, starting with novelty. Novelty is the true concept of the great teachers of modern philosophy and it can be thematized starting from the Judeo-Christian notion of creation. In contrast to the Hellenic systems that present an eternal and immutable world, for biblical thought the cosmos results from an original action, the creation by a transcendent God. Creation itself remains inconceivable in classical metaphysics. It marks the event of something new, which does not follow from something already there and is not explained by reference to eternal essences. Creation is the irruption of novelty into being. But true novelty is not a parachronological idea: it is not sufficient that the created world had been inexistent before its coming to be, rather—and in the end this is the essential—its coming into existence cannot be attributed to any necessity at all! In order to be the creation, strictly speaking, it can only be *ex nihilo*. In other words it should happen without "prior" reason, freely and gratuitously. The extreme difficulty experienced by Scholastic thinkers in their attempt to explicate the Creation stemmed from their vision of God, principle and core of intelligibility. God is perfect and nothing at all can be added to perfection. Here the world cannot be a counterpart, a complement to God, a mirror holding out to him his image, serving him as partner in dialogue and love. But precisely, Christian thought involves essential elements of such a conception of the divinity. The Christian God is Trinity, existing eternally in a life of integral and perfect exchange of its Three Persons. It therefore enjoys an autarky, a sufficiency in its perfections that imply the freedom and gratuitousness required to make a true work of creation.

If the Trinity allows us to conceive the radical freedom of God, the absence of all "reason" necessary to set in motion the work of creation, another major obstacle stands before its philosophical thematization. Creation, causing to occur what was not there previously, seems thereby to add something to God. But precisely because God is perfect anything "added" to him comes around to rendering him imperfect. This conceptual barrier to the notion of creation can be jumped over only on condition of a rereading of the very idea of perfection. A perfect being is the one that is and does what is possible for him by his essence and which is not able to do and to be anything else. Yet this conception of essence makes him a kind of slave to his own essence. Some believe in the necessity of making the perfect capable of passing beyond his perfection, but what about his *falling short* of it? Doing and being all that he can do and be is implicated with a naturalist conception of the Perfect. But why lock up the Perfect in the chains of a very clarified, formalized *physis*; why subject him to the necessity of his own nature? The highest and most worthy notion of the Perfect comes down to recognizing in him the freedom to do *less* than he can do, to consent to be *less* than he is according to his nature. This notion of perfection will be offered by the other essential theme of Christian dogmatics, the Incarnation. The coming of the Word into the world signifies that he subjects himself to the limitations of matter and assumes the weaknesses of human nature. The Creator God who is master of the world renounces being all, assumes flesh, and takes on the form of a servant.

The centuries of Christian thought have not made the best metaphysical use of the high theological theses of Creation and Incarnation; the Hellenic philosophy suffered no veritable expansion or refoundation before Kant. It is undoubtedly true that with the Cartesian cogito a massive opening, a violent gap appeared, which refigured the metaphysical role of subjectivity, but it is only in and through the transcendental idealism of the Critique that Metaphysics is effectively renewed, realizing a true expansion. In Kant transcendental subjectivity is conjugated on two registers, time and freedom. From now on time is conceived as a sui generis power of conceptual structuration and freedom understood in terms of its unlimited sovereignty, which nevertheless operates according to an integral rationality. In both cases it is a matter of "variations" of the foundational metaphysical intuition that overcomes the imprisonment of the intelligible in the chains of necessity. Time ceases to be an evanescent instant or blind flux and freedom is permanently disassociated from contingency. Even more, these two acts of rescue are not mere attempts at rehabilitation, but signal the birth and elaboration of new intelligibilites by virtue of the central category of the Critique, *the a priori synthesis*. By contrast with analytic judgments where the concept of the predicate explicates only what is contained in the concept of the subject and synthetic a posteriori judgments where the predicate marks something new in relation to the subject and of which the novelty arises from experience and not the subject itself, synthetic a priori judgments advocate for the event of novelty at the level of the predicate which, without being deducible starting from the subject, still occurs in an a priori way. The a priori synthesis translates a metaphysical "situation" where what happens does not necessarily follow from what is given, all the while remaining linked with it on a conceptual level. The necessary implication of predicates by their subject is surpassed in favor of a profound connection of another order. This means that "the convertibility" of necessity and intelligibility cedes before a metaphysical vision in which being is understood as containing an originary "more" and novelty and superabundance can and should be claimed in a *strenge Wissenschaft*.

3

The first and capital moment of the expansion of metaphysics is when becoming is reintegrated into the heart of being, possibility opens up into fecundity, necessity is vanquished by freedom and justice is subsumed under love. In other words, it is a matter of "unlocking" being, which is no longer conceived starting from the immutable order of nature but is found enriched by a power of infinite novelty, a novelty which, all the while being unforeseeable, that is, not deducible, establishes itself with an integral intelligibility.

Being no longer knows how to be only what it is *able* to be. No longer does it depend on its essence or rather its essence is precisely the germ of a going beyond it: a going beyond every given because a going beyond itself. Being is "heavy with the future" but a future that is not simply a mechanical unfolding or necessary actualization: the *more* that happens through the process of becoming is truly new. Being is not condemned to recite a lesson prescribed to it from the beginning but is the very power of articulating its discourse according to rules not given in advance, though which impose themselves with a tranquil force. The real is more and other than the explication of the ontologically given, it is rather to be understood as an infinite, perennial fecundity. This fecundity is not only the power of bringing into existence virtual entities but also and above all the serene and joyous power of ceaselessly performing the coming of the new. In brief, the real is understood as the reign and regime of superabundance.

Superabundance as metaphysical principle is the sovereign other, the victorious counterpart to the stingy economy of justice—a justice, that is, that founds and controls the order of nature in which everything occurs according to inflexible rules and all the relations among beings are governed in obedience to an implacable *do ut des*. Justice is the regime of reciprocity and, as such, it is opposed to the superabundance that precisely indicates an overflowing, a going beyond what can and should be required. In its way justice is blind: it does not proceed through choice because it has no choice. Justice has to follow the given order of reciprocity. Consequently justice ignores and excludes freedom understood in its essential determination as indeterminate choice between two or more possibilities. But precisely as power of indetermination, freedom bears some affinity with superabundance. Freedom is definitely not contingency, it has its reasons for its choices, but its reasons can very well be reasons that "reason does not know." This means that in actuality decisions can be made in favor of what is not best, the most powerful, and richest for the choosing subject. Thus freedom negatively enacts the logic of superabundance: it chooses and does so in the knowledge of the lesser cause. Starting from this moment an entry-level metaphysical affinity appears between freedom and love. Freedom is the power of a non-necessary choice, a choice, therefore, that is not merely a function of something higher, and love is always love of another, of another as other, and therefore implies an activity for this other, in service to this other, gifts and sacrifices for this other. In the last analysis—and here their relation is perfected—love, according to its ultimate truth, is a category of superabundance. The eidetic condition of superabundance is marked by quantity and unforeseeability. It implies an unlimitedness, which has two faces: an as it were quantitative face, where there are no limits given in advance of what suddenly arises out of superabundance, and another face of radical unanticipatability that is not deducible from its activity. This unanticipatability does not simply stem from an absence of regularity. Unanticipatability and indeducibility surely mean that what happens happens according to principles and rules that do not entail essence, but which are nevertheless found fecund within the world and apply to it. But the surging up of love passes wholly beyond this economy. When love in its sovereign freedom consents to choose less than it could demand, it does not make only a restricted use of its natural egoism, of its perseverance in its own being, but comes down as its own opposite or adversary. Love's renunciation is not a simple limitation of the ontological option for itself, it derives from an option for another. Love of enemies appears to be a limit case of love pushed to extremes from its natural eidetic moments. In reality it is the metaphysical paradigm and moral principle of all love.

Love of enemies is the paradigm of love because love in its metaphysical truth is disinterested. Its highest moment, the very accomplishment of its disinterestedness, is service to the one who gives me nothing, who even takes from me what I have, who wrongs and wounds me. Surely love seeks a response; it pursues proximity to the beloved, but the truth of love is to love without reason and therefore to begin to love before the other has loved me, even before he has any reasons to love me. Love is always "in advance," but this anteriority, this temporal precedence, is only a symbol of its ultimate gratuity. This gratuitous nature leads love to break with justice, or rather, to come out of it: love is born as rupture with justice, and thus with reciprocity. The essential non-reciprocity of love appears in its two main forms, gift and fidelity. The gift should not result from the superfluous but rather the necessary, nor should it be a simple transfer of goods and services, but a true tearing apart of the fabric of exchange. The gratuity of the gift does not simply mean that it should surpass all reciprocity, for to be truly free it should even allow for and accommodate ingratitude itself. Fidelity is an exemplary example—a manifestation par excellence—of love. In its truth love is without reason and this absence of reason does not only characterize its occurrence, which precedes the affection of the beloved, it also determines its persistence when the beloved no longer loves and does not himself remain faithful.

Introduction to Metaphysics

The unconditional nature of fidelity radiantly translates the essence of the love that is a recapitulative category of this "unlocked" ontology in which the *more* and the *otherwise* are integrated into the eternal and necessary being: they will prove to be poles and principles of intelligibility. This "otherwise" is related to being not only as the movement of its becoming and this "more" is not articulated simply according to quantity: they manifest and witness to a marvelous subversion of *anankē*-being that is unfolded through the subsumption of contingency by freedom. And freedom perfects itself in love, allowing an entity to surpass itself and to be surpassed in favor of another. Love rips open the straitjacket of reciprocity and institutes a new law of relation among beings. Yet the event of novelty does not stop with this refounding of relations among entities already there: the unlocking of being is not confined to the horizontal but wants to be equally extended in the vertical. Freedom-love bursts out of the reciprocity of given beings, but it will also take responsibility for the coming of new beings. The expansion of metaphysics begins with the emancipation of being, of beings *from* necessity, but it continues with the rereading of individuality and singularity. If contingency has been capable of liberation by its transposition into freedom, a rescue of the individual and particular is equally foreseeable. This will take place through a complex metaphysical process in which moments of being and moments of essence—the world of fecundity and that of meaning—are engaged in a common work.

Novelty subverts being bound up in itself by means of freedom breaking out in love. In and through love being does more than be certain about itself—it is galvanized, going so far as to be turned against itself: the opening up of necessity permits a diminution amounting to a self-opposition. Love is the artisan par excellence of the first expansion of metaphysics. But metaphysics has a second great moment of expansion and ontological subversion: the event of the image and birth of the singular. It is always a matter of descending movements, first of the essence diffracted into the image and then being which engenders the singular. The diffraction of essence is accomplished when new entities come into the world. The truth of this novelty was negated—doubly—in Hellenic metaphysics. The image was conceived as a contingent instance of its original, its form, and therefore deprived of true being. Above all it passed as a kind of reflection of this form, a passive reflection that innovated nothing over its original, but simply represented a tiny fraction and isolated attribute of it. This was so much the case that the image only possessed a "counterfeit" being and manifest only an infinitely poor and incomplete *eidos*. However, the wind of novelty that shattered and unsealed the ontological imprisonment will be equally felt in the category of the image. The image as psychological or ontological category is revitalized starting from the image in its aesthetic sense. The artistic image rejects the condition of weak reflection of a tiny portion of essence and denounces the pauperization of an ectype condemned to be only one among a myriad of shadows of the archetype. In the aesthetic register the image—every artistic image more precisely—is a deterioration of its original, but of the kind that constitutes in its own way a sketch of the whole archetype. In other words the image of art profits under the regime of novelty, and, all the while remaining faithful to its original, it presents an unprecedented version of it. This version always seems to add something to its paradigm while forever remaining in its wake.

The unlocking of Essence, every adumbration of the movement from novelty to the work will bear decisively on human intelligence. The pscychological-ontological image leads to the artistic image, namely an image that is not passively received as a partial copy of its original, never simply representation but always autonomous presentation. And this victory of presentation or representation allows for a rereading of the image in general and above all of the Image par excellence, the imaging principle itself, consciousness. In his *Spaetphilosophie*, Fichte uses the image, the *Bild*, as true symbol of Consciousness. *Bild* is simultaneously ideal reflection and power of formation, suffice to say, an original instance of the a priori synthesis understood in a general sense. Consciousness is related to the world and therefore judges it, but its judgment equally expresses a power of innovation.

The artistic image therefore enriches the conception of the image and makes possible the attribution of a sui generis condition of intelligibility for subjectivity, which is from now on neither docile mirror nor opaque screen but rather always falls within the same jurisdiction as its "objects." Yet is this enhanced status of the subject sufficient to "found" a multiplicity of subjectivities? In the metaphysical expansion of the conception of the image one can see that conscious and knowing subjectivity creatively reflects and gathers together the world of Essence. But does this synthetic power of unification legitimate and justify the effective plurality of subjects? Does it finally only come under a para-existent transcendental subjectivity that "accompanies" worldly consciousness, underlying every judgment, but nevertheless carries no ontological weight? In sum, does the expansion of intelligibility of essence allow for the deduction of the plurality of entities?

Subjectivity as image, or more exactly, as imaging principle, can be augmented into a plurality. Classical metaphysics in which intelligibility is locked up in itself teaches that multiplicity is constituted by entities that possess no difference or proper "originarity" and which are more or less interchangeable. Hence the ecological crisis caused by the destruction of things conceived as malleable because replaceable at will by industrial production. Hence the political and social regimes in which men and women are finally only statistics, defined not by themselves but by their role in economic functioning and the engineering of social life. But the expansion of metaphysics implies a vision of individual entities that shows and establishes autarky, the sui generis value of the individual, the entity, the member of an unlimited series. In other words this means that the singular being should possess an ontological condition that makes it irreplaceable. But "the irreplaceable," originally a techno-economic category, should be reread in light of moral and metaphysical imperatives. Entities are replaceable inasmuch as they are situated in a quantitative register, but also when they are conceived in light of their function. Ultimately an entity is replaceable when it receives its role and meaning starting from a relation of abstract and impersonal justice. Popular wisdom says that the cemeteries of the world are full of irreplaceable people and this vulgar irony is right—to a certain point—for does a truly irreplaceable worker, storekeeper, professor, doctor, general or senior civil servant really exist? Once these individuals have exercised their role to the satisfaction of their vanished client, they will certainly be missed, but someone or other will be found to replace them, who, having the appropriate competencies, will cause them to be forgotten. But among friends, spouses and children it does not work this way. Of course they will share in this peopling of cemeteries, but precisely as friends, spouses, or children who cannot be forgotten because they were truly irreplaceable.

Replaceability means interchangeability. A being is interchangeable, meaning exchangeable for another, when considered not in itself but according to the function it exercises or the service it renders, in other words, starting from the evaluation of the qualities and properties it possesses. Evaluation leads to discernment of value and value is characteristic of a being, in fact what is most proper to it because it expresses the essential. But evaluation is not adequate for the understanding of a being precisely because it claims to know its own worth and pontificates on the value of another being. But this other may be worth as much or more than he himself. The economy that governs this world is founded on the exchange of those who are equal, and it approves of and encourages the abandonment of those who are less than others.

The autarky of an entity, of a being in its individuality cannot be based on considerations of having (in the Marcellian sense) that allow, even enjoin comparison.[1] Comparison is a category based on the relativity of the thing compared, on its relativity to another thing, but the autarky of an entity implies that it is seen and considered in itself. However, the unique situation in which a thing is considered in and for itself is when it is *loved*. Decidedly, our infatuations, sympathies and affections, in fact, our entire psychological and moral comportment towards beings and the things of the world, is influenced—in every determined appearance—by their qualities and properties. But qualities and properties are not exclusively proper to a being. Love, in the strict sense, should not pay attention to what is not proper to a being: one should not love the other because he or she is blond or brunette, weak or powerful, rich or poor. Love can be muddled or diluted, covered or mixed in inextricable ways with considerations of having, but its proper intentional object is not of the order of possession. One should not love the other because of what he has, one loves him in and for himself.

The instance par excellence of love is creation. God does not create a being for this or that reason: the creature does not even exist, how could it possess within whatever there is about it that makes it "interesting" to the creator? It can be created only because it is loved for itself, even before it effectively exists, and thus even before it

1. Cf. G. Marcel, *Being and Having*.

possesses any quality or property, any wealth or capacities. And the counterpart or reflection of creation is procreation, a call to existence that should never be motivated by any consideration of interest, but only by the love that is gratuitous by nature. Of course, love is addressed to a being with an essence, endowed with qualities. Yet this essence and its qualities are so to say circumstantially concomitant—necessary, but not sufficient conditions for love. Parents are frequently—and stupidly—asked: which one of your children do you love the most? The only correct response to this incorrect question is "each of them." The parent should love each of his children the best and the most. This love that, without being divided, is addressed to a plurality institutes the ontological condition of the singular, assigning to it its *sui generis* intelligibility. Classical metaphysics thought it could deny the intelligibility of particular beings, dropping them insofar as they were only incomplete reflections of an essence, faceless members of a multitude. But love recognizes the singularity of what is only a member of a series, establishing it as a valuable being in and for itself, and thus as *unique*. Children that are each an object of maximal love are unique, notwithstanding their plurality. The uniqueness of the child influences in a quasi-retroactive way all beings, and starting from it one can and should discern the intelligibility proper to the singular.

4

The uniqueness of a being asserts itself starting from the bracketing of considerations of having, qualities or properties. But this does not simply mean that love is addressed to a being simply because it exists. Indeed, the suspension or diminishment of every value does not call into question the continuous and persisting meaning of an existing being, yet a being exists only in and through specific modalities in which it represents and gives itself. Love seems to shelve considerations of intelligibility. In reality it manifests itself as a reinterpretation of intelligibility. Rather than relating itself to essence, it aims for the *eidos*. The essence, the material essence, which, for classical metaphysics served as the answer to the question about what a being is, is in the last analysis only a formalization or generalization of quality or property. Without actually breaking the link with the essence of classical acceptation, the *eidos* bursts its borders in favor of larger vision of quiddity. Above all, it takes account of the metaphysical condition of the free being. The love addressed to a child as wholly unique is not a consequence of the configuration of its qualities and yet it discerns and valorizes the manners and modes in which this uniqueness expresses itself, develops and maintains itself. The quiddity proper to a unique living being in time and space is found before it and in company with other unique beings. It cannot be restricted to a static set of qualities. Instead, it is a matter of the articulation or proper structuration of its existence in space and time. It is equally related to the principles and form of its will. In other words, the unlocking of being by novelty is doubled through an extension of essence through *eidos*. Hence the arrival of the *new intelligibilities* in the wake of Kant, which can only be brought to completion through a phenomenological metaphysics. The intelligibility of space is a function of its capacity to shelter and nourish a plurality of relations among beings of the world, especially among free beings, and it is deployed through the orders of dimensionality and directionality. The intelligibility of time is founded on free and loving fecundity, the principle as well as instrument of its power of innovation that shows forth and punctuates an eidetic of *time*. The will's intelligibility, rather than necessitating, sensu stricto, an eidetic articulation, presents and actualizes itself according to the higher logic of the opposition between good and evil.

Space has typically been conceived by classical metaphysics as the principle of exteriority. Frequently assimilated to the material and bodily—pejorative categories for philosophies of Hellenic inspiration—the spatial serves as cypher and symbol of immobility, hence also as site and force of inertia. But it is equally the occasion and dimension, even the artisan or lynchpin of alienation—until such time as it appears and imposes itself as the principle of *rarity*, that very soul of conflict and war. Yet this contempt and millennia-long mistake will end by being surpassed and vanquished from the moment that the spatial is awarded the status of a priori condition. Henceforth the door is open towards its reinterpretation in positive terms. Space is projected by distance, which is the principle par excellence of the acknowledgment of the autarky of others. To establish distance in relation to a work of art is required in order for its beauty to be made manifest to the contemplative gaze. Above all, distance is the *conditio sine qua non* of respect before things and men. Respect stems from the maintenance of a distance towards and before another. Respect precludes trespassing in the sphere of another, trampling on his flowerbeds, or even walking all over him, knocking him over, and quashing him. It commands patience towards the other and inspires piety towards things and persons, institutions and traditions. This spatiality manifested and expressed by respect is articulated according to an entire logic, or better, an eidetic of which the two principle moments are direction and dimension. Spatiality does not designate an indeterminate homogeneity, but a sui generis power of structuration. It is the junction of directions that incarnate its active and projective aspect; it is also the collection—or better—the system of dimensions that make it manifest according to its direction, the "milieu of the given," and even the site and force of welcome and protection.

The second instance of the new intelligibility is time. More than space, time has always been conceived as a negative category. It is the principle par excellence of finitude and at the same time the manifestation par excellence of absence of meaning, as well as root and architect of corruption. Condemned to flow by as a violent flux and without structuration as well as fallen into disrepair in a set of instants without density closed in on themselves, time will finally turn out to be a guardian, despite itself, of the immutability and eternity proper to intelligibility. But the Kantian revision of time according to its apriority emancipates it from its ancient servitude and makes it capable of playing a "positive" essential role. Henceforth time is disclosed as laborer for the fecundity of being. It is the principle and architect of the novelty that unlocks necessity, allowing the promise to be announced and opening the way before the philosophies of history. But in order for Time to be capable of undertaking these noetic adventures, it must be given an eidetic where each moment of time has its own weight and specificity. The three times will no longer be conceived as successive moments along the same line but as specific *eidē* independent of a given place along the trajectory of Chronos's flux. The past will no longer be a type of burden and treasure defined by the oblivion of what has come and gone. On the contrary, it will register a presence at the heart of the present, a presence with specific colors and values. The future will no longer be a non-existent fountain without effective impact: it will haunt the present and intervene in its structuration. And the present will cease to be a punctual reality—or rather unreality—a place of ever-evanescent passage between what is no longer and what is not yet. Henceforth the three times manifest their own structuration and from this starting point they will establish a system that structures Time—a structuring in which this world is no longer given as mere place of instantaneous passage, but, still impermanent, it appears as the atmosphere and dwelling place of intelligent and free beings which occupy and develop it.

5

Space and time constitute the milieu and the weft, the principle and the very deployment of finite existence, but of a finitude that possesses its own resources and which is above all detached from the sphere of the inanimate and non-free. Things and material entities are structured by material essences, passively receiving their intelligible structure; they are born and come to be through these essences. Things are different for free beings, which are certainly defined by their essence, but their definition is not consequently a determination. Spatial and temporal eidetics punctuate and structure the existence of beings that do not passively live their quiddity, all the while receiving, as it were, from the outside what they are. They autonomously form and articulate their own future. Time and space constitute the human psycho-physiological sphere of existence. This existence certainly stems from the category of finitude, but the eidetic structures of space and time inscribe within it the markings of an authentic intelligibility. Yet man is not only a psycho-physiological being. His finitude contains a power that surpasses it on all sides. *Anthropos* is determined by finitude even if he masters its logic, but man is also a free being and exercises his freedom through his will.

Freedom is exercised in and through time and space but it is independent of them, it originates in another metaphysical register. The villain, the criminal, the one who has wronged another, sinned against another or others, he feels guilty, he is aware of having done wrong and would love to be relieved of this burden, liberated from his culpability: he aspires for forgiveness. One asks for forgiveness for an evil act one intended and carried out in the past. The request for pardon is born out of a recognition of an evil deed carried out, of a particular action or omission that occurred in the past. In its full truth, forgiveness is sought by and for the person whole and entire, and what he seeks is not conceived as situated in the past. One certainly asks for forgiveness for offensive words or an inflicted wound: these words were proffered yesterday or before, even six months or six years ago. And the kick in the head or stab in the back suffered by the other was given on a day in the near or distant past, but always on a given day. Yet if one seeks forgiveness for a wicked action carried out in a past moment, one seeks forgiveness *now* and above all one seeks it for oneself as one who is situated in the *present*. Feeling remorse, one repents of his bad past action of which he would like to be free, for he suffers in the present. And if one always suffers from a past crime, this is because it has not removed itself from oneself, but continues to adhere. The action of the crime is past: I did it; I no longer am doing it. But if my physical action falls into a bygone past, I continue to feel the bad action as my own in the present. I am the author, the subject of the crime and if I take that on myself this is because I see myself as continuing to accomplish it—accomplishing it, that is, in the *will*.

The request for forgiveness testifies to the deep awareness of continuity, to the radical homogeneity of the will. Beyond every vague desire to put right the material and external consequences of the bad past action, one aspires to heal oneself and thus to a healing of the whole person. And this healing will only be accomplished by the will exercised in space and time (but the truth of which is located beyond space and time). The extra-temporality and -spatiality of the will comes from the exclusion from it anything psycho-physiological (the force of desire, vigorous affection, ardent aspiration or powerful impulses). Strictly speaking, if the will is power and act, it is not a faculty but reveals a sui generis plane of being. It doubtlessly possesses a certain dynamism—one could even say that dynamism is all that it is—and it has an efficacy, but which is not exercised on a physical or psychological plane. To the degree that the will is action—and it is only such—it is intention. Intention formulates the radical dynamism of desire, its ontological condition of ceaseless transcending of the self, and simultaneously its truth of being realized through a direction, of being deployed in a direction, or better, being only a direction. Intention is a single and undivided reality, without fragmentation or levels, but at the same time is absolutely determined. The doctrine of the will as pure intention seems to stand in proximity to or affinity with the apophaticisms of certain phenomenologies. Yet if it takes its distance from (material) being, it does not slide into a negative ontology. Instead, it manifests a metaphysical variation, even a metaphysics of being other than "material" being, and it manifests in particular a return from above to quiddity.

Contrary to the other register of finitude where theoretical intelligence, perception, and imagination work, the world of the will is not structured by a plurality of eidē, but only by a duality of principles. The will is intention and intention is either good or evil: in its deepest truth, it does not admit compromise or degree but evidences a formal unity and perfect homogeneity. The will desires to split into two integral universes, each manifesting (or rather *is*) good or evil. In and through Good and Evil differentiation, that is, Essence, finds its realization. Beyond multiplicity, beyond qualities and material properties, and beyond the temporal and spatial eidē, the ultimate realities of the good and evil will do not scatter themselves about in partial moments but exist in an unlimited and undivided unity. Good and Evil are as the highest instances of Essence, but also the moment when Essence seems to realize an originary synthesis with Being. Good and Evil are nothing but form—the good will like the evil will are the structures, or better, supreme archetypes, decanted from out of action. And action is a sign of being, even when any material efficacy is bracketed. Suffice to say that the first sketches of the Expansion of Metaphysics may be brought to fruition through Good and Evil as ultimate categories.

Introduction

1.

From its far origins in Greek antiquity, philosophy has sought to say things inaccessible to other disciplines of knowledge. It begins its investigations in the natural world and slowly rises up to what is supposedly found beyond this world. It wants to put the sciences in their proper place and to put itself at the center—as much to surpass the sciences as to found them. It claims to be the central, principal, and first science. But establishing itself as the center and mistress of every rational activity is a risky venture with a high cost. Philosophy believes it can expand its hold on the real, deepen its vision, and universalize its intuitions, but periodically it is constrained to prune these ambitions to the root, to restrain its aspirations, and to demarcate (and therefore restrict) its territory. The majority of purges are followed by a restoration. Subtractions lead to expansions. Yet every expansion proves to be an ambiguous conquest. Philosophy can be pleased to have managed to penetrate realms previously closed off, to have wrapped in concepts zones of the real that seemed impermeable to universalization and formalization. But unfortunately this extension represents only a false victory because the expansion of the thinkable pays the high price of a leveling of its condition. The Critique leads to the Encyclopedia, but if Absolute Knowledge can claim for itself the integral penetration of the real, the real it illumines is only homogenous and univocal: the expansion of intelligibility passes through the abandonment of Transcendence. Even more, this victory of Reason is in the end completely ephemeral. The various interrogations of philosophy's reach end in logical positivism, an analytic philosophy hardly content with ratifying and bringing to completion the dispossession of philosophy from its pretensions to reach the "bottom" of things. Here it is even denied the capacity to talk about anything that has always been most important to humanity. The Critique thought its solemn power and duty was to prohibit philosophy from scrutinizing the things of Heaven; now even its capacity to talk about the things of Earth will be disputed. Philosophy should stick only to what can be expressed by "natural language." But natural language has no grip on the essential, in other words the most profound realities: being, truth, good, and evil.

The Expansion of Metaphysics

Philosophy should keep quiet because what it wants to say—and has always wanted to say—is unsayable. It has a native proximity to quotidian language and "logical" discourse, which precisely disqualifies it from the power to signify the transcendent and normative. It would be better if it gave the word to Poetry and Religion, which in their own way and according to their proper intelligibility are fit to speak about what is "unsayable" according to the criteria of natural language. But since Plato we know that the Logos is not jealous: the human mind is truly capable of thinking the essential things. And the vocation of Philosophy, a discipline with specific intentional objects, is to formulate and express these thoughts. Philosophy is not a logic of the sciences, or a poetics of the concept, or a mythology of *eidē*: it is a speculative and descriptive discourse on the structures and potentialities, the values and promises of the real.

2.

Philosophy is a discipline of generalization and universalization. It wants to decant the essential from the diverse domains of the real by way of its great branches of ethics, epistemology, and aesthetics. But beyond these regional discourses is found metaphysics as their principle. In a simple yet perfectly adequate way, Descartes defined metaphysics as "the root" of the tree of philosophy. It denotes the principle, origin and therefore something that is at the base, in the depths, where in its original linguistic sense the *meta* means after or beyond. According to ancient historiographical tradition, the editors of the Aristotelian corpus placed the work of *Prima Philosophia* after the treatise on Physics and subsequently this branch of philosophy that is situated *beyond* the empirical and the particular and which is as the foundation and paradigm of everything else is termed *metaphysics*. Metaphysics teaches the first principles of all knowledge. It knows the essential in the contingent, the universal through the particular, the stable at the heart of the ephemeral, the permanent as the source and support of the changing. Metaphysics has two ultimate intentional objects, being and essence. It is concerned with the supreme fact that the real *is*, and with the supreme content, *what* it is. It is therefore a science of being and of essence, and the entire history of philosophy is only an immense variation on the respective relations between these two ultimate first principles of the real.

Traditionally, the doctrine of being is called *ontology*. For certain great Aristotelians as for some famous representatives of phenomenology, ontology enjoys a primacy in relation to every doctrine of *eidos*. Ontology is the true first science, it is the keystone of the "essential thought," it, and it alone, is able to counter the failures and ravages of western metaphysics, which suffers, since ancient times of the "forgetting of Being" (*Seinsvergessenheit*). Submerged by the empirical or blinded through meditations on the divine, or even hypnotized by the infinite details of an eidetic, the doctrine of ideas or the casuistry of eidē, western metaphysics loses view of the essential, the First, to wit, Being—which alone can save it from the diverse avatars

Introduction

of nihilism: scientism or mysticism, logicism or empiricism. In reality, however, the high discourse of essential thought cannot hide the limits and deficiencies of a science of Being. The philosophy inclined to adorn itself with the "arrogant name ontology" (*Critique of Pure Reason*, B 875) had already warned.[1] The Critique condemns complacency towards ontological speculation and this denunciation is legitimated by two equally sufficient reasons. On the one hand, Being in its immensity and absoluteness wipes out and annihilates any vague desire to understand the particular, the singular, the new. On the other hand, existence, a synonym for being, is not a predicate, it therefore cannot contribute to the analysis and description of the world and therefore to the increase of knowledge.

Metaphysics is tempted to speak only of Being, which it ends up conceiving in terms of a radical univocity, and it believes it can and should consign essence to its proper place, namely understanding it as a secondary and subordinated condition. Essence is only a grammar of the real while the subject, the energy, the principle and end, the source and telos of this grammar is Being. This at times fascinating vision of metaphysics does not lack a certain grandeur, for it seems to offer a coherent and unified interpretation of reality. Yet it has its limits and faults, which the history of philosophy insinuates with sublime dexterity. Metaphysics begins in Athens not in Elea, on the banks of the Ilisos not on the shores of the Tyrrhenian Sea. It does not take flight in the Eleatic verses on Being; its date of dispatch is with the Socratic discussions on the Ideas. It is not an accident of history but an immanent justice, a wise ordinance of Providence if you like, that almost all the dialogues of Plato are conserved while the great poem of Parmenides survives only in fragments .

Contrary to the pretensions of ontological theories of diverse obediences, in metaphysics Essence plays a central role distinct from that of Being. In fact, the deficiencies and faults of the classical doctrine of essences are due to the limitations and excesses of ontology. Doubtlessly, great philosophers have been able to evade the prestige and fascination of Being. Many hardly make it a theme at all, bracketing it out of their reflections, and some see in it only a "complement of possibility,"[2] a simple "accessory to essence."[3] Notwithstanding these prudent limitations, the notion of Being will have heavily mortgaged the heritage of western philosophy, and instead of a Forgetting of Being, we should rather have to complain about its exaggerated hold on Metaphysics—especially because, in the wake of Aristotle, *Ens* and *Actus Purus* were assimilated to each other, being was fatally united to actuality. The reinterpretation of being in terms of actuality had the two-fold end of clearly marking the unlimited

---

1. References to biblical books, famous writings of antiquity, and the *Critique of Pure Reason* are given in line. The reasons for this are as substantive as typographical, for it intends to emphasize the background and role as point of reference played in my thought by the great philosophies of the western tradition, especially Kant, and by Christian theology.

2. Wolff, *Philosophia prima sive ontologia* § 174, 143.

3. Thus Al-Farabi: Gilson, *Le thomisme*, 55.

dynamism of this foundational principle of reality and of providing a positive notion of its perfect homogeneity. Being has nothing to do with an (even supreme) essentiality, it is and only is act. Consequently it is like the seamless garment of Christ, perfectly continuous, immaculately white. But this undivided actuality stands at the origin of the deficiencies and excesses of metaphysics. The lofty speculation of the Schoolmen established the philosopheme of the perfect actuality of *ipsum esse*. Unfortunately, this notion that is the keystone of classical metaphysics easily converts into its contrary: actuality, supposed to be the reason and principle of an integral explanation of reality, sinks into a supreme factuality. The ontological doctrine of the *actus purus* struggles with jealous obstinacy against any intrusion of contingency, whence the reinterpretation of Being in terms of Necessity. The absolute actuality that is Being is unconditioned; it excludes any possibility of non-being or being otherwise. Yet if the identification of Being with necessity is able to prevent it from breaking apart, subjected to change, to degrees, in short, to impermanence, incompleteness and partiality, it condemns it at the same time to an imprisonment, immobility, and sterility. The *ipsum esse* is necessary and is necessarily what it is, but precisely this unconditionality is the cipher of an ultimate limitation. The *Ens necessarium* must be. It must be what it is and how it is. This absolute actuality and incandescent intelligibility derives in the last analysis from a supreme powerlessness. Being is necessary and necessarily what it is but this necessity has not been "chosen" or "assumed" by it; it fell on it from the outside; it achieved this state "incidentally." Being as *actus purus* is only therefore a synonym for *anankē*, principle and ultimate accomplishment of fate, a false necessity—the ultimate truth of which is contingency.

Speculation's insistence on the unconditionality-necessity of Being leads to an impasse. In fact, it is detrimental to the cause of ontology. And it can be redeemed only through disassociating being from its double, necessity, and then proceeding to reinterpret its actuality. Speculation should itself take on the task of reopening Being locked in on itself, and this unbolting will bring about an ultimate enrichment of Being, in the place of its restriction of power, infringement against its perfections and aggression against its intelligibility. Actuality will see the restitution of its primitive root of potentiality; infinity and universality will celebrate their blossoming in the particular and concrete. Ontology, instead of condemning metaphysics to an ignorance of novelty, will on the contrary open it to the horizon of fecundity and singularity. Fulfilling in an unprecedented way its role as First Philosophy, it will be rethought starting from and by means of the great categories of freedom and love. There is more: this positive subversion of being does not confine its work to the area of ontology sensu stricto, but registers an extraordinary impact in the world of essence. Essence has always been understood as the counterpart of existence: existence is the act of reality for which essence is the content. Yet to the degree that being is conceived through the actuality that excludes all novelty and limitation, the quiddative can be represented only by material essences that are like so many particular diffractions of the one Essence of Being. The qualities, properties forms and ideas fall completely under the jurisdiction of this zone of *quoi*, this *Was* that describes the *what*, the *Dass* of necessary being-actuality.[4]

But along with the opening of ontology, the unbolting of being, comes a restructuring, an enrichment of essence. Being, understood as principle of novelty and singularity, calls for new regions of description, hence the birth of new branches of the eidetic: time, space and the will. The subversion of ontology leads to the expansion of being and the expansion of being allows and requires the expansion of essence.

3.

An expanded metaphysics makes it possible to understand areas and moments of reality previously considered inconceivable, impenetrable by philosophical thought. It opens to conceptual speech what had previously been taken for unsayable. This extension of the reach of metaphysical saying is a function of its reinterpretation of intelligibility. Metaphysics continues to move within the intelligible, to deal with the Ideas, Forms, and Phenomenological Essences, but it is the status of its formulations that will be modified. Philosophy continues to try to describe and explain reality by providing coherent and systematic reports on its findings, but it allows and—at least tacitly—demands plurality. Not a relative plurality emerging from the root of an absolute universal-unity, but a plurality every instance and sample of which possesses a sui generis validity. This plurality proper to Metaphysics is manifest "first" in a "negative" way: philosophy, the philosophers, can lay claim to rationality, to the truth, but their claims appear essentially open ended. Conceptual discourse follows a strict and profound logic but it makes the best of statements that are not ultimate, it elaborates highly articulate theories that do not, for that reason, come to term and reach a final conclusion. Naturally the openness of philosophies, this negative acceptance of plurality, leads to plurality in a positive sense, that is, to many philosophies, multiple metaphysics that each lay claim to truth. But what matters here is not the pretension of this or that philosophy to the truth—after all, could a philosophy be conceived that does not lay claim to that?—but this legitimation of a plurality does not at all amount to the admission of relativism. This validity of a plurality of philosophies manifests itself through the refusal of a singular metaphysical principle of explanation of the world. It implies a revision of the theory of truth.

Great philosophers like Spinoza or Hegel wanted to deduce the edifice of concepts from a common foundational principle, but the required departure starting from a single and unique point can impoverish reflection as much as force it to hold one-sided meanings that from time to time end in conflicts with good sense. Contrary to these radical variations on the genius of Laplace, philosophy should abandon the

---

4. Schelling, *Introduction à la philosophie de la mythologie*, 519.

dream of an integral system, of a complete explanation of every nook and cranny and all the structures of reality. Instead it should be inspired by the thinker of the *Cogito*: it is not necessary that the "first principle" to which one appeals, be "such that all other propositions can be reduced to and proved by it, it is enough that it can serve to discover many things."[5] It should profess with the first known writing of the author of The *Critique* that the whole of knowledge cannot be deduced starting from "one truth."[6] The renunciation of a unique principle for the articulation of reality does not amount however to a prudent withdrawal from reason, it is not the same as a recognition of defeat, like the reminder of the inherent limitations of our finitude. To trade in this way a foundational principle for a plurality of particular principles manifests a new conception of rationality, of intelligibility, which is a function of a theory of philosophical truth much different from the classical "conformity of mind to thing." The truth of a philosophical idea does not consist in its condition of being a reflection, trace, or copy of a "real" thing, the truth of a philosophical judgment does not mean that it presents and represents events as they "effectively" unfold. Metaphysics is not a technique for producing copies of originals, but a discourse for elaborating and offering images that, all the while being related with relevance and fidelity to sensible or intelligible "things," is able to claim a sui generis originality. Analysis, philosophical reasoning, does not amount to making photocopies of reality, or practicing the art of extracting the universal from the particular, or abstracting the formal from the material. Philosophy is certainly supposed to recount reality, but this recounting is nothing less than an autonomous recitation, possessing its own specific intelligibility. Philosophical discourse, the themes and theses of metaphysics, are not hypotheses or paradigms like those elaborated by the sciences. The status is neither relative nor of temporary, provisional significance: the dialogues of Plato and the treatises of Aristotle do not constitute a collection of intuitions and half-baked ideas of restricted validity, limited to a historically given period. The plurality of philosophies means that the great metaphysics eternally conserve their "power of signification."[7] The ideas they conceive and proclaim bear a load of perennial truth.

A philosophical idea corresponds to an entity, idea, or relation of the ontological order; it is a reflection, or rather, an irradiation of it. It presents a valuable analogy with the Phenomenon of the *Critique*. Phenomena "correspond" to noumena; they are appearances to be conceived as relative to a thing in itself, but one cannot reach thetic knowledge of this counterpart, which is a univocal knowledge because registering a real continuity with the intelligible "original." The philosophical idea cannot presentify or reproduce in its own way "its" noumenon, but it does make use of a power of referring to it and signifying it. But this power of reference and indication is in no way a capacity for unifying conceptual refractions of the *intelligibilia*. The

---

5. Descartes, *Lettre à Clerselier, Oeuvres* IV, 444.
6. Kant, *Gedanken von der wahren Schätzung... Schriften*, Akademie Ausgabe I, 9.
7. Merleau-Ponty, *Le visible et l'invisible*, 139. (See *The Visible and the Invisible*, 103.)

Introduction

philosophical idea can and should claim to "correspond" to its ontic counterpart, but this correspondence has nothing to do with similarity. Philosophical formulations are not fragmentary and incomplete effects of originals in the sphere of the concept, but flashes of light where the Meaning of the form, the transcendent essence, is found transposed, transubstantiated if you like, in the metaphysical universe. Philosophy, in other words, cannot claim knowledge of things and essences as they are "in themselves" but has however a sufficiently adequate view on them to be able to be dazzled by their light.

Decidedly, the philosopher attempts to discern more clearly the transcendent aim of his discourse. He clearly admits that his concepts are not an adequate retelling of the original, but he does claim an affinity between the archetype and ectype. But, precisely, philosophical utterance is a very particular kind of ectype: it is not an incomplete sketch of the whole, nor a diffraction which, like a Leibnizian monad, partially but adequately reflects the whole from its own particular perspective. One should rather say that metaphysical utterances apply to intelligible realities like a multiplicity of representations is related to the Kantian Aesthetic Idea. The transcendent entity that philosophical concepts transcribe is an infinite overdetermination; philosophical ideas each claim to deliver a presentation of the Idea whole and entire. The philosophical utterance argues for its fidelity to the sublime principle of meaning; it intends to shelter, as it were, the latter's radiance. It exults in the power accorded to it to capture and reformulate the lightning flashes of Essence—all the while being evidently aware that if its way of transcribing and proclaiming them is true, it is nevertheless not the only true one, that if the image it claims to be of the Original is faithful, it still does not exhaust the richness of this Original.

Philosophical formulation constitutes confident and exultant discourse—but also humble and sober—where the human mind articulates and deploys this specific conceptuality that allows it to formulate and share its living vision of intelligibility, of its reality, structures and moments. An expanded Philosophy or Metaphysics comes with the unbolting of actuality, source and resource of novelty, describing its successive moments and forms and it studies its eidetic structuring. Decidedly, this division between the act of being's appearance, integrating and appropriating the richness of potentiality, plurality and singularity, on the one hand, and the exposure of great eidetic regions of reality, namely the spatial, temporal and the will, on the other hand, does not at all entail the profession of an absolute scission between being and essence. The ontological and eidetic are definitely written according to two different grammars but they are ultimately reconciled in the activity of the Will. The will reveals a particular moment, a specific face of the mind, but it is also the promise, call and presence of the Good, which occurs through its activity, but which also and above all signals the irradiation, the uninterrupted work of that which—or rather, the One who—maintains the real and gives it its meaning and its end. Metaphysics is the chronicle of the occurrence of novelty, which is at the same time the advent of meaning. But the opening of the self through the liberation of potentiality and the deployment of intelligibility are conceived only on the basis of the paradigm and supreme energy that is this Other, this hearth of transcendent superabundance without which reality would only be a powerless immanence, locked in on itself.[8]

---

8. The companion volume to the treatise that follows is *Explorations metaphysiques*. Paris: L'Harmattan, 2012, a collection of studies composed over a thirty-five-year period that prepared for the great themes of this text. Its introduction [included in this English edition—WCH] briefly sets forth the conception of philosophy that unfolds here.

BOOK ONE

First Philosophy

I

The Image

The Nothing of Subjectivity

There are three domains particular to man: art, religion, and philosophy. In art one expresses oneself, proposing truth. In religion, one is guest to a higher truth. In philosophy, one wants to understand oneself and the world. This understanding is first negative, or rather, differentiating. One knows oneself as other with regard to the world, but how to conceive this alterity? One would like to define oneself, but in what terms? In order to be defined, traits, images, and concepts should be drawn from the world—but, precisely, the self should be marked off, or better, stand out from the world. To conceive and articulate oneself one must describe oneself, but any element of a description issues from the milieu from which one wants to escape. Following negative theology one could be tempted to build a negative anthropology; but just like negative theology, in a negative anthropology we ultimately delude ourselves. To draw a theory of traits or unfold a litany of characteristics, the various eidē that one is not, comes back to defining oneself starting from what one pushes away and negates. Description concerns positive content and whether one enumerates and expounds them by negation or affirmation, this fact does not change. The yes and no make the decisive difference for the will, yet they have no quiddative, eidetic weight. Whether I affirm or deny one hundred thalers, the affirmation and negation are related to the same essence.

The eidetic negation seems to lead to an impasse. The essence of man cannot be formulated taking what is given in the world as a starting point: it is a distinctive essence, of a radically different order from worldly essences. How then to express this essence when every way leading to it appears blocked, when all the eidē are off the beaten path? The only thing left is to pick back up negative theology, resort to a negation, but of a very different and more radical kind. From here man will no longer be explained as this or that but will instead be called nothing, or, more directly, it will be said that he *is* nothing. The moralists and religious thinkers of every time and place have unfolded the intuition of nullity, of the nothingness of man. However, this intuition is the child of a "comparison" with the Eternal, or more simply with the forces and powers of the World and thus without taking into account the metaphysical originality of man, the place and the purpose of the investigation. This insignificant speck and void of misery and tragedy has nothing at all to do with the "nothingness" of man taught by the philosophers. From Boehme to Sartre, and actually from Aristotle, man or more precisely his symbol or eidetic truth—self-consciousness, the will, in short, subjectivity—is articulated through variations on the vocable "nothing." With the fascinating naiveté of an imagistic discourse, Jacob Boehme speaks of the will as "the paltry nothing" and the *Critique* says again and again that the condition of zero-density of self-consciousness is the "nothing" of time which is the very essence of subjectivity. Fichte teaches that the self is nothing, like "a point," which Hegel terms "a void." And Schelling passionately proclaims that freedom and human subjectivity do not exist.[1] Finally, in the middle of last century, Sartre defined the for-itself as *not being* the in-itself and thus as being *nothing*.

The vocable "nothing" is proclaimed with force and feeling. But it is truly a technical term to denote the metaphysical condition of the subject insofar as it does not come under the jurisdiction of ontology. The self is nothing; in other words, it is not added to the things of the world like another link on a chain. Time, which is the material from which the self is woven, is not a being but a form; freedom is not at all a power rebellious to the law of nature; the subject is not one thing among others, not even a super-thing. The nothing, the void of subjectivity is discerned and understood in relation to entities, to the world's contents, but it is not a member of the entities, it does not belong to the world's contents. Rather, it designates a para-ontological mode of being, something like an eidos without qualities or traits. Yet the nothing is not univocally formulated: the subject possesses two ways of being things, the contents, the in-itself. Either it denies and then recreates them, or welcomes them and sees being in them. In both cases it is a matter of a native indeterminacy, but which can be developed in two completely different ways. The subject can be made manifest through the pathos of an anarchy of essence. It can also yield to the ancient image of the blank tablet capable of receiving any impression.

The nothing of subjectivity is exempt from every determination, even of the highly intelligible kind: it contemplates no eternal essence. Essences belong in the last analysis only to the order of the given and the subject endures the influence of nothing from this order. What it has it gives itself, when and how it wants. The subject is for-itself and the for-itself does not come from elsewhere, it is not born from the womb of the in-itself. It has neither beginning nor end, it never happens, and above all it is not the product or fruit of any causal relation. Essences pertain to the world, to the given

---

1. For references, see Vető, *De Kant à Schelling II*, 283 and n. 62.

whereas the subject, being nothing, points only to the new. It is nothing of the given world, but its vocation is to become all, namely, to call into existence what it is not and to give itself what it has not.

The for-itself, manufacturer of values and creator of essences, is kind of like an anthropological avatar of the *magister veritatis* of philosophical theologians, but one could equally understand it as the exalted counterpart of the humble Aristotelian *nous*, the soul that is *quaedammodo omnia*. The soul is all things: it can *be* so potentially because it is not so actually. It can be *all* because, in itself, it is none of these things. It is a blank tablet capable of any inscription because it does not bear a single one and a receptacle allowing any content because it possesses none. The subject is an opening, a receptivity, a welcoming. It is open to the outside, it receives contents, it welcomes the eidē. How? The self's welcome appears as the highest instance of hospitality, but with an essential qualification. True hospitality implies at least the residual, discrete presence of the one who welcomes, visible traces of courteous preparation and the certainty that, if something is lacking or out of place, the host, who remains near and ready will act to remedy the deficiencies, fill the cracks, repair the defects. But consciousness is not related to its contents in this way. It is tempting to think of self-consciousness as another instance of consciousness in general, tacitly and imperceptibly accompanying every occurrence of consciousness of the world. Self-consciousness would be the "universal Witness,"[2] faithfully present during each mental event, accompanying the birth of every image. However, to attend in this way the occurrences of mental contents and to continue to be present to them only very imperfectly corresponds to the self's metaphysical role as accompanist of the eidē. A warning lamp may not shine for a long time, remaining as it were in a state of potentiality, but when it is time to light up it flashes vigorously. The witness is not always visible, he may not be present, but he is always found as it were in the neighborhood, or even, tentatively absent, he can be summoned anytime. To be precise: the capacity to be summoned constitutes his essence. But the self never lights up and it cannot simply be summoned at any given moment. In other words it does not appear like one more entity, an additional content. Self-consciousness is neither host nor witness. It is not described as having been present at a given moment beside its contents in order later to retire, waiting to return when summoned. Simone Weil said that "mind...is something that erases itself owing to the fact that it exerts itself."[3] The flaw in the production, the error in reasoning marks the blurred intrusion, the inappropriate presence of the agent that properly functions only when making itself absent. Do we have to imagine that the subject is able to make some clandestine, illegitimate but very real forays into the midst of its contents and that it is by rectifying these deviations that it gives itself over to reduction? One is naturally inclined to consider this conjecture but in reality

---

2. Sankara, *Commentaire aux aphorismes sur la brahman*, II, 3, 7, in Hulin, *Sankara et non-dualité*, 73.

3. Weil, *Cahiers, Oeuvres complètes*, vol. VI 4, 490.

it is a fantasy. The mental states where we think we notice the presence of the subject through disorder and deviation are not unsuccessful moments of the reduction from which the subject has to withdraw in order to exert itself in a truthful way. The reduction may seem to trade itself in strong and weak moments, in occurrences of perfection and imperfection. In reality, the self-effacement required has no degrees, it shows a sui generis mode of being, a clear homogeneity in relation to anything that is or can become its content, entering into its condition. The mind can not effect at every moment a phenomenological bracketing, but the very being of the subject of which it is the exertion no less consists in a reduction, a continuous one.

This integral negation that is the logical consequence of the nothing of the subject should not, for all that, remain an apophaticism. After showing that the subject *is not* through the account of *what* it is not, one must try to say *what* it is. How? Self-consciousness is present to consciousness but this presence gives itself as a pure absence. Every mental state, every datum in our mind is unfolded against the invisible background of self-consciousness, which accompanies consciousness as its necessary correlate. An invincible amnesia seems to dominate every thinking, conscious being, making it incapable of truthfully grasping the for-itself of subjectivity. A famous anecdote related by a former student of Fichte eloquently illustrates the natural incapacity of the mind to perceive the insubstantial nil-condition of the subject. "'Concentrate,' said Fichte to his students, 'go within yourselves; nothing external matters here, but only yourselves.' The audience was thus urged to go into themselves. Some changed posture and stood up; others withdrew and closed their eyes. Fichte continued: 'Think of the wall.' The audience thought of the wall and this seemed like a great success to everyone. 'Have you thought the wall?' asked Fichte. 'Then think the one who is thinking the wall.' It was very curious to see the trouble and confusion this injunction seemed to create."[4]

The innate incapacity to apprehend and consequently to describe subjectivity constitutes an important lesson for our investigation. It is not enough to be content to repeat that the self is nothing, to reiterate the affirmation that it possesses no content of its own. Instead another way to conceive it must be found than by eidetic description sensu stricto. If the self is not one eidos among others, how is it possible to read it as a quality, content or essence? The self accompanies all of its content; it is wed to them; it even is them. Instead of asking what it is, of trying to give a definition of its *what*, it would be better to ask about the proper way that it is its contents. In other words, to ask: *how* is it its contents?

We have always had an acute awareness of the difficulty of conceiving the self: "My selfe the hardest object of the sight," exclaimed the poet.[5] One then makes recourse to various subterfuges of the imagination, reveling in the invocation of the

---

4. *Fichte im Gespräch* (Stuttgart-Bad Constatt: Fromann, 1992), 17.
5. Donne, *The Poems*, ed. H. Grierson, I. 272, in Ellrodt, *Les poètes métaphysiques anglais* I, 103n20.

interiority where intuition, the feeling of depths, the hidden and protected private realm deteriorates into realist metaphors of vast spaces at the heart of the self, interior places, abysses functioning like receptacles. One takes inspiration from the high mental-spiritual faculty of the attention in order to show the condition of pure reduction in which every half-light, every vague potentiality disappears and the mind is no longer anything but active attention, undivided intentionality. But in each of these cases, the elementary metaphysical truth of the sui generis condition of subjectivity irreducible to any given content is transgressed. The monist temptations of every human culture, their profound inner tendency to engulf themselves in animist, pantheist, and ecological continuities, find their secret but wholly faithful transcription in the inclination of philosophers to include subjectivity in one way or another in the universe of virtual and actual contents, to subsume the correlate of all contents under the contents' eidetic regime. But these multiple examples of a pluriform dogmatism, these diverse occurrences of a feigned or sloppy reduction fail their purpose. They offer a range of material variations on the metaphysical specificity of the subject while the *how* of its being that is sought lies in the formal order.

The sense of dejection and frustration before the failure of these attempts at eidetic description were very predictable: subjectivity simply does not submit to eidetic description sensu stricto. To understand the *how*, the psychological path is attempted, articulating the subject in terms of strong or weak, acute or subdued, continuous or intermittent, etc., up to the point of reaching the last resort: to recall the invincible feeling, the *evidence* that the subject acts and exists and that it does so in a specific way. To spare ourselves from these rear-guard battles, which are played out well short of the reduction, we are left refusing to consider essence at all and to consider the subject more straightforwardly. The subject is for itself, returns to itself, and is conscious of itself: in other words its being is split in two. But this doubled existence should not be conceived in terms of primitive arithmetic. It designates the accession of a second [*deuxième*] but in the sense of *second* [*second*].

The *second*-second is a sui generis phenomenological essence: not being a numeral in the etymological sense, it is preferred to the *deuxième*-second when the idea of repetition takes precedence over that of rank and when what occurs is not a simple reflection of the first but registers a distinctive sense. The *second*-second is like the new form of a unique thing: at death we are closed in a casket but this first disappearance from the world of the living is followed by a "rapid forgetting, the second death shroud."[6] People often speak of a second nature, a second youth, or a second innocence. In reality the *second*-second does not mean only a particular manner of repetition but a quasi-unique reiteration which is not and even cannot be followed by another. *Second*-second replaces *deuxième*-second when only two objects or entities are under consideration: it is always a *deuxième*-second but also always a unique one. The uniqueness of the *second*-second presents itself as the theme of *my* second. My

---

6. Lamartine, *Harmonie: Le premier regret*.

second supports me [*mon second me second*] and to "support" [*seconder*] involves a mysterious fecundity. At first glance it means to help, to assist and therefore to complete my action, and the leap will easily be made from there to the notion of a kind of repair. But the eidetic vocation of a second is not to fill in the gaps or dot every "i." The spatio-temporal imagery that makes the *second* the successor to the first, a *deuxième*-second following a first, manifests only an incomplete diffraction of the self-splitting which, despite every disparity or distance, conceals an authentic metaphysical correspondence. In its truth the second is neither behind nor beside the first but it *is* the first in its own way. Beyond its various acts of assistance to the first, the second can reach the point of replacing the first, but one entity is only able to replace another only if it corresponds to it in one way or another. The correspondence can take on the form of reflection or reproduction, and thus of conformity, but is still not reduced to the status of a trace or copy. The correspondence-conformity that reconciles difference with identity and the new event with repetition is the proper mode of being, the *how* of this nothing that is the subject.

Distantiation of the Ectype

The subject succeeds the object, it repeats [*redit*] it, but the mystery of subjectivity that is this *re*-telling [re-*dire*] is above all an original saying [*dire*]. The subject recalls the world, loyally puts itself in its train, but this loyalty that endures every trial is not a blind obedience or servile repetition. Subjectivity molds itself to the contours of being without clinging to its internal structurings and edges. The designation of the subject as nothing translates the perplexity of the mind before a phenomenon detached from the in-itself, by problematizing the primitive simplicity, and claims to invoke it in its integrity, all the while transposing it into another metaphysical register. Self-consciousness is the faithful correlate to its contents but it is through a *creative* fidelity that it is related to them. But the self's creative fidelity is evidently not of the psychological or moral orders. To the degree that it designates the appearance of something other in view of its contents—and therefore the event of the new in relation to the given—it discloses a level or rather an entire regime of being different from that of the given, from the in-itself, from primary being if you like. Before primary being, after or rather *according to* it, there is the second being of the *image*.

The image is the veritable spoilsport of classical philosophy. Ignored, or rather, obscured in Elea, the *eikon* appears in Athens and ever since it has ceaselessly confused the philosophical order, undermining certainties, relativizing absolutes, endangering promises. The image claims to be a reflection of its archetype, but the rectitude of a reflection does not signify the exactness of a copy. The image has—or rather is—a high aspiration to re-present being, yet the appearance it provides eloquently illustrates the formidable difficulties harbored by the aporias of the *Sophist*. The multiple disparities registered by the image in relation to its original provoke ontological explications in terms of a contamination of Being by non-Being when the interpretation of this undulating and ambiguous reality should be sought through metaphysical analysis of the mysterious syntheses of Same and Other.

Consideration of the mode of being of the image probably should not presuppose a hermetic separation between these two great philosophical visions: links exist between intuition of nothing or of the lesser, on the one hand, and of what is otherwise and deviant or false on the other hand—above all when it is a matter of readings in which the native alterity of the image is delineated in a negative register. The elementary vision of the image is inspired by a naïve realism. The image is very far from the powerful massiveness of the rock and of the inflexible resistance of steel. It has neither weight nor layer nor depth. It is what it is on the surface; in fact it is all surface. It is common to call the image a "mirror" in order to suggest its ontological indigence and inconsistency and it is often noted with compassion or disappointment how the image is "pale" and "weak." The everyday conception is that the image is a vitiated mental repetition of an effective, vigorous sensation, something from the outside deprived of all living spontaneity, a kind of impoverished aftertaste. Ultimately the image is conceived as the echo of its archetype; an echo can only enfeeble, diminish and disperse the original sound. And philosophy's task here is to serve everyday life by transposing these impressions into concepts: it attributes a "remainder of being" or "diminished being" to the image.[7] The image is "in" space and the primitive realism of this spatial vision is reinforced by the interpretation of the *eikon* as phenomenon of surface in order to push it into the condition of superficiality which, taken literally, would amount to stripping it down and depriving it of all reality. The image is on the surface or better, is only surface, but even this condition of being all surface withers away and dies with alarming speed. In order to be able to identify this, so to speak, reality in free fall, more and more precisely and completely, three-dimensional plans will be drawn: the image surface is indefinitely thinned down in order then to be dissolved into an extension without any density. An infinitely fine skin, the image becomes a reflection deprived of being that philosophical abstraction completely finishes off by portraying it as a non-being.

This non-being translates a quantitative-ontological conception but the metaphysical truth of the non-being proper to the image is that the image is not itself: its being or essence consists in being related to another that it reflects. Consciousness can be defined in terms of intentionality, as reference to an object; the image as such seems to consist only in this reference. It is only to the degree that it references another, its archetype; its being is even reduced to this reference, which exhausts it. If it exists, it exists only in the act of referring to this other that it is not. This condition of being-other than itself is reinforced, exacerbated to the point of paroxysm. The archetype can become absent or even cease to exist. Yet the foundational relation with the original that has disappeared continues to constitute the very being of the

---

7. Averroës, *In Metaphysic*. VI. com. 2.

image! It is tempting to celebrate or praise the image's fidelity even to its death but this metaphysical nostalgia retains a deep ambiguity. When the original falls into the yawning abyss of non-being, the ectype persists; it attempts to continue on, to keep a foothold, to save its place, to play its role. But the disappearance of the archetype makes questionable to a certain degree the rectitude of the imitation. The image can no longer recharge itself by plugging into the original, it is returned to itself, to its own internal resources. From now on incapable of receiving, of internalizing the nourishing warmth of its other, it is forced to draw on its own depths. Yet the displacement and effacement of the original is not the unique cause of the disparities in imitation, resulting from the inadequacy of the image to the original. The likely accidental but inevitable disappearance of the archetype is only an indication—certainly spectacular but not exceptional or unique—of the metaphysical situation marking the origin of the deviations of the image. The shift in meaning of the archetype, being reflected towards an indeterminate *sheol*, towards the opening expanse of an abyss, draws media-like attention to the development of philosophical thought starting from the least being, from non-being towards a being-otherwise, towards deviation, falsity. If the image has been understood as a "diminished" mode of being, it is especially in the sense of a decrease in conformity, but the completely quantitative intuition of the decrease has its metaphysical truth hidden in the alterity. In other words: to explain the native deficiency of the *eikon*, the category of weakness must be set aside and that of the deviant, the fake, must be picked up.

All the while protesting its vocation to fidelity, exactness, and rectitude, the image by its nature aspires to imitate its original but is condemned only to realize its promises imperfectly. The ectype is separated from the archetype by an ontological abyss that the imagination is inclined to represent under the guise of a simple distance internal to the same world: this would explain the acute weakness of the reproduction, the loss of accuracy inevitable in every attempt to make a copy. Yet with the support of spatial intuition, the homogeneity of the distance is based on the elementary but very real heterogeneity of disparity. The image is not only separated from its original by the no man's land of a calculable distance, it finds itself isolated through a distance that attracts it. In other words the image is not a pale reflection of the original. It is not only condemned to inaccuracy, but fatally suffers from the deviation.

Philosophical reflection on the image was born in the thematic context of imitation, which is often a shady operation, even, frankly, an immoral enterprise. It produces hollow phantoms and deceptive illusions out of things that themselves are not dangerous or treacherous simulacra. The native vocation of imitation is to make instructive and useful similitudes, but this honest, labor-intensive activity is on the lookout for and perpetually menaced by a deterioration into harmful chicanery. Instead of imitating the archetype and exemplar with humility and abnegation, it is mimicked in the form of a double counterfeit. For classical philosophy and the culture it inspired—an inspiration never absent from thought—the innate tendency of every imitation, the hidden horizon of every image, is at best deviation, at worst falsity.

The inevitable disparity between the image and its object, between the ectype and its archetype will make it appear most often and most spectacularly in a negative light. However if the disparity is especially the origin of inadequacy, malformation and counter verities, it can also lead to something positive. The ectype is not condemned only to diminish and deform; it equally disposes of authentic possibilities of enrichment. It can highlight the original in unexpected ways or strikingly emphasize one or more of its traits and aspects. Because of the perspective from which it arises, the disparity allows what is contemptible or shameful to be covered with a modest veil. The vocation of the *eikon* is to focus on the riches of the being whose structure, color and contours it reproduces. The image can therefore become a brilliant expression of the original, making us forget the clumsiness, blemishes and the grey areas. It can also seem to iron over the wrinkles, fix the imperfections and reduce the inequalities.

The vigorous and powerful images as found in great works of art have, so to say, the capacity to step across the gap between archetype and ectype. "A firm and sharp thought," wrote Sainte-Beuve, "necessarily carries its expression along with it. Unaffected souls. . .have just the right word and often the only word."[8] A tacit presupposition of languages and cultures is that idea and expression are situated over a fatal gap, that there is an abyss that separates them; only the works of the greatest artists make a lucky exception to this natural inadequacy. But the virtue of the image is not exhausted through expressing or making appear the being of the other to which it refers. It does have a kind of ascetic vocation of effacing itself before the manifestation of the archetype, but this vocation can take many different forms. The image has a preparatory role in description as well as definition. It certainly "cannot be the idea but it can. . .cohabitate with the idea in the sign; and if the idea is not yet present it respects its future place and make its contours appear in the negative."[9] It can equally announce future realities. Like those *figurae Christi*, the events and persons of sacred history preparing the advent of Christ, some images prefigure ideas, contributing to their effective coming. The image can play a quasi-prophetic role in relation to the reality it foreshadows, but the accomplishments for which it prepares and serves as a vehicle are not unveilings that destroy mysteries, but rather revelations that do them proper justice. The gap to which the image gives birth and by virtue of which it subsists, recalls the "moral" obligation inscribed within it to ensure that the founding distance remains. The aspiration to express solitude would never be able to invert the metaphysical asymmetry that constitutes it. An image is always like its archetype whereas the archetype is never like its image. It is an essential teaching of theology that creatures resemble God. But another, and just as essential, teaching is that God does not resemble them. The idol appropriates all the light of the archetype in order to

---

8. Sainte-Beuve, *Causeries de lundi*, 17-12-1849. *Oeuvres* (Paris: Garnier I), 179.

9. Lévi-Strauss, *La pensée sauvage*, 30.

focus it on itself; the *eikon* expresses and manifests another beyond itself, but without ever capturing and confiscating that which it represents.

The Autonomy of the Image

The image reproduces its original in greater or lesser ways. It can express it only in an effaced, deficient and truncated manner. It can equally put it under a magnifying lens, providing it with the means of becoming visible, of becoming brilliantly evident. If the image's presentation makes the archetype run the risk of seeing its truth deformed or obscured, it also carries the possibility and hope of a more and more adequate representation. However, whether the re-production and re-iteration is precise or imprecise, approximate or adequate, unsuccessful or successful, the condition of the image remains that of a reflection of an original, in short, one of dependence in relation to another. A dependence that not only expresses a necessary relation to its partner but also signifies the lack of its own metaphysical status. The image is supposed to be only a reflection, but the resources of the reflection are found outside of it in the being that it reflects. The notion of the *nothing* of the subject conveys the impasse of explication, or rather, radicalizes and formalizes the data. If the subject—and thus the image that shares its condition—is nothing, this should not be taken in the sense of a privation or an actual void. The image is nothing in the sense of the nothing of the condition of being. Yet instead of shutting down the analysis, the designation of the subject and the image as nothing dramatizes the interrogation. The image is nothing but this nothing is not of the same eidetic family as weakness, dimness or even as the mirage or inconsistency. In a way one could very well say that metaphysics is born with the idea of the image. To conceive the image leads us to presuppose something beyond it; to understand a reality like the image implies the acknowledgment of another reality, which is more than the image. Hence the arrival of the principal dualism of metaphysics, the vision of the two worlds, that of the image and the original, of appearance and being. The being is primary and archetypal, the image is secondary and it is subordinate according to both essence and existence. The image repeats its original according to being but in a diminished, diluted way. It similarly repeats its essence but with deficiencies, abridgments, and confusion. This conception or "doctrine" is as old as the world and it continues to enjoy the favors of everyday language, but this quasi-consensus of the commonplace concerning the hierarchical relation of archetype to ectype remains cruelly deficient, unfounded to the mind of the philosopher. The image is other than being, but in order to be truly other, it must fall under another metaphysical register. Its multiple insufficiencies can recall this alterity but they do not yet count as examples or instances of it. If the image is less than the archetype or deviates from it, it always constitutes its avatar. But metaphysical investigation cannot simply be content to rubber stamp the subsumption of the ectype under the archetype: it aims at nothing less than the affirmation and demonstration of its authentic originality.

The Image

The question of the condition of the image receives its conceptual formulation in the dialogues of Plato, but this manner of thinking is parceled out between the oh-so natural thesis of the dependence of the ectype on the archetype and the disconcerting intuition, the difficult discernment of its metaphysical autonomy. It is obvious that the image should reproduce the traits of its original: if it did not would it still be an image? But still, should it reflect all of its traits? This is unrealizable, both *de facto* and—what is most important—*de jure*. Absolute precision in reproduction can never be reached, and if (impossibly) it was, then we would have not a perfect image of the original but the arrival of another original, the double (*Cratylus* 431 b-432d). To escape this impasse Plato thinks he can and should point out the limits of reproduction. The production of images is an exercise of imitation but "mimetic art touches only a small part of things" (*Republic* 598b). We recognize as an image of a thing only what represents its colors and form but this presentation can only be incomplete. The image does not yet cease to be one if it lacks an element of the original; well to the contrary it cannot and should not contain all its traits (*Cratylus* 432c-e).

This theory is suggestive and even seductive. It seems to conform to good sense and is founded on the genre of the equitable compromise, which should be able to reconcile opposed conceptual exigencies. Unfortunately it is destined to remain unsuccessful because the solution it envisages is unsound and inadequate. One thinks he can do justice to the image's vague desire for independence by liberating it from the necessity of an integral conformity to the structure and elements of the original but the metaphysical autonomy of the image cannot be reduced to the condition of being emancipated from the obligation to display *all* the traits of the original. Incomplete, partial, and selective conformity to the archetype can impose itself as an empirical last resort, but it does not yet indicate an autonomous, sui generis metaphysical status for the image. The image certainly could be given the respite of less difficult conditions, a loosening of its obligations. But even so this reduction of material exigencies would in no way affect its persistent dependence on the archetype, its regulated and weakened but nevertheless continuous and effective belonging in the world of being. The image would always be a part of the web of beings while metaphysics requires the attribution of a proper status to it.

Plato himself clearly discerns the issue, and indicates, in a few hesitant but infinitely fecund words, prospects for the solution. Resemblance does not really exist, but it nevertheless has some form of existence. It really is not except that it really is an image (*Sophist* 240 b). The image is in other words not a *being* although it is an *image*. In the ontological context it is nothing, nothing of a being, but it registers an undeniable reality for the *eikon*. The image is therefore different than being, but this difference does not only designate a negation: it transcribes also an affirmation. One should certainly remember that the image *is not* being, but it is equally necessary to spell out and unfold the proper reality to which the negation leads us. Not to be being is evidently a foundational attribute of the image, but this negation should not be emptied of its proper eidetic meaning and fall back again, powerless and empty, into ontological immanence. The image reflects being as that which it is not. But this secondariness of essence, this relationality of origin also connotes a sui generis pole of reality. The image is; the image is itself and it is; it is itself in not being being. This leads us to say that it is *otherwise* than being. It is otherwise in two clearly distinct but complementary ways: one according to existence, the other according to essence.

The other-being of the *eikon* according to existence is called "appearing," according to essence it is called, sensu stricto, "image." The demonstration or rather, showing-forth, of the metaphysical autonomy of the appearing was successfully completed by Kant and his successors, the phenomenologists from Husserl to Marion. Establishing the autonomy of the image according to essence, advocating for the image as image, still waits to be accomplished. The image has been overburdened by accusations of evanescence and infidelity. These should not be rejected but refuted by clarifying its metaphysical condition in which its vocation of resemblance is envisaged in light of its relationality. The image certainly does not have to reflect the same traits broadcasted by the archetype, reproducing all the elements constitutive of the original. Nevertheless, the autonomy of the transposition is conceived only starting from the relation that establishes and constitutes the reality of the ectype. The image falls within the universe of similitude but it bears more conceptual importance than resemblance, which is only the quiddative or eidetic dimensions of the image, belonging to it from the vantage of its contents. But if the image is truly a collection of elements, a configuration of traits, then it is not a content, a unidimensional reality locked in immanence and deprived of any transcendent referent. The image is not such because of the structural moments recognized as identical, similar or analogous to the structural moments of another entity, but because it registers a constitutive relation to another being. A very old and venerable "argument" says that there is nothing more like an egg than another egg: but can we say that one is the image of the other? But a son is the image of his father. He can resemble him less than one egg does another, but while the similarity of eggs only connotes their being occurrences of a kind, without a relation of belonging to one another, of dependence, briefly, without a connecting link between them, the son is son because of a foundational relation emanating from the father.[10]

Distinguishing in this way the image from resemblance allows us to safeguard the essential component of the *eikon*'s "reference," the condition sine qua non of the metaphysics of the image as image. This metaphysics has been drafted by a philosophy while its site of origin and eidetic locus is found in theology: the second philosophy of Fichte is considered a doctrine of the Image, but in Christian Trinitarian theology the Image gains access to its ontological plenitude. Here it is set apart as symbol and principle of a sui generis universe that is the object of a true *Secunda Philosophia*, the brilliant and autonomous counterpart to a Prima. Fichte is the philosopher of subjectivity, of the I designated as nothing, and the entire second period of his thought is only an

---

10. St. Thomas Aquinas, *Summa Theologiae* I 93 a. 1, concl. and ad 2.

immense effort, an unceasing attempt to revive the conceptual thinking of the Subject, the hypostasized ectype of an apophatic archetype that it seconds but from which it remains separated as far as the heavens from earth. The ectype is named Appearance or Image and if the Image is truly the Other to a primordial Absolute, it is nevertheless not deducible from it. The philosopher insists that we do not need a descent of the Absolute to the Image but only a rising up from the Image to the Absolute.[11] The primary purpose of this prohibition seems to be to safeguard the transcendence of the First. In actuality what is in play here perhaps even more is the protection and defense of the autonomy of the Second. The Image corresponds to the Being, it is the reflection, the projection of its riches, but it is a projection or fulguration "per hiatum." As the Being of the Image is not caused by the Absolute, its eidetic contents cannot be deduced from It. The Image is, it subsists, but we do not have to find the time or place of its birth. It is knowledge and wholly knowledge: said differently, it is the Image and every attempt to discover an explanation for its advent is destined to fail. There definitely exists a succession, a series of images where the Image is broken up into smaller equivalents, but which still does not constitute a *historia*, even a conceptual one. Images describe, if you like, they confirm the articulation of the Image, but they do not accompany its eidetic progression.

The late Doctrine of Science, Fichte's second philosophy, claims to be a conceptual meditation on the Mystery of the Logos, the Word of God. The Image-Appearance is the Logos event, the Word that reveals and displays itself. But if the doctrine of the sovereign autonomy of the Appearance represents a grand apology for the originary reality of the second, it does not yet constitute a justification, a metaphysical legitimation for its vocation and condition as image. The Image is not constructed in layers starting from Being; it comes forth so to speak as a *deus ex machina*, rising up like Pallas Athena in full armor. The Image constitutes a sui generis metaphysical universe, autonomous before the world of being, creating a duality that dramatizes the Fichtean terminology that opposes *Bildsein* to *seinsein*, image-being to being-being.[12] The extraordinary Fichtean idea is an original and unprecedented attempt to conceive a metaphysics of the Image as such. It develops and unfolds without any concession the intuition of a perfect symmetry between the First and the Second. It refuses any implication and deduction—any genealogy—that could compromise the autonomy of the ectype. Nevertheless, it constructs this autonomy in a negative and merely defensive way. The Image is autonomous, constituting an integral world, a universe sufficient to itself, but it is neither integral nor self-sufficient as image despite being only image. The Appearance is the authentic other to Being even if it is only appearance; the ectype has its sui generis truth, like the archetype, despite its ectypal condition. But to conceive the Image in its truth, in the plenitude of its metaphysical autonomy, a positive approach must be adopted. The Image constitutes a metaphysical autonomous world

---

11. For all that follows, see Vető, *Nouvelles études sur l'idéalisme allemand*, 79–94.

12. Fichte, *Wissenschaftslehre 1813, Gesamtausgabe*, II 15, p. 149.

precisely as image, it is not the symmetrical partner to being despite its condition as image. *This* primordial intuition is not that of the Doctrine of Science: it emerges from the speculation of theological reflection on the ecclesial teaching that expounds the dogma of the divine Trinity.

Theology has constructed the dogma of the Trinity starting from discussions on the Word that reflects and expresses the Father—a theologoumenon of extremely significant philosophical import. The Word of God is not only the expression of a person but is the supreme instance of *expressio*: it is equal with the Father and "all equality has its exemplar in the equality of the Son";[13] it resembles the Father and by this fact it constitutes "absolute resemblance."[14] These variations on the foundational intuition, the primordial conception of the Word as ectype of the Father, wish to translate the supreme mystery of the Second Person. Dogma professes that the three divine persons are equal in divinity, each person being "as much" God as the others. The first divine person is the Father, the second is the Son, who is his exact representation, his Image (Heb 1:3). But the Son not only exercises the "function" of reflection, of reproducing the Father; on the contrary, being his image constitutes his very being. In other words this Person is, in what is his own, the image, the perfect image of another. Thus the intimate essence of this entity is referred to another. Yet—and this matters above all—what seems to be an ontological *ascesis* of faithful adequation to the other, the first, is revealed precisely as the nature, the specific, originary, sui generis essence of the second. The Son is divine Person as image; his own divinity consists in this image-being. Theological speculation leads to the establishment of a supreme paradigm of the image. The Image is from now on conceived as the figure of an autonomous metaphysical universe. If entities, beings, are so many instances of Being, images are the same for the Image.

The Artistic Image

The metaphysical autonomy of the image was conceived out of theological considerations; its place of birth is the image-being that is the Second Person of the Trinity. But this high dogmatic speculation reached its conceptual completion during the iconoclastic crisis and bears essential import for the veneration of icons. The Byzantine iconoclasts who sought to restrict the role of images in worship stem from the theological posterity of Arius, denier of the divinity of the Son. Yet the veneration of icons is recommended and justified by the doctrinal position of orthodoxy, anxious to defend the absolute equality of Son and Father, thus of the Image and Archetype.[15] This means that if the deduction of metaphysical originarity of the image is accomplished in a theologico-ontological discourse, it has an immediate impact on the artistic *icon*,

---

13. St. Bonaventure, *Sent.* 1, 31, pars 2, art. 2, 3 ad. 7.
14. Raoul Ardent, *Speculum universale* VII, 14 in *Dictionnaire de Spiritualité* VII, 2 col. 1426.
15. Schönborn, *L'icône du Christ*, 30.

the pictorial image. The metaphysical theme of the image, the image, so to speak, "in general," has appeared in the context of the Platonic discussion of the limits and exigencies of artistic action, starting from the interrogation on that imitation in which artistic creation supposedly consists. After the crucial digression on the theological reformulation, it returns, explicitly and definitively, to be deployed in the problematic of the image, whether pictorial, sculptural, literary, or musical.

The image is a doubling and it is comprehended starting from that originary doubling that is subjectivity. The subjectivity that doubles the world adds nothing to it—or rather, it is added to the world as a nothing, and the image that is the consequence or production of this nothing reveals its dimensions and hidden potentialities. It is born under the sign of flawless conformity but it will realize its vocation to fidelity only by being unfolded in dissimilarity. The subject believes it can and should stick to the contours of the given, explore its expression, mold itself to its structures, but the limitations and ambiguities of such a "program" quickly appear. The subject is the given's other but it is such only quasi-naturally, like one given thing among others, a superior given, but a given nonetheless. The truth of the subject is surely found in its extraction from the given, but the subject is ignorant of its truth, or rather, it is conscious of it only in an implicit and inarticulate way. The founding separation that is the very being of the subject constitutes it as the image of a given, but the subject will accomplish or realize the metaphysical meaning proper to its image-being only by surpassing its condition as a faithful copy and servile double in the direction of an autonomous secondarity. The images secreted by theoretical intelligence are only so many occurrences at uniform distances in which the subject exchanges itself and continues on as it represents nothing new relative to the given. For the supreme truth of its alterity and originarity to appear, it must freely produce images at will—images that illustrate and intensify its fecund secondarity.

Mental images, the contents of consciousness are situated within the subject; these do not represent a truly new given. From the point of view of existence, they are only simple continuations of this double that lives in and through them. Regarding essence, their condition is apparently—but only apparently—different. All that is perceived is dependent on realities, given entities of which it is supposed to be—and only be—the double. Doubtlessly, the perceived image can "lack" its original, reproducing its contours and structures only in a deficient way. Indeed—and this is even more important—the perceived image can be understood as a particular interpretive framework that filters the "objective" components from the archetype. In other words, perception follows the articulation of the given, but it follows it in its own way, according to the constraints and distortions proper to it itself. In the two cases the ectype certainly suffers a gap in relation to the archetype, but this gap is regular or constant: in and through it the ectype remains in direct dependence on the reality that it filters; it continues to fall within the world that it is supposed to reproduce. Things begin to get foggy however, as soon as we "climb" from perception to imagination. Imagination produces images that seem to represent the new, but if, crudely, the imagination is tantamount to an overflowing fantasy, if it seems like a power for generating the novel, for eliciting the incredible, briefly, for producing the new, the philosopher will not fail to call it back to order. By obstinately returning fantasy back to the outer court of the given, it dispels its illusions and shatters its dreams. Imagination believes itself to be the mistress of the unexpected, it strives to promise the unpredictable; in reality its fireworks prove to be only simple variations on perception. Even in fantasy or hallucinations, one is always only drawing from the given. The rich exuberance of fantasy is admirable, and yet that is not a sign of an authentic fecundity. If the imagination appears to trade in novelties, its activity is only one of discovery, never creation.

The highest and most brilliant instance of the image is the artistic image: the image seems to gain access to its truth in literature, painting, and sculpture. The work of art does not stay confined in the psychologism of the subject, it detaches itself from it or rather, it rises up victoriously, adding itself to the given, even taking a position over against it. Yet for millennia the proper activity of art was never designated as imagination but *imitation*. The artist strives to imitate his model and his public thinks it can and should judge and appreciate him in proportion to the success of his efforts: critics celebrate the greatness of the novelist whose characters seem to be true flesh and bone, men and women who surround us and walk among us; they bang on about the merits of the sculptor who is able to reproduce in rock or bronze the most minute details of the human body. And we all know the anecdote of Zeuxis who painted grapes with such fidelity that the pigeons took them for "real" grapes and landed on them in order to eat them. The entire millenary history of naturalist duplication seems to have reached its telos in the Barbizon School whose paintings brought the art of imitation to its apogee. The texture of the trunk and branches of the tree, the color of its leaves, the misty shades of the atmosphere that bathes the vegetation are all reproduced with consummate artistry. But a peasant of Beauce addressed the truly fatal question to one of the great masters of Barbizon, Théodore Rousseau, painting a tree in great detail: "Why are you painting this oak since it is already there?"[16]

Naturalist imitation obeys a logic that, pushed to its extreme, results in the pure and simple doubling of the model. But the secondarity that is the image's ideal is not capable of inspiring copies or traces; the process that causes an ectype to appear is not cloning. Reflection on art wants to avoid the term "imagination," overloaded with impurities, evocative of the arbitrary, the impermanent or the deranged. Thus it chooses imitation. But despite appearances, *mimesis* is not a univocal notion. From the beginning in Plato, reflection admits that even mimesis claims a selective conformity. The image should certainly reproduce the object, and correspond to its structures, but with a correspondence that concerns only a small aspect of its characteristics. However, it is not only a matter of quantitative limits of fidelity. Already Aristotle, although considered the master of naturalist aesthetics, ends by subverting the simplistic credo

---

16. Gilson, *Peinture et réalité*, 226.

of conformity of image to object. The Philosopher considers music the most imitative art: yet music tends the least to duplicate an existing reality. And none other than Aristotle has left us the famous line where the original ambiguity of *mimesis* clearly stands out: "It is less of an error not to know that the doe has no horns than to paint an unrecognizable picture" (*Poetics* 1460b). A factual error is not yet a "bad" imitation. Agreed. Then what makes it bad or good?

For millennia the schools and manuals of art did their best to furnish a response by dispensing principles and formulae of "good imitation," although this response is not situated on the technical plane. More precisely, instead of explaining how the image manages to correspond to the original, another question should be posed: that of the foundational relation to the archetype that presides over the occurrence of the ectype. The ontological condition of the image is that of secondarity, but in art, the secondarity of the image contains a gap, even a dissimilitude. From its distant origins in the Magdalenian period, art has been obsessed with fidelity and adequation to the real, nevertheless from the beginning it has lacked basic requirements for naturalist conformity. And this lack is not a result of weakness or powerlessness, but rather by virtue of positive metaphysical imperatives. It goes without saying that artistic creation involves an essential dose of technical dexterity and artistic accomplishment, but just as modern painting is not a vast conspiracy of people who do not know how to draw, so also the arts of great ancient or medieval civilizations are not the poor stammerings of humanity's infancy. From the cave paintings of Lascaux and Altamira to the canvases of Miro or Klee, expertise, technical virtuosity, have never been absent from painting, but instead have been placed in service to ends that transcend them.

D'Alembert thought he could proclaim that music unrelated to an object is only noise, but the desire to trace copies, and even the aspiration toward *ancilla naturae*, has never been able to account for the true genesis of the work of art. There is an incantatory rhetoric that has always chanted the glories of strict conformity to nature, but some great, though more or less isolated, voices have managed to raise themselves above the din in order to remind us of the essential metaphysical difference between the beings of nature and works of art. Goya was so bold to say that "the artist is able to remove himself entirely from nature,"[17] while Baudelaire spoke of the "simple and luminous language of art." And twentieth-century artists would resolutely take the side of breaking links with nature to the point of brutally declaring: "Nature is one thing, painting another."[18] Modern art wants to cut the umbilical cord that attaches the artwork to some correlate and it will end by demanding a radical autonomy in relation to any tutelary archetype in order, at least, to bracket external referents, if not to realize a total emancipation.

17. Charpier and Seghers, *L'art de la peinture*, 314.
18. Bissière, *T'en fais pas la Marie*, 113.

From Dissimilarity to Auto-figuration

The ambiguous logic of the artistic image translates a mysterious synthesis of the same and other: the image is as much itself as something other than itself. This means that the image cannot be image without returning to another than itself. The metaphysical condition of the image implies this return; nevertheless the movement described by the synthesis that constitutes it inclines to break with the correlate, therefore to a kind of flattening or self-imprisonment. The artistic image is supposed to be the faithful double of the archetype, but the balance bends in the direction of an ever more problematic fidelity, ultimately breaking with the very idea of resemblance altogether. The native difference between the image and the model is "first of all" observed and then—consciously or unconsciously—rules of fidelity are sought at the very heart of the dissimilarity. The painter asks himself how intervals between colors may directly indicate the contours of solid objects. The poet seeks to express the force and tenor of emotions through rhythm and rhyme. And yet, not denying the essential correspondences between the moments of the image and the elements of the model, the attempts to establish rules remains extremely aleatory. In painting and sculpture of course one seems to be able to proceed to a work of analysis starting with natural forms: the work of art is only able to be an extract, review, or digest of colors and given forms. But this conception quickly reaches its limits. In architecture, that wonder of the structuration of space, there is hardly any relation between the work and its signified; in music there is nothing else but a kind of affinity, an indeterminate sympathy in relation to its contents. The difference between the arts, that appear to exercise their essence through naturalist predispositions, and the others that come to light under a regime of heteronomy evident by their relation to a model or to no given content at all, does not in actuality reach the essential. According to a sonnet of Michelangelo, the sculptor thinks all he is doing is liberating the figure sleeping in the marble. In fact his activity is one in which the apparent preexistence of the image in the world interferes in no way with its naturalist transposition by the artist. The picture portrays its subject from the starting point of what is given, but its truth as image has nothing to do with the submissive reproduction of a model. The hundreds of Sienese Trecento Madonnas obediently follow the iconographic rules of their time and place, but within this multiplicity of doublets and synonyms the differences between the mediocre pieces of anonymous painters and the magnificent Virgins of Duccio clearly jump out. One "observes" with amazement the wide gap that separates the masterpiece from the laborious work, and would really love to "explain" it. But if there is an explanation it does not derive from material considerations that want to confirm and measure degrees of conformity.

Modern painting requires us to accept a truth of the canvas that is not like that of the universe of things. All art contains a native component of unlikeness in relation to the model, a relation that is only mediate, indirect to its correlate. There seems to be no discernible derivation of the work of art from its sources in the world, just as Paul Klee remarked that we do not require the tree to form its branches on the model of its roots, so why think that the painting should reproduce the objects that surround the artist? Ever since Schelling especially, aesthetics allows, even demands a certain discontinuity between the model and the work, the signified and the signifier; it protects itself from taking symbols for allegories. The work of art is a signifier without a clearly discernible referent. Or even: it is a phenomenon only indirectly expressing its noumenon. Artistic creation would certainly be able to take place without the existence of a correlate, some "external" reality. Yet the correlate is less a model to be reflected than a springboard that allows a takeoff, a ladder that once used is discarded, leaving no trace on the quiddity of the artwork. Renoir starts to paint on the seashore but his nudes have nothing to do with aquatic immensity and the teachings in the works of geology Cézanne studied before touching brush to canvas leave no visible imprint on his *Montagne Sainte Victoire*. In the last analysis one can say that in the realm of art resonance takes an even formal precedence over causality (Valéry). The language of the poet certainly does not represent an empty exercise of ideas devoid of meaning. Poetic speech is not without relation to thought, but it is a very unique relation: words are "haunted" by thought, "like the tides by the moon."[19] The artistic image is not a windowless monad, it reflects its correlate, but only as a mere echo.

There is a quasi-consensus out there that believes that for want of doubling or imitating entities, artworks *express* ideas, values, emotions, or even that the artist creates in order to express himself. But connoisseurs and above all the exasperated artists reject this hypothesis and frequently take refuge in paradoxes. Madame de Staël said: "Those who do not love painting in itself very much attach a great importance to the subject of the piece."[20] A half-century later, Flaubert contends that if he writes novels it is because he has nothing to say. And with her typical radicalism Simone Weil drives it all home: "Some churches express piety: these are ugly churches. But a beautiful cathedral expresses nothing."[21] The violent refusal of expression, the angry denunciation of any message or idea, of any teaching that the artwork is supposed to telegraph or advertise, will be translated positively into the demand for radical autonomy, in other words, in the auto-figurativity of the work. The paradoxical thesis of no content, of the non-signification of the artwork will be replaced by the affirmation of its sovereign independence where the metaphysics of the Image is realized. The work truly has content, it bears a message, but it neither announces nor expresses that itself.

The admission of indirect correspondence, of deep heterogeneity and therefore of dissimiliarity, gives way to focus on the signifier: in other words, we are witness here to an extraordinary instance of the phenomenological reduction. The Romantic myth of inspiration and the Kantian concept of the genius are only variations of this

---

19. Merleau-Ponty, *Signes*, 71.
20. Mme de Staël, *De l'Allemagne* II, 32. (Paris: Firmin-Didot), 378.
21. Weil, *De la perception ou l'aventure de Protée*, in *Oeuvres complètes* I, 138.

huge bracketing of every referent and correlate. If the artist is supposed to create without preparation or anticipation, this is because nothing should pre-exist the work, not even in the mind of the poet or composer at the origin of sonnet or symphony! This disappearance of every reference (which yet remains constitutive of the image as such) imposes itself as the keystone of the aesthetics of abstract art, but already an ancient, Roger de Piles felt he must observe: "painting is only accidentally historical."[22] Clearly the picture is never a mere pictogram of the essence. In fact, one could even state with only a hint of exaggeration that representation has nothing to do with art, that the Image in the various arts is a Second that can go without a First.

Already in classical aesthetics, the inherent beauty of natural entities is asserted without their being put on ice in order to be taken as presentations or expressions of something other than themselves. Gold or light has always been thought beautiful in itself, just as colors have been thought significant in themselves: did not Matisse create some of his most famous paintings by cutting them up into pieces of different colors? The painting doubtlessly keeps some links with the worldly given, notwithstanding the level of its distance from natural morphologies. This natural integration nevertheless yields to the exigencies of auto-figuration established by the work of art. Visitors to museums and readers of poems or stories quasi-instinctively understand the work in light of worldly entities, but the work is related to empirical things only on condition of being itself auto-figurative. The things of the world exist according to their own eidetic order, but a second eidetic, that of art, of the image, is found to be sponging off of it. Cézanne warned his admirers not to confound artistic objects with "real" objects. Braque insisted that the intentional object of pictorial action in a still life is not the velvet of peaches but the velvet of the painting itself. And someone remarked in the presence of Matisse that the women he painted did not look like "actual" women. He responded: I paint paintings, not women!

The words of the poet but also the novelist grow like vegetation; the lines and forms of painting launch, soar, unfold and are tangled together according to a sui generis logic. If classical aesthetics was thought capable of tracing the genesis of temples and palaces back to caves and primitive huts, the truth of those sublime works of frozen music like the Doric column or Gothic nave is not of the natural or utilitarian order. In its metaphysical essence art is a radical and continual distancing from nature: it puts together the image in a thousand ways and the image realizes itself to the depth and degree that it frees itself from the influence of the given. However, beyond every occurrence, every artistic manifestation, the confirmation of this movement of emancipation, the eidetic accomplishment of the auto-figuration finds its paradigm in the Image that is the Son of God, whose very being is to be an image. The Son is the ultimate redemption of the Image, a non-indigent, autonomous Second.

Secondarity is reached in its fullness only in the theological paradigm of the Son, but it ceaselessly haunts Art, being present in one way or another in all true art,

---

22. Piles, *Cours de peinture par principes*, 38.

even when it imagines itself falling under the jurisdiction of representation. Yet the elucidation of the metaphysical autonomy of the artistic image, the advent of an image that is only an image, will only take place in non-representational art. Like intentional objects without external referents, works of abstract art are missing any relation with a correlate. Non-representational art appears as the paradigm of eidetic phenomenology: it produces concrete eidē. Abstraction in art is like a victory over every *Hinterwelt*. Attempts to find the model, thereby going "beyond" the work are condemned, prohibited in the universe of the non-objective painting in which the pictorial form gives only itself to be seen. Not being the singular instance of a universal, the work is not a spokesperson for the essence, but rather its blazing appearance. Art is always a spectacle and the spectacle aspires to be taken for the reality or, at least, to make us forget it for a fleeting moment. All painting, and abstract painting in particular, is an activity of visibilization. The invisible suffers the most radical and most literal of reductions, which repulses it into the darkness when the visible rises up, imposes itself everywhere, occupies the interstices of the real and clogs up the horizon. With profundity Hegel taught that the finality, the metaphysical truth of art, is to display existence as true in its very appearance. In painting and poetry, and even more clearly so in music, the essence becomes inseparable from manifestation, even being absorbed into it without anything left over. To use a resolutely spatial language: in art everything is at the surface and if this is the case then the image as such is at the surface. Or rather: it is only surface. Now the surface certainly includes in its essence the intuition of a depth but the reduction that it perfects and incarnates is radical. The surface as spatial eidos is not a void without proper thickness but a three-dimensional reality in its own way. It is a figure of the Image and it allows us to understand the metaphysical meaning of the Image more fully. The Image is conceived with the background of an archetype, but an archetype from which it is fully emancipated.

II

Newness: Premises and Regressions

Renewing Newness

Man, a free and intelligent subject, seeks to express himself, and in being expressed, to express the new. The first instance of this novelty is the image, but this is a very relative novelty, full of reservations and conditions. Intelligence forms the image but only in relation to something else, an existing thing. Or, at the very least, the image conceived by the mind is mortgaged by a dependence in its very emergence. The truth is that its metaphysical condition is deeply ambiguous. The image displays a double reference or distance. It is distant from the thing to which it is supposed to refer, but it is also in a certain way different and distant from the subject that forms it. A minimum amount of autonomy should surely be afforded to it to the degree that it must be other than the reality in order to be its image. But this native requirement, foundational for representation and reproduction, means that this other-being is completely deprived of its own content, that it is in truth only a division into two that excludes by its very nature every possibility of constituting a ground, any attempt to aspire to a sui generis density. The paradox of the image is that in order to be it cannot possess anything of its own. And this being without having is, needless to say, a very meager condition. The image is evanescent. Banished from the three-dimensional world, it shimmers and floats along unstably, but above all it is confined in the interior space of the senses, imagination and memory.

The image manages to escape its confinement to the interiority of the mind through the fabrication of images, especially the work of art. Yet it continues to be ripped apart by contrary necessities: cut into wood, drawn on paper, or painted on canvas, it suffers an undebatable ontological independence, but which (it was thought for a long time) had to pay the high price of radical dependence, that is to say, imitation. Of course it is true that fidelity to the given even in the strictest naturalism is largely fictional. It always appears starting from a basic self-sufficiency. And with abstract art, the image completely cuts the umbilical cord that ties it to the archetype. The banal truth of its ontological independence, of its existence, numerically different from any physical or moral origin, is from now on in service to a metaphysical autonomy in relation to every given, to any external and anterior content. The image of art is no longer simply a "thing" as real and as subsistent as physical things, but it also rejects every reference to an external correlate, to an eidos other than its own. The work of art is a signifier of which the signified is well and truly itself. In and through it the image is liberated from its native servitudes and gains access to an integral autonomy. It constitutes a second world, with its own existence and its own essence. Having detached itself for good from its author, it represents the occurrence of the new, the birth of an authentic novelty.

Images effectively constitute a second world, a kingdom of the new. Yet this instituted and consolidated novelty can certainly be positioned opposite or rather on the fringes of the *already* given world. All the same, it is missing the essential condition of innovation. The image is established; it cannot establish itself. It is created; it is deprived of the power of creation. Though called into existence through freedom, by virtue of its metaphysical status it is ignorant of freedom. The work of art is the result of an aspiration, a labor, an uprooting, but in and with it a brief adventure of creative freedom expires, stopping the work of innovation. It is born at the end of a dazzling self-surpassing, but in itself it will no longer have anything to do with any kind of surpassing. Prodigious fruit of the action of its author, it is henceforth detached, located at a distance from itself. The image of art is outside of the subject, the creator, as well as of the spectator; it is situated in the world, and if it enjoys a durability shared with the elements, it is, however, deprived of every connection with freedom.

In order to transcend a shackled, powerless novelty, assigned to the past—as is appropriate for the image, an external entity—one must turn within the self to rediscover there the creative power. It will be found on a level which is neither that of an independent existence nor that of a sui generis configuration. By contrast to the elitism of artistic production in which the new is given only to the *chosen few*,[1] an innovation exists of which everyone is capable and to which everyone is obligated: namely, the perpetual renewal of free moral action.

In opposition to the image that in one way or another suffers a difference, a distance in relation to the subject, freedom is *in* the subject—not, of course, like the seed within an apple or the traveler in a bus. The "in" does not signify a local or localizable interiority: it has no topological bearing but harbors a metaphysical meaning. Freedom denotes a sphere that is proper to me, that I do not share with other beings, even if they can matter to me. It includes my corporeity and exists in continuity with other freedoms. It is—or at least can be—constantly outside itself and its condition of being

---

1. [These words in italics are in English in the original. –WCH]

situated "in" the subject indicates only the core from which it emerges and rushes forth, from which its activity emanates and diffuses.

Freedom is the highest instance of novelty, of renewing newness. The novelty it establishes is less about the eidos than the existence, or, more precisely, it manifests itself in a how, an "otherwise" that includes existential and eidetic elements. Freedom expresses a profound yearning and power, a desire to change, therefore, into a different being. One wishes to exist *differently* than before. It is to want to surpass the modalities and forms, accents and preferences of our past and present existence; from now on one will exist and therefore feel and act *differently*. But this existing differently is not only the form of a reality numerically identical with what precedes it. The feeling and above all acting differently connotes a new sensation and a new action and therefore new realities other than those that heretofore subsisted. The novelty proper to free action, creative novelty, opens a metaphysically unforeseen dimension: something falling within the universe of the eidos possesses *eo ipso*, or rather, *is* by its essence a reality, an existent. Free action can evidence a continuity with what precedes it, but it no less represents a maximal separation or change, the upsurge of a moving act of creation. The acting *differently* becomes apparent through a reality, another entity. One lived until then in a condition of oppression, in blind submission, in a state of servile conformity. The separation, in other words, the awakening to autonomy, the adoption of a critical attitude, the refusal to continue to collaborate can be deployed only through an apparent continuity with the past; they are by nature groundbreaking moments, acts of rupture, and they are brought to completion by being translated into the actual appearance of a new reality.

The being-otherwise that arouses—or rather, *is*—moral decision is a new reality. The truth of its novelty lies in its moral condition. Only what falls under the jurisdiction of freedom has an authentic possibility for being-otherwise. But moral freedom should lead along a straight path the one situated between chance, accident and caprice, on the one hand, and necessity, determinism and destiny, on the other. In order to be "moral," action should involve a real possibility for being differently, but also a correspondence, a conformity to Sense. Kant called freedom an "inconceivable concept": how to think a reality the very definition of which is the capacity to be otherwise than it effectively is?[2] This is a reality in which the foundational truth is un-anticipatability, or rather, un-deducibility, but which should no less obey the strict exigencies of rationality. One should not be able to read the free act in the entrails of the given, to discern it at the heart of the present. Yet at the future moment of its appearance, it should impose itself with the full weight of metaphysical and moral evidence. The metaphysical problematic of renewing newness is how to be otherwise than one is—not in the sense of a quantitative alteration or even an ordinary qualitative change. Neither is it a radical division, witness of a brutal facticity and dramatic

---

2. Kant, *Akademie Ausgabe* XXVIII, 1315. (*Akademie Ausgabe* will be cited hereafter as *Akad.* in the footnotes.)

vulnerability. It is not exhausted through the analysis of prodigious developments or spectacular metamorphoses, or in the dumbstruck contemplation of ruptures and fissures. True innovation finds its intention and purpose in paradoxes and contradictions that expose the limits of classical ontology and which cannot be "resolved" by dialectic. In the renewing newness of free action there is instituted an unforeseen and unforeseeable reality that is not implied by or contained in the being of the subject, but which should no less be understood in and through terms proper to the subject.

Becoming Less than Perfect:
The Withdrawal of God and the Descent of the Son

True novelty that re-news is commonly understood as a development, an enlargement and an addition. The new that appears is supposed to be added to what was already there. The advent of the new is doubtlessly able to imply and entail—and most often it actually does so—a loss or a reduction, but these local and partial losses and diminishments are understood as the price to pay for the enrichment. The diminution is only apparent; the loss proves to be finally like a transfer or rearrangement. The deaths that the birth of the new entails are only provisional and thus fictional; the life that passes through some "rough patches" comes through it unscathed and in fact even strengthened. But this economic logic of sacrifice, this pedagogical discipline of the enhancement of our way of living falls short of the proper exigencies of re-newal. True novelty only occurs at the price of ruptures: losses immediately compensated, debts converted into assets constitute only so many prudent investments to protect the old things. Addition and growth are not essentially opposed to re-newal but they are rather found beside the fruits of moral action, or more precisely, next to its ends, its correlates. In fact, the primitive moral intuition of humanity is rediscovered here: moral action, understood in the sense of good action that improves the lot of the other, rendering him service, offering him gifts. However, on the side of the agent, the subject, the new most often seems like an exhausting and painful effort, an expense and therefore a diminishment.

Eidetic—or rather, empirical—analyses of moral behavior insist on "division" and "deprivation" as essential ingredients of the virtuous act and behind the description of the behavior, the story of the action, one really rediscovers on the intentional plane decisions to restrict aspiration, slow down ambition, sacrifice projects—in other words, self-delimitation. But how to think the diminishment of which these moral acts are only so many instances and variations? A heroic effort or renunciation of a possession are certainly losses but they are not only one-off: these losses have a bearing on our physical, social and economic being. Do they not then have a bearing on our being as such? It is doubtlessly not necessary to confound being and having, but everyone knows that from a particular vantage point what affects having will also affect being. The loss of a precious object does not yet modify my economic situation, but if a stock market crash reduced to nothing the block of shares I own, my economic being is shaken or reduced. As the result of an accident I have to undergo surgery to remove a finger, but I have not yet become an invalid. But if it is my forearm that has to be amputated, I will henceforth be disabled. If, starting from a certain degree of loss a privation in having is transposed into a privation in being, it is only because ultimately having is rooted in being. In other words, the diminishment of my possessions inevitably translates into a diminishment in my being. But how can my being become less; how can it be diminished?

The question of the possibility of decline in general appears here, starting from the analysis of the eidetic descriptions of virtuous behavior. It is first related to one-off instances of loss leading to the interpretation of the impoverishment and deterioration produced by these instances. The inventory of things snatched or stolen from us gives way to the intuition or rather the assessment of the weakness, destabilization or contortion of our very being. There is therefore deterioration. It is first discerned on the quantitative plane, then envisaged as affecting "quality." But all this becoming-less is only a sub-species of the general metaphysical reality of being-otherwise—but a kind that is not brute and naked, not merely a matter of change. Beyond the reduction in quantity and the modification of quality, a more essential and more primitive being-otherwise is found, the principle and eidetic root of all modification, but which makes possible the disclosure and explication of the full range of particular instances of being-otherwise.

After millennia of theogonic narratives, philosophy finally identified the question of the birth of the world, the occurrence of the finite, through an interrogation of the First, the Principle, the Divinity. The first is supposed to be perfect. It contains all in itself; it is sufficient. It has, or rather, is pure actuality in itself: why would it exit itself in order to act "elsewhere" and in view of something other than itself? The First is complete, undivided, integral. How would it have anything to do with something beyond it? It harbors no need to be related to something different than itself. Even more, its relation to such a reality would not merely be useless and superfluous but impossible because degrading and diminishing. Because of its perfect being, the principle is not capable of doing or undergoing something new, something supplementary. The perfect is, so to say, a closed circle, locked in on itself. If it does something that it would not have done before, it is lacking something. The First should not be able to "do" anything beyond or on the edges of its effective existence. Ancient philosophers—and not only the ancients—were not capable of reaching the idea that God can be occupied with finite beings, and even know them, for the good reason that he was not capable of producing them, of causing them to be. Classical philosophers in their ontotheologies disclaimed in every way the difficulties, impossibilities, contradictions and paradoxes that the conception of a Creator inevitably entails. The joyous and generous gift of being to the creature appears to constitute an admirable growth in being. This is certainly the case—for the finite creature, but not for the Creator, the

Newness: Premises and Regressions

infinite Being. Envisaged on the plane of "representation" ever since the birth of the world, God appears surrounded by new being, additional beings; he therefore seems to be enriched. But the truth is that the creation gives no enlargement to God. If God were perfect, if God were "all" before the creation, and thus *without* the creature, he cannot become any richer. Ultimately, as Simone Weil said, "God and all creatures is less than God."[3]

Classical ontology of the necessary being as pure act found itself unable to overcome this conceptual blockage; the great Scholastic Aristotelians could only take record of it. It was left to the imagery of the theosophists, mystics, and poets to face the paradox. Some say that the creation is an abdication of God, a true "sacrifice."[4] Others find at the very heart of the divinity the "virtue" of temperance: an infinite Power that imposes limitations on itself is "more infinite" than unbounded power![5] But the intuitions and scattered formulations of isolated thinkers will be, as it were, surpassed or rather recapitulated by the great theologoumena of kabbalists: *Tzimtzum*.

The Hebrew term *tzimtzum* means an act of withdrawal for the sake of the advent of the created universe. Rising up in the primordial Being is the will to create the world. It contracts itself, withdraws into itself, and the empty space thus produced serves as a receptacle for creatures. The withdrawal of God was a leap, not a process—but not a once and for all leap; it is ceaselessly repeated. It unfolds through an infinity of contractions, of different *tzimtzumim*, or rather, the *tzimtzum* occurs in a myriad of degrees. The immense ontological imagery of the Withdrawal of the divinity presents the creation—that instance par excellence of being-otherwise—as a self-limitation and thus as a reduction of the Eternal. How is this possible? The primordial Being withdraws in order to give room to creatures and this withdrawal is a restriction, a diminishment. However, if the Kabbalah "describes" the withdrawal of the All-Powerful, if it presents some fascinating accounts of it, there is no attempt to analyze its ontological structure in order to discern its metaphysical meaning. The divinity becomes "less" than it was and this becoming less is not a cosmic accident: it is motivated by Mercy, one of the primordial attributes of God, but speculation hardly asks about the relation between the "less" and the "otherwise" that the *Tzimtzum* establishes, the divine withdrawal allowing the advent of the new.[6]

The metaphysical theme of perfection's becoming-less receives a subtler and more radical formulation in the kenosis of Christ, premier theological paradigm of the renewing newness at work in the "diminishment." The conceptual motivation for the great theologoumenon of the Incarnation of the Word, the coming of the Son into the world is found in the themes of the descent, the debasement and sacrifice that find

---

3. Weil, "Formes de l'amour implicite de Dieu," in *Oeuvres complètes* IV 1 291.
4. Baader, *Werke*, II 83 n.
5. Traherne, *Christian Ethics*, in Ellrodt, *Les poètes métaphysiques anglais* II, 341n84.
6. See Scholem, *Les grands courants de la mystique juive*, 277 sq.

their most striking and most spectacular formulation in the Hymn of the Letter to the Philippians:

> Who, though he was in the form of God,
> did not regard equality with God
> as something to be exploited,
> but emptied himself,
> taking the form of a slave,
> being born in human likeness.
> And being found in human form,
> he humbled himself
> and became obedient to the point of death—
> even death on a cross. (Phil 2:6–8 NRSV)

The hymn expounds in a suggestive abridgment the foundational vision of Christianity: the Son of God was made man. The story of Christ begins with a contrasting vision if there ever was one: becoming the newborn child on the straw of the stable while the angels sing the "glory of God" (Luke 2:14). It seems to come to an end with the Crucifixion, but a "crucified messiah" is a "scandal for the Jews, foolishness to the Greeks" (1 Cor 1:18). Feeling scandalized by Golgatha, being bluntly struck by the madness that seemingly emanates from the insufferable and risky tragic adventure attributed to the Most High, is a *normal* reaction for "natural reason." How can the Most High appear as the lowest, life as victim of Death, the Master of the world as slave?

If the God of the Bible is the creator of heaven and Earth, the God of hosts, "high and holy in his dwelling place," he is also "with those who are contrite and humble in spirit" (Isa 57:15), "hidden" in the midst of his people Israel that he accompanies in exile (Isa 44:15). Jesus, Son of God and messiah of Israel, will extend this work of humility, which will unfold hidden and new dimensions within it. He seeks the company of the poor and the weak. Although one of his titles is the "King of Israel" he assumes the "condition of a slave." The Judge of the World will be executed as a criminal. "Mighty Prince" (Isa 9:5), he comes in the "weakness" of the flesh (1 Cor 1:24). From his birth in the manger at Bethlehem to his death on a Cross, he lives in humiliation, which will be prolonged after his death by the Eucharist where he is "reduced to the limits of a morsel of bread."[7] Moses was called the most humble man who ever lived (Num 12:3), but the humility of Christ is of another order. It cannot be expressed by excessive ascetic practices, nor even by daily, elaborate humiliations, but it is truly a unique humility—a humility exercised by someone who, by virtue of his "equal rank with God" has no reason to humiliate himself.

Physical suffering and moral and social humiliations already seem to be ill fit for a being of the status of the Son. But with the sacrifice on the Cross, the Death of Christ, a new ontological level is uncovered that promises to deepen reflection in this

---

7. Bérulle, *Notes et entretiens*, in *Oeuvres complètes*, 5.37.

exceptional paradigm of renewing newness represented by the Incarnation. Death is the sting, or rather the symbolic form of finitude, the principle and culminating point of all the flaws that undermine imperfection: how could it then touch the perfect? In order to be perfect, the perfect should reject all contingency but death is the culminating point of contingency, the paradox where the contingent actualizes its essence through its very disappearance.

The Christian church has always fought numerous heresies that, incapable of sustaining contradiction or paradox, wanted to dilute in one way or another the effective reality of the Incarnation. Either, on the one hand, the Son was a man, certainly extraordinary, exceptional, enjoying a totally unique relation with the Father, but nevertheless only a man, whose death was not the Death of God, or, on the other hand, he was not truly human. The Docetists of diverse stripes always do their best to evacuate the mystery from the Cross: the coming of the Second Person of the Trinity in the flesh is only an allegory; his death was only the definitive return to the other world from where he descended for a time. But, unfortunately for the Docetists, the gospel account does not corroborate their fantasies. After the resurrection, Thomas continues to doubt and declares: "Unless I see the mark of the nails in his hands, and put my finger in the mark of the nails and my hand in his side, I will not believe." Jesus later says to him: "Put your finger" in the mark and "reach out your hand and put it in my side" (John 20:25, 27). The glorified body of Christ bears the scars. For Marcion the body of Christ was only a phantom, but the Orthodox Church sings in its Matins for Holy Saturday: "God was placed in the tomb!"

The death of Christ is a supreme manifestation of novelty. It represents a qualitatively different degree of novelty from the range of quantitatively different modalities of divine being-otherwise found in his sufferings and humiliations. The death on the Cross shows the radicality of the kenosis; it is the proof (as it were) of the entry of the finite into the infinite, of the rupture and division at the heart of the unity and continuity. Dogmatics inquires into the motivations and structures of the kenosis and especially its subject, properly speaking. Was the impassible divinity itself made passible? Was it the Second Person of the Trinity or Christ in his Humanity? But the discussion of the Abasement as philosophical paradigm is only indirectly concerned with these questions. Of course, it must take account of the Trinitarian dimensions of the kenosis, its presupposition or prefiguration on the level of the relations among divine Persons, but it is essentially preoccupied with understanding the Descent of God as archetypal instance of being-otherwise, of being-less.

The Epistle to the Philippians represents the kenosis as annihilation, the Son's humiliation and obedience unto death, but these diverse biographical moments, the diverse mysteries of the life of Jesus are, so to say, epiphenomena of the root-mystery of the Incarnation. The rhetoric of preaching and the discourse of piety are essentially addressed to the Passion of Christ and thus contemplate his humanity. But the prize and the meaning of all the dolorous mysteries is to be found in the eternal difference that unfolds at the heart of the divinity. "The Lamb was slain from the origin": does this mean that "the Crucifixion of God is an eternal reality,"[8] that "the historical Golgatha is rooted in a "metaphysical Golgatha"?[9] The eternity of the crucifixion, the metaphysical Golgatha are images, speculative images if you wish, that express the Incarnation, but on the level of the concept the Incarnation is the highest archetype of becoming-*other* as becoming-*less*. It is already very difficult to conceive that a finite being can wish to become less but its plausibility and possibility seems even more incomprehensible when one is talking about the Absolute, the Perfect. Piety and Christian preaching cannot get enough of contemplating this mystery: "Life descends in order to be killed; Bread descends in order to be hungry; the Way descends in order to be tired on the path; the Source descends in order to Thirst."[10] It celebrates the humility of the Most High, the patience of the All-Powerful; in short it states on all registers the great "definition" of the Apostle: "strength is manifest in weakness" (2 Cor 12:9).

The Incarnation is the becoming-less that is not a quantitative weakening, a second-degree diminishment. It should be understood as the event of a true novelty, a leap. Most often the possibility of rupture, the capacity for a leap is attributed to the finite being, subject to accident. But the leap of kenosis, the becoming-less of the Son has nothing to do with the troubled contingency of the accident: if it signals an ultimate fact, it nevertheless does not fall under a facticity, even a supreme one. The annihilation of the self of the Son celebrated by the epistle is not of a limited rationality or a partly glimpsed meaning. It is not simply a concession of Reason to Revelation. The Incarnation truly obeys a logic, but *this* logic is not of the ontological order. The idea of a perfect becoming-less is rejected by "natural reason" because it seems opposed to the very principle of non-contradiction. One does not remain oneself in becoming another; one does not remain perfect by plunging into imperfection! Yet if the kenosis has never been "welcomed" by classical philosophy, it nevertheless proves to be a matter of an integral intelligibility. Christ's cry of distress on the Cross is not the sign of a rupture in the union of the two natures because the dying Son continues to be faithful to the Father. The inequality and rupture are ontological categories while fidelity is a form of the will. In fact, fidelity does not belong to the metaphysical register of being, but to that of love. And the essence of God is neither being, nor perfection, but love (1 John 4:8).

Later theoreticians of the *tzimtzum* resolutely emphasized the voluntary nature of the divine withdrawal.[11] The act in which the divinity withdraws is not a spontaneous movement of its being but a free act of its Mercy to make room for the creature. Kenosis is a voluntary state of the Second Person of the Trinity as such, which is not

---

8. Weil, *Cahiers, Oeuvres complètes* VI 3 279.
9. Bulgakov, *Du Verbe incarné*, 159.
10. Augustine, *Sermon* 78, 6 (PL 38, 493).
11. Scholem, *Zur Kabbala und ihrer Symbolik*, 149.

at all opposed to the essence of God. Well to the contrary, the abdication it expresses is the supreme actualization of the divine essence—not its negation. A Patristic text voices this: "The descent of God is a kind of excess of power in which there is no obstacle to what seems opposed to his nature."[12] The nature, or rather essence of God is Love, and is made flesh, enters the world.

Thinking the New: The Power of Synthesis

The kenosis of Christ is the advent of a novelty, but all novelty that is not a stroke of luck or mere accident should be capable of conceptual exposition. The non-accidentally new represents something original, even unforeseeable, but once it appears it should be possible to account for it. The new should be understood as a condition B coming from condition A without being able to make out that it is entailed by A, deducing its configuration from the structure of A. A crucified messiah is a scandal for the Jews and folly to the Greeks but the Passion of Christ does not appear as an implication of the Pure Act. The weakness of the Servant is hardly compatible with the Almighty Lord of the World. But once understood as beyond actuality and power, God can and should be conceived as love: the kenosis that is the Incarnation becomes intelligible. The intelligibility of the new that is the same spirit of life and the work of Love is understandable starting from a metaphysical logic centered on the conceptual comprehension of novelty. In other words, the ontologies of necessity and the logics of identity (briefly: the procedures of analysis) should give way to a philosophy founded on synthesis, more precisely, on the *a priori synthesis*.

Since Leibniz, philosophy has divided logical judgments into analytic and synthetic groups. An analytic judgment is only a dissection of a given concept, its clarification. It pursues no other result but to discover the implications of the concept, implications that, while being *given*, remain hidden, obscure, latent. Analysis begins with the concept that it penetrates from all sides, illumines and unfolds. It is not a production of the new but an explication of the given. It lays bare the hidden wealth of the concept, unveiling from its moments and elements a clarification that illumines the obscure gaps between its structural points. In its own way analysis is excavation, in-depth study, which can certainly lead to a challenge to our presumed knowledge. Nevertheless, the new that it brings about is only accidental; it is new for a mind that has not yet evaluated what it has before it and does not yet have the means to complete this task. Analytic judgments can provide information that precipitates dramatic changes in the world. The new that analysis brings to light can surprise and shock, but in the end it is still simply the *not-yet- known*, the *not-yet-familiar*. Like all judgment, analysis attempts to get beyond the monotony of the identical and to unmask

---

12. Gregory of Nyssa, *Or. cat.* 24 (PG 45, 64).

concealed tautologies. It believes it can traverse unknown paths, make progress, and go further than before. In reality it runs in circles, remaining in one place.

The other great form of judgment is synthesis. Synthetic judgment is not content to elucidate the given; it also aspires to complete it through something "more." If in an analytic judgment the predicate adds nothing new to the subject, only explicating it in one way or another, in synthetic judgments the subject discovers itself linked to a predicate that it does not contain within itself, but which it should look for and find elsewhere, beyond itself. Synthesis is the connection between subject A and predicate B, joined to the subject from the outside. The subject may very well assume this predicate but it does not imply it through its essence. B is connected to A only in an external way: the subject does not hold the predicate within its logical structure; it receives it from experience. Before the pure logicality of analysis, synthesis seems like an empirical category. If analysis is the domain of "pure" knowledge, of logic and metaphysics, synthesis does not share its reign in the domain of empirical knowledge, especially history and natural history. The opposition between the two registers of knowing can also be represented in the terms a priori and a posteriori: analytic judgments are a priori while synthetic judgments are a posteriori. These definitions pertain to a kind of philosophy that deals with universal and atemporal knowledge, but Kant will refuse to let them remain this way. The Critique first challenges metaphysics in order to re-establish it subsequently in a more rigorous and stable way—and the key of this re-establishment is the idea of the a priori synthesis.[13]

Classical philosophy, the sciences and metaphysics are constituted by analytic propositions. If they were not their apodictic purity would be compromised. But Kant thinks that this purity can be guaranteed in an infinitely more fecund way through synthetic judgment, on the condition that they are a priori. The question of a priori synthetic judgments is the central question of the Critique, the very problem of metaphysics. Before attempting the demonstration of this possibility in proper form, the Critique presents examples of the effective exercise of the a priori synthetic use of the understanding: "Every body has extension" is an analytic judgment because I do not have to leave what is contained in the concept of the body in order to demonstrate extension. I only have to break down the concept in order to run into the predicate of extension. Yet when I say, "all bodies have weight," the predicate is not found in the general concept of a body. This proposition is therefore not analytic but synthetic, but it is no less a priori: weight does not follow sensu stricto from the concept of the body, but it is recognized by the mind as belonging to it. Or again: "Everything that happens has a cause" is a basic principle of any intellectual operation, but it is not of the analytic order. In the concept of some B that happens, I think of an existence A that precedes it. Analytic judgments can be drawn from that. But the analytic conception of this succession does not yet correspond to a causal relation. What is supposed to be the cause is a different concept from what happens, from the effect; its representation

---

13. For this interpretation of the a priori synthesis, see Vetö, *De Kant à Schelling* I, 61 sq.

in no way contains the effect. Nevertheless, my mind understands A as producing B and the producing itself in a certain order. In other words, the understanding finds outside of the concept A a predicate B that is foreign to it and yet is reckoned as bound to it. The attribution to a subject of a predicate that does not belong to it is a synthetic act and when this attribution is both rational and necessary, it is an a priori synthesis (*Critique* B 12–13).

The a priori synthesis accomplishes a radical reformulation of conceptual interrogation which signifies a remarkable expansion of *a priori* knowledge. It is a "paradox"[14]—a fecund paradox that asserts nothing less than the conceptuality of the non-conceptual, and the jurisdiction of the paradox is the shift of the investigation from the concept to the judgment. Because logic is supposed to be the logic of the concept, because *a-prioriness* is inevitably a synonym for analysis, it is only once logic expands over judgment that knowledge can appropriate the synthesis. The *Critique* begins the investigation on the possibility of the a priori synthesis in order to be able to explain the validity of science, that is, the impact of our understanding on the external world. But the implications of this extension are more general. As principle and instrument of science, in other words, of "pure" knowledge of the world, the a priori synthetic judgment is the symbol of the mind's step outside of itself. Yet the horizontal and therefore spatial character of the step outside of itself is only the epiphenomenon of a more general and more radical movement, namely, the projection of the new. With analysis there is nothing new because, ultimately, it only removes the screen separating subject and predicate, or rather reduces it to being only a transparent mirror by which the fundamental equality of subject and predicate is revealed. However synthesis attests to the non-coincidence and native heterogeneity of the initial terms that it gathers together and reconciles by virtue of the copula. The copula, simple sign of identity, of pure function, which, in analysis is without its own density, "becomes" in synthesis an authentic third, an original term of the proposition.

The a priori synthesis is a power proper to judgment and is related to the movement which takes shape from the subject toward the predicate. On the plane of representation this movement is conceived as a self-building bridge, the spanning of a distance. Overcoming the distance requires power and a formula: a power to effectuate the bridging, a formula to structure it. In reality, it is not a matter here of two elements but one alone: the third that ties together the subject and predicate is the copula, but the copula is an existing thing, or rather an act of existing, structured and structuring. The a priori synthetic judgment is enacted in the theoretical and practical domains and the mediating third of the copula comes from time in the theoretical register and from freedom in the practical register. In theoretical judgment, the understanding represents the world in terms of synthetic relations of the number sequence, substantiality and causality, which are so many ways of moving from the subject to the predicate, of tying together A and B, of establishing a connection between the given

---

14. Kant, *Akad.* XXVIII, 393.

and what is not yet given, and of instituting it by a conceptual structure. Kantian time is no longer the child of Heraclitus playing a board game, but the extraordinary power of the mind to give coherence and direction in judgment. It is neither a blind overflowing flux nor consecutive points following one another in deadly monotony. To the contrary, temporal movement is a progression from past to present and from present to future, a progression that is neither brute flux nor simple explication of the past, a pre-programmed unfolding without history, but a projection that aims for the new through thinking it.

The a priori synthesis also vivifies the practical domain. It shows the subject the soundness of subordinating any selfish motive with respect to the Law—for the Law's sake. It also especially furnishes the subject with the force and power to realize this subordination, to make it effective. The finite rational creature is the subject or, if you like, the agent of an imperfect will, "affected by sensible desires," which by its nature is able to be incited only by selfish interests, but it is commanded as if it were an "intelligible" being in possession of a "perfect will."[15] The emblematic formula for practical reason, the moral will is the Categorical Imperative: it pronounces the sublime obligation to act only according to an absolutely universalizable maxim. Universalization is made conceptually possible on the plane of meaning through the comprehension of the radical primacy of the Law, its unconditional value *in itself* and *for itself*. It is realizable through the power of freedom, counterpart in the practical sphere to the motivation of innovation that constitutes time in the theoretical sphere.

The Categorical Imperative commands us to obey the Moral Law willed in and for itself, and this obedience brings about a division. But the division, a movement within immanence, is surpassed and overcome by a tearing open: a tearing open of the closed circle of the self which entails opening to the exterior, exit from the self, exodus for someplace else. This tearing open is the phenomenon of novelty but to the degree that it is performed and articulates itself according to the Law, the new that it establishes is an emergence of Form, a birth of Meaning. The a priori synthesis, theoretical and practical, incarnates the high philosophical intuition of the superior unity of Form and Novelty. It is the cause of and, in the strict sense, a category of "the theory of knowledge," but if it reinterprets the theory of judgment this is because it unveils the presence of a metaphysical reality, namely, a hidden power that spans the distance between the subject and the world, the given and the new, an articulatory power, a gushing forth that is legislative.

In the last analysis, if the finite subject is capable of judging in a synthetic a priori way, this is because it is itself synthesis—a priori synthesis. The condition of all rational thought and moral action is the continuity of the subject, a continuity which is neither a banal analytic identity of atoms nor an incoherent succession of leaps and ruptures. Called to a finite and fragmented existence with death as the ultimate horizon, the subject should be understood as ceaseless self-production—as a "departure" from the

---

15. Kant, *Akad.* XXIX, 606.

given in order to reach the new, a new that happens through sudden appearance or epiphany but that nevertheless is established with a consistency with the former. The self-faithful but innovative appearance of moments that mark the history of the subject has as its deep source the memory, woven from contents that detach themselves from a background all the while remaining tied to it. Memory is the undisturbed but also expressive side of the continuity of the subject; the dramatic and actively creative side is freedom. Memory and freedom are the two basic forms of the synthesis that is the being and acting of the subject. They allow the accession of the new, albeit a new in intelligible continuity with the old. With them the subject is given starting from itself. Thought and action produced by the subject producing itself show its constant exit from itself that is neither alienation nor mutilation. They represent the act of crossing a distance that is the trajectory of the new, which does not detach and disassociate itself from the subject out of which they emerge.

The Thorns of Analysis

The a priori synthesis allows the renewal of metaphysics because it modifies the given of pure knowing. Through it knowledge is extended beyond traditional limits, but in the first instance it is only an addition (albeit massive) to analysis. It has not yet questioned the indispensible role and essential importance of analysis for knowledge. However, interpreted starting from the potentialities and accomplishments of the a priori synthesis, analysis will reveal its limitations, even its poverty: a sterility that can invert itself into injury and aggression.

Analysis is an indispensable element in every investigation. It allows the discovery of what is hidden, the clarification of the obscure, the explication of what is latent. It is the supreme way to untangle confusion, to unfold and stretch out the twisted, briefly, to allow the unapparent to come to light, to unfold hidden structures. Analytic judgment refuses any aspiration to reach what is not contained in the concept. However, it claims an integral capacity to excavate the concept and to expound its moments and implications. Analysis is ignorant of a substantial part of the real that escapes it, but it firmly and strongly declares its unconditional rule over the sphere that is properly its own. But this recognition of its limits and sober modesty in ambition, should not obscure the harmful potentialities and humiliating perspectives of an enterprise that refuses the new and is condemned to be locked within itself.

With analysis the intelligence moves in the closed space of the concept. It is sheltered from the unexpected, protected from any foreign incursion. Here the copula is only an extra; it plays a minor role. In the analytic judgment the intelligence should not provide any true effort: in the impossible scenario when it happens that it goes beyond itself, it is still content with a, so to say, purely grammatical, non-existential role. Analysis proceeds only to establish inventory lists for reason; it increases neither its capacities nor its possessions. No one would have thought that the sterility of analysis stems from its a priori condition, that the cause of reason's infecundity is its purity. Apparently, pure theoretical reason has *pure* hands, but does not have *hands*...

However, the sterility of reason is not attributable to its purity, its apriority. This is more clearly seen in the universe of practical reason. The Categorical Imperative is a synthetic a priori proposition, it commands the following of a maxim the reason of which is not found immanent to the subject. However, the imperatives of prudence are only analytic. Under the rule of prudence I look for happiness, and once happiness is fixed as the goal of my will, every means to access this state become the necessary object of my intention. Whoever desires an end desires the means, and between the end and the means as the two terms of a practical proposition there is a simple relation of analytic implication. The mind should engage in no real effort in order to exit itself; the predicate, namely, the will that desires the means, is contained in the subject, the will that wants the end. But if the mind can remain thus in itself, if it describes only an immanent movement, this is because, to the very degree that it is given happiness as an end, it is alienated, has left its own a priori sphere. To remain itself the will that is practical reason should follow only a priori rules, drawing on its own resources. Yet happiness is only an empirical concept that does not emerge from out of practical reason itself. Indefinable by knowledge in an a priori way, it can be rigorously prescribed to the will. In giving itself the imperatives of prudence the will moves in a "contingent" sphere. But the contingent is good and well the a posteriori. All the while being analytic propositions, the imperatives of prudence fall in the last instance under the jurisdiction of the "synthetic a priori" use of reason.[16] The analytic character of judgment falls into the hands of immanence; the banal good-heartedness of reasonable maxims is in blatant opposition to the high rationality of moral detachment.

The infecundity of analytic judgments is not a function of their a priori nature but of their immanence—an immanence that is locked in on itself, a closing the truth of which is exclusion, a boundary that not only indicates where the subject ends but which functions like a barbed wire fence, opposed to the other. Analysis refuses the new, it contents itself with the given. But this eminently reasonable attitude does not pass the test of reality. One tries to confine oneself to one's own circle by excluding everything that does not belong to it.One would like to create the light; all the light in one's own sphere. Then one feels safe, and would not trade this safety for any adventure or promise. Yet the transparency, limpidity, the placid and peaceful clarity of analysis end up being read—by others as well as by the subject itself—as sterility. And sterility is not the assessment of the non-appearing of the new; it is a deep affection that the subject of analysis undergoes with bitterness and spite. Sterility is felt as a threat and experienced as a curse. It destroys the however reasonable equilibrium that prevails in the sphere of analysis and plants the shadow of impoverishment and dearth in the middle of harmoniously linked structures. It uncovers the shortages and fear that want to supply the arms of aggression in the closed and clear space of analysis.

16. Kant, *Fondements de la métaphysique des moeurs. Oeuvres* vol. 2, 317s (*Akad.* IV, 448).

The sterility that shows itself to be the truth of this form of immanence that is analysis appears to itself and to others as an eidos of negativity, and this for the good reason that by nature it involves threatening behavior and aggressiveness. Plants and trees bear leaves and where the water is plentiful the leaves are large, thick and fleshy. They convey the security and vigor of vegetal being which sends out delicately designed and well articulated shapes. They also exhibit a robust vitality, constituting a profuse repetition of the plant itself, which, without being detached from it, seem to have their own proper existence. Even more, leaves constitute the natural manner of expression by which the tree and the bush relate to their environment. They constitute a system of foliage that offers a place of protection for insects and birds, shade to filter or receive the light of the sun. Leaves are, as it were, the exterior outline of the tree and they are also like the clothing or perimeter of a being, which, while demarcating its reality, mediate its relations with other natural entities. A plant is located in the context of other plants, in relation with other inhabitants of the fields. The harmonious richness of its foliage is like the expression of a welcome to others, an invitation addressed to them.

Yet some plants are deprived of foliage. The Cacti of sub-tropical deserts dress their trunk, they even wear bright, multi-colored flowers, but they do not wear leaves. The cactus only very rarely shelters bird's nests. It has no leaves, only spines. It extends a welcoming shadow only very parsimoniously. In place of smooth leaves, pleasing to touch, it puffs out spines like darts that point, prick and pierce. The leaves decorating trees are fed by strong and regular rains while the spines growing on cacti manifest a poverty of irrigation, the constant threat of drought. The cactus has available only a minimum of liquid, which it receives irregularly. It lives in indigence and therefore without security. The necessities of life cause the cactus to tighten its extremities. It has to manage closely the precious liquid that keeps it alive and therefore may only yield the least possible surface to evaporation. Fleshy leaves, even flat and slender ones, pointlessly intensify the loss of fluids; the plant must reduce their density and thin them out. The result of this constriction is the metamorphosis of the leaf into a spine. With the same length the spine exposes infinitely less surface to evaporation than the leaf; it is only an extension, a minimal excrescence of the plant. The tip at the end witnesses to the optimal attenuation of thickness which tries to squeeze the third dimension until it is nearly subsumed under the second. This transposition at the sharp tip shows that we are not simply dealing with an impoverished variant on the leaf but its transformation into an aggressive form. The plant wants as much as possible to curtail its expenditure, therefore diminishing the places and means of contact with what is not itself. It suffers the acute awareness of its tenuousness; it is in anguish, terrified of being affected, cut into. This desperate flight from encroachment takes the form of a pressing back into itself. The cactus turns towards itself and seeks to close every door to the outside. But the inevitable external face of this closing down is its aggressiveness. The spines of the cactus are the consequence of its obsession with security; they demonstrate the metaphysical relevance of the moral intuition that self-love is never neutral, that withdrawing into oneself is always the exclusion of the other. Apparently the analytic judgment expresses only the modesty of an attitude content to explore the given. In reality this withdrawal that implies the refusal of novelty is sterile and sterility proves to be exclusion. Charity is commonly spoken of as reasonable self-love; love should begin with oneself. But if love of self begins with oneself it also ends with oneself. Even more, it is not content to seek its own good, but inexorably opposes the good of the other.

Nature: Variations on Immanence

The sober rationality and beautiful lucidity of analysis is only a cover for a wounding sterility that ends up secreting spines. Analysis is not only powerless to break out of the locked enclosure of immanence, it equally involves an aggressive egoism. An analogous transposition/deterioration lies in wait for the great metaphysical principle of Nature. Nature has two senses but unifies them in the end. First, nature is a near synonym for essence, a more leafy and fleshy expression of the metaphysical category. But it is also, and primarily, understood as the external world that surrounds us, the cosmos seen in the unique continuity of the living and non-living. The logico-ontological definition of essence and the marvelous balance of spaces and creatures of the external world are both subsumed under a deadly indifference.

When someone speaks of the nature of a being, he intends to indicate what is essential to it, that without which it is not what it is meant to be, that without which it ceases to be what it is or rather, ceases to be at all. Nature is almost the eidetic translation of definition; it contains the indispensible elements and characteristics of a species of entities or rather, it is their conceptual description. However, the "positive" component of description, the enumeration of the moments proper to the species, the organic unfolding of its elements, has its negative side or counterpart. Nature shows not only everything that rightfully belongs to a being, a member of a species. It recalls on the one hand that the being *should* contain these elements and moments or otherwise face no longer belonging to the species. On the other hand, it also prohibits against transgressing the strictly defined limits of a configuration, against its venturing outside of them, going beyond itself. Nature offers a generous line of credit but it also brandishes an inflexible interdiction. It furnishes the means of becoming what one is, but also marks with intractable jealously where one should not aspire to go. It incarnates everything that has happened to a being to actualize its potentialities, to accomplish its purposes, but it also traces the limit inscribed in its heart in order to prohibit it from going any farther, in order to wall it up in itself. Nature is supposed to connote the initial share of a being, its proper powers and possessions, but it equally confirms its radical dependence. It shows what one can do and be, but it recalls, sometimes surreptitiously, sometimes openly, that this "can" is an "ought," this possibility is a necessity. Throw nature out the door and it will return through the window, says the proverb. In reality, these monads that are the entities, instances of nature, have no windows. The openings that they desire or that they think they make are not even true cracks or gaps but simple, blind links of the mechanism that constitutes them and of which they do not understand the function.

Its nature prohibits a being from surpassing itself: it exercises a tyranny in its regard that is rendered as violence towards everything that it is not, but which amounts to violence towards itself—a violence that, by recalling it to the strict limits inscribed in its being, reveals its radical powerlessness to reach the new, to claim a true fecundity. For westerners in our day, nature is reckoned as a wonderful place of renewal, a vast space that invites us to rest, to refresh and renew ourselves. But for the majority of humanity, it was and continues to be a perilous place where threats abound to what they have been able to build and consolidate over millennia of voiceless effort and persistent labor. Nature is not only the habitat of savage beasts, but also especially the lair, the home of frightening forces: floods, earthquakes, volcanic eruptions, ready at any moment to destroy cultures, roads, buildings, all that has been wrenched from the earth with blood, sweat, and tears, at the cost of immense unknown effort. These traces of savagery and irruptions of violence are however only the epiphenomena or accidental, contingent moments of the violence brooding in the depths of nature, or rather what it *is*. Nature can spread in local explosions or peripheral conflagrations: these lightning flashes are only like masks for a fundamental immobilism, fickle modalities of a turbulence that is really only the strong and sure refusal of any effective development. As in the obviously extremely abstract universe of analytic judgments, in the oh-so harmonious and well-ordered realm of nature, the perfect coincidence of terms, the regular development of forms is only the cipher of a fickle, superficial structuring. Nature seems to deploy series of well-formed and clearly determined figures and events, but this precise and valuable articulation does not signify an authentic differentiation. Nature seems to be incessantly becoming, or rather *is* becoming. In reality it is not going anywhere because the truth of the differences that it displays are found in Indifference—the secret work of which is the bracketing of the other or others, or rather their active negation and obliteration.

Indifference is a tolerably ambiguous idea. It denotes a situation of non-engagement, of neutrality. But what seems at first to be laudable impartiality can only be a contemptuous impassivity, a cruel insensitivity. The indifferent does not intend to mortgage the freedom of its options. Yet instead of expressing scrupulous reserve, its refusal to take sides is most often the sign of a cruel disinterest. The "cold indifference" of the egoist is castigated and the novelist goes so far as to speak of "that death of the heart called indifference."[17] The hardened Stoic takes pleasure in preaching the noble attitude of indifference towards whatever is not in one's power, but the *apatheia* of the Sage denotes above all the absence of a stir of compassion. The philosophers love to

---

17. Balzac, *Béatrix*, 565.

read indifference into the essence of nature. Nature follows its course without allowing itself to deviate from its prescribed trajectory. It obeys immutable laws; it only carries out a single program across a motley multiplicity of events and individuals. It is an immense purveyor of existences, an inexhaustible source of births, but this entire sequence of entities emanating from it show the price to pay for preserving the remainder or rather not having to consent to any advent of the new. Few philosophers have thought as much and with as much passion about Nature as Schelling, but he is the one who recalls that "nature is the most indolent beast" as it "loathes separation."[18] By separation he means what comes down to a true detachment, an authentic emancipation. Some revel in denouncing the so very mechanical relation between cause and effect. But if the effect ineluctably follows the cause with any freedom, once it happens it is autonomous—the umbilical cord tying it to its principle is cut. Yet in the substantial relation, the accident can truly boast a distinct existence, can appear as a spark that has escaped from a primitive bonfire. In reality its autonomy is artificial: there is no true reason for its occurrence; its emergence is only a contingent and temporary appearance. The accident remains submitted to the substance, which recovers it without remainder. "The dark substance consumes" beings, the individuals that issue from it.[19] Kronos devours her children.

This dramatic vision of nature as the implacable enemy of its offspring truly corresponds to the metaphysical structure of *physis*. Yet it rarely imposes itself on human intuition. Its cruelty, its intolerance to the autonomy of others, its violent refusal of what is different, are apparent and visible only in its peripheral manifestations. They are no less expressions and clear instances of the refusal to open that is only a face, the external aspect of the same metaphysical reality of which continuity is the hidden essence. This is the continuity that, under the appearance of relativizing difference, its more and more complete subsumption under sameness, constitutes a resolute opposition to any withdrawal, any *tzimtzum* that gives place to what does not yet exist. Nature can at times be convulsive, overflowing, or flooding. In its truth it is the kingdom of the Same which, forced into movement and subject to becoming, nevertheless struggles to preserve continuity. In order to persevere in its being, the same is ready to make every risk, it resolves to take the winding path of history, even accepting the unknown ahead and its inevitable adversity. Continuity is the supreme form that the same assumes in and through nature, with the unique specification being the all-around defense of the metaphysical status quo in the face of the irruption of the new, the impediment of its encroachment on the analytic immanence of the given.

It is in the intelligent creature that nature should have to face the threat of subversion, the apparent discontinuity that *anthropos* drives into the *physis*. Nature is destabilized by humanity, a breach in the continuum of living beings and principle of the deconstruction of the scale of beings. Science strives to find the missing link

---

18. Schelling, *Werke*, III 324 n.
19. Hegel, *Encyclopédie des Sciences Philosophiques*, I § 151; Add. 586.

of a half-animal, half-human being but the true missing link is human being, and in its eidos it must remain such forever. Beyond the narrow and rather late circuit of cultures inspired by the religions of transcendence, the community of essence between humans and animals has always been professed, as it is today. Animals would only be the pre-history of humanity from which it has been only partly extricated and which it continues to bear the imprint and the goad within its affective gut and the depths of the mind. Humanity may well be the culminating point of the line of evolution—only a beast more successful than the others. The fairy tales of long ago and the sermons of ecologists today ceaselessly remind humanity that it belongs to the animal kingdom. The borders are tenuous; the lack of impermeability and the theory of species is never a reversible path: any disentangling of humanity from the animals is hardly a detachment. The path of return remains open. After death, according to its merits or demerits, the featherless biped will live on as an insect, reptile, bird or quadripedal mammal. The doctrine of transmigration rings the bell on any conception that takes the sui generis originality of man too seriously. Instead of returning to the dust, humans return as animals; the brief moment of his sovereignty and freedom has ended. Vegetarianism, whether ancient or modern, Eastern or Western, has a metaphysical affinity with the doctrine of transmigration and is an ideology distilled from the intuition of the continuity of life. It warns us against the destruction of life that is different from our own only by degrees, not according to nature. It strongly rejects the consumption of animal meat, which cannot be very well distinguished from human flesh. Without a doubt, how could we be insensible to the sufferings inflicted on beasts, especially before the sordid processing of livestock in the service to an ever more pronounced taste of a meat-filled diet? Nevertheless, if the suffering of beasts is the object of a legitimate emotion, the compassion felt in this situation could only be established on the inacceptable metaphysical principle of the continuity of living beings, of a Benthamite moral community of humans and animals. Sweet Julie in Rousseau's *Julie, or the New Heloise*, demands that the annoyed fisherman throw their catches back into the waters, but Christ, the Easter Lamb, never gave a similar order to the fisherman on the Galilean waters.[20]

If vegetarianism cannot be maintained as a metaphysically founded doctrine, this is because there is a gap, a radical discontinuity and unbridgeable distance between human and animal. Without intoning unfounded and problematic hymns in praise of the glory of humanity, the one formerly called the crown of creation is effectively a being apart, possessing a unique dignity. The difference separating the free creature from other living beings opens a new direction in the world, interrupts its faultless continuity and smashes through its sterile immanence. Humanity, a free being, is a representative of alterity, of the other and is unlike the long chain of well-defined species, the entire parade of entities that punctuate becoming in complete submission to the power of instinct. Within the succession that they constitute, the beings of nature

---

20. Philonenko, *Jean-Jacques Rousseau et la pensée du malheur* II, 94.

are subsumed, subordinated to each other, whereas humanity is resolutely proclaimed an end in itself—which exists and subsists only to the degree that it stands on its own legs, and this self-assumption is only a succession of ruptures in which the subject ceaselessly masters and exceeds itself. Nature is definitely the place and foundation, the *Grund* for all this surpassing but the surpassing disturbs and tears through the artificial peace of immanence. Humanity is clearly located in the forest of living beings, but it is a tree with roots in the sky (*Timaeus* 90a). It is a killjoy to the calm circles of cyclical nature, the source of a hemorrhage that weakens the *physis*. With *anthropos* new winds of change penetrate the cosmos, a fecund disorder shakes the immutable structures of nature that lacks liberating novelty and is only one immense analytic judgment, the supreme form of infinite immanence.

Limits and Pitfalls of Justice

Nature is an infinite, self-unfolding process. It abhors separation and if it consents to release particular beings it is only in order to be able better to engulf them thereafter. The supreme figure of all immanence, nature is the principle of the negation of the different, of opposition to the new. In order to be able to surpass this deadly egoism, metaphysics works to unblock the frozen confinement of the *physis* and prepares this loosening through the metamorphosis of *Chronos* into *Dikē*. Nature on the cosmic plane—where each being exists according to its own nature—tends to close on, to sink into itself. In order to break this lawless egoism, or, if you like, a single law, namely the *conatus* that causes every being to persist in its being, metaphysics rethinks nature under the figure of justice. In this way it thinks it overcomes exclusion and masters violence. Justice wants to hinder or even break with the ontological regime of which the unique principle and driving force is power in favor of an order that hinges on what is owed to each. The eidetic principle of justice is *suum cuique*. With justice beings receive their due, they act according to a reciprocity that should assure equality and equity.

The "due" is what comes back to a being—what comes back to *it* as such. It means the detachment of an entity from nature, its disassociation from it. The due reveals, as a being's emancipation, a state in which functioning according to its nature amounts no longer to the mechanical exercise of the role that falls to it because of its membership in the whole: a condition where the entity ceases being the link of a chain and reaches autonomy. Yet emancipation remains illusory and autonomy does not amount to a true break with immanence. Justice is practiced according to an unalterable order; it is finally only a superior reflex. What it distributes and the events it makes happen are only so many examples of analytic judgment. In its eidetic essence, justice truly seems to imply a relation in which a collapse in the whole would be prevented by relation to another autonomous entity. Justice allows a being to recover its due through compensation, transfer and acquisition of property, briefly, through instances of reciprocal action. In reality, reciprocity proves to be a fictional duality and the exchange of favors from various transactions between partners serves only to obscure the persistence of an ultimate homogeneity.

Before being an ethical and metaphysical concept, justice was originally a juridical notion. At the civil or penal level, justice renders each his due, performing an activity originally stemming from rectification and restoration. Justice does not intend to make an unprecedented situation occur, it has no intention of bringing about a new given. One gives justice to someone who has been wronged, and essentially, someone can be wronged in two ways: either in relation to one's goods or in relation to one's person. Justice in the realm of possessions seeks the restoration of a past condition altered by illegitimate procedures. Someone has been deprived of his property, prevented from enjoying the benefits due to him. Justice is rendered when the good that has been stolen from him is restored or, in default of this damaged, ruined, broken, burned, lost good, a good of equal value is offered to him. The insistence on "equal value" is the keystone of every procedure of justice. The one who has been injured demands compensation that can only come about by means of an object or service equivalent to the good of which he has been deprived. If restitution is not the direct work of the responsible party, the fraudster or the thief, it is the work of a third party, the judge. But as Montesquieu suggests, the role of the judge is "null." He is not there to establish a new situation of property but simply to reestablish the former one. The judge only appraises the loss and gauges the damage. In other words he is only supposed to uncover the usually easily quantifiable extent and scope of the lack and order that the gap be as it were plugged up by something that will completely fill it. Judiciary action can be hesitant, merely conjectural, surrounded by uncertainty, it can be awaited with fear and hope, and yet for all that it must utter only analytic judgments.

If criminal justice seems to be running on different paths than those of its sister, civil justice, it too ultimately cannot and would not want to be liberated from its roots in analysis. Penal justice also partakes of an essential parallelism of equality and proportion. It punishes but it wants to punish *justly*: the sentence must correspond to the crime! Doubtlessly, with realities difficult to quantify and to measure, the penalty struggles to be determined, but even when the primitive rule of retaliation no longer subsists, the punishment is intended to be proportionate to the offense. Crime injures an order. Order must be restored and the complex and complicated criteria that govern judgment determine the fitness of the penalty and aim to placate and to make amends, to punish and to remunerate, in short, to *reestablish* order.

In civil law as in penal law, the art of judgment consists in the meticulous calculation of equivalencies, the price of the object ceded, the punishment of the offense perpetuated. The commodity and its price, like the transgression and its penalty must fit with one another or rather constitute true replacements for one another. Judgment is a skillful extrapolation; it is placed in a domain where the essential eidetic difference of two terms of the operation is offset by the qualitative and (especially) quantitative identity of their content, their value. Justice wants everyone to answer for his works: evil for evil, "Blow for blow! Blood for blood! Misfortune for the maleficent."[21] But judgment is to be repaid in given situations and it must *set a cost for* its operations. The ancient law of retaliation demanded "an eye for an eye, a tooth for a tooth" and in commercial transactions a field is to be valued according to an exact equivalent in gold powder or silver bar. The probity and artfulness of a judge, in other words the justice of his verdicts, are a function of an evaluation that is supposed to be only an excavation, the dis-covery of a relation, a hidden but very real proportion between the crime and the punishment. Partners in a commercial transaction want to determine as closely as possible the correspondence of the value between the merchandise and the price. The seller considers himself satisfied when he obtains a payment equivalent to the current "market price" and the convict, while asking his lawyer to appeal, is able to recognize the justice of the judgment. But it is not a matter here of simply discerning with precision the exact amount of the penalty, but in a certain way, of understanding its moral necessity even from the perspective of the one who is subject to it. The penalty is imposed and if so, this is because it imposes itself. Its self-imposition is a function of an adjuration toward right and wrong, even if, as Hegel thinks (but not only Hegel), it is sought and demanded by the humanity of the criminal, by his dignity as a moral agent responsible for his transgression.

The quality and quantity of acts that occur through justice are like the consequences that follow from the premises of a judgment. But it is not just that the eidetic fact of all these equivalencies is determined, but the very fact of their occurrence also appears necessary. Justice is an immense machine, at times Kafkaesque, what it does it carries out quasi-automatically. Greek tragedy depicts with incomparable power the fate that is exercised in the destiny of its heroes. Men and women think they choose, decide, and then act according to their choice. In reality their actions are parts of wholes, configurations that surpass them on all sides; their actions will lead to consequences that they had neither foreseen nor desired. Orestes thought he decided, that is chose, to exercise justice by putting to death his mother, but matricide is a crime that starts the disastrous mechanism of a succession of tragic events. The Euminides sleep but the crime awakens them—a dramatic expression if there ever were one of the sober and severe principle of law: with every case of injustice a rectification is necessary. Talk about "immanent justice" is common, essentially to designate the difficulties that entangle the imprudent, the fastidiously proud, but especially the deceitful and the vile. It is exercised within an individual existence where one inadvertently falls into the pits one dug for another and the traps close on the one who prepared them. Hamlet says with an acerbic irony how "this is sport to have the engineer hoist with his own petard," and Laertes concludes, somberly, "I am justly killed with my own treachery."[22]

---

21. Aeschylus, *Les Choéphores* 313–14 (translation quoted by author is from Claudel, *Théâtre* I, 924).

22. Shakespeare, *Hamlet*, 4. 206–7, 2. 307.

Shakespeare presents here examples of "immanent justice." In reality, justice is always immanent and what is designated *stricto senso* as "immanent justice" is only a particular figure in which the automatism of *Dikē* is exercised quasi-explicitly. A metaphysico-moral synonym for the very prosaic category of causality, it translates the vision of an ontological machinery that implies and demands that possibles be realized, that every possibility be actualized, in order simply to give way to the actualization of what follows it. Justice expresses the fateful connection between cause and effect, the iron link between moments of the cosmic process that the powerful intuition of Presocratic thought glimpses under the sign of a cosmic expiation of incurred debts (Anaximander). The theme of debt is particularly suitable for suggesting the double nature, metaphysical and moral, of justice. It harbors continuity, a strict implication, but also an imputation: it is therefore a contract appearing as an obligation. Debts are to be done away with: a debt should be paid, that is, settled. An individual—or a country—impoverished or imprudent, can drown in its debts, but real debts are not simply a matter of money. The gravest debts are ones contracted towards persons. A person is offended, wounded, or killed and this initiates a deadly process. Justice has always demanded a noble indifference towards competing parties; it pretends even to wear a "blindfold in order to see nobody in its verdict,"[23] in order not to be tempted to lean in favor of on or other of the litigants. The blindfold covering the eyes of the judge is a powerful symbol of impartiality. In reality it connotes the blindness of justice, the blind course in which its process unfolds without making any exceptions, a misleading expression to designate a progression that overturns and crushes anyone in its path. Justice is supposed to be incarnated by the tribunal that exercises it. But the tribunal, the "Tribunal of the World" is capable of being only a cipher for the succession of cruelties and crimes of the "History of the World." Here we are waiting for the appearance of the blind and implacable process against Joseph K and the other accused, a process where "the procedure...gradually melts into the verdict."[24]

Justice is a regular process, unfolding according to a strict order; after all, it is only the exercise, the very translation of the law. Unfortunately, the regularity and justice of *Dikē* is not only accompanied by a brutal indifference and blindness, it can also be inspired by inexorable hate. The end of justice is indemnification and satisfaction but the need for satisfaction is often accompanied by a violent resentment. *Dikē* requires the payment of debts, the expiation of faults, but expiation is only the convex face of a single reality of which the concave face is vengeance. Vengeance is a process that is initiated starting from an intolerable offense, but it is initiated necessarily and is propagated unstoppably. Actors of vengeance can be carried away, often despite themselves. Those to whom the task falls to perpetuate it can no longer understand the sense, the reason that moves and motivates this violence; they would love to be removed from it but they are unable to be. One wants to repay evil for evil and through

---

23. Ronsard, *Premier livres des hymnes. De la justice*, in *Oeuvres complètes* vol. 2, 164.
24. Kafka, *Am Dom*, 289.

this to destroy it, but instead of being annulled, it is perpetuated. A vicious circle of reprisals is engaged: the act that was supposed to render justice initiates the escalation of vengeance. Vengeance doubtlessly has a vague affinity with the most legitimate law, some even call it the primordial form of law, or the first revelation of a consciousness of law. It is certainly said that the one who takes revenge takes justice into his own hands, but most often the vendetta is demanded by the community; it is understood as a social and moral duty. Unfortunately, if vengeance can appear as the restoration of a shattered equilibrium, the very action by which it thinks satisfaction is brought about and the tear patched over, the process is reinitiated and the cry that awoke the Eumenides is heard again. The vendetta seeks to, and seems to, effectively repair the wrong that is suffered. However, it is in fact the motivation and instrument of its perpetuation, of the continuation of this process of a bad infinity.

Vengeance is the culminating point of nature and immanence, it is the hidden face or rather the nocturnal side of justice. Francis Bacon calls it "a species of savage justice,"[25] and indeed, it is the ultimate figure of *Dikē* and, if you like, it stems from what one could call the natural history of free beings, "a natural history of humankind."[26] Justice has been explained until then in the register of immanence, the mechanical, a necessary implication and automatic unfolding. With the works of vengeance it seems to be done with the well-programmed software and to part ways with analytic judgments. The cruel malignancy of its outpouring, the dark power of the passion that animates it demonstrates access to its kind of freedom and therefore opens to the new. Vengeance would be equivalent to an internal transposition of immanence and novelty, in short, to a tearing apart that the sameness would accomplish through its own resources. However, this tearing is only fictitious because if the beings that newly transgress in each act of vengeance are truly free, their freedom does not yet fall under the category of a true opening. The freedom that is at work when vengeance surges forth is perhaps authentically culpable but the compulsive fury that makes it act is only a metaphysical variant of the theologoumenon of the servile will. Nature seems to writhe in order to escape its imprisonment and shatter its enclosure in the supreme monad, yet by not surrendering itself to sacrifice, to the exit of the kenotic self, it cannot accomplish any true rupture.

Reciprocity

Justice is the last failed avatar of the unsealing of immanence: its regular and rational deployment ends up proving to be an obsessive forging ahead with the same program. The failures of successive openings are discouragingly observed. The identity of the motivation for these relapses of immanence is speculated about: it may be found in the indeterminate multiplicity of phenomena that succeed one another. One will try

---

25. Bacon, *Essays IV. Of revenge*, in *Works*, 12, 92.
26. Fichte, *Die Prinzipien der Gottes-Sitten-u. Rechtslehre. Gesamtausgabe* II 7, 450.

then to break the locking mechanism, to shatter the circle of analysis by abandoning the multiple series of succession in favor of horizontality, of the simultaneity of the two terms in mutual relation. Philosophy wants to climb out of the deadly immobility of the Same, to break down the barriers of the Totality. It calls for the appearance of difference, the appearing of the other, in short, the irruption of Infinity. It presumes that the whirlwind of phenomena may be surpassed by the symmetrical relation of two beings that face one another and who subsist only as they act with an integral reciprocity. The reciprocal relation of two free creatures would be the responsibility of the liberating movement, the principle and paradigm of all original novelty. The relentless inevitability of the processes of immanence appears to be a function of the irreversibility of relation that binds successive phenomena. It should be replaced by a relation of mutuality in which the terms are two partners that neither impose nor endure domination in relation to one another. They should exercise parallel and analogous actions, in other words, be situated in a reciprocal relation. By reciprocal, I mean any action or relation, given the two terms A and B, that is exercised or subsists both in the direction of A to B and B to A. Reciprocity would be the very cipher of the highest relation that can prevail between free beings, causing them to flourish in their profound vocation of original innovation.

Reciprocal action is well illustrated in the domain of dual transactions whose truth is the exchange. An exchange is an operation in which one object is traded for another of equal value or meaning. An exchange in chess happens when each side takes and loses a piece. In the basic commercial process of exchange, bartering, one gives to his partner an object in view of receiving something having the same usefulness or importance, the same value. If the eidetic description of exchange necessarily consists in the mutual transmission of at least two entities, two different possessions, under a physical and legal transfer, each of the partners retains his property. However, this unchanged condition, this ultimate non-occurrence of the new not only characterizes the objects of exchange but also its action. Exchange is the ancestor of every sale, and it remains the hidden principle. The sale is only half of the total operation: the complete exchange breaks down into two successive sales. I sell something, and with the price obtained, I buy something else. From the point of view of the jurist, this is a matter of two operations that refer to two agreements, whereas from the point of view of the economist, sale and exchange are a single and same thing.

Reciprocity seems to be a true life preserver for this difficult philosophical enterprise of removing the partitions of immanence. It replaces the implacable, irreversible succession of entities subject to one another by the beautiful simultaneity of equals. But strangely, what is seen and wanted as mutual aid and respect of two sovereign beings winds up relativizing the autonomy of partners, as a matter of fact, by dissolving and obliterating their self-sufficiency. The properly metaphysical scope of reciprocal action receives a remarkable illustration in the admirable Hegelian account of the Absolute Relation. The absolute relation has three moments: substantiality, causality and reciprocal action. If in the first two moments a substratum exists, an asymmetry, in short, an excess in one of the terms over the other, then within the third, reciprocal action, the two partners enjoy a complete equality. There is no longer subordination but coexistence, the harmonious coordination of two passive and simultaneously active realities. In fact, instead of two entities, it would be better to speak about "one" single reality that unfolds. The two that face one another are only homogenous sections of "a relation locked within itself." The two terms are doubtlessly not the "same," but the difference separating them is completely "transparent." In other words if at the "origin" the terms of reciprocal action are supposed to represent the core of life proper to the All, in reality they are reduced to a homogeneity, to an ultimate "identity."[27]

Throughout its economic and logical manifestations, reciprocal action seems to return to the path of analysis, to relapse, or rather to bend back into immanence. Once more the hope of access to true novelty, to the regime that governs the a priori synthesis, is frustrated. The immaculate symmetry, the harmonious equality between terms only obfuscates the continuity of the same; it does not really undermine the reign of the totality. As a last attempt to vanquish the power of the immanent, the same, reciprocity must resolutely be rethought in terms of the effective relation of two free beings as such. Love is the supreme relation between free beings, a relation that is complete and thus spreads over the entirety of their existence and acting. The union of lovers is therefore only a superior instance of reciprocal action. It also seeks an integral mutuality, a true reduction of the lovers to unity, yet with the safeguard of the flourishing of the proper core of their being. Love is not only a figure of reciprocity but sublates it, conserving its marvelous transparency without sinking into homogeneity, into the continuity of immanence, the circle of analysis.

Love is the highest figure of reciprocity, manifesting its perfections but also enlivening its contradictions. The succession of natural phenomena obeys the law of causality: the effect follows the cause and their connection is limited to determined aspects of their being. Cause and effect necessarily touch one another, but—if you want to use topological metaphors—they only touch through certain extremities, the causal process concerns only some eidetic moments of their ends. All the while being an implacable progress, justice establishes only partial relations among phenomena. Things work differently within reciprocal action, in love. The terms of this relation, the lovers, are not limited to partial contact; they should not be able to maintain spaces between them. A short formula of one's story of love has been attempted: "he gave me his heart in exchange for mine."[28] This exchange, symbol and motivation of a superlative act of sharing, entails sharing everything else.

Contrary to friendship, love aspires to the union of bodies and therefore to a complete and unconditional unification of the lovers' being and having. It allows the contemplation of the other's nudity: this immodest suspension of modesty, that

---

27. Hegel, *Encyclopédie* I, § 155, 154, p. 402s; *Science de la Logique* 2, 293 sq.
28. Scarron, *Don Japhet* IV, 1.

marvelous "gift of Zeus to men" (*Protagoras* 322c), is the powerful symbol of the collapse of the walls of separation, of the suppression of any kind of reservation. Lovers should not keep secrets from one another. They must explain their preoccupations and reveal their intentions. Even more, they want just as much to unveil their past, its moments of glory or pain as well as shame. What is done cannot be undone, yet it can be shared and thereby be illumined in a new way or even undergo a kind of transubstantiation. The profound aim of the confession of past failures, like stories of experiences and triumphs, is the retroactive transformation wherein a sharing in the present is revitalized and reinforced by a communion in what has happened. Ultimately one is not content to exert effort to relive one's past in another, to transfer, in other words, what has happened through and for me in the sphere of the you. One obscurely feels, is convinced, persuaded, that one has been created for the other; one thinks one can read in the stars a predestination that creates a shared destiny.

The predestination to the other that lovers think they discern leads logically to marriage where "there is a single soul in one flesh." But this means more than an utterly complete intimacy. Conjugal union is limited neither to being nor even to the eidetically essential having of the spouses but extends equally to the greatest and least moments of daily life. Spouses are duty-bound not only to "faithfulness" but also to "succor and assistance." In other words, they must realize a unity without fail, an active and efficacious complementarity in every domain of life. Yet here the difficulties arrive and a profound ambiguity appears within this absolute relation that forms between lovers.

Complementarity is the nerve of the relations among things in the world relative to each other, but when it is exercised between *two* beings, it can lead to an exclusivity that is the source of heartbreak and conflicts. Lovers seek their salvation in each other. They are ready to give all but they expect to receive all as well. There is something unconditional in this giving and receiving. One wants to give everything and to give completely and one expects the gift to be received in the same way as it is given, namely as the expression of a total commitment that one receives and treats with a corresponding total commitment. But this requirement of reciprocity, however reasonable, is the fatal curse that influences the amorous relationship. I sincerely believe in the altruistic radicality of my action but the gift that I lavish is subject to an eidetic slippage. I desire to display generosity in order to satisfy the needs of the other; I therefore provide things and offer service. But it is possible that the true telos of the gift is not the succor of the recipient but the satisfaction of an aspiration of the giver. I want to aid and succor the other but this other has become to me such a unique and exclusive good, that by doing him good I end up doing *my own* good. One is not necessarily aware of this inversion, of this curving back onto oneself of one's affection, but the signs of exasperation, impatience and even ingratitude that the other manifests witness to a change in the relationship that will not fail to translate into confrontation and discord. I notice that my partner's response is insufficient or even wounding and this stinging observation allows me to see more clearly and to go farther. He did not respond as he should have to the perhaps excessive but sincere expression of my affection. Even more, this shortcoming in the reaction lies at the root of an insufficiency in his action towards me. I have done "everything" that should be done, I have given "everything" that I had to give, but he has not given as he should have. He did not give enough. He gave with reticence. He kept things for himself, and held them back because he held back himself, and precisely for this I rebuke him.

The eidetic description of the amorous relation emphasizes the sharing of everything, which, accomplished, would be the soul of it, but the requirement of the unconditioned can only be unfulfilled. I expect the other to make a clean sweep of all that he has and of all that he may possess in order to be able to provide me with some moments and elements of having that I covet. But the expectation is condemned to frustration. The other is not able to give everything that he should give, he can object to offerings and sacrifices and above all he can appear to deviate, to go astray, to deceive. Jealousy, whether "justified" or not, it does not matter, is the symbol or rather the unhealthy end of reciprocal action that renounces the shopkeeper logic of sacrifice only to perish in the allegedly pure and perfect complementarity of an existence between two partners. Jealousy is like the emblematic manifestation of the contradictions that haunt the relation of love. When one is unconditionally won over to another, one is jealous of this other, in other words, one suspects that he departs from the unconditionality of love that should correspond to our own and become its counterpart. Jealousy is provoked by the slightest shortcoming to perfect and complete fidelity, whether observed or imagined, but it compromises itself in its occurrence because it destroys its own purpose. I experience jealousy towards the other who by this very fact appears as no longer being unconditionally my own. But at the very moment that he seems to me (really or potentially) unfaithful, he must necessarily cease being the counterpart, symmetrically corresponding to me as loving unconditionally.

Logically, with good reason, one should say therefore that justified, legitimate jealousy can be felt only toward someone who in fact is not, or is no longer its proper object. But this is not the only paradox of this catastrophic passion. Jealousy is supposed to be a movement emerging from the (obviously threatened) equality of partners: it often comes from the fear of being wounded or betrayed. It is an obsessive anxiety that can take the form of a persnickety tyranny. It should be motivated only by the occasional aberrations of the other, but most often someone is "consumed" with jealousy: one is never completely reassured of a true symmetry within the reciprocity of love (however paradigmatic it may be). Jealousy must exclude love, or at least suspend or weaken it. Yet gnawing doubt and stinging suspicion make good company with the transports and ardent exaltations of affection. In fact the most astonishing and spectacular eidetic moment of this passion is its strange self-sufficiency—more precisely its metaphysical condition of being self-founding and self-continuing. Jealousy can certainly be awoken by an action, a particular event from the spousal or amorous realm but very often it burns and rages in the absence of any external fuel. As Emilia said to Desdomone: "souls. . .are never jealous for a reason; they are jealous because they are jealous. Jealousy is a self-engendering monster, born from out of itself."[29] The jealous lover's impossibility of justifying himself, of designating and clarifying the cause or occasion for his passion seems to attest to the irrationality and absurdity of this affection. Actually it powerfully illustrates its proper condition of coming into the world through itself, of not being the effect, the product or the fruit of anything preceding it or outside of it. One cannot justify jealousy as the logical rational result of an antecedent, and neither does it lead to a consequent, to an autonomous effect that subsists outside of and other than itself. Not coming from a peaceful origin, it likewise very rarely engenders positive or constructive effects. As La Bruyère says, it is "a sterile passion."[30] Yet one must be careful: this sterility is not to be understood according to the meaning of a pragmatic moralism because it also and above all possesses a metaphysical meaning and scope.

Jealousy is sterile because the exquisite complementarity of lovers offers only a further figure of immanence. The symmetry and mutuality of two free beings was supposed to break the continuous action of the succession of phenomena but this ideal reciprocity proves itself to be a curving back onto itself. The meaning, the metaphysical aim of the reciprocal action that is the elation of lovers is the rupture of Sameness but it seems to constitute a Whole in reduction, a totality written in lowercase. Spouses in love are united in everything, share everything, assist one another in everything but the ceaseless mutuality that penetrates and animates their being and acting ends up presenting only an exemplary, executed instance of being locked in on oneself. The marvelous complementarity of lovers constitutes a splendid edifice, but such a novel monad is still without windows. The lovers are one, but this One only gazes on itself, its eyes are always turned inwards.

In so far as it rejoins the circle of analysis and falls down into the continuity of immanence, the true Absolute Relation (that of lovers) suffers the absence of an authentic innovation. Love wants to perfect itself in complete complementarity, the unconditional reciprocity of two beings, but it is nevertheless condemned to exhaust itself and to conclude—or rather, to be concluded—in sterility. But sterility is not only immanence and powerlessness. It is truly the existential face of analysis, and everybody knows that analysis grows thorns—towards both the outside and inside, as instruments of internal division and the arms of external conflict.

Jealousy is a particularly violent, inordinate form, involving excesses or rather heartbreaks that lie in wait for lovers, but it is not their unique form. The reciprocal relation of love can also take the form of a duel that takes place in a closed field, increasing the lacerating power of the blows exchanged. The vicissitudes of these most intimate enemies that lovers and spouses can become are spread over the pages of

---

29. Shakespeare, *Othello* III 4 159–62.
30. La Bruyère, *Les Caractères*, in *Oeuvres complètes*, 338.

novels and short stories: they seem to constitute a substantial part of the explorations of moralists. However, if confinement can drive the couple locked in on itself to internal conflict, it can also give to them, like a poisoned gift, an inclination for aggression towards the outside. Concerning a relation of integral complementarity where the two partners cloister themselves from anyone else, we should be happy to speak—in a very precise determination—of "egotism of two." The two exclude every third, but the exclusion is not a simple demarcation of spheres. The I is supposed to swell and to spread out and by this fact to encroach on others, but there is also an internal encroachment proper to the couple. The aggressive desire for growth at the expense of others is definitely not the exclusive privilege of sterile unions, but it seems to be a proper potentiality appearing on the horizon of infertile couples. Psychologists and moralists try to take account, in empirical terms, of the unclear affinity between sterility and aggressiveness but these conflicting impulses, these tendencies to conquest have their metaphysical "reasons."

Sterility is the matrix of conflict. It is the consequence or rather the faithful expression of a blind movement of self-continuation of which peaceful analyticity is ultimately only a deceptive mask. The same that advances remains the same at the price of refusing, even obliterating others, if it must. To be sure, the same does not deny itself every expression, but the structures it provides itself constitute only so many variations of immanence. And if in the course of its development immanence seems to accommodate forms of novelty, even its highest moment, justice is finally only the defense, or rather the self-defense of the continuity that claims to be interrupted. The mechanical process by which immanence is unfolded in nature proffers an infinite multiplicity of entities. To the degree that they only punctuate the frame of Nature's self-continuation, they exist according to justice, but they still remain below creative freedom. The reciprocal relation of two lovers should interrupt the blind procession of *physis-dikē*, but as it confines itself to the complementarity of exchange, it remains a form of immanence, analytic judgment. It was thought that love as perfect reciprocity of absolute relation would "resolve" the confinement of justice. In actuality, in and by this reciprocity, immanence reveals its flaws, the inevitability that condemns it to enter into crisis. Jealousy witnesses the illusions and limits of complete symmetry; sterility attests that the integral and exclusive exchange of partners leads to a blockage. Reciprocity seemed to present the promises of an interior maturation, a self-surpassing of justice. It ended up showing and demonstrating the impossibility of a natural opening of immanence.

III

Newness: Figures and Paths

The Horizons of Potentiality

Philosophy tries to overcome the deadly immanence of nature by transposing the mechanical unfolding of justice into the wonderfully proportioned complementarity of lovers. Unfortunately, the operation is destined to fail. At the end of a succession of figures, one would think one has broken the spring of the mechanism and triggered the movement of opening, of self-transcendence. The accounts of justice are cleaned out and nature is pushed back into the night of indifference that is its truth. You can chase off nature but it will return because it has never really left. In its moral and juridical meaning, *Dikē* is perceived as victory over revenge. Yet in its metaphysical truth it is always only the supreme figure of "pure avenging reciprocity" of which the union of lovers may appear as the true fulfillment.[1]

Leading nature beyond itself is the proper project of metaphysics, but it is an arduous task, littered with traps and mined, especially, with contradictions. Philosophy likes to display the movement of transposition of analytic immanence into synthetic novelty. In other words it wants nature to go beyond itself, but starting from itself, always remaining near itself. The Incarnation of the Second Divine Person has been defined as the mystery where one becomes other, all the while remaining oneself, but *physis* hardly disposes of the power of freedom and *Dikē* cannot help herself to the instruments of love. Since Parmenides philosophy has not stopped challenging the dogma that rejects a third way between being and non-being; it wants to conceptualize this first and fundamental Excluded Middle. Yet as it conceives and formulates this process bearing the marks of a shaky compromise, it fails to get off the ground, to pass beyond the pejorative sense of Becoming that is generally imperfect and at times

---

1. Girard, *La violence et le sacré*, 47.

deceitful. The fate of ancient philosophy, the ball and chain attached to its feet since the Eleatics, is the vision of becoming as below actuality and being; a potentiality that is simultaneously contingency and violence, bloodless possibility and blind excess. Since the Neoplatonists what has always been sought is a way to overcome this fate in order to glimpse an active potentiality, a *dynamis* that by its nature would be a capacity for growth, a positive aspiration, a movement towards what is other and better than itself. But it is only in light of the great theologoumena of the *tzimtzum* and the kenosis that a transposition can be envisaged where the Same would overcome itself starting from itself, and where the Totality would open up from within by means of its own proper sources. In other words it will need patiently to explain the figures and the eidetic promises of Potentiality. From the overflow we will pass to superabundance and from difference to direction, with the exodus, self-exit and self-surpassing as ultimate horizon.

From Superabundance to Tearing Away

The march toward novelty is accomplished under the sign of potentiality, of an active potentiality that is not the simple actualization of the possible, a making explicit of what is given. The initial attempts to unseal immanence passed through the development, the unfolding of structures that were contained, or rather, pre-contained in nature. But the beautiful regularity of the unfolding is ever only the exercise of Analytic Judgment. The development of becoming according to its rules and its own resources could never kindle something truly new. Another way will then be tried: starting from the primary and elementary intuition of growth and the advent of excess, the opening up of the Same as Superabundance will be envisaged—a superabundance that is neither an overflowing of a blind self nor a flooding starting from an overflow, but rather an effective self-surpassing.

The surpassing of immanence towards newness will have superabundance as its first form. The life that overflows every side is superabundant, but one that is benign and peaceful—certainly unforeseeable, or rather, non deducible, but not mere improvisation or light caprice. In superabundance a being enlarges or expands itself, it is surrounded with a halo but one that is not merely a nimbus or aureole. Superabundance is substantial, fleshly, an enrichment of the given that is truly added to it. It is the sign of a good-natured prodigality, but which will ultimately barely concern itself with producing or effecting permanence or independence. The figures of superabundance are without a doubt not simple excrescences, parasites on a self that would not manage to maintain its natural rhythm and measure. They constitute a true periphery where the self is completely present, even if it does not obliterate the difference between center and periphery. Superabundance is the development of the center towards the periphery, or rather its prolongation in the periphery. The phenomena of superabundance cannot be disassociated from the being that gives itself over to the joy of blossoming, above all because the spontaneity of this growth is not from the automatic reflex of instinct. In fact, superabundance at times, some would say at its best times, comes from exuberance, albeit exuberance with a light critical accent. Superabundance is a remarkable self-unfolding; it is like the middle way between blind overflow and planned production where superabundance seems to bring about this beautiful equilibrium. It weakens the natural prolongation of the self but steers it toward an excess where the overflow is converted into consequences that seemed to evade the superabundant without however constituting another entity, a new reality. If generosity is the predicate of the superabundant subject in an a priori synthesis, exuberance is only a simply elaboration or unfolding where the a priori synthesis fights the analysis.

Superabundance means movement towards the outside, but the progression towards the outside is not a circumstantial or limited habit or gesture. It certainly exercises itself at the extremities of a being, at the borders of what it is not, and yet it does not amount to external contact, a simple "local" movement. Superabundance is the first phenomenon of the exit from the self, but every exodus, even the most rudimentary, has its origins in the depths of the being. The placid immobility of immanence is first disturbed and shaken by a movement, a flux that wells up from the interior. Before appearing at the peripheries of an entity the flow of superabundance invisibly takes shape in its internal spaces. Superabundance is either a sudden upsurge or eruption. The sudden upsurge is the first but still very primitive, elementary form of the exit from the self. It is only a quick and delicate rough draft. In a very visible and clear way it displays the non-instinctive character of true superabundance. Through the imagery of an unforeseen emergence and sudden advent it implies the impulse to go beyond oneself that a being is concerned with. But the upsurge pays a stiff price for these first eidetic appearances of rupture. If it anticipates the exodus of generosity through a beginning as a *deus ex machina*, then the freedom of the self-exit is irremediably jeopardized by the contingent, fortuitous character of this appearance. Even more the evident detachment of the phenomenon from the depths of its origin goes along with the retention of these accidental colors. What has surged up is planted there where it is found but one does not see very well why it is located there nor for what reason it remains there. The phenomenon of upsurge spectacularly points to the gap or crevice opened up in the heart of being, of the in-itself, but its emancipation in fact remains bereft of meaning.

The upsurge is an authentic form of superabundance, but only partially does it justice. It certainly manifests it, albeit in isolation and dispersion. A second and more balanced eidetic form of superabundance is eruption. An eruption has the same vivacity and vigor as the sudden upsurge but it surpasses it through harmony in the flow, a protected presence at the very heart of the blossoming. Being a sudden appearance, eruption doubtlessly suffers from an impenitent elementarity, but at least it does not peter out in isolated occurrences. The flame erupts from a lighter, lava from the crater, blood from the wound: one is always dealing with phenomena of Hegelian immediacy. But the immediacy is always found, so to say, redeemed: the eruption certainly has no reason for its existence that will have served as detonator for its advent, but its very movement seems to attest to a first surpassing of the spontaneity of matter, a condition that prefigures freedom. The eruption is like the eidetic precursor to generosity. An eruption of feelings can be in itself only a figure of excess, but it is no less an organic moment, an indispensible element of a generous heart. In fact, the distinction between superabundance and generosity passes through degrees: superabundance draws its own border but it does not grab hold of these emanations and defluxions, it does not worry about jealously retaining what emanates from it. Superabundance only pushes further out its own borders, but these are like margins, the elements of which can if necessary be detached from the central body. What is essential is not that the superabundant preserves everything that surges up from it, but that it not dry up, that it continues to erupt.

Eruption is a profusion, a prodigality not encumbered by calculation and located beyond every economy. It is the instrument of the advent of something new, but to which corresponds no diminishment or disappearance. It has nothing to do with justice, skimpy and stingy, the justice that "gives no gifts" and which is only what it is, no less—and above all—no more. Superabundance is like life: it surges and resurges, it erupts and re-erupts. In other words, it is inexhaustible. It can leave its emanations on the edge of the road, abandoning what it produces, but this frivolous waste does not decrease its movement nor encroach upon its unfolding. Superabundance is like life: what surges up and erupts in it does not weaken it, does not diminish it, does not compromise its integrity. Like all true life it exudes a freshness—a freshness that is not a lower degree, a gradation of cold, a freshness that is not a matter of a given season, but rather the air or native atmosphere of every revivifying eruption. The freshness of a being, an event, a complexion or a word, are like the eidetic moments of "youth" (not understood in the chronological sense). As is often said, youth is not a matter of years, of a certain distance from a beginning, but rather it expresses a condition of non-degradation, non-deterioration, of a non-exhaustion that is in fact inexhaustibility.

The freshness in a young being is a sign of a good state of health, or rather the positive and promising manifestation of an intact vitality; it extends and indicates the fecund self-mastery of life "at its peak." In other words it corresponds to the "creative" aspect of the inexhaustible, but creativity is never simply reprise or repetition. It certainly does not have as an explicit eidetic moment, direction towards this or that, nor the production of multiple disseminated parts, but it is also not infinitely unfolding, a *kinesis* that would never have started and never have come to an end. Instead it is like the growth of a plant that perpetuates itself through a self-extension that is self-elaboration, a true creative evolution. Creativity is constructive evolution, a progression through successive syntheses according to its own timing, but this maturation and enrichment is not locked in itself. Creativity doubtlessly does not have as its intentional aim the accession of individual entities, but it is a flowering, and as such it should result in fruits. Fruits mature and then fall and then can be collected. But the essential is that they are less taken as planned outcomes, automatic and necessary results of a process, than as phenomena that creativity entails and that happen, if not in a contingent and fortuitous manner, nevertheless freely. Justice does not give gifts, yet superabundance is strewn along its paths. It is not that it pursues transcendent ends, that it intends or wants to give gifts, but, at times a playful power, it tolerates and even surreptitiously favors what is unjustified. The upsurge and eruption of the superabundant do not have much to do with work or labor, useful production or sober economic calculus. They would not want to stop punctuating their operation with moments in which they consent to suspend their progress and above all to give up its consequences. Superabundance has an innate tendency towards celebration, it loves to give feasts where the grandiose and liberal distribution of goods indicates a first sketch of exit out of oneself, already beyond the necessary unfolding of justice, but still below love's self-surpassing.

The feast is the greatest distance that superabundance can allow and assume in relation to itself, but it does not yet represent an authentic surmounting of immanence, a true self-exit. The feast is without tomorrow, it accomplishes the suspension of the natural course of things, but this suspension is totally momentary, ephemeral. It produces some theatre actors, but theatre only brackets real life for a short time. The feast wears masks, plays roles, reverses or inverts situations, it professes to give rise to something new, but it never definitively brings it about. It is only the ultimate avatar of creativity, of superabundance, in other words instances of development that do not manage to halt the flow of becoming. It has been said that superabundance anticipates generosity, but in order for it to accomplish it, to call into existence even some simple elements, it must be willing and able to agree to the position of something other than itself. Ultimately, superabund0ance is a headlong rush where the same pushes back its own borders, but this multi-form pollen, these myriads of fragments, flakes or scales that detach themselves from it and disperse, fill up only an area of which it remains the substantial center, the unique autonomous entity. Free exit from the self presupposes the subject's acceptance of differentiation, but for the eruption to transform itself into a fertile self-surpassing, it must recognize the other within itself.

The figure or rather the elementary principle of every being-other is Difference. Consequently, the sublation of superabundance by generosity seems to lead reflection to pose and to assume difference. Difference appears as the condition, the heartbeat, the core of every existence that asserts itself starting from the cosmic process. But despite all of the accomplishments of its dialectical deduction, difference does not really manage to distinguish itself from diversity. The metaphysical principle for the existence of singular autonomous beings, for the advent of the new, is sought: a newness that is filled with meaning. But difference is not the principle or manifestation of meaning. Difference is a fact, a dull and crude ontological fact, it is authentic but it does not have its own intelligibility. Difference can lock an entity up within its own confines or, above all, it can demarcate and separate entities, but it is only a factuality without meaning and without promise. In its eruption a being can come across and bang into difference, it can finally even obliterate it or at least trample on it. But difference remains a facticity, an exteriority. The platitude claims: one must respect difference, any difference, whatever it is! Yet the intentional object of respect is truly an end in itself, an autonomous reality, a focus of meaning. Difference is not found within this universe. To have to respect difference, more clearly, a being that is different than me, in the last analysis means to respect it because it is different than *me*. But the fact of being different than me does not yet tell me anything about this being and is incapable of saying anything about it. Or rather: it says loudly and clearly that it is not like me and therefore defines it in terms of me and only in terms of me. Despite its apparent condition as principle of alterity, Difference does not really separate itself from Sameness. It is a category that certainly dramatizes Limit, limit as it is imposed from the outside, but that cannot be read as an intrinsic moment of our being and thus effectively as a self-surpassing. In its banality and radical indigence Difference is ill suited to found alterity. This role can only be reserved for Direction, a category where the sense-less condition of the limit is overcome by the *towards*, the indication of orientation and sending on mission.

Direction certainly entails difference but a difference that is, so to speak, superior and which conquers its native condition of facticity. It is not able to be a tension or effective movement, but it is under the sign of the *towards* (the towards of orientation), which suggests an aspiration, a throbbing that represents a certain eidetic advance in relation to difference. Direction and difference both pertain to the spatial. However, whereas difference seems essentially to be located in a banal and indistinct horizontality, direction implies a differentiation that underlies and prepares for the founding opening of the exit from the self. Direction is not found but it is impressed on you. And it not only causes the observation of the configuration of a distance but it constitutes the spatial structure of an élan. In reality, direction is like the skeleton or prefiguration of this same metaphysical-moral reality of which the exodus of the self-exit will be the definitive enactment.

Difference and Direction respectively constitute an eidetic framework for the two great figures of Laceration and Tearing Away where an advancement towards an opening to the work seems to be accomplished in subjectivity. Laceration is, in other words, the translation of difference into an effective movement. It is no less caustic, vigorous, or (if you like) radical than tearing away, but it represents a moment of progress where one is not yet capable of surmounting or departing from oneself. Division nearly shares in the poverty of facticity, the horizontality destitute of difference. It is practiced flush to the floor, or rather, in an interiority without horizon or finality. Laceration can only be a simple laceration of the skin. It nevertheless represents an infringement of the integrity of being, though a crude and local one, and while being apt to wound or to disfigure, it is not a moment or inner cause of a profound alteration, especially one of which it would be itself the principle. Laceration is a phenomenon of contingency wherein a being struggles against what occurs within its immanent world, though immanence denotes here only the implacable mechanism that outstrips and overtakes the singular. Pascal distinguishes between the enemies of the church outside of it and those within, "who lacerate it from within."[2] The "internal" condition is not here a cipher of meaning or genuine appropriation. Laceration is located in the bowels of a being, but it articulates only the failure to collect and to master oneself. It can lacerate a living being only on the surface, but even when it happens internally, at the heart of its organism, it is precisely a sign of its non-self-mastery. Laceration can translate some authentic efforts in order to surmount them and perform a self-exit, but as always in the universe of difference, the limitation that one is subject to, a limitation however real and effective, does not amount to a true, disappropriative exit from the self.

Laceration is accomplished on a horizontal plane, in the absence of a *toward*, a sign of direction and orientation; it is a condition without opening and without telos, not only when one is subject to it from the outside but equally when one imposes it on oneself. Spouses disunite, "separate themselves," as they say, but the reflexive character of the expression is precisely a sign of imprisonment, of a movement without meaning or hope, and of convulsive but finally sterile efforts. Things are different for *tearing away*, which could count as the first breach of immanence, the first occurrence of a true exit from the self. While laceration is conjugated in the accusative, a sign of immediacy and brutal continuity, tearing away conserves a space for the adverb, for the sake of being able to insert a distance between the subject and predicate. Most often one tears oneself away *from* one thing and tears oneself away *to* another: there is, as it were, an interplay between the action and the result. Rightly understood this interplay is very serious: one can tear out the desperate fugitive from his hideaway or tear out a pound of flesh from one's defeated adversary. Tearing away would be a true synthetic a priori movement that extricates itself from missed attempts to surmount analysis. In order for it to be considered an authentic instance of the a priori synthesis, it must originate within subjectivity *and* make possible this subjectivity's going beyond itself. In other words the tearing away must emanate from the subject, emerge from it and be undertaken by it. On the other hand, it is an action in which the subject turns against itself and does not merely renounce trifles or suffer scratches. In order for an attempt to surmount the self to be taken seriously, to count as a true self-surpassing, the self cannot try to keep all its property: one cannot make an exodus weighed down by weapons and baggage. He must abandon at least a part, an important part, of his possessions. In its truth, self-extraction is a costly activity, and it costs much more than the possible compensation. It is neither an impulse nor a fit of rage. It is hardly an irrational adventure. It is a process, an activity in which the expenses are able to

---

2. Pascal, *Pensées,* 858, in *Oeuvres complètes.*

be, if not completely calculated, at least foreseen in their magnitude. What counts is to know and to accept an activity that costs dearly. According to every human calculation, one risks not breaking even. But, as a Puritan preacher said, "When men's expenses... exceed their receipts... they cease spending."[3]

Self-Exit and Self-Surpassing

The self-extraction that moral subjectivity decides on opens the path to the kingdom of newness. It expresses itself in the two great figures of self-exit and self-surpassing. Whether I exit from myself or surpass myself, I accept the call of the Opening, I obey the injunction to unlock Analysis. But Opening is a complex idea; it is the cipher of a difficult, ambiguous reality. The path of opening directly connects a concealed extension of the self and a hemorrhage of the subject. My ponderous egoism demonstrates valiant and vigorous efforts in the moral action that I engage in in order to surmount my nature and condition. From where could these efforts emanate if not from the *conatus* subverted by service to others, but which remains truly the energy of the self? How to avoid the experience of self-tearing away being used for self-extension by means of sacrifices, especially of the inessential? In short, how to resolve this squaring of the circle that is the continuation of the self at the heart of the rupture of the self? The symmetrical counterpart to this apparent impossibility of obeying the kenotic command of becoming other, all the while remaining the same that one was, is the danger of the radical loss of self. "God," says the Cherubinic Wanderer, "has the character of pouring himself into the creation."[4] But just as God does not cease being God when pouring into creatures, so the free creature called to surpass itself does not have to disappear or lose itself. But if someone takes the praiseworthy discontinuity that he preaches to the letter, does he not risk depriving it of its subject? In order to be effective and not an act of stratagem, the exit from the self must not be a pure defluxion, a hemorrhage. The imprisonment in immanence is doubtlessly overcome only through the opening, but the great injunction to de-nucleate must be balanced, if one wants to correct it, by safeguarding the possibility of keeping *its* promises, of welcoming *its* other—briefly, of remaining itself through self-abandonment.

The structure of this 'becoming-other while remaining itself' is a supreme instance of the a priori synthesis that is perfectly illustrated by the kenotic paradigm. "The attribute of God" is to pour himself into the creation but kenosis stems from the verb *kenein*, "to empty." Through his suffering and death, but already in his Incarnation, the Second Person, instead of holding himself back in order to protect what he is and has, is emptied of himself and pours himself out. However, to be emptied and to pour himself out do not mean to lose. The two pitfalls to avoid in the formulation of Christian dogma, a fortiori in the conception of kenosis, are the diverse Docetisms

---

3. Shepard, *The Parable of the Ten Virgins*, in *Works* II, 285s.
4. Angelus Silesius, *Le pèlerin chérubinique* II, 132.

as well as excess in reading Christ's cry of dereliction on the Cross. The body nailed to the Cross was truly the body of the Incarnate Son. Yet the Passion and Death of the God-Man does not mean a true ontological rupture between the divinity and the tortured. Beyond differences in theological explication of the subject properly so-called of kenosis, in what manner it is attributed to the Second Person, how it affects the hypostatic union, the two natures, what matters is that the subject of the kenosis is the Incarnate Word who continues to be God *and* Man through all the forms of debasement and privation that he assumes. The spear that strikes the crucified makes blood run from his side (John 19:34) but the blood that pours out does not signify the dissolution of the divine-human subject but rather its continuity, its effective permanence. The wounding of his side like an opening: an opening that unlocks the subject and through which he exits from himself, but which is also the place and moral force of his presence in his going beyond himself.

The newness of our acting requires tearing away. Yet the drama of tearing away, a violent action, a costly activity, does not yet adequately express the radicality and totality of creativity. In every extraction we are doubtlessly torn away from ourselves, undergoing an experience that may affect us in our whole being. Nevertheless, the accomplished and definitive character of the act suggests the metaphysical fiction of a duality, the at least momentary advent of a scission of the person, a doubling of the self into contrasting selves that are certainly temporary but also vigorous and efficacious. Tearing away is heavily associated with a partial operation that removes from me a fragment of my flesh, a member of my body. Totalizing imagery, however, is better suited for the logic of going beyond the self. Moral action is proper to the individual, but in its paroxysm it leads to a kind of bogus twin-making. I intend to overcome *myself*, but the I does not accept any reduction, a reduction to a part. If the moralist thinks he can explain the exercise of true virtue as "control over his own heart,"[5] this is because the heart is not an organ of the body, it very well stands for the I itself. Combat not only produces "localized wounds,"[6] it represents total war. It takes place between the soul and the body, between what is best in me and what is the worst, or more precisely, between two men within me, the I that I am and the I that I should be and would like to be. However powerful and suggestive, this vision falls only under the regime of "representation," and if the expansion of metaphysics neither can nor should renounce the use of metaphor, the diverse metaphors of twinning do not do justice to the a priori synthesis that structures the work of creativity.

Tearing away should not be retained as a figure of true moral action because it risks reducing it to a partial operation. Twin-making sections out or dissolves the subject that must remain the same while becoming other. By still using the discourse on "the self" one most closely corresponds to the exigencies of the a priori synthesis and remains most faithful to the profound logic of kenotic opening. The two

---

5. Rousseau, *Lettre à M. de Franquières*, in *Oeuvres complètes* vol. 4, 1143.
6. Milton, *Paradise Lost*, XII, 387.

primordial figures of renewing action are self-exit and self-surpassing. They are both manners of acting, operations attributed to the same self, precisely inasmuch as it remains the same. The wholeness of the movement assumed by the subject is joined together according to a spatial understanding where the opposition between direction and difference implicitly reappears. Self-exit appears to be enacted horizontally, in the dimension of difference, whereas self-surpassing carries the imprint of direction, in the case of direction towards what is above.

Without a doubt differentiation according to spatiality does not affect the essential, which is for the two figures—self-exit and self-surpassing—their complete and definitive condition. An exasperated person is said to fly off the handle but this has little in common with the immense separation denoted by self-exit. Flying off the handle designates a violent and sudden movement full of ardor and emotion—but essentially provisional, temporary. And above all it designates a movement that instead of translating the truth of a person by expressing a free but deeply rational progression, unveils instead a moment in its life where it had escaped from itself and momentarily skipped the continuity and therefore comprehensibility of its project. Well to the contrary true self-exit means a total investment of the self under the form of a total disinvestment or withdrawal from what has up to then seemed important, precious, even essential. Self-exit is a synonym for leaving. It also corresponds to deserting and above all to abandoning. It is an exodus, which has a range of moments and figures. Exodus is made starting from the habitual, the familiar, or rather, the native. It contains dramatic connotations: one is constrained by the force of circumstances, the severity of time, and above all, by the harshness of men. It can certainly be imposed on us by our own choice, by a decision, but which, despite not being without reason, exudes coercion. In any case exodus is sorrowful and confusing. It causes you to leave your points of reference, possessions, and friends. It causes you to trade the known for the unknown, to forsake the familiar for the foreign. It forces you to abandon the security of your world for an unexplored universe. Exodus is the spatial translation of a rupture in the temporal order. The I lives peaceably within a harmonious continuity of the three times. It tranquilly enjoys the present when the present is a continuation, an organic, logical development of the past. Above all it can enjoy the sweetness of the present because the future in preparation promises to be the fruition of labors past and present. Self-exit takes here the form of a rupture between the two first times and the third. It is the irruption of the unforeseen and the unpredictable in our zone of security, a rupture that is not like enduring a natural disaster, a sudden inundation, but one provoked by oneself, summoned by one's own voice.

Opposed to the cyclical movement of nature and to every starting point that one wishes to be only provisional, self-exit is conversion. One turns one's eyes to another— and turns them for good—to the same degree that one succeeds in turning them away from what was, until then, one's own. The journey of Ulysses ends by bringing him back to his native Ithaca and the last great philosopher of the past century opposed

Abraham's departure from the country of his forefathers. This is a departure that is a break with his family and his gods, a journey that will lead him to a far-off, unknown country. Self-exit is like this peregrination that removes you from your origins and does so definitively, without return. But if the removal in the horizontal leads to the sealing of the separation, in other words, if the definitive character of detachment is essential to self-exit, then self-surpassing exercises another way of opening, the unlocking of immanence. Self-exit realizes a bracketing of the self and its possessions, coming down to, if you like, their neutralization, whereas self-surpassing teaches us of their small value in relation to what it enjoins us to attain. Above all it brings about and causes us effectively to reach this surplus of value that it presents and promises. Self-surpassing contains inscribed on its eidetic essence direction towards what is above. The above is like the spatial cipher of elevation and sublimity. But what finds itself raised up to a better position than it formerly occupied does not leave behind its first faltering steps, its imperfections, but causes them, as it were, to profit from what is newly acquired, penetrating and transfiguring them by the spirit of its new condition. Self-surpassing is a particularly striking example of a gradual transformation that, through the sublation of the old by the new, illustrates the reorientation of the immanent towards the opening through a subtle economy of creativity in fidelity. While self-exit is like a bracketing of what one formerly was, a conscious and determined forgetting of the past, in self-surpassing one retains the relation with the self that one intends to surmount. It is an accomplishment but it remains rooted in its origins, a victory but one that retains a continuity with what has been overcome. Properly understood, this continuity is not accomplished at once but should be understood as a constant renewal. Self-surpassing is not a singular battle but a constant fight, an ever-renewed struggle. It is certainly a fight careful to avoid a relapse but which above all aims to go farther and higher. Plato already taught that "the good man is stronger than himself" (*Republic* 430 e) and to the degree that he becomes that, he becomes it through fighting and incessantly winning victories over himself.

Freedom

The drama of moral discourse likes to appeal to spatial imagery, which seems singularly apt to express the call to the movement of going beyond. In order to signify the properly moral moment, that of the injunction and response to the call, creativity assumes with partiality the figure of the ascent. Yet direction, in the present case upward direction, is only one of the eidetic aspects of this transformation of which growth is another essential face. Growth is progression, enhancement, enrichment: it appears as a natural process, mixed with and propelled by life. One speaks of growth in various virtues; one hopes to grow in perfection. Growth is a synonym for maturation, but maturation is not simply development. Trees mature, thanks to favorable climactic conditions, whereas humans grow through experiences, in adversity. The "positive" sense implied by maturation is neither of the quantitative nor qualitative orders. It is not a matter of a quantitative accumulation nor even of a qualitative approximation of perfection. Growth means the procuration of a more, or rather, the access to a more, but this *more* is neither a numerical accrued value nor a more faithful configuration of an essence. The more that one desires to obtain certainly corresponds to a potentiality on hold, but this is neither a lack to be filled nor a need to be assuaged. The mystery of the more is that it seems to be a response to a call of nature but which is not able to be given in the same terms of as the call that provokes it.

The more is supposed to be the reasonable solution to a problem, without being prefigured by what is given. It is expected, but cannot be found through anamnesis or deduced maieutically. A violent impulse issuing from the entrails of nature calls for its desires to be satisfied; one can experience a screaming lack longing to be filled. Inversely, one can be pushed towards the exterior by a movement, an action that goes out and rises up within us. It has always been thought that man was a being defined by lack, a being with cracks in it, undermined from within, destabilized by faults and gaps. Anxiety would even be its specific difference, translating itself into the feverous search for hobbies and in the incessant effort to do and to acquire. But in the same way that the regularity without exception of the process of justice is only a mask for the egoism of the essence of nature, the diverse ways that we hurry to plug the gaps and satisfy desires are only another face—the dynamic face—of *physis*. In terrestrial beings other than man these diverse ways that the conatus is exercised are adequate and proportionate ways to conform to essence. But man, an alien and unique being, a being in excess, has a different relation to its essence. The essence of rocks, plants and animals is found in actualizing their nature, whereas "the nature of man has not been created in order to stay within the terms of nature,"[7] *its* nature, but to exceed and surpass it.

Life already carries a propensity to come out of itself, to give itself a perpetual halo and an excess. Intelligence is, as is well known, nothing in itself. It is only an intentional tension, a perpetual quest and a conquest of images, eidē, in short, realities other than itself. But the true response to the "questions" of nature is not to try and find within a plurality some kind of prolongation of the self. It says loudly and clearly: "leave yourself, surpass yourself." These two great separations are ruptures on the ontological as well as eidetic plane. The advent of the new is a leap that no power of nature could accomplish and the figures that it assumes do not count among the eidē proper to life in its immanence. The being-otherwise that is creativity is inaugurated in the *reign* of freedom.

It is through freedom that potentiality sublates its primitive condition as simple possibility. Through it the rescue from contingency and the bracketing of the arbitrary are accomplished. Freedom is a properly ontological category but is rethought starting from the great notion of the a priori synthesis. In the terms of Kantian orthodoxy,

---

7. Bérulle, *Oeuvres de piété* 204, in *Oeuvres complètes* vol. 4, 85.

freedom is the practical corollary of the Third mediator represented by time in theoretical judgment. In reality one could understand it as the truth of all synthetic mediation, the foundational moral force of the a priori synthesis. The a priori synthesis is the power of creativity proper to subjectivity, a creativity that, all the while being a leap, a rupture, briefly, indeducible, establishes itself with structure and meaning. In and through the a priori synthesis subjectivity is given a path to take, a trajectory to follow. Freedom is the power that allows the path to begin and to be accomplished while apriority prescribes its limit and discerns within it its structural steps. To the degree that it is unanticipatable and indeducible, freedom "has no essence,"[8] but it constitutes to some degree the distinction, the gap between being and essence. It is certainly not the good: after all, the principle of every morality is that the creature is free to desire and to do *evil*! It is nevertheless a *conditio sine qua non* of the good: if freedom is the possibility of separating from oneself, of surpassing oneself, the good is the accomplishment of this possibility as self-diffusion. The eidetic essence of freedom is the possibility of choice, but this possibility is finally only the moral instance of the primordial metaphysical category of the power to be otherwise, the power of creativity.

Augustine defined freedom as "*novitas*,"[9] and effectively, nothing is so new as that which is free, or rather only the free is truly new. Beyond the false or merely relative newness of the Image, a true newness is found perfected in self-surpassing. Moral action is the authentically new action: emerging from the leap of self-tearing away, accomplished by the rupture of self-exit, it appears rootless and insubstantial and it brings about the unexpected and the autonomous. From a properly metaphysical point of view freedom is the great adversary of the principle of sufficient reason. It has the lightness of things that should not worry about watching their backs, to the degree that they do not depend on any kind of background. Freedom is exercised "without support and without springboard,"[10] and it serves, in other words, as an effective manifestation of a prowess of which this habitual liar Baron von Münchhausen speaks, who can even extract himself from quicksand without any outside help.

Philosophers and theologians are always repeating that freedom is a leap, but what kind of leap is it? It is represented as a detachment from the given, an extraction from nature. We have a natural tendency to think of the leap as a passage starting from A and arriving at B, occurring within the realm of nature, an immanent newness. Immanence is like a springboard from which the leap breaks away, but the truth of the leap is precisely that once executed its springboard is destroyed. The young Schelling felt compelled to remind his readers that "no infants are born free,"[11] that we are not free from the very beginning, but that we become free. How? Originally, freedom is

---

8. Sartre, *L'être et le néant*, 513.
9. Augustine, *De Civitate Dei* XII, xxi, 3.
10. Sartre, *L'être et le néant*, 560.
11. Schelling, *Ideen zu einer Philosophie der Natur. Werke* II, 12.

understood as the effective power to go to the Agora, the power of the male Athenian citizen to go where he wants when he wants. This same primitive idea of the possibility of non-restricted movement is at the origin of the great theories of metaphysical freedom that, essentially, are only so many variations of the question about the terms in which one could think the "effectiveness of the will in nature," the human influence on what it is not, outside as inside oneself. But it is precisely this conception of contact between freedom and what it is not that leads to various paradoxical and insoluble difficulties for the interrogation on the external efficacy of the will, that is, on the causality of freedom in nature. However, if one must believe in this causality that is seen at work every moment, one still cannot conceptualize it. Hence the shift of the interrogation into the moral sphere where it is essentially a question of freedom's self-determination. It is thought that freedom influences nature, and does so through the determination that the willing subject gives itself. The moralists, Stoics of diverse obediences, are hardly mistaken when they exhort us to struggle against our inclinations and to subdue our natural tendencies. Freedom is a battle, but an internal one. It does not have to be born out in an elsewhere that ineluctably escapes us; it is confined to the arduous and oh-so exultant task of self-subjugation, of coincidence with itself.

In its strict metaphysical meaning freedom emerges from itself and this self-engenderment has as its very logical corollary that it should only be able to develop itself within free beings and inasmuch as they are free. A rigorous conformity to this vision doubtlessly entails inextricable difficulties. It should rather be conceived as a regulative, not constitutive, concept; it should illumine and inspire the thought of freedom without being able to translate itself completely in our interpretation of free action at work in the world. In fact, the apparent impossibility of doing justice to the requirement, however "logical," of being able to develop itself only within free beings, opens the way to a true revision of the idea of freedom, involving the acceptance of shifts in its absoluteness. In order to avoid these shifts being taken for inevitable compromises, for observations of fact, briefly, for the fatal encroachment of the empirical onto the metaphysical, one could or should expound them starting from consideration of correctives applied to freedom analogous to those to which the classical conception of perfection has been submitted. The perfection that was seemingly excluded from any being-otherwise, any more or less, ended up accommodating abasement and withdrawal. In fact abasement, the power-to-be-less, shows itself to be like the highest ideas of perfection... but if the perfection of the perfect must be able to admit of some exemptions, imperfections, enervations, then also the pure spontaneity of freedom could invite limitations and self-limitations.

In its metaphysical essence freedom is indivisible: it cannot be damaged or delimited and above all it must only happen through and starting from itself. Here the lesson of kenosis would be particularly instructive and useful and above all easier to allow: contrary to the perfection that is proper only to the absolute being, freedom is attributed to finite beings. Kant said that the idea of "human freedom is even more difficult to conceive than the freedom of God."[12] It is the unconditioned within the conditioned, the infinite within the finite. Freedom is the supreme power, or, if you like, the very being of the finite creature. Finitude spills over into freedom. Notwithstanding its irreducible difference from being-in-itself, it cannot be thought without taking context into account, abstracting from its roots in the psychical, the physiological, and the social. If freedom is essentially an incessant gushing forth, a perpetual new beginning, a radical self-resumption, it can also escape from itself. In short, it can get lost, or rather it can lose *itself*.

Freedom is supposed to be an indivisible élan, a homogenous reality. Yet in order to be effective and real, a difference between project and realization must insert itself: without condition or obstacle or context, our freedom would only be a dream. Freedom falls within the for-itself that is only a void of being and which would like at every instant to make of the past a blank slate. However, just as the future is reached only through the Caudine Forks of circumstances, one is freely renewed only on the foundation of the past that grounds us and entirely surrounds us. Context, of course, is less a guardrail and gravity than nourishing soil for the efficaciousness proper to freedom. Conjugal love springs from given circumstances and natural determinations assumed by a mysterious, unforeseeable and ineducible choice. It is realized in a permanent relation with an infinite horizon. The doctrine of the indissolubility of marriage presents a supreme example of the radical seriousness of freedom: freedom is truly a faculty of choosing and yet the ceaseless actuality of choice signifies its constant creativity, not its incessantly being brought into question. As Kierkegaard said, freedom is not an aesthetic but an ethical category. Instead of being a playful and consequently immanent exercise restricted to the interior spaces of the subject, it is the self-exit, the self-surpassing that is renewed in order to be reaffirmed.

The self-exit that underlies conjugal commitment is a "positive" example of the power of freedom but in life teems with negative examples where the unconditional power of freedom leads it to its suspension or very extinction. Moral activity can be conceived as a leap, a rupture, and therefore something essentially instantaneous, but extraction cannot be represented by the lone punctual dimension of the instant. It spreads out like a line that increases in thickness. Bad actions make a man bad, and yet a bad man is not only the author of misdeeds. The bad blow of transgression extends itself and takes on flesh in the irreversible rupture it incites within personal commitments. Passions and vices and, in fact, the villainous character and badness of the human heart cannot be transcribed into a mosaic of misdeeds. These are not necklaces where the black pearls of depravity, hate, and cruelty are strung together. The evil will is not a collectivity of evil volitions, but a permanent figure that malignancy animates or rather in which it expresses and unfolds itself. All the great figures of the alienation of freedom find their principle or paradigm in the servile will of theology, to wit, a freedom that freely lost itself. Those who hold to an absolutist theory

---

12. Kant, *Akad*. XXVIII, 609.

of freedom as unalterable spontaneity, a power that perpetually gushes forth, have never justified the unfortunate phenomenon of a subjectivity completely sunk into an engagement to the evil it had nevertheless freely chosen and accomplished. Man was created with the usage of free will, and it is this very free will that inverts itself into the servile will. If, however, freedom has had the power to engage in a course of action, why must it be that henceforth it no longer disposes of the same power to disengage itself from it? Theologians are always presenting some suggestive analogies in order to make this self-destruction of freedom more plausible. Augustine recalls that a man has the strength and resources to "kill himself" but once he commits suicide "he can no longer return to life."[13] Kierkegaard tells the story of a child who was given money in order to buy a good book or a toy. He opted for the toy but later wanted to exchange it for the book. But the shop-owner he had seen was inflexible: "when you had the money you were able to buy the book instead of the toy," but now it is too late, the toy has no value; you cannot take back your money in order to use it another way.[14]

The powerlessness to get a refund for spent money, to rediscover the life that was taken away from oneself, are suggestive illustrations of the paradoxes of freedom, paradoxes that cannot be resolved by persisting in the "absolute," unconditioned vision. Things will be different once the essential moment of self-limitation will have subverted and indeed enriched the perfection of our foundational faculty. In reality, the power of creativity is considered as a near synonym for freedom that requires in a certain way a measure of limitation. Creativity presupposes and implies inexhaustible superabundance and then ceaseless renewal. But newness is not only ceaseless activity but also accomplishment. What is truly new will not devolve to the old; the new condition to which one has passed will be acquired for good. The birth of novelty recalls the lightening flash. It appears as a true epiphany, but it is not a kind of ontological firework show. The passions, the vices, the evil heart, and finally the servile will witness in their distinct ways to the consistency and permanence of the new. One could doubtlessly find indecorous or absurd the so very exciting advent of the new that one calls for and fervently celebrates taking the form of a temporary or permanent plunge into evil. But we must yield to the evidence that the new is not necessarily and always good, that malign novelty is possible.

Meaning

Consistency and permanence are not only contingent figures, harboring the possibility of newness, they are essential for its advent. The new is not only a flash of lightning, it is also a fire that continues and endures. And the new is not only a burning fire, it is also light and form. The consolidating permanence witnesses to the seriousness of newness; it is even the *conditio sine qua non* of its radicality. But there

---

13. Augustine, *Enchiridion* 30.
14. Kierkegaard, *Miettes philosophiques*, in *Oeuvres complètes*, 7, 16n.

is no permanence without structure. Metaphysics attempts to conceive the rupture of immanence accomplished by self-surpassing. The source of this self-surpassing is freedom. However, if freedom is not exercised within a horizon of meaning then the leaps it accomplishes are only blind spasms of becoming. Classical philosophy was doubtlessly very cognizant of the perils of a rapprochement between freedom and *dynamis*, but it was not going to be able to navigate this without accounting for the truth of the essential creativity proper to freedom. Classical philosophy always sought to unfold freedom along a straight line between necessity and contingency and to avoid the two pitfalls of determinism and chance. It wanted to remove it from the definitive shortcomings of becoming and to hold it back before the abyss of the irrational. Attached as it was to the integrity of freedom, its immaculate purity, classical philosophy wanted to disassociate it from the limitations corollary to finitude. Since the Stoics, metaphysics did not want to admit that true freedom could be something other than rational, and it ceaselessly professed that acting freely and acting rationally are synonyms. However, this very ambitious discourse ended up handing freedom over to the aporias of Perfection. The unconditional capacity of freedom to choose continued to be professed, but given the absolute prescription of its rationality, choice was reduced to being only a dot affixed to an 'i,' a yes confirming a necessary solution. Freedom is able to avoid the pitfalls of perfection only by reinterpreting it starting from the a priori synthesis. Only the a priori synthesis allows us to conceive the new according to the fullness of its being, in all its structural consistency.

Compared to the sub-temporal immobility of analysis, the synthesis represents the advent of novelty within judgment. But the a posteriori synthesis accedes to the new at the cost of the renunciation of the concept. It adds to knowledge but it adds only some empirical data. The a priori synthesis is a self-exit of the subject towards the world and one that leads to the rational, the intelligible. The a priori synthesis constitutes the unity of self-consciousness that the *Critique* calls transcendental apperception: "apperception" *is* "the categories."[15] In other words it is the thread of these pure concepts like causality and substantiality in and through which the subject spans the distance separating it from the predicate. The predicate is not implied by or contained in the concept of the subject, but nevertheless it is discerned and understood as belonging to it. Said differently: the new that the a priori synthesis accomplishes cannot be deduced from the subject but still imposes itself with an evidence full of rationality.

The a priori synthesis is the true metaphysical source of the rationality of newness. It expresses an action that is "unforeseeable but hardly arbitrary."[16] We pass from one moment to another of our existence through events and actions that, without being foreseeable, are not irrational. Moral action is initiated through acts of extraction but these apparently punctual antecedents unfold through a parade of rational and intelligible consequences. Christ appears as a "lightning bolt" (Matthew 24:27) but

---

15. Kant, *Progrès de la métaphysique en Allemagne. Oeuvres* 3 1226 (Akad. II, 271F.).
16. Weil, *Cahiers. Oeuvres Complètes* VI, 3, 125.

his life and his death are the faithful realization, the accomplishment of the prophetic pronouncements. The storming of the Bastille was the result of a sudden riot and those who participated in it hardly foresaw the events to which it would lead. Nevertheless the flight and arrest of Louis XVI, the abolition of the monarchy, and the end of the *Ancien Régime* were already lurking in the background of this popular uprising. History is woven from these kinds of facts from which unfold consequences that can be understood retroactively as arising "logically" from unpremeditated ruptures. In reality our entire personal existence is sculpted out of these structural novelties. When someone is engaged to another in marriage, they sign, as it were, a blank check that still has perfectly consequential and rational implications. They promise assistance and fidelity without being able to predict how they will be in the future, what their circumstances will be, what might happen, and the evolution of the personal tastes and interests of each. But this enormous, in fact infinite margin of possibility does not compromise in any way the effective exercise of the engagement of persons. One cannot predict how one's promise will be fulfilled, one cannot foresee the modalities through which fidelity and assistance will be manifest. However, one will feel oneself obligated to reaffirm the faithful engagement within various situations and one will be able to put into practice the obligation and the call in particular directions and behaviors.

The adage "unforeseeable but not at all arbitrary" and the formula "both inexhaustible and moderate" illustrate the metaphysical fecundity of the great idea of the a priori synthesis.[17] It provides a true conceptual foundation, if not to pluralism, at least to plurality. In mathematics only a single right answer can be given to any given question, but in other domains of knowledge and existence many a priori solutions can be envisaged. The "sensible" condition of creativity fits perfectly with the possibility of a plurality of judgments. In fact, it implies, even demands this plurality. Creativity can only concern itself with the realm of existence, of the advent, in other words with the ontological arena. If not it would only be an affair of leaps and ruptures but not the establishment of the new. The novelty of the new does not consist in a second—or third or umpteenth—emergence from a first but in the appearance of another essence, the advent of a change on the eidetic plane. Our analysis of moral action made us understand that the new that comes about must have meaning. But one can and should go further: it is not enough to say that novelty must be meaningful, but also and especially it is necessary to proclaim that the new that comes about must *be* and must *exist* as a new meaning.

The theme of the "new meaning" is first explored by rereading "contingency." Once again this is inspired by the logic of the unlocking of perfection. Metaphysics has always opposed contingency and necessity (necessity read as complete integrity, regularity without fail and absolute rationality). But if the contingent is the contrary to the necessary it is nevertheless neither fragmentary, nor irregular, nor (above all)

---

17. Quotation from Claudel, *Le poète et la Bible I*, 475.

"irrational." The contingent does not necessarily stem from the essence but it can be conformed to it. The movement of the a priori synthesis is the output of the contingent, of *meaning* that is "contingent" because indeducible.[18] It is a questioning that receives its meaning and significance starting with the answer it arouses, that is, starting from a very particular eidos, one in which contingency is transfigured by freedom. The a priori synthesis finds its fullness in a meaning other than the one in which its movement is involved. It is the metaphysical source of creativity—of the creativity that appeared to establish itself through a free and rational self-surpassing. But in the strict sense of the term creativity reaches its end in judgment and moral action. Even if the subject is surpassed through judgment and action, its self-exit only ultimately represents a kind of halo, a reality apparently detached from the subjective body but which does not yet constitute an entity that is truly other. The artistic image is only a grand expression of the self; the moral work that realizes the self-surpassing still remains mid-way between the subjectivity and the new meaning for which it calls. This new meaning, this effectively other meaning, is another being, another subjectivity, a newness capable of creativity.

Love

The new meaning is another being, another free being. I find it; I encounter it. Yet this is not enough: I must recognize it as such. This recognition cannot be reduced to a mere locating, a kind of observation: it is realized in and through an engagement with regard to the other. The prehistory of the recognition is the liberating self-exit. It is an opening, but it does not signify a flight or a hemorrhage, or even the well-controlled exodus motivated, provoked and accomplished in accordance with an end. It can suggest unheard of efforts, unanticipated experiences on the part of the moral agent, but it is as much reception and expectation as action and operation. The recognition of another free being as other and free is made through an opening, "an unarmed opening":[19] the self-exit is enacted before and for another. The effective recognition of another is love. The quintessence of this love is the self-exit "towards" him—love is naturally ecstatic!—but the ecstasy does not yet make of love a unilateral action. In its eidetic nature love is not a heroic and solitary act, an epiphany confirmed by the experience of time; it is a relation. It cannot be expressed in a formula or published, yet it implicitly entails a response, even if deferred or refused. However, the call for a response, whether eloquent or inaudible, has nothing to do with the demand for reciprocity. Love must destroy the process of justice, to yield its sovereign place to the disproportionate, the unreasonable, to the gratuitous. It is then comprehensible starting from the two great themes with deep metaphysical affinity: the gift without veritable counterpart or proportionate object and of the asymmetrical relation. True

18. Jüngel, *Gott als Geheimnis der Welt*, 29.
19. Balthasar, *De l'integration*, 261.

love never arises from the universe (certainly respectable, but skimpy) of justice; the links and relations that it involves are mutually unequal.

The self-exit of love should be understood in substance from the deepening of Potentiality. Much philosophical effort has been spent attempting to isolate and identify the meaning of the idea of possibility. But these must not be allowed to impair our discussion of potentiality. Potentiality is more than possibility: it is aptitude, capability: "a capability that contains, preserves and protects"—and above all fecundates.[20] In other words, the quasi-negative notion at the origin of *possibilitas* should be articulated with a positive emphasis. Yet this enrichment or transposition into the positive is not yet enough to provide a metaphysical base for the enterprise of love. Love is not content to unlock the process of justice; it intends to situate, to initiate its movement towards it starting from a new ontological given. Despite numerous occurrences that are meager, destitute, shaky, in short, partial, it is an unconditional phenomenon that attests to and reveals above all its unforeseeable and inexplicable advent. Love forces the connoisseurs of the philosophies of suspicion to despair and it exasperates the adepts of the investigation of causes. It comes like a flash of lightening; it appears "out of the blue." In fact, it is not simply a matter of a factual impossibility where the birth of love is explained: the explication of love presents an impossibility that is not only *de facto* but also, above all, *de jure*! It is a reality that brings back into question, even challenges the principle of sufficient reason. Instead, it refers to a "principle of *insufficient reason*"![21] The absence of a principle of sufficient reason, tying it back to a "principle of insufficient reason" only reveals the immense metaphysical paradox of the possibility of the impossible. In order to surmount the process of nature, of justice, in order to break away from an "economic horizon," forgiveness must "forgive the unforgivable" and the invention related to "what does not appear possible," the departure, is enacted as a displacement in order to "go where it is impossible to go."[22]

The possibility of the impossible is the metaphysical horizon of love—of love as the principle of the unconditional gift, non-reciprocal service. Measured in light of the impossible-become-possible, the surmounting of justice achieves recognition from rationality. The possibility of the impossible underpins a range of actions present within each life, even the most simple, in the most banal existence, but which otherwise struggles to find their explanation, their justification in the conceptual order. Human society is structured by the application of the principle of justice, but the relation among humans implies every day operations that send *dikē* back to its native *physis*. We throw ourselves into actions without reason, render to one another unsolicited actions, do more than is strictly necessary, and, reciprocally, accept that others render to them what is not owed to them or that they are given less than what is theirs by right.

---

20. Bérulle, *Oeuvres de Piété* 37, in *Ouevres complètes* vol.3, 125.
21. Marion, *Le phénomène érotique*, 137.
22. Derrida, *Papier Machine*, 507, 516; Derrida, *Sauf le nom*, 63.

Love is like a vast fairground for asymmetrical action, but it is even further a process in which poorly enumerated (or rather, unquantifiable) products are exchanged.

From time immemorial "altruism" was at work in the world. Servant-like, even sacrificial behavior is a fact of Natural History: throughout the ages myriads of creatures have had to abandon their own life so the world and other beings could continue to exist. However, these withdrawals and sacrifices, often painful and awe-inspiring, are effectuated in view of the development or preservation, if not of the individual, at least of the species in which it takes part. All these living beings short of freedom constitute chains of nature of which they are only links, or organic moments; their divisions and extractions, however poignant and dramatic, do not yet qualify as authentic self-exits. The submission of living beings to a sacrificial finality in service to the ends of a species does not yet amount to a break from the mechanism of the natural process, nor to an opening where a being abandons or leaves itself in order to receive another. To the degree that it is a matter of activities in which the animal enacts and realizes something with very little or no compensation, the "material" content or eidos called "amorous gift" seems to show itself. Yet it lacks the "formal" factor that alone can ratify the authenticity of love, to wit, the free consent to be and to receive less than one is able to or should receive and be.

Animal altruism—but also much behavior and many acts of human altruism—does not truly correspond to the great logic of the possibility of the impossible. It is the unfolding of the possible, a step in the realization of biological ends and of the advent of social schema. Even more, altruism, including even the sacrifices of all kinds, can simply be the principle and source of interested operations, of true transactions of exchange within human economies of relation. Directly or indirectly, this entire range of natural altruistic actions serves the interest of the subject whereas true love, charity "does not seek its own interest" (1 Cor 13:5). Love is disinterested, but this disinterest is not negative, ascetical, cold, impersonal, or abstract. Love can hide itself behind the masks of modesty, discretion; it can keep quiet about its disappointments and pains, conceal its losses and failures; it remains an activity that deprives its author of the accidental, but above all it wrests him of the essential. Love is more than a passion. Nevertheless, it must suffer. It consents for its flesh to be cut into and for its being to tattered and torn.

The eidetic description of love hardly does without traits of the emotions or passions like so many external reflections on disproportion. Love is self-exit and if this exodus is not necessarily something disorganized it experiences only a little respect and patience for frozen harmonies and sterile equilibriums. By the commandment to "pay your debts," the call to accompany another two miles when he asks you to accompany him for one mile, the principle of insufficient reason subverts the natural order of justice. Justice gives everything it is supposed to and it also demands everything that is owed to it. Love settles for less, much less when one owes it and it gives more, much more than it is obligated to give. In fact, love not only establishes the disproportion but in a certain way it banishes the very idea of proportion altogether. Any human activity is supposed to be enacted in view of a specific end that serves as its reason: love is the affection that is exercised towards the other; it provides a reason and gives a meaning for the subject. But authentic love, taking the full stature of its metaphysical truth, measures itself against the effacement and recession of every meaning and every reason. One gives to the poor, the sick, the indigent without asking anything in return, but at least these powerless and disparaged beings exist. However, the creation, the call to life, the end of the operation, the correlate of the gift does not yet exist. The highest, or rather purest form of love is creative love, which is not content to give a large gift to a tiny being, but to give it its very being.

Creation is the true paradigm of love to the degree that the necessity and quest for proportion are excluded: strictly speaking, only what is free is love. But one can—and it is actually commanded—to go farther than the abandonment of care for proportion, inspiration by gratuity alone. In its fullness love is not content to approach those who serve us poorly and love us little or those who do not love us at all. We must also love those who hate us and who fight against us; we must love our enemies! Some are tempted to represent love as an effusive energy, and pure, gratuitous love as the outpouring toward an end that only appeals to us a little bit or not at all. But charity also implies that we orient the effusion toward an objective that not only lacks a motivation, but is, so to say, *anti-motivation*. It is not enough to love the one who does not attract us, but we must also love the one who loathes us, who fights us off, even the one who hurts us. If *ascesis* is an apparently "virtuous" behavior in moral eidetics, this is because in and through it we show our unique aptitude to challenge our native selfish spontaneity by renouncing the appropriation of beings and things. Yet this "aptitude" for discipline, privation, and renunciation has an equally positive face. We cannot be content to limit or restrain our spontaneity. We can and even must put it in service to ends that are frankly oppositional or hostile. Patristic authors remarked that by contrast to reptiles and to various ferocious beasts, humans, created in the image of God, are capable of "not turning away from those who do them evil and of loving those who hate them."[23] This power of facing someone, of taking part against one's own interests is the supreme faculty that allows us to surpass immanence, of making judgments other than analytical ones. In other words it is the anthropological node, the "natural" substrate of the immense moral metaphysical program of creativity that is Love of Enemies.

Love of enemies is the commandment that the Sermon on the Mount pronounces in the context of the abolition of the ancient rule of an eye for an eye. Instead of conforming our conduct to the adage, "an eye for an eye and a tooth for a tooth," we are ordered to consent to be deprived of what belongs to us and commanded to let someone take our coat when they ask for our tunic, to turn the other cheek. Even more, it enjoins on us the radical commandment to bless those who curse us, to pray

---

23. Maximus the Confessor, *The Ascetic Life* (PG 90, 917 B).

for those who persecute us. The injunction, *Love your enemies* very clearly intends to give a deathblow to the economy of justice, the universal and immemorial regime of reciprocity. But it aims for more than its abolition: it constitutes a true inversion. Since the dawn of time, humans, from their slow and very gradual emancipation from the grip of Nature, have thought they are supposed to be friends of their friends and to do good to those who do good to them. But this reasonable and noble quintessence of natural virtue is challenged and condemned without appeal: those who only love their friends are no better than "the sinners" who also "love those who love them" (Luke 6:32). Conformity to the natural regime of moral reciprocity certifies the subjection to the process of justice, a condition where one neither can nor wants to be released from this blind sequence, to be torn from this iron mechanism. An ancient exegete—himself a martyr—comments: "If you love those who love you, then what are you doing new? . . . If you lend to those from whom you hope to be repaid, than what are you doing new?"[24] Love is as old as the world, yet it alone is the source of novelty in the world.

Sacrifice

Love brings newness about; it inaugurates a new regime of being and acting. As such it implies both the unconditional and the definitive. Novelty is not only a spark and a lightning flash. The action of love cannot be exhausted in the brief movement of a provisional abandonment. The gift and loving service convert into self-exit, which is a definitive transposition: self-surpassing is an effective victory over oneself; its operations have "no-return" inscribed onto their essence. All of these elements of alienation and self-extraction find their paradigm in Sacrifice, the supreme figure of the "radical" conduct of detachment, dispossession, and disappropriation. In its historical origin, sacrifice is a phenomenon, an eidos of religion. A man offers a sacrifice to the gods, yet this renunciation, this abandonment has its proper finality: it is not a matter of an utterly wasted gift: something in return is sought. One endeavors to conciliate the divinity that could be offended by one's being and acting. This is a difficult world, full of traps (transgressions occur without necessarily being aware of them) and hidden boundaries (one trespasses on territories belonging to another). Sacrifice hopes to coax the divinity, to make it lenient, helpful. In its primitive eidetic essence, sacrifice is only a phenomenon of economy, an instance, perhaps strange and twisted but nevertheless authentic, of justice, of *do ut des*. Yet by virtue of certain essential eidetic moments, like the invaluable character of the sacrificial object and the accompanying violence of a *definitive* operation, the mercantile category of sacrifice can be slowly eroded by love.

The sacrificial object was normally an immaculate beast, the first fruits of crops, in short, costly and choice objects. The customary requirement of precious quality

---

24. Justin Martyr, *1 Apology* 15, 9–10.

attests that the sacrifice is not a lesser evil, an activity of lesser importance: well to the contrary, it is of intimate concern to the subject. If the renunciations and trials of love are designated as "sacrifices" this is because tearings away that are *costly* to the subject are always involved. The "extraction" dimension is perhaps even more manifestly present in the violence accompanying sacrifice. Animals are immolated; their blood flows. But this primitive violence finds its completion in the flames: one is not content to slaughter the victim; it must be burned. The rite of consuming with fire counts as a primordial eidetic trait of sacrifice, but the seeds of transition to the metaphysical-moral sphere are best observed here. The fire that reduces the victim to ashes shows the definitive character of the operation, its dispossession, the radical alienation that lies at its heart. If sacrifice is, so to say, predisposed to serve as a figure of love, this is because it connotes a rupture of analogous scope to that of the opening, the self-exit of love.

The character of definitive alienation proper to sacrifice is indicted starting from the immolation and reduction to ashes of the object. In reality the essential is not the transfiguration, the non-return of the object, but rather the non-return to itself of the subject. The alienation of one's possession, without counterpart or payback, signals the disengagement of the subject from the net of reciprocity and from immanence as well as its access to novelty. In fact, the dispossession cannot be limited to the material sphere: an even infinitely costly sacrifice with immense efforts, dangers and risks can apply to only a conservation or reinforcement of the powers immanent to the subject. The gift one pours out should not come from the "superfluous" but the necessary (Luke 21:4). It is not enough for it to be voluntary or supplementary; it must sink its teeth into the vital. The bite of the wound is necessary but it is not because of a superior or exalted dolorism. Suffering is an essential criteria for the effective exercise of love. It prevents the self from rejoining itself through and beyond the intentional objects of its action. The ultimate seriousness of love appears in the radical seriousness of sacrifice. Love must be prepared for an unlimited succession of sacrifices, none of which should allow it to bend back onto itself. In order to exercise itself love must be able to retain itself in its activity. But this self-conservation has nothing to do with a kind of journey taken in the midst of reefs and currents where one is assured to find at the end one's native Ithaca. It is more a matter of imitating Abraham, who left his home country not knowing where he was going and without seeking a return. The ultimate seriousness of love is its unconditional engagement in each of its operations, its abandonment at every moment to the demands of its correlate, its other. The destiny of a loving subject is to travel the entire range of possibilities, to submit itself to an incalculable number of tests. The subject must subsume itself to all the predicates that the judgments of love present to it. In fact it must bracket its subjective condition; its vocation is even "to become the predicate ceaselessly, without becoming subject."[25]

---

25. Nishida, *Le lieu*, 81 (translation modified by Dalissier, *Anfractuosité et unification*, 483).

Non-return to self is essential for the "definitive" condition of sacrifice. It is grasped and displayed through the investigation of the motives of the subject. But if passage through this psychological research is necessary for an eidetic study, the subjective truth of sacrifice is also above all attested through the more traditional way that considers the subject as such an object of sacrifice. One finds oneself led to give, to abandon goods and possessions of various kinds, to tear oneself away from parts of one's being. But through and beyond these partial abandonments and fragmentary gifts, the self is intended as the supreme object of sacrifice. Sacrifice must be unconditional, but the various partial realities that I give up are so many conditions of my well-being, even of my being itself, the sole reality that is not a simple condition but belongs to the unconditional, the self, principle and substrate of everything I have, and all that I am. It is true that political and moral passions, or more simply the circumstances and engagements of our personal existence can make us renounce our life without this signifying an absolute rupture, an unconditional and definitive gift. But apart from these limit cases of deviance or intoxication, the gift of one's life is the only gift that no discernible advantage can compensate; it is the supreme sacrifice that alone represents—literally—the way of non-return.

For the Greek as well as the Christian, sacrifice of one's life is possible only through love; it is realized and sealed by this love. Plato solemnly declares: "To die for another, only those who desire this truly love" (*Symposium* 179b). And the Christ of St. John adds: "There is no greater love than to give one's own life for one's friends" (John 15:13). Sacrifice of one's life is the highest instance of this "helpless opening" that is the principle and source of all true newness. In it the reign of justice ends and through it the life of love is inaugurated.

Double Asymmetry

Sacrifice appeared to be a true realization of love, a phenomenon centered on the free subject as subject. Yet the free being is not only the subject of sacrifice but also the supreme intentional object. It is true that we always talk about sacrifices accomplished for our own personal development, for our physical, intellectual or moral perfection. We are also able to consent to heavy and cumbersome sacrifices in service to a moral or religious principle, but essentially it is for another or others, for free beings that we sacrifice ourselves. Sacrifice highlights the purpose of the creativity proper to love, to wit, its opening to another meaning and through the eidetic necessity that this "costs" me. It dramatizes the seriousness of the extraction. But if the free being is the necessary end of the exodus of the subject, it is only its stationary end. It is like a reef against which the waves of self-surpassing die out, but which remains itself nearly unaffected and passive. On the other hand, if the gift of its life is the archetypal phenomenon of action and love, it constitutes an immense paradox: nothing attests with as much authenticity the serious and definitive nature of exodus as the self-exit without return, but must the definitive nature of creativity be sealed by an event wherein the subject that loves, the loving subject itself disappears?

Sacrifice writes, so to speak, the first pages of the eidetic history of Love. This is an imperfect history where the ephemeral-punctual action of the subject has as its other the un-affected, the un-open other, its intentional object. It is the very meaning of novelty that requires these figures of isolation to be surpassed. The definitiveness proper to the new rejects the temporary and demands the stable, the permanent. But permanence does not occur simply through the uninterrupted succession of instants, through the incessant renewal of moments that constitutes the fabric of affection. It equally demands a response in the horizontal realm. The fervent repetition of the confession of love emanates from a subject and if these ardent words can be cast into the void, their native purpose is to be received or rather welcomed by the recipient that is the other subject. The confession of love can be a line extending into infinity but in order for it to be incarnate in duration, in permanence, it must meet a corresponding other in the spatial realm. The mystery of the recognition of the other has been compared to the theologoumenon of "*creatio ex nihilo*."[26] But all true creation is "continuous"; it is a continuity that acquires, in its occurrence, recognition and love in the confirmation by the other in which the opening is established by relation.

The most complete and consummate form of the relation of love is conjugal union, marriage. In it the helpless opening is organized and consolidated. But at the end of the process of justice, a relation of love has already been observed. It seems like the culminating point, the most perfect instance of this entire natural theory of humanity marked by immanence and confinement. *This* relation of love—even when it appears in its superior form of marriage—has been judged and condemned as the consummate manifestation of mortal reciprocity. Justly designated as "dual selfishness" unmasked in its noxious sterility, it appeared as the ultimate step into a dead end. Does this mean that Relation has no place in the vocabulary of novelty, that Reciprocity itself cannot receive a meaning that would allow it to be sublated by the vivifying enterprises of love? Said a different way, can we rethink the perfect complementarity, the integral exchange, the immaculate symmetry of actions and payments in order to redeem them for the sake of employing them in service to novelty? Could we reread (and in what terms) the dual relation in order to ward off the danger of relapse into the blind mechanism of *dikē*, into the brutal process of the *physis*? Conjugal union shows an essential eidetic affinity with the relation of love that prevails in the universe of justice though it boasts two radical differences. On the one hand, it possesses as principal source and as the principle of its metaphysical regime a complementarity, not abolished but from now on explained starting from a double asymmetry. On the other hand, the exchange that extinguishes the currents flowing from partners is worked loose by fecundity, by procreation. Asymmetry, like fecundity, brings to an

---

26. Jacobi, *Fliegende Blätter* 2, in *Werke* VI, 177.

end a condition of repetition that the intensity and richness of the interaction of lovers managed to obscure and to hide.

Reciprocity is first loosened, so to speak, in order to be subverted in a more profound way. The possibility of this loosening and subversion is implied by the very genesis of the conjugal relation: with the receding of the custom of arranged marriage, the contingency of the encounter of future spouses is imposed as the epiphenomenon of the essential gratuity of unconditional engagement. If the refusal of incest survives in a world so inclined to break with immemorial norms and prohibitions, that indicates that anything pertaining to the mechanical, the determined, and the necessary in the emblematic relation between free beings is rejected with an accumulated intensity. Unconditional, definitive, and insoluble commitment does not obey the principle of sufficient reason; it is strictly unjustifiable and unmerited. It is like a magnificent building spanning a gap, built over a void. There is no link of analytical predication between two loving beings; their relation is born out of a free crossing of the distance that separates them. Yet spanning a distance does not at all mean to eliminate it. Love always crosses the gap between the two terms of the relation, but it cannot and should not want to abolish it. The distance is the elementary breach in the coincidence of the terms, the surviving alterity within diverse elements fused together that compromise the freedom of the engagement, relativizing its truth, its moral scope.

Distance introduces room for play, space for movement in the coincidence that is only an eidetic moment of the same immanence that articulates and unfolds as reciprocity. Reciprocity will be subverted by a reinterpretation under the sign of the asymmetry that safeguards the complementarity of spouses. In a certain way, the distinction between difference and direction is rediscovered here. Distance effectuates the unsealing of the horizontal while asymmetry enacts it through movements towards. . . The perfect reciprocity of the relation of love manifests itself through the admirable complementarity of services and tasks, of tastes and feelings. It protects and safeguards all through the dispossession of its virtue—or rather its vice—of confinement and enclosure. The ultimately material principle of complementarity is reinterpreted in light of the formal principle of Love, that supreme eidos that sublates the material essences of conjugal life. Beyond all behavior and every particular feeling proper to conjugal union, Marriage is the relation of unconditional necessity. And reciprocity, even when it surpasses the sphere of various benefits, even when it is "reserved" for the most profound plane of relation between spouses, is not apt to accomplish the unconditional. On the contrary, it confuses it through contradiction and drives it to paradox. The relation of love is based on the integral mutuality of terms: I ought to do as much for the other as he does for me. But if this necessity seems to be clear from the point of view of relation, it can be questioned starting from the *terms* of the relation. Love does not seek its own interest; it therefore must place the interest of the other, of the beloved, before its own. It does not care about what it receives in return; its ambition is to do all that it can and all that it should for the other. The one who loves cannot remain content to do only as much as his other does; he must do more. One always considers oneself more responsible than the other; one thinks one has to do "one step more," to have always "more to give."[27]

This conception of love is proper to lovers, to spouses. But spouses are always two. Consequently both must consider and live love in the same way; each should want to go farther, to do more than the other. But does this not mean that one must do more than the other and the other must do more as well? We wanted to overcome the completely quantitative exigency of equality, the reciprocity of actions and responses, but do we not here end up recovering just this? In the first place, it seems proportionality has been broken: I owe the other *more* than he owes me. But if we follow this line to the end—and we must—then the other owes me *more* than I owe him. This means that beyond the apparent difference between the two instances of "more" it seems that we are led from the new back to reciprocity—to that despised reciprocity from which we have sought to be liberated, the intimate mortal enemy of the unconditional relation. In reality however the parallelism of attitudes that produces the two apparently analogous instances of "more" is artificial. In place of re-enclosing the couple in a sterile symmetry, it allows them to free themselves from the last vestiges of deadly reciprocity.

True love, unconditional love requires that each love the other more than oneself and therefore do more for the other than for oneself. If we take this prescription literally, in a purely quantitative way, then we end up not only in the prison of reciprocity but also slide into absurdity. If the other owes me more than I owe him (and inversely) then we both owe to the other less than the other owes us. The logic of love entails that each owes *more* and *less* than the other. This paradox is avoided only if we resolve to abandon any quantitative vision of the more required by love in order to rethink it in terms of a fecund asymmetry. The more that love demands of me does not represent a greater quantity: it does not imply a greater weight or a stronger movement. In fact, it has nothing to do with quantity, nor even with a given action. The more that I require of myself does not mean that I compare what I do with what the other does or that I want to gauge the intensity of my action in light of his. If I intend to do or to give more than the other does or gives to me, then this amounts to me prescribing *myself* a task, compelling *myself* to serve in order to give a benefit. My more is certainly pronounced in the context of my other but it is not calculated in terms of a benefit that comes from him. In fact, this more is not calculable or quantifiable at all: it expresses the highest commandment to turn from myself and to another. The analogous call to action to the other has nothing to do with some kind of reciprocity. Just as my action was not aroused by an action on his part, his action is not provoked by an action on my part. Our respective actions are autonomous without being dissociable. The are integrally conceived in and through myself and himself, but they are impossible without the presence of the other. The two terms of the couple subsist only by virtue

---

27. Levinas, *Autrement qu'être ou au-delà de l'essence*, 134.

of a correspondence that is a communion of two—two centers decentered by a double asymmetry.

Faithfulness

The supreme relation which is that of lovers clearly requires the equality of its two terms and this equality seems to imply the reciprocity of feelings and actions. However, if equality is an essential eidetic aspect of Relation, then in the last instance it is only a consequence or moment. The truth of the supreme relation, the primordial nerve of the link between lovers is unconditionality. Love is the victory over justice. It opens up the mechanism and plants with sovereign freedom spaces of indetermination in nature that represent and express gratuity, the source and soul of the unconditional nature of the commitment. The commitment of lovers is a gift. Lovers give all that they have to one another; above all, they give *themselves* to one another. This gift of self to the other is constructed in durational time. But from a metaphysical viewpoint it appears as an all-powerful instant. To the very degree that the instant appears to be sub-temporal and therefore non-temporal, it is reputed to have gone beyond duration. The amorous relation, marriage is the most durable relation precisely because its ambit is located beyond all duration. Lovers consider themselves predestined to one another from the beginning of time and they want to love each other until the end of time. They swear eternal fidelity. Faithfulness profoundly expresses the metaphysical meaning of the amorous relation: it connotes a trail through the pathways of duration, a trail that determines and animates this unconditional vow that constitutes its genesis. Faithfulness is the translation of the unconditional into the infinite multitude of conditioned moments; it causes to spread out in the succession of time what had emerged at the heart of freedom: love. It prescribes behaviors and acts of service: it gives color to the feelings and gestures of lovers. Lovers, spouses have to convert at every moment their infinite engagement into actions and individual events. Fidelity constitutes the basis of these advents, or rathe,r the principal eidos of which all that happens are simply so many lesser instantiations. One could write a kind of dictionary of all these feelings and encounters that express and accomplish fidelity, which share in it and constitute the prism through which it is read. Yet the principal face, the privileged appearance of faithfulness is its continuity in time. Faithfulness is the emblematic manifestation of unconditional engagement, but nothing presents such a suggestive image of the unconditional than the permanence of a decision, the pertinence of a choice through time and despite its fluctuations. Lovers vow, "Nothing will separate us," but this nothing that belongs to the order of things means above all that there cannot be a moment in which the link that unites them will be mutilated or broken. In reality the nothing that is from the order of negation announces the "positive": notwithstanding the inevitable advent of events that threaten it, the amorous relation will endure forever! The life of lovers, of spouses is full of pitfalls likely to weaken their relation, conditions and events that ceaselessly arrive but which were unforeseeable. The resulting order demands some extreme shifts that the lovers will be incapable of making. But even in the absence of unforeseen disasters, the course of time fatally undermines certainties, cools affections and exhausts emotional resources. Yet faithfulness means precisely that obstacles cannot put into question the infinite commitment of the spouses. What is most at stake with the idea of fidelity is its attesting to the possibility of a relation which, founded and constructed on freedom and gratuity, can no longer be questioned. In its realized, perfect form, the relation of lovers appears as an indissoluble union of which faithfulness is the subjective translation.

Indissolubility is the metaphysical truth of the amorous relation and through the fidelity that it implies and requires love assumes a moral face, a face of duty. Spouses have the obligation to remain faithful. But until when? The most facile response, the evident response is: one should remain faithful as long as the other does. Love calls for love, faithfulness for faithfulness, and if the other stops loving and being faithful, why should I continue to love and to be faithful? Despite its passionate character, its enslaving power, love is a phenomenon, even the highest phenomenon, of freedom. It emerged out of the commitment of my freedom and freedom comes to live in and through it. The amorous relation is a mutual commitment of freedoms and when the other removes himself from the relation, breaks his promise, does this not release me from my obligation? Does it not return to me this visible or invisible ring that supposedly seals our vow of fidelity? I have been loved and I have loved, but you have broken your promise and you no longer love me. Betrayed, I am tempted to cry out: "You no longer love me? If so, then I will take back my freedom, my independence, and I will no longer love you." But if misled and betrayed, someone is moved to stop being faithful to another, this is because his love was not unconditional but depended on the love of another. The one who freely, unconditionally loves does not wish to fall in step behind infidelity, into non-love of the other. Well to the contrary, he declares: "You may no longer love me, you may be unable to, but "I *must* continue to love you!"[28]

The true freedom of love is to continue to love even when there is no longer a "reason" to. Great loves claims to be stronger than death. Spouses love their other even after he has died: how then should one love the other while he is still alive? But the question is less, should I love the other who no longer loves me? It is rather, could I love him? In fact, the love of the one who no longer loves us will appear as the paradigmatic example of love, of love in its fullness and of which the other forms of love are lesser moments. The survival of love in the disappearance of its "object" exemplifies unconditionality, an unconditionality that illustrates and confirms the very genesis of this relation. It is thought that in every amorous affection one of the lovers has loved first and the other second, that one called and the other has responded. In actuality, according to its metaphysical truth, love is never a response because one has always loved "from the beginning" (1 John 4:19)—for the good reason that if love is

---

28. Kierkegaard, *Les oeuvres de l'amour*, in *Oeuvres complètes* vol. 14, 38.

unconditional then it can never be provoked or established by something given, by something quantified. Love must occur spontaneously, independently of every particular consideration; its spontaneity is nearly the empirical expression, the material token of its principial freedom.

To love from the first is the founding moment, the eidetically determining aspect of unconditional love. Love emerged without why, without demanding a counterpart, without requiring a response. It is the unmotivated and uncaused upsurge that is prolonged through the days, months and years of conjugal union. It is the promise of continuation and irrevocable commitment. The yes proffered by nascent love is not only a flash of lightning but is perpetually resaid and the indissolubility only names or, if you like, defines, this condition of perennial reiteration, this "creative fidelity" that draws out of itself the power of persevering, and persevering as a fecund eruption.[29] The promise of its condition of eruption is the act of each of the two lovers, the spouses, declared independently of the action of the other. Each understands himself as having loved first, each must say and repeat his yes, without waiting for the other to say and repeat it himself. The double asymmetry of the metaphysical condition of lovers is the place where the break with reciprocity is accomplished, where nature is vanquished by freedom and where the process of justice is loosened open. The indissolubility of marriage announces the definitive victory of novelty over repetition, of the a priori synthesis over analysis. In short, it proclaims the advent of the truly unique transcendence of love.

Towards the Third

Faithfulness is a paradigm moment of the opening of immanence and in fact reveals the two great realities that allow the victory over nature: freedom and love. To be faithful is to be faithful to oneself but also and above all to another. To be faithful is to be free to surpass oneself, which is effectuated through love. Free action is the effective exercise of the a priori synthesis; freedom is the power of creativity. The free man vanquishes his inclinations, brackets his interests, wins the victory over his natural being. However, ultimately these new things come about inside the free being while the self-surpassing that is love is always realized with reference to another. Freedom and love are categories of the "more": they witness to the presence within us of a power that allows us to surpass ourselves, a power situated within but which refers to something outside. The a priori synthesis furnishes the grammar, so to speak, of self-surpassing, but ultimately it is inexplicable starting from itself. More precisely: the a priori synthesis shows that we always have within enough to go "farther" (Malebranche) but this immanent power must indicate a transcendent counterpart, or rather, principle.

---

29. Marcel, *Homo Viator*, 176.

Transcendence appears on the horizon only with the emancipation of lovers from the reciprocity that locks them into a perfectly determined face to face, one that is therefore without novelty, and is sterile. Faithfulness breaks, or rather, forgets and surpasses reciprocity. It refers to an external, transcendent dimension. In an apparent paradox, faithfulness is a unilateral relation. It is an exchange where each of the partners functions and acts independently of his other. The other doubtlessly "owes" fidelity to me, but it is not on account of his faithfulness that I remain faithful to him. As a phenomenon of love, faithfulness as it were inaugurates the fecund asymmetry that alone makes possible the victory over nature. It is the glorious countenance that catches love in the relation of lovers, the manifestation of this self-exit in which the other, removed from the terms of a necessary process, establishes himself in his self-sufficiency. The faithful lover is like Eros ceaselessly shooting his arrows—arrows, not boomerangs that return to him. They are planted in the heart of the other in order to tell and retell him of the lover's unconditional commitment. The asymmetry, of which gratuity is like the moral nerve, discloses the deep truth of fidelity: it teaches that the other is a sui generis reality, that he not only functions as a term of Relation but that he represents, that he is, an end in himself. Faithfulness is doubtlessly a step in the metaphysical history of Relation, in the process that leads it to its definitive opening. Faithfulness brings about the unsealing of Relation but it is only a first and very incomplete moment. Reciprocity certainly no longer reigns; the "epoch" is over when Relation was all and the terms, which are only a function of it, were nothing. Henceforth we have reached a state where the terms have found their independence, their self-sufficiency: each of them loves unconditionally; each is unconditionally loved. Yet this metaphysical emancipation of the two components of Relation still constitutes only one moment in the story of Renewing Newness. Like the freedom that is the source only of a novelty confined within the free being itself, faithfulness signals only a novelty come about for two beings that constitute the Relation. The Love that is exercised in and through faithfulness, reshapes the relation of the two free beings or rather, it subverts it, breaks its seals. But it does not cause it to undergo a modification that refers to a newness with an ontological scope. The asymmetry incarnated by faithfulness does not yet reach this duality of beings apparently existing according to the regime of reciprocity. The necessity, the quest for reciprocity that continues to haunt the faithfulness of one and the other will be exorcised for good only through opening to a third.

IV

The Singular

The Third

Faithfulness signifies the advent of the autonomy of the two. Within it the symmetry of reciprocity is transposed into the asymmetry of love. Yet if faithfulness marks autonomy, the self-sufficiency of two, it does not yet actually introduce a third. Rather, it announces it, but only implicitly, starting from the breakup of reciprocity. Faithfulness cannot say anything about a third but simply reveals the impasse one reaches if one wishes to remain with two. The relation of fidelity obliterates reciprocity. It is founded on the parallelism of two existing beings according to the regime of the unconditional, but it almost thwarts itself as relation. The two are related through an unconditional love, but one does not access the other, or rather, it self-surpasses toward it but without reaching it. The self-exit of faithfulness is much more effective than the a priori synthesis practiced by freedom: when the intentional object of free action remains the self itself surpassed and overcome, in this first great "moment" of faithful love, the self-surpassing is directed toward a true other. Yet if the self-exit is made here in accord with another, it remains a self-extension that aims for the other without truly reaching it. The unconditionality of faithfulness implies the bracketing of both the reply and the non-reply of the other. In other words if faithfulness gets the two out of reciprocity, it is at the cost of its quasi-reduction to an isolated condition. The other is really reached only with the advent of a third that exorcises every threat of a fall back into reciprocity and equally prohibits reduction to monadic isolation. This third will be the child in whom the self-surpassing belongs to true newness.

Reciprocity closed in on itself has been unlocked by the asymmetrical love of spouses, but their love will realize a true self-exit only through the advent of the child. The duality that is only the prolongation or rather repetition of a superior power of sameness must be subverted by a veritable or effective opening to another. This other in and through whom the opening is realized is the child. Children represent an alterity shielded from mutual exhaustion as well as from reduction to the monadic condition. The birth of a child is an ontological event that brings about novelty in its totality. However, if the new is truly an ontological phenomenon, then like every ontological reality it is conceived and understood starting from its metaphysical structures. The metaphysical structure making possible the unlocking of immanence and access to a truly new and renewing alterity is asymmetry. This metaphysical principle of asymmetry founds the relation of fidelity of lovers but it will be fully at work only in creative and procreative love. The eidetic category corresponding to it in a particularly appropriate way is the third, which will show what it really is as the truth of the child.

Since the beginning of time numbers are given a metaphysical, religious and moral scope. Beyond their numerical value they take on sui generis eidetic value. The One has always commanded a religious respect, ceaselessly symbolizing the origin, and simplicity, wholeness, primacy, superiority, even perfection. As for the Two that initiates the numerical series, it was almost naturally ready to take on the role of symbolizing all other numbers, gathering in itself and signifying the indefinite multiplicity that follows the one, succeeding the first. But the meaning of this multiplicity is not univocal. If one is naturally led to feast on the richness of the multiple, to celebrate the proliferation of beings, the infinite range of nuances, the inexhaustible multitude of layers, then for a philosophy enamored with the intelligible and the totality, multiplicity appears as degenerating layers unfolding from the One, deviations from the perfect, a fragmentation of the whole, an explosion or implosion of the totality. The multiple rips apart the seamless garment of being and the numbers that punctuate and denote its parts, its fragments, are so many powerless and unfortunate witnesses to this imperfection. In his unwritten doctrine Plato opposed to the blessed and perfect Monad the Dyad, the Two as principle of dispersion, even of decomposition and destruction. But these unfortunate associations, this execrable heredity of the Dyad efface themselves in western philosophy even if the dualisms of diverse makings and unequal radicality continue to prejudice the metaphysical appreciation of duality. The eidetic story of duality seemed to have turned towards a definitive rehabilitation last century with the philosophy of intersubjectivity, clearly formulated and explained in the "dialogical" thought of Buber. Dialogical thought celebrates the richness and profundity, the fecundity and intensity of the I and the Thou. But precisely this exaltation of the two first persons happens at the expense of the third, which is cast into the Sheol of abstraction, superficiality and exteriority. The I and the Thou, the One and the Two are located in a demanding and exalting face to face in which the Three designates only the instances and indistinct, indeterminate occurrences without face and without depth of an exploded, dispersed multiplicity. Living under the constant threat of passing into an exclusive reciprocity, the exchange and dramatic interrelation of the First and the Second seems to occupy the entire scene of signification. The Third, effaced and forgotten, is condemned to the unfortunate destiny of in-distinction. The three is thus the third, the excluded third in the literal sense of the phrase, the eidetic number for realities deprived of true eidetic significance.

This pejorative vision is not the only reading of the three in the history of philosophy. Above all, under the inspiration of the Christian mystery of the Trinity, philosophical and theological speculation has often taken pleasure in constructing triads. Triads, especially in the immense Hegelian system, serve as principles and sources for the construction of diverse areas of the real, constituting active frameworks for the unfolding of the concept. But instead of exploiting the metaphysical potentialities contained by the eidos of the three, speculation on triads and ternaries has risked falling back again into the prison of immanence. Hegel speaks of the "great instinct of the concept" that rediscovers in triplicity the power of synthesis.[1] However, the synthesis under consideration here does not truly correspond to the leap of novelty. Instead it represents a dialectic that redeploys in another register the same analytic logic governing the reciprocity of justice. The synthesis reconciles the thesis and the antithesis, but if the reconciliation is not without fecundity then it results in and necessarily occurs starting from the premises of which it is the accomplishment, the shared apotheosis. Synthesis is the truth of Relation, but the absoluteness of relation harms the autonomy of its terms. In the last analysis, if the Hegelian Three manages to avoid the pitfalls and traps of the Two, the Dyad, then it will only repeat in its own way the perfection of the One while the number, the eidos three holds its own potentialities in order to read the multiple or rather the plural.

The three represents a plurality that avoids the exclusivity of the two without falling into the dispersion of the multiple. Christ promises to be present when "two or three gather" in his name. Two *or* three: numbers are named that are situated at the beginning of the numerical series and therefore possess a preeminence. But it is not defined or circumscribed. The equivalence of the two and three indicates an opening toward the multiple, but the opening does not lead to a submersion, to a dissolution in the infinite succession of a series. On the other hand, the proper position of the three, its respected even exalted position in numerous religions, its specific grammatical situation in certain languages, indicate the possibility of a middle way, a third way if you like, between the deadly reciprocity of the two, of twos, and the limitless and groundless dispersion of an infinite theory of atoms and instants. The three is able to constitute the symbol or rather the eidetic key to a plurality able to accommodate asymmetrical relations among its elements. It represents an exceptional alternative to the scorching exclusivity of the two. However, if the plurality subsumed under the three is not subject to the obsessive pursuit of reciprocity, it is not, for all that, condemned to frigidity, to the neutrality of non-engagement. The third is not a reality whose vocation is to situate itself in the margins outside of the unique and exclusive drama played out between the I and the Thou. It has nothing to do with the unfortunate neutrality of the One, or with the indigent indistinction of a multiplicity

---

1. Hegel, *Leçons sur l'histoire de la philosophie* vol. 7, 1863.

of faceless instances and occurrences. Well to the contrary, it powerfully shows the possibility and the actuality, the promise and the parousia of the magnificent plurality of autonomous singular beings that are whole in themselves but also harbor fecund openings. These are singulars provoked into and maintained in existence through asymmetrical love.

Distinction and Differentiation

The three refers to the multiple as place and succession of singulars and it aims to "save the appearances" of the multiple. Of course, this rescue is not self-evident, above all because the singular, as such, is an ambiguous, ambivalent reality. The singular value of moral behavior or the uncommon beauty of a woman, landscape, or fountain is praised. At the same time individuals stand out when they are made a fool of by ridiculous behavior. The moralist encourages us to behavior that distinguishes us but does not make us stand out. The vanity and folly of coveting a "spirit of singularity for the sake of having the ridiculous advantage of not thinking like everybody else" is criticized.[2] Again, the "incomparable disorder maintained by ten thousand singular beings" is denounced.[3] Singularity is expressed with a light psychological and moral accent, but essentially it seems to correspond to the ontological category of individuality, a reality that classical philosophy since antiquity has ceaselessly denounced. The individual is only the privation of the universal and as such it is, in the best case, of miniscule worth and has, in the worst case, a gross defect. It is then a deviation that violates the order and harmony of the cosmos. The individual is only a furtive shadow, a floating cloud that progresses for a moment before dissolving without a trace. It is a kind of elementary and precarious reality, which is certainly distinct from other realities. Its distinction, however, is restricted to the inessential. Philosophy denounces the inessentiality of the individual and it ends up drawing the strict conclusion that "basically, each individuality is only a special error, a misstep, something for which it is better not to exist."[4]

At the origin of these denunciations is found the diverse metaphysics of Form in which the individual is understood as a de-multiplication of the universal, of essence through matter—in other words by virtue of an entanglement with the non-intelligible. This is a vision that inexorably leads to the conception of the unintelligibility of the individual. Yet precisely, the ultimate end of philosophical discourse on the singular is to reestablish the truth and eidetic dignity of the non-universal that, in turn, institutes and guarantees its value, or rather, its uniqueness and irreplaceability. The investigation wants to liberate itself from the heavy heritage of a medieval philosophy

---

2. Bourdaloue, *Sermon sur la religion chrétienne*, in *Oeuvres*. Paris: 1716 in *Singularité*, Robert, *Dictionnaire alphabétique et analogique de la langue française* 6 (Paris: Nouveau Littré, 1996), 264.

3. Valéry, *Monsieur Teste*, 94s.

4. Schopenhauer, *Le Monde comme volonté et comme représentation* IV, suppl. 41, 1920.

tormented by the impossibility of giving God knowledge of individuals, of the influential posterity of scholastic speculation that jeopardizes the discourse on the individual and the singular by refusing to give it its proper eidetic impact. But if the impenitent Aristotelianism of Thomas and his posterity seems to prohibit forever the metaphysical foundation of the dignity of the singular, then the Scotist haecceity represents a fecund inspiration for the exploration and construction of the individual. Haecceity announces the sui generis intelligibility of the singular and seems to anticipate the disassociation between intelligibility and universality practiced by phenomenology. Neither the notion of haecceity nor Husserlian eidetic exploration yet resolves the question of the intelligibility of singularity. Neither provides a true "deduction" of the singular. Yet they mark the path to the establishment of a new idea of singularity, according to its plural unicity.

The basic ideas about the status of the singular insist on its condition of being distinct from other realities, especially other singularities. Whether it is found in the middle of a landscape or at its periphery, whether it occupies a vast horizon or is hidden in distant corners, the singular demands an essential solitude: it is detached and separated from every other being. But this spatial separation, the necessity of a distance by relation to all that is not itself, does not yet exhaust the alterity of the singular. This alterity, even in its most primitive, most rudimentary acceptation, is not just topological. Neither is it simply "numerical." It is much more necessary that singularity be reduced to simple ontological alterity. This means that to characterize singulars separation remains insufficient, just as distinction is inadequate to found them. The singular is not just distinguished from other singulars: it also must be differentiated from them.

Differentiation is certainly also a distinction, but it possesses a superior power. Ultimate distinction designates only the separation from another. Its heart and soul is distance. But distance is neither within what is distinct nor within that from which a reality is distinct. Yet differentiation is founded on singular beings themselves. It is essentially a matter of quality, of property and, as such, it can be described and defined, whereas distinction, a brute ontological fact, can ultimately only be affirmed. The difference between beings is not determined by something situated beyond them but belongs to the observation and description of these beings themselves. However, if differentiation is a function of the eidetic givens proper to the different beings themselves, it can still be relegated to the extrinsic domain, whereas the realization, the proper truth of difference belongs to the intrinsic order.

Extrinsic differentiation of beings can belong either to the quantitative or qualitative orders. When it is quantitative, reference to the property, the quality is certainly undeniable but it is submitted to considerations relativizing its significance. Beings are defined, evaluated and appreciated starting from their properties and this evaluation leads to attributing to them a worth. But if the consideration of property is an indispensible ingredient of evaluation, the price or value of the object is not determined by virtue of this property, but in terms of the presence or absence of other beings having the same properties. The qualities of an object stand at the origin of its use, at the base of its role that it is susceptible to play in a given situation. Nevertheless, its importance depends on the frequency or rarity of its occurrences. In a country with a closed economy possessing emerald mines, the most beautiful emeralds negotiate a relatively low price. However, if this closed country has difficulty importing computers or cars, computers with a weak performance or cars of a low-end brand sell at a high price. What is rare is expensive. If in the philatelic universe the Mauritius Post Office Blue of 1847 or the Round Stamp of British Guiana of 1850 are the most expensive in the world, this is not because of their beauty, or the perfection of their design, but for the one and only reason that there are only two of these blue *stamps* with the effigy of Queen Victoria and only one of these tiny round bits of paper put in circulation in 1850 by Her Majesty's Post in Guiana.

The economic value that individualizes and singularizes represents the most radical extrinsic differentiation and it obeys the same logic as that which jeopardizes in an irremediable way the reciprocity between free beings. Reciprocity implies equality of services and benefits, but this equality is commanded by the absolute relation that empties its own terms of meaning. Something analogous occurs with the differentiation produced by rarity. Rarity does not completely abolish the quiddative truth of the things evaluated but it ends up translating it into monetary terms. It could be said that a human collectivity and its members are inclined, even constrained, to dedicate a certain sum of money to a category of objects of consumption or to a category of services and price. In other words the value of its objects and its services is calculated by simple division—namely the division of the sum in question spent on the available number of objects and services. This reduction of autonomous realities to their common denominator, their "universal compendium" has always been felt to be something offensive. Money certainly has no odor but it still provokes distrust and denunciation. Doubtlessly the declamations of the baseness, toxicity, and impurity of financial considerations and of the role of money are largely stamped with hypocrisy, with bad faith. Of course, this does not preclude a profound truth. If, thanks to the use of diverse means of monetary payment, exchanges have become easier, more rational, and if this fact renders all our actions simpler and more efficacious, then the consummate monetization characterizing modern and postmodern life manifests a radical reductionism. Contemporary society has elaborated an immense, novel catalogue of available things—objects and services—but this at the cost of an effacement and even true bracketing of their proper eidetic reality. This imaginary catalogue, however omnipresent and immensely influential, contains an infinity of precise descriptions of entities that are immediately returned, reduced to something outside of themselves, other than themselves. In its rudiments, extrinsic differentiation is almost perfectly under the influence of quantity, of a fictional, "inessential difference."[5]

5. Hegel, *Jenar Systemfragmente* III. *Gesammelte Werke* 8, 5.

The Singular

Extrinsic differentiation according to quantity—despite objections and exceptions that occasion personal attachment to an artifact of daily use, to a plant or an animal—is commonly accepted in the world of objects. The things of nature and especially man-made entities share in the immense totality of eidetically different realities but with a finally homogenous, common essence. However, the quantification does not seem to apply in the world of free beings. Slavery and prostitution, the reduction of an autonomous individual to the condition of a quantified and monetized, exchanged being is a moral scandal. Nevertheless, the moral scandal of these "institutions" only emphasizes in a particularly crude way a universal metaphysical anomaly: the definition of a being in terms of something other than what it is in itself.

By refusing to assess a being quantitatively, extrinsic differentiation is supposedly overcome. A thing is no longer defined according to the frequency of realities bearing the same properties as it, but in terms of its properties as such. Flowers are red, green, or yellow; soups are spicy or bland; poets are abstract, eloquent, or hermetic (setting aside more vulgar examples like the preference between blondes or brunettes). Yellow tulips are contemplated in ecstasy—even if they number among the thousands—although among them is a radiant solitary red tulip. A brunette among half a dozen is still admired even when blondes are rare in the southern country where one lives. Assessment follows a definition according to proper traits. Nevertheless, what is proper is not yet necessarily intrinsic. Well to the contrary, property belongs to the universal, the general (this is a thesis of classical metaphysics): substance, individual substance—so teaches Aristotle—is a "possessor of properties but is itself not a property" (*Categories* 5, 2a). Redness and blondeness, blandness and spiciness, are properties, but they are not *exclusive* properties of their subject. In fact, these are predicates and as such, they can be affirmed of an indeterminate number of subjects. One subject can be distinguished from another by virtue of its possession of a quality, but this quality is a property that can be found in another. And in this case one ends up, as it were, back at square one. I love spicy soup but only have a choice among several dishes of pottage. I will end up choosing one, probably the one that tickles my taste buds without scorching my palate. I will have made a reasonable choice, that of the "best" available soup, but still, I have fallen back into evaluation according to quantity.

In reality it is not necessary to emphasize the quantitative aspects of quality in order to understand that the differentiation that it represents is not truly intrinsic. When I characterize someone as artless, another as naïve, a third as insightful, I am not defining them in terms of a knowledge of the singular being that they are but in relation to qualities they possess. The relation is practiced starting with a universal, the property that I can relate to a universal other. The end I seek is to grasp the singular, but singularity is submerged, or rather, bracketed by the general. Differentiation according to property receives its prestige thanks to the ancient heritage of the doctrine of essence. But paradoxically, if the quiddity, the essence of a thing is one of its indispensible constituents, even *the* indispensible constituent, it is still not truly intrinsic.

Property belongs to Having. However, if a being cannot subsist without having properties, the components or elements of this having still do not exclusively belong to it.

The decisive proof of the extrinsic condition of the evaluation of a thing by rarity or frequency, that is, by quantity, is that the reality thus defined as an instance of Having, is exchangeable and transferable. In other words, it does not have a core that is unconditionally its own and only its own. Yet the definition of a being by character traits, to wit its qualities and properties, delivers it over to an analogous external determination. The distinction between two blocks of butter at a market stall is made in terms of the obviously external and homogenous category of quantity. The judgment that differentiates two flowers of different colors is not exercised in terms of an external common category, but it no less subjects the two realities to an evaluation by extrinsic criteria. In a first moment (which suffices to establish the metaphysical status of a being), the singularity is defined and determined in terms of the universal that is its property. In a second moment (which proves to be particularly significant for rational, free beings), the definition by property is subsumed under a choice decided by Comparison. The evaluation of the value of a good leading to a commercial transaction is made by a simple observation that begins with a homogeneous, quantitative given that is clear and visible. The evaluation of beings possessing different properties does not dispose of such a unified grid of interpretation. Yet it is practiced as the deciphering of an ideal, utilizing an invisible but sovereignly present and universal scale, a scale that serves as the external, hidden common denominator for beings that are, according to appearances, different.

Intrinsic Differentiation

The singular is defined by virtue of a differentiation, but an *intrinsic* one. Said differently, the singular is not singular because it represents a quality or property in an unprecedented, especially significant, or exceptional way. Exceptionality still refers to an external series of beings or occurrences, realities other than the singular itself. The singular is not an entity that forcefully represents a universal unless it is a sign. But a "'sign' is that which, apprehended, brings something else to awareness."[6] It is what it is only in terms of the reality to which it refers, whereas, precisely, the singular refers to nothing but itself. The singular is not interpreted starting from a context. Of course, it is not hermetically closed to what surrounds or rubs against it, but all that it encounters is what it is, only to the degree that it takes responsibility for it, integrating it into its organism or into its sphere. The singular carries its meaning in itself. Heidegger cites an old German text, *The Peasant from Bohemia*: "As soon as a man is born he is old enough to die."[7] But the profound and largely obscure truth of the proverb is not only that there is nothing absurd about dying at twenty years of age, but

6. William of Ockham, *Summa Logicae* I, 1.
7. Heidegger, *Être et temps*, 197.

that ultimately nobody dies "too early." Life is not an enterprise possessing its meaning outside of itself. Even cut down in the prime of life, one does not stop constituting a totality.

Every true whole is not the sum of its parts, but their organic unity—a unifying and not unified unity. It is a whole-being established and maintained by its own principle, a being, in short, having an intrinsic unity. The secret of singularity is found in this intrinsic core that is at the base of everything universal and general in the singular. One could say that a singular is a simple substrate to which properties adhere. Is it then the substrate below or beyond properties and which constitutes singularity as such, a deep core, stripped of everything external and accessory? To take the substrate as the truth of the singular proves to be an untenable hypothesis. Singularity is not only existence but also essence; it is inconceivable without a minimum of quiddative elements. Substrates, the *bare particulars* of analytic philosophy, are only brute ontological facts, examples and instances of this merely numerical difference that, ever since the formulation of the Leibnizian principle of indiscernibles, philosophy has resolutely rejected. The idea of the substrate has always been considered an evident and indubitable metaphysical category. But the substrate as such, "in itself," is ultimately an abstraction: it only ever exists as the root or support of its properties. In other words, despite the strong inclination for human thought to take shortcuts, to bracket "details," to concentrate only on the "essential," philosophical analysis has clearly shown that the singular is not only its substrate but is rather the substrate *and* the properties that, so to speak, grow and unfold out of it. These properties and qualities could be considered simple accidents of the singular substance, yet this substance, like every substance besides God—as is well known since Aristotle—cannot dispense with accidents. This amounts to saying that if the singularity of a being is determined by virtue of what is exclusive and incommunicable within it, one still cannot skip over the presence of universal components. Well to the contrary, properties, the paradoxical designation of general, universal realities belonging to the singular, make up part of it. Even more, without wanting to reduce the singular to being only a packet or "*bundle*" of properties or even to the string that holds together the totality, it can be conceived only as a reality that (necessarily) has its moments and elements. The metaphysical meaning of singularity is the way in which a being gathers and unifies its elements.

A singular substance cannot be, cannot subsist without possessing properties, qualities. But are these properties, the quiddative components of the singular determined in terms of "its complete notion," or does the necessary adherence of accidents to the singular go with the indeterminacy of its accidents?[8] In other words, if the singular necessarily possesses properties, are the properties it possesses contingent? Before entering this problem, we will rapidly proceed through an investigation that will delimit the sphere of entities susceptible to qualify as singular (and without any

---

8. Leibniz, *Remarques sur la lettre de M. Arnauld*, 109.

prejudgment about the answer to the question "how does the singular posses, that is, unify its elements"). A singular being contains elements, it shows properties, but the properties are universal. The diverse beings of the world display different colors, possess various qualities and talents, contain different potentialities. However, this infinite multiplicity of quiddative elements is only a multiplicity of universals. The beings of the world can constitute microcosms, each different from every other, and yet one always finds in them only universals. They are distinguished from one another by specific blends of these universals, but the specificity of the configuration of common qualities does not yet refer to a principle of another metaphysical order than the property. In the terms of classical metaphysics: whether individuation or singularization is attributed to Form or Matter, it is always false. If the singular exists it can only come from a principle that, all the while being bound to the universal, remains heterogeneous to it. Once again, Metaphysics ought to make a Critique of the analytical, the homogeneous. It ought to revive the struggle against immanence; it must indicate the limits and pitfalls of Nature. As was the case in every other register of self-exit and self-surpassing, true singularity also has its roots and sources in freedom.

Freedom is here exercised as the surpassing of the homogeneity of the universal, as the extraction from determination by the property that is not truly proper to us. Only free beings are truly singular: a metaphysical fact most cultures manifest by the attribution of forenames. Plants and animals are designated only by their generic name. Of course, pets, circus animals and work animals sometimes receive a forename, but if they are honored in this way, it is by virtue of their association with humans. Like the most beautiful tulips, the largest whales and the juiciest oysters are designated only by their generic name. We may speak of a tiger or giraffe, of a shark or a crab, but these are like last names, which by definition are attributed to an actual or potential plurality of like beings. The forename, the proper name realizes a designation in which the signified and the referent are one and the same. The proper name corresponds to the intuition of a unique situation: the incommunicable identity of a being is imposed with evidence; it subsists without any kind of mediation belonging to another. The forename expresses the limit situation in which a reality is perceived in and through itself, known according to its being, not according to its having, and where event its seizure is extended to having.

The forename is the appropriate designation for a unifying unity of properties, of a unification that reaches an independent integration distinct from every other. If singularity can be affirmed only of intelligent and free beings, this is because they alone are capable, not of suppressing or obliterating properties, but of rereading them in terms of a figure or rather a paradigm that surpasses them. Properties are universals and, as such, they represent something heterogeneous to the singular that possesses them. In other words, if a being is without metaphysical leeway in relation to his properties, it cannot be a singularity. But no being can be what it is apart from its specific traits. However—and here the great metaphysical adventure of singularity occurs—humans, rational animals or animals endowed with language, possess, as animals, common properties. Nevertheless, they have a specific relation to the properties of the species that they are. They certainly have no leeway in relation to the presence within them of human eidetic properties, of the biological and psychological character traits of *homo sapiens*. However, they dispose of a leeway in relation to the distribution or rather composition of traits belonging to their *humanity*. This humanity is an eidos unlike any other animal eidē. Of course, the individual of any animal species registers disparities and variations in the configuration of its specific traits, involving a range of degrees of their eidos. But the degrees of the eidos "human" are of an altogether different nature. The human eidos is not only descriptive: it also registers a prescriptive dimension. The biped without wings is defined as human and yet a human is enjoined to behave humanly whereas it does not occur to anyone to require a dog or a cat to behave in a truly *canine* or *feline* manner.

This free being man is able to constitute a singularity because the prescriptive dimension of his eidos carries the possibility of an unforeseen unification, namely, a unification of properties by an a priori synthesis. The a priori synthesis is the framework for predicates that do not necessarily follow from an essence but are chosen and assumed in accordance with an intelligible order. The singular that is man is the sovereign principle of order, of the unity of its properties; it singularizes (as it were) through its face, by the unforeseen configuration of its properties. However, this particular configuration in the horizontal, in the spatial, is not only the artisan of an unforeseen figure but also the source for a renewing continuity. The a priori synthesis that unfolds in and through time causes man to win a supreme victory over Becoming: he can remain himself without remaining "the same." The operations of analysis can support and accomplish sameness, whereas the synthesis, more precisely, a priori synthesis is the source par excellence of ipseity. The synthetic power at work in freedom is not content to found and conserve the harmonious configuration of properties as stable and permanent givens, but equally institutes and animates the dynamic continuity of moments. The singular happens as an ineducible flash of lightning, but it is also and above all an unforeseen history.

Syntheses of Singularity

The singular is the synthesis of predicates by the subject. But to the degree that it is a matter of an a priori synthesis, the belonging of predicates to the subject is in no way deducible—not even for an ultimate understanding. Scholastic interrogation on contingent futures is located in proximity to this problematic but falls short: neither future nor present predicates are—because they cannot be—implied by a free subject. Hellenistic and medieval metaphysics teaches the radical heterogeneity of substance and its properties. A substance is irreducibly itself; it can never become a property, whereas its properties can belong to other substances. Leibniz thought he overcame this residue of contingency, this space of irrationality by the idea of the Common Notion. A substance, that is, a subject, contains a certain number of predicates, but the predicates it contains are only and can only be its own. Given predicates can belong only to a given subject; they can never be attributed to another. Predicates are glued to the subject; they belong to it and cannot belong to any other subject. We are capable of not discerning the necessary affiliation of a predicate to its subject, but a more diligent and penetrating exercise of our mind or superior gaze of our understanding would comprehend their necessary link.

The idea of the Common Notion is innovative. It is a unique moment of reflection on the singular, but, in the last analysis, it represents a fall back into the universe of analytic judgments. Predicates, it teaches, are able not to appear with evidence like necessary, logical moments of the subject, but even if they are not truly within the reach of the finite intelligence, deeper investigation will not fail to reveal their implication by the subject. But here precisely the deficiency and radical misunderstanding of the Common Notion manifests itself. The singular is the unforeseen joining of its properties. The subject's exclusive implication seems to do justice to the singular, individual condition proper to this unification. In actuality ignorance here continues of the two essential moments of the implication of which the singular is the principle and source: the singular is not related to eidē properly so called and the synthesis that realizes it is a priori.

The singular that gathers its properties is not a unique super-property added to the other properties. It is not a superior or first eidos collecting secondary eidē. It is a subject that can never be a predicate for the good reason that it does not belong to the world of predicates. Predicates are objects of description whereas the truly singular is correlate only to a nomination. It is the object of a nomination, it responds to a name, because it is Subject. In fact, the secret of the singular is found in correlation, the relation between the Subject and its predicates. Predicates do not constitute scattered and contingent impressions of the Subject, a Having that the Subject gathers, piles up and moves at will or disposes of arbitrarily. They do not fall to it, either, through a kind of inevitability; they are not assigned to it by an internal or external necessity. The subject is, or rather ceaselessly effects, the synthesis of its predicates, a synthesis that is a priori. The singular is—only—this a priori synthesis through which diverse properties constitute a single and whole being. The subject realizes this integration through a particular, or rather *singular* manner. It leaves its mark on its predicates, giving them a specific color, shaping them in an unforeseen way. The freedom at work in this unification causes the predicates to happen to the subject in an unanticipatable way. Yet, they are perceived as suitable and appropriate, possessing a metaphysical affinity with it. The subject does not contain or rather does not pre-contain in a virtual way its properties but finds them, welcomes them and integrates them into its universe. Doubtlessly, the properties thus seized and taken charge of possess traits and colors that seem unforeseen and belong only to unique occurrence of the eidos, and may not be confounded with the moments of another subject. However, the unforeseen, the incomparable within the quiddative moments of a singular is not of the order of contents. The unique synthesis that assigns them to a given subject does not yet modify their universal condition. From a material point of view, the properties of a given subject are not only its own, but may be effectively found in other subjects.

The a priori synthesis constituting the singular is sovereign in relation to its contents. It chooses and assumes them, and once it has done this, they belong to the singularity that synthesizes them. And they belong to it so radically and properly that the presence of quiddatively the same realities within a second or third entity, in a singular B or C does not affect their authentic belonging to a singular A. A color or a tone, a word or an idea can very well characterize two or more singulars. What matters is that they are integrated into a subject, penetrated, recreating the synthesis that constitutes them. Fashion tells individuals to wear very similar, almost identical clothes, shoes, gloves and hats. Many share the same line of production. But taking advantage of the same sales does not yet mean that I am dressed like my neighbor. My principal items of clothing are differentiated by accessories, haircut, jewelry: the Indian villager who wears a sari exactly like her sister-in-law wears it in her own way, in a singular manner.

The principle of indiscernibles is here illustrated and very pertinently validated. There are leaves and flowers in a garden not only numerically distinct. But there are also individuals glimpsed through the configuration of these possessions, all this essential having that serves as their clothing. But these occurrences, which are despite everything fairly external to singularity, can be deepened in the direction of phenomena where synthesis is manifested in the form of a more immanent, or rather, further intrinsic structuration. Poets and novelists share the same language and dispose of the same vocabulary: especially when they are contemporaneous they use words according to extremely similar thetic and affective valences, hear them with the same tone and order them with the same grammatical rules. However, writers that draw on the same linguistic treasury display very different styles of writing. A word count in a *corpus* teaches that each poet or novelist or dramatist, but also each philosopher selects the materials for his text in his own way and integrates them in an unforeseen way in his writing. Writing style is precisely the singular configuration of predicates accessible to each locutionary subject, integration into a unique totality of properties, however general. Style is the cipher for a synthesis of imagination, feeling and design that has apparently never taken place before and will never take place in the future. It constitutes a spectacular manifestation of the thesis that the subject remains itself without remaining the same. Detailed, quantitative studies are susceptible to present the development or evolution of a style, the slow transformation of certain constants, the nearly imperceptible modification of formulas, the weakening or intensification of accents. But, notwithstanding the transformations and emphases, and the erasure of accents or the dramatization of certain urgencies at the expense of others, style preserves its continuity. The singular is a synthesis and this a priori synthesis is effected not only horizontally but also vertically: a singular reality is not only the configuration of spatial components, but also structuration in time. Style seems to be the very cipher of permanence and stability. In fact, it is the emblematic expression of the singular, of this free subject that is history, a history that is only its own and that alone will tell of it.

Style is the external expression of a singularity from which it is separated and frozen: after all it is realized only through an act of proffering words and above all recording them on paper. It is like the prolongation of the writer, both a consequence or product and something more intrinsic to him. But other exteriorizations of the singular being are found that are not disassociated or separated. If artists are differentiated by style of their *oeuvres*, the singularity of women and men is perceived above all by their face. The face is certainly what is most "characteristic" about a person; someone is recognized above all by his or her face. If other parts of the body are normally covered by clothing, they are general, common, alike among a multiplicity of individual humans and are therefore predisposed to receive the uniform that comprises every item of clothing. Vestments can certainly accentuate the forms of a body, yet they play a quasi-role of disindividualizing (which is considered normal, obvious, and appropriate). However, when one covers one's face with a hood or veil one yields to an anomalous practice, most often dubious, that invites mistrust and censure: one acts to obscure or to hide, in short, to *mask* a truth. But when the vestment effectively or symbolically molds to the body, the mask, even if it adheres closely to the face, is opposed to the truth. A mask expresses a ritual or theatrical role and therefore works toward the recurrence of universals through individual occurrences. The mask expresses and accentuates the general, the common. It brackets the singular. A face becomes a mask precisely when it seeks to hide wealth or indigence, worries or joys that are its own. The face is a "form," though every form is not yet a face. Humans have faces while animals have only muzzles. The French language multiplies synonyms in order to disqualify the singularity proper to the face; it produces expressions wherein the dignity of the human form, appearance and incarnation of freedom that makes humans singular, is betrayed in favor of sliding into the general, the stereotypical and the routine. The French speak of a *jolie frimousse*, a "pretty face," and a *bonne bouille*, a "nice face," or of a *sale gueule*, an "ugly face," but also of a *trogne*, a "look," a *tronche*, a "mug," a *trombine*, a "pan," and a *binette*, a "kisser." In this way are we not invoking the contemptible practice of characterizing a person by their features? Whether pejorative or banal these expressions miss the truth of the Face that appears, the shocking form of a free being's singularity. The friendliness or violence of these expressions seems to belong to a totally different register from the scholarly attempts to read the content or message of singularity by studying physiognomy. But if the traits of a face provide an important lesson, they mediate feelings and character, and are in the last instance universals, properties that, taken in themselves as true eidē, can play the role of a mask. The old practice of phrenology seriously claimed that the structure of our skull determined our constitution and allowed one to read through it the structure and potentialities of our personality. However, taken to its ultimate consequences—as readers of Hegel know—phrenology results in understanding the spirit as if it were bone.

Of course ossification and generalization must be avoided, and therefore various kinds of deadly abstraction, if instead of thinking of the traits of the human face as so many gradations of a phenomenological essence, they are seen and read according to the singular configuration that gathers and constitutes them as a sui generis whole. The face appears as the external or even spatial expression of our being, a fixed and frozen entity. In reality, it is formed in and through time—time understood as the free self-articulation of our existence. The wrinkled face was sculpted by what happened to it through its life; it is the trace or translation of which this life received and assumed the experiences that happened to it, the trials it endured. The face shares the human body and, as such, it shares the biological destiny of the *soma*. But the body has a history that is neither dissociable nor differentiable from the history of the free being of which it is the body. The face is this aspect of the body through which the body lives most directly and intensely this singular life, registering with a blindingly obvious evidence its effective, incarnate singularity.

Levinas spoke of the Epiphany of the face. The face is as much expression of the singular as manifestation, a manifestation that, all the while referring to a singular, complete totality surpassing it on all sides, appears valuable in and through itself, emerges without us having to conceive something that founds it, its principle or substrate. The face is, so to speak, the supreme cipher of the singular, of the free, historical being that it is. The critique of big capital, of the banks, of world capitalism discourses about the "faceless corporation" analogously to the way Kafka's posterity does about the process of the State, of faceless bureaucracy. The face or visage is ultimately the true cipher of the singular, its most faithful "representative." Someone hurls insults to my face; I receive a physical or moral "slap in the face." My face expresses what is most proper to me; in and through the face the body goes as far as possible as the singular being, the singular in its properly free, moral dimensions. The face translates in a particularly adequate and suggestive way the synthesis that is the being of the singular, the synthesis that gives consistency and meaning to the elements that are its traits. However, the sovereignty of the synthesis can take an even more complete form. The face is a figure of singularity in which the components and properties, all these eidetic universals, are combined and qualified by virtue of the subject that is the source and artisan in the true sense of the configuration. Nevertheless syntheses exist in which the unifying link, the connection among the elements plays an even more intense role, carrying out even more radical interpretations and integrations.

Psychoanalytic treatment is a particularly propitious place to identify closely the sovereign synthesis that founds and animates singularity. It illustrates in an exceptionally clear way the two moments, the two essential elements of this synthesis: the subject cannot dispense with predicates but the meaning of its predicates entirely depends on it. And this dependence is so integral that the subsistence on the eidetic plane in no way hampers the modification of meaning. Someone suffers a psychological dysfunction, he or she has a problem with memory, experiences dread and panic, is incapable of completing simple actions or gestures. The encounter with a certain person or animal, going to a certain place, certain sounds strikes him or her with a kind of paralysis. Beyond this dysfunctioning, these psycho-physiological blocks and wounds, he or she experiences anguish, is eaten up with remorse. Usually this dysfunction, these wounds and blocks like anguish and remorse come from time immemorial: the subject has forgotten *when* they began. He or she has forgotten *how* they began. At the beginning there is an act or event that disappeared from consciousness and the cure is found in rediscovering it. Subjective life is a succession or series of events that is neither continuous nor complete. Treatment consists in long meetings in which one patiently enters into the past, follows the twisted thread of events, tries to populate deserted regions, to fill in gaps. It is essentially a process of restoring lost memories; its end is to find the initial moment of a break, the act or event that caused the dysfunction. This act or event has fallen below memory, slid out of the reach of consciousness; one wants to find it and place it in the train of moments of the subject's life. How surprising and disappointing to find that the discovery of the founding moment of the perturbation is not yet enough to restore harmony and peace. Healing requires bringing this moment of the past to light, but it also requires a reconquest, a reintegration. The forgotten moment did not simply slide out of consciousness like a coin fallen through a hole in the pocket or a piece of paper taken by the wind. The forgotten moment has been obscured by the subject; its restoration requires reappropriation. It is possible that my circle of friends knows all about the distant event that triggered my psychological dysfunction. Granted. Now I "know" what lies at the origin of these wounds. Thus the successive series of memories of my life seems restored. However, this material restitution of an absent memory does not yet reestablish the integrity of my memory as such. The disruptive fact was certainly a moment in a series, following on and preceding others. Yet the subjective series is not a theory of atoms, of disconnected points; it is the thread of a synthesis. The reappearance of the forgotten memory and its reinsertion in the place where it was originally located is not enough to heal the break in memory because this is a material operation whereas the forgetting is a suppression, thus an intentional, voluntary act. In short: one cannot make it back to the beginning, reaching the place of the past where the subject can, in its own strength, reintroduce the obscured memory into its subjective synthesis. The sameness of the eidos and the same position in temporal succession must pass through the crucible of re-appropriation in order for memory to carry the day over forgetting, for division to cede to the harmony of reconciliation, and for peace to be found.

The Singular

From the Singular to the Unique

Discussion of the eidetic category of the three initiated investigations that would allow the surpassing of the individual has led us to the Singular. The singular is distinct from every other entity. Or rather, it is found differentiated from them. But true differentiation is only intrinsic: it is the work of the a priori synthesis. The foundation of the singular by the synthesis permits the definitive surpassing of the paradigm of the indivisible: a being is not singular because it cannot be separated or divided, but because it has in itself, or rather that it is itself, the active source of its unification, its subsistence, its functioning, in short, its own existence. The synthetic condition of the singular allows us to reconcile the perennial with the changing, being with becoming. The singular is not a one-time thing, but a being living in time and freely existing. To understand the singular as a synthesis that unfolds itself and does so in its own terms (this is the very meaning of its a prioriness), starting from an originally quidditative spontaneity, cuts short every attempt to assimilate the singular being to the individual, to an entity only numerically different from every other. But in a way at first disconcerting, the true synthesis that institutes and protects singulars as intrinsically different from each other does not exclude the possibility of the advent of two or many singulars identical according to content. Seeing the primacy of the a priori synthesis in relation to its predicates, the same predicates, even the same material correlation of identical predicates, could lead to the birth and subsistence of numerically different singulars. The four figures of singularity, the individual's manner of dress, the style of a writer, the human face and the recovery of buried memory, illustrate the phenomenological thesis that the subject can remain itself without remaining the same. But they equally attest that the doctrine of singularity goes farther still, that it can lead to more radical conclusions. If the sameness of predicates is not required for the subject to remain itself, this is because in the last analysis, in the strict sense, it has nothing to do with the continuous identity of the subject of the synthesis. *Selbstheit* is so little identical with *Gleichheit* that the latter is irrelevant!

The result of this entire investigation offends common conscience, attached as it is to quidditative considerations seemingly more apt to recognize and discern singularity. But the comprehension of singularity beyond all having, its interpretation as synthesis that short-circuits considerations of content, calls for new research. The singular appears to adapt to a plurality of occurrences of identical contents. There are thus many singulars with the same content. If this is the case, the deepening of the essential, of the proper intrinsicness of the singular, ends up detracting from the articulation of the real. Differentiation alone allows a true founding of the singular, but pushed to its farthest implications it abolishes distinction. In other words, it leads to a situation in which the proper intrinsic synthesis hidden in the depths of a being becomes the principle and source of an appearing entity registering only a numerical difference in relation to its neighbors. The doctrine of the singular nourished the ambition to go beyond the principle of indiscernibles. In fact, it seems to fall short of it.

These contradictions and paradoxes attest that the aporias of singularity are hardly resolvable but give every appearance of being perennial. One tries to bypass them but they end up being surpassed thanks to the introduction of an idea with metaphysical affinity to the singular. The singular appears in the context of meditations on number; it is related to and allied with the one. Another theme, this time explicitly numerical—that of the unique—joined to the singular will lead to the definitive victory over the universal and general, secret accomplices of immanence. The singular still owes its unity to extrinsic differentiation whereas the unique, the intrinsic, will be joined to the extrinsic without itself becoming extrinsic. The unique seems inseparable from the one, but unicity is not a category of arithmetic. The one, an atomic, limited reality, exists independently of every other reality; it is an entity of dispersion, of ir-relation and ir-reference. More precisely: it is only one—not a unity or unification, whether intrinsic or extrinsic. The one is short of the singular, which is unity, intrinsic unity, differentiation from every other thing by virtue of itself, but a differentiation that, being and being only intrinsic, cannot ward off the peril of sameness. Said differently, the singular is different only for itself, whereas the accomplishment of difference requires it also to be for another. Adequately understood, this being-different for another is not of the material, quidditative order. The unique is a singular, but all singulars are not unique. Those that are, are not by virtue of specific character traits, but thanks to an external, transcendent constitution. The singular does not have properties that render it unique; it can only be *acknowledged* as such. And the acknowledgment can only come from the outside.

The acknowledgment that establishes the unique must be the sovereign fact of an external reality. It chooses one singular among others. Yet this "election" must not be able to be either contingent or necessary. This "election" and "differentiation" would be necessary if it follows from objectively definable criteria. It can only be the result of a "comparison" and, as such, it represents a fall back into the extrinsic.[9] It must not be contingent any more: an arbitrary choice can distinguish and put aside a being but in this case, the essential links between the unique and the intrinsic would be cut. The unique would be simply an entity grasped and set aside irrationally, and therefore a reality with a condition, by its nature temporary, revocable at each moment. And this would doubly interfere with the unicity of the chosen which could be neither unique *in itself* nor *for another*. On the one hand the temporary condition registers the absence of continuity, the proper identity of the chosen, the preferred. On the other hand, engagement in election is required in order to make it an authentic, proper action of the being that chooses.

---

9. Jüngel, *Gott als Geheimnis der Welt*, 443.

The Singular

Things

The aporias of singularity lead to unicity. The unique is the singular in which the two differentiations, the intrinsic, coming from within, from the singular itself, and the extrinsic, that of recognition by another, meet and are realized. The unique as the singular is an entity that, paradoxically (if thought according to the designation "unique") is one among others. In fact, by its metaphysical essence the unique contains a return to a plurality of entities, in the context of which it shines as unique, against the background of which its unicity flares forth. This native dependence of an at least virtual plurality seems to allow the possibility of the unicity of any being. After all, every being, independent of its essence can share in a plurality! However, in the strict sense the unique occurs only in the context of singulars and in the large sense only in relation and with reference to a singularity.

The unique is related to a numerically different entity and the latter are either material things or free beings. Everyone agrees that the highest instances of the unique are among free beings, but how to doubt the possibility or rather the effective reality of the unique among things? We could be tempted to distinguish inanimate material beings and living beings and to situate unicity within the animated creation. Yet the thesis proves itself null. Even if we find examples of unicity more easily among living beings, cats, dogs, and horses, we must yield to the evidence: we can be attached with exclusive devotion to an inanimate material object, a stone, a crystal or even an artifact like a shirt, a hat, a pipe, or a cane. But whether we are concerned with inanimate or animate "things," we can speak of "unicity" only as a function of a kind of sublation of the thing within the free synthesis of singularity. If a kind of devotion is experienced for a doll or a rock, this is because they are associated with proper moments of singularity. One is passionately attached to an artifact because it constitutes an essential component of our manner of dress or to the furniture of our family house. Someone appreciates and differentiates from every other a stream or a rock because they remind us of our youth or of sites from our daily walk. The eidetic character of things considered unique, what they are in themselves, are clearly conditions for our designation of them as "unique" but they are only necessary, not sufficient conditions. For the thing determined by its eidetic traits to be recognized as unique, it must belong to the project of my life, it must be a part of the synthesis that constitutes my history. The same thing goes, a fortiori, for the living things that surround me, my pets or work animals. The spontaneity of superior animals doubtlessly contributes to our appreciation of them and experience of them as unique, but this spontaneity, anticipation, or prehistory of freedom ultimately has value only by virtue of its association with the synthesis that constitutes a human singularity.

The impossibility of attributing unicity to things in a full, authentic sense will be seen more clearly through a more detailed analysis. Material inanimate things are either works of human action or beings of nature (metals, minerals, components of the soul or elements of the atmosphere). The products of human work are themselves divided into two categories: artisanal works or products of mechanized industry. The artifacts of artisans register at least an infinitesimal difference in relation to one another. They appear as so many variations of an eidos. They are produced with more difficulty, and hence less frequently, whereas the products of machines are identical (barring accidents) and can be numbered quasi-infinitely. The ease of their multiplication favors waste: the products of modern industry are apparently inexhaustible, so why would I make the difficult, expensive effort to economize what is so easily replaced? Also the similarity, the near-complete absence of individual traits hardly tempts me to retrace their genesis, to tie them back to their source. The object is located, so to say, on the surface; it appears without its own thickness or link with something other and more profound, more original than itself. However, the shadow of unicity continues to fall on this universe of multiplicity and dispersal. Contemporary environmentalism echoes this presence or rather this necessity that haunts the world of waste, setting humanity face to face with the threat that puts into question the very conditions of life of post-industrial societies. Environmentalism in its original inspiration is the care and defense of nature; it attempts to make us aware of the value of artifacts, all of them, even the most insignificant or banal, the most easily produced. In other words, the intuition of the integral and sacred character of an immense organic All, gathering and unifying the inhabitants of the cosmos, is a powerful goad for the investigation of the metaphysical status of the "singular." By accompanying it along the path it follows, may we reach the "unique"?

The claim of value, of the meaningfulness of natural objects implies, explicitly or implicitly, reference to Nature as principle of value, source of meaning. We may marvel at orchids or otters, sycamores or dolphins. Yet this appreciation is only emotional or aesthetic where any direct or indirect attribution of unicity entails metaphysical reference to the foundational synthesis of the singular. Although the correlate of impassioned feelings and the object of ardent veneration and fervent admiration, Nature has, or rather, is not such an a priori synthesis. *Deus sive Natura* has never been able to summarize the singularity of its modes .

The quasi-mythological intuition of Nature is a very effective motive for action and appreciation but on the conceptual plane it does not replace the principle of singularity and ultimately of unicity that is the a priori synthesis. We are then constrained to turn to the theme of the exhaustion, the inexorable increasing scarcity of resources. Environmentalist discourse here has only to do with an empirical, contingent figure of rarity, but even as a metaphysical idea, rarity cannot justify the unicity sought. Rarity expresses a screaming lack, an inadequacy, a lethal insufficiency. It is a negative category. Unicity, however, is a supremely positive category. It is the essential: if unicity presupposes singularity as intrinsic differentiation, rarity is a notion defined precisely in extrinsic terms. The rare and the unique can include one another, can materially coincide: a unique object is evidently a rare object. Yet a rare object is still not necessarily unique. Rarity is a function of an empirical, contingent situation: when the crops fail or their transport system halts, the market is poorly stocked and certain commodities become rare. With curricula changes, the knowledge of classical languages can become a rare phenomenon. Yet this rarity disappears with the reestablishment of a transport system or with curricula reform. Markets inundated with fruit and an increase in degrees in ancient languages put an end to the rarity of prunes or of professors of Greek. This does not intrinsically change the nature of fruit or professors.

The demythologizations of Nature—more precisely, the awareness of its metaphysical insufficiency to found singularity and thus to justify unicity—does not have import only in the world of inanimate things. In the last analysis rarity not only replaces the sacredness of Nature in the realm of artifacts and basic materials, it ends up being discerned as a powerful reason for attempts to valorize living beings. The defense of vegetal and animal species is inspired above all by an acute intuition of their sui generis value. Yet in the absence of the a priori synthesis within these beings themselves as within Nature (their principle and their all), a shift comes about in the philosophical legitimation of their protection in the direction of the prevalence of the theme of rarity, even for living beings. It is true that the increasing scarcity and immanent disappearance of certain animal and vegetal species has always been and continues to be the main theme and source of environmentalist discourse. What is "new" is the conceptual clarification that the absence of any reference to an a priori synthesis puts rarity front and center in the argumentation and at the same time qualifies and nuances the idea.

The defense of living beings, plants, and animals, concerns species, not individuals. We worry about the significant drop in living individuals of a given animal species, we take note of the illnesses destroying important trees of a certain forest. Imbalances in ecosystems are monitored; proper proportion between wolves and caribou, or seals and sharks is sought. But we must remember that this care never concerns individual animals or plants but their species as such. We do not think to defend the life or health of a living individual, but if we do we are concerned with the health of the whole. Even if an animal species reaches the extreme limit of extinction, even if there is only one individual left, all our concern, however impassioned, that motivates this animal's defense is not a matter of it itself but of the entire species that this animal represents or is the anonymous specimen. Unicity presupposes singularity and singularity presupposes intrinsic differentiation. But the defense of species is formulated in quantitative terms. If the evaluation of living beings, the interpretation of their diversity is made in the name of the sui generis value of a species and therefore of a form, an eidos, it is not practiced according to the criteria of differentiation but of simple distinction. Environmental philosophy is not only incapable of reaching the unique, it even ends up remaining below the conceptual exigencies of the singular.

BOOK ONE—FIRST PHILOSOPHY

The Work of Art

Like living beings industrial artifacts do not seem to fill the required conditions for unicity. Artifacts can always be multiplied and living beings are by definition members of species. A category of entities may apparently be capable of vindicating unicity. While constituting an indeterminate multiplicity, works of art seem to fill the required conditions for being understood as unique. They represent an unprecedented and immaculate synthesis of their moments and elements and there is nothing like them. The idea of course, or rather its empirical concretization, carries a certain confusion or imprecision. If there is no difficulty found in distinguishing between works created by an artist and a series of objects produced by a machine, the delimitation of the artwork in relation to a handicraft is more difficult. And above all, how to determine the criteria of differentiation among works created by artists? In short, how to differentiate masterworks from less accomplished works, creations of genius from the works of mediocre painters and poets? The answer can only be pragmatic, but of a pragmatism founded on metaphysics. If the taste of an epoch—or rather its bad taste—prevents the discernment that recognizes and sets apart the masterpiece, it is nevertheless usually recognized when seen. At least, it should be and we should not forget that in this realm judgment is hardly an affair of the number of voices, of the majority or unanimity of those who vote.

If the philosophical theories that formulate the unicity of the work or its author, the artist, are relatively recent, there has always been an awareness of the exceptional value of great works. Zeuxis knew—and he was not the only one to say it—that the great artworks are priceless. Two thousand years later Kant will reserve the condition of "pricelessness" in its fullness and in an integral way for the moral person, but the attitude of the Greek painter attests to the germ of an analogous intuition. A painting has no price if it cannot be exchanged with any other entity. It possesses an irreducibility ultimately of the metaphysical order, a double irreducibility, external and internal. The external irreducibility of the work of art means that it is never the double of another entity, never an instance or specimen of a series or a species, never the individual realization of an essence. As far as its metaphysical interior irreducibility is concerned, it means that its perfection is recognized.

The true work of art is perfect. As is well known, perfection denotes a metaphysical condition in which nothing can be added or subtracted from it. Manufactured objects can always be made more resistant, more solid, more performative. As regards living beings, a flower with a sublime scent can always be conceived as emitting an even more sublime fragrance and the fastest horse in the world could be made faster through more perfect training or by means of a better diet. Things are different for works of art. Our intuition of a masterpiece is precisely that it represents an accomplishment that can neither be improved nor enriched. One finds oneself fascinated, enchanted standing before the work; one desires to alter nothing about it because one cannot conceive of altering anything about it. If the poet takes days, weeks, even years perfecting his verse, if he does not stop working until the perfect work or line imposes itself, this is because he pursues a condition that, without being able to explain why, brings an end to his labor, for it has reached perfection. In fact, the impossibility for the creative artist to explain why he has made a modification, why he has "chosen" a color or a nuance, a word or a line, shows that there is no criteria, no external ideal determining the work. The artwork is a whole that is neither the sum of its parts nor the substance or substrate of its accidents; it is a totality for which the absence or modification of an element would constitute a mutilation or rather a destruction. The strange servitude of the creative artist who seems to have no latitude in the choice of component elements of his work has as its counterpart the deep desire of the spectator to change nothing, the satisfaction, the profound peace with which he welcomes and contemplates the work. Who would think of changing a verse of Keats, who would imagine the nave of Conques Abbey with higher pillars and wider spaces? As Diderot—that very assiduous visitor of the Salons—remarked, the painting is not like a "stew to which we can always add a pinch of salt!"[10]

Perfection is a necessary, negative condition of unicity. Other negative conditions chain together in order to reach, quasi-imperceptibly, demonstrations through properly positive reasons, even, if you like, sufficient reasons. The artwork reveals a truth, but if there is a domain in which the ancient formula *adequatio rei et intellectus* is without pertinence, it is that of art. Without being hermetically sealed from the outside, inaccessible to every other reality than itself, the work of art truly has its truth in itself; its truth is immanent to it, its own. Schopenhauer said that "the work of art is never false," and he was right.[11] The true work of art is never false because it has no model or end on which it depends or that it has to realize through representing and reproducing the lineaments and elements. Reflection on the image emphasized its sui generis intelligibility, its range of self-figuration: the image is an autonomous Second that signifies and has worth independently of a First. The perfection discerned in the work repeats in its own way this intuition of the bracketing of all referentiality. More precisely, the artwork can have a referent, a model, even a signified, yet it remains no less a signification without legible referent. In its naïve banality the question of the farmer from Beauce remains the greatest: "Why paint the oak-tree since it is already there?" The answer passes through the demonstration that the very premises of the question are erroneous: what the landscape portrays has never been there before; and it is not something that appears simply at the same time as the work is realized.

Art supposes and presupposes non-referentiality conjugated in various registers, but instead of taking the risky and fanciful path of wanting to demonstrate that the painting or novel does not correspond to a model, that the figures or non-figures lack proportioned eidetic correlate, it is better to try to expose the intrinsic harmony of

10. Diderot, *Oeuvres esthétiques*, 796.
11. Schopenhauer, *Le Monde comme volonté et comme représentation* I, § 8, 131.

the work, to understand the complete synthesis that establishes it, to start from the investigation of its becoming and to decipher the conditions of its advent. The aim of the reflection is the demonstration of the autonomy, the self-sufficiency of the work. In its occurrence, however, this autonomy not only concerns the relation of the work to the outside, to what it is not, but also and above all its relation to itself. Hegelian aesthetics insists on the non-priority of form in relation to content. Its famous formula is that there is no perfect form without a perfect content. This thesis may seem banal or self-evident but it hides unexpected depths. It seems to teach the simultaneity, the parallelism, the coincidence of the two great metaphysical components of the work, but above all it opens the way to the understanding of the non-precedence proper to art, both the non-precedence of the work in relation to itself and the non-precedence of the artist in relation to himself. More simply: the work is neither conceived nor conceivable before being created, and the artist neither plans nor calculates; he does not follow anterior or external models.

The form dominating artistic production should not be conceived as a mold preceding the content, and if the great work of art involves a high technical perfection and a rigorous regularity, it never follows a rule laid out in advance. Otherwise, it would be one instance among others of an archetype, while it is truly a singular, different from every other. Recall the painter from Ubeda in *Don Quixote* who never wants to divulge the subject of his painting before finishing it; he must first guarantee the success and therefore fidelity of the reproduction.[12] But if the bad painter is afraid of missing his target, for the lack of skill and true draftsman talent, the great artist cannot represent his work in advance for rather different reasons. He is incapable of foreseeing the result of his labor simply because this result does not yet exist independently of his action. Instead of lying about the painter or poet contemplating the archetypes or, more prosaically, consulting manuals of style before getting to work, we must comprehend and admit the paradox that "the idea truly does not reach the artist until he has effectively revealed it."[13] Those who frequent the arts, like those who study them, end up realizing the non-foreseeability and non-deducibility of the painting or poem, and consequently their apparent and paradoxical independence in relation to their author. A truly original work is "of a *vegetal* nature; it rises up spontaneously…it *grows*."[14] The vision of the vegetal, organic condition of the artwork has the goal of rejecting the idea of its dependence on plans or calculations of its author, of explaining its advent in terms that are only its own, of taking account of its continuous subsistence according to an equilibrium and a sui generis order. The work is certainly the product of its author but it detaches itself from him and cannot be explained except in and through itself.

12. Cervantes, *Don Quixote* II, lxxi.
13. Baader, *Werke* II, 195.
14. Young, *Conjectures on Original Composition*, 12.

The Singular

The vision of the autonomy of the artwork in relation to its author is present in a number of aesthetic theories. It receives a particularly suggestive expression in the famous formula of the New Critique: never trust the author, trust the text! Insistence on the radical self-sufficiency of the work is opposed to various causal or ideological "explanations" of artistic production and it ends up depriving the author himself of every authority to explain or comment on it. Nevertheless in a paradoxical way the autonomy of the artwork comes precisely from the action that gives it birth. If one cannot conceive a content, an essence preceding and therefore determining the work, this is because the artist who creates it is also not submitted to the exigencies of self-precedence. The discourse of modern aesthetics on genius, on the great artist (notably of Kant)—and the true artist, sensu stricto, is only the great one—represents the genius as exempt from all dependence on external or anterior law. The genius is spoken of as an inspired being. But at first glance and in the proper sense, inspiration means subjection to the external. To be inspired means to possess a sui generis power of creativity but "to possess" does not yet amount to "having at one's disposition." Well to the contrary, if the genius is inspired this because he is submitted to a power that surpasses him on all sides. He certainly has to justify the validity, the truth of his work to nobody, but he depends absolutely on the sovereign source from whence his inspiration comes.

Anecdotes and stories about the lives of artists happily represent them as bound hand and foot and delivered over to the power of inspiration that suddenly "falls upon" them in an unforeseeable and above all irresistible way. In reality the apparent dependence of creative genius on an external source is above all the cipher of its independence in relation to every criteria and every foreign end in the synthesis that constitutes it and that it unfolds. The creative genius—so they say—does not calculate and does not follow pre-existent ideas or models when he sculpts, composes music, or writes poems. It is certainly not a matter of lightning strikes to the head or leaps into the dark, but his actions are one, united and undivided. The artist can doubtlessly spend endless amounts of time on his work with the utmost devotion, enriching it with countless detail. However, the infinite plurality of empirical moments of production does not yet compromise the integrity and unity of his project. The project makes up a whole, but its condition of being a whole does not signify the absence of a period of elaboration more or less prolonged. Rather, it designates the undivided mastery of the author over his work. They say that a talent can do what he wants, but the genius "only" does what he can. The creative artist is not like Leibniz's God who chooses and creates one among an infinity of possible worlds. The genius does not choose; he does not even find himself before possibilities that he can compare. He can pass through a period of confusion or rather, indetermination, but this disappears when the Work appears and imposes itself. The Work causes the ideas that have crossed the artist's mind not to occur, it makes impossible the possibilities that nevertheless shimmered before him.

Here we find ourselves before the non-precedence of the artist to himself that corresponds to the artwork's non-precedence to itself. It is the source and principle of the accomplished form of singularity. However, the work of art is not only a perfect singularity; it is also a specimen, an authentic instance of unicity. This is the case precisely by virtue of the implications of the non-precedence to himself of its author.

Historians of different arts strive to discern the relations between artists in terms of influence and sometimes even imitation. In reality, imitation cannot prevail in the universe of artistic creation. A work can be reproduced or copied but it cannot truly be imitated for the good reason that the authentic artist, the artist in the strict sense of the term can only trigger or initiate the total process of creation on the occasion of each new work. A multitude of gothic churches and realist novels exist, yet none of these edifices of gothic style are a simple variant of another, none of these family sagas are merely enhanced or weakened versions of another. And the impossibility of imitating another is, so to say, an illustration, a secondary instance of the primordial impossibility, the genius of imitating *oneself*. The artist is so preoccupied with his work that in the process of writing or painting he seems to forget everything else, his other works, his preceding works. You would think that this forgetting is only a simple utilitarian bracketing accomplished by the pragmatic functioning of his psychologism. One should not be diverted from the present work by past work in order for what one is doing now to have a chance to succeed. One has to disregard the past in order to exclude everything that risks interfering with the concentration required by the present. Yet in reality, beyond any utilitarian end, the forgetting of other works reveals the metaphysical truth of artistic creation. If each painting, as Schelling said, "opens the intellectual world,"[15] this is because "each painter revives for each new work the entire enterprise of painting."[16] The path leading to the Work is littered with sketches and drafts. Yet these attempts do not simply represent a preparatory stage, an imperfect state of the completely realized work. Instead each in its own way is an autonomous work. Despite the absence of moments and components present in the final version of the work retained by the artist, despite their fragmentary condition, hurried nature, despite the taste for the provisional that accompanies them, many sketches of great sculptures and painters are works of art in their own right, not merely ladders cast into the abyss once the ascent to the summit is accomplished. Most often these multiple moments allowing the reconstitution of the genesis of the Work are doubtlessly consigned to museum storerooms. Locked in closets and boxes, they seem to serve henceforth only the cause of documentation, the study of the genesis of another than themselves that alone matters. However, it happens that wise curators show sketches and drafts among their paintings. Both the Grand Louvre and the Alte Pinakothek of Munich have dared to consecrate, if not a great hall, at least an entire room to the sketches and drafts of Rubens!

15. Schelling, *Philosophie de l'Art*, 60.
16. Merleau-Ponty, *Signes*, 75.

The Singular
Works of Art

The necessity for the artist to revive the entire process of creation at every new work is the principle and cause of the unicity of the work of art. Every work is a harmonious whole, an organic singular, complete in itself. Even more it is a singular that is incomparable to another, which has nothing like to itself. In short it is a singular of which the perfect autonomy founded on intrinsic causes "completes itself" through external principles. This is the renewal of creative action. However, if this necessary renewal guarantees as it were the unicity of the work, this unicity will have its limits. Works of art constitute a multiplicity of unique realities, but these seem to fall back into the condition of simple Distinction. They are located next to one another without encroaching on one another. Yet this peace of unmovable, impassible realities is only the absence of any relation, the lack of all contact while in its highest incarnations the unique reality, or rather, unique realities can and must constitute a plurality of beings with proper links among them.

The first collections of art, contemporaneous with curiosity cabinets, piled up works on top of one another without reserving a minimum of adequate space that would allow the viewer to focus on each. In the museums of the last two centuries the situation changes: conditions of presentation are improving; the contemplation of the work is aided by its spatial enhancement. No longer desiring to exhibit the entire collection, only "important" works are presented, which are shown in such a way that they can be seen and admired, set apart from the rest. Presentation doubtlessly takes into account chronological order, and even themes of a painter, but these criteria of classification, these theoretical, didactic preoccupations are secondary. The essential principle of presentation is of the spatial, not the thetic order. Paintings are suspended on white walls that both set apart and enhance the work. A lone painting is located on a given portion of the wall, with no other paintings above or below it. It is separated from others by a distance allowing uninterfered contemplation of a portrait or landscape. The whiteness of the wall is an additional factor that helps concentration: it expresses and manifests the neutrality of the environment, contributing to the enhancement of the painting; its colors and forms impose themselves more easily in the absence of any given pictorial exterior.

The parallelism and non-encroachment, in short, the pacific coexistence prevailing in museums is proper to the unique being of artworks, but it also shows their metaphysical limitation, a limitation explained by the synthesis that founds them. The artwork is born out of a synthesis; it is an authentic unfolding. But if it belongs to a synthesis, it does not itself realize it. The artwork is synthesis by proxy; it is the prolongation, the continuation of a synthesis. The creative artist is a supreme instance of the a priori synthesis that he constitutes and exercises and of which his works are so many occurrences. Each work is an authentic expression of the synthesis that continues within it, but which exists there in a frozen and accomplished form. The creative action of the artist finds its completion in the work but the point is that the work represents a completion, an end, a resolution. The sculpture and the poem, the sonnet and the cathedral receive or welcome the synthesis that is the act of the artist's subjectivity. This welcome is all that they are, and as such in a passive, blocked way. They welcome in order to preserve, but not in order to give back; they listen and receive faithfully, but without the capacity to proffer a response. The creative synthesis celebrates its accomplishment in the work, but it is still an accomplishment without redundance, without return. In short, it is an immortal accomplishment, but without life, autonomous but without freedom.

The deadly reciprocity of lovers prey to jealousy shows the flaws and pitfalls of impenitent duality, of a relation of exclusivity between two beings who merely complete and perfect the relations of immanence proper to Nature. This unfortunate duality is surpassed by the plurality of works of art, but these works represent only rudimentary specimens of the Third. They constitute a multiplicity, but these multiples, the first authentic instances of the metaphysical category of the unique, are situated in an innate ir-relation; they are only ones along with others, with an existence separated by a no man's land, voids without the power of articulation. The plurality of uniques doubtlessly marks a certain progress over the process of mutual exhaustion of terms in a natural relation, in a relation of justice, but it does not yet signify access to the vivifying sovereign gratuity of love. Results of the action of innovative freedoms, these unique singulars enjoy an authentic autarky. But deprived of any aptitude for mutual interaction, they are also deprived of all creative fecundity. These entities that birth themselves out of a priori syntheses are not in a position to respond to the creative action that constitutes them or to resume it and extend it around themselves. Fruits of creativity, consequently having the metaphysical condition of newness, the singulars that are works of art possess no power for creativity. Offspring of their author, these beings of color or stone, of sound or rhythm, do not relate to it as to a parent, and they do not move towards one another as towards brothers. Beyond justice but still short of love, these entities have not yet reached the metaphysical fullness of Uniqueness.

V

The Unique

Asymmetrical Love

The investigation of unicity ends with the artwork as the first example of an authentic unique. However, if the condition of not having anything like itself is founded on an intrinsic differentiation, it is completed only through an external, extrinsic differentiation. Masterpieces are indeed unique but their unicity has no external significance. More precisely, their unicity is relativized by contingent considerations quasi-belonging to the order of rarity. The truly unique does not and cannot have a price, but paintings and sculptures do have a price. If the museum housing them exhibits them with a neutral co-existence, the market of art subjects them to comparison and (by virtue of comparison) to assessment and evaluation. And evaluation will compromise and subvert the peaceful coexistence of artworks which will end up being represented as a plurality of entities in competition. However, true unicity, the unique in its fullness, is irreducible to any evaluative assessment and this is the reason that it is allowed to constitute multiplicities of which the members maintain organic links. Before artworks coexisting in the false peace of the museum that only obscures the echo of the competition of the market, the paradigmatic truth of the condition of free beings is the child, procreated by a descending and therefore asymmetrical love: the child, or rather *children,* in fraternal community.

The artwork belongs to the universe of the synthesis but only to the degree that it prolongs and manifests a synthesis. It is only a reception when it should be a response. And evidently, only freedom can be a response. Said differently, in order for the singular to be unique, to enjoy the status of unicity in its fullness, the creative action that from the exterior gives rise to it must become intrinsic. Instead of simply prolonging the exterior and anterior synthesis that calls it into existence, the being of "unique" metaphysical status must institute and unfold another synthesis, one proper to it, that of response. Yet it is necessary to know that response does not yet mean reciprocity. Reciprocity neutralizes, obliterates true a prioriness, overloading the newness of the synthesis and causing it to fall back into immanence. In order to palliate this danger, the phenomenon of "marriage" has been rescued through exhibiting it not as a reciprocal action exhausted in a *do ut des*, but as two independent actors acting according to newness and integral gratuity. But if this duality of entities, this independence of action saves the self-transcendence of free beings, these freedoms remain always confined in themselves. They therefore prolong in a certain way the immanence that should be avoided at all cost. Immanence can be broken in the strict sense only through a self-exit more radical than any victory over oneself. It was first glimpsed in the negative "version" of self-sacrifice, dying in the place of another free subject. But the accomplishment of self-exit here amounts to its actual obliteration, while philosophy calls for a self-surpassing that endures all the while being a true ontological leap. Self-surpassing, self-exit is the birth of a child in whom two freedoms go beyond themselves. The birth of a child is a brute ontological fact, the advent of a new substance. Yet this novelty can and must receive an explanation, a deeper interpretation. Birth should not be understood only in terms of a new, isolated entity; it signifies and manifests an expansion of the philosophical notion of the a priori synthesis. The a prioriness of the synthesis expresses a tearing away and strictly speaking so does the procreation of a child. Procreation indicates that in its highest accomplishment the a priori synthesis is carried out not within but *outside* the subject. The child comes into the world, the umbilical cord is cut, the child grows up and leaves its parents: this presents the highest instance of self-surpassing, of the self-exit of free subjectivity.

The effective and enduring self-exit has as its counterpart or correlate the response of the creature called into existence. Yet this correlate is not symmetrical: it is asymmetrical, and doubly so. Procreative action is a descent while the response is an ascent. And above all, procreation is first in relation to the reception in the procreated, who in the strict sense only responds to it. Procreation is a work of love and the astonishing truth of love is that it is always naturally asymmetrical, and as such by virtue of its metaphysical-eidetic constitution. "God loved us first" (1 John 4:19). He has loved us first because he *is* love. The lover loves; he only loves: this amounts to the condition of loving first. The one who loves only loves unconditionally and one does not love unconditionally if one is only responding to the love of another. In order to "save" the phenomenon of the love of the two lovers a double asymmetry had to be posed, the two loves in which one neither completes the other nor is completed by the other. Thus there is an asymmetry in the parallelism. But a more astonishing and more evident asymmetry is at work in the loves that link up *procréateur* and *procréature*. It seems to be provoked and governed by the love emanating from the one that calls into existence. The "empirical" evidence, the witness of every society of every era is that, with some exceptions, the love of the parents for their children is stronger than the love of children for their parents. Descending love has its counterpart in ascending love, but even in this very particular physics, climbing is less natural, more difficult than descent.

The metaphysical truth of love is that it is unconditional and first, and this truth determines its essential forms. Love is by definition a relation to an intentional object but very paradoxically the intentional object according to its quiddity is not its proper determinant. Usually the one who loves will appreciate, venerate, and adore the beloved; nevertheless, it is not because he is venerable or adorable, possessing some intrinsic value, that he should be loved. In fact the paradigm, the purest occurrence of asymmetrical love, of the love that loves first, is *creation*. It is *ex nihilo*. The asymmetry is so radical that it not only marks the absence of the possibility of a response, but the very term of amorous action does not exist, and must be produced. Creation out of nothing, this primordial manifestation of love prefigures all authentic love and it powerfully influences the logic that governs it. Love is pure in proportion to its asymmetry, and the strongest asymmetry prevails in the case where its correlate, its intentional object is the most disproportioned, the least susceptible or apt even to form a hint of reciprocity. The call to love the widow, the orphan and the stranger, in short, the poorest and the weakest, does not only follow from a high moral intuition, it is also conformed to some eidetic necessities. If in the strict sense the correlate of love should not be defined, given in advance, the finitude of our condition enjoins us to find the closest approximations of this eidetic non-given in the minimums of having. In reality these suggestive approximations serve to illustrate the paradoxical logic of love: its unconditionality and asymmetry bring about the bracketing of quiddative factors in its correlate to the point of rejecting the predicates of this correlate precisely in order better to found its unicity.

The essential, primordial paradox of love is that what matters to it must not be able to furnish quidditative reasons to prove and to affirm its importance. In fact, it seems that an inverse relation is found between "the value" of a being and its aptitude to play the role of correlate of love. It seems to follow that the correlate, the most appropriate object of love is precisely the unlovable. Free, gratuitous, and asymmetrical love that loves first would have to approach the one that is not lovable in itself. Ultimately the one is lovable who *is* not lovable. The lovable *would be* the unlovable. The paradox seems to be somewhat attenuated if we say that what matters is to love and love must love without distinction, no matter what, or rather no matter whom. In fact this attenuation indicates the path to follow in order to understand and live with the paradox. To say that the unlovable is the lovable is not only a logical contradiction, it is equally opposed to the logic of love. If love is first, if it founds its object and provokes its predicate, this foundation and provocation cannot depend on anything in what is founded and provoked. But the unlovable condition belongs to the object, it is truly proper to the correlate. As for the second formulation, defining the correlate of love as any object, as anyone at all, is also unacceptable and incorrect in itself. At first glance, to say that what matters to me is anything at all is no less absurd than saying that the lovable is the unlovable. Nevertheless, there is here a difference that proves decisive: "to matter" has nothing to do with the quidditative givens of the correlate, of the object; it relates to the loving subject, it connotes a theme proper to it. In fact, it suggests the sovereignty of the subject who has loved first. It contains implicitly a return to the gratuity of asymmetrical love. At this moment the purity and unconditionality of descending love seems assured: it does not depend on the quidditative givens of its correlate; it does not depend on, is not determined by the correlate's value. But if this return to the exterior safeguards the asymmetry of love, the flawless gratuity of love, it seems to miss the essential element of the intrinsic in the unique. Unicity is certainly the condition of being unique before the one who calls, yet the gratuity of the call seems to compromise the structures patiently extricated from singularity. Under the pretext of the radical asymmetry of love, the truth, the autonomy of the beloved is bracketed, forgotten, rejected.

Against the ancient objections to the radical gratuity of love, which must be love of choice, of predilection, we will proceed to reinterpret the metaphysical category of singularity. Singularity is the a priori synthesis that constitutes a being. The being is and acts according to this synthesis that animates, gathers and determines its quidditative structures. However, the essential dimension of the proper synthesis that founds a being is not found in the properties and qualities that it constitutes and orders. The synthesis should first be intrinsic and only secondarily of a particular quiddity. It constitutes and governs the material moments composing a being, but it *is not* the structures and order of its components. The true synthesis, synthesis in the strict sense is and is only the a priori synthesis, and, as such, it is not the simple formula expressing the mutual relations among elements but rather the principle and active source, the framework of their articulation and development. The a prioriness of the synthesis signals its sovereignty, an intelligible sovereignty by relation to its quidditative moments, but it also and above all expresses this constant self-surpassing through which, by virtue of which, the free creature persists in its being. The singularity that alone allows unicity consists above all in this proper manner of self-exit, of surpassing that makes possible a free being's response to the call of love. And it is in the wake of this unicity that the free being will be a part of a multiplicity of entities related with one another.

The Child

The representative category of the unique singular is the child. The child is not taken here in the sense of a reality of the biological or social orders, which would denote a certain age and be subject to becoming. Pallas Athena emerged from the head of Zeus fully armed, Adam, the child of God (Luke 3:38), was born an adult. A child can be a nursling as well as adult man or woman: the condition of childhood is not a matter of age, but that of a sovereign action leading to a reception. Bérulle rightly speaks of the "state of childhood," which is effectively a condition with a proper and permanent character. Educators have too often been tempted to see in the student only the future adult, considering their pupil only as a kind of larva that will emerge as a butterfly only as an adult. In reality, the deep principle of all true education is the one professed by Rousseau: "let childhood ripen in the child." There is certainly nothing fixed and definitive in the child. Nevertheless the child is a whole, but a whole that ceaselessly grows and develops.

A wise pedagogy respects the singularity of the child, its sui generis truth. Nevertheless it only glimpses or comprehends it as *a* moment in a personal history. The moment can be protected against encroaching external finalities, removed from the tyrannical requirements of the future; it no less remains a stage amidst other stages of our development. But the phenomenological essence, "child" possesses the eidetic moment of "stage" only secondarily; it hardly depends on temporal considerations, even if purged of every chronological factor. The content and metaphysical range of the category of the child are defined by the syntheses that are their principles and sources. The image of the child is certainly that of a young being, but this empirical and contingent vision fades before the elementary analysis of its structural moments. The child is a being that comes from parents and which remains so despite the passage of time, the vicissitudes of the moment or changes in circumstance. The child is called into existence by its parents: procreation is in the image of creation; it is also, in its own way, an evocation from out of nothing. The radicality of the call that leads to a new ontological given, namely, the advent of a being that previously did not exist, has a counterpart in its unconditionality. The child is procreated not in order to play a role, to render some service, to fill a gap, but so that a new reality happens, a being that has never yet been seen, that replaces nothing and no one and that nothing and no one could replace. In other words, every child is a chosen one, a unique. Yet by definition children are *many*. They constitute a plurality that is like a happy middle term between the violent immanence of the dyad and the dispersed multiplicity of effects or products. This plurality is that of brothers, a non-quidditative expression of the relation among men. It is the synonym of the other non-quidditative expression, the neighbor. Neighbors are like trees in a forest: they coexist in a living and welcoming horizontality, whereas the condition of the child suggests with particular emphasis that these plants certainly have different roots, but that each grows from on high.

The majority of past legislations, civil or religious, distinguish the firstborn from other children, attributing to them particular rights and duties. The firstborn, the one in whom the ontological leap of newness happens in a meteoric way, seems to have a specific role, to enjoy a proximity to the parents, the origin, that is no longer the case for the others that follow. Yet if the "firstborn" is an authentic eidetic moment of the *child*, it is a moment proper to every child, not only the one born before others. The coming of the first is doubtlessly a first in the life of the parents; it inaugurates a new generation; it can modify from top to bottom a political or economic situation.

However, in itself, as such, every birth (the second, the third or the sixth) is of the same metaphysical nature. A birth is always an absolute beginning, a breach in the circle of immanence.[1] Every birth realizes a self-exit, a radical self-surpassing. The children that incarnate this unsealing, this exceptional unlocking, are instances of the same condition, the same dignity. They each "merit" being called first, not just the one that appeared before the others. Every child is ultimately a firstborn and should be understood and treated as such. Each opens a new page, as it were, in the Book of Life, a page that tells a new story, different from every other.

Paternity: Creation and Procreation

The child constitutes a breach in immanence; in the child the relation of lovers is perfected and which is realized only to the degree that it is unsealed and opened in self-exit and self-surpassing. This self-exit is a leap, a light that suddenly appears, but this advent of the new is hardly like a lightning flash or a spark, a kind of epiphany. The child certainly barges into the world, but not like a comet that appears on the horizon only disappear into the void a few moments later. The appearance of a free being ruptures the horizon, but it is above all the advent of a novelty that perdures. It is symbolized by the "instant" of coming into the world, birth. In reality it involves a gestation and history. The child is procreated by parents and procreation, like creation, while being in its own way ex nihilo, is also preservation . . .

The child is the fruit of the union of two parents of different sex and the eidetic differences of paternity and maternity have always been insisted on. These differences are and will always remain irreducible despite all social and historical conditioning but nevertheless, from a metaphysical point of view, the two procreative beings enjoy the same status: namely, that of calling into existence a being and then of continuing to sustain it and help it along towards its realization. Instead of the unfortunate neologism of "parenthood," it would be better to use the term "paternity" to connote the procreative status of the father *and* the mother—not in order to attribute priority to one of the two parents, as it happens, to the father, but for the sake of signifying the non-immediacy of human procreation where the obligatory reference to the biological and the natural is joined with its essential support through freedom. Maternity is a dear and *solid* value, to the degree that it has the certitude lacking in paternity and above all because it seems evident, intuitive because instinctive. People of every civilization and writers of every era do not hesitate to adumbrate parallels and analogies between animal and human maternities; the majority of religions celebrate the mother goddess, origin of all things, generous source of all life. Things are different for the biblical religion where God appears almost never as mother, not only to spare him from sexual connotations, but above all to enhance, to ensure the freedom

---

1. See Hannah Arendt, *The Human Condition*.

and gratuity of his creative action: the bringing forth of the world is creation out of nothing, not emanation. Maternity is a phenomenon observed in the simplest way; it implies limitations and actions, duties and joys that nature itself seems to trace with a sure hand. Gestation in the body of a mother, nursing, and then, in an always diminishing but real manner, diverse caretaking activities traditionally associated with maternity all manifest an immediacy that belongs to immanence. Certainly maternity also involves a learning process: if it is very natural, it is not for all that purely and simply immediate innate. It equally has its trials and struggles; it must be embraced anew each day. Yet for the cultural and moral conscience of humanity, for primitive reflection of women and men, love of a child is imposed on a mother as the exercise of an analytic judgment while paternal love, apparently not obvious, must so to say be learned. The stories in all kinds of literature abound with passages in which the mother "recognized" with natural joy the nursling given to her. But the great novelist had to "clarify" that Jean Valjean "saw Cosette every day and felt paternity be born within him and develop more and more..."[2]

Paternity is a relation constructed through time and by conscious, voluntary effort. It is the cipher of the non-immediacy proper to procreation, and this in both negative and positive senses. Negatively, the non-immediacy of paternity shows that it is a relation that is not "self-evident," that it is not naturally reached. The child is neither carried by the father, nor is a biological existence continued between them through the umbilical cord. But precisely, since the child is not immediately tied to him, the father can and should be related to him only mediately. Paternity emphasizes the essential obligation for *nurturance* proper to parents demonstrated first by education. However, if education does not consist in immediate actions, it is still in its way marked by a certain naturality. It must be exercised toward a young being, still malleable and above all imperfect, incomplete by virtue of its age, in other words belonging to a natural, biological state. Frequent conflicts between school and family betray the ambiguity of education, an institution where the biological and the cultural, the immediate and mediate are still found in a difficult union. The parent and the teacher cannot decide between their roles because the parent is and should be an educator. But if paternity implies education as a share in the nurturance commanded by his native non-immediacy, nurturance goes much farther than adolescence, it is extended through one's entire life. Animals are occupied with their young and protect them for a period of time, but once their young have reached a certain level of maturity, they abandon them and no longer acknowledge them. For animals, infancy and the condition of being a parent are only natural realities, limited within time. Things are different for humans who remain children and parents, children of their parents and parents of their children for the duration of their lives. In other words, Childhood and Paternity can be conceived as true metaphysical categories.

---

2. Hugo, *Les misérables* IV, iii, i, 897.

Paternity is the highest metaphysical category of the synthesis that sparks forth another, others, and it has its model and origin in God. Saint Paul speaks of the "Father from whom all paternity draws its name" (Eph 3:15): the heavenly Father is like the archetype of all earthly fathers; divine paternity is the principle of human paternity. We speak with deep suggestiveness of "procreation," an image or reflection of "creation." Creation is the supreme act of bringing forth something; it is done starting from nothing and not for one reason or another. God does not create in order to fill a void; he is neither determined nor necessitated to create. The source of the work of creation is always generous love toward the free creature, never any need in the creator. God, as a theologian said, "does not create by indigence but indulgence."[3] And to the degree that creation is ex nihilo, free and gratuitous, it must be within each creative action. Every free creature should be thought as called to existence through a constitutive act of the same radicality; it is the work of the same total freedom, a gift of the same pure gratuity. Consequently, it possesses the same validity, the same reality, in short, the same unicity.

In the image of creation, procreation should be free and should spark forth unique beings. Every birth, every act of the constitution of free life is like an irruption in the world that neither motivates nor necessitates a "reason." Procreation is an act of donation and as such it responds to no calculation: it is a sparking forth, a complete innovation. It represents a beginning and consequently an affront inflicted on the slavery of the eternal return of the same. As an irruption in the world, birth upsets the world's economy. An authentic and true gift, it provokes a new given. Each free being, every "procreated" that happens is a gain, a plus, but not as a simple addition, something added to the preexistent, to what was already there: the child is always a new departure. Yet the coming into the world of a new human is not a kind of cosmic epiphany, a sudden precipitation; rain and hail fall but the child does not because, contrary to *Dasein*, it is not and must not be "thrown" into the world. The child is not conceived as "emanated" from a maternal source or as an effect of a production. The fruit of begetting shares with the effect of a cause separation from its principle, emancipation from its origin. In other words the radical and gratuitous call to existence of procreation has a correlate in the response, a response as free and gratuitous as the procreative love itself. But how can the radical sovereignty of the sparking forth be reconciled with the autonomy of the one resulting from it? Taken generally, this is a question of the theological order, but which will be repeated (with vigorous and deep resonance) in the register of finite freedom, in the universe of procreation.

The all-powerfulness of the creator and the freedom of the creature seem to make up an irresolvable contradiction. If the creator is all-powerful freedom, the creature can only be powerless servitude. The contradiction could be mollified through quantification, proposing 75 percent sovereign freedom for the first with 25 percent autonomy for the second. Or we could even climb to a more balanced situation with 100

---

3. Wolleb, *Abridgement of Christian Divinity*, 57.

percent + 100 percent. Yet freedom is not susceptible to quantification. The sole way of resolving the contradiction is to renounce every attempt to decide between opposing parties and to grasp that true sovereignty is not only reconciled with autonomy but that it calls for and requires that the latter be affirmed. Schelling wrote that God is not "so indigent that he can create only according to general ideas," each of his works is the realization of a unique essence.[4] Kierkegaard will go further: "only the all powerful God" is sufficiently powerful to be able to tolerate in his presence a being that is independent from him, capable of escaping him."[5] This vision of the all-powerful sovereign is a striking instance of the fecund rupture with logic and perfection; it directly connected with the metaphysics of newness. It alone permits an understanding of the truth of paternity that is not only free and gratuitous sparking forth but also tearing out and emancipation. Humans are all too tempted to procreate in order to ensure themselves when they are old, to have a son or daughter to succeed them or even simply to establish an intermediary, a screen, a barrier between death and themselves. But the truth of procreation is precisely not to consider the child as a means but as an end, of wanting it for itself and of putting it forth through itself. Paternity harbors latent and poorly veiled conflicts: the parent would like to have a child, and have him or her be this or that, and not as the child would want him or herself to be. Another is wanted but another who is not truly other, other on its own terms, but rather as an alterity chosen by oneself, an alterity integrated into the world of self, in the circle of oneself. But as Levinas recalled with profundity, "the alterity of the Other is in him, and not by relation to me."[6]

Paternity is a gift founded on an opening; it is the sparking forth of another which implies a ceding of space, an allocation of a place. In its own way it is a phenomenon of *tzimtzum*, with nevertheless the immense difference that it is not simply a matter of retreating in order to leave a void, but of calling into existence a singular being. Procreation is in its own way a sacrifice, but it is not an abstract, general renunciation, but a call to love addressed to a specific other. And it is precisely through this condition of ceding a place for another that it illustrates the supreme mystery of creative donation where the proffered gift constitutes an abandonment, an effective alienation without returning to a diminution, a mutilation of the one who proffered it. The procreated is detached from the procreator and confirmed in its ontological autonomy. Nevertheless instead of being valued as a subtraction, an injury to the integrity of the procreator, its autonomy constitutes its realization.

Of course God, the heavenly Father, alone, cannot be moved or reduced through the manifestations, the particular instances of his pro-creative action. As for the finite being of man, he can never be completely free in and through another, despite his unfortunate efforts, very often pathetic and tragic, and above all noxious and vicious to

---

4. Schelling, *Werke* 7, 190.
5. Kierkegaard, *Tagebücher*, 239s.
6. Levinas, *Totalité et infinité*, 121.

keep the engendered in submission. The father certainly has an authority procured by his ontological condition as principle of the child, but by its nature this human authority is poorly used, perverted and abused. In order for him to respond to the call that brings him forth, the child must be able to unfold himself and he can only do so if he can offer words that are his own. As education, paternity is continuous creation, but this power is put in service to the child; it must fit closely with his own dispositions and ends. Paternity is a call to existence ceaselessly offered. It is a particular, unique call, and as such it can search for and expect only a unique response.

Monads

Some parents have only one child, but usually children are multiple. In fact, as will be seen, they constitute a specific plurality. Parents have multiple children and they love them. It is tempting to ask them—and this is a question they often pose secretly to themselves—which of your children do you love the most? But this is a terrible question that should never be asked. De facto, it risks causing jealousy and resentment among siblings, causing unease and bad conscience in parents. De jure, this question should not even be raised because it is inappropriate, ethically deficient. It is also and above all incorrect, even metaphysically absurd. Loving more, loving best are quantitative and comparative judgments whereas love is neither a matter of quantity or comparison. It is believed to be a good thing to insist that I love each of my children in the same way. But if the intention animating the reply is merit-worthy, the expression used is unfortunate and inexact: children are different in age, sex, gifts, and accomplishments. How could I love them in the same way? Changing the expression by saying, I love them each *as much* as the other belongs to the same reductionism as before: it is only now an explicitly quantitative version that translates the naïve and pernicious assumption that love is measurable, something a child can "justify" or "merit," something that could be numbered and is miraculously the same for each child. A more appropriate response would be to take hold of the question in order to turn it inside out. You ask me which of my children I love the most? Maybe this seems strange but the answer is: each of them. I love the most strongly not the eldest or the youngest, not the little brother or the big sister, but each one. I love all my children; I love each of them "the most."

The expression is paradoxical and touches a logical contradiction. In reality it faithfully expresses the paradoxical truth of procreation. I love each of my children the best, the most, not in the sense (or rather the non-sense) of loving them each better than the others. I love each of them in an unlimited, unconditional way. The original paradox of procreation is that it involves unconditional love and therefore aims at a plurality of beings, and uniquely aims at each of them. And the comprehension of a being as "unique" rejects any comparison. Comparison is the principle of choice, of the choice of one among others, but procreation is not a choice among possibilities that one would weigh and evaluate. It is a sparking forth that has nothing to do with deliberations of choosing among a plurality of pre-existent models. The procreator is himself not so indigent as to be constrained to bring forth the child as an individual instance of a universal. Children constitute a plurality, which should not be conceived as the sum of elements, of a set of components it completes. Finitude, the limitations of human existence doubtlessly cause the experience of desiring a daughter when one has only sons or vice versa. Yet in its metaphysical truth the asymmetrical love that brings forth a new being does not take account of the rest. It is addressed to this particular being as if it were the only being in the world.

The free and gratuitous choice of giving life and then being related through an integral love to the one that you have called into existence is constantly threatened by the temptation to *compare* beings that are essentially unique. The comparison of entities conceives them as constituting a potential whole—a whole that would be the sum of its parts. Quantitative comparison is the obvious source of all judgment of a love articulated in terms of more and better. To the plurality constituted by our children corresponds an amount of affection that is parceled out in proportion to the being and value possessed by each child. In other words children would not be loved in themselves, by virtue of what they are and what they signify, but in terms of their part in the whole, and therefore in terms of a reality external to them. This (quantitative) comparativist conception is a radical distortion of procreative love. It is like the sinister shadow drawing behind it the supreme work of procreation. In reality it is only a disguised instance of pathological, heteronomous love in which a being is not loved in itself but by virtue of external, alien ends.

When the comparativist conception is worked out according to the more and the better, to quantification, the influence of extrinsic considerations that found unicity are easily discerned. Things are clearly different when love is differentiated according to quality, when the love that one feels towards a child is determined and specified in terms of the way that one incarnates the possibilities of perfection contained within the human essence. This conception of procreative love seems to be associated with very respectable metaphysical references. In reality it signifies the reduction of the unicity of the free being that is man to the condition of an ectype understood and evaluated in terms of its archetype. The differentiation of procreative love, the motivation of procreative action starting from qualitative considerations, recalls the Leibnizian vision of monads and beyond that, the medieval metaphysical legitimation of the particular. Translating the high logic of the principle of indiscernibles, Leibniz's monads are each incomparable, irreplaceable entities since they occupy a perspective that is theirs alone and from which they reflect—in a way distinct from every other—the Absolute. Each monad represents in its own way the Absolute: it cannot represent it like its neighbor does. It seems to play a unique role that no other is in a position to play. This conception doubtlessly sanctifies the unicity of the monad, but this unicity remains ultimately extrinsic. The monad is one and unique but only because there is no other that can assume its vocation, the task proper to it, to reflect the Absolute from a given perspective. The monad is truly an irreducible unicity, but its unicity remains imperfect because it is defined by virtue of its condition of a reflection of a moment of the Absolute. Consequently its unicity does not stem from itself but from something external. The limits of the unicity recommended by monadology are seen when one realizes that in its metaphysical truth the theory of monads offers ultimately only an exceptionally suggestive variation on the classical deduction of the particular. The particular, the finite has worth only to the degree that it expresses the universal, but a finite being, by the fact of its finitude, its incompleteness, its essential fragmentariness, is not apt to reflect the universal. Only a multiplicity of finite beings added together, complementing one another would be capable of it. In the world of finite materiality, therefore, each essence, each idea can and must be diffracted in a multiplicity of individuals that are so many gradations from the eidos. Classical metaphysics belongs to this way of deducing the particular, of legitimating the individual, only under the condition of an obligatory reference to a universal and therefore at the cost of relating it to something external and anterior to it.

Ectypes and Copies

Recourse to properly metaphysical considerations in order better to understand the meaning and conditions of procreative action has led us to contemplate it through the prism of the relation of archetype and ectypes. Like the particulars of the Aristotelian Scholastics, Leibnizian monads are only ectypes of an archetype, and philosophy's attempt to ensure their validity assumes the cost of turning to the archetype they represent. This means that ectypes in their multiplicity suffer a hemorrhage of value, their profound truth deserts them, emigrating into the archetype that they reflect. This denucleation of essence and flight of meaning is the hidden teaching of the classical philosophies of the West. It shows the intrinsic limitation of their potential for the deduction of the singular as well as for, above all, the foundation of the unique. It casts its shadow on the attempt to think metaphysically the categories of childhood and paternity. In reality however, this destabilization of discourse on paternity in light of the pitfalls of the doctrine of ectypes proves to have a salutary significance. It will correct the aim, or establish the true purpose of procreative action, and through this correction it will contribute to the metaphysical deduction of the unique.

Procreative action is burdened with a latent egoism; it likes to brag about the altruism of its work, the pure generosity of its donation. In fact, empirically, human paternity aspires less to realize itself as *tzimtzum* or kenosis as it tends—alas—to repeat and confirm the immanence that reigns in Nature. Procreation aims for the advent of the new, it puts nevertheless everything in play to subvert true innovation. Parents are rapturously transported before the little being that has irrupted into the world, but in order to protect themselves from the dangers of the unheard of, the surprises of the unexpected, they seek to reassure themselves by ardently looking for resemblances. In reality the quest for resemblances encouraged by family and friends comes under the jurisdiction of a deeper aim. It is a basic element, a native moment of the work of procreation: it only dilutes a fundamental ambition to find oneself in the child. One can judge oneself harshly, be discontent with his accomplishments, skeptical about his gifts. What does it matter? We wish to continue, to prolong ourselves and the supreme manner of this extension is the procreation of this other self that is the child. Consciously or not, we aspire to make the pro-created, the new being, as close as possible to the old, to make the child resemble the parent as closely as possible, to make the son the faithful image of the father. But it is precisely around the true meaning of the term *image* that the metaphysical drama of paternity is played out. Paternity is the bringing forth of unique beings, in what sense then could we seek to find ourselves in this image that the child reflects to us? A reinterpretation of the idea of the image, adapted to the condition of the unique imposes itself on us, and we must exclude from it the traditional doctrine of the ectype, and above all that extreme instance of the ectype that is the copy.

The quest for the unique leads to the rejection of the ectype since it only has value in terms of its archetype. The supreme form or rather the native idea of the ectype is the copy. If there are many situations or vocations in which making copies is necessary, both the action of copying and its result are severely judged and even call for contempt. Strictly speaking, the copy is traced, even if it is not obtained through an act that presses paper or cloth against an original of wood or stone, of metal or terracotta. The aim of the copyist, the intentional object of his action is the faithful reproduction of the original. Nevertheless, fidelity naturally slides towards servility here. The copyist strives to follow with a maximum of precision the lines and colors of an external reality, but while admitting, even admiring the success of his efforts, one is tempted to censor the attitude characterizing his action. In fact one cannot disassociate between judgment of the subjectivity of the copyist and the object, the copy produced. More precisely, one admits, finding perfectly appropriate and normal that a copy machine spits out a multitude of copies of the document under its lid, but when it is a free being that performs the act of copying, suspicion arises. Copying is an ambiguous action: it certainly has as an eidetic source the desire to reproduce, to repeat. Yet the judgment is that the docile execution of the task takes a good amount of servility and reveals a lack of imagination and an absence of initiative. In fact, one can, and often must, go even farther in the critique. In its primitive eidetic essence copying is an operation where one is generally put in service to another. In reality, frequently it amounts to attributing to ourselves what does not belong to us, and consequently to be taken for what one is really not. The legitimate intention of reproducing the other can be supported by the culpable will of appropriating for oneself what belongs to the other. Every copy is obviously not the fruit of a fraudulent intention: after all, are not young painters encouraged to go to the Louvre to copy the paintings of ancient masters?

But—and this is an infinitely more common case—students copy during exams in order to appear and to be judged better and therefore other than what they are in reality.

The copy is the supreme ectype, the ectype in the strict sense. However, where the ectype is not yet judged as deficient, the copy can be outright condemned as pernicious. There is slippage of judgment and appreciation therefore, which is going to get worse, even according to the very logic of the quest for the unique. A singular becomes unique through the love of another: the eidetic constitution is a necessary but insufficient condition for unicity; it still requires an external action. The copy so to speak builds on this lack of intrinsic meaning because it dramatizes its circumstances: it is no longer the reflection of a partial aspect of the archetype but the integral reproduction of its original. But the complete quidditative correspondence can be striking, perfect, but it cannot for all that attenuate the condemnation that the copy not only shows a metaphysical insufficiency but it continues to encroach on the original. In fact the encroachment of the act of copying is not only of the quidditative order, it is a phenomenon of which the reality and the significance cannot be defined in terms of simple considerations of exactitude and similarity. The good copy is the work of a good copyist, skillful and precise, capable of faithfully and adequately rendering the lines and colors of a work. But the supreme instance, the morbid apotheosis of the copyist is the counterfeiter. Yet it must be understood that the counterfeiter is not only a vulgar copyist: he does not servilely reproduce a given work of art but produces his work after the style and manner of a particular artist. The image of art born out of the action of an artist prolongs within it his own synthesis. The counterfeiter is not content to imitate the artist's material results, he intends to quasi-appropriate the creative synthesis. Suffice to say that through the discussion of the theme of the counterfeiter, philosophical analysis surpasses the doctrine of the ectype, centered on the material correspondence between the image and its original, on the precision and virtuosity unfolded in the execution of the copy and reflection definitively slides to metaphysical and moral considerations—considerations proper to the investigation of the unique, of which the paradigmatic accomplishment is the child.

The Shadow and the Double

The phenomenon of the counterfeiter is an important step in our difficult investigation into the constitutive structures of unicity that has been waylaid by the image. It shows the insufficiency of merely quidditative considerations, which should be surpassed or rather completed by ontological, metaphysical analyses. The study of unicity struggles with the pitfalls of the ectype, the copy but it would still need to contend further with the experiences of the doubling of being. Procreative love certainly has an inclination, a temptation to gaze into its reflection, but its native aspiration is to bring forth an existent that is truly other. Yet the other thus intended is another in which it wishes to find or at least dreams of finding itself. Searching for resemblances wants to break with the unfortunate temptation to copy. It goes directly towards the existence of a being that, while being an authentic other, is not foreign, another that is "*alius*. . .but not *alienus*."[7] The bringing forth of another in whom one continues oneself appears as a doubling, but the child cannot be a double because like the copy, in fact, even more than the copy, the double proves to be an ambiguous, dangerous, impure reality—as we will now see.

Procreation in the most elementary sense is a doubling of entities. But does not numerical doubling amount *eo ipso* to the advent of a "double"? Procreation is conceived in the image of creation precisely in order to avoid succumbing to the temptation to represent it as a simple emanation. The pro-created should in its own way prolong the procreator, albeit according to an essential discontinuity. Birth is separation, disassociation, and we must not think of its fruit as an entity that circles around the procreator like a planet around the star from which it emerged. No true substance remains tied to its source, dependent on its principle: it can certainly reestablish a connection with it but this will be a new relation, a new condition. The power and richness of a being doubtlessly demonstrates a kind of overflow of its borders. Saints have halos; eminent persons of diverse vocations are encircled by a kind of aureole. And the radiance spreads around its subject a halo with force, intensity and vigor that heralds him and at the same time protects, witnesses to and hides him. Yet the variations of radiance are ultimately only extensions of an already existing entity, whereas procreative call cuts even the thinnest and finest links between the principle and its descendants. The separation and disassociation with the result of our action is not evident: just as we surmount the natural tendency of our mind toward analytic judgments only through ceaseless effort, we do not easily vanquish the instinct for immanence. The procreator will vigorously protest against any association with old *Chronos* gobbling up his progeny, but the stages leading to the *alius*-child begin with the shadow, which is hardly a real other.

The shadow is the first moment of the productive work where the mirroring of the reflection is consolidated, coagulated as it were into a separated entity. It is already disassociated from the object but it is not yet determined truly to detach itself, to pull itself away in order to take an autonomous course. A being's shadow surrounds and accompanies it, but this remains ambivalent. The shadow aims to reflect its object faithfully, but at the same time it will always remain—a shadow. It is supposed to reproduce the being from which it emanates, yet if the reproduction aims to be faithful it is far from complete and precise. To the contrary, the shadow is furtive and imprecise, possessing an imprecision that is not simply absence of details, diminishment of contours but also a veiling and a contortion. The shadow suffers a native weakness, but it is also changing, transitory, even deceptive. It always remains dependent on the "actual" being of which it is so to say the counterpart. Night is the shadow of day, death

---

7. St. Thomas Aquinas, *Summa Theologiae* I. 31 a. 2 ad. 3.

of life, the old person of the adult. And do we not generally say that a deteriorated, injured or impoverished person is "only a shadow of themselves"?

All these connotations and negative, pejorative traces are found in the *double* where the entities of the order of the image celebrate a certain realization. The double is the image in the ontological order, in the full reality of its being. Yet the ontological element is qualified by quidditative moments. We could say that the double is the existing copy or the shadow capable of being completely detached from its object. In reality the double is not distinguished from the copy or the shadow simply by its autonomous condition, by being a rightfully existent entity. The double has its quidditative, eidetic, sui generis moments differentiating it from diverse variants of the ectype, but this quiddity is not something added to a common ground shared with the ectype. The double is an ectype but its ontological condition influences the configuration of its essence. It possesses properly quidditative moments but which can be attributed only to an effectively existing being. The double is infinitely more autonomous and incomparably more independent than the shadow. In fact, it enjoys the same ontological status, the same degree of existence as the being that it doubles. However, on the plane of existence it registers a clear dependence on the "first" being; it belongs to the secondarity proper to the Image, but the secondarity is pronounced here with a negative accent. It is a purveyor of corruption, hiding a threat that manages only with extreme difficulty to hide a predisposition, even a native metaphysical inclination for evil. Like duality, the category of the double signals the presence of two beings. Yet where the duality is content to pronounce the fact of two coexisting entities, with nothing left over, without touching and without mattering to one another, the doubling that leads to the double engenders two beings related to one another and registering a relation of essence—a relation where the first seems to find in the second all that eidetically constitutes itself, but which is nevertheless the founding relation through which the second is brought into existence, qualifying it as different in an irreducible and, above all, irreversible way.

The double is a natural reality; twins are known in every human race. But precisely, they are recognized as such only among humans. Even more, for the majority of societies, the existence of twins does not constitute a "neutral" phenomenon. The suspicion of twins, the maleficent character commonly attributed to them, eloquently witnesses to the sui generis metaphysical signification of the phenomenon of the "double." The metaphysical logic governing being and becoming, the action and value of the double is admirably elaborated by Stevenson's famous novel, *Jekyll and Hyde*. A literary interpretation seems to overcome the difficulties of a properly conceptual discourse on the double. London—the story begins—is in a state of shock: a little girl is brutally attacked in the street and a venerable member of parliament assassinated.[8] Clues lead to a certain Edward Hyde, a strange person living under the protection

---

8. For the references to Stevenson, see Vető, "L'unité et la séparation du bien et du mal: Jekyll et Hyde," in *Le mal*, 263–79.

of Doctor Henry Jekyll. The reader is led through the circumstances of the birth of Hyde, the difficulties and growing threats that Jekyll must face, ultimately learning of the disappearance of Jekyll and the suicide of Hyde. Edward Hyde is the "protégé" and "favorite" of Jekyll, but the connection between them is much more enigmatic. The beginning of the novel presents the young man as the doctor's "son"; later he is designated as a "part" of him. Ultimately the novel calls him his "twin." The novel as a whole is like a report on the ambiguous relation of these two persons. One is conjured by the other but ends up exercising an increasingly harmful influence on him, to the point of challenging his personal identity.

Hyde is like the alter ego, the "second self" of Jekyll. The doctor wanted to live out experiences that his social situation, his aspirations and moral convictions prohibited him. He begins to manipulate chemical substances in order to effect a kind of disassociation from himself, to take on a second physical appearance. But the use of an impure form of the mixture leads to the advent of Hyde, who comes into the world so to say by accident. The novel is like a large game of hide-and-seek: when Hyde is there, Jekyll disappears; and where Jekyll is, Hyde does not dare to or cannot stay. Each influences the existence of the other, but they cannot co-exist. At the end of the story, Hyde commits suicide: the existence of the double, of an illegitimate reality is not truly justified, is always susceptible of being put in question, almost destined to a premature, violent, disappearance. But it is not only the being of the double of Jekyll that is burdened with non-being: deficiencies and contradictions emerge whenever the discourse could lead to a description of essence. Hyde is a "faceless" being; he can neither be named nor described. He is designated with a neutral pronoun, treated like a *creature*, an indeterminate term that brings along with it a strongly pejorative accent. The person, the man Hyde is not deprived of structure, of eidetic constitution, but he seems to draw on the quidditative elements of his other, Jekyll. Hyde is "co-extensive with Jekyll in every aspect of his life." He is of the same substance as the doctor; the difference is found in their intentions, their deep designs. This *formal* difference co-existing with a *material* identity is registered up to the level of the routine, the habits of the individuals. The writing of the young man is the same as his guardian, only "angled differently." This allows him to have his own bank account, while drawing on Hyde's. He practices a sort of permanent embezzlement that has its counterpart on a higher plane: the doctor, shocked and frightened, observes that this other he called into existence seeks the same sordid adventures, the same pleasures prohibited him. However, what was only "indecent" in Jekyll is "monstrous" in Hyde. The novelist describes with somber exaltation the shady character traits and sordid deficiencies of Hyde where the insufficiency of being and of essence always turns into perversion. Hyde is "an incurable scoundrel," "an intrinsically bad being"; he "has nothing human" and carries "the signature of Satan." In other words drawing forth the other as distorted procreation can only lead to misery and to evil—not only for the double but also for the first, the original. At the beginning, Jekyll was able to incorporate, if you like to incarnate himself in Hyde and, when he wished, to retake his primitive form, his original condition. Yet with the passage of time he loses this power and will begin to be uncertain about his own identity. He no longer dares to say "I" but only "he." His appearance is altered; he becomes a "stranger" in his own house. At the end of the story the good doctor Jekyll is constrained to admit that the doubling has gone wrong and that the wicked Hyde is "also himself." At the same time his deep feelings toward this creature change: henceforth he fears his protégé, and even hates him. And he is hated in return.

Stevenson's story is scattered with various occurrences of the double: he speaks of "doubleness," "double life," and "double existence." A neutral adjective, the double tends towards a negative, pejorative meaning. Doubleness blurs the lines, makes recognition difficult, yet the confusion thus initiated is not simple misunderstanding or disorientation. The adjective "double," is not only a numerical value, it is not only the designation of a duality but bends back onto itself to denote the action, the condition, the very being of a single individual incapable of self-surpassing in order to draw forth another. The chubby baby has a double chin, which we all delight in. Double windows are installed in an apartment to economize the heating bill. But before a double-edged sword, distrust is established and it is intensified when a two-faced person is encountered or when dealing with a double agent. All these phenomena of the "double" find their completion, their monstrous realization in *duplicity*. Contrary to simple falsity, duplicity signals an attitude of acute dissimulation, an internal doubling become malignant. The counterfeiter wants to put himself in the place of another, tending to usurp his role, whereas the duplicitous man suffers an internal scission; he lives duality, *his* duality is lie and contradiction. Duplicity is certainly only an "internal" phenomenon proper to a sole being. Nevertheless in occurrences of effective doubling it announces illegitimacy. The call to existence must be authentic and therefore effective and generous. It cannot and must not be content with a partial gift, a limited, conditional drawing forth—with, in fact, a "material" gift. The call desires to draw forth another that is *truly* other, not like "duplicate of myself."[9] From within ourselves the doubling is strictly rendered as alienation: it signals two kinds of conduct or behavior, one normal, the other pathological. And the internal doubling is itself no longer as such neutral or normal. The double is the clone, a being without proper center, therefore an entity that does not enjoy autonomy, a true existence in itself. One would think that the ontological leap calling another to exist suffices to found it, but the numerical difference (the principle of indiscernibles applies here also) is not yet differentiation. A being deprived of its own center, of a sui generis synthesis, is condemned to remain as a parasite of the other that brought it forth, and the weakness of its means, the insufficiency of its autonomy ends up turning into misfortune and evil.

---

9. Husserl, *Méditations cartésiennes* § 53, 99.

The Unique

The Image-Child

The two major examples of the drawing forth of an autonomous other are the copy and the double. Insufficient foundations are found in both cases. The copy is constituted from an insufficient and radically poor foundation on the plane of essence: the copy claims to possess only what the original possesses. The peasant from Beauce, the interlocutor of the painter of Barbizon was right to question its validity, its reasons for being. The act of copying possesses almost no relations with procreation: despite its actual limitations and imperfections, it has as its intentional object the advent of an autonomous being, the birth of a new entity, while a copy boasts of having avoided the work of innovation. Regarding the genesis of the double, the emphasis is on existence rather than on essence. A strong quidditative conformity and a faithful resemblance of the double to the first seem quickly validated. The goal of the operation seems effectively to be the drawing forth of an autonomous other. Unfortunately however, the desire to work towards the advent of an authentically independent other is no longer present. Procreative action gets lost in obscure, poorly marked paths of conditional calls to existence, and if the beings it engenders can satisfy the biological and juridical definition of the *child*, they are still not radically different from the act of cloning.

Beyond the copy and the double, another second has to constitute the intentional object of procreation, namely, the image. Within the Trinity the Son is the image of the Father who engenders him. Similarly human paternity is a drawing forth of an image: the child is procreated in the image of the father; the son is image of his father. The highest instance of the image is accomplished in the artistic image. The truth of the artistic image is the self-figuration that permits it to surpass the aporias of reproduction, to avoid the pitfalls and traps of figuration. Yet the self-figuration is still a *hapax*, a paradox that grips philosophy as it persists tying the analysis of the image to quidditative considerations. Through self-figuration, the artistic image is confirmed in its sui generis truth, but the condition of this rescue is the radical disassociation of the image from every First of which it would be the Second. The non-figurative artwork is the clearest and most authentic manifestation of self-figuration: it is the supreme image but an image where every relation to an imaged is bracketed. The non-figurative artwork seems to be the true paradigm of the image. In reality it is only a superior degree of the eidos "image." Naturally, the investigation of the image moves into the universe of art, of production, like nature, but one can surpass the paradox of self-figuration by steering the investigation towards the universe of relations among free beings, namely, the world of procreation and paternity. At the end of this reinterpretation, the pro-created, the child proves to be the true paradigm of the image. It proves itself to be thus under the condition that the eidetic analysis is freshly resumed. The aporias and paradoxes of the image are the results of the investigation in which the eidetic is identified with the quidditative. Normally, an image presents something in its quidditative moments. A portrait is supposed to reproduce the facial characteristics of a woman or man, a novel describes the moments of existence and character of members of a family, while a still life shows us the petals of a flower and the leaves of a tree branch. According to this vision, in order to be an image of his father, the child must reproduce his physical traits and evince similar psychological dispositions, bearing traces of his family heredity. Ye the human eidos is not a collection of figures or biological, psychological, social, and historical components. These are properly quidditative traits of a being, but the eidos, more particularly the human eidos, is not a sum of quidditative elements. Its quidditative components stem from this phenomenological essence but they do not constitute it. In non-free creatures the eidetic is exhausted in the quidditative, but in a free being, a man, it presents only its structure, an important but non-essential articulation of characteristics.

The classical definition of man, taught by the Aristotelian tradition, is the *rational animal*. Rationality, reason is the essential characteristic of man, the characteristic that makes him what he is. However, man, the singular free being cannot be defined in terms of a faculty, a property, something ultimately quantifiable. There are men who possess a very powerful reason, others whose reason is weaker. Psychology applies tests that determine one's intellectual quotient, the "quantity" of intelligence that a human possesses. Freedom is not susceptible of being understood in a quantitative sense: no one can measure my freedom or his own in order to give a definition or numerical formula. Freedom can have a genesis, a history, but it does not have degrees. The same thing must a fortiori apply to love, which is the realization, the actualization (supreme in fact) of freedom. The procreative action proper to man seeks the advent of new beings, eidetically the same as their procreator. But the goal of the human being that is freedom and love is another being endowed with freedom and love, another that *is* freedom and love. Procreation is not the drawing forth of entities that possess certain properties or attributes, but the calling forth of beings that are loving and free. And it is important to see that one is not loving like one is blonde or brunette, an excellent swimmer, or good at math. If one insists on recalling that love is not a property, this is order to cut off any attempt to understand it as a "faculty." By their nature, the faculties have a plurality of intentional objects. Sight is related to the entire spectrum of colors, touch can feel, brush, or rub against a multiplicity of things. Intelligence, that "blank slate," can conceive an infinity of objects both inclusively and without being affected by them. From the perspective of memory it appears as a receptacle, a treasury in which the faculty receives an infinite plenitude of objects. Things are different for love, which is by definition related to one "object" and can have only a single "correlate," not by passionate jealousy, but by virtue of its metaphysical structure. Just as "God adds nothing to the idea of faith" (there is no sense speaking of faith without its intentional object),[10] the beloved adds nothing to "I love." I cannot say that I love without including the one that I love. More precisely, the one I love cannot be conceived in itself, *minus* "I love." Otherwise love can have many different intentional objects and

---

10. Marcel, *Journal métaphysique*, 40.

consequently its unconditionality would be compromised. This eidetic impossibility of conceiving love, effective love, the love exercised by, or rather, that is a free being (as determined by characteristics, by quidditative elements of its intentional object) intersects with an impossibility of the moral order. Montaigne's magnificent formula is often quoted: "Because he was he, and I was I." What is he saying here if not that when you love someone, you love because you love? The love of another is "*causa sui.*"[11] Love, like the Rose, has no reason outside of itself. The reasoning that desires "to explain" love lacks its supra-predicative essence. One does not love another for one reason or another, and one cannot conceive the love one experiences as having an intentional object other than the one it effectively has. The moral and eidetic impossibility of conceiving or positing another intentional object other than the one love effectively has is translated by the intuition of the irreplaceable and the inconsolable. The child with a broken toy is not consoled by the promise of another. "There shall be no other toy... Behold the cry of love."[12] Someone wounded by the loss of a spouse cannot speak of another who could take the place of the departed. He is inconsolable, which means that his love was not addressed to qualities or properties of his spouse but to the "hacceity" of the "person."[13]

Love is a supreme a priori synthesis; its predicate cannot be defined in quidditative terms. It is a judgment that has ineducible results. It is an action that rushes towards an end that it cannot justify, but which nevertheless perfectly fits it. Procreative action is love and in fact the supreme paradigm of love in its free, gratuitous and asymmetrical condition. It wants to draw forth an autonomous other, of which it in no way seeks to prejudge the quidditative configuration. But precisely, it is through this asymmetrical love, without the goal of drawing forth a likeness according to essence, that procreation succeeds in calling into existence a sublime reflection where the parent finds itself in another, in *its* other. Any non-free, non-gratuitous act can only lead to contingent, conditional productions, to substances that are ultimately only accidents. Gratuitous action alone permits its end, its engendered not to be submitted to determination; it alone can draw forth an entirely free being. In its disinterestedness, in its radically free aim that brackets every property and quality, which proceeds to total quidditative reduction, the procreator is engaged in the supreme adventure of bringing about an autonomous being that is independent in relation to itself. One finds oneself standing before an immense paradox, that of a free drawing forth through the procreative act. The paradox of this free drawing forth that love alone makes possible is that the abandonment of the aspiration for reunion in the quidditative allows the appearance of the response on the eidetic plane. The truth of the procreator is the asymmetrical love that seeks no recompense and it is precisely as perfect renunciation of recompense that it calls to existence another that will also

---

11. Jankélévitch, *Traité des vertus* 2, 214.
12. Marcel, *La métaphysique de Royce*, 63s.
13. Jankélévitch, *Traité des vertus* 2, 230.

individually exist as source of asymmetrical love. Yet love is never in general but always in particular, or rather, in the singular; it is addressed to a unique pro-created. Consequently, the (asymmetrical) love emanating from the one drawn forth happens under the form of a free and gratuitous response. In its truth, procreative action is the ardent desire for the autonomy of the other called into existence. But it is precisely this ardent aspiration for the advent of an autonomous other that allows it to find in the other a loving response.

In reality, the procreative vow does not simply aim for the advent of another that can be the source of an asymmetrical love addressed to any free being. Without a doubt the parent knows that his child could love and will truly love others than himself. In fact, he wants him to be capable of experiencing love for others far away, unknown, even non-existent, unborn. However, as his love is not related to any free being other than himself but to the one he engenders, the asymmetrical love addressed to this being brought about by virtue of it, could and should incite this being to turn towards and respond to his procreator. The love of the child for the parent remains gratuitous and free; it is not required by virtue of a logic of necessity, but is nevertheless imposed through a logic of congruence. Love is by its nature asymmetrical, but asymmetry does not mean non-correspondence, non-correlation. Love is gratuitous, but gratuity does not mean contingency. Love is the exercise of a synthetic a priori judgment; its end is not immanent to it. Nevertheless it must be recognized as reasonable. Indeed, love of father and mother is reasonable and fitting because, independently of its empirical manifestations, the conditions of its genesis in duration, it is original and unconditional in its metaphysical truth.[14]

The Unique Ones

Discourse on the unique led us to the child, the goal of the asymmetrical, unconditional love of the call, the source of an asymmetrical love no less unconditional of the response. The child is the result of the discussion on the unique, the paradigm and highest example of the unique. However, by its eidetic nature, the gratuitous, generous

---

14. In the last analysis, the "rationality" of love for the procreator finds its origin, its truth in its metaphysical condition: it is certainly a response but also a call. The asymmetry of true love can be translated by a great disparity of intensity of affection between those who love but it essentially amounts to its originarity. In the same way that love of the beloved for the lover is conceived as original, as appearing first, the love of the pro-created for the procreator also has a fundamental dimension of originarity; it is also in a certain way first. The parent calls the child into existence, the call to be his child, but an analogous call, no less original, equally first, emanates from the child. Just as the child is not child without being loved by the parent, the parent is truly parent only as intentional object of the child's love. The child addresses this call of love to the parent, or rather, he is this call. He is the call in a certain way from before all thought and all explicit feeling. He is call by his existence as a child. And it is through this originarity, this native gratuity, that he "justifies" and supports the perseverance and deepening of procreative love of father and mother. The original call of the child is a deep mystery of the human condition. Ultimately, it is still only a counterpart, or rather a "second" of the divine mystery of the call of the Son through which the Father is Father within the Trinity.

love that aims for the child cannot be exhausted in a single, solitary correlate. The intentional object of procreative love is not the child but *children*, a plurality. There are of course families with one child but children are so to speak, by definition, many. If the child is unique, are children also? How to conceive of a plurality of unique ones?

The paradox of a plurality of uniques should be read in light of another paradox, that of the non-quidditative truth of the image that refers to the conception of the singular as the bracketing of having, of qualities and properties. The singular possesses quiddity—how could it not? It has properties and qualities but qualities and properties are predicated only in terms of the synthesis that constitutes the singular. The singular has predicates, but it is not the singular that it is by virtue of its predicates. Similarly, the unique also has predicates, but it is not the unique that it is through its predicates. Inconsolable love gave clear witness: love is addressed to the person, not to his attributes and properties. The person, the subject is so sovereign in relation to all its quidditative components that the very radical alteration of its quiddity does not put into question its haecceity. The child can become a criminal, the spouse can develop dementia, but they nevertheless remain the intentional object of the unconditional love of their procreator or their spouse. In both cases it is a matter of a unity that surpasses the quidditative. Nevertheless, their respective situations are different. The bracketing of the quidditative is the preliminary condition of all true unicity, but the unicity of the spouse is nearly continuous with the immanent unity of the singular while the unicity of the child, more precisely of children, is situated in a totally other metaphysical register. Procreative love rushes towards the child from the outside and only by virtue of this external action is the child constituted as unique. The unicity of the procreated is not a function of an internal synthesis proper to the unique: if there can be many unique ones, the reason is found in the asymmetrical unconditional love of procreation.

Procreative love ignores every quidditative element that could prohibit the advent of a plurality of unique ones. In the absence of a quidditative determination, the procreated do not encroach on each other: they are neither incompatible nor sites or occasions of superfluous duplication. Children are loved for themselves, not for a role that they play or that others play less well than they. More precisely, they play no role at all, for there is no duality, no space between their existence and their essence: these coincide and leave no room for incursion or replacement by another. Children are not occurrences of an essence, individuals constituting a genre. They are rather like the angels of medieval theology of which each, in the absence of elements that diffract their specific essence, presents in itself a whole entire species. Appearing through a descending gratuitous love, by virtue of an "election" that differentiates, without being based on a "comparison," children constitute a plurality in which each member is an integral whole, or rather, an end in itself.

Children are uniques in relation to the descending love that constitutes them and if the essential relation that determines them is built up through relation to the procreator, these uniques are also principles of horizontal relation, of relations with other uniques. Children are brothers and as the child is paradigm of the unique according to its unicity envisaged according to its relation to the procreator, the brother is the paradigm of the unique as member of the plurality of uniques, considered in its relations with other uniques. The relation among brothers is exempt from the necessity of deadly reciprocity that spies on conjugal love. The "beautiful name brother...full of delight,"[15] designates a condition of freedom in dependency, of unicity in affinity. One can certainly be the friend of his brother but the Brother is not the Friend. One meets the friend at a given moment of his existence: of course, habit and circumstances help him; one nevertheless becomes friend only through a free choice while the origins of brother-being are lost in the night of procreation. In fact, they are not lost because the source from which brothers came continues to animate and nourish them. Contrary to affection among friends that depends entirely on the freedom of two friends, the love among brothers possesses a base, an external and anterior root of their existence that spares them the attempts and adventures of finding another and which liberates them from every consideration of complementarity, of reciprocity in this other. Brothers belong to a plurality that the same creative vow has called to existence; they are naturally turned towards one another, but this ontological affinity does not yet predetermine them to exclusive links and exchanges with one another.

The relation among brothers and sisters is constructed on the common base of procreative action that constituted them and always shines over them, but which has as its counterpart the native difference among these unique ones. While in friendship parallelisms play an important role (despite the possibilities of gaps of condition, taste, interest and similarities), the category "brother" precisely excludes these quidditative factors. Friendship can hardly abstract from these attempts at intrusion, the reappearance of sameness while the metaphysical category of brother firmly refuses the temptation for nostalgia of the double. Other children born of the same procreator who called me into existence must not be either shadows or clones. The mistrust and even fear that can be felt before the twin demonstrates the rejection of these achievements of singularity and unicity. As has been rightly said: we seek, we wish for "a brother" not "a mirror."[16] Their radical singularity, their unicity of essence determines the relations among brothers. They are not monads related to the Principle all the while perfectly ignoring their fellow creatures. Brothers are not only located beside each other. They are not blind, hermetically sealed; they have windows, almost as if they are all windows through and through. Unlike paintings in a museum or individual members of an animal species, they are not entities closed up in themselves separated by an ontological no man's land, but beings differentiated and linked together by relations of love.

---

15. Montaigne, *Essais* I, xxviii, 191.
16. Shakespeare, *The Comedy of Errors* V, 1, 418–19.

The theme of the relation among brothers and sisters could inspire political and social philosophy. It is equally apt to fructify metaphysical discourse on the plurality of "thirds," a multiplicity that is neither incoherent dispersion and infinity nor duality exhausted in an exclusive reciprocity. But it also and above all serves as paradigm for the definition of what is and must be a free being. The free being is part of a multiplicity of free beings where each is called to existence by a free and gratuitous procreative action. And it is part of this multiplicity by virtue of its aptitude and irreplaceable, unique relation with each of its neighbors. But this aptitude horizontally turned towards its others should be understood beginning with the Response that it can address to its foundational Other, its vertical Other if you like. The eidetic truth of man cannot be exhausted by an ultimately quidditative factor, a category from the order of Having that is the understanding. The power of autonomous legislation recommended by Kantianism's definition of free being transposes the discussion onto a superior plane. Yet it remains insufficient, or rather, inadequate. The legislative power inscribed in the heart of each of us explains the free creature in terms of a perfect universality, but freedom and above all its effective exercise, love, is not located on the universal or even unconditional plane. Love is a unique act of the procreator; it is addressed to a unique being and the response that it can draw forth is also unique. The essence of the free procreated being should be defined in terms of asymmetrical, descending, unique love that constitutes it and in doing so invites it to respond through free love. The Response to the procreator has as its counterpart the relations towards our brothers and neighbors, but these relations, or responses if you like, have their principle and paradigm in It.

More than an impersonal power, without the appearance of universal legislation, the aptitude to respond to procreative love is the essential eidetic moment of the free being. But how to delimit the aptitude to the response? More precisely, if I am a man to the degree that I know how to give a proper response, my own unique response to the love that called me into existence, how to determine, to define conceptually the beings capable of giving the response? The Call constituted the possibility of the response, of ascending love, and the effective aptitude to respond should be understood through the dependence that locates the creature, in other words, starting from the sovereignty of the First Love.

The Love that calls to existence draws forth beings that are its images and therefore capable of responding to it, but the love is unconditional and does not require a "proportioned" response, not even an effectively given response. The imagistic condition of the procreated, namely the principle of the possibility of ascending love does not depend on a level or quidditative degrees of properties or faculties, of thresholds of intelligence or physical aptitude. In fact, the highest moral-metaphysical intuitions of humanity have been able to highlight the power and efficacy of the asymmetrical love that draws forth in the most indigent and most deficient instances of the image. The commandment to respect and care for the "stranger, widow, and orphan" (Jer 22:3) powerfully recalls their condition as complete recipients of the descending love that draws them forth. And while the moral scandal and metaphysical absurdity of slavery is eliminated, both canonical and secular law already distinguished between the juridical personhood refused to the slave and his condition as a human being, principle, and end of love. The plantation owners of French America were hardly interested in promoting or even allowing marriage (and therefore the foundation of families) for their slaves, but an ordinance of Louis XV solemnly decreed that slaves, created in the image of God, must be allowed to unite in the sacred bonds of Christian marriage. But more than the social or economic condition, the intellectual conditions and their principle source, the conscience, seem to play a determining role for the recognition of the uniqueness of a human being. One is unique by virtue of the unconditional call to existence and one must be able to address to this unique call a unique response, but how to respond when one is not able to understand, to conceive the response? Are the little child, the mentally ill, the comatose patient able to recognize the call that has drawn them forth, and consequently, are they able to respond? And of what power of response is the embryo capable?

The response of love is not an exact formula to be precisely articulated in speech and above all it is not a one-time act. All love, ascending love included, is a whole, a state, a condition, and its non-exercise or rather the momentary impossibility of its effective exercise does not yet compromise its truth, its reality. The conscience is certainly an essential moment of the eidetic of the free being, but it does not exhaust it. The dream continues on in the wakefulness it inhabits, and the unconsciousness cannot be disassociated from the consciousness that is comprehended and structured starting from it. Nobody thinks that the humanity of a being is suspended or obliterated during sleep. To kill someone while sleeping truly brings about the death of *that* person and our moral condition suffers no interruption even when we cannot confirm or annul the choice that determined it. The villain remains "a villain" and the just remains "just. . .while they sleep."[17]

The extreme case, the dramatic example of the apparent inaptitude of response to the call is the embryo which seems to be found short of any structure, deprived of all power allowing it to recognize the call and to engage in a response. The unborn child is deprived of every physiological and psychological element that would anticipate (even remotely) the appearance of consciousness, the exercise of freedom. Scarcely a being, nearly deprived of form during a certain period of its existence, how can the unborn child be capable of claiming the condition of image? In reality, in it the unconditional descending love drawing forth the unique comes forward and shows itself with the greatest force. The necessary condition of the unique is the internal synthesis of singularity; the sufficient condition is the external and anterior call of love. Despite the absence of all morphological evidence the unborn child remains a singular different from every other: the fertilized egg contains a complete DNA program; from

---

17. Nicole, *Instructions théologiques et morales sur le symbole I*, 190.

conception an entire series of genetic messages is programmed; from the beginning of fertilization the embryo sends biochemical signals that the maternal organism knows, receives, and recognizes. Despite the radical dissimilarity between the elementary cellular reality and the future human being in full possession of its faculties that emerges from it, every egg contains from its fertilization the essential information that animates the individual and guides it throughout its life. But notwithstanding the entire range of scientific proofs demonstrating and confirming the singularity of the unborn child, it cannot be recognized as the image of the procreator and consequently as unique starting from the love that draws it forth. In its eidetic truth, procreative love is unconditional and the unborn child, this image nearly without form furnishes the paradigmatic intentional object of asymmetrical descending love.

The eidos "image" that constitutes the metaphysical essence of humanity is not a material content. It is not inscribed in the one drawn forth as an objective, immanent structure but rather comes from the drawing forth itself. And the drawing or sparking forth is an a priori synthetic action, an élan, a self-exit towards another who cannot be something attractive, desirable, or even deducible, definable. The insistence on the radical absence of all "proportion" in the one drawn forth in relation to the one who draws forth only highlights the authenticity of descending love that is procreative action. It attests to its radical asymmetry, its perfect unconditionality. Gratuitous love, the first love of procreation is at the origin of the unique, of the unicity of the unique shards of a white hot light in indignity, poverty, and passivity, finding its paradoxical archetype in the formless being that is the unborn child.

BOOK TWO
Eidetics

VI

Space: From Homogeneity to War

Material Essences and Synthetic a priori Eidē

The first five chapters of this book sketch a first philosophy. The discussion began by reworking the Image, which spells out and confirms its autonomy. Then, thanks to the notion of the a priori synthesis, Novelty was integrated into the metaphysical universe. Finally, the a priori synthesis equally permitted the conceptual construction of asymmetrical love leading to the deduction of the Singular as Unique. These are three instances of transgression, or rather, surpassing of taboos of classical philosophy. And the parricide continued down a fruitful path: after passing the prohibitions of Parmenides, certain teachings of Aristotle are bracketed, or rather, rectified. And through the inspiration of Kant and with the revitalization afforded by themes from biblical theology, the image is no longer an evanescent and unfaithful copy, the new ceases appearing as an illegitimate and impossible breach of the body of the present and the singular is celebrated as the highest example of the entity.

The expansion accomplished by the three moments of redemption, the image, the new and the singular will be completed by the reworking, or rather, expansion of the doctrine of essences. The discourse of classical metaphysics essentially concerns material *essences*—essences constituting superior forms of quality, glimpsed on the intelligible plane and responding to the question of the *Was*. The essential can be situated on the plane of the universal, of conceptual abstraction where its genesis is located, being always related to a *quale*. The opposition between essence and existence is posed with force and clarity but quoddity always has its counterpart in quiddity. And this is reached at the end of an investigation by nature analytical: the apprehension of a content in itself, without relation to another thing, the description of an isolated eidos, a homogenous atom-monad, closed in on itself. Husserlian phenomenology enlarges the field of eidetic description and surpasses the unarticulated and inexplicit limits of discourse on essence. Henceforth the moments of the will as forms of space and time constitute eidetic instances just like colors or sounds, metals or plants. Phenomenology thus tacitly extends the investigation to eidē of the synthetic kind, but in reality Kantianism already reached this expansion. Despite its roots in Wolfian scholasticism, the *Critique* hardly speaks of *essences*. It concerns instead the concepts that are either empirical or pure and the pure concepts are the Categories. But the categories are instances of the a priori synthesis. The category is a noetic élan, a predication accomplished through and at the end of a trajectory of reason. The universe of the categories does not coincide with the eidetic one that makes Phenomenology possible; it does not exhaust the possibilities of a vision of the eidos, surpassing the narrow limits of quiddity. Intelligibility, or a priori craftsmanship, cannot be denied to the emotions and to values that are not material contents. Similarly, if the *Was*, the *quid* are generally predicates of a judgment affirming a state of fact, a truth, there are yet some formulations that, without indicating "true or false, are nevertheless perfectly meaningful."[1]

This expansion of significations must be taken into account. It amounts to a substantial advance on the positions of classical philosophy. Yet, the expanded metaphysics does not include the indeterminate totality of essences that Phenomenology tends to describe. The eidetic it practices is as it were selective, taking into account only the eidē of synthetic a priori craftsmanship and unfolding them in the context of an organization inspired by the Critique. In a late text Kant declared that "there are two hinges on which [metaphysics] turns: *First*, the doctrine of the ideality of space and time. . ." and "*second*, the doctrine of the reality of the concept of freedom."[2] It is therefore in fidelity to the Kantian inspiration that the "eidetic" part of the Expansion of Metaphysics is related to the proper intelligibilities of space, time and the will.

The immemorial reflection of humanity has always seen in space and time the impassable limits of our power, the irrevocable shackles of our action and philosophy sought to raise these perennial intuitions into concepts. Space and time characterize the finitude of the creature; they are the framework of our condition. Space is the place and instrument of the borders of our action, obstacles against which our efforts shatter. And time signals the brevity of the moments imparted to us, the unaccomplishment that threatens our endeavors. It is also and above all the cipher of mortality, the essence of our condition, the horizon of every project and every human end. Put differently, and conceptually: time and space are tied to finitude, constituting the law and source of materiality, or rather, of the sensibility that is the mode of being of our finitude. Material essences chop up and describe a universe structured and governed by intelligible laws while time and space are only "accidental principles"

---

1. Stroll, *Twentieth-Century Analytic Philosophy*, 175.

2. Kant, *Progress de la Métaphysique en Allemagne. Oeuvres* 3, 1263. (Akad. XX, 311. "What real progress has metaphysics made in Germany since the time of Leibniz and Wolff?" *Theoretical Philosophy after 1781*, 397.)

of the configuration or advent of things.[3] Classical philosophy is a discourse on the order and coherence of the real, while time and space are only supreme ciphers of Dispersion.

This pejorative vision of time and space prevailing in the philosophical tradition prohibits any attempt to found novelty and the singular in metaphysics and it condemns thought to understand any continuity as simply contiguity, to take history for a simple becoming, and not to know how to distinguish works of freedom from the consequences of contingency. Western philosophy truly remains "a footnote to Plato" (Whitehead). In other words it manages only to read the finite from the vantage of the infinite, it discerns in things of the Earth only weak and deficient reflections of the realities of Heaven, when it does not subsume them in the flames of Hell. This interpretation of the spatial and temporal, the pitfall par excellence of every metaphysical investigation, is surpassed by Kantianism. The *Critique* keeps the vision of space and time as forms of finitude but rethinks and reinterprets them. Time and space are always forms of sensibility but they are its a priori forms. The temporal and special always remain inseparably tied to dispersion, but they broadcast its coherence; they always constitute the horizon of multiplicity but they make possible its subsumption under unity. Space and time are defined as, respectively, the a priori form of external and internal sense. They become the law, the directive and organizational principle of the sensible that they revitalize starting from the intelligible. The sensible is thus "rehabilitated"; it no longer carries the stigma of dispersion. It is the very condition of the eidē of finitude, of a finitude that is neither cut from the infinite nor opposed to it, but which receives its proper, sui generis foundation, starting from the intelligible.

The Forms of Dispersion

Philosophy as popular wisdom has always considered space and time as parallel realities, as metaphysical categories with analogous structure and roles. The poet speaks of "this double sea of time and space,"[4] and the philosophers are happy to expound them as the two great moments of the same category of the imagination while the pure concepts belong to the understanding. In fact time and space constitute not only in themselves counterparts of intelligibilities, they indissociably found and structure things. Direction is an essential eidetic moment of spatiality, but it also implies a potential progress where one passes from one moment to another. Consequently, the very essence of the spatial implies the temporal. A spatial thing, a *res extensa* does not exist unless it occupies a position in time and therefore possesses duration. Space is a system of an infinite number of *heres* that can be realized, actualized only *at the same time*. Here and there are certainly determinations and moments of space but ultimately they prove to be temporal-spatial phenomena. The *here*, abstracted from

---

3. Boethius, *In Porph. comm.* II, 3.
4. Hugo, "La pente de la rêverie," in *Oeuvres poétiques* I, 773.

the *there*, can be conceived "in itself" as purely spatial, but how to define the "there" if not as the place where I am not *yet*?

Space and time are connected and inseparable. They constitute the two essential categories that structure existence. Philosophers have always compared them starting from their configuration, in terms of their essential aim. In its ambition to "deduce" them, post-Kantian idealism opposes space to time as the delimiting indeterminate sphere at the borders, like the force of expansion in relation to the force of contraction (Schelling). Space is the area where the real, so to speak, spreads out; time is the straight channel where it is interrupted and concentrated. The things of space enlarge themselves, occupy their place, take up volume, whereas time contracts and above all establishes them in movement, in forward momentum. Space can be represented as a vast, unlimited domain where beings subsist in a lazy and placid coexistence, whereas time appears as the obsession with progression, the whirl of an intensity that carries beings in a forward flight. Metaphysical analysis has its counterpart in a vision, an intuition where the two forms of space and time end up designating the two universes of nature and the person (Novalis). Space corresponds to the world of beings short of freedom, while time is understood as the principle and source of freedom itself. Space is the place of a movement that is merely kinesis, a movement that remains "local" even as it includes some displacements and irradiations that can be measured or expressed only in light years. Time is the framework and goad of actions of an innovative scope, even when their unfolding is effected in modest circles and results in fractional changes.

The opposition of time and space leads ultimately to qualifications and evaluations susceptible to establish a difference of value, a hierarchy of relevance. Ancient philosophy seems to have attributed a certain priority to space, the *chora* appears to play a more important metaphysical role than *chronos*. But modern thought takes the side of time. Time becomes the form of the internal sense, the necessary filter and therefore true "superior" to the spatial domain of the external sense while being transposed into the supreme principle of history. Time is also the form and principle of intimacy and individual subjectivity as of the formation of subjective community. And space, place of obstacles and weights, sphere of bindings and conflicts, ends up appearing as a "reactionary" principle.[5]

This modern devalorization of space is doubtlessly susceptible to being called into question. If time exercises an unavoidable mastery over space, simple experience attests to the primitive consciousness of space, of the being-in-space that is constitutive of self-consciousness. This primary, foundational fact can and should be conceptualized. The subtle descriptions of the novelist will come to the aid of philosophical analysis. The novelist recalls with exquisite simplicity that when someone wakes up at night, he does not know where he is or who he is. This is the source of a fecund

---

5. Bloch, *Philosophy of the Future*, 120.

education: to ignore space amounts to ignoring, in a certain way, oneself![6] And indeed, when the victim of an accident regains consciousness, "returns to himself," he asks: where am I? who am I? In other words, primitive interrogation on self-identity seems indissociable from the awareness of being in space. As for the "moral" register, the sphere of Value, becoming aware of the ecological crisis, the realization of the precious character of the given world, must relativize the priority of time. It will mute the exclamations celebrating the breathless advance of Progress, the technological stranglehold on the cosmos, the exaltation before the advance of the Noosphere in order to give time to stop, to sojourn in the places where rocks lie quietly and trees grow.

Indeed, if these evaluative comparisons are not without philosophical value, the essential is to unfold the sui generis manners by which the two great spheres of space and time join and structure an eidetic multiplicity. "Temporal and spatial beings lie in dispersion...they constitute a system of exteriority," a universe of "the *Ausseinander*."[7] Space is the universe of multiplicity, of dispersion according to being-beside, coexistence, and time according to being-after-one-another, succession. These two regimes of dispersion seem to express an analytic order, where the gaps and distances, crevasses and openings ultimately constitute only variations of repetition, instances of sameness. But space and time are not simply receptacles, or even forms of flux. They represent, above all, systems of distribution of place, principles of organization, and structuration of positions. Time and space not only house the beings they contain, they also impart to them their place, and in terms of this place determine the way that these beings stand out against the background of a whole and express the modalities of their relations with other things. But this signification, this vocation of systems of dispersion presupposes a synthetic a priori craftsmanship. If classical thought believed it could interpret the spatial and temporal according to the analytic unity of homogeneity, modern philosophy projects a synthetic a priori conception of the two forms of sensibility that will allow the unfolding of an eidetic proper to each. Even more, an analytic reading of space and time is not only inexact and insufficient, it is also at the origin of mistakes and misinterpretations of a significant metaphysical and moral bearing.

Extension and Exteriority

The expansion of metaphysics passes through a reinterpretation of space involving the constitution of a spatial eidetics. But even more than time, space seems recalcitrant to the concept, or rather, it seems to be situated below the concept to the degree that it is as such the domain of the absence of structure, lacking any intelligible configuration. Space is the vast receptacle that contains me, an unlimited extension surrounding me on every side. I cannot conceive myself or things otherwise than in space, but

---

6. See citations of Proust in Bollnow, *Mensch und Raum*, 181s.
7. Husserl, Ms D 8 (1918), in Claesges, *Edmund Husserls Theorie der Raumkonstruktion*, 37n.

can I conceive space itself? In ancient thought space is the synonym and paradigm of formlessness; it receives any and all beings without respect of persons, and it contains and houses the most diverse entities with complete indifference. But precisely, what is at stake in reflection on space is the conception of indifference. Indifference is a function of extension constituting the spatial and extension seems to be a limitless and unstructured reality. Lacking an external border, space registers no principle of internal structuring. It is deprived of any power of self-structuration. And here we find the basic ambiguity of the spatial: it is extensive, but is this sprawling character a simple extension, or is it rather an expansion? If it is only extension, it lacks form and figure. Because the placid extension is truly its site, the drama proper to the spatial is that the extension naturally transposes itself into expansion; the inherent indeterminacy of the spatial reveals itself as principle of destructive violence against the figure.

The spatial is self-extended; space is thus constituted through extension which leads to a spreading out. Space extends in all directions; it lacks borders, and, so to say, spreads itself out. A naïve, quaint conception represents it as a container, a receptacle, in order to distinguish it from everything found within it, entities with shape and definition that it houses. But the vision of an immense bag or cauldron, chest or cabinet is far too infantile and imperfect: the vagueness proper to the spatial hardly fits with the diverse imagery of variations of an immense box. Space is strictly indeterminate; it cannot be qualified in opposition to that which it contains, which is structured and therefore contrasted to it. No, space is simply an extension to which one cannot and must not give borders. Instead of presenting it as a cosmic container, it is better thought as a milieu or ontological ambiance. It is the transparent medium where beings are situated in simultaneity and hence an immense area without articulable structure. As soon as the sensible intuition of the *chora* is thought through in an intellectual conception of the milieu and as a translucent and homogenous area, one approaches the genesis of the idea of objective spatiality, the truth of which is mathematical space. "Space," writes Simone Weil, "is the solitude, the indifference of things. . .even Christ's crucifixion is no more charged with significance than a falling pine needle. . . The body of Christ occupies no more space and occupies space in no other way than any old tree trunk."[8] Space is the area for all external realities, it extends in all directions but possesses no proper center. The absence of a center explicates the fundamental intuition of the spatial as devoid of any preference, of all innate proximity. Space has no center from where someone could contemplate and classify things as a privileged observer in terms of distance from their respective position. This conception of space demands a flawless objectivity, the absence of any hermeneutic by nature relativistic but this ultimately amounts to the refusal, the renunciation of any eidetic structuration. Space is without a point of coagulation; it registers no relief or escarpment, no ravine or pit. It is flat and smooth, opposing no obstacle to the gaze or to movement.

---

8. Weil, *Cahiers. Oeuvres complètes* VI, 3, 84.

In itself it is only a flat and peaceful terrain without history: man is located in it but it is neither visible nor perceptible.

The primary intuition of this smooth environment that is always equal to itself is at the root of the mathematical idea of space as infinitely divisible or rather is infinite divisibility itself—and this because it is homogenous. The eidetics of every stripe are a function of differences and heterogeneities, of flickering discontinuities, but the spatial is a domain, in fact the supreme domain of continuity. The spatial that is extended spreads out, and it does so in every direction in the same way, without registering any difference in the multiple moments of its unfolding. Of course the continuity proper to space does not prohibit us from noticing segments, marking out parts. But segments and parts can be various lengths; they are still of similar make. Space is the universe of homogeneity, a whole composed of parts of the same nature, or more precisely of parts without any nature. The spatial is a shining example of the same, which in its fundamental truth is the enemy of the figure. Figures, whether natural or traced by a human hand are located in space; they are, as it were, cut into space. Yet despite their inscription in space, their radical spatiality, figures are incompatible with the spatial in its objective sense. Homogenous space consents to release the figure that, almost despite itself is constrained; it looks only to close up the gap, the cut, the wound that has been inflicted on it. In an infinitesimal moment it reestablishes the continuity caused by the unique articulation.

The conception of space as infinite, pure divisibility means that if the spatial has a structure it is quantity. We have already seen that quantity is an "inessential difference." The quantitative truth of space, the structuration of the spatial in exclusively quantitative terms, attests to its paradoxical condition. Space is only the context or place for relations among beings, but these beings, these things are reduced to being only instances of quantity. Space appears as "the relation of things having no relation."[9] The absence of relation manifested by mathematico-objective space discloses its pre- and anti-eidetic nature. On the level of intuition, the spatial in this perspective is presented as a boundless flow in which no structure can be discerned. On the level of the concept it registers the absence of any structuration, any inherent hook where the noetic regard can be hung. Contrary to the tireless flux of time, space appears only as a serene flow. But it is a flow. The spatial flows for lack of a center that would govern its unfolding. For the idealists, this centerless condition of space amounts to the absence of a proper concept. If space is the principle of beings that distinguishes among them no specific difference, this is because it also lacks a conceptual focus. Ultimately the absence of any relief, the *smoothness* proper to space is only a figurative expression for the native flatness of the spatial. In its condition of unlimited flow, of an unarticulated essence, space is all surface where everything slides and nothing is fixed that would constitute a structure.

---

9. Sartre, *L'être et le néant*, 241.

The intuition of this sliding and limitlessness has a flavor of placidity but it ultimately leads to a less pacific vision in which the flowing of extension is transposed into exteriority, namely, into an eidos that, all the while being a cipher of indeterminacy, of unstructuration, already dons negative aspects. In its primitive sense, the exterior is that from which I am separated by a distance, that which is therefore not under my control and does not share in my circle. But to say that a thing does not belong to my sphere does not simply mean that it is outside of my jurisdiction, beyond my reach. The exterior is what is located in an elsewhere, as not belonging to us; it is what is experienced as foreign. But the being that is foreign to me is not only an entity outside of my sphere but also a being that it does not matter what it is, which is indifferent to me. It is therefore what I could like, or use and abuse. In its canonical definition, space is the form of the external sense. But the peaceful neutrality of this a priori Form of Sensibility harbors some virtualities and threats of bad processes and bad handling, in short, of transgression. Exteriority is not only cipher of a position outside of my sphere, it also carries within it germs of separation, premises of scission. Exteriority is a category of the universe of indifference. But if indifference is truly a synonym for neutrality, then neutrality is only a fictitious impartiality; it always carries a core of hostility. At first glance the spatial is simply located below the activity of structuration. But unfortunately the absence of structuration is not an absence of the power of structuration but also implicitly contains a strong inclination to affirm a difference by attacking another.

From Indifference to Hostility

Objective, mathematical space is homogenous; it is the sum of parts of the same nature, pieces different only according to quantity. Movement from one part to another implies no novelty but is a simple, unbroken progression. The respective relations of moments of space is the object of an analytic knowledge where the mind is confined in the circle of the same. But recall that analysis is not a mechanical procedure, not only a peaceful and placid movement. It can equally constitute a journey on a path filled with thorns. We rediscover these thorns in a quasi-literal way in the study of space. Homogenous space is the totality of always equal parts; ultimately it is the sum of points. But the metaphysical status of the point is like the hinge around which the interpretation of the meaning of the spatial turns. Space is the coexistence of an infinity of points and yet the point is intuited under the form of a little, colorless speck, of minimum extension. Strictly speaking the point does not even appear as a speck, with even the smallest amount of extension. Rather, it represents an abstraction, a function in itself deprived of true extension. The point will have its truth less in and through itself than through the multiplicity that it constitutes with other unextended points. This conception of a pre-ontological or rather ante-figurative status of the point illustrates the traditional meaning of Analysis in its greatest radicality: analysis is the noetic operation where the mind proceeds only into the milieu of realities of the same order, and describes an immanent movement that implies no leap. But there is also another, very different conception of the point: instead of considering it as the unidimensional reality below being, one of its elementary significations could be rehabilitated, namely its role of constituting the extremity of a line. The point that marks the extremity, the end of a line is not simply a dot on an i, the spatial particle that completes a bi-dimensional moment, a ray, a stick, or finger. The point can also constitute the extremity of a line that tends towards—more precisely, it can indicate and signal a direction. In and through the point located at the extremity of a line its proper spatial role is played out: it *points* in a direction. And by "pointing," the analytical is no longer synonymous with a false peace. The point that points can be the end of a sharpened stick, the tip of an arrow, the point of a dagger. It is thus like "a spur," the sharpness of a dart, and therefore "a *point* that pierces."[10]

The point of the point, the point as point is like the narthex of the noetic edifice where the homogeneity of space is ordered to deliver its deadly truth. The point is not an unextended, insignificant moment of the spatial but is the point of the sword that cuts the smooth surface of space, tearing apart the false harmony among beings. Mathematical, homogenous space is the principle and receptacle of beings existing side by side, but the being beside the other in dispersion constitutes only a factual coexistence; it is the milieu and place only of a truce, less foundational for a true peace than the expression of an armed neutrality. Homogenous space is the universe of indifference, but the indifference neither resolves nor reconciles differences. It covers and obscures them. It can keep a peace, but one that involves only a precarious and therefore provisional equilibrium. Divisible, homogenous space houses beings located next to one another but deprived of place, of a proper place, they do not fail to spill over into each other, to encroach on the domain of their neighbor.

Things in space do not form an order according to concepts, a system in which different beings are tied to their neighbors, placed in their respective structures. The entities of space constitute an aggregate instead of an organic whole. Instead of being united in a rhythm of articulated multiplicity, they are simply located next to one another. They do not constitute a functional edifice, with floors and rooms, frames and pillars, but a kind of jumble of stones, "without form, without contour, without floor, without ceiling," a heap of bricks and planks, but "no stair, no spiral, no banister."[11] The beings of space do not form a structured society with members each having a role. Their principle of being-together is not an élan, an eidetic trajectory, provided with energy, but a pure *also*. It allows them to be listed in an accidental, contingent order and is, even so, not the source of their ordered distribution. The absence of all true configuration causes things as it were to float along beside one another with a true no man's land among them. The result of this passive and lazy "action" of the "also"

10. Casey, *Fate of Place*, 67.
11. Hugo, *La légende des siècles*, LIV, *La Vision de Dante*, 661.

is that things lie in space without being demarcated by precise limits providing them with a task to accomplish, a meaning for which to exist. Things float, but this does not mean a movement or an action. Things are left floating, an attitude that is the faithful expression of the inertia prevalent in this world. But the inertia of the spatial derived from the absence of determination, the lack of structuration, does not connote simply a condition of passivity. Inertia is only a face of indeterminacy that is also the principle of violence: the floating manifests a deficiency, that of a proper place. But the one deprived of a place will also be led to encroach on his neighbor.

In fact, the floating is not a simple balancing or oscillation with a minimum of displacement, without a true modification of my state. To the degree that I am without proper place (according to the analytic vision of homogenous space) I can continue to be there where I am located only through inertia, by virtue of an accidental play of circumstance. Even if from a topological point of view I subsist in a precise location, I persist in a given place, I am still not attached to a fixed pole or anchored in a supporting and protecting ground. The apparent immobility and fixity of a being in homogenous space is finally only the anticipation of an inevitable displacement. United by the structureless "also," the things of space can only capsize and drift. But unfortunately the drifting does not only mean the loss of an individual's bearings, it also means its spilling over onto others. The entities of space are like drunken boats that sway and keel over. And in keeling over, they always bump and crash into their neighbors. This violent drifting is a faithful expression of the concept-less condition proper to the spatial. The a-conceptual spatial, deprived of its own core that could animate and guide it can be located only outside of itself. The encroachment on others precisely expresses this condition. The spatial being, a piece without structure or face of infinitely divisible space is therefore doomed to spill over and finally to escape itself. This loss of self appears in two forms: the drifting entity can be driven to touch, wound or drown its neighbor, but it can also attempt to enslave or replace it. And it is this second possibility of the Analytic Regime that proves to be particularly mortifying and perverse.

These unstable entities are as if lost in space: their incapacity to find a proper place to stop and to affix themselves manifests itself as a mistake that leads to a lie. Tossed about in the empty and sterile extension, disequilibrious and confused beings are seized by vertigo and darkly think that it is the fault of their neighbor that condemns them to this wandering. Unarticulated space is deprived of light; it is an opaque world of shadows where "each figure says to the other that he is bad, that he is hostile to him and the cause of his anxiety. Each thinks to himself: if the other did not exist, I would have peace and yet each one is wicked and false."[12] Each of these spatial beings thinks that "hell is other people" and that the other is the source of his misery. He will try to rebuff him, to wound and annihilate him. Not finding his place, he is convinced that the other has usurped him and yet again he tries to take it back.

12. Boehme, *Sex Puncta Theosophica* IX 2.

War

Unorganized, unarticulated space, principle of violence and conflict, is a glimmer of Chaos. After Aristotle, philosophy tried to understand chaos as empty space. Empty space can welcome or accommodate all kinds of entities, but if it houses them, it nevertheless contributes nothing to their structuration and organization. Well to the contrary, passive and apathetic towards the things they contain, it becomes the principle of disorder to the things it contains, principle of the disorder that prevails among them. In fact, "emptiness" is far too neutral and placid to characterize this sui generis principle of confusion. It is glimpsed as an external and primordial "darkness," a receptacle for disoriented beings that in their wandering and drifting must crash into their neighbors. But this inevitability of discord and conflict causes to appear the spatial as a world without law, and consequently, as matrix of conflict and war.

The void of chaos has its truth in indeterminacy, confusion, and in the disorder of its inhabitants, a disorder finally revealed as hostility. Jung spoke of chaos as the world of "inimitia elemontorum": the indifference proper to the spatial is the germ of conflict.[13] Homogenous space is that of an undivided state that ignores the pretension of the individual to an area, a region of its own. The naïve apology for a primordial time sings the praises of an epoch where no land is fenced, no pastureland delimited. In this happy time—or rather within this blessed space—beings were not yet folded back onto themselves, they did not timorously occupy any fragment of land, and were not constantly on guard against external threats, haunted by premonitions of an aggression that would prejudice the integrity of their sphere. They did not covet with greed and envy the possessions of their neighbors. And this for the good reason that for them "one's own" did not exist. In reality, however, if the primitive undividedness implies the community of goods, it signifies also and above all the absence of difference between mine and yours, mine and his. It less signifies the peaceful enjoyment of shared goods and more the absence of safeguards before the explosion of personal lust, the overflow of ambitions without hindrance, pillaging and slavery of anything that one could capture, the occupation of another's place, the confiscation of things by which he draws his subsistence. "Before" the primitive Contract that founds private property "there is nothing to which man has a right."[14] If each has a right to all, this is because nobody has exclusive ownership of anything.

To have nothing of one's own signifies anarchy where no possession is sure: the bogus freedom of sharing everything actually leads to a situation where nothing is guaranteed to anyone. A system in which all possessions are absolutely shared has never been and never will be seen. Tools and toys, tables and furniture, or even the family house itself are usually removed from collective ownership, even in the most collectivist systems. Yet a still incomplete realization of homogeneity-equality is

---

13. Jung, *Mysterum Coniunctionis* 2, 143.
14. Hobbes, *Leviathan*, cap. 13, in *English Works of Thomas Hobbes* III, 118.

enough to derail the social machine. In fact the abolition of private property from the essential tools of production and distribution already entails that instead of acquisition and serene enjoyment of necessary goods there is shortage. A socio-economic regime in which one does not work for oneself, where individual efforts of industry do not end in our own enrichment but only in the enlargement of the common good, inevitably turns into an ineffective accomplishment, and not only for technical, empirical reasons. Exclusivity of property seems to be the condition sine qua non of a well functioning economy. Economy is based on exchange and one cannot exchange, that is, transfer ownership of what does not exclusively belong to him. It is very unfortunate, however, that the unconditional principle of exclusive private property and the effective or at least virtual access of all men to property—aside any moral or political consideration—does not yet suffice to guarantee effective and equitable distribution of goods. Forebodings of a general ecological crisis reveal the insufficiency and exhaustibility of our planet's resources. Yet if the primary materials and energies of the universe are not infinite but show themselves to be limited, the reasons or *the* reason is not found on the empirical plane. Common sense may seem the most shared thing in the world, but the goods of this world can never be appropriately shared. They are insufficient and their insufficiency is not only a matter of quantitative deficiency. One can certainly try to enumerate what is now lacking and may be lacking in the future but this general and inevitable deficiency has metaphysical roots. If no regime of production ensures a perfect procurement for everyone and if no system of distribution protects us from lack, this is because even if they move away from one another, humans will never have enough space. The spectacular multiplication of consumable goods will never abolish poverty and shortages. Said differently, space in the peaceful homogenous sense is under the law of Rarity.

In this application to the spatial, the category of rarity of Sartrean origin manifests the impossibility that indifferent, infinitely divisible space can guarantee the autonomy and integrity of the beings it houses within. This spatial (and temporal) world is the universe of rarity where independently of the extension of his sphere, of the value of his possessions but also of the excellence of his talents, one is capable of realizing himself only at the expense of his neighbor. We are commanded to love our neighbor, but unfortunately this love is opposed to nature and contradicts our primitive inclinations. In his primeval condition, the human being encroaches on his neighbor. Homogenous space lacks the principle of structuration that would assign each his place, imparting to each his own possessions and perfections in order to safeguard himself. Jealousy and envy most often experienced towards one's neighbor are a function of the perverse homogeneity of space that behind the mask of faultless equality and of a just and peaceful neutrality proves to be a sinister indigence. Pure space offers us nothing by which we may guarantee our autonomy and protect our security. Well to the contrary, instead of attributing to the inhabitants of the earth a proper place, instead of providing them with a face, a proper physiognomy, it condemns them to vegetate in a space of deadly indeterminacy. Unable to assert myself securely in a place of my own, unable to point to a precinct where I dwell, incapable of drawing my face with its own figure, I can possess much, but I can never possess enough, I will be happy to stay somewhere but I will never feel secure.

Rarity is the somber truth of finite existence, the hard law that limits and frames being-with, the being-together of men. "Narrow is the world and *wide* is the mind"—says the poet: "Thoughts gently rub/But things harshly crash in space/Where one occupies a place the other must withdraw/Who does not want to be chased must chase another."[15] A legion of angels easily sits on the point of a pin, but for men to coexist in the same space each has to retreat into a lesser space than what corresponds to his needs, talents, and merits. Rarity reveals and attests to the complexity of the spatial order. It is clearly seen that the false homogeneity is condemned to failure: indifference engenders difference; neutrality engenders conflict. Yet even the most energetic critique and bracketing of indifference is not enough to eradicate scarcity, envious competition, and mortal jealousy. Rarity signals the end of a fantasy, that of the peaceful homogeneity of space, but it forcefully illustrates the survival of an unwavering opposition. Continuity turned into discontinuity is supposed to eliminate the floating, halt the drifting, and prevent the encroachment. Said differently, the spatial would be cured of its tendency to destruction through its fixation on place and form. But unfortunately the fixation is always incomplete and (above all) provisional. The alterity and exteriority proper to the spatial as such cannot be abolished. The intrinsic weakness and tight limits of this enterprise of limitation of the unlimited is manifest in war.

The rarity that is the source of the encroachment on the other, on others, is not ultimately a moment of quantitative essence, it is manifest only partially in a physical register. It not only inspires fear of the absence of objects, of materials and gold but is also, and above all, the violent desire to dominate and surpass the other. In fact rarity is witness to a forever unsatisfied aspiration: we always desire more than we posses and we desire to have what we do not, or rather, to be what we are not. Unlimited, space encourages, even favors this smooth overflow without relief and cracks. War is the supreme moment of that drifting, the truth of which is aggression. War is a continual and immemorial phenomenon of the human condition; it appears to be anticipated in the animal world and is also attributed to the gods. Despite the elementary violence of its events and actions, despite its unlimited nature, war is a composite reality, an incongruous *synthesis* of indifference and difference, an ambiguous quest of a self-surpassing immanent to the spatial. The proximate causes that make war break out can doubtlessly be very different: war is waged in order to abduct the spouse of a king or to assassinate an heir to a throne, to annex a city or to prohibit pilgrimage. We are obliged to initiate a conflict for reasons of prestige, for objective economic reasons, or in virtue of ideological preoccupations, but essentially, war always turns around

---

15. Schiller, *Wallensteins Tod* II, 2. *Sämtliche Werke* II, 435.

questions of "Territory."[16] A great dose of violence, more or less gratuitous, doubtlessly motivates the initiation and continuation of conflicts, but its intentional object is territory, a portion of space to defend and conquer.

Territory is a part, a portion of space, a given piece, delimited as such, and seems opposed to the pernicious homogeneity of mathematical, homogenous space. However, the phenomenological essence, *territory*, shows the ambiguity and complexity of the spatial. The attribution of a given territory, the enjoyment of a portion of space, formed and molded by history, the possession of a territory recognized by other States as proper to a State is only imperfectly and temporarily sufficient to assure peace. Territory is a synthesis of the unlimited and the limit, and yet it is a dubious, precarious, even incongruous synthesis. Its telos is the appeasement of desires and above all the guarantee for a community of men that they may possess a place to fill up, a domain to make fruitful. Territory is supposed to be the portion of space where a human community, a nation can realize its natural tendency to stretch out and extend itself, giving free course to its innate drive to expand. And this in well-defined and clear limits—consequently not encroaching on its neighbor's sphere, and without prejudice against their rights. Unfortunately, if territory is the necessary spatial form of a State, if it is the unique possibility for taming the savagery of space, in order to give an articulatory limit to homogeneity, it is also the occasion and principle reason causing neutral indifference inevitably to slide into chaos and war.

War for a territory has two essential moments or components: the persistence of the unlimited within the limited and the imperfection, deficiency of limitation. Territory is supposed to have put an end to the infinite extension-expansion of homogenous space, but the deadly indifference like rarity continues to cast its large shadow over all. War lies in wait, always threatens because the however imperfect articulation of space by territory cannot withstand the violent current of expansion. The truth of indifference is not the peaceful and smooth reception of contents, but a space of craving. One has certainly received a territory furnishing a vital space, but the *Lebensraum* belongs naturally to expansion. One possesses a domain, an area, a territory, but one always wants to possess more. The true motivation of war is the desire for expansion. How to subject that to a limit? In other words, across and beyond its territory, a State harbors a desire, a more or less hidden but never extinguished or satisfied lust to occupy additional territory, to enlarge itself. The persistence of the desire for expansion, notwithstanding the limitation-articulation in territory, shows the irrepressible survival of the craving that is the hidden truth of Homogeneity, the profound nature of the Analytical, but it also refers to the defects and malfunctions of limitation. States are guided by a voiceless and violent desire to expand in space and this diffuse craving converts into a desire for expansion that motivates the acute feeling of the inadequacy of one's territory. The apparently infinite and indefinite impulses to expand, to conquer other territories receives a rational formulation, a conceptual

---

16. Ardrey, *The Territorial Imperative*.

justification starting from comprehension of the fact that the limitation leading to the establishment and delimitation of my territory from that of others is not "just," is not "correct." To speak in Hegelian terms, the territories of States are not conformed to their concept.

The non-conformity signifies that what I presently possess, my present public territory does not truly correspond to my concept and that the territory of the other, my neighbor does not correspond to his. War is the rectification by violence of an inadequacy that is felt, then affirmed and spelled out on the conceptual level. War is commonly seen as the attack of one State on another and consequently as an overflowing, a unilateral outpouring. In reality, the overflow is not so unilateral. If, empirically, and from a chronological point of view, the overflow of A onto the territory of B triggers hostilities, thus provoking conflicts on the metaphysical plane, the overflowing of warfare is bilateral. More precisely, it is the potential or actual act of all the inhabitants of space. The sally of Francis I is well known: my brother Charles and I want the same thing: Milan. France covets the possession of the great Italian city that the Empire also covets. But France and its king are only particularly striking singular instances of the drifting that lies in wait for spatial entities. Every being and, a fortiori, every State aspires to possess a part or the totality of other States, and thus territory is never but a fragile and provisional compromise between the unlimited and the limited. In other words the phenomenological essence "territory" exemplifies and incarnates the ambiguities proper to attempts to articulate the noxious homogeneity of Space, the difficulties encountered by attempts to think the moments of the spatial order.

VII

Spatial Eidē

Beyond Homogeneity

The vision of space as an area, an atmosphere, a homogenous milieu, infinitely divisible, and neutral leads to encroachment, conflict, and war. And it leads to war even when the infinity of homogenous extension is limited, when space is subsumed under territory. Territory cannot pacify the bellicose nature of the spatial: it is a determination of space but a merely quantitative one that does not permit it to transcend its analytic condition. But the solely analytic articulation of the spatial is not only principle and source of catastrophe and conflict, it is more simply deficient as well as insufficient from the metaphysical point of view. Homogeneity is not an essential attribute of space as such; homogenous space is not the whole of what space is. "Objective" and "isotropic" space doubtlessly remains a necessary reference and salutary corrective to any reflection on the spatial, but it constitutes only a kind of preamble because it cannot be developed and unfolded in order to found a spatial eidetics. The temporal unfolds the given as changing, mobile and variable, whereas the spatial exposes it as heterogeneous, even contrasted to it (William James). But the heterogeneous and the contrasted are principles, or rather premises of an eidetic regime that stands out against the uniformity of extension glimpsed under the primacy of homogeneity, in the occurrence of quantity.

Philosophical reflection can take three paths in order to establish the eidetic regime proper to the spatial. The first path is the most traditional: instead of formulating and enumerating eidē, properly so called, the spatial is articulated according to determinations that remain confined in the world of material essences. One meditates on the differences of our perception of visible space, between night space and daytime space. Here the spatiality of specific colors is described. The pitfalls of the vision of quantitative homogeneity are certainly avoided but one does not yet conceive spatial eidē properly. The second path begins with a principle of opposition within space in general, between total space and its partial moments. Said differently: the emergence of locality perhaps place and form are envisaged as moments, determinations standing out against the background of an unlimited, or rather indeterminate extension. Finally, the proper system of spatial eidē is installed, directions and dimensions are unfolded starting from a center implicitly or explicitly posed. Directions and dimensions constitute, as it were, the "logic" of space, and the multitude of anthropological significations of the spatial open up here, as well as the moral bearing of reflection and meditation on space.

Space and Color

Understanding the dangers and deficiencies of a purely quantitative conception of space leads philosophy to a more profound articulation, to qualitative determinations of the spatial. One is no longer content with the domestication of the *chora* by homogeneity, but conceives, so to speak, variations of a single space. Reflection appeals here to resources of vision. More precisely, instead of leaving space to float or shiver in an indeterminate grey, it is thought in terms of color. Lines and contours in painting are faded or effaced; they seem even to disappear: differentiation is provided by colors. A painting is a collection of spots that divide up pictorial space. Of course, if color is the supreme milieu of the pictorial; it is no less an essential factor of the natural and artificial universe. Without being moments of space in themselves, colors have an impact on our perception of space. Bright colors make a room seem larger; dark colors constrict a room, making it feel cramped. It is not necessary to take color as a properly spatial category: even if all red objects are square and all square objects red, this does not yet mean that red is equal to square. In fact, differentiation by color is only a secondary phenomenon, almost peripheral to spatial analysis. After all, colors are only material essences: they give a corrective to the purely quantitative reading of the spatial, but do not yet constitute authentic instances of the eidetics of space. Things are different for the diurnal or nocturnal phenomena of space, which are no longer particular material quale but seem to "cling" more faithfully to space in its continuity of unlimited extension.

In fact, it is nocturnal space that holds the greatest eidetic promises. Daytime space reflects homogenous space, imitating or rather doubling homogeneity in its own way. Daytime space is continuous, fully transparent, and visible. It does not contain any hidden pits, snares, or abysses, and it does not impede the progression of movement or gaze. Bright space is a space with other people, a domain of co-existence, even conviviality. It is a context of exchanges, a place of encounters. As homogenous-mathematical space, it is the receptacle of beings, but adds to the pure passivity of reception a dimension of active accommodation. Diurnal space constitutes a subtle variant of emptiness, which is one of the faces or essential aspects of objective space.

Or rather, it attests that the absence of contents, of determined entities within it, does not yet jeopardize the density proper to the spatial. But this immanent, essential density shows itself in a most striking way in nocturnal space. The dark space of the night is not empty; it is full of obscurities that are its own proper content. Nightfall is announced by twilight. But twilight where colors are effaced, or rather fall into indistinction, is not empty—an absence, a non being—but something material that seizes and carries us. Nocturnal space is more material, more *stofflich* than the light of day: it blurs and limits my vision, it almost adheres to my members, to my body, it weighs heavily on me and slows down or obstructs my progress. In short it prohibits me from moving about freely. I am, as it were, locked inside it, mixed with it. This space appears to possess no other dimension than depth: it is layerless, without strata or degree. Nocturnal space is not entirely deprived of clarity but the few lights glowing there are indistinct, situated at no determined distance. Even more, beyond the indistinctness within its sphere, nocturnal space, without being truly closed or locked, registers a inexorable lack of any completion: it is without horizon or perspective. It provides an image, a startling reflection of homogenous *spatium* in its native undifferentiation. Like objective, mathematical space, nocturnal space is also unlimited but possesses no direction at all. It is, so to speak, the reflection in the finite of the indeterminacy of the grand continuum of infiite space.

The light and the dark, diurnal and nocturnal are instances of the doubling of space, particular shadows of the formal universality of the spatial. Light and dark are also samples of material essences without, however, constituting true instances of structuration. Like dark space, bright space is an obedient ectype, without relief or escarpment, without the structure and limitation of objective space. They inaugurate an entire series of phenomena that qualify space through determinations that yet remain universal and featureless. Fog and snow are these phenomena in which the spatial is explicated by concrete universals that are material without being essences properly so called. Fog and snow enjoy a noetic proximity to light and dark but also register an authentic eidetic autonomy. They present spatial phenomena, or rather, worlds, deprived of borders and directions. Without being manifestations of confusion, they are nevertheless principle and source of an absence or loss of orientation. If in the dark night the voyager is led astray, in the fog and snow he is paralyzed, brought to a stop. The fog makes things lose their determined contours; things escape into the elusiveness and end up assuming a disquieting, threatening aspect. Fog surrounds and envelops beings on all sides and thus separates them, making them distant from one another. "It is strange to wander in the fog—Every bush and rock is solitary—No tree sees another—All are alone."[1] Fog disorients us by enveloping us and separating us from other beings, whereas the snow makes us lose the path through the abolition of distinctions. Snow is a fullness of light that is fatal for the visibility of things. The immaculate whiteness of the blanket of snow covering the ground possesses a clarity

---

1. Hesse, *Im Nebel*, in Bollnow, *Mensch und Raum*, 187.

that is too bright. It obliterates and dissolves every difference, especially that of the high and the low, heaven and earth.

Figure and Place

Dark and light, fog and snow are types of space; they are "spaces" that adhere to Space and if they reflect and represent it, they do not yet represent the true eidetic forms of the spatial. If eidetics is more than a doctrine of essence, this is because the world of eidē is larger than the qualitative universe, even when qualitative is understood according to a formal universality. If colors play an important role in the perception of space, they are always only material essences. By appealing to nocturnal and diurnal space, it seems that we have been able to surpass the "qualitative" sensu stricto: the brightness of the day and the darkness of the night are not only colors—and this not by virtue of the infra- or supra-colored condition of darkness and light. The diurnal and nocturnal are like components, essential ingredients of atmospheric, climatic moments and also of cultures and even cults. Yet the atmospheric and climatic, the cultural and cultic can be found in another register: even so they do not belong to the spatial and consequently they cannot work as principles of the eidetic articulation of the *spatium*. These are the same considerations that relativize or bracket the far too simple discourse on a plurality of spaces. Many revel in multiplying spaces with a tidy, specific consistency. Oneiric space is studied next to and in opposition to the space of "normal" perception, the space of the dancer is envisaged as different from that of the member of the orchestra. Sacred space is supposed to contrast sharply with profane space. Primitive space is assigned certain prerogatives as a truly anomalous system before the sober and utilitarian, petty and prosaic spatiality of the universe of transport networks and trade. We certainly cannot deny the effective diversity of our systems of spatial perception: we feel and sense that we live in the middle of spaces that interlock and are tangled up with one another. Ultimately, however, they are truly a function of principles of articulation that do not fall under the *spatium* as such.

Only the analysis of the spatial in itself leads to the establishment of an eidetics of space. The spatial seems to consist of two manners of intrinsic structuration. The first travels the paths where space divides itself, the other examines the moments where it is articulated in and through itself. The immanent articulation of the spatial is realized in the universe of direction and dimension, and which constitutes the most rigorously authentic part of a spatial eidetics. The idea of an immanent, intrinsic division of space represents massive progress over the infinite divisibility of homogenous space. The sui generis specificity of the spatial has nothing to do with the quantitative division where space suffers the totally external influence of quantity. Space is not divided into portions where "more" or "less" represent only external variations imposed on an indistinct matter. Space is certainly divisible, capable of being split up, but it is not a matter of dissecting a homogenous continuum into pieces of the same nature, or of cutting into pieces a noetically undifferentiated mass. Space must undergo a division leading to the discernment of truly different parts. The intrinsic division-differentiation of the spatial is done according to magnitude, form and locality. At first glance, magnitude seems to belong to quantitative considerations that one would like to avoid but as we will see later, with analyses accomplished at the very heart of the auto-articulation of the eidetic, in its truth spatial magnitude is not a category of quantity but a descriptive, morphological concept. But form and locality are the truly essential categories of the auto-division of the spatial, the intentional objects of a properly eidetic conception of the division of space, of the demarcation of its parts. Form denotes the phenomenon of the construction of an entity within space, starting from the spatiality of space. Place indicates the demarcation that space unfolds starting from itself, the determination that permits the reception of forms.

The efforts of modern philosophy to break from the external visions of the forms of sensibility in order to recognize time and space as sui generis eidetic principles constitute attempts to rethink the vulgar vision of a filled receptacle, of time as a receptacle of points-instants and space as receptacle of atoms. To overcome the unfortunate picture of the filling of a container, a completely external and poorly articulated process of the installation of entities within it, the successive dispersion that is time will be conceived as duration while the dispersion into the simultaneity that constitutes space will be seen as the establishment of forms. Form is the most general notion to designate the entities contained in space. Yet if "form" is an elementary category of our thought of space, it no less registers a native ambiguity. Form can be related to and is truly related to all material entities, to all beings contained in space, but in and through itself before any application it denotes only a proper moment of the spatial. Forms sensu stricto are geometrical forms, planar or tridimensional, but form is inevitably also attributed to entities that shelter space. Phenomenology distinguishes aspect and position, two givens proper to every perceived being, but if position preserves spatiality in its immaculate purity, the spatiality of the aspect is unfolded according to a system of compromise. The form is first and above all a spatial moment, the sui generis moment of the auto-division of space, but surreptitiously and inevitably, as Aspect, it registers a collusion with the material, the qualitative. In its primitive truth, form is a manner of self-division practiced by space but in each effective instance of this partition, the part or portion assumes a determination of the qualitative order.

Notwithstanding the compromise between the spatial and qualitative that quasi-generally prevails in its concrete examples, form is truly an authentic theme of spatial eidetics. Form means the external determination of a thing, the more or less defined aspect of an entity, a silhouette that clearly stands out against the horizon but which, as such, seems to lack precision or rather detail. Indeed, its condition of exteriority and schematic generality that skips over the details confirms and corroborates the designation of form as proper category of the spatial. It is a matter of determination, but of one that appears and emerges external to a thing and which represents the whole, or rather, the contours of an entity. More simply, it represents "the relation between the extremities of a body."[2] It is a determination not equivalent to a general structure of an entity or a form in the Aristotelian and Scholastic sense, namely, a formula for the essence, a bond holding accidents together, a thread for predicates. It is therefore a determination that does not belong to the qualitative register. As for the absence of precise articulation—this self-donation that, without being vague or effaced, passing over the details in order to present itself in "its general contours"—it too witnesses to the native independence of the form in relation to quality, to the material moments of its condition as Aspect. Exteriority and general determination, lacking details, play an important role in understanding the spatial truth of the form, but this takes shape above all through the metaphysical distance separating it from the Image.

Form seems to belong to the same universe as the physiognomy and morphology of the Image, but the image is a category of attribution while form belongs to the order of description. Evidently the image also is an object of description, but description is not sufficient to establish it. We have certainly seen the complexity of the relationship between the image-ectype and its archetype. However, if on the metaphysical plane the Image can be thought of as having cut the umbilical cord tying it to its "original," then according to its phenomenological truth, it always contains a reference to. . . If it is not a reproduction of something else then it is a self-presentation, an auto-figuration. But form reproduces nothing; it symbolizes nothing, neither something other nor itself. The form is a silhouette without any return to something beyond, outside or within it. It harbors no meaning beyond, outside or within itself. Form is no longer a signification: it is evident, perhaps perceived and thought, but it signifies nothing. It is not a reference to another or correlate of a counterpart. But it is a supreme instance of an autonomous intelligibility, to wit, of spatial intelligibility.

Form is a category of spatialization where the spatial submits to an external determination or to a division that is eo ipso differentiation. However, the locality and in its train, place, position, and situation are notions belonging to the spatiality of space as extended. If form is an entity standing out against the background of extension, the locality is a portioned and parceled-out reality. Forms are clearly something other than space whereas localities are spaces within Space, little spaces within large space. Yet to call locality a little space does not amount to a quantitative qualification. Locality is doubtlessly a measurable, quantifiable part of Space, but its vocation is not simply about cutting and dividing up space. Locality is instead the elementary auto-criticism of extended-space, the positive censure that it exercises on itself. Locality undermines so to say the internal homogeneity of space. It is the simplest, the most elementary manifestation of its potentiality to give birth to a multiplicity where the extended exists and subsists according to principles other than that of pure and naked extension.

2. Locke, *Essay Concerning Human Understanding* II, xiii, 168n.

Book Two—Eidetics

The beginning or more precisely the principle, the root of locality is the *here*, which is the most elementary moment of space. Like site, it is a little space, with a littleness without quantitative implication. It is the first appearance of the site, the rudimentary beginning of its genesis. Or rather, it is a non-consolidated site, evanescent because incomplete. It is tempting to consider the here as a point in space, but this analogy is dubious and in fact erroneous. The point is part of a quantitative continuum, an elementary part of extension, but it is itself without any extension. It is ultimately a simple abstraction. However, the here in its precariousness and indigence is already something actual. It is the first manifestation of the sui generis reality of the *spatium*, a result of a distribution that is also a direction. By contrast to the point, an intentional object of an analytical judgment, the here is conceived only as the signified of a synthetic judgment, the end of an élan, a movement, a projection. Form can still show itself to be non-intuitionable, imperceptible, without association with quality, whereas the here is an instance of the spatial alone, its first pure and naked instance. The misunderstanding that assimilates the here to the point is dissipated when one understands its condition of return that is both the principle of authentic spatiality and source of its indigence. The here can be glimpsed only by virtue of the comprehension of space according to its spatiality. It does not appear through cutting a quantitative mass but starting from the intuition of a continuity with a center. Already in itself, a here is a center, a center in the measure where it results from an elementary and primitive distribution of space "around" an entity, an activity, a function. But deeper reflection will understand that the here, that each here, despite their apparent autonomy, is a function of a "common" center. More precisely, the here is the first manifestation of the auto-distributive condition of space that establishes its moments through a synthetic link with other moments. But in addition to this elementary rooting in a common referent, the here also bears a fundamental native relation to another center that is particular and lateral like itself. Considered in itself, as such, the here is only an abstract difference, or even something absolutely impermanent because provisional. Space stops for an infinitesimal moment in the here, but a here receives its consolidation only from another here that conserves it as a *there*. In fact the here is never only in itself but always a function of a there that is its correlate and its contrary. The there is located at a certain distance from here, it is separated by a gap that is like a permanent critique of the here but also a permanent invitation to go to its there addressed to it. The there seems second in relation to the here; it implies a distance to be crossed. But this secondarity that suggests a condition of ulteriority has its own metaphysical originarity. As the *you* "follows" the *I*, the there can seem to happen "after" the here, being located at the end of a path taken by the here. However, as the *you*—notwithstanding its secondarity—takes part of the very being of the *I*, the metaphysical (and physical) reality of the here implies the there.

The here and the there are inseparable. They constitute an effective part of space, but not of truly extended space. A line rushes from here to there; it can retrace its steps or miss its end and wander. The here has its truth in the there and the there obtains the heart of the here, but the reality of this reciprocal implication is very meager. A certain difference is definitely registered in relation to quantitative divisibility, but its condition as a line causes the here-there couple to be an itinerant, not a habitant or resident of space. The auto-division of anticipated space begun by the here-there finds its realization in locality, which is the truth of space. In its absence the *spatium* overflows, bursts and consequently returns to dispersion. The site, the "universal here as such,"[3] actualizes the eidetic telos of the here, consolidates the unsubstantial couple of the here and there and thus permits the realization of the auto-division of space: locality will not only be a portion but a true condensation. Locality is a part of space according to its truth of distribution-orientation. It should be thought of as starting from a center, and it too constitutes a center, one that extends out but which is not simple extension. Locality appears thus as a supreme example of the spatial in its eidetic truth. Yet a reinterpretation of "site" will relativize the purity and integrity of this eidos. The iteration of the here towards the there and from the there towards here seems to imply a minimum of temporal dimensionality: the here is not yet there and in order to reach it there must be time or at least a metaphysical prefiguration of temporality. Yet the locality that occupies a place not only needs time in order to extend itself and spread out in the portion of extension reserved for it, it also needs to remain there, to continue and endure there.

The intuition of a temporal or rather para-temporal component of locality, "calm identity of space and time,"[4] means that if locality is an effective moment of the auto-division of space and therefore an authentic category of the spatial, it is no less exempt from a certain native heterogeneity. Time seems to be a metaphysical element of the advent of locality and this genetic, heterogeneous moment could be at the origin of the inevitable compromises with quality. Locality is a properly spatial moment of space, an instance of its auto-division. But locality is not only part of space as space, it is also the principle of reception of form. Form characterizes the auto-division of space giving birth to entities, and locality also stems from the auto-division of space and receives form. Sensu stricto, this doubtlessly does not yet compromise the pure spatiality of locality: locality could be considered as the auto-division of the spatial encountering and containing its structuring content, form. In reality, however, the acceptation of form does not stop at form as such. Locality is always understood as the location of something or someone: a battle site, a place where a family house is located, a place where lovers meet. There are holy places and places that exude terror, secluded, lonely places, and others where the spirit of the age seems present and active. A locality is always the locality of something, but it carries a necessary reference to an extra-spatial component that seems to constitute it as such: locality is simply a space detached from Space while an area is qualified. But this qualification is not necessarily

   3. Hegel, *Encyclopédie* II, § 261, Add. 364.
   4. Ibid., § 261, 201.

an articulation in terms of "quality." More precisely, if locality seems to share the condition of form by registering an apparent collusion with material essences, deeper analysis reinforces instead our understanding of the *locus* as an authentic instance of the auto-articulation of the spatial.

Locality is quasi-synonymous with "place," but if "locality" seems to denote a part of space that receives and takes in a form or quality, then in the eidos "place" the relation-reference of this content is different. Locality is certainly the locality of a person or thing, but the entity it contains seems to suffer rather than produce its situation. A locality is assigned or allocated to the being it contains. It surrounds it on all sides, yet this being, if most often located close to the center of the locale, is still not the active organizational principle for the space that shelters it. Yet "place" registers a strong connotation of belonging: beings have their place; they can cede their place or take the place of another. A space saved for someone in the theater will be lost if he is late. This strong emphasis on the belonging of place to a being corresponds to a properly spatial relation, not to the quantitative order. A part of space is my place, not because I am located there but because it is from me, my physical situation, my body that the links of force and orientation begin to tear out this fragment of extension from Space. Locality finds its realization, its metaphysical accomplishment in "place": place is truly the locality of an entity, but this entity is not simply encompassed by and preserved within it. Place is also principle and source of organization, the structuration of space, of the distribution of Space into spaces. The genesis of locality-place starting from the entity located at its center completes the presentation of the auto-division of space. This auto-division is not a simple quantitative partition or even a cutting up of Space into a multiplicity of parts in terms of their material quiddities. The entity contained by the locality "produces" this site: through its central location it is the principle and source of the place surrounding it and that it penetrates and dominates. Space is therefore effectively divided in terms of the spatial by virtue of the thing found at its center. In other words, if this elementary moment of space that is locality appears ultimately as differentiating according to material essences, the truth of this difference is not qualitative but spatial. . .

We still have to revisit the relation of the spatial to the quantitative. If the category of locality is unfolded without reference to the quantitative, when it is called "place" one cannot bracket the native quantitative component of extension. Locality is only able to be a spatial moment resistant to measure, place always implies measurable extension, or at least something that is too much or enough, excessive or sufficient. In other words, as in the philosophy of time, it does not overlook measure. Spatial noetics, while critiquing the attempts to mathematize the spatial, must take note of the ultimate indissociability of the quantum from the *spatium*. Of course, the quantitative has only a secondary role: it is subordinated to the spatial and only, as it were, a concomitant factor. This is very well seen in the eidos "place." Place is the name of locality when it is a matter of emphasizing the constitution of this part of space starting from a center, principle, and source of organization and distribution. But this is not a center in the mathematical sense, equally distant from every point in the periphery. The center is not defined in mathematical terms, which would lead us back into the conception of abstract homogeneity. It is instead the moving nucleus, the dynamic node of forces and directions that extend and project a space, and it performs these actions by assigning to them limits, borders. One can doubtlessly measure the permanent or temporary distance between the center and periphery, which is the principle of site, constituting its distance from itself, but if this distance is susceptible to measurement, it still does not express a relation that belongs to the order of extension.

Extension and Expansion

Space possesses a proper eidetic that articulates its manner of being specific. Analogously to the Heideggerian discourse on time that is not, but which temporalizes itself, we could say that space is not but spatializes itself. Spatialization is the unfolding of an intelligibility that expresses the auto-articulation of the specific mode of being of space. Kant defined space as "an infinite given magnitude" (*Critique* B 39). This infinity is not related to quantity and has nothing to do with the condition of measurable being. Instead it indicates an unfinished state, an incompleteness. Space is not a *compositum* but a *totum*: it is not the sum of thinkable or given unities; it is neither a collection nor aggregate of elements. It is a very peculiar totality. Space can be cordoned, sectioned off, but the elements that result from this division have no autonomy: provisionally, or rather artificially separated, they expect only to fall back into the whole. But if the division of space is such an infertile, even pernicious procedure, this is because the sectioning of the *spatium* cannot be conceived as practiced on a body with firm contours, on a complete reality. Space—like time—is "an incomplete whole."[5] It is therefore something open. And the opening that signifies this incompleteness implies an invitation to go further, to go towards another.

Traditionally, beings in space are designated as *res extensa* and space itself as *extensio*. But here a phenomenological reading could avoid the impasses and pitfalls of the ancient consensus. To define space in terms of extension seems nearly self-evident, and yet it is an insufficient and erroneous definition. Extension is rather the expansion of a quality. For example, an extension of whiteness is found in milk, of darkness in ground poppy seeds. In other words that which is "extended" is a quality and thus a material essence. But the eidē of space are not material essences. Extension as diffusion of a quality and thus finally a homogeneity only perpetuates and illustrates an analytic conception of the spatial, while here also one should seek the enlargement of the eidetic in the direction of the synthesis a priori. Instead of extension, *diffusion* is the term that seems most apt to translate the mode of being of the

---

5. Gent, *Die Philosophie des Raumes und der Zeit II*, 347.

spatial. Diffusion expresses a certain autonomy of the spatial while extension carries a dominant accent of passivity and heteronomy. The being, or being that is extended slackens, it allows itself to flow. It certainly spreads into the terrain, domain, or locality where it is extended, but this is a gain that does not stem from an internal center and, above all, that constitutes a process where nothing new happens: neither stepping nor leaping over a distance, nor a decision to go in the direction of another and thus no election of a direction. Expansion powerfully registers an active profile. It is an irresistible progression that especially accomplishes the new to the very degree that it emanates from a proper center. Extension seems properly to integrate flat surfaces in horizontal continuity with its point of departure or even rushes down hills according to the respective slope of the sites that it traverses. Expansion certainly seems to prefer the horizontal and it unproblematically undertakes a descent, but it also even possesses an aptitude or native aspiration to surmount obstacles to go against the grain or towards the above.

Expansion is opening and as such it prefigures in its own way the a priori synthesis. The a priori synthesis is always a mediation between A and B that implies the bridging of a gap, the resolution of a difference. The spatializing progression passes beyond the continuities of the homogenous and breaks with the monotony of analytic repetition. But this is possible only on the condition that an effectively different end is aimed for, other than the self. Yet according to its primitive phenomenological truth, diffusion is the source and spring of exploits and accomplishments, but which can appear more like the elements and steps of an advance of the Same than the moments of a path leading to another. Expansion seems to reject forcefully the slippery continuity of Analysis, but is it not ultimately only a more vehement, passionate variant of extension? The path of expansion is fraught with danger or rather thin of vanquished obstacles, but has this effective progression truly reached the status and condition of an analog to History? Expansion certainly registers a notable difference from extension, but does it not measure the depths of the same metaphysical condition as extension, albeit doomed to public contempt, burdened with the impenitent form of homogeneity?

The purpose of the discourse that detaches and differentiates expansion from extension is to found the sui generis metaphysical condition of spatial eidetics. But this is possible only if one manages to extract a proper phenomenological essence from expansion that is irreducible to analytic homogeneity, an eidos of expansion definable in purely spatial terms, without any dependence on heteronomous considerations. The curve represents the supreme eidetic instance of a spatial uncontaminated by quantity.

Curves

The curvature of space is the principle-prefiguration of curves. It eloquently attests to the irreducibility of the spatial to continuities that would involve the analytic homogeneity and the condition of being measurable, and therefore subject to quantity. Curved lines are perhaps the purest instances of the spatial, of the proper, specific moments of spatialization. Contrary to the straight line constituting the shortest distance between two points, the line drawing sinuous twists and turns displays a sovereign independence in relation to any moment, every extra-spatial element. The curve is an ambulant whole that can certainly be divided up into parts, but complete division of it would be fatal. When the parts of the straight line are of the same nature as the line itself, constituting faithful eidetic samples of it, the portions of a curved line register a difference, a heterogeneity in relation to the curve. The curve is perhaps the first and most authentic instance of the spatialization of space and through its variants it unfolds an entire range of degrees, of *Abschattungen* of this eidos where the spatial structures itself without mixing with material or quantitative ingredients.

The curve, this pure other, this primitive counterpart of the line, translates itself into an entire procession of secondary figures. It can be sinuous and serpentine, or draw zigzags, or take an undulating or spiral-like form. The sinuous line is the most elementary degree of the curve where, recalcitrant to any framework or external structuration, it appears according to a radical irregularity. The sinuous line is an unfolding that neither modulates nor articulates the presence of any law or aspiration to a term: like streams and rivers before going through dike and diversion, like many measures of "rationalization" and "regulation," the sinuous line, the "fluxous" line (da Vinci), draws twists and turns where space happily lives a sovereignly sufficient life.

The sinuous line is the curve still according to its irregular articulation that is a true "irregulation." With the serpentine a certain tendency to regularization appears. A serpentine route indicates curves that are part of a Curve, but it is a less capricious partition than that of partitioned-up sinuous curve. The serpentine illustrates the essential curvature of the curve, but it attests to it and instantiates it through portions that are less divisions than stages. Said differently: if the serpentine does not yet break the integrity proper to the curve, its indivisibility into similar pieces, then it is possible, permissible for it to arrest itself at a given moment of its evolution without breaking up the incomplete whole that it constitutes. The serpentine signifies the first breach endured by the primitive undivided spatiality of the curve, but it does not yet connote its effective partition. This will happen with twists and turns. In their native, indeterminate plurality, twists and turns mark the first sectioning of the curve. They represent a division or rather fragmentation of the curve. They register the irregularity proper to the sinuous but in a more violent way: after all, only a species of primordial violence can take account of the partitioning and the fragmentation that this first figure suffers as space spatializes itself! The relation of twists and turns to the sinuous curve is, moreover, completely original. None of the twists and turns can hold as a shortcut of the curve, unless they register an affinity with portions of the homogenous. However one can consider them as analogs of the sinuous that represent this elementary eidos of the spatial in the dispersion.

The sinuous and serpentine are the two instances of the curve, of the continuous unstructured reality, while twists and turns are rather the unstructured as discontinuous and divided. Yet the vocation of the spatial, its native aspiration remains, despite all, the immanent articulation that appeals to heterogeneous elements. Space does not receive the principles of its articulation but spatializes itself. Undulation and the spiral are the supreme moments of this spatialization where the line-curve manifests its profound potentialities in order to unfold itself from within, in order to diffract the curvature according to a metaphysical progression. They are so to speak mediated by the interlude of the zigzag which, despite its provenance in the world of straight lines, does not slip into the quantitative and remains resistant to homogenization.

The zigzag is so to speak a sample of the straight line, lost in the world of pure spatialization proper to curves. Or rather, it represents the unique occurrence of the line sharing the elementary, original condition where the Line "exists" still anteriorly to any compromise with measure, rejects any vague desire for subsumption under the analytic. The zigzag denotes a movement, a path where broken lines form alternatingly protruding and retracted angles. But if the angle effectively stems from the eidetic universe of lines, the zigzag of which it constitutes a constitutive moment marks above all a decisive step made in the articulation of the line. The unstructured character of the sinuous and the serpentine has ceded place to the plurality of twists and turns, and yet twists and turns do not constitute true structures, they are only simple fragments. The aspiration for articulation breaks the line, which is decomposed into twists and turns. The zigzag will mark the return of the continuous line, but this time under the form of a rough outline of articulation. It must be insisted that it is only a matter of a rough outline because the sequence of different moments composing the zigzag obey no regularity. They say drunks walk in zigzags, and that boats that sway end up zigzagging in violent winds.

Yet these unequal distances in the progression of the walker and the ship do not yet make up a structure, they do not yet punctuate an order. Things will be different with undulation and the spiral, which mark the effective advent of a moment of spatialization where the curve as such acquires the rudiments of structuration. The undulation of hills in a landscape correspond to a structuration where the line bends into a curve in some moments or steps that, without being regular or implying measure, obey an order, express an (uncertain) style, hesitant but effective, the self-articulation of the continuous. Undulating hills arise starting from valleys from which they do not abruptly separate. Yet they are clearly, visibly separated from them. The order of undulation, the succession of hills and valleys depends on no arithmetical principle. The distances between valleys and hills are not the same and the heights of hills are not identical. However, the sequence of elevations and extensions is constant and none of the hills is too much higher than the others. Undulation softly and discreetly approximates the regularity that the spiral will complete in the direction of an accrued exactitude. The spiral is defined as a curve turning around a pole from which it draws away. This drawing away can be effectuated towards the below or above or even horizontally. The essential is insistence on the fixity of the point from which the curve departs and the regular character of the movements that compose the line as it moves away. The bends of a mountain path are the premises, the stuttering anticipations of the spiral. The smoke rising from a fire unwinds in a spiral and the spiral staircase is almost the realized example. The spiral is a way of being extended proper to the line. It traces enlarging circles or ovals in a continuous way. Here the line continues to celebrate its access to immanent structuration, without mingling with arithmetical elements, without allowing moments of measurement to irrupt within its structures.

Undulation and the spiral are consummate moments of the pure spatialization to which correspond movement-actions on the anthropological plane. Spatialization unfolds itself without the intervention of external, heterogeneous factors, notably those that come from homogenous quantification. Movements equally exist that, without being deprived of all order and structure, are realized without being useful, without obeying logics other than those within the givens of space. From the beginning of time humans have taken paths, moved from one location to another. Usually these movements cross a portion of space in order to reach a locality near or far. But there are also paths that move from one locality to another but do not aim for a locality as the necessary end of a route. Humans, even those deeply occupied, have always gone for walks, and who does not like to go for a stroll when the occasion presents itself? Strolling and walking are "actions" undertaken without haste, abandoning oneself to feeling and to the spectacle of the moment. The stroller is ready to stop and to linger. He "advances" but he is easily diverted; he wanders without any specific end or objective. The stroller uses space without an anchor point or place to hold on to. He can certainly overcome certain obstacles, scale rocks, jump over ravines. But what matters is never the end but taking the route itself. In its original form the path of the voyager is less pilgrimage than peregrination. He can certainly pursue an objective, a locality as the end of his travel, but this will prove itself provisional. He will stop near a rock or a cross, in a grove or on the edge of a stream in order to catch his breath, recover his strength. But these pauses are only temporary. For the stroller who survives in the voyager, the monuments of history and the views of nature are only pretexts. He wants to wed the forms of space, not to reach its localities.

Ultimately perhaps the purest form of movement that seeks to adapt itself to space is dance. The dancer does not actually go anywhere; he hardly changes his place. The dancer does not move in a direction; he follows no end. In walking one moves *through* space, but in dance one is happy to move *in* space. Dance relates neither to the past nor to the future; it is pure presence, without any history. It is a sequence of movements that obey a rhythm and are satisfied to take place, to be in space. The dancer can dance for hours but he does not want to go anywhere. Yet his non-advancement, non-progression is not a sterile agitation of useless forms. At the end of his action, the dancer is located nowhere but at his starting point, and yet he does not just go in circles. He accomplishes in his own way circular movement, which is according to the *Timaeus* the most divine movement.

Center: Symmetry and Asymmetry

The sui generis reality of space manifests itself as spatialization. It is an articulation not governed by the quantitative-homogenous. The homogenous denotes a continuity without an ordering according to quality or hierarchy, in other words an analytic structuration other than the spatial, or, if you like, below the spatial. Spatiality rejects the principle of analytic distribution and is manifest by eidē that belong to the regime of the a priori synthesis, eidē that articulate space according to a difference. The elementary spatial moments like the serpentine or undulation seem to reject any hierarchy in their moments. All kinds of sectioning out can be done, and in the serpentine one can divide up undulation into undulations without the dividing up or sectioning out being done starting with a particular, special element, a moment that would command the others. Similarly the stroller wandering on the trails or in the bush, the walker taking a ramble without a precise endpoint, apparently has no middle point. He does not read the trail map starting from a place where the trails start. Yet a central axis, often ignored, obscured but very real, is at the origin or principle, at the bottom of any form of space, of every undulation and peregrination. It is the center that is the forgotten point of departure of all structuration. The hidden source of spatialization is already clearly discerned in this elementary eidos that is the spiral. It will be seen as the essential truth of symmetry. And it will above all be shown with force in the principal spatial eidē of dimensions and directions.

The paths in space that mold the forms within them can manifest a sincere forgetting, even a sovereign contempt for every "objective" goal and end and yet they are described starting from an orientation, whether virtual or actual, and the orientation always starts from a mobile or fixed center, in other words from a form of space, or rather a locality in space. This locality is the center for which all the rest is only peripheral. This center can be understood according to its generality like the Earth but it instantiates and manifests itself effectively in one's own body. Phenomenology has described and analyzed with detail and an admirable penetration the central situation of one's own body, its priority in relation to other bodies, and the way in which it is found at the origin, at the base of spatialization. Man is not in space like a piece of fabric in a box. He *inhabits* space and inhabitation means not only a kind of intimate subjectivism: one's own body is not simply found leisurely in space but it constitutes the center where the great eidetic moments of spatialization begin to unfold themselves. One's own body occupies a particular situation in relation to other surrounding bodies and to portions of space where these bodies are found. "My body

Spatial Eidē

is the pivot of the world...the end...towards which all objects turn their face."[6] It is truly the permanent point to which every spatial relation seems connected, but this does not yet signify that it is condemned to immobility and unalterability. It is rather a point of reference, a node of moving significations out of which spatial forms unfold themselves in their diversity. The body is center and principle of orientation, principle and source of the immanent structuration that is spatialization. If modern philosophy, above all since Kant, has so favored time over space this is because the exteriority attributed to it as its essential metaphysical element condemns the spatial to a poor, unarticulated eidetic. Time stops being celebrated by the philosophies of subjectivity because, ultimately, it is the scheme and paradigm of history, to wit, of a reality moving towards an end. It is thus deprived of meaning. Time is the milieu of all signification, the principle of all difference, the "horizon of Being," whereas space in its massive exteriority is, as it were, cleaned out, denuded, dispossessed of all essentiality. But the phenomenological reading of the *spatium* makes possible and favors its quidditative rehabilitation. Deprived of a center of reference, space is no longer driven into homogenous indistinction, to "inessential" quantitative difference. A concept not necessarily of the topological order, the center makes spatialization not the flow of a rushing torrent but the development of a rich multiplicity of forms—a multiplicity of which the first very elementary but also very striking instance is symmetry.

Symmetry is the ordered relation of parts to each other and to an entire form. It is the regular distribution of parts around a center, an axis or a plane. Hence the variation between the axial symmetry between stem and root and the bilateral symmetry among leaves. Symmetry denotes either the equal distribution of different things or a distribution into identicals. In its most common definition symmetry concerns a work or a thing divided into two equal and like parts. It is the mode of distribution in the space of like elements. One can observe the symmetry of the human body, of our hands, or among the halves of our brain, or even among the windows of a house or the rosebushes of a garden. Yet "symmetrical" can also denote contrary and contradictory realities. Negation is precisely symmetrical to affirmation, even if opposed to it in form. Symmetry also designates exact correspondence in form, size and position of opposed parts. It could be defined as "the similarity of juxtaposed things within a dissimilar milieu,"[7] or, to the contrary, as a "homogenous merging...of unequal determinations of something in relation to another."[8] What is essential in the meeting of opposites or the differentiation-distribution of identicals is that we are always dealing with a relation where the formal determination, the determination according to space brackets the material, quantitative or qualitative differences. Before and beyond the universe of material essences, symmetry marks the irreducible originarity of the spatial eidetics.

6. Merleau-Ponty, *Phénoménologie de la perception*, 97.
7. Wolff, *Math. Lex. Gesammelte Werke* I, 11, 1343.
8. Hegel, *Cours d'esthétique* I, 144.

An even stronger and more prominent metaphysical role than the symmetrical relation is attributed to the relation-opposition of left and right. An opuscule from 1768, *First Principles of the Difference of Regions in Space*, nearly marks the turn of modern philosophy and the true beginning of the expansion of metaphysics. Here Kant unfolds the creative results of a reflection on left and right. Normally, two entities, substances, and subjects are identical when they are the same according to quality or quantity. But everyday experience refutes this position held by immemorial philosophical consensus. The appearance of our hand in a mirror appears to be a faithful reflection. However, our physical hand does not match its reflection. On the other hand, we have two hands and feet with practically the same structure-configuration and the same surface. They are therefore identical or at least strongly alike according to quality and quantity. However, if I try to put my left foot in my right shoe it will be too tight and hurt my foot. And if I try to slip my right hand into my left glove, my fingers do not find their place; it will not work.

The symmetry between two like or unlike entities is the work of space. Beyond all identity and difference in terms of quantity and quality or in other words of material essences, the symmetrical relation reveals the eidetic significance of space by this extra- or super-quidditative "more" determining the appearance of phenomena. But the relation between left and right is significant in another way from the eidetic point of view. It adds not only a supplementary interpretation of things; it does more than simply subsume them under a new grammar. It reformulates them, causing them to undergo a true metaphysical metamorphosis. The two asymmetrical elements, the left and right entities show with simplicity their material identity. Each hand has five fingers, both palms are of equal surface. Yet this native material identity submits to a difference that becomes radical. Entities withdrawn from space, or rather glimpsed through a bracketing of the spatial, immediately slide into identity, fall back into a peaceful sameness, yet display as left and right a total alterity. The elementary opposition between left and right attests to the essential significance of spatialization. Left and right are eidē irreducible to the condition of material essences. They equally loathe every attempt at reunion through analytic homogenization. They powerfully witness to the unfolding of the spatial through the a priori synthesis. They are the ends of a predication, not deducible according to content, the concept, but which nevertheless has its intelligibility and predication in a sui generis way. Left and right demonstrate the eidetic regime of the spatial: in its non-conceptual nature space is principle and matrix of noetic syntheses.

Dimensions and Directions

With the left-right opposition, the "phenomenon" of asymmetry, we have been able to get a sense of the eidetic range of space, its reality, sui generis truth, irreducible to quality and quantity. We could then try to systematize the manners of the unfolding of space, the principle and source of its power of articulation. We have passed through the spatial eidē like the sinuous, the serpentine, undulation and the spiral. These represent particular instances of the auto-articulation of the *spatium*. Space *is* not; it spatializes itself and spatialization has two basic categories: dimension and direction. They disclose the fundamental manners of the structuration of space as such, and consequently from an extra- or supra-quantitative point of view. Nevertheless, spatial references to quantity or rather to a pre-quantitative component, anterior to measure—size and distance bearing witness—cannot and must not be forgotten.

Space spatializes itself. It articulates itself through eidē where the expansion that is almost the very metaphysical nature of the spatial is intuited in its diverse variants and moments. Space can extend or rather spread out in itself, without registering a gap or void, a hole or internal fissure. It unfolds according to its *dimensions*, then. However, space is not only itself, or rather, it should not only be examined in itself. Space spreads itself out but in doing so it is affected by another than itself. It is the locality where beings are situated; it is the rim or enclosure surrounding them, the arch or dome that envelops and protects them. The structure of space related implicitly or explicitly to one or more objects that it contains or applies to is called *direction*.

Dimensions apparently constitute the primordial moments of the auto-structuration of space. Dimension concerns space in its totality. It is integrally present there and it suggestively alludes to the primitive massiveness of space, leading one to consider it an undivided reality, an integral entity. If direction bears a call from elsewhere, an élan that drives towards, dimension reminds us that before being related to something else, to a beyond, space is first the substrate and source of the immanent movement to being, to beings. The Ancients insisted on the indissoluble links between matter and dimension. Dimensionality constitutes matter and is inseparable from it. In fact, all the while struggling against it, it shares to a degree the metaphysical weight of matter, to wit, immanence and the quantitative condition. The elementary way of space's self-articulation unfolds in dimension, but the spatial appears here without perspective or goal. It spatializes itself according to the proper modalities of expansion that are its mode of existence. But it obscures every element, even rudimentary ones, of the intentionality proper to the a priori synthesis. This primitive spatialization that is dimension—still incapable of separating itself clearly from affiliation with immanence—maintains an ambiguous relation to quantity. We have been able to define dimension as the measurable extension of a body in different directions, the magnitude that measures the extension of a body in a given direction. In fact, many make generous use of it, without any discrimination, by designations in which the category of magnitude proper to dimension does not avoid a facile and diffuse subsumption under quantity. We speak of a body of small dimensions, or an edifice of large dimensions, but we also speak of a project of small dimensions, or an affair of large dimensions.

The three dimensions of space, height, width and depth, constitute the universe, the cosmos, in their massive immanence, their seeming independence of every subjective moment (Eph 3:14). But space equally possesses another essential principle of structuration that, exempt from any quantitative reference, belongs to the subjectivity of the subject that orients itself within it. This principle is direction. Direction also unfolds itself according to a plurality that constitutes above and below, before and behind, left and right. For Phenomenology direction represents the pre-mathematical condition of space; through it physics is distinguished from mathematics. From an eidetic point of view, direction signifies a superior step of spatialization. And through it space surpasses the condition of imprisonment proper to dimension. Direction causes the indivisible space to explode, causing it, as it were, to sprawl out by distinguishing it from the forms it contains, and, above all, it plants within it the goad of an élan, a progression, an aim. Interrogation of movement and orientation in space begin with the question: "where are you going"—that is—"to what place?" But the essential aim undergirding it is, "in what direction?" Contrary to dimension, direction has a differentiation from intentional aim as a basic ingredient. On the plane of the spatial it anticipates the moral-metaphysical surpassing. Of course, it is the principle and source of movement, but one that is not only kinetic, animated, and projected, determined and oriented by an intentionality if not an intention. In fact, direction, in its verbal form "to direct," is easily joined to the rational. It is a way for language to express potentiality, or rather the proper task of subjectivity for this category of eidē that constitute the framework or spatial grammar of constituting the new.

Contrary to the dimensions that seem never to interfere with one another, which never surpass their condition of native simplicity and remain below subversion by relation or composition, direction claims the power of inversion that we have already seen at work in left and right. Left and right contain this irreducibility that anticipates in its own way the irreversibility proper to time. And above all they practically constitute an exclusive principle of phenomenal determination. In fact, direction, the directions, possess this "virtue" of qualification that furnishes a death blow to metaphysical limits and, regarding quiddity, on the plane of material essences alone. Direction and the directions dispose of a sovereign power of the interpretation of things: they are the principles or essential rules of a spatial grammar. For a noetics of understanding that knows only material essences, a portrait remains the same whether it is nailed to the wall upright, with eyes above the chin, or flipped upside down, with chin above the eyes. Things are different for an "expanded" reason, assuming all its native dimensions: for it, or rather, before it, an inverted painting will have an inverse meaning. Similarly, the understanding does not register any difference between the inverted image of a face and one seen right side up, whereas spatial eidetics will register two different contents. As Merleau-Ponty succinctly said: "to invert an object is to remove its signification."[9]

9. Merleau-Ponty, *Phénoménologie de la perception*, 292.

Spatial Eidē

Magnitude and Distance

Dimension and direction are the essential principles of the spatial, intuited according to its native condition as that which is in expansion, which spreads itself out. Dimension appears to concern only space, as such, whereas direction designates an articulation of space as relation to an object or a locality that it contains. It is a matter of eidē that do not belong to the quantitative, yet spatialization has no locality without reference to quantity, and the role of quantity is seen particularly well in the two great eidetic moments of the *spatium*, magnitude and distance. If direction and dimension first concern space as such, space in its undivided integrality, magnitude and distance are essentially realities situated in space. Things are perceived which populate space as magnitudes, whereas the movement traveled by spatialization is read as distance.

Distance is the eidos that appears through the near and the far; magnitude is subdivided into smallness and largeness. This definition shows that the eidos magnitude, which can be large or small, cannot be taken for a reality of the properly quantitative order. Magnitude corresponds to mass, but to a mass conceived in its continuity: it can even be defined as consisting in "the successive repetition of the homogeneous" (*Critique* B 300). But here homogeneity signifies less the metaphysical construction of sameness than the absence of roughness, escarpment and relief that troubles the smooth continuity of the tridimensional body extended in space. Magnitude is a spatial, not mathematical notion and it results from the absolute valorization that touches only the thing itself without consideration of context. In a certain way magnitude is a non-mathematical reality, extending itself in space. It is a distant analog of the singular as such, conceived outside of all comparison in its radical irreferentiality. In fact, a thing is understood as large starting from itself, and the entrance of objective, arithmetical considerations cannot modify this interpretation. But if magnitude denotes what can be enlarged or diminished, this is because large and small are defined before any objective, numerical point of reference. Some things are large in themselves, while others are small, and they are conceived as large or small independently of any measure or comparison. Upon arrival in a foreign country or disembarking on an unknown island, a mountain on the horizon can seem large even if "objectively," according to sane and sober comparison, it is only a moderate hill. And inversely, a bush can seem very small, when, in reality, it is rather of a "moderate" size, just as a man or woman can be considered "small" when they are in actually situated in an average or superior percentile according to demographic statistics.

The metaphysical independence of magnitude from measure, quantity is, so to speak, "inherited" from its roots in dimension. The three dimensions that seem above all concerned with space in itself are located in things, inhabitants of space. Physical things are bodies and "all bodies are marked out by the three dimensions" (*Physics* 209a). But if dimension marks and describes the particular way that a body—that is a magnitude—is extended through space, it survives, it continues to be the same when quantity changes. A house of four floors is located in height, yet if an extension adds two further floors, this will hardly modify its situation of participating in height. Dimension, incarnated by magnitude, even while implying a reference to quantity, is finally independent of it. However, distance that represents in a certain way a counterpart of direction, of a spatial eidos however little affected by the quantitative, seems more directly tied to quantity and submitted to measure. Distance separates two forms or two places, and it is first of all intuited as a line that begins near one entity in order to arrive at another. The most salient phenomenal characteristic of distance is its condition of being located between two things: it marks the separation of these beings but secondarily also their relation above the gap that lies between them. Distance reveals the abyss, it constitutes a narrowed, reduced, abstract expression of it and to the very degree that it seems to exorcise the elements of depth from the interval, it is flattened into a surface and finally narrowed into a line. But the path leading from the distance-line to measured distance is adopted quasi-naturally by thought, accomplice from the beginning with the seductions of the quantitative, fascinated by the history-less and simple smoothness of the Same. Distance appears then as a kind of Trojan horse of quantity within the spatial: it is in and through it that the homogenous and the analytic infiltrate the spatial or rather reveal a presence that the eidetic would have loved to ignore or obscure. However, if distance is still the Achilles heel of the spatial, the aspect by which the *spatium* the most recalcitrant to the metaphysical exigencies of the synthetic condition, it possesses also strong and solid foundations in the spatial according to its own extra- or rather supra-quantitative truth.

The constitutive moments of the eidos "distance" are the near and the far and it is only an incessant variation of distantiation. Distantiation expresses the subjective-moral nature of distance, of the distance taken in regard to another and that one would like the other, others, to take in regard to oneself. But distantiation is a function of moral, subjective factors. We place ourselves at a distance through discretion and we expect that others will not draw too close to us, that they will leave an empty space between us, in short, that they *move out of the way*. In daily life we prefer to have a minimum of our own space; the *Lebensraum* is not only a political invention, a dull ideological slogan! When we climb on a bus, we don't want others to huddle up against us; in line at the ticket office we try to make sure that those behind us do not press too closely against us; we want to avoid touching and falling on one another. The distance we think we should keep with others and that we want them to keep with us doubtlessly can hardly be measured. Civility will have nothing to do with arithmetical studies and ethics will never be an exact science! The distance required by a certain person in a given situation depends on social and personal, cultural and historical factors. Each person, every free creature can and must surround itself with an aura that is a certain extension of its singular, unique being and that corresponds to its outside edge, the proper periphery of the center that constitutes it. But the aura is nothing but a variation of distance—an essentially linear figure—under the form of a luminous emanation surrounding and enveloping it.

Beyond the essential role it plays in daily life, distance is equally a supreme factor in artistic perception. The beautiful is what pleases without interest; we must not touch the statue, the painting must not be inspected too closely: otherwise vision becomes blurry, contemplation is impossible. Distance is also and above all a physico-metaphysical condition of the moral life. *Suum cuique* clearly entails erecting barriers around what is owed to me. However not only justice but love ought to be master *of* distance. In love, the neighbor doubtlessly should come infinitely close to me, but what is a true proximity if not the constant surpassing of a respected distance, consequently scrupulously maintained?

From Breadth to Remoteness

Magnitude and distance powerfully illustrate the presence of the quantitative within the spatial, reminding us that, implicitly or explicitly but in a very real way, quantity influences spatialization, the spatial eidē leave themselves wide open to measurement. Height and depth certainly do not escape the grip of measurement but breadth is probably the dimension where the spatial properly so called is the strongest and most clearly articulated by the quantitative. Breadth connotes the expansion of a body, its condition of being extended more or less strongly. But it is an expansion determined by direction. In fact, it can even be defined according to an orientation, namely that of the observer standing in the horizontal dimension, parallel to the shoulder line. From phenomenological vantage breadth first denotes a certain abundance, even superabundance. It is subdivided into wideness and narrowness. And narrowness makes breadth undergo a compression or shrinking. According to its meaning as unlimited expansion, wideness in the primitive sense covers a vast domain and signals a latitude, that is, an absence of constraint. It implies the power to take generous initiatives, a generosity where the largess of views and intentions goes along with an absence of ultimate precision, or rather a certain vagueness of detail. Without being referred to a precise cyphering of its goods, "to have significant means" signifies having more than necessary in order to maintain one's life and well-being. And La Bruyère spoke of that kind of oversize dress of "rustic people" who were "shod widely and roughly."[10] He suggests that we dress in a loose, poorly fitted way.... Through all its variations breadth shows itself to be an authentic, essential, primordial eidos of spatialization, but like the two other dimensions, perhaps even more than them, it hardly favors an analogous articulation to the unfolding of material essences.

The very poor, very summary articulation proper to breadth can be attributed to the native immanence of distance to this dimension. But dimension, the dimensions

---

10. La Bruyère, *Les Caractères de Théophraste*, "De la rusticité," in *Oeuvres complètes*, 45.

are not only contaminated by quantity but also mixed with elements coming from direction. In fact breadth articulates itself according to four of Aristotle's six directions: left and right, before and behind. We have seen left and right to be instances of direction with exclusive spatial eidetic purity. They are not at all susceptible of admitting quantitative considerations: one could be higher, or ahead, or further on—but not more left or right. However before and behind constitute forms of direction where the eidetic spatiality enter, so to speak, into collusion with the quantitative where the eidē of space lend themselves to measurement, allow an essential qualification by the quantitative. Before and behind are doubtlessly first and above all phenomenological essences with spatial determination. "Being before" signifies being on the same side as a person or thing's face and being behind is to be on the side opposite this face. But before and behind bear other potentialities than spatial signification. "Behind" is not related necessarily to a situation compared to a single and same body, the center of a field of perception. Someone could hide behind another person or a door and we could equally say of our interlocutor that his eyes shine with peculiar brilliance behind his glasses. There is something analogous with "before," which is also no longer confined to the primitive eidetic determinations of Direction. Things situated in relation to a human face are often said to be "before" it. One could also be seated "before" a jug of foaming beer or taking an oath "before" God. Ultimately these are instances of spatialization in which the quantitative, the measurable, originally absent, can surreptitiously insinuate themselves. To force someone to walk behind you is at best to drive him back into second place, and, inversely, you can say to someone beside or behind you: go on past me, since you are in a hurry. This amounts to saying: go first!

Another and much more powerful interference of measurement happens when the direction of "before" is seen under the form of movement. Before is thus transposed into "ahead." To go ahead corresponds to a progression where a given place is left behind, where one emerges from a situation in order to complete a task. The ambulant kind of before, someone ahead taking to his heels, betrays a sliding from the topological toward the kinetic, but always within an eidetic regime of the spatial order. You can see that the before-ahead is condemned, if not to subsumption under the quantitative, at least to subversion by measurement. But measurement manifests the fullness of its power, perfects its omnipresence only through the rereading of the line going ahead as a *straight* line. To go ahead amounts to going straight, adopting by one's walk a direct path, a straight line. The straight line is the contrary of the curve or the twist. According to a Portuguese proverb recalled by Claudel in "The Satin Slipper," *Deus escreve direito por linhas tortas*, "God writes straight with crooked lines." But if the transposition of the curve or twist into the straight line is possible for God, it is apparently not within the reach of humanity. The curve is a different form of space than the straight line and no amount of twisting will make it straight. Well to the contrary, the curve and the straight line can be reread in anthropological and ethical terms that deepen and further articulate their primitive eidetic condition. To go backwards, towards the rear, is frequently judged as reactionary, sometimes cowardly, usually lamentable, while going ahead is considered an exalted act, a movement and progression that exudes optimism, displays a forthright courage. Even more, the straight line, the straight line as such, not only harbors a potentiality of eschatological priority, it can be indeed read in properly moral terms. By contrast to mistakes and culpable distractions, to the act of evasion made by weakness, to the deviation of the sinner, which are so many inopportune spatial forms, the straight line shows and attests to the clarity of intention of the good man, his undivided devotion to the Cause, his strong and serene concentration in his progression to the End.

Progress straight ahead has as its "objective" and goal, the horizon toward which it unfolds itself. The horizon, an extremely rich spatial eidos, contains and shortens an entire spectrum of moments of the articulation of the spatial and at the same time reveals the problems and difficulties of the eidetics of the *spatium*. The horizon is an absolute frontier that certainly cannot be surpassed but which does not limit us. It is an end, an inaccessible limit but also a space that waits for and invites an approach. The horizon is given, but one that is mobile and ceaselessly withdraws. It contains the essential category of the far and also, therefore, the near. Near and far possess a fundamentally quantitative element, and yet they are nevertheless not determined by quantity. Near and far certainly imply potentialities for being measured but these are ultimately recalcitrant phenomenological essences, intractable to being enumerated. Near and far are eidē of an essentially subjective kind. They do not express an "objective" distance at all, capable of being expressed in meters or kilometers. Far does not signify an interval, length or distantiation. It is not frozen, but given, and given without stopping, without being fixed. The far is the horizon, or what is on the horizon, and just as space is through spatializing itself, the far is through moving away—not by situating itself ever farther away, but by keeping itself as far, affirming itself as remoteness. And the near similarly is through drawing closer, but this drawing closer does not make it "objectively" closer, in other words at a measurable distance. Like the far, the near is doubtlessly susceptible of less or more. Sometimes we say: this airplane is getting farther away or this storm is getting closer and closer. But this less and this near belong to a non-arithmetic regime: they do not correspond to a certain number of identical unities and thus a certain quantity but to two different structures of our spatial perception. Touch implies linkage, but it does not constitute a kind of culmination or apotheosis. Otherwise it would end up shooting itself in the foot. To the same degree that it implies the abolition of distance, the bridging of every gap, touch leads to the dissolution of the near, its subsumption without remainder in a given entity. However, the maximum diminution of the gap in touch does not yet ring the death knell of the near. The rapprochement continues to accommodate a disposition, an inclination to letting up, and it neither excludes nor destroys a hidden tendency to slide. Near and far constitute an eidetic couple of which the reality, the sui generis specificity depends on their irreducibility to quantity. If the far and the near depend on quantitative considerations, then one could be expressed in terms of the other. Yet as a phenomenologist remarked: "Three nears does not make a far!"[11]

Far and near are phenomenological essences irreducible to quantity, to the measurable, even if they are inseparable from some moments in deep affinity with quantity. The phenomenologist observes that "directions of orientation in a straight line, like directions of distance that put in perspective, lead to a limit for disappearance by shortening. . ."[12] A self-evident fact of our perception is that the two principal moments of breadth, the widening and narrowing of a field, go together with remoteness and drawing together. Briefly, reference to the quantitative, to the pre-quantitative if you like, pervades the heart of the spatial. Even more, this native affinity, these essential connections with the realities relating to the quantitative equally apply in the anthropological and the moral spheres. What is near seems to everyone more important than what is far, and a science, *proxemics*, unfolds around a law according to which distance from a reference point reduces and weakens phenomena. The idea of the neighbor is the axial theme, the flagship principle of Christian morality, but the structures and moors of all societies, instead of requiring that all be treated as neighbors, seem almost founded on a maxim which, without very often being clearly expressed, nevertheless remains quasi-universal. To wit: we can and should only love the one close to us. The one far away, the stranger is not only an object of indifference, but also of fear, contempt, even hate, whereas the one close by, usually close by blood but also by other often conjectural and accidental and yet vigorous and efficacious considerations, is the cynosure of our respect, the hinge around which our affections turn, the source and end of our actions. Man should love each of his congeners, such as sisters or brothers. In reality, he thus loves only a tiny part of humanity, a handful of men and women. We should love generously and efficaciously those located far away from us. In fact, interest, respect and above all love are exercised in our world in inverse proportion with the distance of their intentional object by relation to our heart.

Beyond these very simple and obvious repercussions of the forms of the spatial in terms of their rooting in the quantitative, the spatial has also connotations, a moral bearing according to what is properly eidetic. The straight line is certainly the shortest distance between two points, and it is therefore imposed already for utilitarian, pragmatic reasons, but also as the paradigm of a moral attitude. It is at the origin of the moral intuition of "uprightness," in other words of noble simplicity, probity, and honesty in our action. The near and the far also have anthropological-moral connotations, certainly less clear and univocal than the straight line, and yet still suggestive and persuasive. The far, especially qualified as *remote*, is the principle and source of any psychologico-moral dialectic. The far represents the reading of a place, an event, a person as located at a certain distance. We are separated from what is far from us and it takes time and effort to reach it. However, the intuition of the far, the remote, does

11. Strauss, *Vom Sinn der Sinne*, 409.
12. Husserl, "Notes pour la constitution de l'espace," 55.

not correspond only to the assessment of this separation and our becoming aware of what we can and should do to rejoin that from which we are separated. The far exercises an influence and fascination for us. It reminds us of our vocation not to remain confined in a given place, absorbed in routine occupations. The far is in an elsewhere that we have not taken hold of, but it always affects us. It is like an analog of why, it reveals the void beyond our fullness, its silent call gives birth to a hollow place within us. The far is frustrating but also promising: it shows we are imperfect, but imperfection also has as its counterpart the possibility and vocation of being fulfilled. What is far is most often erased, poorly visible; it nevertheless exercises a powerful fascination. It is like the bite marks of mystery in our being which we ceaselessly seek to decipher. We certainly could see the distance separating us from what is far as a straight line, but the remote has an essential aspect of the cheerful, the funny, and also the adventurous. It loves detours, enjoys taking poorly marked trails, and sinuous, even tortuous paths. In other words, all the while espousing sober and virtuous manifestations of a laudable progress, the far seems to have a weakness for the world of the most primitive spatial eidē.

The sinuous and tortuous express in their own way the essentially elusive, inaccessible condition of the remote. The remote is like the horizon, an unsurpassable frontier that does not limit us because it is itself moving. The essence of far is not a distance more or less long, but separation: to remain far, the far must recede. The far is certainly the counterpart of the near, but it seems to harbor its own eidetic potentialities without any correspondence in the near. It is *other* to the near, but their relation is hardly that of a mechanical reciprocity, a servile symmetry. In order to remain near, the near must not—and cannot—become ever closer. In fact, it must even conserve within itself a moment of the far. The other should be made my neighbor, without blocking my horizon. I must maintain a distance from him. This is not only to protect my autonomy but also to respect his. The true neighbor should retain his remoteness, if not he ceases to be other. The far and near, the faraway person and the neighbor should be considered in a genetic reciprocity, but they contain value in themselves, according to their own irreducible eidetic sui generis truth.

Depth

Of the three dimensions depth is nearly the most "dimensional." It provokes few attempts to reduce it to another dimension. It certainly has an aspect of vastness and it seems to bear an affinity with the vertical, which is the soul of height. Yet it has very little of the horizontal proper to breadth. Contrary to breadth and height by which things are juxtaposed to one another, depth is the dimension by which they conceal themselves. The two other dimensions haunt us, they make themselves, so to speak, felt as absence, while depth attests to itself as presence—a massive, powerful presence that is naturally protective but at times scary and menacing. Thanks to depth we have a foundation in space that allows us to hear the calls of the remote and height, to follow their leads and to obey their injunctions. Depth possesses a spatiality that is, pardon the expression, more spatial, more purely spatial than its sister dimensions. This is why it also clearly appears, and is hardly susceptible of being transposed and distorted into direction. In fact, depth is resistant to articulation and it certainly bears (like other dimensions) a germ of structuration in opposites, the deep and the shallow, but it is not at all prepared for further structuration. It lacks the procession of derived eidē, like those constituting near and far, before and behind in the context of width. The imposing and radiant spatiality of depth makes it "the most existential of all dimensions" and a true "participation in the being of space beyond every point of view."[13] Depth immediately reveals the links of the subject to space to the very degree that it is almost exclusively related to the perceiving subject. Width and height essentially concern the relation of one thing to one another whereas, depth is centered on their relation to me.

Neither height nor depth displays a propensity for articulation and structuration, but depths seems to nourish a solid mistrust towards its own structurations. It is bound up with the night where it stretches out, receiving and enveloping things without framework, surface, or true distance in relation to the I that lies at its center. Depth has an elective affinity with the dark, the black. It integrates or engulfs beings, dissolving them in its atmosphere, extending over and around them a non-transparent veil. It is like a blanket for things, or rather like an immense overcoat that does not allow their traits or contours to appear. Merleau-Ponty vigorously and subtly analyzed the role of depth in relation to the beings that it envelops. Depth can contain and accommodate a multitude of singular beings, without suffocating or marginalizing them. It can equally be centered on a singular, bracketing every other thing. But this bracketing is only provisional; it is a fiction produced by a simplistic thought. In fact, depth offers the simultaneous presence to things that, however, excludes them. Within it everything is seen in its place precisely because they obscure one another. From a metaphysical point of view depth can include compossibility. Compossibles are organized according to quidditative affinities, essences where each has its place in what Kant called "the transcendental totality of predicates" (*Critique* B 600). However the tridimensionality of existing beings makes them incompatible with each other in the physical universe, "this *narrow* world. . .where things harshly crash into each other." In its own way, depth alone allows the accommodation of these in-compossibles in space, making them appear without being mixed up, without their suppressing or repulsing one another.

Depth has strong affinities with the dense, the thick. Yet density and thickness are eidē foreign to every limitation and donation of meaning and are finally realities of a simplicity and analogous homogeneity to the quantitative, while depth does not permit a flattening into an ultimately analytic condition. Depth, of course, registers a

---

13. Merleau-Ponty, *Phénoménologie de la perception*, 428.

Spatial Eidē

flawless continuity but which should be understood in terms of an élan—one that is certainly not garish, sparkling or sensational but which powerfully rushes forward in order to traverse a gap. Expansion into the opening, its traversal, a noetic synthetic a priori condition proper to depth possesses something of the unfathomable, but of an unfathomability nevertheless pointing to intentionality. The unfathomability of depth can be as much a protective shelter as a consuming abyss. Depth does not juxtapose the beings that it accommodates: it envelops them. Nature has endowed certain animals with carapaces or shells, and it has taught birds to make nests. It has littered the hills and mountains with caves that protect living beings, and the shelters and dwellings erected by humanity imitate these caves. These are constructions where roofs and internal and external walls are only the shell surrounding and hiding an interior that is always a specimen or instance of depth. Humans inhabit the depth that harbors and protects him. Hölderlin opposes to the "wresting" nature of time the "enveloping" character of space. Space is "the friend of being," the "nest," the "fold,"[14] and depth, this space of space, is the most powerful source of the *spatium* for sheltering and defending the beings it contains.

The poets and philosophers celebrate rest and peace, in short the warm security that the quiet depths of houses ensure to men. Yet this security constitutes, as it were, only "half the story." Depth is not only where the fugitive hides, a recess to shelter the poor or sick. Habitations are not only huts and houses, hovels and palaces. They are also tunnels with dark and narrow trenches, forgotten dungeons, labyrinths. At first glance one would think that depth is covered with negative connotations when it shrinks and narrows. Yet the narrowing is not an aspect or degree proper to depth, but rather a marker along the path where depth abandons, leaps, and escapes from itself. But the sui generis frightening and menacing character of depth emanates from it when it exists in its fullness. We speak of the "horror of a deep night" or of the "deep unfathomable passions." Depth is certainly a source and principle of phenomena that shelter and protect, but it is also at work when we feel that everything is crumbling and collapsing, when the walls crumble and boundaries are erased. In fact, depth seems simply to have *become* an aspect of protection. In its primitive nature and original condition it is opposed to all security, every guardrail. It surrounds us on all sides without directly touching us, without coming close, but if it is perceived as distance, this is only because it defies every measure. Unfathomable and measureless, depth is a gulf, apparently without bottom that attracts us and draws us in. *De profundis clamavi*, writes the psalmist. His cry is the complaint of the creature dislodged from his own place, held against his will in a foreign and hopeless place. In truth however, the horror proper to depth, its negativity, properly speaking, is not a matter of being principle of exile, but as subversion of all location, obliteration of every place.

Depth pushed into its entrenchments, depth in its own eidetic truth does not connote a locality situated very low or very far away but which is located nowhere, or

---

14. Bachelard, *La poétique de l'espace*, 188, 92, 99.

rather corresponds to a place which is not truly one at all. It is a form par excellence of the without-place, which is not simply the absence of place but active opposition to every place. In its truth recusant to every place, depth is an *abyss*. The abyss is anti-place in two ways: according to essence and according to existence. Place is a category of articulation and structure, and the abyss rejects every structure. If depth can manifest itself at times as compossibility, it regains even more frequently the appearance of violent disorder. In numerous mythologies and cosmologies, the primordial abyss, the gulf preceding the cosmos or found below it is designated as *chaos*. Chaos is the receptacle, or rather principle of confusion, of limitless intermixture, perceived according to its active acceptation as a vortex. It is revealed then—in a highly paradoxical way—as the proper eidetic form of the anti-eidetic. It sows disorder; provokes perplexity, turmoil; it jeopardizes efforts to buoy being by essence; it condemns to failure every attempt to orient oneself, to "sort things out." Regarding the second and certainly more spectacular manifestation of the anti-place moment of the abyss, the way according to existence sticks closely to the eidos "depth." Depth-abyss is an unfathomable depth, a bottomless depth. Being engulfs itself and incessantly sinks without reaching the bottom and it drags down beings in its haste to find the bottom. In its strong physical sense, the abyss is "gaping." It appears as an immense open mouth that swallows everything that approaches it, as the source and principle of an irresistible suction that sucks up and consumes beings. Depth in its meaning as abyss provokes anguish and vertigo. Vertigo is the fear of falling into the abyss, of being dragged away by the murky waters of chaos. It is ultimately only a variant or physiological sample of the metaphysical affliction of anguish. Anguish before the abyss of depth corresponds to the intuition of space as void. The void is not a simple absence but the "phenomenon" proper to the nothingness of space. The *spatium* has a metaphysical vocation to be articulated and anguish corresponds to this "nowhere" that is the cipher of the spatial in its morbid un-articulation.

Height

Each dimension bears a scission, a division into two: breadth into wide and narrow, depth into deep and shallow. Height also divides itself into two opposed faces, but which distinguish themselves from the related elements of the two other dimensions. While breadth and depth are divided into properly dimensional moments, height is divided into directions. Its two faces are the directions high and low. This complexity of structure, this native compromise of expansion according to volume with direction to the vocation "of spanning a distance" is a fundamental moment of height and we will see that it lies at the origin of the metaphysical specificity of this category of the eidetic.

High and low are opposites but (at first glance) are defined only in relation to an imaginary vertical line of which they designate the arithmetically different portions.

Spatial Eidē

The low seems to correspond to a lesser, modest portion of the line, while the high designates a very large part of it. In reality, this quantitative interpretation of the moments of height is extremely deficient: after all, there are "very low" realities that could be measured, enumerated according to so many meters or kilometers in the same way as very high things! If you want to remain faithful to the elementary vision of high and low in their opposition, it is better to interpret them starting from their relation to gravity which is the principle of all vertical movement. The low would thus be that which is conformed to the proper direction of gravity, the high which is opposed to it. This reading of the two great moments of height has the advantage of being conformed to the eidetic specificity of the idea. In its own way it will contribute to the non-quantitative understanding of space. Instead of analytic homogeneity of measure according to number, a kind of irreversibility proper to the spatial is encountered. Gravity goes in a specific direction, towards the low. It does not tend toward the opposite direction. And the entire dialectic, or rather the entire eidetic, the entire metaphysics of height takes its origin, finds its specificity starting from this vigorous asymmetry.

The essential asymmetry of the two vertical movements determined by their relation to gravity is at the origin of the eidetic message of the high and low. The high is not simply the symmetrical counterpart of the low, but it signals the sui generis alterity of one in relation to the other. The high doubtlessly implies the low and vice versa: there are no mountains without valleys or valleys without mountains! Yet if the high registers a primacy, a moral superiority, the low enjoys a metaphysical priority. We tend naturally towards the low: to go towards the high represents a particular effort, a push against nature! We could say that the low is the innate direction for all beings, while going towards the high signifies going against the current. This state of metaphysico-eidetic fact could be called on by the theologies of fallen nature, the philosophies that profess that man is naturally perverted, alienated, or at least fallen into languor, inert and indolent from birth. But without being engulfed in theological or moral speculations, the qualification of the high by its original relation to gravity largely determines the perspectives of philosophical analysis of this dimension of concomitant realities.

The high connotes a movement against gravity and demands a sustained effort. Parallel to this unnatural, enhanced and boosted, elevated and climbing conception of movement towards the high there is discovered the proper sphere of height, of instances of height. The phenomenology of religion observes the universal and quasi-systematic association of the high and the sacred. The gods are located on Olympus, God is in Heaven. And when the Most High wants to encounter man, he meets him on the mountain. He commands Moses to climb Sinai and wait for him to descend and give him the tablets of the Law! But if Yahweh does not want to descend all the way to the plains, it is not because he balks at the distance but that he considers the high places, the summits as particularly appropriate for commerce between Creator and creature. The mountain possesses eidetic specificities that predestine it for a moral vocation. It has a particular atmosphere; the air is pure, the views are unobstructed. The landscapes of mountains are of a sublimity that predisposes them for action at a remove from the everyday, surpassing the ground level of our normal preoccupations. The mountain is like the topological, geographical condensation of all these aspirations and behaviors suitable for the conduct of the one who moves against gravity by ceaseless effort. Authentic moral action is born out of an elevated spirit. It is exercised by a being possessing a deep intuition, a being that neither bends nor yields, but which remains standing amidst tribulations through exposure to assaults of multiple temptations.

The high refers to an aspiration to climb, to climb without stopping. The lover of mountains is enamored with heights, heights that are always higher. The high shares with the far away the native metaphysical condition of the unaccomplished, the state of being open towards, of progression. The aspiration for the infinite is inscribed in these spatial forms: space, let us not forget, is "an infinitely given magnitude"! Height aspires to rise to the peaks, to ever-higher summits; it is attracted to and fascinated by this infinite "more." In reality the passion for height is a manifestation of the desire for the infinite of which a partial translation—if you want to narrow it to a somewhat devalued form—is the quest for the inaccessible. In fact if the quest for the inaccessible belongs to the universe of the high, it constitutes a peripheral, one could almost say perverted phenomenon of it. As respectable as this quest is, as noble as is the aspiration, it must always evoke the shimmering and fanciful that leaks out of and derives from the far away, whereas the high, the high in its metaphysical truth, always retains its entire dignity because it remains "serious," always serious. To the very degree that it corresponds to a crosscurrent movement, the high remains indissociably tied to moral effort, more precisely to an effort that has its sources in the subject itself and that the subject ceaselessly unfolds and renews. The supreme phenomenon of the high is ascension, and ascension contains an irrepressible moment of spontaneity. We speak of the ascension of a liquid in a pump, but also of the irresistible ascension of a charismatic public figure. And ancient theology defined the Ascension of Christ as a rising to heaven "by his own power." In each case, the rising of the ascension is effected by virtue of a force possessed by the agent and exercised in and through it.

The "serious" and "spontaneous" moments of the notion of the high can receive a topological translation in the leap, in the tearing off from the ground, the take off of elevation into the air. The low also registers a leap, a rupture with the location where it is found, but in a lesser way. Everyone doubtlessly slips from time to time, which causes us to fall lower. More generally, the Fall has sent Man, all men, towards the low, towards a servile sphere, a domain of the crushed spirit. But the hurried changing of places, the crossing of levels proper to slippages, to the movements of beings that fall, are less characteristic of the low than of a gradual descent, a slow collapse. To better understand the meaning of "low"—especially its negative connotations, but of an ultimately limited negativity where the trifling and pitiable play a more important role than the wicked and the horrible—we must clarify its meaning in relation to depth. It is tempting to confound low and deep, but the low is the extremity of a vertical line and occupies only a limited place whereas there is nothing momentary or limited about the deep. It fills much more space. The low breathes in the atmosphere of the small, the narrow-minded. The low or base, like its substantive, lowness or baseness, refuses in its own way an entire theory of negative realities. Both designate first a world of dubious, deficient morality, or rather a world of immorality. Lowness-baseness characterizes an entire cortege of phenomena like degradation, abasement, inferiority. But all this immorality is explained and in part excused or even attributed to attenuating circumstances, starting from its topological roots. How to perform high and noble actions in this "base" world? How can we walk uprightly instead of falling lower and lower "when the low, heavy sky pressed down like a lid?"[15] How to avoid the temptation to cheat and defraud when I am forced to sell my goods at a "base" price? How to keep from snatching something that no one is guarding, a being that nobody protects? And in another, non-moral register: The exhausted and starving needy seek bread in a "low," that is, quiet, voice and the authors of a decadent epoch write in "low" Latin...

The low is certainly opposed to the high. The two denote contrary visual perceptions and intuitions, but in this sense, a metaphysical difference is added to the radically different value of forms of height. In its proper condition the high is secondary to the low because the low flows naturally in its being whereas the high involves the exercise of effort to be brought about. Yet this secondarity can be rethought and requalified. The high and low are not only opposites, but also register an asymmetry that finally devalorizes the low, revealing its dependence on the high. The act of rising has an energy, a force of spontaneity as its source whereas the low does not lower itself but is allowed to fall. This means that the low cannot raise itself, climbing by its own resources, whereas the high descends when it wants and is not altered or compromised by this abasement. Baader writes: "The high knows and penetrates the low...whereas the low does not know the high."[16] In fact the high enjoys a positive vulnerability that allows it to accommodate its contrary. The far away ceases to be far away if another approaches it, but the high remains such even if the low meets up with it. A weak being uncertain of itself should fear losing its identity through proximity or contact with another that risks destabilizing it and eventually causing it to descend even lower. Yet a strong being, sure of itself, a being that resides, maintains itself in the heights has the luxury of looking for another, weaker being to bring up to itself, to receive and to take in.

This asymmetry has a strong metaphysical range. Once again one sees a form of space referring beyond itself, beyond the eidetic domain where it is situated. Depth, as

15. Baudelaire, *Les fleurs du mal* LXXVIII.
16. Baader, *Werke* XIII, 115.

we have seen, divides and unfolds into two opposed moments: the envelopment that protects and the abyss that draws in and engulfs. The duality of the protecting and the abyssal prefigures on an eidetic plane the primordial metaphysical scission in the two great areas of good and evil. However, the asymmetry of the two faces of height, the irreversibility of the low with the high prefigures the mystery of kenosis. The power of the high in relation to the low, its condition of *capax inferiori* is manifested by the Ascension of Christ. "He who has descended is the same one who has ascended" (Eph 4:10). The one with the power to descend to the earth retains the power to climb to the heavens. Yet it is not here a matter of the power to do more or less, but the power *to be* more or less. The expansion of metaphysics has as its foundational principle the potentiality for the auto-surpassing of the perfect: the perfect is so perfect that it can become imperfect; it is so itself that it can become less than itself. The perfect is not condemned to remain perfect, that is, itself in its given essence. It is possible, it is permitted for it to go beyond, or rather below itself, to admit its opposite into itself, even to become it. The mystery of the Incarnation in its deep kenotic truth is the power of God to become other than Himself all the while remaining himself. The Most High descends, joins himself to the below, becomes it, all the while remaining the Most High. It is this supreme metaphysical potentiality that is found inscribed in the spatial eidos of the dimension of "height."

VIII

Time

Change and Corruption

The second region of eidetic expansion of metaphysics is time. Like space, time is a category of dispersion and it has also been represented in negative terms by a quantitative and abstract conception. This quantitative and abstract conception of time belongs to pre-critical classical thought. Reflection on and analysis of time is not lacking in "dogmatic" philosophers but it is truly present in them only in order to make a scapegoat out of the deficiencies of sensible knowledge and to be established as principle and source of the shortcomings of finitude, of the evanescent and the provisional, in short, of the instability of things in this world. Time, wrote Schelling, is "the bad conscience of every dead metaphysics."[1] Indeed, particularly because of the absence of an adequate conception of time, the pre-Kantian systems were not able to ground in concept the great metaphysical themes of subjectivity, freedom, and history. Classical philosophy has always had a strong predilection for space: think of Spinoza for whom space is one of the two known attributes of Substance, whereas time is only a pure *ens rationis*! For classical western thought, space is the location and source of stability and conservation, whereas time is the principle of modification and change. Ancient thought liked to associate time with irrationality and chance: it is an infant playing backgammon! But it equally represents it under the dark flag of an implacable destiny: it is the hidden face or the proper source of the blind progress of fate. Irrational contingency and ceaseless necessity, foreign to all sense, are the two faces of *Chronos*. And this doubly privative and negative vision seems to be imposed on Christian thought even though it is rooted in the mysteries of the Word come into time, in a theology nourished by the stories and interpretations of the History

---

1. Schelling, *Philosophie de la révélation* III, 128.

of Salvation. In his reflection on the three times and the history of the City of God, Augustine doubtlessly accomplished in his own way a rupture with Hellenic anti-temporalism, but Scholastic, Cartesian, and post-Cartesian thought all drowned (as it were) the Augustinian intuition of an authentic metaphysics of time in an abstract ontology. Time is "rehabilitated" only with the advent of the *Critique* which makes time "one of the hinges" of true metaphysics, the sense and structure of transcendental subjectivity. Hegel the philosopher of History defines time as "the concept being-there" and the most powerful philosophy of last century, that of Heidegger, will celebrate it as the horizon of Being.

The metaphysico-moral appreciation of time plays a decisive role in the comprehension of its structure, but inversely, the eidetic analysis of temporal structures has a powerful impact on the metaphysics of Time. In fact, a true eidetics did not appear before the Kantian rereading of time: the diverse "dogmatic" speculations were only able to elaborate a weak conceptuality of temporal structures, being limited to a mechanical, abstract interpretation of the three times and with concepts essentially belonging to the quantitative order. The classical vision of time begins with the sense and realization of its brevity. The time apportioned to us is brief and insufficient and even this (however congruous) portion of space and time is undermined from within. Time is the cipher of impermanence. It denotes the impossibility of foreseeing and therefore controlling the future, for those in our condition. But it is not simply a matter of the powerlessness of our hold on the world. Time is not only the cause of our non-mastery over the external, it is also and above all the sign and symbol of our non-mastery over ourselves. It signifies that everything escapes me because "at each moment...I escape myself."[2] Time is partially linked with change, but change is not a neutral ontological category, but the sign of a profound disquiet that reveals a disharmony, the presence of a hostile *no* within every *yes*, a violent opposition to all stability and all peace. In the last instance, change is only the simplistic, banal designation for becoming, for a reality founded on contradiction, or rather which is itself a contradiction. The time that is becoming, or, if you like, the face that becoming turns towards us, reflects and expresses the ceaseless peregrination of the no in the yes, of non-being in being. It is "the being that, in *being*, *is not*, and that, being *not*, is."[3]

Nietzsche speaks of "the innocence of becoming" but common sense, and its interpreters, the classical philosophers, were instead in agreement with Anaximander: existence in time seems to be an expiation and consequently a punishment that causes fragility and imposes suffering. Time is the principle of change, of the change that is everywhere and dominates all things, the change equivalent with corruption, the corruption that directly or indirectly causes all imperfection and ambiguity and which leads to the ultimate catastrophe called Death. In fact, corruption is not only comprehended in a vertical sense, but also horizontal sense: it not only brings about

---

2. Montaigne, *Essais* I, xx, 89.
3. Hegel, *Encyclopédie* II, § 258, 197.

destruction at the end of a certain flow of time, but it undermines it from within, starting now. It not only happens in the future, it is already active in the present. The diverse modalities of present corruption doubtlessly lead to a future destruction but, in anticipation of that, they weaken, decompose and reverse the condition of beings in space now. To the degree that temporal existence amounts to non-control and non-mastery of the self, it is at the origin of diverse imperfections. Life in time is characterized by "Irresolution, Ambivalence, Indecision, Incompletion, Incompleteness, Misfortune,"[4] and therefore by an entire cortege of privative realities located as much in the wake of falsehood as in that of disease and destruction.

Time is thus the principle and source of decompositions and fragmentation, and thus of weakness and disease. Nevertheless, it is also glimpsed as an ultimate power, the entire source of all that happens, the master of all things. Time houses beings, presiding at their birth and driving them towards their disappearance. People are born, grow old and disappear in time and its condition as receptacle containing and embracing all things, its power to dispense and take away life is not well distinguished. Time, as principle of uncertainty, weakness and nullity, is also a power, a supreme power that manages and dominates beings and things. Time shelters a double essence and it is because of this duality, these two components and faces, that it has been so poorly conceptualized and above all assigned opposed (and uniformly negative) attributes. Ultimately the final privation of force or supreme power of destruction, time is seen as principle and synonym of Death. Living creatures in time are mortal and their plans, works, and aspirations are located under the shadow of death, a shadow that powerfully affects the conceptual analysis of forms and moments of time, grounding and determining the unfolding of its eidetic structures.

Power and Powerlessness of the Now

The most elementary vision of time is that of a flow. Time is a stream, it flows and is running, and, at first glance, one does not even realize that it harbors a direction. The intuition of this flux is that of an evolution, which, meandering peacefully or powerfully spilling, effectuating—in both cases—is a progression that can only be conceived as irreversible. The first representation articulating this flow, this flux, will discern within it a before and after through which is discerned a tripartite structure, that of the past, present, and future. In fact, it is less a matter of a structure than a procession of realities that each manifest an evident difference in relation to the two others, but that thought takes pleasure in representing as terms of a simple succession. The past is what was before, or rather formerly, the future is what will be afterwards, or rather later, and the present is only this provisional moment where, without truly stopping, time marks the distinction between before and after, the past and the future.

---

4. Baader, *Werke* XVI, 552.

Book Two—Eidetics

Common sense and classical philosophy faithfully witness to the triad of times, but without attributing to them a truly eidetic specificity. The past, present and future are hardly three different eidē, but rather three stages of a single flow and they are barely distinguished according to their placement within this flow. The past is its beginning, the present its milieu, the future its progression, its advancement. Beyond their differentiation according to the progression of the arrow of time, the three times show no properly eidetic distinction. They each compose a moment, a point, an atom of time with the same metaphysical condition. From a quantitative point of view, the past and future are doubtlessly very different from the present, and they equally register a certain difference in relation to one another. The future is "composed" of an infinity of temporal moments, of an open infinity, whereas the past is equally enumerated as countless moments supposedly begun but which no longer constitute a present infinity. However the present reveals a radical indigence: it is also a world of temporal atoms but ones that end up being united by a specific uniqueness. One could experience the feeling of weight, extension, and depth of the present, but before the gaze of Analysis it will end up revealing its truth in the representation of only a single temporal atom, a singular point of time.

Time flows or rather it is running. It is a pathway, a progression, but it does not yet indicate any determined direction; it is a current that advances but without showing a clear direction of movement. However, if one stops to examine it closely, one "sees" that it comes from a before, a far away, called the past, and that it is going towards another far away, the future. And "between" the two far-offs is located the observation site, the point of departure of the ways going rearwards and forwards: the present. The gaze turned rearwards discovers the past, a reality that is not, or rather, is no *longer* one. The past is that which is no longer, the disappeared, the gone, the definitively gone, and the mystery of the past is that what has disappeared has left traces that cannot be erased. The double face of time vigorously shows itself in every metaphysical or moral, popular, or scholarly interpretation of the past. It is powerless and powerful: a vanished, annihilated reality that no power can bring back to life. God can make something happen and prevent something from happening, but can he make what happened not happen? But this disappearance, this non-being influences what is; it penetrates and determines beings. The past is a ghost without a body, a disappearance without substance, but it also represents an infinite weight, the very weight of Time.

To continue to use a spatial metaphor, the past could be represented as located on one of the banks of the river of "time," with the future on the other. But can we truly say that the future "takes place"? Taking place means being somewhere, but—precisely—the future is not located anywhere because it is not, that is, it is not *yet*. The future is the location of aspirations, but aspiration is doubly related to non-being. It is in an indefinite elsewhere, far beyond us, and it "is" there in a perfectly indeterminate way. The future is this not yet there that can be anything, which does not depend on the goodwill of men and is difficult to see as submitted to the laws of nature. The immemorial reveries of divination, astrology and fortune telling attest to the intuition and powerful conviction of contingency, and therefore the undeniable unforeseeability of the future that cannot be revoked but at best allows some breaches and ruptures. And this, even if for the mechanistic necessitarianisms it contains a sequence of moments as implacable as those of the past.

The third modality of time is the present, the observatory on the two others and their point of demarcation. But the present also shares the double condition of all temporality, and perhaps even more strongly than the past and future. The ambiguity between being and non-being, of anterior and ulterior proper to the past and future results in a veritable exacerbation of the opposition in the universe of the present. The present is the sole reality sensu stricto, the sole of the three times that effectively exists, but the present in its condition as instant, as now, is also something without density or weight or perdurable being. For certain philosophies like Stoicism but also for a vulgar pre-philosophical ratiocination, the present is real, in fact, the only of the three times that actually exists. And, inversely, there have been those who have sought to deny the effective reality of the present. The present is something added to something, the object of discourse or sensation, but it possesses no content of its own. It corresponds to the copula of an analytic judgment, but the copula is never a predicate. This condition of non-essence doubles up as that of non-being. Philosophers have always meditated on the present as unstable and evanescent instance, on the present that disappears as soon as it is formulated. Boileau writes: "the moment that I speak is already far from me... We are far from ourselves at every apprehended moment."[5] Contrary to the strong existential meaning attributed to *presence*, the present, as such, seems like evanescence itself. But despite these negative existential connotations, this lack of any proper material content, the present is not deprived of all efficaciousness. It fills the office of mediator, of ferryman, of necessary passage between past and future. It is also the artisan of separation. Sadness and fear pin me to the present, which does not prevent me from invoking the past or of leaping into the future. But this fixation not only breaks the continuity of my history, it also tears apart the links I can have with another. The sting of pain isolates me, torture can cause me to betray another and the anxiety of death erases my aspirations, brackets my ambitions, it tears me from care for the world and solidary with my neighbor, even with those whom I love. At the approach of death, I am so obsessed by this atom, this strata of time without thickness that I no longer have time for anything or anyone.

By surpassing the intuition of the flow and the discernment of the before and after, the articulation of time leads to the three times. And, strangely, despite its apparent infra-temporality, its lack of a true duration, it is the present, the elements of the present that impose themselves as the essence of time, as its first eidetic truth. The present is the thin layer or rather infinitesimal point of the now, which happens

---

5. Boileau-Despréaux, *Oeuvres complètes*, Épître III; Épître V.

but only for an instant, which is there but can never be fixed, without even having the time to repeat, or even to say that it is and that it is now. We remember that if after Heraclitus we cannot step into the same river twice, for Cratylus we cannot even step into it once. "Now" is the truth of time, its proper essence, but it is not truly an essence. It is not only without a stopping point but also without essence. "The now is night."[6] In other words it emits no light; no meaning shines from it. And above all it is or lasts so briefly that paradoxically it seems to fall below time. The poet speaks of "the instant…this point, this time without time."[7] The point is without extension, in its occurrence it is without temporal extension. In other words its punctuality condemns the now to a quasi infra-temporal condition. An extensionless point, the now is an atom entirely separated from all, closed in on itself. It is a first obvious fact that time is continuous, but since Aristotle philosophy has professed that "it is impossible for a continuity to be formed from indivisibles" (*Physics* 231a). The present-now is an atom without link to all that is other than it, to any other atom; it is the principle and paradigm of discontinuous time escaping from itself. The theme of the being-other-than-itself of now-time is not the result of a conceptual dialectic. It does not intersect any longer with the intuition that is found at the origin of the metaphysical themes of appearance. The now is not simply a time that happens not to be fixed, a time that, so to speak, is struck with wanderlust and is always on the move. Well to the contrary, its atomistic condition makes inexplicable the process of time, its progression, its continuous unfolding. Quantum physics explains that the electron leaps from one place to another in a discontinuous way. But if the exteriority proper to the material can cope with discontinuity, the world of the subject, the supreme sphere of time cannot accept it. Subjectivity certainly knows rupture, the leap, but the leaps that it accomplishes result from itself; they happen by virtue of the a priori synthesis that the subject is.

The now-atom can express the powerful intuition of indigence; it does justice to the feeling of the fragmentary, of the rupture proper to finitude, but it leads to an impasse in the discourse on time, a double impasse, moral and ontological. The discontinuity that establishes the atomic conception of time destroys even the idea of moral responsibility and it is the principle of an ontology where beings can persist in their being only by virtue of an external principle. The reading of time in terms of a rhapsodic succession of instants without connections, obliterates the continuity which allows me to make promises, which forces me to pay my debts, and which makes me capable of recognizing the actions of my past as mine, and to form projects concerning the future. The absurdity of the conception of abstract time, of atom-time, is powerfully manifested by the feeling of remorse, of repentance, which attests to my consciousness of having been the author of my past actions. The request for pardon that I can formulate signifies that I consider myself to be the same person who had

---

6. Hegel, *Phénoménologie de l'esprit* I, 84.

7. Donne, *Complete Poetry and Selected Prose*, 692; quoted in Ellrodt, *Les poètes métaphysiques anglais* I, 89n33.

accomplished the misdeeds in the near or remote past and who would like to be delivered from them. The acute consciousness of moral responsibility, the good or bad conscience that I experience is the "proof" of my moral continuity and constitutes the counterpart to an ontological continuity whereas the vision of atom-time is the very principle of all ontological and moral heteronomies. It can certainly be the source of a profound piety, of the feeling of being maintained in existence by a transcendent being: after all, if the creation of the world was a sovereign act of God, should it not always be required for the continuous existence of his work? The reality, however banal, of sleep symbolizes, so to speak, our powerlessness to maintain ourselves by our own powers. One knows the old Jewish prayer that thanks the Most High for having carried us across the abyss of the night. . . But this deep intuition of the fragility and precariousness of all finite existence can be exacerbated and lead to more and more radical theories of continuous creation, doctrines of the divine sovereignty that obliterate the creature's ontological autonomy. The theologoumenon of unlimited sovereignty has always made a good bedfellow with the nominalisms of various stripes. And the teaching on the atom-time is precisely a nominalism. It refuses to attribute essence and existence to anything other and more than the isolated point without true extension, without duration.

The Infinite Divisibility: Work and Money

The now-instant is the paradigmatic notion of a vision of time that refers to moral and ontological heteronomies. But the atomization of time is not problematic solely because of its implications and consequences, it also does not adequately express our native intuition of time itself, our elementary conception of the temporal. The idea of atom-time appears following large "successive" steps of the comprehension of time, namely, the flow, before and after, its structuration in three times. But the instant, principle, and source of temporal evanescence—in other words responsible for time's powerlessness to gain access to being—also falls short of essence. Put another way, if we do not manage to conceive of time, it is not only because "we never have any time" to grasp it, to "arrest its flight," but also and above all because it lacks structure allowing us to define it. The instantaneous, atomic condition of the now offers some elements of time that can no longer be considered minor, but their condition of being located at the ultimate limit, disposing only of a tiny reality still furnishes only an external pre-quidditative common denominator. Modern reflection—actually already Aristotle—wants to regularize this untamed condition of the atoms of time, and failing to assign them a properly eidetic structure, it tends to impose on them a uniformity, one that will be only quantitative and therefore abstract. The nows can mark unequal temporal values, atoms can be longer or shorter, but they become completely measurable and measured. Of course, the now is originally the elementary moment only of the present, but for lack of an intrinsic, eidetic differentiation of the three times, the instant transposed into a measured moment becomes the common element of the three times. The quantitative uniformization defuses the subversive charge of evanescence and manages to deceive the foundational intuition of the continuity of the *tempus*. The three times constitute a *continuum*, a line that one could cut up, portion out however and, indeed, *whenever* one wants. People have always complained about the insufferable length of days and hours, but also of the tragic brevity of time given to us. From now on the respective intuitions of the lengthiness and brevity of time will be transposed into measured, quantified portions of a line.

To render measurable, to mathematize time constitutes a victory won over the atom, over this chaos of evanescence and this opacity of self-closure. Yet it is a Pyrrhic victory. The uniformization according to the quantitative allows the use of time, its integration into rational discourse, but the price of this integration proves to be prohibitive. The caprices of the instant are certainly halted, its sovereignty is bridled, but the reduction of the now volatile to the abstract regime of the quantitative does not yet amount to a true eidetic reading of the structure of time. Instants are no longer radically heterogeneous atoms, but are submitted to the general condition of measurement. However measure reaches them from the outside, it is not a function of an interior source, an intrinsic principle. It is an emblematic category of quantity, but we cannot forget that quantity represents an inessential difference! Measure does not join the articulations of portions of time; it is like a coat thrown over them, even a straightjacket that disciplines and masters them. The arithmetization of time comes down to rereading and rearticulating it, but this rereading is the transposition of the flow, of the movement of time into an external, abstract representation.

Arithmetically divided time is an essential factor of the rationalization of existence. It increases the efficaciousness of the social organization and productivity of work. But the augmentation of the efficaciousness unfortunately has as its counterpart the equalizing uniformization of action and life. Money is its symbol and source. Moralists and social critics have always denounced the dangers and harmful effects of money, the rapacity of those who seek it, the baseness, predacity of its agents and servants. They hold forth against money, the root of all evils, the principal factor of the corruption of social life, and yet the true culprit of all these derivatives is not money, but time. More precisely, uniformized time, principle of the alienation of beings that reduces them to being only instances of an abstract equality and interprets them starting from a ladder of quantitative value. Money is truly that *compendium universale*, the counter-value of all things. "Every man has his price," observes the disillusioned moralist, but if men have their price this is only because the things of their world each have their own price. And if each thing has its price, then everything existing on earth can be expressed in terms of price. And Price, at least indirectly, refers to Time.

The price of something signifies the quantity of money needed to sell and to buy. Money is a general instrument allowing the exchange of things for one another. The exchanged things are estimated to be of the same usefulness and importance.

Bartering marks the stammering attempt at evaluation where a thing or concrete service is conceded against another thing or service. The arrival of money will introduce a third term into the exchange, an abstract term by which the two others are evaluated. Originally, money is also a concrete thing, made of silver or gold. But with the arrival of bank bills, checks, and wire transfers, this third "thing" loses its concrete thinghood and is more and more reduced to abstraction. The slow substation of monetary transaction for the diverse kinds of bartering is a function of a reinterpretation of things and services as *merchandise*. To understand something as merchandise means no longer thinking of it in itself, on its own terms, but as virtual or actual part of an external and abstract whole. Merchandise is an entity that can be exchanged for another and therefore which has its truth by virtue and according to its place within a universal system of useful realities and an enumerable utility. Things as merchandise are expressed in terms of money. Money is the "representative" of "universal merchandise."[8] But the merchandise (the value of which is determined in monetary terms) is not a material thing, an object of wood, rock or metal, nor a personal or administrative service, but a social abstract relation. The monetary value of things produced and exchanged is the result of a complicated and invisible operation that reinterprets things according to their role, their utility within the relations among members of a social body, but ultimately these relations are relations of time.

That the producers or providers of service are paid per service rendered or hourly, weekly or monthly, their remuneration is always calculated according to time—not according to *their* time, the time that these individuals have effectively employed in order to make an object or perform a service, but according to a social, universal time. A journalist or supermarket cashier is supposed to work as many hours per week as a high speed train conductor or a top State administration official. Nevertheless, for the same duration of labor the first examples may earn three or five times less than the second. Kant wrote that money "is *for men the* universal *means of exchange of their industriousness*,"[9] and yet if this diligence, this industry can require the same quantity and the same intensity of effort in different kinds of employees, they do not reach a salary of the same amount, the same quantity of money at the end of their labor. Instead of being evaluated in and from itself, the work is reduced to the condition of merchandise of a more general and universal kind. This entails the obliteration of the thing and the dehumanization of man.

In the period anterior to the Industrial Revolution, man always had before himself things that he considered capable of serving a purpose. But if every material entity is understood as susceptible to becoming an instrument of a need or human pleasure, the things of nature, like the things of art, remain surrounded by respect. They are given but not in an unlimited quantity; they are not produced and possessed only at the end of a ceaseless, difficult effort. An elementary rarity is the metaphysical regime

8. Marx, *Manuscrits de 1857–1858 ("Grundrisse")*, Première partie, 79s.
9. Kant, *Métaphysique des Moeurs* § 31, in *Oeuvres* vol. 3, 548.

of the thing that one appreciates and tries to conserve and if necessary repair. Numerous businesses used to be dedicated to fixing broken things, the repair of cracked pots, torn clothing, broken spades and hoes. But with the advent of an ever more powerful and efficient industry, we stop repairing things—for it is not worth the effort! The work required for the repair of a broken object approaches and even surpasses that required for the production of a new object. Consequently, instead of repairing the object, it is thrown away and replaced. This massive modification of a relation between humanity and things from time immemorial seems to signal a huge human victory: the thing loses its autarky and becomes malleable, exploitable, and dispensable; humanity disposes of it at will, at our pleasure. The evolution of the conditions of work thus entails a true destabilization of things that, having fallen into the Provisional, witnesses to the sovereignty of time, arithmetized and uniformized. Yet this domination of uniformized time over things leads also to a tyranny over humanity—more precisely, to the tyranny of abstract Time over personal time.

The reduction of things, of products of work to human temporality has always been an essential element of economic and social relations, but it is completed by globalization that, under the appearance of a faultless equality, can lead to violent inequalities. Globalization accomplishes the reduction of the time of one man to that of another. The lowering or improvement of customs barriers, and the decline in cost of maritime or air transport lead to the fragilization of the industries and agricultures of underdeveloped countries. As the nineteenth-century Indian weaver working manually was incapable of competing with the textile manufacturer from Manchester, the farmers of sub-Saharan Africa today are almost defenseless before the products of western agribusiness. Modern production requires infinitely less time and effort than traditional production and therefore the products it delivers to the supermarket are much less expensive. Consequently, the traditional artisan or farmer must dedicate much more time to the production of the same merchandise, and their time is therefore worth much less, often many times less than that of their "modern" counterpart. This inequality of the time of men in the same business doubles in the inequality of the time of men in different lines of work. This has certainly existed since the social division of work, and in fact since the beginning of Humanity. But the economic conditions of the modern market systematize and aggravate it. The value of the time of a certain work is a function of the valorization of the time of other works. The infinite diversity of works is surreptitiously reduced to a basic uniformity. These works are each producers of merchandise but the merchandise expresses "the undifferentiated human work . . . the quotidian reduction of concrete works to a common force of human work"[10] which corresponds to the "time of work socially necessary" for the constitution of merchandise, and thus an abstract and tyrannical Time—tyrannical because abstract.

---

10. Schmidt, "Verdinglichung; Vergegenständlichung," 610.

Time

The Unfolding of the Given

The reading of time as infinitely divisible establishes a properly arithmetical vision of it. Time becomes masterable for practice and conceptualizable for theory. Through its arithmetical divisibility it surpasses the condition of heterogeneity-discontinuity of the now-atom in order to accede to the homogeneity of an infinity of similar, identical moments. This uniform time has as paradigm and supreme manifestation the time of socially necessary work. But this abstract *tempus* proceeds with a cortege of failures and violences in its wake. It is supposed to constitute the order of all that unfolds within it. In reality, it leads to the fragilization and undifferentiation of things as well as to human impoverishment and enslavement. The resemblance or rather profound identity of its measurable particles represents a pre-quidditative definition of time. Unfortunately the metaphysical truth of this identity according to the quantitative is only a matter of sameness. *Tempus* flows, is punctuated by before and after, divided according to the modes of time, but all this differentiation remains superficial, even fictional. We could bend the discourse of the dividable towards the same, but we would not avoid the damage done by this blind rationalization of the temporal. We would not overcome its heterogeneity by putting on the straightjacket of homogeneity. The uniformity or rather uniformization does not yet amount to a true structuration, a harmonious articulation. This classical and *analytic* discourse on time is condemned to powerlessness. Moving within the flat and arid regions of the pre-quidditative, it can only remain below a true eidetics of the temporal. In order better to understand the deficiencies of these unfortunate attempts of articulation through the homogenous, common to all pre-Kantian philosophy of time, we must continue to explore its metaphysical implications.

The *universal compendium* of the "time of socially necessary work" is a form of abstract time, glimpsed according to simultaneity or rather coexistence. More precisely, it is *tempus* reduced to the present. Yet the perennial truth of time, the universal intuition that we have of this reality, is not that of a flat board of the present but of flow, succession. The advent of perfect homogeneity that the abstract time of work announces and accomplishes, so to speak, spreads time out in the present and makes it clear, transparent, and continuous, but of a continuity that is only the unfolding of the given and lacks true novelty. Existence in time that one would complain or be happy about is understood by the creature as the location of the unexpected, even the unforeseeable, of that which astonishes and shocks, of that which one can neither divine nor deduce. Time is a river. Its progress certainly only obeys its own laws, but the chance happenings of physical nature as well as the initiatives and efforts of individuals and whole peoples are able if not to divert its course completely, at least to plant some new formations, some islets of the new. But the time of sameness effaces, even suppresses all vision of historical time: what happens may surprise us, we may not accept it, or may struggle against it, but we cannot modify its progression. This time is not history but *fatum*, destiny—of which nobody can avoid the consequences and with which nobody or nothing can interfere. It is not susceptible of modulation by variation, but a perfectly coherent fabric of events that cannot be embroidered, a succession of good and bad things that cannot be evaded. In fact, Destiny is the name for the unfolding of the time of sameness according to its immanent acceptation, whereas Predistination is its designation starting from a transcendent perspective. Destiny designates the unfolding of the same without discerning within it an external principle, whereas predestination attributes a supreme power to Spirit, a "decision" to the Divinity for beginning the course of moments and determining its structure. In both cases, what was would not have been able to be otherwise, what is cannot be different, and what will be must happen.

In fact from the metaphysical point of view destiny and predestination represent only an external variation on Time. Whether the determination of the unfolding is intrinsic or extrinsic, immanent or transcendent, what matters is that it is always only a matter of the given. Here we rediscover the theme of justice, the interpretation of judgment, of *Dikē* in terms of *Chronos*. If justice is ultimately only a transposition of vengeance, time is the medium of its procedure. And the violence of this procedure, this explication of Justice understood as expiation is nothing other than the auto-propulsion of the same where, once its time is gone, the given is overcome and suppressed. While the compendium marks the coexistence of sames, destiny-predestination is the cipher of their succession, a succession that is related to the uniform and which also takes place in an inevitable, necessary way. The Leibnizian formula is well known: "the present is pregnant with the future." The future is separated from the present only by a distance on the temporal line, but its content is already there, under the form of virtuality, of preformation within the present: "the future is" already "there. . .rolled up" in the present.[11] It is coiled up and waits to be unrolled. Chryssipus already wrote: "The flow of time is like the unwinding of a rope that brings about nothing new but develops what was there previously."[12] The present succeeds the past, and the future the present in an inevitable, mechanical and necessary way. Because the elements, portions of time are metaphysically identical, the same; nothing prohibits the passage from one moment to the next. This passage, as it were, is obvious: it can take place in difficult, dramatic circumstances and yet it does not represent anything new. It only makes explicit what is implicit, un-veiling the given.

This theory of time as the unfolding of the given is at the heart of the Kierkegaardian critique of idealisms, whether Socratic or Hegelian. All those idealisms of perfect Logic, of complete Encyclopedias ultimately transcribe only the immanent movement of the concept that punctuates philosophical anamnesis. Idealism envisages the conceptuality of the world which, seen horizontally, gives the transcendental totality of all predicates and, understood vertically, unwinds according to a perfectly rational

11. Bergson, *L'Évolution créatrice* 341, in *Oeuvres*, 784.
12. Chryssippus, *De divinatio* I, 56 in *Oeuvre philosophique*, vol. 2, 1397.

progression, and envisages and promises a complete making explicit of all meaning and signification. The Absolute Spirit is supposed to animate the good unwinding of this triumphant cortege of contents, but unfortunately it registers disturbing affinities with the (not very sly) demon of Laplace. The flux of time is held back on all sides, its twists and turns are straightened and the velocity of its different stages is ratified. The unfolding of time from sameness is a supreme parade of Analytic Judgment, but here also novelty, the surmounting of the self can be enacted only by the a priori synthesis. Analysis sinks into the Given because it lacks true differentiation and immanent articulation. It conserves continuity by engaging all of its powers, but by sliding into the uniform it compromises its creative vigor, evacuates its essence or its innovative truth. Arithmetized, Uniform Time claims to render justice to the basic structuration of the three times but it remains powerless to found a true temporal eidetics. Here you can clearly see that the a priori synthesis not only concerns the life of judgment but also that of eidē, or more precisely, that the eidē are not simple sections of the quidditative but instances of judgment. In the occurrence of the specific manners of judgment the course of Time assures the crossing at each instance of the gap separating one from the other two tiniest moments. Philosophy will do justice to the innovatory truth of Time only through the discernment of specific moments where the progression of time accomplishes its articulation. There is conceptual interpretation of the Newness only in terms of a true eidetics of *Chronos*. We could then step twice into the same river, but (with time unfolding according to an organic continuity) each of these immersions will be different.

Repetition and Rythm

To conceive time as the simple unfolding of the given deprives it of one of its essential components, namely, newness. But the ontological category of novelty has differentiation as its counterpart, or rather as its condition on the plane of essence. The foundational intuition of Time is that of flow, of a river. Yet the flow is truly a succession, and all succession involves distinct moments. For the progression of time to be more than a simple unwinding of what is coiled up, a mechanical explication of the given, it must be seen as a succession of different things. The first difference doubtlessly discerned in the course of time is anterior to its articulation into moments. This first difference adapts to the homogeneity of arithmetical, divisible time and in fact can be expressed in quantitative terms. The first difference, or rather differentiation of *tempus* is that of speed. Time can flow slowly or swiftly. Its course can be a barely perceptible progression and is here barely distinguishable from stagnation. It so fully takes its time that it almost seems to be stopped, "suspended midflight." But *Chronos* can also advance quickly. It can run distances with maddening, breakneck speed. Instead of marking moments and steps it seems to tear through its stages. Obsessed with the aspiration to cross the most space possible, fast time claims to be, as it were, immediately future, but this at the cost of bracketing every landmark and excluding every possibility of differentiation. However, speed and slowness still remain resolutely below all structuration of time. In fact, if from a phenomenological point of view both can manifest an eidetic sui generis reality, from a metaphysical perspective they constitute only instances of one and the same category: speed is a lesser slowness and slowness is a lesser speed. These are authentic representatives, servants of homogeneity. But in order to do justice to the truth of time, we must glimpse its essential potentialities for heterogeneity. Time is succession and succession can be only different moments. But more quickly and less quickly only take the pulse of time's course; they do not punctuate its progression.

The preparation, the properly termed pre-history of succession is repetition. The unfolding of the given is arrested or rather suspended; the course of time endures an interruption. But this interruption is only momentary. More precisely it serves, and only serves, the appearance of moments. The first appearance of moments is still done according to the economy of sameness and it does not yet amount to an introduction of heterogeneity within the homogenous. In fact, the first example of succession is not yet conformed to any criteria or quidditative rule, it obeys no principle of structuration. This first and most elementary kind of succession is repetition. Repetition is the return of the same, a return the frequency of which is not determined and the location is not precise. Repetition is the first victory that time seems to have over itself: time is assumed here to possess an articulation but it is not yet truly one. It is only an interruption of the flux, redeemed by an initial action, but deprived of intrinsic rationality. In fact, repetition is interested only in a single thing, the return of the same, without caring if it obeys only a simple regularity or if it is done according to a meaning. Repetition hardly violates the smooth continuity of the homogenous, it only, as it were, scratches the surface. It displays a great neutrality or rather renounces all signification in advance, but this abdication of responsibility will pay a stiff price. Repetition easily dons the colors or rather the non-color of monotony. It is deprived of all pretention to differentiation. Like a stupid student, it repeats its words; old and senile, it drools. It possesses the art—or rather the absence of art—of vexing and ultimately exasperating. It doubtlessly has inscribed within it some negative "powers." It causes the spines of analysis to burst forth, made sharper and more dangerous by tautology: "I repeat!" inaugurates the discourse of the intolerant; the injunction "repeat what you said" distills the threat. There is doubtlessly imparted to it a certain creativity by ricochet. If repetition most often leads to boredom and makes us yawn, it remains true that "the gestures of an orator that are not funny in particular, cause laughter through repetition."[13] But these colorful exceptions do not truly change the greyness of a parade of advents where the same wants to effect change without reaching the constitution of difference.

We are often asked to repeat what we said so our interlocutor can understand us, but the repetition only very rarely brings comprehension. The one who repeats is

---

13. Bergson, *Le rire*, 26, in *Oeuvres*, 403.

short on his capabilities; he does not understand himself very well, does not clearly conceive what he thinks and says. Repetition is condemned to fail to accomplish true efforts and works of conceptualization; it seems hostile to meaning. It mumbles formulae and tends to clichés. Instead of deploying the constitutive moments of an expression or phrase, it prefers to represent them as is. To all appearances it arrests the effort of research and is content to recall the given. In reality, repetition's hidden face is monotony. And monotony stupefies and causes despair. It does not nourish thought and prevents consciousness' return to itself: where can we, where should we stop in this homogenous fog? Where are the landmarks and guardrails to grab onto? From which edge or escarpment, islet or sandbar of time may we seek a place of rest? Can we find an observation tower? The misery and deep noxiousness of monotony is that it interferes with the power comprehension. The monotonous unwinding of time is deprived of reliefs where the mind can come to rest: the flux of consciousness is endured absent of a knowledge and discernment of the chain of successive moments. In other words, the consciousness of time is lessened in order to endure the sequence of the arithmetical particles of *Chronos* without structuration, the mechanical operation of seconds and minutes.

"Superior" forms of monotony doubtlessly exist where repetition is delivered from the misery of the a-conceptual and accedes in its own way to the universe of meaning. Liturgical psalmody or sacred dances of certain archaic cultures are sublime occurrences of the repetition of the same that is here revitalized starting from a bountiful heterogeneity. They are privileged instances of monotony integrated into a subtle movement of the redemption of meaning. However, at this moment monotonous repetition surpasses itself and is transposed into an authentic structuration where the succession of the same is subsumed under the vivid progression of rhythm. After crude time, time interrupted without reason and irregularly, and the repetition where interruption obeys the order of sameness, this "form of fluidity"[14] represented by rhythm is the first instance of a structuring interruption. If repetition is the monotonous succession of identicals, of sames, rhythm introduces succession according to difference. It is either the return according to longer or shorter intervals of unities of identical time or the advent according to equal intervals of equal and unequal unities. Rhythm *sensu stricto* is an aesthetic category, more precisely that of music and poetry. In music it measures and regulates the relation between dissonants and consonants; in poetry it is above all related to the order of plurality of syllables. In ancient poetry rhythm is as it were assisted by meter, that element of measure for verse composed of two "feet." However, while rhythm, which for modern aesthetics is only "the formed movement" still anterior to all concretion, can very well do without meter; meter has use and life only within rhythm. Rhythm seems to represent a radical rupture with repetition. It trades identity for difference, it vivifies the dreary uniformity the monotone. In short it surpasses the homogenous in the direction of heterogeneity. Its innovational

---

14. Benveniste, *Problèmes de linguistique générale*, 327ss.

scope notwithstanding, rhythm remains an instance of differentiation of the quantitative order of time. It certainly introduces difference within sameness, but this alterity does not yet come from the eidetic structure of *tempus*, and is only a variation on the abstract uniformity of arithmetical time. In fact, the category of rhythm is expanded in other spheres than time sensu stricto and it is this expansion that will confirm its confinement in the quantitative through the introduction of heterogeneous moments.

Rhythm is located in the world of nature as well. The succession of seasons manifests a supreme form of rhythm: it involves a regular procession of different contents. With its freshness spring melts the frost, unfreezes the numbness of winter. It lavishes flavors and lights; it flourishes and disappears in its turn before the heat and harvests of summer which itself withdraws or rather dissolves in the enervations and witherings of autumn, where life droops, tightens and falls. The procession of seasons displays a certain inevitable monotony, but the irregular appears within the regular, difference within the uniform. The fires of alterity burn within the night of sameness and break up the greyness of monotony. The regular alternation of the seasons presides over agricultural labor and makes the difficult condition and countless servitudes of the worker tolerable while the work of the chain laborer, all the tasks and chores where repetition undividedly reigns, brutalizes and alienates.[15] The changing of the seasons seems like a provision provided by nature in order to mitigate the pains of the daily human action, but human society always inserts or interposes in the passage of days some breaks, intervals that plant rhythm within it. Human life—the central theme of *Works and Days* (Hesiod)—is the unwinding of days and years where man is called to the daily repetition of humble tasks or more elaborate actions, it does not matter. But the religious, social or familial Feast interrupts repetition. The feast is essentially the reinterpretation and restructuration of the present starting from an event, a form of the past that is commemorated. Commemoration evokes a moment external to the unwinding of daily life, of the same, from which it tears our gaze, refocusing it on something different. The feast subverts the homogeneity of the flow. It interrupts the daily activities by prescribing the suspension of routine work undertaken for the preservation of life. It orders other activities, essentially ritual, liturgical actions and it is most often accompanied by entertainment, games, even excesses, celebratory meals, or orgies. Excess of food and especially drink are means—certainly primitive but nevertheless very logical, very appropriate and very efficacious means—for this rupture with utility and routine. They symbolize the exuberant aspirations of Life which consents from time to time to bracket the exigencies, the meager and pindling needs of survival.

The discovery and constitution of rhythm within the temporality of natural and cultural phenomena enriches and diversifies our consciousness of time and yet still does not surpass the conception of a uniform, abstract time. The homogenous

---

15. Vető, *La métaphysique religieuse de Simone Weil*, 133. (*The Religious Metaphysics of Simone Weil*, 111.)

is elaborated and modulated but it does not give itself the forms it takes on; it only receives them from the outside and they remain extrinsic to it. Time is certainly structured, but it is in function of and starting from its contents, not by virtue of itself.

The Irreversibility of Death

Rhythm and its cultural translation, the feast, represent a very important moment of the efforts to overcome the homogeneity of time, but they run smack into its irreversibility. Irreversibility is the ultimate principle of the conception of abstract time, but it proves equally to be a *conditio sine qua non* of the articulation of time, of History. Time is flux, a flow, but the flow does not merely mark an un-arrested fluidity or progression, or an infinity, or even a "bad" infinity. The flow of time is *irreversible*. This means that you cannot return to it, you cannot turn back its path: each of its moments is definitive. A certain number of forms of the decisive, of the immodifiable, conducive to what happens in time exist. There are irrevocable judgments, unreimbursable debts, irreparable injuries. Imprescriptible crimes and the unforgivable sin are commonly known. It is always a matter of something that has taken place, which has happened and cannot be remedied or undone, something with a fateful efficaciousness of which the action cannot be stopped. But irreversibility is the core, or, if you like, the seat of all ineffaceable realities.

The irreversibility of this "completely incomplete" reality that is time is anterior to all division and all structuration, and in fact to every consideration of interruption and cessation. Time flows, it flows by, and you cannot catch it or put your hand on it. Even if you manages to do so, it serves no consequence. You can touch or brush against the flux, or even dip your hand in the river, but it continues to flow. It progresses, flows through mountains and valleys; at times it overflows. Irreversibility qualifies the whole of the flux, but it does not denote it only according to its totality: it is irreversible as a whole, but its irreversibility affects each of its moments, everything that it drags along and carries. Time is the procession of events, but "everything that takes place in it takes place only once."[16] The truth of the temporal is that what occurs happens only once. Each moment of time and what it contains is unique. Said differently, this blind and unstoppable torrent, this violent unwinding apparently neither avoids nor respects any reality that it finds on its path. It is also the very principle of the ultimate seriousness of every singular reality. The flux of time seems to annul and obliterate everything that is stable. Nevertheless, this ultimate subversion of permanence equally founds the value and price of singular realities. *Chronos*, cosmic category par excellence, is also—in an indirect, hidden and obscure way—the principle of History. And it is the master and source of Death. Death is the emblematic

---

16. Spengler, *Der Untergang des Abendlandes*, 127.

example of temporal existence, the paradigm of all change, the change that "realizes" its essence in its very disappearance.

Irreversibility is an essential moment of time as such. But this does not mean that nothing can bring the flow to an end. Rather, it means that what happens in and through it is not submitted to any regulation or condition. More precisely: the dramatic sense of the irreversible is not that what happens in time is destined to remain forever but rather that what it dismantles can never return to existence. And death is precisely the dismantling par excellence that can never be repaired.

Time, our lifetime leads us to death in an irreversible way. It is the ultimate and inevitable horizon of our life but it is a horizon that is not merely located far away, in the future. Everyone knows that "no one is too young to die" and a commonplace saying is that if death is the most certain, its hour is the most uncertain. Death is the principle of our fragility, our precariousness, of the impermanence and contingency of our existence. Whether conceived as coming from beyond, coming towards us, or as rising up from within, falling upon us, or ripening within us like the worm in a fruit, it destabilizes us. As Epicurus said, "concerning everything else, it is possible to obtain security, but with death, we, like other men, live in a city without walls."[17] Humanity lives under the shadow of death, a profoundly ambiguous condition. Attention to and anticipation of your death can push you into the arms of despair or into the cynical hedonism of *carpe diem*. It can equally lead you to recall the ultimate seriousness of your actions and endeavors. Since you live only once, everything you do carries a weight. And, above all, everything you do not do now cannot be accomplished later!

You can doubtlessly not fear death, face it with serenity as "the blessed passage," the end of all misery and suffering, the way of access to definitive peace. You can also find refuge in certain doctrines or beliefs such as reincarnation, which relativize the seriousness of death and advocate for a continuation that removes its sting. On the other hand, like the patriarchs of the Old Testament, old men having completed their course, you could welcome death "happy and full of days" (Gen 25:8). You can still find consolation in the conviction that death is "a piece of the order of the universe,"[18] that it takes part in the great cosmic process of Nature. But if philosophies and religions can be a support before the face of death, if they can make the moment when its sword falls less bitter, less frightful, it is still usually understood as a catastrophe, the ultimate catastrophe in fact of our condition. You cannot justify or explain it. They say death is "egalitarian" but this shows precisely its irrationality. It strikes without discernment, regarding neither age nor merit, without taking into account the usefulness of the individual or the consequences of his or her disappearance for others. On the other hand, if death is inevitable, it comes "like a thief in the night," unexpectedly, always too early or always too late.

---

17. Epicurus, *Sent. Vatic.* 31.
18. Montaigne, *Essais* I, 20.

Time

Death's coming at a time when it should not, too early or too late, shows its inopportunity, its incongruity and absurdity. Death is certain and inevitable; no one can escape it. Yet it is neither normal nor natural. It is not a native reality; it does not share in the primitive structure of our condition. Death occurs as the consequence of an accident, somehow a banal accident, but usually a culpable accident, referring to a moral responsibility. According to the Bantu people, in the beginning death did not reign, it was brought about because of an unfortunate failure. God sent the chameleon with the message of immortality, but the very slow animal came late and stammered. Or a man found a large squash, opened it without any reason and Death, which was locked inside escaped. According to other accounts, the disobedience of a woman or man triggered the series of events leading to death.[19] But even if it is related only to some very trivial prohibitions, the disobedience traces the marks of culpability. Death happens at the margins of the original order; it confuses the structure, contrary to its intentions. In other words it constitutes a tear in the tissue of the world and as such, it must be read as the translation and consequence of a hostile, rebellious intention. "God did not create death" (Wis 1:13) says the Bible, and the Christian tradition ties it to the appearance of the Devil and sin. In one way or another, it should be understood as the consequence, the sanction, and the punishment for a transgression. Our world lives under this threatening shadow but at the end of history when the time of God is instituted, "death will be no more" (Rev 21:4).

The disappearance of death at the end of time is only the "realization" of its essence: death is what should not be and therefore it realizes itself in the act of one's ceasing to be. In "primitive" societies (but not only) the death of a man is never conceived as natural. A cause is sought, most often through another person, by poison or witchcraft, or even in the deceased himself because of a fault or transgression. The unnaturalness of death expresses the irrationality of its essence. We do not comprehend it when another dies, and above all we cannot imagine ourselves dying. The difficulty of conceiving the irreversible end of an existence translates the incongruity, absurdity, and even the impossibility of death (in the very face of its effective truth). Death seems impossible to us; it opposes all our expectations and aspirations. It seems deprived of meaning. Above all it is opposed to the order governed by Justice and the Good. And this acute feeling, the irrefutable conviction of the impossibility of this most certain reality, possesses a deeply philosophical reason for its existence. In addition to the invincible intuition of the incompatibility of this terrible evil with the Sovereign Good, death is also rejected because it represents an irreparable break in the rationality of finite existence. Death seems truly like the absolute bankruptcy of all being and all temporal action. Yet, notwithstanding its terrors and horrors, it presents itself as the perfect accomplishment of Time. The classical vision of Tempus is determined starting from the perception of the flow that can be regulated through its arithmetization but the ultimate truth of which remains its irreversibility. Yet death is the supremely

---

19. See Vető, "Le rôle de l'homme dans les mythes de mort," 77sq.

irreversible. However, precisely as paradigm or phenomenon of the accomplishment of the irreversible, death lacks meaning. It presents to thought irrationality and absurdity; it entails imprisonment and despair in our outlook and action. Classical philosophy leads to the comprehension of death as the truth of time. Yet this conception of death as imprisonment, as division from others, as principle of absurdity, is only the result of a mechanical metaphysics, of an interpretation of time that remains below a truly eidetic interpretation. If someone holds an inadequate conception of death as the realization of time from a metaphysico-moral point of view this is also because he failed to conceptualize the eidetic structure of *tempus*.

IX

Times

Towards an Eidetic of *Chronos*

The results of the interpretation of time in terms of a divisibility of a homogenous reality has lead to a double impasse. Death was the very essence and meaning of time, but death itself is deprived of meaning. To understand time as the horizon of meaning-less death reveals the indigence and bankruptcy of every classical conception of *Chronos*. There is doubtlessly no relation of direct implication or automatic derivation between the epistemological analysis of time and the "metaphysico-moral "results" of this consideration. However, let us recall the adage, "a tree is recognized by its fruits." The fruits of this interpretation of time practiced by philosophers from Cratylus to Laplace are as meager as they are bitter. The theory of time as irreversible flux having as unique articulation the repetition of the homogenous finds its realization, its truth in the dark and savage intuition of the irreversible. Irreversibility seems to do justice to the "flux" essence of time, and it even anticipates the nature of direction. Nevertheless, it prohibits it from any possibility of articulation and condemns it not only to remain below Meaning but to be violently opposed to it. The only way to remedy this downward slide of the philosophy of time is to submit it resolutely to analysis, the study of its sui generis eidetic structure. The interlude of the Feast has shown that the homogenous is susceptible fecundation by heterogeneity, that the introduction of true diversity can breathe meaning into the Continuum of portions of the same nature. But the rhythm that time receives from the feast originates from outside of it: we certainly find time fitted with articulation, but one proper only to what takes place within it, to its contents therefore, and not to the container that it itself is. Yet the proper articulation of time must come from time itself. Kant's important discovery was that time is not a concept but an intuition. In other words, it cannot be submitted to a structuration in properly conceptual terms, that is, in logical terms or in terms of material essences.

Kantianism will pull the wool over the eyes of classical theories of time because it intends to explain it according to its eidetic, immanent, sui generis structure. As space spatializes itself, time "temporalizes itself."[1] It contains or harbors an armature or rather a noetic structure that cannot be translated into "theoretical" categories but only described by enumerating and analyzing its proper eidē. To do this it is first necessary to rise above the mathematico-atomic vision of *Chronos*, whether dynamic or static, Heraclitean or Newtonian. Time is not an unwinding of the same, but an unfolding of the unity of the same and the other, an original a priori synthesis differentiating and structuring itself in a multiplicity of particular syntheses. There are three great moments to this rereading of time that do justice to its true "timefulness,"[2] to the eidetic becoming of temporalization. First, the truth of time is not in the flow of the homogenous, but is found within the living unity of heterogeneous duration, its auto-differentiation. Then, the heterogeneity obeys laws where the synthesis of the same and other, of the one and multiple is enunciated and manifest through a plurality of temporal relations. Finally, the "horizontal" articulation of *tempus* according to different figures of the relation between succeeding moments gives way to the edification of a "system of the three times," namely the exposition of the proper manners to Time as it gives itself an eidetic structure through present, past, and future.

Duration

We doubtlessly cannot and must not bracket the image of flow and flux: after all, it is our first intuition of time our foundational intuition. What is required is an essential rectification: instead of explicating the flux according to the false rationality of the continuity of the same, we must integrate the other within it. In fact, the philosophical explication of the flux by the line—the arrow of time—is incorrect. To represent a stream as a straight line is an illegitimate process. First, because rivers do not all and always flow downstream by taking the smallest distance between two successive points of their progression, but also and above all because a stream is not a line. If a phenomenological essence of the spatial order is used to symbolize the flow of time, we must not make recourse to a bi-dimensional reality, but to a phenomenon of the material world that does justice to the irreducible intuition of the tri-dimensional in the flow. Time is not a point projected ahead, an atom cast on a trajectory. It is rather something broad and thick, something that takes the trouble to advance, but advances by spreading, by "taking its time" to the very degree that it inhabits space. The stream of time is not a meager rivulet and, above all, not a streak of water without an extension. Progression is certainly an eidetic moment proper to time but it should

---

1. Heidegger, *Être et temps*, 253.
2. Whitehead, *Modes of Thought*, 64.

be represented as embracing and bringing together at each moment of its advance a multitude of lines, or rather parallel states. Put differently: *Chronos* is not the forward flight of the same but the majestic movement of others in unison, gathered and reunited in the same. People have always taken pleasure in describing time in terms of violence, haste, intolerance, and exclusion, but the deep truth of time is Peace, yet another expression more significant and edifying, for the three very prosaic notions of coexistence—understood not as contraries and opposites but different, heterogeneous realities. And the designation of time according to its reconciliatory nature of the same and other is *duration*.

Bergson of course elaborated the philosophical category of time as "lived duration." The teaching on duration is the key to the refutation of objective time, of clock time. Duration demolishes the quantitative, the abstract, but also the punctual, the evanescent. It reconciles permanence and change, evanescence and continuity. And it does this through the discernment of heterogeneities that institute within the flow a plurality of differents in continuity, differents that "pass" into one another without dissolving, states that are distinguished but do not separate from one another.

In opposition to the evanescent instant, to the punctual now without thickness, supreme form of the infinitely brief, duration is the cipher of permanence that interprets length. It continues and can only continue for a long time. Duration is always "a long duration,"[3] endless and perennial. Do we not say of an old friendship that persists through the passage of time that it *endures*? Do we not end the telling of a story of a relationship uncorrupted by the succession of years and events of life that "their love has endured"? However, the length of these relations does not signify simply that they have traversed intact a great number of years: this would be to fall back into mathematical time, that of the clock! If duration consents to be counted, it cannot be enumerated. It does not designate the sequence of temporal moments, and thus a line. It connotes rather the permanence of feelings, of intentionalities. Permanence signifies continuity, not the conservation that is finally only a form of repetition, in fact of the repetition of the same. Conservation watches out for any compromise with the other, the different; it rejects any interval between the portions and sections of time. But through the anguish and fear in the face of interruption, it emanates apprehension for the winds of alterity.

Contrary to conservation's indigence, permanence—with scarcely a concealed glimpse at persistence or perseverance—betrays the dynamism of duration that (like all true dynamism), has its roots in sameness wed to alterity. Duration celebrates the uninterrupted continuity of its unfolding, but this unfolding is no longer an infrastructural flow. The unfolding describes the mutual relation of realities in movement. It causes a plurality of quantitatively different elements to unfold, but which are, even so, not separated distinct realities. Duration is a process that becomes strained, that tightens and can be intensified. Its moments are like vibrations of light: distinct from

---

3. Husserl, *Die Bernauer Manuskripte*, 135.

the luminous source itself, its uncut "shining," they still do not enjoy an existence, an autonomous "being there." Duration is "a succession of qualitative movements that blend, penetrate, without precise contours."[4] In its Apollonian, diurnal sense, duration is like the rainbow where each color shines in its proper splendor, standing out clear and pure in the horizon of the total phenomenon, but not separated from its neighbors by a neatly traced border. In its nocturnal sense, duration recalls the dream: it is a succession of moments and elements with an affective tenor, of an existentially different flavor but which are nevertheless united and embraced by the continuum without precise separation of the dream. Duration as structure and movement of the unfolding of the heterogeneous represents an identity but one that is not flat, one that is an active coincidence with itself, a coincidence where the identity manages the difference that it sublates, where the same welcomes the other with respect and attention and the one reconciles, pacifies and unifies the multiple. Duration is the positive vision of becoming: *dynamis* is ultimately entrance into a sure haven. *Chronos* as duration is a majestically flowing stream, a spacious path, a life where one remains near oneself, all the while extending before and behind. The source of this reconciled and reconciling life of Time is the synthesis in its greatest unifying and creative generality, the synthesis that alone allows the traversal of the interval, or rather transfer from the same to the other, the synthesis that allows the leap towards heterogeneity without being a leap into emptiness—in short, the synthesis that resolves the ancient paradoxes of becoming and time, forging a pathway between the before and the after, a bridge connecting them together. However, if duration witnesses the reality of the bridge and makes possible its traversal, it still does not provide any key to an explanation of the passage. The synthesis of duration witnesses to a mysterious affinity of heterogeneities, but it is not capable of elevating them into the concept. It reminds us that the link between its moments, its heterogeneous states, is not a simple line without extension, but a link having its own thickness and depth. But it can only give up before the task of conceptualizing the connection that it nevertheless effects with ease and security.

Synthesis and Schema

Duration is the first form proper to the flow as synthesis but it still registers only one of its metaphysical components. It is the existing unification, the unification in process but it does not yet mark out and elucidate the articulating, structuring nature of the unification that is the truth (if long obscured or rather rejected) of time. Time is not a line, an indefinitely extended point in ceaseless flight ahead, but a direction, a progression following a rule, or (more precisely) gives itself the rule that it imposes on its moments and contents. It is neither a river in which one cannot step twice or a child playing backgammon. It is a power that establishes permanence as the source and

---

4. Bergson, *Essai sur les données immédiates de la conscience*, in *Oeuvres*, 70.

framework of intelligibility. Novalis' formula is well known: "time is the concept."[5] While lending permanence to beings it also constitutes the principle proper to their articulation.

The pejorative, privative ancient conception glimpsed *Chronos* as dispersion, dissipation, but the discovery of synthesis as the crux and power of time allows us to surpass the unfortunate and deadly abstractions of the punctual vision. The flow of time can certainly be envisaged as a sequence of points, but in order not to fall into a destructive segregation and to be delivered from the instant's condition of the non-existence of the now-atom they must form a series and thus prepare the advent of the first authentic form of time temporalizing itself. The series in itself denotes only a sequence of points. For it to register a true continuity, a linking relation among elements, it must appear as their ceaseless and integral unification, as, namely, a synthesis. Principle and root of every ulterior synthesis, this synthesis is apprehension. The points, elements, moments not only follow one another but are tied together. Even more, the relation does not affect only two neighboring elements, one anterior and one directly posterior. The series of apprehension designates the foundational enigma of temporality: the mind that progresses takes its path through the individual instants that succeed one another, knowing them at the same time as being a part of a unity, a continuous movement. The finite intelligence is not capable of considering, of thinking multiple things at the same time, but self-consciousness is based precisely on the enigma of apprehension where a plurality of elements are embraced in one gaze as forming a series that that moves forward. The lynchpin of Kant's transcendental deduction is Apprehension. The synthesis of apprehension gives the mortal blow to the punctual conception of time and it is the first and paradigmatic example of the temporalization where the multiple is subsumed by the one without renouncing its multiplicity or falling into dispersion.

Apprehension inaugurates the process of temporal forms leading to the expansion of metaphysics. In and through it *Chronos* consents to be transposed from stream to synthesis. Yet the continuity in Apprehension that gathers together the parts of time in a living totality requires the concurrence of a second form of the synthesis. Apprehension embraces and gathers a sequence of moments that will have appeared one after the other. But this gathering together takes place in a given moment where the other moments will have already fallen into the past. And apprehension implies precisely that these past elements are always there, *reproduced*. Reproduction alone allows Apprehension to hold together the atomic components of Time's unwinding. Only because of it that in order to locate or recover a past moment of consciousness we do not have to descend into the wellshafts of the past but can *now* embrace in our gaze what has passed, seeing and perceiving past things as given a share in the present.

Apprehension and reproduction manifest the power of temporalization as the ingathering-conservation of the multiple. They allow the comprehension of

---

5. Novalis, *Das allgemeine Brouillon*, in *Schriften* 3, 428.

permanence as a dynamic continuity, in movement, and above all in a movement that clearly wears the specific marks of the primitive intuition of Time as before and after. Permanence is still a primitive form of duration while the syntheses of apprehension and reproduction surpass duration and transpose it from unwinding to unfolding. But the definitive surpassing of duration will only take place once the unfolding reaches articulation. This will happen through the synthesis of Recognition. Apprehension and reproduction explain the continuity and coherence of the work of gathering together proper to time. The mind apprehends the moments that follow according to their connection and it apprehends them by virtue of the work of reproduction. But the integrated series of instants is not only a phenomenon of the register of existence; it equally has its dimension of essence. Each series apprehended by the mind is like a melody, which is always a configuration of notes, words, and syllables. To discern the melody of the series, to be assured that the reproduced series corresponds to the succession of sounds in the order that they take place in the time of its constitution, we must have the means to *recognize* it as such. This means that besides its continuity, or its unfolding according to duration, it must also appear according to the truth of its articulation or structuration. Recognition is also an authentic form of time that temporalizes itself, which unwinds and continues, but the continuity is here manifest only on the plane of content, of essence. With this third elementary synthesis time effectively reaches the Concept.[6]

The triad of apprehension, reproduction, and recognition realizes the metamorphosis of duration into synthesis and consequently reveals the intelligibility of time. Yet the intelligibility proper to time does not signify a conceptuality that arrives from the outside. It is not an affair of material essences, of logical categories that are imposed on a recalcitrant *Chronos* in order to enframe and halt its overflowing flux or to articulate its indigent sameness. The synthesis makes an intelligibility appear that separates and unfolds the plurality of eidē, immanent forms of time temporalizing itself. A privileged way to emphasize these eidē is indicated by the Kantian teaching that displays the truth of the categories of the understanding through the transcendental schemata, notably the schemes of substantiality and causality. The empiricist critique thinks it can demolish the ancient metaphysico-logical edifice of the categories, deconstructing the rational validity of the respective relations between substance and its accidents, cause and its effects. But what is definitively understood on the plane of the concept sensu stricto will be rediscovered and re-established through the discovery of an eidetics of time.

Since Aristotle, one of the essential distinctions of philosophy is between substance and accidents. Substance designates permanence and accident designates evanescence. Substance remains, while accidents appear and disappear. From a logical point of view, it is always subject, never predicate. More precisely it is a reality that can never be conceived as belonging to another reality as predicate. It is tempting to

6. Kant, *Critique de la raison pure*, B 180–84.

conceive substance as a solid, permanent reality, a thing, an entity that is and remains there, that persists and subsists, continues and endures, while all around it a galaxy of impermanence is observed, shimmering ephemerals that flash and disappear, returning to non-being in the next instant. Yet the representation of Permanent and Impermanent situations among or beside one another is insufficient, even erroneous. Substance is not simply surrounded by the circle of accidents but rather constitutes their center, principle and source. Accidents not only form a court or periphery around Substance, they are *its* accidents. Their reciprocal relation is not a simple contiguity, but effective connection. And this effective connection clearly represents the scheme of substantiality. In the mysterious depths of consciousness the mind has the intuition of a like that, beyond all description and definition, in the absence of any mark, any material content, ties together a permanent with one or multiple impermanents. But this link, this admirable connection is not only like a rope thrown over a gap in order to establish a connection between heterogeneous realities. No, substantiality not only ties permanent and impermanent but it makes the impermanents derive from the Permanent and represents them in dependence on it. Time rushes forward, starting from Substance towards the accident. Its élan does not flag. The relation continues and endures. It is not simply a fact of a long and stable duration, but a duration that does not stop effecting a relation of dependence. The accident continues to exist by virtue of the substance that maintains it as accident, as contingent, without an immanent reason to continue. The para-conceptual connection of this scheme effects the rescue of the eidetic moment of the irreversibility of Time by joining it with an element of articulation. The scheme of substantiality is related to a subject that is always subject and never predicate, and it is therefore based on the intuition of the irreversibility of a link. But this irreversibility does not merely mark the impossibility of a return, of a turning back, a reversal. Irreversibility does not connote the movement between undifferentiated terms, but between those clearly defined, namely, the permanent and impermanent. And these different realities do not perdure in an external way, but they unfold according to an intrinsic relation, or rather they *constitute*, they *are* an intrinsic relation. The scheme of substantiality is referred to the intuition of an irreversible relation of different moments where the different that follows is maintained by the Different that precedes it and is maintained by It as different. The second different, the accident is, and is such by virtue of the first different, substance. In short, the scheme of substantiality designates an eidos proper to time temporalizing itself, namely an irreversible succession according to an order.

The scheme of substantiality is the first authentic manifestation of the intelligibility of time. It corresponds to a relation of determination, according to content, but this determination still remains relatively rudimentary. Substance determines accident but the dependence of the evanescent on the permanent is still related only to the level of existence, of effectiveness in respect to two heterogeneous realities. It does not yet seem to concern their properties, their essence. The scheme of causality will remedy this deficiency. The question of causality is perhaps the most important that can be posed in order to be able to orient oneself in the world of finitude, of entities in becoming. We understand very well that an entity comes about because of another according to the principle of identity, but how can we conceive the birth of a thing starting from another according to a rule that is not that of identity? Put differently: "how should I understand that since something is, something else is?"[7] With every fiber of its native rationality, the intelligence tends to apply an *analytic* grid of interpretation onto the relations among things, more particularly to their genesis, but we are always running into beings and events that by themselves explain particular syntheses according to which "to something A a completely different B is posed according to a rule" (*Critique* B 122). This "rule" is an essential moment of the eidetics of time. It can be discerned and conceived only by virtue of the scheme of causality.

The scheme of causality designates a relation in which the second term, the effect, does not only follow the first, the cause, but "is posed by it and ensues from it" (*Critique* B 124). A rule, that is, a line is presented to consciousness, unfolding in an irreversible way and according to a certain order. The line runs from A to B, a particular B determined by A. The scheme is this progression (unrepresentable by a concept and yet clearly perceived) that goes in a given direction in order to reach a particular term. This term, the effect is not contained in the other term, the cause. Yet the movement that concatenates starting from the one can lead only to the other. This scheme is in other words a direction intuited as a route that arrives at its end, leading to its result. It is a line not an arrow on an endless flight; it is the trajectory of an occurrence, the advent of the other from which it has separated but which it also carries with and in itself. The effect is not given, as such, in the cause, but when A surmounts its condition as point, as atom, it expands towards a concrete, determined B. The scheme of causality is a powerful instance of the eidetics of time. Consciousness experiences, produces if you like, the authentic intuition of a movement of time that is pure progression but also effective structuration. And it is structuration precisely as progression. The structure that occurs is not given from the beginning; neither is it found at the end. It is prepared, as it were, in and through the movement that celebrates its own realization in it.

The scheme of causality marks a decisive moment in the eidetics of time, in which the movement of temporalization blossoms in its intelligible truth. If the relation of substantiality already reveals the power of the articulation of time then its destiny to conceptualization is confirmed by causality. Causality reveals the order in becoming, a progression from anterior to posterior, the advent of a second authentically other than the first, but an advent according to the concept. In fact, causality conceived as scheme, as an eidos of time is an essential example of the a priori synthesis, the emblematic idea and category par excellence of the expansion of metaphysics. The a priori synthesis is a connection between subject and predicate where the predicate follows

---

7. Kant, *Grandeurs négatives*, in *Oeuvres philosophiques* I, 300.

a subject without being entailed by it. In other words it is a connection explained neither by the subject nor predicate, but contains the third term of the judgment, the copula. In analytic judgments the copula is only an *ens rationis*, simply playing the role of an equals sign, constituting a kind of transparent glass where the subject is reflected in the predicate. It will find its truth in the metaphysics of time. In fact, we could say that the copula is time, time temporalizing itself. It ties the subject and predicate and does so in a fecund and creative way. The copula is the active mediation between A and B. In it A does not contain B in a conceptual way, but still produces and projects it as B. But this creative vocation, creative on the properly conceptual plane where the copula finds its exemplification or rather realization in the scheme of causal succession responds to the age-old question: how to understand that since something is something else follows?

The emphasis on causality as the eidetic key to the expansion of metaphysics ought to lead to its rehabilitation. From post-Kantian Idealism to contemporary phenomenology, modern philosophy has severely judged causality, understood essentially as efficient causality. Modern philosophy floods it with accusations of mechanism, automatism and conceives it as the supreme instantiation of bad infinity.

The law of causality is supposed to dominate or rather tyrannize the phenomena of nature but also the structures of social life. Entirely ignorant of difference and heterogeneity, it subjects the world to an analytic order that excludes dynamism and therefore prohibits novelty. No one can deny the soundness of these accusations. Positivisms and scientisms of all stripes have reduced causality to being only the principle and source of a universe submitted to a "third rate" necessity, the synonym of the indigent regularity of the unwinding of the homogenous. The philosophies of suspicion have used it as the supreme instrument of the "explanations" that have deprived the works of the mind of all originality, all sui generis reality. These explanations come from an obsessive desire to show and demonstrate the new's determination by the old, the flowing of the other from the same. Yet the metaphysical truth of the causal relation is not the punctuation of the repetition of the same, but, to the contrary, the articulation of the succession of heterogeneities. This succession is fecundity and thus the establishment of the new. Contrary to substantiality, cipher of a relation where the First, the Permanent produces its accidents only in order to reabsorb them thereafter in itself; the cause engenders and gives birth to its effects with an autonomous existence in view. The accident only temporarily, momentarily subsists while it is maintained by substance. The effect is definitively liberated from the ontological tutelage of the cause. It is set free in order to fly with its own wings, to get by all alone and especially in order to be at the origin of its own continual development.

BOOK TWO—EIDETICS

Past, Future, Present

The schemas of causality and substantiality appear as the first authentic examples of an eidetics of time. They have allowed "the rescue" of the primordial intuition of the irreversibility of the course of time. The substance-accident relation and the cause-effect relation are the sui generis manners of the articulation of time, the structures that in a certain way relativize and curb the irreversible. Time temporalizes itself by adopting a movement that cannot be reversed, inverted. Nevertheless, it should not be seen as the flow of a stream. Represented this way the course of time does not appear as a place and source of a maturation, but rather as the drive towards the realization of a blind destiny. With the schemas that qualify and determine succession, the irreversible receives a structure, and above all, with causality, it finds an endpoint. The effect can certainly never become the cause and consequently the direction of movement of the succession of time is not susceptible to inversion. On the other hand, *Chronos* is no longer constrained to be only a rushing ahead. It will enjoy from now on a repose in the effect, a certain completion in which it consents to the subsistence of what issues from it thus curtailing the ceaseless resumption of the evanescent for an effective fecundity, for permanence. In other words, because of the schemas time manages to overcome the absence of articulation proper to the vision of a condition of homogeneity. However, if the schemas deliver up a first result for a temporal eidetics, it is still limited: the schemas represent rules according to which the succession can be qualified, but the principle of this qualification does not belong to time sensu stricto. The schemas represent the conceptual potentialities of time, the ways that time is susceptible of being subsumed under the concept. But by their plurality that so to speak coexists within the temporal matrix, they constitute only a "*horizontal*" eidetic regime when it is a nonetheless a matter of "creating a new kind of...vertical intelligibility."[8] This type of vertical intelligibility proper to time is nothing other than an eidetics according to the three times that in their descending order constitute the simplest, most primitive, and most original division or articulation. More precisely: as old and as original as the intuition of irreversibility is that of the before and after. However, the dual difference of before and after "passes" naturally into a ternary differentiation that leads to the birth of the three times.

The "system" of the three times plays a qualificatory role in relation to the primitive distinction of before and after, analogous to the relation of the schemas to irreversibility. "God has placed within the human heart the totality of time" (Qoh 3:11). This totality is constituted by the past, present, and future. The task of the eidetics of time is to decipher this "network of intentionalities" that the three times constitute.[9] Meanwhile we must conceive them first according to the ways they are reflected on the plane of *Weltanschauung*. In reality, very often the comparison concerns only two

---

8. Merleau-Ponty, *Le visible et l'invisible*, 322.
9. Merleau-Ponty, *Phénoménologie de la perception*, 477.

of the three times, the past and future, a fact that reflects the "asymmetrical" situation of the present, its specific condition, the whiff of non-originarity that they seem to radiate.

The differentiation of *Chronos*, of flux and in fact even of duration, into three times with an eidetic and ontological specificity, bursts the shackles of the given and presents the immanent ways Time surpasses the monotony of the homogenous. Before and after, the first monuments of the differentiation where time, as it were, speaks itself in order to give itself an articulation, are consolidated into forms that are also sections, portions of its course and modalities of its auto-structuration, its temporalization. The first differences that time imposes on itself are before and after, which, despite serving as adverbs proper to the past and future, announce and anticipate them. In addition to realizing the closure of the duration into an eidetically structured time, the past and future suggest and symbolize attitudes and human aspirations; they indicate and characterize modalities of the life of the mind. By contrast to perception, which is glued onto the given present, memory is the faculty by which we are turned to the past and imagination allows us to throw ourselves into the future. The past gives us resources and the future harbors hidden energies that we hope to bring into our service. These two times doubtlessly indicate and manifest also the distance from the truth of the given, of escaping from its constraints, of drilling an opening through which we can escape from the difficulties and prosaic servitudes of the present. The past is the place, or rather the temporal component of the intentionality of remorse and the future is an inevitable part of the intentionality of fear. We would love to exorcise the shadows of our past, and, inversely, to protect ourselves from the preoccupations and threats of the future. We are doubtlessly here dealing with moments and attitudes that seek to reach, to turn us towards sections of time that have effectively happened, as well as to moments that have to happen. Nevertheless, the past and future are not only durations that have effectively happened and will happen but categories, intuitions of themes that crystallize and hypostasize elementary moments of temporalization, independently of any belonging to an effectively given section of duration. We can turn ourselves nostalgically to a past that is originally gone and which has therefore never effectively taken place; or we can yearn for an originally hidden future that we have always been deprived of, which will never take place but for which we still always yearn. In addition to being spaces where existence had been or will effectively take place, the future and past are original dimensions of being in becoming, a condition where the ultimate seriousness of event and occurrence, of decision and resolution is softened or rather relativized by the possibility of a forward or backward flight. "Afterwards and beforehand are terms created by freedom itself," says phenomenology.[10] This is certainly true because through them the flux suffers its first articulation, the irreversible acquires its original structuration. However, in themselves, self-sufficient in their unrepentant duality, they constitute one of the ultimate

---

10. Sartre, *L'être et le néant*, 566.

resources of the posterity of Parmenides, of all philosophies that do not lay down their arms before the simple truth of the Becoming that *is*, and therefore of Time that effectively exists according to a sui generis structure. In an unexpected but ultimately very logical way, the anathematization of Becoming leads to the rejection of all thickness proper to the present, bracketing and even obliterating it for the sake of drawing together the past and future. But it is important to realize that this drawing together of two times that excludes the third is not a neutral or innocent intellectual exercise. Its telos and hidden (but living and active) plan is the refusal to face up to the present in its sui generis eidetic dimension. This refusal is, so to speak, the metaphysical source of pre-Kantian and pre-Husserlian doctrines of time. Unfortunately for them, the crux of all the truths about *Chronos* are found precisely in the phenomenological comprehension of the present, the non-punctual, non-evanescent present of duration.

Making the present a dead end betrays what we could call the Parmenidean penchant innate to the mind, the malaise of the intelligence before this mysterious synthesis of the point and duration. Yet, how to stop seeing the past and future as two separated times? And how can we avoid considering this enigmatic time that is the present? Out of the three, it alone "effectively" exists and yet it always evades the scrutinizing eye of analysis. In reality, the comparisons of the three times can take account of this ambiguous condition of the present, but most often they reflect the "positive" intuition of the present, its foundational role in relation to the two other times, its own dimension, its specific extension and native affinity with duration. We effectively speak of the flight into the past and the march into the future while the present evokes a sojourn, a rest, even a delay. Considered from an "epistemological" point of view, the past is related to knowledge, to acquired, accumulated knowledge, while the present is rather the location and source of feeling and the future, the ontological dimension of potentiality, lending a hand to desire and duty. Or even, envisaged starting from the anthropological associations of our consciousness of time, the past appears to provoke melancholy for its ever-evaporated riches and the future appears as source of terror before the dangers and threats to come. But whether a matter of the past or future, these phenomenological essences designate conditions where we are deprived of means, where we find ourselves in a state of privation and powerlessness, whereas the present appears as the dimension of creative actuality. From the starting point of the intuition of its actuality, its condition as duration, in the occurrence that is less "the flow of a stream" and more the "stationary rocking of a sea,"[11] and therefore starting from the conception of a present that resolutely avoids the traps of the atomism of the now, we can understand and explain the system of the three times, this "network of intentionalities" that constitutes the framework of Time.

---

11. Ellrodt, *Les poètes métaphysiques anglais I*, 408.

The Present: Duration and Differentiation

The division of three times constitutes the true eidetic structure of Time and implies that the present is not something simply intercalated between past and future without itself possessing a certain extension in duration, which is a translation of its specific intentionality. In other words, it would be necessary to break once and for all with the punctuated vision of time that makes the present "a mathematical abstraction," "an ideal limit" between what is now and what was before.[12] It is tempting to rediscover the metaphysical place of time in duration. After all, we find and conceive a present that extends and spreads out! However, the present is a time, and the notion of a plurality of distinct times seems opposed to the intuition of duration. The present is a time situated after a first and before a third while duration rejects division, ignores an effective order of succession. The present doubtlessly can correspond to a section taken from duration, understood as a moment or portion of it. But, precisely, this sectioning seems to separate only a homogenous section of duration whereas the present translates or rather consummates the heterogeneity contained by time. If a true eidetics of time cannot be content with this grouping of elements and states that is duration, this is because the differentiation into three times corresponds to the relation between three different intentionalities. In other words, the present is neither a reflection of duration nor phenomenon of encounter without thickness or extension proper to the past and future. The solution to these difficulties, the reconciliation of these apparently contradictory noetic requirements is found by unexpectedly recalling the point: the point will be injected into duration in order to give it determination. But the condition for this good use of the point is a rereading of the now. In the various Heracliteanisms, the now is an undivided and unextended atom. However, in the phenomenological theory of internal time consciousness, the now is not an extensionless atom but the impact and mark of the *Urimpression*, the original impression consciousness is subjected to that emanates from a sensation that, although indivisible, is nevertheless understood as extended and spreading out in duration.

The original impression can appear like a meteorite, a sound, a light falling into consciousness, affecting and striking it. In fact, it harbors moments of difference that predestine it to differentiation. The now is already difference: its originality comes from the trace that deepens the original impression. But a trace is always a trace of something other; it returns beyond or rather below itself. Even more, the difference is not only the genesis of the *Urimpression*. It also establishes its effective existence. Sensation is a piece of the sensible that touches me: the now is not an atom, an unbreakable point, but the encounter between consciousness and that of which it is conscious. This native duality is the base for the possibility of differentiation exercised by the present. Notwithstanding its punctuality that seems to deprive it of articulation,

---

12. Husserl, *Leçons pur une phénoménologie de la conscience intime du temps*, 56. *Husserliana* 10, 227, in Bernet, *La vie du sujet*, 223, 221.

the present possesses an ontological authority over what precedes and follows it. It is certainly the border between what precedes and follows it and separates and delimits them, but its role is above all one of discrimination and determination. Through and in it potentialities are actualized, choice is made between possibles, promises are fulfilled and desires are appeased, but it is equally in and through it that fire becomes ash, the loud noise echoes weakly. The present is the unique authority that presides over the future's coming into existence and it always serves as authoritative interpreter of the past.

Despite the traditional reading, the present can be considered as a "differentiating" relation, but this efficaciousness of differentiation of the exterior intentional object finds its truth starting from the question: how can a present act be related to an extension that extends beyond itself? Or rather, how to conceive a subject that exceeds itself? The subject can exceed itself to the degree that the now does not contract into a punctual instant, but includes a "longitudinal" intentionality (as Husserl taught) where it is both itself as well as the retention of what precedes it and the protention of what follows it. We must not forget the simple truth that the present enjoys a privileged place in relation to the other times. Every act of perception is accomplished in the present. The perceptive experience of the present, "presentation" is the foundation of all consciousness of time, awaiting it like memory follows from it. The eidetic essence of differentiation like the ontological privilege of present perception makes possible the definitive surpassing of the reading of time as an atomic now. It has been said that this dimension—or rather, non-dimension—of *Chronos* that condemned it to struggle *to be*, to fight have the right to claim effective existence in duration, is sublated in the vision of the present as power of differentiation and as site and force of active, intentional gathering together. The present that distinguishes past and future by reuniting them in itself, by making them the two other figures of the soul's "distention" (Augustine), appears from now on according to its truth as duration and domain. The present is not immobile, inert or frozen but registers a true movement. Here the primitive intuition of the flow finds its value. The present, as Heidegger said, is an "ecstasy" proper to time temporalizing itself, with a specific, sui generis "movement" that, despite its native indivisibility, adapts to or rather completes itself in the gathering of the multiple. The now is a link to its own other, to those proper others that have gone and are to come. Without forsaking or deserting itself for the future, the present is thus a horizon that is not given, but being given; it appears as extending itself and regathering its petals into a kind of bouquet. But more than a horizon of expectation, it is a receptacle and site of reception. It is a bay where the waves of duration co-exist, a field that embraces the gaze that gathers and unifies what occurs simply contiguously. The present is in this way the force synthesizing coexistence and succession, and is therefore like a shortcut to the entirety of time, of time itself in its essence of integral becoming.

The present proves to be therefore the power and principle of differentiation, active unity of the One and the Many. In other words, we attain "a concept of the present that is not passage but in which time rises up and reaches its rest (*Stillstand*)."[13] However, once the victory over the now-point is accomplished, respect of the multiple assured and the salvation of the specific intentionality of the present effectuated, we must now take account of the *other* aspect of the present, that which flavors it with eternity. The native affinity of the present with the eternal can doubtlessly be only an illusion, a non-sense at best and a catastrophe at worst. Yet if thought must apply all its powers to reject the noxious assimilation of the present to a frozen immobility, it is neither permitted nor possible to avoid meditation on the millennia-long reflection on the association of the present with eternity. The dominant tradition of pre-Kantian thought disapprovingly judged moving time from the standpoint of the lofty idea of the *nunc stans*. Put differently: its task was to establish a metaphysics dedicated to the pillorization, the dispersal, the evanescence, in fact the non-existence of the three times, and specifically to what is intercalated between the others. But another association of eternity with time exists, constantly invoked but curiously unexploited, that expressed by an elderly Plato: time is the moving image of eternity (*Timaeus* 37d).

The Moving Image of Eternity

The moving image is a vision of time that has been hardened, even travestied into a privative conception. Time appears as evanescence before stability, turmoil before peace, lack against plenitude. Its flow is only an unfortunate deprivation from the majestic permanence of the *aevum*; the succession of nows manifests only the impossibility of the gathering together; the moments and sections of time are only like the tearing apart and fragmentation of the seamless garment of eternity. Opposed to the "single, eternal age of the world the face of which is without wrinkle. . .and smile always even and full,"[14] time is only a sarcastic grimace decomposing into a sequence of trembling and vacillating instants. Tied to the *aevum*, introduced as if by a stingy left hand, time appears like "the winter of eternity."[15] But this conception of time is a result of an ontology of the image where the ectype is only the sad imitation of the Archetype, the projection of the One into the dispersion of the multiple. Yet as we now know the image is not the imitation of being but its autonomous *second*. The image does not participate in its original in order to unfold it in a partial and imperfect perspective: it doubles it, but in terms of an autonomous structure, with a sui generis configuration of moments. If time is not eternity, it no less represents an authentic *second*, its riches can be understood as having their source in eternity. But it does

---

13. Benjamin, "Über den Begriff der Geschichte," 702.

14. Crashaw, "In the Glorious Epiphany of Our Lord," in *The Poems*, 255, in Ellrodt, *Les poètes métaphysiques anglais I*, 414.

15. Baader, *Werke* II, 121.

not merely manifest these riches in a weakened, alienated and denatured way, but incarnates them otherwise, in its own way, its "mobile" way that is not impermanent becoming but temporalizing synthesis. The idea of the moving image of eternity holds good for each of the three times, but it is the present that best illustrates its eidetic range.

The present is the emblematic, paradigmatic time: it reunites the two opposed faces of *Chronos*, evanescence and infinity. The present represents the infinitesimal "quantity" of time: it appears, but immediately disappears. Contrary to its elder brother and little sister it possesses no space of time to in which to abide. On the other hand, in opposition to its siblings, the present is ultimately the lone portion of *Chronos* that currently is, that effectively exists instead of only having been or being ahead of us. The inclusion of eternity in the eidetic universe of time will allow the support and ultimately reconciliation of these contradictory visions of time. The conception of the instant as "atom of eternity"[16] signifies the redemption of the punctuality of the now. The intuition of the plenitude of the phenomena of the present corresponds to the vision of the present as unique effective reality.

The ceaseless efforts of Husserl to do justice to the intuition of the "now" as a phenomenon of duration, his analyses of the specific intentionality that permits the instant to be extended or, if you like, to exceed itself, finds its metaphysical foundation beginning with the interpretation of time, and more specifically the present, as image of eternity. The now-atom is a fiction of hair-splitting rationality that is rejected and refuted from the perspectives of metaphysics and phenomenology. The analysis of the present in terms of a "longitudinal intentionality" receives support and assistance, confirmation and reinforcement from metaphysics. The instant is no longer a point, an *ens rationis* but the site and result of a synthesis: the notion of the moving image of eternity expresses an encounter between eternity and time, between what is, so to speak, beyond duration and what is found below it. The instant is no longer a being that does not stop disappearing but receives from now on a constant vivification on the part of Permanence itself, which lends it a hand and assimilates it to itself. It certainly retains its acuity, immediacy and native simplicity, but all this is reinforced, deepened. The instant is in fact a supreme example of the synthesis that constitutes the truth of subjectivity. It is intuited in accordance with its weight and understood according to its irreplaceable uniqueness. The hedonist proclaims *carpe diem*, but in the final analysis it is perhaps a matter of something other than a self-abandonment caught up in the momentary. The instant is the sole "thing" that truly belongs to us, over which we have power and influence. Above all it is unique and irreplaceable. Counterpart of the singular, of the unique, the instant cannot be exchanged for anything else; it has no price. It never comes back, not only because the course of time is irreversible, but also and above all by virtue of the principle of indiscernibles. As there cannot be two beings merely different numerically, there cannot exist two instants

---

16. Kierkegaard, *Le concept d'angoisse*, in *Oeuvres complètes* 7, 188.

that are distinguished only by the fact of their respective place against the background of duration. Each instant in history has its specific revolutionary chance; each instant of salvation history is "a little gate through which the Messiah could make his entrance."[17] Of course, the synthesis of eternity and the evanescence that points to the instant is not limited to an infinitesimal portion of time. The instant is in a certain way the paradigm of all the moments having a depth through duration, of all the moments that convey a rupture, that mark an event, that signal an occurrence. Christ speaks of his "hour that has not yet come" (John 2:4). "My hour" is the accentuation of the "now," of that great "now" where "the mystery" of God will be manifest (Col 1:26). In fact, each life, even the poorest, the most monotone, is scattered with nows, instants in which the ephemeral and the permanent celebrate their espousal. It is not a matter of lumps of time, wreckage hampering the flow of the flux, but proper instances of the auto-articulation of *Chronos*, moments where the temporalization that is time is registered with a particular clarity.

The vision of the instant as a veritable "atom of eternity," of the time that is like "a *vase filled* with perfumes, sounds, projects and atmospheres,"[18] rescues the truth of the present by resolutely suppressing the conception of the punctual now. This victory over the punctual is an essential step of philosophy in its quest for a better comprehension of the eidetics of the present. But this enhancement of the thickness proper to the present can entail a kind of triumphalism that almost takes it for the unique effectively existing reality. The past no longer exists: why bother with it? The future is not yet: why take time to think about it? We cannot respond to these disillusioned questions simply by presenting a present with density and weight, a present that does not pass and appears without being on the way to disappearing, a present that endures without flowing by. A moving image of eternity, the present is an intentionality having a proper space; it is an ontological reality that seems to be all-encompassing. The present endures, and it seems to do so without limits. It has neither beginning nor end; it is a *nunc stans*. Incorruptible, without cracks and without stain, it is always equal to itself. Yet this present colored with eternity risks compromising the *temporal* truth of this time, trading living duration for lifeless immobility, joyous actuality for a grey, toneless ataraxia. However, if the ontologies that explain time as *privatio aeternitatis* or (same thing) as a weak participation in eternity are incapable of taking account of the concept of the living present, the metaphysics of the "moving image" makes possible the interpretation of the present in its truth of longitudinal intentionality. And pending the analysis of simple forms drawn from common anthropological funds we will have recourse to eidetic elements of the theological order in order to illustrate the phenomenological essence of the "present."

The present is a moving image, not of an Eternity of Absolute Being but of the eternal life of God in the loving procession of his three Persons. Reflection or rather

17. Benjamin, "Über den Begriff der Geschichte," 704.
18. Proust, *Le temps retrouvé II*, in Poulet, Études sur le temps humain I, 430.

effect of the Trinitarian mystery, the liturgy progresses according to a sui generis intelligibility, according to a logic that assigns to it an integral articulation and a full signification in each of its moments. Image or Second of an eternal life, it unfolds a perfect presence, it allows the living of "a present that suffers. . .no deficiency and which is complete in itself."[19] The liturgy of the Church reflects this other liturgy that unfolds the life of the Blessed. This liturgy is essentially a vision, the beatific vision that is like duration, the continuation of "an instant that neither comes nor goes."[20] The blessed vision is the contemplation of the attributes of God, the "moments" of his life. It contemplates the Mystery whole and entire, but in a finite way it "adequately" sees it in its Infinity but with a knowledge that will never be exhausted. The *visio beatifica* prefigures and exemplifies the present seen in its proper intentionality. The present is not the fixation of a sole, isolated reality, but the taking-together of a plurality of moments. It does not succumb to dispersion and does not include gaps and fissures, even if it is related to the multiple. In other words it is a supreme example of the synthesis that—without being fruitlessly curved back on itself—gathers and unites the heterogeneous in a complete and perfect form.

Pleasure

The present contains essential components that risk appearing as extra- or (more precisely) as infra- or supratemporal. Implicitly or explicitly, it possesses essential traits of autarky, of harmony with itself, of the ultimate and final condition of its intentional object, even if—however—*noesis* and *noema* can be differentiated in the state of the Present. These are non-temporal elements of nature that are ultimately proper to the instant, but the eidos "present" is not the "instant" and every effort must be made to avoid falling back into the vision of the now-atom. Like the other two times, the present has its sui generis eidetic truth that will be confirmed and reaffirmed starting from the consideration of its metaphysical (or rather anthropological) counterpart: *presence*. But presence has a primitive, original form that is pleasure. And while being a form, a supreme manifestation of the in-differentiation proper to the instant, to the *nunc stans*, pleasure equally possesses as constitutive elements of its phenomenological essence "the action" of persisting, the feeling and certainty of continuing, and even the awareness of the unification of a plurality of elements that open the way to the comprehension of this longitudinal intentionality as synthesis.

The classics denounce pleasure for its primitive thoughtless character, for its blindness, and they remind us of the human powerlessness to hold onto it, to retain it. Pleasure entirely fills us, it possesses us, and it excludes the consideration of everything external to it. It encloses man in himself, closes his eyes and shuts his ears to all that is located outside of him. It confines him in the present instance, and it takes away

---

19. Lacoste, *Expérience et absolu*, 71.
20. Thomas Aquinas, *Summa Contra Gentiles* I, III, lxii.

any smidgen of a desire to recall and study the past. Above all it deprives him of any power to foresee and project the future. In its own way pleasure is a paradigmatic illustration of the ambiguous potentialities of the instant: the instant is a faultless totality but also a radical powerlessness. It brackets every intentional object that is virtual, not yet possessed, by means of closing in on itself. It manifests and parades a joyous unity with itself but which is ultimately only absence of self-differentiation. In pleasure the subject is in perfect agreement with itself, but the *with* of this "relation" does not correspond to any metaphysical reality. It is effaced by the absence of the object that would stand over-against the subject. Pleasure is apparently an isolated punctual reality, without relation to any other. It is in a sense the ultimate form of Analysis where the coincidence of two conceptually identical but numerically different terms gives way to a continuity-unity that connotes the absence of all duality between essence and existence. The absence of differentiation between content and container, *noesis* and *noema* is seen very clearly in the quantitative conception of pleasure. When centered on the theme of pleasure, moral philosophy thinks it must—and can—be unfolded through "a hedonistic calculus," the appreciation of pleasures according to their strength and weakness, their degree. And indeed, if poets and spiritual writers discourse on the softness, sweetness, or power and excess of pleasure, this is because, essentially, the unique quidditative differentiation that can be practiced in this domain, is measured by "intensity." Colors are differentiated as red, blue, yellow, and green; trees are structured as trunks, branches, leaves, and roots; yet men and women attempting to take account of their pleasures know how to catalogue them only in terms of their intensity.

The necessary reading of pleasure in terms of degrees, according to its intensity, is the sign of a homogeneity that does not sit well with the synthetic condition of intentionality proper to the present. But there are some instances or, if you like, some kinds of pleasure where this homogeneity is almost redeemed by virtue of the reinterpretation of the sameness of affection—the affection that blossoms or rather is clarified in autarky, in the self-continuation of presence. Every pleasure manifests the feeling of a deep agreement with the self, or rather an undivided presence to self that is not tasted only in an isolated instant, but possesses a deep motivation, an intimate tendency to continue to prolong itself. Kant said that in every pleasure is discerned "the awareness of the causality of a representation respectively to the state of the subject and to the intention of *retaining it there*. . ."[21] It is tempting to see in this innate tendency of pleasure to prolong itself only a kind of stretching of the Same. In these unconscious depths pleasure seeks to endure, and duration itself is not yet an eidetic category sensu stricto of temporality. A universe of pleasure is found, however, where the deadly homogeneity of undivided sensation is conjugated in terms of a separation, a differentiation. In elementary, paradigmatic pleasures, those of the senses, the homogeneity of affection is confirmed by the possession and assimilation to self of the

---

21. Kant, *Critique de la Faculté de Juger*, in *Oeuvres* 2, 978.

object. Sexual pleasure, like the pleasure of eating and drinking precisely expresses a situation in which the phenomenological paradigm of the original impression (according to its condition of being beneath differentiation of *noesis* and *noema*) is exemplified and confirmed on the plane of existence by a coalescence, an identification with the object. The ambition of sexual pleasure is a body, more precisely, the effective possession of this body. The perhaps asymptotic but very real truth of pleasure is the becoming-one with this other body, in other words, its reduction to the condition of continuity with my body. Orgasm is the cipher of this unification where the autarky or rather the auto-teleology of pleasure sinks into in-difference. In other words, pleasure as such, as reality of the analytic order remains irreducibly foreign to the metaphysical condition of the "present" intentionality.

We could mollify this infra-intentional condition of pleasure if we succeed in discerning even within the undividedness, the immediacy, the instantaneity, a separation, a duality that causes the identity to be transmuted into the prefiguration of differentiation, where the fusion, the coalescence opens into Synthesis. The supreme example of pleasure where the unity is seen despite, or rather through the separation is the pleasure experienced during the perception of beauty. In its classical Kantian definition, beauty is what pleases without concept and without interest. The a-conceptuality of the experience of beauty is an essential condition of the sui generis specificity of aesthetic pleasure, independent of any didactic consideration, any doctrinal principle and criterion. The criterion of "disinterest" expresses the aesthetic experience's irreducibility to ethics or utility. But from a properly metaphysical point of view, the bracketing of interest signifies respect for a certain duality. The phenomenological essence "pleasure" announces dominance over the object, its possession and ultimately its inclusion-integration into the subject. The culminating-point of pleasure, in fact, pleasure in the strict sense, signifies this fusion-undividedness where the immediate celebrates its realization. However if in aesthetic pleasure we are not dealing with possession and inclusion, this is because the pleasure we experience is motivated not by possession but by the contemplation of the object. It does not aim for its existence but its simple form. The pleasure of the senses is literally domination over the body, grinding of food by the teeth, the caress of the palate by drink, whereas artistic emotion is chaste: it rejects all physical contact. The one contemplating a painting takes trouble not to come too close to it. He seeks the point, the position in the space where he can best see it and this amounts to the introduction and observation of a distance between the work and spectator, a distance that alone allows him to see the painting in the autarky of its form. "Distance is the soul of beauty," said Simone Weil.[22] And indeed, it is the sine qua non of all artistic contemplation. It is the physico-physiological condition of vision but also, and above all, the metaphysical principle of this pleasure without concept and without interest that accompanies aesthetic judgment. Someone looking at a temple would like to welcome the form within the mind without adding to or

22. Weil, *Cahiers. Oeuvres complètes* VI, 3, 348.

subtracting from it. In fact, the evident absence of any inclination to change on the quidditative plane has its counterpart on the plane of existence. The one contemplating the temple does not want to possess or handle it. It is sufficient that the temple is. Or rather, he ardently desires that the temple continues to be, and this independently of all relation to him, the spectator.

Of course, this deep desire to change nothing in the object either according to existence or essence, fits perfectly with a certain movement, a certain modification of the contemplator. Contemplation endures and it is always the same object that is contemplated as such. Yet to contemplate a painting for a long time has as one of its basic purposes the emphasis of neglected or effaced moments. Continuing to look at the same painting causes diverse lines and forms, nuances and spots of color to appear with an ever-greater clarity and acuity. The elements and moments of the work are elucidated and imposed with an increasing force and articulation before the gaze of the contemplator. And one effectively has the impression of always seeing further. But this "seeing further" is rather the cipher of a "seeing better." Stopping before Tintoretto's *Coronation of the Virgin* in the Louvre, you first see the canvas top to bottom, left to right. You perceive and behold multiple spots of color that slowly individualize and begin to impose themselves as forms. You are tempted to lock your gaze longer on one or another of the forms and the detail of their vestments or faces that begin to stand out against the background of yellow and blue clouds. You gradually become aware of all that the painting represents, its four superimposed series of characters. Below, a line of blesseds, above, important people from ecclesial history. At the very top, in the middle, the Virgin surrounded by the Apostles, her Son placing the crown on her head. To the degree that you contemplate the work, the more and more clearly you see the figures. Yet it is not a matter of a reinforcement of our vision of the details, of an accrued knowledge of the painted surface, of a more and more acute knowledge of the lines and forms. Contemplation surpasses this articulatory vision in order almost to perish in a globalization where forms seem nearly to dissolve into patches, or rather, gathers the structural elements in a whole that is imposed with a renewed, intensified depth. It illustrates in a spectacular way the hidden action, the incessantly veiled exercise of the three cognitive syntheses that result in the appearance of the image or form, the form in its truth, its entirety.

This analysis of contemplation permits the rediscovery of the theoretical structure of perception. But what is from an epistemological perspective the construction of an image is from a metaphysical point of view the advent of a dynamic reality. The pleasure accompanying or rather supporting and animating the establishment of the image, its powerful and integral appearance, is a synthesis that gathers and unites— but not only: it maintains the union, even assures its continuation, and momentarily even its intensification. We *stop*," Kant writes, "to contemplate beauty, because this contemplation strengthens and reproduces itself."[23] The pleasure experienced before

---

23. Kant, *Critique de la Faculté de Juger*, in *Oeuvres* vol. 2, 982.

the beauty of art or nature, this pleasure in its autarky and synthetic constitution, registers and exemplifies all the positive moments of "present" intentionality. In its own way it illustrates the native immediacy of the Present, but it explicates it in light of the Synthesis. There is nothing ephemeral, immediate about aesthetic pleasure. There is nothing punctual about it; it is not a trembling, floating atom of sensation. The pleasure of beauty, like each authentic occurrence of the Primordial Impression spreads itself out and extends itself. Its extension in duration is not a simple flow, but a vigorous effort of the gathering together of elements within the instant, the linkage of instants on the framework of becoming. Even more, this linkage is not simply the maintenance of equally intense affections, it can also blossom into a sequence, into a theory of sensations that reaches a *crescendo*. Elementary form of the present, pleasure is certainly an undivided totality, an impression imposing itself in one total swoop, a state that continues without referring to anything anterior or posterior. But it is also a movement, an affection in operation, a victory always won.

Peace

Pleasure is a primitive and emblematic figure of the present, located on the plane of sensation, and on the psychological plane. Peace is its near counterpart on the moral plane. In both cases it is a matter of states manifesting an autarky and an apparent absence of articulation, but of which analysis can still reveal the originally synthetic nature. In fact, the ethico-political category of peace finds it origin in *rest*. The apparent univocity of the notion must not obscure the potentialities for plurality of composition. It is tempting to understand rest as *absence* of action. But does this absence simply mean non-action or should it be understood as result of a stopping of movement, but a stopping that does not take place necessarily once, at a given moment? This question is highly relevant to the metaphysical truth of peace, the transposition of the neutral, everyday notion of "rest": like Rest and yet more than rest, Peace can have, like the temporal eidos of the *present*, passive and active acceptations. The passive acceptation is seen through the moral-spiritual category of surrender and the active acceptation through political peace between States, and, ultimately, in the religious feast of the Sabbath.

Surrender is a psychologico-moral attitude that expresses indifference, disinterest. It is above all the absence of all effort and tension, a supreme manifestation of the passivity that can be found in certain moments of our existence, or rather, that characterizes our behavior, our relation to others and the world. Essentially, *these* figures of surrender are catalogued in the register of moving, even culpable weakness that humans can display. But surrender can also appear as a noble figure of confidence, of love. And, above all, it can connote a certain vision of spirituality. Masters of the French School advocate surrender [*l'abandon*], an Abandonment to the Present Moment that is neither *ataraxia* nor fixation on the instant. The present moment is the paradigm of the presence of the Will of God and Abandonment denotes the wholehearted conformity to this will. The religious soul desires to discern the will of the Most High amidst the cacophony of the world; it loves to be "sure" in its grasp of it, sure of discovering it in order to obey it. But the will of God is known only in and through what actually happens in the course of the world. And of everything that occurs, the most clearly visible is the present moment. "What happens at each moment bears the imprint of the will of God." Pious souls want to recognize the divine action in the events of the world, in the moments of their life, and "each moment gives it to them whole and entire." The soul must be satisfied by "the divine fullness of the present moment"; it must "be content to bear the present moment as if there was nothing else to look for in the world."[24] This integral attention, this wholehearted conformity is clearly not an isolated movement, a unique act, but rather the continuation of the same "genial act" in duration, conceivable also as a succession of uniform acts. What matters is understanding that the simple and uninterrupted *fiat* of adhesion to the will of God implies, or—if you like—contains all the assents through which it is unfolded. The acts of abandonment, this multiplicity of acts flowing from a "single but present disposition," gather together and penetrate one another in order to constitute "a perfect concert."[25] The disposition to abandonment announces, so to speak, all the acts of abandonment that follow it. It is exercised as a synthesis of different and successive acts.

Abandonment to the present moment is a supreme form of presence, a peerless illustration and realization of the *Erstreckung* that constitutes longitudinal intentionality of the present. The counterpart or "positive" synonym of abandonment is peace. Peace of the soul, like that of society, of peoples, seems to be almost an a-temporal, natural given. In reality, peace has nothing to do with a "natural state" of the body or mind, nor with the state of Nature of the Philosophers: it has never prevailed for long in any culture, even if it has always been very possible, a necessary perspective and horizon for any social existence. To paraphrase Klausewitz inversely, we could say that peace is the continuation of war by different means. It is never natural: for Greek poetry it is conceived as the interruption of war, while according to the Apostle, fighting against the forces of Sin, Christ "makes peace by the blood of his Cross" (Col 1:20). Peace is temporary, fragile; the shadow of its collapse hangs over the joys of the truce from which we benefit. Its interruption, its dissolution into conflict is always threatening. A very long period of peace can make us forget that war always breaks out and is never far away. Peace is most often obtained at the end of a battle and it is a victory that is never permanently acquired. The Rabbis identify peace with creation, but rather as a continuous creation that never stops gathering together and reviving the living forces of nature and history, of defeating and halting powers of destruction.

---

24. Caussade, *L'Abandon à la Providence divine*, 112–16.
25. Caussade, *Instructions spirituelles I*, in *Bossuet, maître d'oraison*, 103s, 123.

Peace is a more active reality than surrender and yet it also is ultimately only a variant of rest. Understanding its truth as non-natural, occurring reality, as ceaseless realization of the synthesis that overcomes diverse, divergent, and opposed forces allows us to emphasize the positive potentialities of this category of presence that is Rest. Giving every appearance of being figure of passivity and inaction, rest is an authentic manifestation of freedom, and this in two senses. Resting means not working, but liberation from labor; the possibility of stopping, doing something else, or even nothing are all ultimately figures of emancipation and liberation. Despite its riches, its authentic dignity, work cannot forget its birth out of the Curse: despite the joys it can give and the results that one can take pride in, it remains a sign of servitude. Rest is thus imposed as a fundamental law; its exercise is an authentic and valuable freedom. But this moral and social freedom has foundations in the metaphysical order. Rest is not only liberation from submission to an external constraint, to another, it also (and above all) witnesses to a freedom in relation to itself. The religious precept of Sabbath rest, a central commandment for Jewish existence, is based on the interpretation of creation. God worked six days in the creation of the world, but on the seventh day he stopped working in order to rest. This seventh day is the Sabbath and the creator "said to man: rest on the Sabbath day as I myself have rested."[26] The Sabbath was instituted in order to do the work of memory, in order to recall that if the works of the preceding days, the creation of the Sun and Moon, fish, birds and mammals, and the creation of Man are each manifestations of the creative power, then ultimately the rest on the Seventh Day reveals in its plenitude the meaning of creation. The creation, in its integral dimension of *creatio ex nihilo*, is the *Tzimtzum*, the retreat of the One who is all in order to give room to what is not. The divine rest following the work of the six days is the supreme manifestation of power in its non-exercise. The incommensurability and infinity of power, the limitlessness of freedom celebrates its realization in the infinite made finite, in the eternal submitting to time. In the rest of the Sabbath the flow, the succession that nonetheless belongs to the very essence of Time is subject to arrest in the instant that endures. The *nunc stans* is certainly the emblem of the present but it is only as victory ceaselessly won. The secret of "present" intentionality is that in it the undivided instant extends itself and unfolds in and through its very indivisibility.

The Form of the Past and Retention

The discussion of the present and its moral-metaphysical forms illustrates the eidetic articulation of *Chronos* but is not yet enough to take account of the profound senses of the intentionalities of the three times. The present appeared as the true destiny of the statement from the *Timaeus* about the moving image of eternity, but a true eidetic of the three times must pass through the conceptual clarification of the before and after.

---

26. "Tanhuma Bresit," in Kasher, *Encyclopedia of Biblical Interpretation I*, 80.

When Aristotle remarks that "before and after exist in time" (*Memoria* 450a) he seems to state a truism, but nothing is more misleading or more fallacious than the common opinion about the signification of these temporal adverbs. Without reflection before is assimilated to the past and after to the future as a primary self-evident fact. But these must not be confounded. Before and after certainly belong to the elementary structure of time. They are primitive eidetic moments of *Chronos*. However, earlier and later are "entirely different concepts" than past and future. One set denotes "ways of being given" in the flux of time while the other corresponds to "opposed directions in the order of time."[27]

"Before" and "after" connote only a situation within time, not an eidetic moment of its auto-structuration, its temporalization. They indicate a movement towards, but do not mark any place. Simply, directions and not true dimensions of time, before and after—all the while being permanent companions to *Chronos*—do not touch the surface of the Flux. Perennially concurrent with Time, without which it cannot be thought, before and after are only temporal forms without specific content. They represent no sui generis mode of phenomenological being. Things are different for past and future, which are not simply portions of time past or to come. But, having their own eidetic content, being modes of specific temporal being, they are autonomous intentionalities. Of course, the future cannot be conceived without positioning it in the to come [à-venir], nor the past without thinking it as sur-passed [ré-volu]. What remains to be understood—and this alone makes possible the elaboration of a metaphysics of time—is: how can what has passed continue to be present? How can what will happen still be present?

The present doubtlessly possesses a radical priority over the other times. It alone, sensu stricto, is the moving image of eternity and ultimately, it alone *is*, is *truly*. Everything that has happened was first present, and all that will happen will only happen as a moment of the present. The past is only the submerged present, the future is anticipated present. As the Scholastics taught, we only speak of the past and future as *"per respectum ad praesens."*[28] But the past is not only present that has passed, but it must also take part in the actual present, the now present. And the future is not only present to come, but lives in its own way in the effective present. The future doubtlessly guides the present, it is its goal, its telos, we could even say its sense, or direction. But it is an obvious fact, a banal first truth that aspirations for the present cannot be conceived merely starting from their roots in the past. The past is no longer but it truly has been: it is the most massive truth, the truth that imposes itself on any meditation on time. And in order to comprehend how the present harmonizes with the future, we must first see its "connection" to the past. Metaphysics is, above all, the study of synthesis, of the modalities where the point is prolonged or rather surpassed. It is the doctrine of subjectivity and the subject is only as it exceeds itself. In ontological

---

27. Husserl, *Die Bernauer Manuskripte über das Zeitbewusstsein (1917/1918)*, 146.
28. Thomas Aquinas, *In I Periherm.* lect. 5, n. 13.

terms, this *excess* is expressed by the question: how to go beyond oneself, how is more and otherwise possible within the perfection of the same? More closely identified, this truth is repeated in terms of the subjectivity that exceeds itself: all of its present and wholly in this present the subject must also go necessarily beyond or below itself towards the past. We will see that the subject is memory, knowledge and history, but it cannot remember and know, it cannot understand itself as history except by virtue of this originally synthetic condition where it is also "behind" itself, all the while remaining in the middle of its now.

The past is the hypostasized vision of the behind-self. The actual being self is, of course, a very ambiguous phenomenological essence. In order to understand it we must first envisage the dimension in a naively topological way. The past is what is behind us. It is made of traces that we have abandoned, burdens that we have dropped, objects that we have let fall. Everything found in the past is far from us, even if the respective distances can be extremely different. Our entire actual experience is composed of "primordial impressions," and the acuteness with which they survive can be located at the top or bottom of a (very extensive, very large) scale. And we are not even taking into account here impressions that have vanished, disappeared, been lost for good. If the sphere of the Unconscious is already immense, the Forgotten is even larger!

The (retained) past, the past that has not lost its relevance, and which matters to and influences the present, is still separated from it by a gulf. And even if it imperceptibly surrounds us, if it infiltrates our present positions, a true leap seems required in order to find it, to connect to it, even to take one's place within it. Despite its pertinence and presence, its importance and relevance, the past is what has gone, definitively *passed* by, and as such it is unalterable, unmodifiable. Man is subject to the temptation to dwell on the past, to ruminate on what he has done or failed to do. He can think of it with rancor or remorse, but he cannot change it. False witnesses and complaisant historians take every latitude in rewriting the past, but they still cannot make what has taken place not take place or even take place in a different way than it did. The unalterability of the past gives it a color or specific tenor. Grey, and perhaps better, black, are appropriate colors for the past. They suggest the fixed and frozen condition of what happened. This discolored appearance and above all this definitively established situation can remove the past from passions and emotions and establish it as the supremely objective place. The past is there, unalterable, always the same. It presents a pacific face and above all an immobility that allows us to study it, analyze it, carve it up and dissect it freely.

This peaceful objectivity and this foolproof stability are organic factors indissociable from the past: if the past is appreciated and celebrated, its objectivity and stability are the main reasons for its many accolades. Objectivity and stability equally contribute to the limitations proper to this time, to what puts it in an unfavorable light in relation to the present. The past, so to speak, deactivates the present and appears to tear it away from living subjectivity. It is like a "For-itself recaptured and drowned by the In-itself."[29] It can represent the domination of Space over Time (Bergson). As past, time depends on space, on the elsewhere, and the past is "the definitive widowhood of every elsewhere. The past less hoards the already given then it closes off the entire future, "the mourning of any possibility for a new occurrence." It does not practice the operation of absence, but its censure: from now on everything has passed; "nothing can happen."[30] The past is like a gate that inevitably imposes itself, maybe arbitrarily, but its arbitrariness falls with the entire weight of the necessary. Here an essential difference between past and present can and must be observed. The past portrays a different face than the present, it is the unmanipulatable, the definitive, while the present entails a latitude for change, a flexibility, an odor of contingency. In reality, both past and present exist through the same original necessity. The present is constituted by the primordial impression that falls into consciousness like a meteor. It "constitutes" the first now, the initial now that necessarily unfolds, and the memory that accompanies it also necessarily coheres there. The necessity prevailing in the advent of memory is doubtlessly not indivisible: it consists of degrees. From Bergson to Husserl the Philosophy of Time is devoted to scholarly exercises in order to distinguish—and dissociate—the first and second memories, the immediate present and the present that is farther away. First memories would be effectively removed from the free action of the subject while second memories may be evoked at will and thus nearly constitute a proper phenomenological essence. But what matters is the presence of the past in consciousness, a presence that can be understood only through and starting from the description of the mode of being proper to the past, of "past" intentionality.

Modern philosophy processes the reality of the past, its effective condition, even actuality. Past being is not so to say "retired"; it has not lost its efficiency or is reduced to an "honorary" condition. The past is certainly *elsewhere* than the now, but this does not mean that, as the result of a fall or escape, it would be lying on the side of the road or sitting like "a rock at the bottom of a stream." The past is not at the center of my effective being, but it continues to fall under subjectivity. In short, it belongs to it. It doubtlessly constitutes a distance in relation to the being of the subject, "but it is truly *its* being not another's that remains behind it."[31] Instead of speaking of the past as being located behind or beneath the present, it should rather be conceived as being situated in the present, effectively taking part in it. But, precisely, if the past is truly found within it then it registers a radical difference from the present. Original impressions are received, perceived, and these are impressions that are subsequently remembered. Memories are therefore perceptions that have entered into the past. They are no longer effectively perceived, but merely remembered. Consciousness can contain original impressions and memories at the same time, but it will necessary conceive the

---

29. Sartre, *L'être et le néant*, 164.
30. Marion, *La phénomène érotique*, 65s.
31. Sartre, *L'être et le néant*, 152–56.

difference between them. The impression is a present perception, memory a recalled perception, apprehended in the present. But "the past apprehended in the present can never be...a real content of an act of perception effectuated in the now."[32] In other words, the now in which I remember and the now that I remember can never coincide.

Present perception and memory coincide inasmuch as a past perception coexists with a present perception. It can nevertheless not represent the survival of the past in memory as a preservation. Consciousness of things past is not a reservoir of bygone events but the vision of what has taken place *as* having taken place. It is not a matter of the accumulation of perceptions anterior to the now, but of their invocation, their presentification as past things. The past is no longer there as it was when it was still present, but as gone, therefore as *past*. The "past" condition does not indicate a period in time but rather a tenor or essence. William James recalls the ancient Christian tradition of "Adam created with a bellybutton."[33] The bellybutton is a sign or trace of the act of cutting the umbilical cord. It symbolizes separation from the past, its surmounting. But Adam was created as an adult, without having ever existed as an embryo within a mother. If he was born with a bellybutton this is because the past does not necessarily denote an antecedent period of life, a chronologically bygone section of time, but rather a condition, an eidos of temporality. The Philosophy of Time always delights in resorting to the example of a sound, a melody previously heard, in order to analyze our intuition of the past. A jingle heard in the past is retained, and if it is retained—thought—then it subsists. But in reality it is not the jingle itself that subsists but the consciousness you had of it. The jingle from the past is not "possessed" or preserved but heard *as* past. The content of the past is not found in consciousness but rather the content perceived in the past is perceived now as a past content. Husserl's famous example: when I remember the illuminated theatre, this does not mean that I remember having perceived it at a given moment, the other day, or the week before, but rather that "'inwardly' I see the theatre as past."[34] In its truth memory does not indicate the given that has been perceived in the past but is instead related to its given being in the consciousness as past.

What is essential in memory is not its material presence in the consciousness but its resurrection under the heading of "having been." Memory can be clear or effaced, intense or faint. It refers to another intentionality than that of present perception. In present perception consciousness is struck with full force by the impression, it suffers it, whereas the "past" tenor of memory renders the situation of a content, a *noema* maintained at arms' length, as an elsewhere. This "elsewhere" is less an affair of a distance than the expression of a tension, a movement of the subject stretching out, extending itself. Elsewhere has a spatial connotation; it faithfully translates the spatializing proclivity represented by the past under the form of a particular space

---

32. Bernet, *La vie du sujet*, 224.
33. James, *Principles of Psychology* I, 641.
34. Husserl, *Leçons pur une phénoménologie de la conscience intime du temps*, 77.

"where" memories are collected and retained. But spatial reification risks obscuring the profoundly active, intentional sense of the past. Like the present, the past is also born from a relation to an impression. However, while the present almost coincides with the impression the past is separated from it. And the efforts of the great philosophers of time, Augustine and Kant, Bergson and Husserl are centered on the how of the separation. The phenomenological notion of *retention* provides the best account of the active, intentional nature of what would otherwise be only a kind of passive, instinctive repetition. Discourse on memory is so focused on the exploits of memory for the sake of resituating, returning what is bygone to the now that it ends up bracketing the specificity and originality of this bygone understood as coexisting with the presently perceived. Yet contrary to the memory that is supposed to make the non-present quasi-present, retention *maintains* the non-present. Thanks to the insistence on the synthetic act of maintaining what has fallen into the past, the actuality of what "is no longer" is reaffirmed without compromising its truth as past. To conclude: retention is the intentionality proper to consciousness of the past. It resolves the aporia of Augustine: the enigmatic presence of the Vestige, something at once present and absent. For something to be present *and* absent the opposition of the Same and Other must be resolved. This happens through the a priori synthesis that allows the Same's access to the Other starting from itself. The retention where the subject exceeds itself is an example, a privileged instance of this self-surpassing of the Same in the Other, which leaps beyond itself in order to find itself in the Other.

Memory and History

Retention is an essential moment of the being of subjectivity in excess of itself. It is an action, an operation through which consciousness surpasses itself, sails beyond, exits itself. But these powerful, dynamic movements are not yet enough to define the self-exceeding condition of the subject. The exceeding certainly indicates a ceaseless effort, a tension, yet it is not an excess, an *elusion* of oneself—something without rule or order. Subjectivity is certainly "condemned" to exceed itself but this condemnation does not amount to destiny that falls to it from the outside. Retention is not something freely chosen, freely constructed or interpreted. To retain the past is neither to be carried by a flood nor to dip into the treasury of past perception. Retention certainly has an essential aspect of accumulation and conservation: in and through it the overflow of the unconscious is avoided, our heads are kept above the flooding waters of the Lethe, and we remain in possession of a panoply of perceptions transformed into memories. However, this conscious and lucid possession of a collection of mental contents, whether intellectual or affective, must be understood as an act of control where the fact or the existential power of sovereignty in selection and conservation is exercised according to the a priori intelligibility of an intentionality. The moments in and through which the subject exceeds itself towards the past punctuates the framework of a unique synthesis, exclusively proper to the subjectivity at work in the retention. This essential and unique work of retention corresponds to what the philosophers and common sense together call *memory*.

Historians and teachers always celebrate memory, but their praises run the risk of lacking or rather masking their appropriate end. A pre-phenomenological, material vision of memory exalts the extension and force within it. It would be a vast store of objects, at best a treasury of precious possessions, at worst a cabinet of curiosities. It is also conceived as a power to revive what is effaced, to reinvigorate what is enervated. But in both cases memory is seen only according to its material acceptation whereas in its metaphysical truth it is truly an intentionality, an a priori synthesis. Memory certainly establishes an actual and virtual ensemble of elements, but the nerve of this ensemble, the active principle of its gathering is the structuring subjectivity. Malebranche writes that the memory is "nothing other than the facility of thinking things we have already thought. . . . The bending branches of a tree that in a certain way retain the facility for being weighed down anew in the same way." A great contemporary, Leibniz, read the passage and did not accept it as such. His annotation says: "There is something else in memory. It is not enough to have facility with thinking, we must judge that we have already thought."[35] Memory is like a repetition or rather a representation of past perception but we still must be conscious of having been the one who received them. Memory is the subsumption of noetic contents under the unity of the subject; it is an aim that gathers up the sum of impressions. But it is not only a gathering together. It is also a structuration.

Memory is the nerve and principle of the identity of the subject in and through its continuity and it is not simply the condition of this continuity according to existence but also according to essence. It is certainly the force by which "past" intentionality is exercised; yet retention is not only synthesis "in general"; it is *a priori* synthesis. It is not merely the power of conserving and accumulating bygone perceptions. It is also and above all the conceptual principle presiding at their selection and their reunion with one another. Memory is like the cipher of the vigilance of the subject that makes sure that the essential, the appropriate, what is fitting to it and representative for it are torn away from forgetfulness, removed from erasure, protected from annihilation. The existence of the finite subject is a constant effort to retain a sense, to maintain coherence before an ever threatening chaos. Memory can have gaps, it can sag, it can even fall into the idiosyncrasy and errors of illusion. But, precisely, these dysfunctions show that it is not a neutral faculty exercised according to the strict laws of a mechanical psychology. Memory has an essential pragmatism that prescribes a necessary genetic engineering. All perceptions are of an equal originality and yet one must greedily choose among them with both harshness and frugality, in accordance with the conditions of a narrow selfishness. It is commonly said that what touches the heart is engraved on the memory, that some events are memorable, while others, much

---

35. Robinet, *Malebranche et Leibniz*, 171.

more numerous, are not. If an event is memorable this is not a result of its own constitution but depends on its relation to the Project of the ego. Out of a near infinity of perceptions only a handful will be "retained." The a priori synthesis has its dynamism and its liberalities, and even potentialities that prefigure, at least on a formal plane, renunciation and kenosis. Ultimately, however, it is the unfolding of a project exercised through self-surpassing that is finally the continuation and perpetuation of the self.

Despite its condition of selection and thus choice, memory retains an aspect, a moment of the automatic, the necessary that its pragmatic, egoistic finality only accentuates. Its unequal, imperfect, fractured and spotty functioning, its negligences and forgettings seem to jeopardize a determinist conception of memory. However, the hiccups and faults, the failures and mistakes of memorization demonstrate contingency. They do not yet proclaim a true freedom. In order to find freedom within Retention, we must turn to that variant or rather counterpart of Memory that is History, that "memory of the ages,"[36] that meandering and intermittent outline of the lights of the past. History: where the pragmatism of memory is sublated by moral passion, bracketed or rather rendered silent, covered over by the shadow of tragedy.

History is a retention, in fact, a supreme instance of retention where a bygone moment is recalled with passion and ardor, with the desire almost to bring it back to life. The past event that one invokes can impose itself on the present, but this constraint always encounters a moral response. The act of the past never "falls" on us; it is recalled or at least received with freedom. Despite its native practice of selection, the facts that memory records can encumber, overload it. Historical events always introduce, register a signifying power and role. This condition of freedom and moral pertinence is seen very clearly in the appearance proper to the historical. The contents of memory—whether imposed without being invoked or appearing as results of effort, an application—unfold with a certain automatism. However, the moments of history become the object of a narrative where, the coherence of the concatenation notwithstanding, the next piece of the chain can never be predicted with certainty. If memory selects a moment that the pragmatism proper to the synthesis that it constitutes will choose as the most appropriate, the most pertinent, then the history that is also a memory invokes and enumerates only single facts. It is rightly said that History never repeats itself. It is the unfolding of the free synthesis that is the identity of the subject. But the continuity of the person is not the persistence of a sameness. By virtue of the a priori synthesis that one is, the identity of oneself is retained despite and through all change: "one remains oneself even if one does not stay the same. . ."[37]

Personal identity is the supreme example of the true being of Becoming, of the organic unity of the multiple. The apparent transcendence of the subject in relation to its contents, to the moments of history that punctuate the synthesis of retention constituting its life can suggest the contingency of its contents, their irremediably

---

36. Ronsard, *Second livre des Poëmes. Excellence de l'esprit*, in *Oeuvres* 2, 469.
37. Tengelyi, *L'histoire d'une vie et sa région sauvage*, 31.

ephemeral condition. In reality the impossibility of being repeated is not the mark of the insignificance and impertinence of the past. To the contrary, this emphasizes and demonstrates its ultimate value, its radical uniqueness. What has taken place once is gone and cannot be brought back into existence. It is an unrepeatable fact. Whether it endured for a moment or a thousand years, it is irreplaceable. A historical event remembered as such is a light forever extinguished, a sound forever muted. It would doubtlessly be tempting to mourn this inevitable disappearance that seems to squash cruelly the pretended immortality of the great deeds of the past: these are unique realities but their uniqueness can be consummated only through their slippage into nothing. But, precisely, the uniqueness receives its veritable metaphysical dimension starting from the contrast between the disappearance according to existence and the signification that remains. The retention that constitutes "past" intentionality is not a physical faculty. Its efficiency is formal, not material. People speak of the "weight" of the past. The expression certainly has an anthropological sense, but it also and above all signifies that despite the inevitable fall into non-being, what has passed can continue to be meaningful.

Protention and the Future

Opposed to the weight of the past, of that becoming that displays a massive and integral factuality, the future, the third of the three times, appears as the universe of potentiality in its two senses, contingency and freedom. People complain that the constraints of things, the absolute power of *ananke*, of the *fatum* that would underlie and undermine the appearances of possibility, would condemn and thwart attempts to act *differently*, to do something truly *new*. In reality, in the depths of our consciousness, in the recesses of our hearts, we remain convinced about the uncertainty of the future, its aleatory character, its essential unforeseeability. The deterministic philosophies of diverse scientisms (albeit already some of the great rationalist systems) thought they could demonstrate the ultimately illusory character of the ontologies of possibility. But common sense and its great ally, Phenomenology, wanted to do justice to commonplace intuitions. The law of the future is indeterminacy, and the intentionality proper to the future corroborates the absence of necessity in the unfolding of the future. With the exception of limit cases of empty memory, occurrences of retention without effective content, "past" intentionality is a *noesis* with a necessary *noema*: Retention is always a synthesis with its material correlate. Things are different for the intentionality proper to the future, *protention*. Like retention, protention is a synthetic unity-continuity of transition with the presentation of the present. However protention is opposed to the clearly and well articulated fulfillment proper to retention and translates an intentional relation to contents of which the entrance into consciousness is immediately occurring, though one is not yet aware of it except non-thematically. In other words, if in the intentionality of the past the aim and the target constitute a reciprocal, well proportioned integration, in protention the target is only signified and promised.

The in-articulation of the future goes along with its uncertainty and corresponds to its eidetic form that does not depend on considerations of effective existence. Prophecy is not related to something like a hidden object to be revealed; the advent of its intentional object is not yet a condition of its truth. One can have an authentic prophetic vision of the future without it being realized in facts. Or inversely, one can seek after things in expectation, count on their realization so that once it happens one can be disappointed and continue to experience restlessness and impatience, feelings that belong to the eidetic form of the future, while the intentional object of the protention will have already been translated into the moments of the present, or even have fallen into the world of the past. This form of the future implies both contingency and activity. Protention is a non-thematized anticipation of what is going to happen, thus of something indeterminate. But precisely as anticipation it presents a primitive form of activity. The vision of the future is marred by uncertainty, but despite being a form of passivity, instead of excluding effort, uncertainty promotes openness and receptivity, and imposes itself as true source of creativity. The unforeseeability proper to the future is not yet improvidence. Instead, it prepares for a flexible but ardent availability. The unforeseen can pounce on me, but it does not overwhelm me for that reason. To the contrary, "I learn to know myself in my response to the unexpected."[38] The positive uncertainty that hangs over the works of the future condemns me, so to speak, to a project existence: to do projects is effectively to create the future, submitting it to our dreams and ideas. And more than the project, the promise is the proper way that the intentionality of the future is unfolding in Subjectivity. The promise reconciles the effective target of the future with the recognition of our limits; it reunites humility and determination, non-mastery and resolution. Humanity has to refuse to preside over its future but without renouncing responsibility for its actions. Humanity must implant fidelity into the field of uncertainty: the eidetic structure of protention underlies the act of promise without "guaranteeing" its effective realization.

Project and promise are instances, manifestations of protention that is a form of self-excess. In fact, they are its supreme manifestation because if retention is really a going beyond oneself, it clings to its object, while in protention one advances, breaks away from oneself. On the material or factual plane the excess of retention is translated by the distance of the object that slowly escapes consciousness whereas the excess of the future is a going ahead that has as "result" the approach, the coming towards it of what it aims for. As Heidegger taught, the future does not signify an instant that is "not yet" real but will be "soon." To the contrary, it is engendered by the action of "being related to" and "being brought towards."[39] The project and the promise illustrate an appropriate and eloquent way of exceeding the self proper to

38. Housset, *La vocation de la personne*, 460.
39. Waehlens, *La Philosophie de Martin Heidegger*, 183.

protention. They show or rather demonstrate that subjectivity is always beyond itself, that in addition to the very evident reality of the present, the future also has its own reality in equally belonging to the subject of the intentional act. More generally, the future is a part, an authentic component of subjectivity. If yearning for the future, the hope or fear of what it may bring, exercises such a strong influence on our now this is because we know that we are going towards the future, that we will welcome into our arms the gifts it brings but also face head on its consequences. In fact, if the "things" of the future ultimately add to our having and modify its composition and coloration, this is because what I *will be* shares in what I *am*. If, in order to avoid going down the path of ontological determinism, it is necessary to avoid saying that the present is "pregnant with the future." We cannot insist enough on the influence and pertinence of the future on what we are now. Whether we perceive them or not tomorrow is present at the heart of today. The belonging of the future to the being of the subject is not only a literary theme, a form of moralist style. It manifests and explains the ontological truth of the free being.

The future shares in my being or rather "there is a Future because the For-itself has to be its being instead of simply being." The being of the present is too thin, too narrow; it must be enriched, completed by a more, by what hides and promises the future: I project myself towards the future in order to complete myself "with. . .that by which the synthetic addition to my present" will complete my being, will make me what I effectively am.[40] The addition of the future, its virtual but indispensable and real belonging to the intentionally existing subject expresses and translates in its own way the ancient idea of the existence of the possible, of the potential, within the actual. The actual alone *is* in the full sense of the term, but it implies, it bears and includes in itself the potential as its own necessary horizon. But the possible must realize its relation to the actual in a synthetic way: the future has a non-contingent, rational relation to the present but it does not result from it in a mechanically necessary way. The protention that makes the future come about while integrating it into the present advances in a hollow space (*creux*) where the *more* is announced that fills in the horizon. This more grants or rather offers leeway (latitudes) but it also implies a possibility of doing otherwise. The project, like the promise has its riches and poverties: it contains superabundance but also uncertainties. We must remember that the intentionality proper to the future is protention. With protention one collects different things and embraces them, and embracing too much cannot be avoided! Like all true intentionality, that of the future is not empty or indeterminate; it does not exist without a noematic correlate. However, the formal moment of the *noesis*, that of the container if you like, remains nevertheless preponderant in it by relation to the material component, that of the content.

---

40. Sartre, *L'être et le néant*, 170, 172.

Hope

With the unfolding of the eidetic of time, of the three times with their respective intentionality, of the demonstration that it effectively contains past, present, and future, *at the same time* if you like, the moral-metaphysical sense and range of time will be renewed. Undivided and unqualified irreversibility is the law of *Chronos*, at once flux and punctuality, flow and repetition of atoms in an integral discontinuity. Death has been shown as the meaningless meaning of flux, the emblematic figure of the Irreversible. With the eidetic articulation of temporalization it will be subject to a reinterpretation. It will be neither less bitter nor less definitive and it will always lack as much meaning. But it will nevertheless signal and symbolize another comprehension of the irreversible. Death will never be integrated into life: if Thanatos and Morpheus are brothers they still retain a radical heterogeneity. Sleep can signal a humiliating subjugation to nature, to the powers of immanence, but it nevertheless remains a vital source for the synthesis that life accomplishes. Death has nothing to do with synthesis: it remains beneath life and the supreme enemy of the continuities that constitute the ontological base of all intentionalities. Yet if death remains beneath and outside of the reunions and renewals that punctuate the life of the subject, it may receive the illuminations that—without integrating it into synthetic continuities—make it appear starting from a new comprehension of the irreversible. The Irreversible certainly remains irreversible but it is nevertheless requested to stop for a moment, to suspend its flight in order to sojourn on the plains of the present. It is equally advised to look behind itself and to contemplate and appreciate the riches of what is retained from the past. Articulated and conjugated by the past and the present, the Irreversible will have a different relation to the future. If it sojourns near the present in pleasure and peace, if it unfolds what is held in reserve in memory, it will transpose the protention of the future into the lofty virtue of hope where the hidden potentialities of the a priori synthesis are powerfully realized. Protention designates an intentionality where the accent is put on the *noesis*, not the *noema*. It is a tension that certainly implies an intentional object, the one *towards* which it tends, but the object is not precise, detailed or unfolded. Hope seems to be of the same metaphysical makeup. One doubtlessly thinks that it will bring about something, that it will make a new object happen, but the tension *towards* is its preponderant aspect. It includes a confidence about what it will lead to. Hope is not optimism. The optimist believes that things "will get better." He believes he has "reasons" for hope; he counts on the appearing of what he has been able to imagine. Taking part in the cortege of Laplace's genius, he is adept in his own way at causal explanation. He is convinced that what he can foresee will effectively happen. The optimist analyzes the present and draws conclusions about the future. He inventories his world and he wants to extrapolate the future based on the results of his analysis. The optimist almost wants to engineer the future, but hope has nothing to do with a science or technique. It is neither the prediction of things that will have taken place, nor the reasoned persuasion that they will (infallibly) happen.

Kant felt obliged to formulate a third essential philosophical question about man's being and vocation: "What may I hope for?" But this formulation is not adequate. We doubtlessly hope for this or that but *that in which* I hope depends on its *what*, its *Was*—as Schelling said—being second to its *Dass*... Hope is a free operation where the form implies matter, being gives rise to having. What matters is that I can hope, not that in which I hope. The content will be given as by excess: represented, it could provoke the absurd and even lead to the pernicious. The question proper to *spes* is therefore whether I can hope, not in what I can hope. The highest intuition of the future aims for the *eschaton*, but eschatologies always succumb to the noxious temptations of gaudily decorating the Expectation of the Coming with the precise calculations and events of the apocalypses. The deadly utopias of the past centuries wanted to impose on history their extrapolations. We all know with what horrible results... A bracketing of determined content is imposed on anyone ready to surrender or rather to dedicate himself to hope. Hope is doubtlessly not only expectation but it is not more than anticipation. Expectation translates the passivity of the mind deprived of horizon; it is an indifference-ignorance that borders on cowardice, less a pacific contemplation than a lazy fatalism. But hope should also be resolutely distinguished from anticipation. The one who anticipates thinks he has rights regarding the future. He must preempt events, force them to be. Said differently, he wants to apply illegitimately the regime of present possession (a regime that is not even truly appropriate to what is and what one has now) to what will take place in the future.

Everything that directly or indirectly belongs to possession is incompatible with hope. It excludes interpolation and rejects domination. Does this mean that it is located entirely elsewhere, that it does not have principle or root located in free subjectivity? Utopia refers to this world, the world in its immanent truth as "laboratorium possibilis salutis" (Bloch). But salvation does not come from a laboratory: it can come only Elsewhere and come to the one who hopes. Nietzsche said that man is an animal that knows how to promise. Is he also an animal that knows how to hope? Of course not, for the good reason that man is not an animal and hope is not counted among his natural faculties. Does this mean that hope has no source in humanity, that it cannot have anything to do with what we are and what we can be "naturally"? No, because we are not locked in our own immanence in such a way that we cannot devote ourselves to this *praeparatio spei* that is availability. Availability nearly establishes the premises and natural principle of hope, but for it to reach the condition of active potentiality, to make room for hope, a leap is necessary. Availability is the cipher of non-mastery, of the dispossession necessary for hope, but it must still mature into confidence, an entirely independent condition from any objective and objectifying aim. It is located and unfolded at the extreme limit of the possibilities of the a priori synthesis.

True hope never lives in the register of certainty, in the light of a security. It is nevertheless always confident. It certainly does all that it can but it knows above all that it cannot do anything great, in fact, that it can do nothing at all. Authentic hope prohibits imagining some kind of continuity between an aspiration and its fulfillment. As Marcel writes, it is "that which fits with what does not depend on us."[41] Indeed, it contains a subtle paradox: at its summit, in its realization, hope is "hope against hope. . .in the night of despair."[42] The insistence on discontinuity and paradox is a modern translation of the theologoumenon *hope*. The three supernatural virtues are located opposite the cortege of natural virtues like prudence, patience and justice. The natural virtues are "possible," accessible at the cost of an exit from self that is its proper realization. The supernatural virtues can only be "infused" into us. With faith and charity, hope is the third of the supernatural or theological virtues. Each is "*totaliter ab extrinseco.*"[43]

The extrinsic character of hope is spelled out by an explicitly theological discourse, which has no less value for a philosophical acceptation. Hope aspires to an advent, tends towards a future, entrusts itself to a fulfillment, which are all forms of ontological transcendence. But at first glance this transcendence seems to pass beyond the limits of the a priori synthesis. The a priori synthesis is the discourse on the different variants of access to the more, to heterogeneity, but the access is always made by virtue of a power proper to the subject. The logic of the a priori synthesis articulates the passage from A to B by virtue of a C that is given neither in A nor in B but nevertheless rises up from within the subject itself. Spontaneity and freedom are resources of the synthesis that allows me to go beyond myself. And if I effectively go beyond myself, if I, so to speak, step out of myself, in short, if I surpass myself, I accomplish this feat always because of myself, by means of my own powers. The discourse on the a priori synthesis insists on the rupture with deadly immanence, but the nerve of the rupture remains internal to the subject. But as figure of the future, hope makes possible an expansion of the synthesis or rather the reunion with or inclusion within it of what nevertheless transcends it.

While having an essential metaphysical dimension of going beyond the self and consequently a surpassing of time, the a priori synthesis is still always transcribed by the ancient syllogism, *A is B*, even if the *is*, the copula, no longer connotes a simple sign of equality but a task to be completed. The Utopian Philosophy of last century wanted to correct the wording by the formula *S is not yet p*.[44] However, if the "not yet" effectively translates the invocation and exigency of a future that would be otherwise, it still does not signify a leap beyond immanence. Despite the obstacles that thwart

---

41. Marcel, *Position et approches concrètes du mystère ontologique*, 73.

42. Kierkegaard, *Pour un examen de conscience recommandé aux contemporains*, in *Oeuvres complètes* 18, 135.

43. Thomas Aquinas, *Summa Theologiae* I-IIa 63 a. 1.

44. Lacoste, "Espérance," in Lacoste, *Dictionnaire critique de la théologie*, 485.

Book Two — Eidetics

and prevent it, what is not yet is on the path of becoming and it will effectively become by means of potentialities inscribed within it. But, precisely, *this* vision of the future is incomplete and, consequently, inadequate. Its intentionality, protention, permits a tension towards for the future and its figures that is quasi-sovereign in relation to its contents. Yet the future is not only protentional progression, a movement of embracing what is not yet there. It should not be conceived only under the form of a going towards, but also as a coming *from*. I not only go out to meet the future, it also comes to meet me. I certainly try to await the other, but the other also intends to wait for me. The intentionality of the future cannot be limited to tension, to aspiration. It also includes a component of welcome and acceptance. But the eidetic moment of expectation, reception and consent to the future permits the expansion of the a priori synthesis. The synthesis cannot only signify a surpassing of self by its own powers. It can equally contain a transcendent dimension. Going beyond the self is always tearing away from self, but it can also refer to the radiance of another than self.

At this moment it is realized that the eidetic potentialities of the Future that define and animate hope lead to a third formulation of the copula of the a priori synthesis. The word that goes from the subject toward the predicate is first stated as *is*, then as *is not yet*. But in light of the integral conception of the future, this word is transposed into a *will be*. The "will be" signifies the going out of the subject towards the predicate as well as the coming of the predicate towards it. In fact, the predicate blurs, dims and is nearly bracketed. What ultimately matters is the movement of going ahead, considered less "in itself" then as sublated in the Coming. This reading of hope certainly surpasses the comprehension of the term in the strict terms of protention, but it also remains faithful to it. If the "Will Be" (see Exod 3:14) expresses the irruption of the Elsewhere that takes up again the curvature of the direction of protention, it retains and reaffirms its two great metaphysical components: the sovereignty of the *noesis* and the erasure of its noematic correlate. Hope does not conjecture but affirms that it does not know what will be except that it will be.

Hope appears here in its authentic condition of radical unconditionality: it is not extrapolation from the future starting from the present, but profession of faith in the advent in the to-come [*a-venir*]. Yet if this invocation of the power of the new corresponds to the intuition, to the aim that underpins the idea of the a priori synthesis, does it not lack an essential component? The a priori synthesis expresses the power of the mind to make a predicate happen that is not implied by the subject, but the non-implication does not yet signify contingency. If a synthesis is a priori this is because it is related to concepts that are not analytically deducible and can nevertheless be affirmed as going with, as conformed to the intelligibility of the subject. But the bracketing of the predicate in the affirmation of the will be seems to ignore all relation of Meaning between subject and predicate, between the one who hopes today and will exist tomorrow.

The paradigmatic instance of the a priori synthesis in its expansion is given by hope in the victory over Death. Time inexorably leads the free being to its end, it is destined and condemned to shatter, to disappear within the irreversible flow. But, precisely, hope says and repeats that the last word is not death or rather that a word will be said other than the one that announces and observes the loss of life. The victory over death is the proof and the ultimate trial of hope: it expresses a synthesis in which reception is the counterpart of the leap and the erasure of every formulated and formulatable content has the presence and persistence of Meaning as a counterpart.

Philosophies and theologies of every time and place have striven to demonstrate human immortality. They teach that the continuation of life, survival, existence beyond the tomb can be proven or ought to be proven. If for the thinker of *Dasein* death ripens within life like the worm in a fruit, in the great rationalisms it is instead survival that ripens within it. The soul is the principle motor of life, but what moves itself, having not begun to be moved, does not have to stop moving itself. In one way or another, immortality is conceived as resulting from elements or givens within life, implied by present existence; one reaches it naturally by virtue of immanent principles. Life is unconditioned spontaneity: how could it be interrupted? Why would it cease? Since the *Phaedrus,* natural reason basks in this edifying discourse, the mother and matrix of ontologies of consolation that strive to explicate the analytic truth of survival. However, the optimism of this metaphysics finds its correctives in the simple givens of our condition. The fear of death, the anguish that seizes us by the throat (independently of our strongest beliefs in survival) eloquently shows the failures of these ratiocinations, the inadequacy of the philosophies that proceed by unfolding within immanence. The rational creature is fascinated by sameness, it considers itself immune to breakdown, and it believes with all of its strength that its identity is forever safe. These seductive certainties can be strong and vigorous, but they lack true metaphysical foundation. The identity of which the unfolding in time is the continuity is not natural: if it is, if it exists and effectively endures, it is not a given but a gift. Immortality cannot be deduced starting from our essence and it must not be sought through postulate or demonstration. I will not die! You will come back! are not very reasonable conjectures but cries that proclaim hope.

Still, the indeducibilty of immortality does not signify that it would be irrational. If on the plane of existence immortality is like a leap, on the plane of essence it registers an affinity, a kinship with what precedes it. Finite subjectivity is not infinite, but it contains an appropriate and logical meaning of not turning off, of continuing to shine. But for meaning to impose itself in existence, the protention proper to going ahead is not enough: it must be subsumed under the reception of the Coming. The Victory over Death is in its own way the ultimate avatar of the a priori synthesis or rather its supreme accomplishment. Hope attests to the presence of Meaning in the subject that totally penetrates it without being divided into little parts, into concrete predicates, into material contents. It is a going ahead, a free, sovereign protention, but precisely by virtue of its freedom and sovereignty it is apt and ready to be transposed into Reception. In other words, if the a priori synthesis is a sign of and attests to the aptitudes and tasks of the auto-surpassing of the free subject, the internal rupture that it knows in advance and that it effectively is can be accomplished only in an expectation that has value only through a leap outside the self.

X

The Will

The Human Self

Modern philosophy understands time as the very essence of man, as the horizon of Being. But time is only a category of "theoretical" thinking: it is certainly the milieu of our existence but it does not fall within the competence of what makes meaning possible, namely novelty. Novelty comes about by freedom and freedom is a form of the will. Novelty unfolds in time but time temporalizes itself through the will. These eidetic forms of *Chronos* become inscribed into existence by the will. The work of free self-exodus is ceaselessly accomplished thanks to the will. The will doubtlessly takes its time emerging from the grip of reason, distinguishing and differentiating itself from desire. Ancient thought only had presentiments of the idea that appears in truth in Augustine and flourishes in the great Scholastic systems. In the work of Kant the will acquires its metaphysical autonomy, which is quickly lost in the Post-Kantians.[1] Schelling (cited by Heidegger with reverential approval) declares: "In the final and highest instance, there is no other Being than the will."[2] Schopenhauer installed the will as the noumenal background of all of reality. Nietzsche wanted to reinterpret all morality and anthropology in terms of "the Will to Power." But these exaggerations, this inflation of the idea is fatal. Instituted as a unique faculty, ontological principle of the real, dominant category of all philosophical reflection, the will loses its proper character, its sui generis specificity and becomes quasi-synonymous with a general equalizing force in which vital energy, impulses and the moral will sensu stricto are subsumed. Superlatives are not absent of course in pre-Kantian thought. For St. Bernard, it is through the will that man bears the image of God; for Dante,

---

1. For a metaphysical genealogy of the will, see Vető, *La naissance de la volonté*.
2. Schelling, *Recherches philosophiques sur l'essence de la liberté humaine*, in *Oeuvres métaphysiques*, 137. Quoted in Heidegger, *Schelling*, 167.

it constitutes the greatest good among all the gifts of God; for Descartes, the human will and the divine will are distinguished only by their range. Kant himself chants the praises of the will, defining it as "the Self of man,"[3] who is by it "superior to the angels without a will."[4] In the critical philosophy, the will is radically independent from nature, in relation to which it registers a clear superiority. Yet the Kantian exaltation of the will has nothing to do with the excesses and exaggerations of the medieval nominalists and voluntarists or the modern vitalists. The will is truly the central power of free finitude to the degree that in and through it the a priori synthesis is unfolded in its plenitude and that analogies of the Kenosis are found within the very self-exit that founds novelty.

Desire

Traditionally the mental faculties are divided into two groups, theoretical and practical. The apparent criterion of distinction is the intentional object. While the intentional object is a being or event conceived as *true*, it is sought by a theoretical power of the mind. Yet when it is apprehended as a *good*, the intentionality is practical. More precisely, our practical faculties are related to diverse, particular goods that are various instantiations of the Good. The properly intentional object spoken of by the practical faculty is therefore the Good, the good in general, and if in every singular exercise of desire a particular good is sought, then through and beyond this singular the Good, as such, is related to the mind. However, this distinction according to respective intentional object is not sufficient to delimit and define our faculties. Theory and practice are not distinguished only in terms of the object of intentional aim but also, and above all, by the way in which it is aimed for. In order better to see something, and thus to describe and analyze it, a distance must be observed. But observing a distance is not simply a technical, pragmatic condition of access to knowledge but equally the expression of a profound attitude of the subject. Stopping and standing still before something translates a neutrality, even an indifference that makes objectivity possible. The knowing subject seeks only to know and understand its object. It does not want to dominate; its goal is not possession. Things are different for the one who desires, covets and wants. Practical *noesis* is not content to be turned toward its *noema*. Ignoring all phenomenological bracketing, it wants to seize, to handle, to possess its object. Practical knowledge is interested: it unfolds like an operation where the noetic is indissociable from the psychological or rather where the noetic as such is of the interested, engaged order. In its material content the intentional object of practical knowledge can very well be equally an intentional object of theoretical knowledge. A pastry is appetizing, but also analyzable in chemical terms. A charitable act pertains to the will, but it can also be described in its conceptual structure, its psychical and

---

3. Kant, *Fondements de la Métaphysique des Moeurs*, in Oeuvres 2, 330 (Akad. IV, 458).
4. Kant, *Akad.* XXVII, 1187.

physiological elements as well as in its legal connotations and implications. All this means that the attitude of the subject of the *noesis* qualifies and determines the condition, the moral intentional truth of a material content.

The *noesis* that in the strict sense aims for its object, in order to know it, to possess and enjoy it, is in its primary, most primitive structure, an impulse. *Impulse* connotes a movement of self-exit but which is the prolongation of the self, not a tearing away from self. The impulse is an ascent, an upsurge starting from the depths of the subject where the subject progresses, continues, puts itself at risk in the literal sense. The impulse ignores difference; it does not look ahead of itself; it is blind, but not because it lacks a particular end. To the contrary, it clearly grasps what it aims for; it knows how to do it, how to overcome obstacles before taking possession. Blindness signifies here the total bracketing of anything that is not the self, everything other than self. The impulse is not given a precise, distinct image of the end to which it propels itself. This movement of propelling contains the end which, so to speak, shares in its eidetic constitution. The violence of the upsurge, the abrupt ascent, the sudden throb must not obscure the metaphysical truth of the impulse, which is still a supreme movement of immanence. The fulguration of desire can appear as a leap. In truth it is only the continuation, conservation, even reinforcement of immanence. Despite the hasty movements, the clamor and the excited movements through which it is translated, the impulse remains a form of nature, a moment where nature perseveres in its being. Despite all that seems like a spurting forth, propulsion, and emergence, the impulse gives birth to nothing new. It is only a moment of analysis, discontent with sprouting thorns, exists and perdures under the form of a violent taking possession.

The impulse is a term, a modern expression translating the elementary forms of the practical faculty. The appetite is another appellation where the stress lies above all on the "covetous" aspect. If impulse denotes the upsurge starting from immanence, the appetite expresses this same upsurge as ignoring or rather obliterating the distance by relation to the object. The object provokes the appetite which tends towards its consummation. Desire is a more general term or rather more distinguished, finer connotation, even if it also contains the eidetic component of domination, possession: it already registers a preformation, an anticipation of the twinge proper to synthesis, of an effective self-exit. Desire is desire *of*, but this genitive that it ultimately has in common with the appetite is articulated by a *towards* that seems in its own way to dilute the violent immediacy of the appetite and above all to make a certain indeterminacy appear that is the source of distance and latitude. The appetites, hunger and thirst for example, can appear, can be exercised "in themselves" without a specific food or meal appearing as their proper correlate. They are still, so to speak, driven to taking possession, a consummation. In the absence of any deliberation, they are pushed towards the good that they covet. Desire is an élan, which, without being free, is not submitted to an exclusive qualification by an object. Above all it remains itself or rather shows itself, attests to itself as itself, independently of satisfaction, of fulfillment. The *towards* denotes a tension of which the eidetic meaning remains independent of consummation. It encourages an overcoming of space but this overcoming is a task, not an effective operation. The eidetic component *towards* is omnipresent in each form of desire, including the forms where the habitual, the permanent, the stable qualify and explicate the impetuosity and ardor, as well as tension and privation. Finally, when desire claims to be in duration, it is called inclination or preference. Inclination manifests the disposition for movement, a constant movement towards a thing or being. Preference expresses the same reality but accentuates permanence. Inclination confesses attraction, even fascination with its object but in a more agreeable, softer register than preference, which is located in proximity to passion, exuding ardor and vigor.

The will that the Scholastics called intellectual appetite also appears as a form of the tension *towards*, of the aspiration to reach an object. In its material reality, every being, in fact every possibility, even that of non-being can become an intentional object of the will. The will aims for its object, but with an particularly strong aim, one that is not merely theoretical, neutral, analytical, or contemplative. The will is related with a mastery, possession in view, but of a very particular kind, one that wants to be total, perfect and without material, physical being. The one who desires experiences the ambition to appropriate what is desired integrally and effectively: without materially engaging with its object the will exercises on it an unlimited influence. The will thus appears as the last member of the cortege inaugurated with the impulse. The tension towards is realized and perfected in the intellectual appetite, through it the aim, the *noesis* is practiced that tends towards effective access to the *noema*. From impulse to the will, the upsurge where immanence is extended and blossoms appears to be unfolded through a panoply of figures of power. If the immobility of *theoria* clearly attests to a non-overcoming of immanence, if the theoretical intelligence is ultimately only the cream of Nature, the practical faculty, with its ardor and vigor, its upsurge and overflow is but an organic part of *Physis* where the grip of Immanence continues and is merely obscured by the violence of the overflowing.

Intention

Like other forms and moments of desire the will appears as a power. Power is a physic-physiological category and, as such, is a given reality. More precisely, it can intensify or weaken but always starting from the given reality that it constitutes. The diverse avatars of the practical faculty, the faculty of desire, are only *Abschattungen* of a power; they only embroider one and the same *dynamis*. They are only forms adorning a libido of an area, a given quantity. Interpreted as libido the practical faculty registers a massive homogeneity: from the brutal violence of impulses to the clear and precise volition, the same energy is always deployed. The essential homogeneity of desire lives in the difference of its successive moments that could be subsumed under the two great steps of feeling desire and its satisfaction. But what apparently matters is that despite the temporal gap and the material difference, to desire and to realize its desire are ultimately movements, operations of the same metaphysical order.

The truth of desire is located on the plane of its simple exercise and registers a certain ontological monism. But this monism in the voluntarisms of various calibers will suffer a first breach in the discernment of a theoretical moment variously present in every occurrence of desire and which is clearly attested to and necessarily conceived in the will. The will is a form of desire that clearly "comprehends" an end, presupposing its advent, for the occurrence of which it labors. If the will is designated as intellectual appetite, this is because in it the desire is given eyes with which to see: in order to desire it is necessary to know, that is, to know what one wants. Comprehension, theoretical conception constitutes the principle of an essential transformation: the blind impulse, sensible desire is transposed, decanted into intellectual desire, into the will. Yet this transposition does not yet amount to a true metaphysical rupture. Impulse continues to exist within the will of which it constitutes the base and the force. Above all, the theoretical gaze's penetration of desire does not modify its desire-being, but at best constitutes its articulation or structuration. *Theoria* certainly signals the taking of a distance in relation to the brute unfolding of impulse, but does not constitute a true counterpart of desire and therefore does not allow the sui generis originality of the practical to emerge with clarity, the proper, eidetic-metaphysical truth of the will.

The will, the practical faculty par excellence does not obtain its proper metaphysical status from the starting point of the category of *intention*. According to common sense, the intention opposed to execution, distinguished from execution only repeats the succession of steps of preparation and accomplishment. An intention is first formulated and that will develop through deliberation on the means employed for its realization, but it is always a matter of two successive stages of the exercise of the practical faculty. In reality however the difference between intention and execution is not simply chronological. In its pre-philosophical naïveté, common sense thinks, or rather imagines that first, one desires or emits a wish without material dimension and then, subsequently this pure, immaterial decision "passes" into a physico-physiological realization. In truth things do not happen this way. First, starting with the stages of preparation, the intention asserts itself and has an effect in a material universe. Above all, with the advent of the result of volition, intention does not disappear. One can doubtlessly be disinterested in (or no longer desire) the consequence of his desire once it has appeared simply because he no longer thinks about it. Insofar as the result concerns me, however, I want it, and I especially do not cease to want it while I execute the operation that made it appear. Execution, in other words, does not follow intention, but accompanies it, is guided and animated by it. The coexistence of intention and execution leads to the dissociation of wanting and doing, to the differentiation of these two forms of the desiring power. Intention is an immaterial expression of desire and the diverse operations of its execution are a material expression.

The dissociation of intention and operation are the work of religion and philosophy concentrated on the consideration of quality, of the moral value of the will. The ancient systems of law are occupied with deciding on punishment, pricing out the appropriate retributions for transgressions considered in their material factuality. Religions prescribe rites and material sacrifices of propitiation and expiation. But a revolution imposed slowly and gradually will enact a moral reduction. Case law will begin to qualify crimes by no longer taking into account only the effective transgression but also the will of the actor. In religion, instead of burnt sacrifice, purity of intention is required. The prophets cry out: "rend your heart not your garments" (Isa 29:13). But the advent of philosophy will complete this first Copernican turn: not content to distinguish action and intention and wanting to measure the moral value of action in light of the sole intention animating it, it therefore leads to the reduction, to intention of the intellectual appetite that is the will.

Moral reflection turns away from physical action in order to center on intention. One certainly encourages the act that one recommends—after all, what would be the meaning of a volition disinterested in its completion? Can we speak of desire without including a desired end? But value, the moral reality of the will cannot consist only in the wanting itself. The charitable person wants to give something to another and wants to do him good, really and purely, from the bottom of his heart. Yet the weakness of his faculties or circumstances prevent his good will being translated into deeds, prevents the good he wants to do to his neighbor from reaching him. Who cares! The good deed does not consist in the effective transfer of an object or the concrete exercise of an act, but in the will to transfer and act. Inversely, ill will is realized even before being put into action, even independently of the action. We are told that "the man who looks at a woman with lust has already sinned" and that "all crimes. . .are completed before the actual deed is accomplished," and that "he who carries deadly weapons and has intentions of robbing and murdering is a brigand even before he has dipped his hands in blood."[5] The logical conclusion of this discourse—drawn by Kantianism—is that the intention constitutes the exclusive truth of the will and must pertain to a metaphysical condition other than impulse. More precisely: the will constitutes a sui generis metaphysical region and as such it cannot be analyzed in terms of an eidetics proper to theory: it has its own intentional order proper to itself.

The Indivisibility and Immediacy of the Will

Dissociated from execution, from anything related to physical, physiological, or psychological movement, the will possesses a perfect homogeneity. Its homogeneity determines its metaphysical condition as from the interior and for the exterior. To the degree that the distinction between intention and execution is obliterated, the action

---

5. Seneca, *Const. Sap.* VII, 4 (*On the Firmness of the Wise Man*, 31); *Benef.* V, xiv, 2 (*On Benefits*, 140).

of the will involves a perfect continuity. The will is not separated from its ends as if they were objectives, objects other to it: its only object is itself. Having itself as object, the will manifests indivisibility and unrepresentability. The homogeneity of the will signifies that it is seamless, invulnerable and therefore always whole, integral. It is therefore autonomous, and ultimately autarkic. Autarky signifies that it suffices for the will to want for its action to be enacted and completed. It involves an immediacy and faultless efficacy.

The perfect homogeneity of the will implies its continuity. The will is doubtlessly not always the same; it desires differently across a register of different numerical volitions. But in each of its volitions it is integrally present. Dividing the will into premises and conclusions is illegitimate, a legerdemain that wants to plant within an indivisible reality the duality of two components that would not be simply heterogeneous according to time but also and above all according to content. But the content of a volition is not divisible into different moments: the same intention is always the principle of life. The intention can be articulated, unfolded into a multiplicity of material, theoretical moments, but its practical truth, its truth for the will no less remains the same. On the other hand, if for the empirical observer the life of the will can seem to follow a rhythm, develop according to the flux and reflux of a psychological tide, the intention does not accommodate itself to an alternation of passivity and activity. As a decision is not separated from its premises, the act of the will does not receive a metaphysical qualification by a diminution or intensification of its psychological expression. The will is an "absolute entity";[6] it is always active. Its activity admits neither moment nor degree. It consists in the approval and consent, and consent can only be in the present.

The indivisibility of the will signifies that it cannot be sectioned, portioned out, cut into a multiplicity of moments and components. But its indivisibility has even more profound implications: it condemns, or at least relativizes the reach of the attempts of the moralist to give the right of metaphysical citizenship to the lowest degree of volition, the tendency, and it cuts short humanist apologetics that desire to justify the one who wants to desire but lacks the power to do so. If the idea of baptism by desire will eventually be raised, what is the meaning of a discourse on the desire of the will? It is "ridiculous to say that 'I want to desire'":[7] "we do not want to want, we want to do. . ."[8] The homogeneity of the will determining its indivisibility equally has epistemological implications. It is not really possible to divide the will into two ontologically different moments, into a "wanting wanting" and a "wanted wanting." Neither can it be doubled into an ontological archetype and an epistemological ectype. If theoretical discourse is powerless to describe the will this is simply because the will does not lend itself to that repetition that is representation. Yet the impossibility of representation above all

---

6. Scotus, *Ordinatio* II d. 44.

7. Voltaire, "Liberté," in *Dictionnaire philosophique*.

8. Leibniz, *Nouveau Essais sur l'Entendement Humain* II, xxi, 23–24 (*New Essays on Human Understanding*, 182).

possesses a significant translation in the moral domain. If someone else can execute in my place acts that are my responsibility, if he can accomplish my works or render my services, he still cannot replace me as willing subject. In the absence of a loved one we can wish to provide relief through some support or service or more simply through gestures and words of comfort but we cannot *love* in his place. Love is an affair of the will alone and another's desire can never count as my own.

The metaphysical aporias of the irreplaceability of the will are eloquently illustrated by diplomatic relations. States are irreducibly unique individuals and their mutual relations are organized in terms of this logic. Material obstacles doubtlessly prohibit a foreign State, or more precisely the head of this State from being effectively present in another State. He sends an ambassador to "represent" him and who enjoys rights and qualifications at least theoretically similar to those of the sovereign that he represents. Embassies enjoy an extraterritoriality, though located in the country where their buildings are erected, they are presumed in the State that they "represent." The question of "representation" far exceeds the sphere of diplomatic relations. It is at the very heart of the political life of every society, and especially democratic society. The function of the State and its provinces, cities and towns is based on the assembly of diverse kinds, each drawing its legitimacy from elections where congresspersons and council members receive their investiture at the end of a vote that establishes them as representatives for a geographical unity or professional group. The parliamentary regime is founded on representation. The citizens of a modern State are too numerous for all to deliberate, to sit in an assembly; they choose a representative. Direct democracy, the practice of frequent referendums still in use in certain Swiss cantons, manifests the political ideal of direct participation. The life of a political community, of a State is animated and determined by a will, Rousseau's general will, which, like every will, remains indivisible and unrepresentable. The election of legislators only gets around the question of unrepresentability by a compromise. The people, the subject of the general will continues to be the custodian of sovereignty, but it delegates sovereignty for a given period to those whom it elects. During this period elected representatives exercise legislative power. Contrary to the ancient Polish Diet subject to the orders and instructions of their constituents, the deputies of our parliaments should not consult their electors during the duration of their mandate. But they cannot ignore their opinions and the possibility of recourse to advanced elections—the Damaclean sword of dissolution—is always suspended over their heads. . .

The unrepresentable nature of the will implicitly demonstrates its autonomy and wholeness. The will as such cannot be submitted to an external, alien law, one it cannot give to itself. Autonomy signifies that, *as will*, the will depends only on itself. This condition of wholly carrying its own burden has a metaphysical counterpart. If the will can only submit to a law resulting from its own legislation, emanating from itself, this moral autonomy is rooted in a metaphysical autarky. Various paradoxes of the Stoics express the autonomy of the will: "the sage is free in his chains" or "there can be no thief of free will" simply mean that the will is unaffected by all that is not its own, that no external event or occurrence can affect it, lead to its innervation of disappearance. You can be forcibly dragged in a direction you do not want to go. You can be forced to act differently than you want and can even be constrained to do things that you would not have done if you were able to follow your own desires and convictions. However, you cannot be constrained to desire what you do not want. Ultimately you want this or that, but you want your own will, and you want completely, wholly.

This essential wholeness of the will, its metaphysical incapacity to be divided comes from its indivisibility. Its "internal" counterparts are immediacy and effectiveness. The will is always in act, tending towards that which it tends; the wanting and the wanted are inseparable. This inseparability is ultimately only another expression of the lofty idea of will as intention. Reflection first liberates the non-physical tension of intention from the physical movement of execution. Then it expulses or banishes execution from the realm of the will. The purification of intention from any material element, susceptible of presenting it as a sequence of heterogeneous movements causes the striking immediacy of the will to appear. The will is not like a physical or physiological machine that one must warm up before utilizing, that would take time in order to begin to work. As soon as it wants, the will wants integrally and whatever a psychologizing moral discourse says, there are no moments where its wanting is stronger or weaker. In fact, this indivisibility, this self-equality of the will must not lead to conceiving it in terms of fulguration, of instantaneous appearance. There is nothing punctual in the will: we would certainly love to localize the moment when an intention was formulated, when we began to desire, but the reading of willing in terms of volitions does not at all mean that it would be the framework for its moments spreading out in time. More precisely: the diffraction of desire into successive moments in duration is not opposed to the affirmation of its immediacy. The upshot of this entire reflection is that desire means to persist and to continue in its being, without appeal to mediation.

Immediacy is therefore the metaphysical condition of the will and this entails its incessant actuality and faultless efficaciousness. It is said again and again that we cannot desire to desire. This means that a situation cannot be conceived in which the will cannot yet desire or desires only halfway. When the will desires it desires contemporaneously and if it does not then it does not desire at all. To will is to approve, to consent, but this consent is present and this contemporaneity of essence leads to the efficaciousness or (if you like) the fecundity of the will.

In fact the will is always efficacious and fecund. Its intentional object is not a thing that would be the end of desiring but volition itself. The drunkard is criticized because he so desperately wants a drink, but the drunkard, as St. Augustine pointed out, does not want a drink, he wants to drink. The object of the will is an action, more precisely, a volition and the volition is not separable from the desiring, in fact, it is the desiring. When you decide to take a walk, you are still separated from your destination by a distance in space and time that can be crossed only by walking many kilometers that could "take" hours. Yet the one who decides is not separated from the "end" of this decision. The physical execution of the decision is accompanied by efforts that could prove difficult and tiresome, while the decision taken most often entails relief, restores the equilibrium of a tormented hesitant conscience. On the other hand, the execution of the decision can be accompanied by unforeseen circumstances and above all it may not succeed, that is, be completed. Yet the act of the will as will must be accomplished. In the juridical sphere a distinction must doubtlessly be made between intention and result. However, before the moral judgment, the intention is considered in and for itself, independently of its material results. The efficaciousness of essence of the will causes it always to be fecund and its "results" resist the erosion of time. One can only admire this ontological invulnerability, this condition where one is as if removed from the grip of contingency. Yet the sovereign efficaciousness of the will contains traps, ambushes, logical and moral snares. The moralist wants to console the man of good will whose action has failed. He is tempted to remind him that once he has done all in his power, if the hoped-for good result does not materialize, the "essential" was the good intention that will never be invalid or lost. In reality this condition of invulnerability, this immediate effaciousness is not only a positive reality: the fruitful tree of the will can also bear poisonous fruit.

The will produces fruits and does so immediately, with a perfect effectiveness. Immanent justice is spoken of in the ethical sphere but its supreme domain is the will. The will immediately bears its fruit, considered as its reward, one that he not only receives after a certain space of time, but that he obtains immediately, at the very moment of his volition. The automatism of vengeance in the sphere of Justice has a superior counterpart in the universe of the free will. The will also lives according to a rule of retaliation but its actions find their recompense or their punishment in themselves. The wicked man thinks he can hide his wickedness, veil his transgression but "the skies will uncover his iniquity," and "the earth will stand up against him" (Job 20:27). Expressed in the imagery of the Bible what is pointed to is the metaphysical condition of immanence of the will. Separated from the veinstone of matter, divided from any continuity with execution, the intention appears here according to its irresistible homogeneity, its unimpeded realization. The good action does not have to be waited on in order to receive its recompense, nor the bad action its punishment. The last judgment, at least in its metaphysical acceptation, is not an affair beyond the grave, but is pronounced here below, here and now, in and through volition itself. Even more, the separation, the dissociation of execution and intention entails the most spectacular consequences. The material act is not simply bracketed, excluded from the proper sphere of desire, and this exclusion still leads to a reversal. The transgression of the one who injures others is turned against him. The crime of Orestes not only awakens the Erinyes, but also redounds on him. The one who mortally strikes another, himself receives, in and through this blow, a different but equally mortal wound. Through and beyond the apparent distance between these two heterogeneities, the physical and the moral, the immanence of the will is exercised according to its perfect immediacy, its integral effectiveness.

Will, Causality, Temporality

Discernment of diametrically opposed metaphysical realities within the same human action dramatizes the distinction between intention and execution, and willing and doing. Orestes' crime of matricide "results" in evil according to two different registers. According to the classical distinction he performed a physical evil, that of wounding or murdering another, as well as a moral evil, inflicted on himself. The physical evil stems from the execution of an action, from a doing, and the moral evil from the decision to kill, from a willing. The parallelism, the co-temporality of the two realities, of volition and physical action is not univocal, not perfect. After all, in a very real sense, the decision precedes the execution. On the other hand, the intention can be considered bracketed during the activity of execution. Above all, it can also be weakened, it can diminish over the course of the material operation. This duality with what it brings with it of asymmetries, imperfect correspondences is of capital importance, has an essential bearing on the great question of moral responsibility. But ultimately this moral problematic should be seen in a metaphysical light. The will is indivisible, whole, immediate, always contemporaneous and efficacious. What is its relation to time? Is it subject to temporality, does it include a temporality proper to it, or is it quite simply removed from time?

In its immediacy, its incessant contemporaneity, the will seems not to belong to the world of time. Execution is unfolded through the theory of links more or less completely connected with one another, with spaces and rifts, moments of great intensity as well as waning. Intention is supposed to emerge instantaneously or rather without its advent being localizable in an atom of time. However, intention cannot obey a structuration according to the logic of time. It does not emerge accidentally, without rhyme or reason. The will is certainly spontaneity, but it is much more. The will does not desire blindly, but with sense. This amounts to saying that if it cannot be expressed in terms of a determination according to the order of time, its advent nevertheless follows a rationale. But are its reasons causes? Common sense—along with the majority of philosophical systems—thinks that willing causes doing, that intention causes execution. The efficaciousness of willing on the doing is evident, even if no metaphysical analysis can specify either the how of this efficaciousness or the order of its successive development. The uncertainties and obscurities of the exercise of determination cannot yet compromise the reality of a causal relation between willing and doing. But can we speak of such a relation with respect to willing itself? Can we say (inspired by a Blondelian distinction) that the willing will is the cause of the willed will, and the willed will is the effect of the willing will? We could doubtlessly bracket every dimension of temporal succession but it only prevents the division of willing into cause and effect, and will entail a radical rupture of continuity of the will and, above all, the end of its homogeneity.

To submit the will to the regime of cause and effect amounts to a destruction of its unity and homogeneity. This also brings to an end a true metaphysical reading that can be only of the moral order. We find ourselves facing an infinity of cases where, at the moment of volition the willing seems not to enjoy an integral freedom. The willing subject can be confused, he may not have at his disposition all the necessary information for deciding knowingly. Or even his action in the present can appear determined by the past. Man would truly "like" to will differently, but under the mounting pressure of acts and events and subject to an inclination become second nature, he no longer seems able to reach a true choice at each instant. He certainly wants evil, his intention is vitiated, he consents to a bad inspiration, but how can this present volition be considered the faithful expression of his will? Now the man wants evil, but he does not want it because he cannot do it (that is, desire it) differently. The present evil-will is only an effect of which the cause is a past determination. And we will have to find the truth of the will in this past determination, not in the present volition. But, founded on a metaphysical theory, this moral conception is absurd and pernicious. It is absurd because it understands one thing in terms of another, and pernicious because it leads to the obliteration of the moral freedom that is still the same principle of every willing, good or bad.

The causal explanation of the act of willing means referring a present volition to a past volition. But to explain a present volition by a past volition is to explain it by something it is not, by something other than itself. One seeks the truth, the meaning of the will, but the meaning, the truth of a thing is "in itself" not in something that "precedes" it.[9] The reality and quality of the will is not found in a past determination, consequently in something that is no longer in it, something it no longer is, but in what it is now, in its present action. We must here also go *zur Sache selbst*: we must describe the will, not what is behind it! Refusing a phenomenological analysis leads to the obliteration of freedom and through it, moral responsibility. If all his action is determined by a past cause, then what can the will decide, initiate, open up? Rigorously determined according to the causal order, the will cannot choose its action but is constrained to function as force of nature or rather a machine. This hypothesis (however fallacious) cannot resist recalling the primary theses of the Philosophy of the Will. The indivisibility of the will does not imply only the absurdity of every attempt to carve it up according to a chronological succession, but it equally excludes a metaphysical reading in terms of activity and passivity, of determination and being-determined. Ultimately, the truth of good and evil is relativized by causal theory. Moral good and evil are of a supreme actuality, and only so. To assign them to a bygone moment of

---

9. Edwards, *Freedom of the Will*, 340.

the past can only diminish and thus compromise this actuality. Good and evil must be wanted now. If they are not then they *are not* good and evil.

Time and Will

The telos of the rejection of the application of causality to the will is the protection of the homogeneity of the will. Here is reformulated on a metaphysical plane what immediacy teaches on the chronological plane. But, precisely, the refusal of a causal interpretation of the act of the will inevitably leads to the question of the relation between will and time. Time is doubtlessly intercalated between decision and execution. Similarly, the physical translation of will falls within time. But what is temporal of the will "itself"? Is the will exercised in time, according to time? Can we will the past or future? Philosophers have always been sensitive to this problem. The distinction between material and formal is addressed at least indirectly to the respective relation of our physical and moral action to time. The matter of our acts, their circumstances and modalities, their components and development occupy the interstices of time, while the formal consideration is enacted through bracketing of every relation to temporality. The material extends into space and it does so according to the order of time. The formal remains apart from all spatiality; it is "elsewhere" and being elsewhere than space has a corollary in not belonging to time. This metaphysical distinction between material and formal professed by the Scholastics and Cartesians will end up being deepened and transposed in to the Kantian opposition between phenomenon and noumenon. The physical and psychic movements of man belong to the world of phenomena, while the action of the will is of the noumenal order. The efficaciousness of his action is at every moment undivided, immediate: "at every instant starting from itself it is the source of its actions."[10] In other words, the will, the will as such, "in itself" is removed from the limitations of phenomenal existence, from all heteronomous causality. In short, "it is not in time."[11]

But how to understand this massive proclamation of the will's non-belonging to time? If the will effectively belongs to another metaphysical sphere than time, it cannot then have a hold on time—namely, the past and future, because the present, at least in its ontological dimension, its traditional, pre-phenomenological acceptation, is truly the location and milieu of the will. As far as the future is concerned, it seems like the supreme domain for the exercise of the will. The will wants, it decides, and its decision will be realized (or not) in the future. Of course, this primary, a-philosophical intuition of the common sense cannot resist the conceptual distinction between intention and execution. Execution takes place in the future, not intention, not volition. And can intention—the will properly speaking, the will in the strict sense—be exercised in the future? Certainly not. We never want in the future. There is a radical difference

10. Kant, *Akad.* XVIII, 46.
11. Kant, *Akad.* XXVIII, 729.

between an action executed because of a promise and an action executed because it is still wanted. In fact, we can want the advent of the will, we can want what we want now to be realized in the future but we cannot will our future willing.

Now a second question imposes itself: can we will the past? The impossibility and absurdity of conjugating the will in the past tense is even more evident than its non-belonging to the future. We can doubtlessly will without any guarantee that this will will translate into actions, but when we do will, we must at least wish that this volition makes an effective translation. Without the effective or presumed possibility of a material realization, an execution of his decision, who could will? But we aptly know that what happened has happened and we no longer have any hold on it. The past can melt away, lose its actuality. What happened in the past can disappear, it can quickly disappear without a trace. Here we are dealing with realities over which the willing exercised now has no influence. We can certainly regret having willed what we willed, we could want to have willed differently, but the will runs into the wall of the past and falls down, powerless to break through. Here we are driven to wonder: does this powerlessness of the will concerning the past signify an absolute impermeability of what has been willed, a complete invulnerability, a pertinence and validity that nothing can disturb? Theology has often posed the question of the limits of God's power. Can the All Powerful Creator of Heaven and Earth change and destroy what effectively exists, what exists now? He could have just as much not created the world or created it differently than he has created it. But can he make what he has created as if it had not occurred (Peter Damien)? This interrogation falls under the problematic proper to theology but there is an analogy with the philosophy of the will.

The immanent unfolding of justice is overcome and surpassed by love. Love breaks the circle of vengeance and inaugurates the new with a beautiful gratuity. But ultimately the metaphysical structure of this rupture can be put forward only in terms of the will. The process of execution can be interrupted; its results can be replaced. What was stolen can be returned and what is broken can be repaired. What is done can be undone. But what has been wanted, can it be un-wanted? Wounds of the body can be cicatrized, healed, but what about "wounds of the spirit?"[12] There is a permanence, even a perenniality of intention that no physical or psychological event can affect. Neither the destruction nor forgetting of its results can invalidate or disqualify the act of the good will, and, inversely, no material reparation can obliterate the transgression accomplished by virtue of a culpable intention. We are taught that both our good and bad actions follow us into the next world. In point of fact, they accompany us now. Recall that the will has an integral efficaciousness; it is always fulfilled. Pure desire for the good is always realized—but unfortunately also pure desire for evil. "The good that exists is mathematically equal to the good desired, the evil that exists to the

---

12. Hegel, *La Phénoménologie de l'Esprit* II, 197 (*The Phenomenology of Spirit*, trans. A. V. Miller [New York: Oxford University Press, 1977] 407.)

evil desired." It is a consoling idea that no true attention, no good is ever lost. But we must also be willing to admit that "no evil is lost either!"[13]

The sobering truth of the exaltation of the effectiveness of the will is that its work—which is nothing other than the will itself—is impermeable and invulnerable. The wear and tear of time can deteriorate the external works of the will, but the will itself remains forever. Before a world of contingent things suffering constant modification and deterioration, the universe of the will subsists untouched. Yet can we be content with this vision, can we assume this so very classical doctrine that makes the will into a prison-fortress, a strange force the power of which is always being inverted into powerlessness? The will can want anything, there is no constraint or obstacle to its action, but it cannot undo its own action. More precisely, it cannot un-want it. Incapable of wanting the past or future and of un-wanting in the present, the will, ambiguously, seems to have an affinity with eternity itself, not with the moving image of eternity that is time.

The Renewal of Desire: The Request for Forgiveness

The theme of un-wanting invokes the call to the sovereignty of the will, to a sovereignty that is certainly supposed to focus on the world but focuses above all on itself. Freedom of the will for the future is doubtlessly of another order than desire in relation to the past. The sovereignty of the will in relation to the future is first displayed simply under the form of its power to modify itself, to want something else and different than it wants now. A deeper and more radical manifestation of this self-mastery in the future is the promise. The promise implies that in a future moment I am going to do what I commit myself to in a present moment. But the eidetic truth of the promise, figure of the will is to continue to will in the future what I want now. And to the degree that the present willing cannot will *for* the future, to the degree that I cannot will my future volition, the promise remains a mystery, or rather a supreme occurrence of the a priori synthesis in which the full use of the copula is imposed, which is freedom. The man that promises promises something and whether simple or difficult, banal or extraordinary, it does not matter! What he intends and wants is not the contingent advent of an object or event, but the continuation of his present intention, a continuation that nothing guarantees or necessitates but which unfolds so to speak from the relation of the freedom of the promising subject to itself. The promise says: the world changes and, with the world, the circumstances and contents of the subject that I am and yet through, even despite these changes, I will not stop having the same intention; I will remain myself.

The promise, a willing concerning the future, clearly manifests the a priori synthesis that is the willing subject. In and through it the sovereignty of the will appears

---

13. Weil, *Cahiers, Oeuvres complètes* VI, 2, 396.

under the form of fidelity to itself. When promising the will says to itself: you will stay the same, or rather, you will always want in the same way! The promise conjugates the sovereignty of the will according to affirmation; it is an illustration, a shining example of the lofty freedom of man towards the future, the future of both things and himself. But another figure of the sovereignty of the will to itself is found, a negative form, that of un-wanting that is crystalized in the request for forgiveness. The request for forgiveness issues from a heavy heart. One feels culpable and is tormented by remorse. One sags under the burden of the past and is haunted by the memory of a crime or criminal volition. The one who feels culpable wants to be delivered from his culpability and aspires to be liberated from his misdeed, to let go of its memory, indeed, to erase the past. Haunted by memories, he is ready to seek pardon, to atone for his transgression. The memory of an offense remains in his memory; he would like to be freed from it, to make a blank slate, to forget. Yet these customary images of the moral conscience are misleading or at least imprecise. Culpability does not signify the presence of the memory of a culpable intention and forgiveness does not come down to the elimination of this troubling memory, to the expulsion of a past reality that remains in the present. Well to the contrary, if the will is affected by a past volition, this is because oddly, but very really, it is experienced as present.

The request for forgiveness wants to deliver the will from the culpable intention tormenting it. However, this culpable intention cannot be understood as something located in a past more or less remote from where it should be extracted, filtered out. There can of course be degrees of intensity to the remorse that afflicts me but the same sense of remorse is not experienced as being related to an object separated from the present, confined in the past. They say that the memory of a crime haunts the murderer, that he sometimes prowls around the place where the murder was committed. But this haunting obsession does not count as a reference to a reality located elsewhere, but instead attests to the presence of this reality now. The return of the assassin does not signify a "reconnection" to an act fallen into the past but the visualization, the making explicit of a continuity with what remains of it, a continuity that ultimately can only result in the great paradox of the metaphysics of the will. If from a chronological point of view and even from the vantage of our psychological economy, our intentions can be considered only as diffracted into far off moments of time, then in a mysterious but very real way, they are in the now. If the bite of a past volition is felt by my present will this is because it is intended *now*.

Like the juridical systems, moral philosophy witnesses to the comprehension of this continuity. The person convicted because of a drunk driving accident is tempted to defend himself by mitigating his incapacity to drive the car well. Under the influence of alcohol he was not capable of calculating distances very well or of steering straight. He ended up losing control and crashing into another vehicle, gravely injuring its passengers. At the moment of the accident he had no culpable intention and in fact, no intention at all. But at a previous moment when he (over-)consumed alcohol he was still lucid and in this state of lucidity he undertook the possibility of a deadly drive. Chronologically, it is clearly a matter of an intention situated in a previous moment. Yet, if juridically or morally a man can be considered culpable for the accident that took place at a moment when the correct execution of this act was no longer materially possible, this is because his intention is supposed to be co-temporal with the execution. This comes down to saying that, from a metaphysical perspective the intention was always present or rather that the subject continued to will it. It is (rightly) said that the request for forgiveness issues from a change of heart supposedly broken from the past: the good intention regretted by the criminal and for which he seeks forgiveness replaces the bad intention of the crime. But, precisely, the substitution can concern only an effective intention, an intention that is still "there." If the intention was confined to the past, it will have already been replaced by the present intention. In other words, it would not exist, would not be wanting anymore. It neither should nor can be the object of forgiveness.

The argument seems forced; it can provoke the confusion of good sense and nevertheless obeys the elementary logic of the moral intuition that it reformulates in metaphysical terms. The sting of a bad conscience causes us to seek forgiveness. But I want to be pardoned now, as I am now, according to my moral present. I seek forgiveness of my culpable intention, of my bad will, which ultimately signifies that my will must be understood as it is exercised now. If the request for forgiveness expresses a change of heart this is because it translates a dramatic realization: if up to now I did not seek forgiveness, this is because I did not intend to break with my culpable intention, I did not stop willing as I willed in and through this intention. The request for forgiveness has meaning only if it is proferred by someone who is understood as continuing to will badly. In this way it corroborates the potentialities and metaphysical conditions of the sovereignty of the will in relation to time. Strictly speaking, as we have seen, one cannot will either in the future or the past. But the request for forgiveness translates the aspiration of the will to un-will, to *be* de-willed. This is possible only at the price of a reinterpretation of its own temporality. Only by behaving as if wanting—and as always wanting—*now* that the will can win a victory over the past.

The request for forgiveness attests to our invincible intuition of the will's creative power. It also teaches its undivided homogeneity and integral actuality. The extra-temporality where the will is immersed is hardly a pastiche of eternity. Our will is exercised, and only exercised therefore through and by means of a constant plunging into time. If the will is denied a simplistic reading of the advent of its volitions into time, this is not in order to bask in a kind of conceptual boycott of temporality but in order to signify the non-instantaneity of the will. Our willing is not a succession of isolated volitions but a powerful current that unfolds. By virtue of the homogeneity of its essence the will can only reject every conception that represents it under the form of a theory of instants, of volition-points. The indivisibility and immediacy of the will does not signify an atomic condition! Yet if the refusal of a parceling out is truly an essential thesis of the Philosophy of the Will, it still cannot count as its last word, its ultimate outcome. If we intend to reject an atomic multiplicity this is in order better to elaborate a discourse on the power of renewal proper to the will. Volitions are one and unique singularities, not separated and isolated atoms but many revelations of a reality that can only be undivided while always being renewable and always renewed. The will is revealed through volitions, not as repetition but rather as reiterations. Volitions constitute, so to speak, the history of the will. They can intend the same thing or something else, it does not matter! The creative power of the will is not at all refuted by the repetition of the same content. The essential is that if it wants the same thing or something else, it wants it anew. "The free man," says Alain, "is the one who, knowing that he just continues an action, knows how to begin."[14] The novelty of the will is not a matter of content. Lovers tell each other everyday that I love you, *ti voglio bene*. If the discourse becomes tedious, the fault does not fall to the one who says it, but to how he says it, not to the *noema* but to the way in which the intentional object is intended.

The creative power of the will is not material but rather formal or existential. Renewal is sought but never acquired in advance. It cannot and should not come about mechanically, automatically. The sun rises everyday but who can guarantee that it will rise tomorrow? Similarly, acts of benevolence and fidelity have multiplied but can we say with all certainty that they will be repeated tomorrow? Addressing our prayers to the Heavenly Father we seek our daily bread, we do not seek bread for the next eight days or for the next year. Manna was given to the People Israel "each morning" for the day that was beginning (Exod 16:21). We cannot "store up" either bread or manna.[15] The Augustinian theologians taught that even perseverance in grace is a work of grace and if it accompanies the "first" grace it still is not a part of it. We cannot establish reserves of either manna or grace. Love is always requested again and given again. The metaphysical nature of the will prohibits the long-term or short-term arrangements. Its renewal should not be envisaged against the background of an internal negotiation of a deal made with oneself. Once again, we must refer to the will's impossibility of willing in the future and its unique possibility of willing in the present, albeit in a non-punctual present, a vast and large present, a present where it "has time" to be presence to self, to sojourn near the self, in a present that is source of its eruption in its indivisibility and radical actuality.

---

14. Pascal, *La pensée d'Alain*, 151.
15. Fénelon, *Correspondance* XVIII, 46.

XI

The Dual Will and Practical Knowledge

Enlarged Homogeneity

Renewal is an essential moment, even the very life of the will. In and through it the will reaffirms its homogeneity without submitting to being locked up in immanence. Willing is only itself, irreducible to any other being or acting, but this being-in-itself does not yet signify sameness. The sublime homogeneity of the will accommodates, even requires alterity. And this in two forms. The will acts with or against another will and is divided, or rather splits into good and bad wills. The first alterity is located on an ontological plane. It appears through the numerical multiplicity of wills. One will encounters one or many other wills. Here we are dealing with a rupture of willing into a duality or plurality without infringing on the integrality of the will. The wills meet, coexist, struggle with one another, and are each complete specimens of the will. They can will differently than their counterparts and yet are still neither more nor less "voluntary" than one another. The confrontation between good and bad wills contains a deeper opposition that transcends the numerical difference: my good will can collide with your bad will, but my good will willing can also and above all be put to the test by *my* bad willing.

The plurality of wills struggling or capitulating to one another like the radical opposition of the good and bad will characterize and qualify the action of willing in its supreme figures of fidelity and forgiveness. But if fidelity is the greatest manifestation of the lofty homogeneity of the will, it still does not appear to get to the bottom, it does not sink into the abyss of the radical opposition between the good and bad will. In fidelity the will certainly encounters at each moment the other will with which it was engaged. But the supreme work of love is fidelity towards another who becomes unfaithful, and this fidelity can essentially draw on its resources only starting from itself. Fidelity is a battle, but one the will gives to itself. Fidelity—like love in general—is a constant renewal of the will. Its daily bread can be assured only through itself. If it passes through divisions and if it finds itself forced constantly to begin anew, this is because it alone is capable of undertaking the efforts that it can out of its own depths of the will. It certainly must make the immense effort of starting anew, of getting going again, of continuing that it will accomplish as preserved creation, as re-creation. But the two ontologically different moments of creative fidelity are not separated by the gap of metaphysical opposition. The renewal closes the register of sameness but the will always renews itself.

Fidelity is like the continuation of one and the same history whereas the work of forgiveness transcends all continuity, even the creative kind. To be faithful is to take a path on the same plane or to go higher, but regardless always remains continuous, whereas forgiveness implies a rupture of the path or a projection outside of its trajectory. Forgiveness certainly aims for the other who has requested it but the request presupposes repentance or is accompanied by it. And repentance is truly rupture and reversal. In and through it the will leaps, so to speak, over a gap and transcends the abyss separating good and evil. In fact the all-too spatial imagery of the leap and even transcending slides into the ontological, whereas the difference between good and evil goes beyond the realm of being. The duality between the will of the one who requests forgiveness and the one who grants it is ultimately only an instance of the possible numerical plurality of wills that are always integral examples of the will. The duality of good and bad wills manifests the radical, irreducible opposition of good and bad intention. Ultimately the plurality of numerically different wills only expresses the metaphysical distinction of the *diversa,* while the duality is the original condition of the *opposita*.

The Wills

The will has an essential homogeneity. The domain of the will is not Nature or even juridical institutions. Objective Spirit receives and welcomes it only in a subdued, indirect way. The force of the will can be experienced when persevering in a difficult sport or technical enterprise, but "the difficulty" is only an indirect translation of the tension immanent to the will. Through extreme effort I can scale rocks or traverse space as a cosmonaut but my will is still not exercised on the cliffs or a far away planet; it is exercised on myself. The homogeneity of the will prohibits it being deployed elsewhere than in its own voluntary universe. Discussing the Gift, Seneca declared: "The matter revolves in a circle within yourself; by receiving you give, by giving you receive."[1] Everything certainly circulates within the will, but does this immanence refer to imprisonment in the donating will? The will that receives gives, and when it receives, it gives—but can giving and receiving be represented as acts of the will that

---

1. Seneca, *Bénéf.* V, viii, 6 (*On Benefits*, 133).

leave and return without touching the ground? Can the supra- or extra-material truth of the will signify that it exists as an island, that its deployment is like the movement of a boomerang that leaves and returns, notwithstanding the difference that the physical boomerang reaches its target whereas the spiritual boomerang affects nothing outside itself and is affected by nothing else? The metaphysical intuition of the Stoics doubtlessly contains a profound truth: The will belongs to another world than nature and because of this it cannot truly touch or be touched by nature. But the sui generis reality of the will, its essential homogeneity does not require its imprisonment. Well to the contrary the will cannot include the status of an ontological island while exercising against an effectively existing other.

The homogeneity of the will would be compromised by its insertion in the concatenation of nature. It remains unaffected by its encounter with an other will as voluntary as itself. The will is "first" exercised towards itself, but it also has a region of unfolding in the encounter with another will or wills. It is exercised either towards itself or towards other wills. And the first case of the figure takes priority over the second. When exercised towards others, *its* others, it does not cease being related to itself. This relation to self proves to be the supreme domain of the division of the will as well as the proper dimension for the discernment-opposition between good and evil. The mutual relation of wills, between the two and then eventually many wills is ultimately only the context for the application of the immanent action of the will or even its prolongation outside itself.

A will can be related to another through either love or hate. Love is the consent of one will to another and hate is its opposition to another. In their truth love and hate affect only *voluntas*, the "material" concomitants of willing do not concern them. It is doubtlessly very difficult to make out, to discern what is truly and purely voluntary from what is not in an affection. Love is most often inclined to recruit heterogeneous auxiliaries for a battle that is wanted and considered pure, without mixture or compromise. During the ecstasy of its pure vice that lacks all compromise even while being yielding within it, hate demands no better than to appeal to the outside in order to assure and deepen its action. Hate is a "pure" affection that can have no external, relative, secondary motive. Yet it is hardly restrained from being subsumed under moveable, pathological heterogeneities. The will is certainly unrepresentable, but it still does not always make a great case for its own homogeneity. Its finite condition, entangled in the psychological and physical that pushes the will to compromises with what is not it, to make common cause with realities that belong to another metaphysical region. The will would certainly love to happen through means proper to it and it would be happy to impel its other hate by the simple unfolding of its own action. But the other is also not of pure will and precisely the non-voluntary in it invites me to impure compromises. When I understand that on the properly voluntary plane I cannot realize my designs because the other, my partner or adversary, or enemy does not purely obey my hate, does not submit his light to my darkness, in short, whatever I want him to do, then all that remains for me is violence. Violence is opposed as such to spontaneity; it is domination of another person, it suppresses, impels and contorts the other. From a properly metaphysical point of view, it signifies the advent and action of non-voluntary factors inserted between wills, in their interstices. The will gives up and exits itself, not in order to give or to serve but in order to grab the other through non-voluntary procedures. Torture is the highest form of the introduction of instruments into the originally voluntary relation, but every conduit where one is not content with one's own resources like the will indicates the imbedding of the will in a universe of instruments.

The orders of law and the state are institutionalized forms of the distance, or rather the tearing apart of the world of spontaneity from the world of instrumentality, the world of violence. The instrumentalization of the voluntary seems to be its inevitable downward spiral into the register of hate, but what about the role of the good will, love? Love wants to be "pure" but it nevertheless inclines naturally towards borrowing artifices and infra-voluntary appendages. To love someone is doubtlessly to love him for the good, and the good of a finite being is not only affection but also possession and pleasure. In other words, giving useful things to the beloved or accomplishing actions that give him pleasure are "natural" to love. A certain heterogeneity is found between love in its voluntary purity and the objects and action that apply or translate it. But this heterogeneity can be conceived as a prolongation of the will where the very materiality, a powerless materiality without the proper truth of objects and movements makes their subsumption under the incandescent action of the will more easily conceivable. However love does not appeal only inanimate instruments but equally enrolls in its service auxiliaries of a confused status. It strives to exercise seduction, excessive, even perverse praise. It wields promise and threat, it does not hesitate to don masks, to bend the truth, even to lie. In short, it uses instruments that, instead of being only wordless appendages, possess a certain autonomy, proving to be impure travesties of the pure action that is the will.

A willing agent, a subject of the will can be subject to violence, seduced by flattery or gifts or more simply by the good services of another—it does not matter. If nobody can steal my free will this is because it is not something detachable, transferable. Ultimately the will is free, *voluntary* only if it is related to nothing outside of itself. More precisely, it can be related to an outside that is of the same metaphysical condition as itself. In fact, even within the objective relation of law, the will remains essential. A commercial contract is spelled out in financial terms and can refer to concrete physical objects. But its truth remains the reciprocity of wills engaged in an exchange. According to its essential definition, the Will is the free will that wants another free will precisely as it wants this free will (Hegel). The truth of the famous master-slave dialectic is that the sole influence a will can have over another will is itself a voluntary influence, relating to this other according to its truth as will. Humans want to influence, to subjugate, to dominate their neighbor and they do not hesitate to use every possible expedient. Ultimately, it is still necessary to remember that "the will breaks only through contact with another will," and that *the will can be conquered only through another will.*"[2]

How to Want More?

The homogeneity of the will expands in order to accommodate the plurality of wills but this numerical difference is deepened in and through the duality internal to willing. Instead of a face-off between two instances of the will, the will sinks into a division, an internal tearing apart. But in the last (as in the first) instance, the object of the will is itself: how then to understand its tearing apart? In reality the internal division of the will accomplishes a kind of stretching of homogeneity on two levels, that of being and that of form, which are ultimately shown to be solidary. The internal division of our will puts in play two different acts. Yet this duality of voluntary action is a function of the duality of the form of the will. Good and bad wills will differently on the ontological plane, but the principle of this difference is the ultimate opposition between how the will should and should not will.

Since ancient philosophy the duality of the will has been amply illustrated. Medea declared: "I understand the magnitude of the evil I am going to do, but my anger is stronger than my reasoning" (*Medea* 1077–79). Nearly twenty centuries later Shakespeare will echo Euripides: "If to do were as easy as to know what were good to do…the brain may devise laws for the blood, but a hot temper leaps o'er a cold decree."[3] These famous texts present the dilemma of the will but they do not do so adequately, according to its radicality. We know very well what we should do but we lament that we cannot act as we ought to. We would like to take account of this opposition by recalling the weakness of the flesh by contrast to the clarity of knowledge, or even by the will's disarmed status, its lack of sufficient resources before the powerful allurement of emotion. In reality, however, the problem does not consist in the impossibility of doing what one wants, but in the strange possibility of doing what one does not want, or more precisely in the paradox of wanting what one does not "truly" want (Romans 7:19). In the terms of the discourse on the Philosophy of the Will this could signify something like: "I want with half of my will what I do not want with the other half," or even, I want in a "superficial" way what I do not want deep down. Moralists and poets attribute the division to the antagonistic action of two faculties or two "men" whereas conceptual analysis will show that it is the same man, namely, the voluntary subject, and the same faculty, the will, that displays an incomprehensible doubling.

The moralist theologian Augustine thematizes in the most suggestive and dramatic way this doubling. "The mind, and no other, commands the mind to will and yet it resists. What causes this monstrosity?" Apparently "my mind does not have

2. Schelling, *Philosophie de la révélation* III, 187.
3. Shakespeare, *Merchant of Venice* I, 11, 17s.

sufficient magnitude to possess itself." I live in combat with myself. . .and this dispersion is made against my will. Yet this was not the manifestation of the nature of an alien mind."[4] My combat with myself happens against my will, but it is clearly a function of another aspect, another moment, another instance if you like, of this same will. Willing is an incessant action that is not a flow but a surmounting. And to the degree that the combat of the will happens in its own interior spaces it amounts necessarily to a struggle of self-conquest. A sober analysis of the struggle demands the admission of two wills within a single will: the reality of two wills is comprehensible only in terms of a moral metaphysics and should be constructed according to the logic of the a priori synthesis.

The moralists ponder the mystery of how to will what one does not want and how not to will what one does want. But the question is reformulated with the help of a generalization, or rather, it is subsumed under an interrogation concerning the being of the will as such. For the Schoolmen the will differentiates desire only according to its intentional object. Desire, the sensible appetite aims for a sensible good and the will, the intellectual appetite, aims for an intellectual or pure good. But these different goods are related in the same way to the two respective desiring faculties: they are the natural objects of these faculties naturally, necessarily tending towards them. However, reflection will show that this parallelism is false. If the two kinds of desire tend naturally towards their objects they can nevertheless miss them. And it is in the way that they can miss their objects that the essential difference between them is located. Desire misses its target when an internal weakness or external obstacle prevents it from coming to a successful conclusion. Yet how can an infinite power like the will possibly miss its object? No one can "steal my free will," no external, heterogeneous power can influence the will. The will can definitely not be transposed into an act, but as will it is eo ipso accomplished. From the moment that it wills, its willing is accomplished. But the metaphysical mystery of the will is that its faultless homogeneity goes together with a necessity for transcendence. When desire desires, it aims for nothing new. Of course, nothing is implicated with it, nothing results from it, in short, nothing can be understood as its analytic accomplishment. Things are different for the will.

The will is not only an ontological power. It is precisely the faculty of transcending the ontological domain. Desire's end is to close the circle of the I, whereas the will possesses the lofty vocation of departing from the given, of surmounting and surpassing the self. The moralist says: man only can be said to be not himself, he "is the sole creature that refuses to be what it is."[5] But an abyss opens up beneath this moral dramatization. Desire's new is not truly new because the future that it beckons is only the logical and ontological continuation of the present. The will's new is truly

---

4. *Confessions* VIII, 9, 21; X, 8, 15; VIII, 10, 22. These citations are found in Marion, *Au lieu de soi: L'approche de Saint Augustin*, 103, 109, 240. (See *Confessions*, trans. Henry Chadwick [New York: Oxford University Press, 1991] 147, 184, 148.)

5. Camus, *L'homme révolté*, in *Oeuvres complètes* II, 428.

new because it goes against nature. For common sense the will is related to the future and this intuition contains an important truth. The future is a radical novelty, a new that breaks with the actual, the present, and the will is effectively the faculty of breaking with the given, above all with the given that is itself.

The truth of this homogenous faculty is rupture, innovation, and not only in an ontological sense. Or rather it must be understood that, strictly speaking, only what surpasses the ontological, located above or elsewhere than it, is truly new. To will is certainly to aim to accomplish something, not as doing but as willing, in other words to make something happen that does not come out of oneself, even that goes against oneself, against what one is. The new containing the metaphysical essence of the will is not what has not yet been, what has never been, but what is other than what has been until now, or rather what is other than what has previously been. True alterity is neither factual nor even solely ontological. In the deepest sense, to will is to will to go beyond oneself. And once it is understood that the self's mode of being is not simply to exist, to persevere in its being, but to seize, to assert oneself, to be for oneself, in view of the self, then the surpassing of the self proves to be the possibility of a going-*against*-oneself. To be self is to have opted for oneself and to will in the strict sense is to adopt a position of independence towards this being-self. Of course, this conception of the will understands it as freedom. To will ultimately signifies power, to be free to will something other than self, even what is opposed to self. Here the fact that the will transcends desire is most clearly seen. Willing is certainly desire but as desiring the non-desirable. And this transubstantiation of the will has two senses: either effectively to desire what is not desirable (a moral attitude that makes possible the freedom that permits our passing beyond our egoism and opting for ends that do not "interest" us), or making the non-desirable desirable, which means binding together neutral actions, even ones that disgust our loving subjectivity (essentially the labor of Respect). Both cases lead to a rethinking of the a priori synthesis.

The great idea of the a priori synthesis was conceived and deployed in the context of theoretical reason. It is the supreme form of theoretical judgment. Synthetic a priori judgments are possible because the understanding has resources for passing from a subject to a predicate that it does not contain through its essence but to which it nevertheless relates in an a priori way. Synthetic a priori judgment is the cipher of the power of creativity proper to the mind, it indicates its aptitude to go beyond oneself by its own means without dispersing in the empirical, without getting lost in contingency. The secret of this self-surpassing resides in theoretical spontaneity proper to human time. Its counterpart in the moral region, in practical knowledge is freedom. Freedom allows the advent of a form of willing that is not, as it were, given naturally. The practical a priori synthesis is the principle, or rather the motivation of the supreme possibility possessed by an imperfect willing that acts like a perfect willing and acts this way without being moved by egoist reasons. But if freedom is sensu stricto the condition of a moral action, in other words according to the law and through respect of it, the metaphysical root of this access to the *more* is found in the eidetic structure of the will. Ultimately, despite its native homogeneity the will is an a priori synthesis through its nature. To will is to aim for an intentional object that if always found beyond oneself; it is to go farther and higher than nature wants to go. The philosophers of Duty—Kant, Schiller, and Fichte—claim that man should never stop, action must always be revived, he must always be going forward. Duty is never accomplished; we always remain unequal to the task. But this moralism represents less a tragic Promethianism than a faithful conceptual interpretation of the will. If the will is condemned to go beyond itself, self-exceeding cannot represent an excess for it. Instead it constitutes a natural, necessary exercise of power that it has, or rather that it *is*. The proper place of the a priori synthesis is judgment but "the will is... judgment in its highest signification that poses the predicate as subject."[6] The metaphysical formula proper to the will is that the will ought to will its willing. More precisely, to will signifies that a subject is related to itself, that a subject that effectively wants, now aims for itself as "another" subject or rather as a subject willing "differently."

Inscribed in its metaphysical essence the will has the necessity, or rather the commandment: the willing subject must leave his given situation in order to will differently. In the moral context where the will is situation in its truth, this means that the will is ordered to will as it ought to will. Kantianism represents this situation by the figure of doubling. The subject in its finite condition wants a will subject to sensible inclinations, dominated by appetencies, obedient to the natural gravity of its native egoism. But this "imperfect will" ought to will like a will would removed from the power of the sensible, a will that is master of egoism, a "perfect" will. Even more it must will simply out of respect for the law because willing thusly is just and good in itself and as such. The possibility of the transposition of an imperfect will into a perfect will is explained in terms of the a priori synthesis. An imperfect will—the subject of the proposition—is commanded to act, to will like a perfect will (which plays the role of predicate). Of course, the predicate is not implied by the subject but still must be realizable by the subject and through the means native to it. The predicate of a synthetic a priori judgment is not conceptually contained by the subject although the subject is still related to it in an a priori way. The a priori nature of the judgment cannot be located "in" the subject or in the predicate, but in the copula tying them together. The copula is here expressed by the verb ought: the imperfect will *must* will like a perfect will. The *ought-to-be* signifies a gap but also the necessary crossing of this gap. This crossing is made possible by freedom.

Freedom makes possible an impossible action, or rather a willing of what one would rather not like to will. It enables the going beyond oneself, even against oneself. The moralists, but ultimately each one of us, knows full well that the good action is difficult, if not impossible. The good action is portrayed as going against our interests,

---

6. Nishida, *Le lieu*, trans. R. Kobayashi, 84 (translation modified by M. Dalissier, *Anfractuosité et unification: La philosophie de Nishida Kitarô*, 449).

as opposed to all that is natural and dear to us. The law (which is always difficult) is obeyed because one cannot do otherwise; we want what we ought to want only reluctantly, and (unfortunately) are prey to spite and resentment. The good action, the truly good willing is made possible only through freedom; it is the free tearing away that allows me to detach from myself, even to oppose myself. Through the sovereign freedom of humanity—and freedom is always sovereign or it is nothing!—that I can will what I do not like, what is not useful to me, even what bores me or is detrimental to me. Ultimately, like love the supreme proof of freedom, its highest instance is in giving up its life. For empirical analysis no motive can appear in man that would allow him to renounce what is at the heart, the root, at the source and quintessence of all that matters to him, namely, his life. However, to sacrifice one's life when honor requires it, or to give it in order to save another is an essential eidetic-metaphysical component of the beings that we are; this supreme gift is (if you like) "conceptually" implied by the loving freedom that is the deep truth of every man. However, this a priori implication can be explained, assimilated, in short, realized only by virtue of the freedom that allows us to leap beyond our own shadow, to actualize the most profound transcendent possibility of our condition. Nothing is more natural than the intuition that in order to be myself I must be, I must live. But this empirical and analytic inclusion drawn from the existential proposition "I am" is bracketed, or rather defeated by the conclusion: following in an a priori way from the being that I am is the power and duty to abandon, where applicable, my life. And freedom is the power that allows the transposition of the simply conceptual interpretation of this a prioriness into judgment, into a true possibility of giving my life.

Philosophy of the Will and Moral Formalism

Freedom is the practical counterpart of time as the power of a priori synthesis. Like the time that is schematized belongs to the subject itself (which is the meaning of its a prioriness) the freedom that allows the conformity of the sensible will to the pure will is also an immanent moment of the subject. However, this parallelism has its limits. Burdened with heterogeneous factors, the spontaneity that is the nerve of the schematization, of the temporalization, finds its limits in the presence of the manifold, of the sensible that remains an irreducible moment of time. The sovereignty of the a priori synthesis is therefore conditioned in the theoretical sphere. Things are different in the practical sphere. Despite the irreducible presence of the sensible within it, the will possesses an unlimited power over itself. Daily experience doubtlessly demonstrates the weakness of the will, its native powerlessness to conform itself to its intelligible nature. Yet the fact of the failure does not compromise the a priori significance of the faculty: the Categorical Imperative wants the moral law to be obeyed that the willing subject gives itself, and the *necessity* of obeying it means—on the moral plane—that it *can* be obeyed. Freedom is this unlimited power making it possible for me to will differently and better than I naturally do, in other words, in a way that is apparently impossible for me. The factual impossibility of conformity of the sensible will to the intellectual will reveals the deepest meaning of the homogeneity of the will. Homogeneity in the domain of nature designates an analytic condition where nothing new can happen. The homogeneity of the will radically rejects all influence or control by the sensible, by the pathological, and is not merely compatible with novelty but calls for and requires it. By willing the new the will is invited to transcend ceaselessly, which can only pass through the sensible that it carries along and penetrates. The great and lofty morality of Christianity encourages the perfect conformity of our will to its normative essence. But nobody can achieve this "ideal of sanctity" but merely "approach it."[7] However this state of affairs has no value as a refutation of the teaching on the unconditional power of the a prior synthesis in the practical domain. Disobedience of the Categorical Imperative hardly manifests a weakness, a simple imperfection, and consequently a limited sovereignty of the will over itself. Instead it enables a reformulation of the teaching on the unconditional power of the will: beside and across from a sovereignty of obedience a sovereignty of disobedience also exists. Freedom makes possible this *more* represented by the tearing away from its naturality against the law, against others. It can also take account of a surpassing of the natural that is not for the universal, for the good.

The homogeneity of the will only relates to the given being, to the real according to matter. It also and above all relates to what is not yet. Not as future, as becoming, but as constitutive moment of willing. The ultimate clarification of the a priori synthesis is reached through the will. The a priori synthesis is movement, not according to its properly kinetic dimension, but in its metaphysico-moral meaning. The movement of the a priori synthesis does not concern the unfolding of the given, the explication of the same; it makes novelty happen and true novelty belongs to the moral order. In its deep nature homogeneity is not only the continuity of the given but also, and above all, the domination of what happens. The proof and the test of the homogenous is that it ties the given to what is not yet given. This link seems like a going-in-advance in the direction of what is not yet. But progression to the future, protection is possible only starting from a repetition of the present, but from a transfigured present that instead of a given that is simply "found" is changed into a given that the will gives *itself*. This "giving itself" is the being, or rather the work of the will. The will assumes the being, that is, it gives it to itself, it will be able to give, to give itself what will be. Through and beyond every given, the will sublates heterogeneity into homogeneity, and one that, liberated from the nostalgia of sameness, appears as unconditionality, as sovereignty.

The unconditional-sovereign designates a stance in relation to the given, to what one is. It designates the departure from oneself, from oneself taken in a non-material, if you like non-ontological sense. The will is unconditional; it wants in sovereign fashion. Its unconditional-sovereignty is a stance of which the intentional object is not

---

7. Kant, *Akad*. XXVII, 1402s. (*Lectures on Ethics*, 108.)

given: the non-self, by its nature non-given, or the self repeated, ratified and therefore transposed into a non-given. The natural repugnance to something other, external, to something that threatens from the outside, encroaching on me, as well as the instinctive adhesion to oneself, complacency to oneself, the innate, immediate attachment to self stems from desire. However, the active consent to another taken for a good or, on the contrary, the conscious choice of oneself as good, as such, are figures of the will. Fear or an irrational antipathy in relation to the other are assumed by the will and slide into hate. But one can equally assume the natural attachment to the self, to the elements and moments of instinctive self-love. Eating, drinking, sleeping, seeking pleasure are natural, neutral functions. But they can become factors and instruments of an egoistic will that brackets others, even encroaches on them and suppresses them.

Sincerity and Rigorism

The sui generis meaning of a moral act, of a voluntary act (or, more simply, a volition in the strict sense of the term) is the surpassing of the given. The will is not defined by what it wants but by the fact that it wants, by the fact that it goes beyond what it has and is, in short, by going beyond itself. Discourse on the will can and should bracket any material consideration. It is essentially a reminder of going beyond oneself, a discourse on the formal. The great philosophies and theologies teach formal morality, but their "formalism" is not an abstraction. Nothing can be richer, more ample, more nuanced than a volition that results from an unconditional willing and which moves very broadly and covers a multitude of details. The moral formalism that is only the faithful translation of an authentic philosophy of the will does not signify the exclusion of the material, the disinterest regarding content. It simply requires a phenomenological reduction to what is *voluntary* in the will. Formalism is most often born in the context of philosophies of the subject, but it is not at all the cipher of a subjectivism. However, moralities that still seem to display clear "subjectivist" signs cannot pass the test of formalism and remain short of the eidetic criteria proper to the will.

Common opinion as well as a great number of philosophies recommend "sincerity" as the supreme criterion of correct moral action, of a morally good willing. One can certainly lack discernment, be blinded by prejudice, carried away by passion, or even do half of what the law requires, or do it approximately, imperfectly, hence poorly. It does not matter! The essential is that what one has or has not done was the object of a sincere will. Sincerity causes to "pass" what could not otherwise happen; it should alleviate failures, misconceptions, wrong notes and barbarities. It represents the necessities of the heart before the hardness of the law; it generously takes account of the weaknesses of the descendants of Adam; above all it is supposed to recall the primacy of intention over action, in short, the light purity of the will in relation to the material heaviness of doing. Yet a deeper analysis will clearly demonstrate the confusion and radical falsity of this argumentation. Sincerity, as such, has and can only have no true moral bearing. One can sincerely desire to eat when hungry and rest when tired. One can equally sincerely desire to cheat in order to pass an exam or even to make the last preparations for a burglary. One can sincerely desire to become a pirate; one can also "sincerely and vigorously desire" the recovery of a sick neighbor in order to resume an adulterous affair with her![8] The enumeration of these cases of the figure where the will is ardently engaged shows how the call to sincerity is insufficient, even fallacious in its quest to approve and justify a volition. The sincerity of desire is not related here to the rectitude of the intention but to the force of the will's engagement. It signifies nothing other than the ardor of desire, the vigor by which one aims for a goal, longs or conspires for an event to happen. The apologists for moral sincerity are rendered culpable through their erroneous reflection in matters of the philosophy of the will. To will effectively, to desire with all one's heart is not enough to legitimate a volition. What counts is what one wants and above all how, according to what end, which intention it is wanted. To will sincerely or ardently designates only the force, the intensity of the will, but intensity measures the quantity of the engaged will while the truth of the will is not quantitative but formal. An engagement of all the forces of our being is not necessarily good. It can be only a very natural perseverance in its being, the sordid consent of the will to this naturality that must be defeated, surpassed.

The critique of "moral sincerity" as quantitative conception of the will reveals the contradictions, the faults of an ultimately "non-voluntary" vision of the will. As by a ricochet it opens onto the path of reinterpretation of the moralities of intention, of the formalist moralities starting from the new understanding of freedom. Freedom is not an ontological force but the power of creativity of the mind, metaphysically qualified by its relation to the given, to nature, to the immediate self. Moral formalism is the child of the philosophy of the will, of the will understood as freedom for moral creativity. It is naturally a doctrine of intention: the moral sense of the will is intention, the position taken in relation to the given. Since the Stoics and the gospel, philosophy has tried to emphasize the primacy of intention over execution, of formal factors at the expense of material ones. The morality of intention reaches its summit in Augustine. It celebrates the lofty virtues of fear and love, but it also makes some sharp distinctions. It opposes filial fear to servile fear, filial love to mercenary love. The true fear of God is not motivated by terror before chastisement but by fear of displeasing, of offending him, in short, of doing what is not to be done, independently of any punishment. Authentic love is not evoked and sustained by anticipation of gain or recompense that the Master could give us, but by the pure intention of doing what pleases him, of willing what accords with the Good that is God. The motivation of pure love is not desire for payment but the service of the Good. If it wants the Good this is not for the sake of its fruits that are consequences of its action but for the intrinsic value of the good action itself. Engendered in a properly theological context, this morality of intention

---

8. Edwards, *Freedom of the Will*, 317.

will be reformulated in all of its metaphysical generality. Moral reflection discusses in what sense an action could be called good if it cannot be willed for its own sake, for the good that it represents. The response to this question is found on the plane of the will understood as love. The truth, the weight, the bearing of a love addressed to another not for itself exclusively but with other considerations, ulterior ends in view can be debated. But the response is simple: "what is not loved for its own sake is simply not loved at all" (*Soliloquies* I, 13, 22).

Moral formalism always appears under the form of rigorism: it is located within the logic of a radical dualism that is determined by the metaphysics of the will. The will is exercised in a perfectly homogenous way. Consequently it is completely and exclusively related to its object. There is no middle way between the option for a being and the option against it: all the options not related to it directly, that do not translate into a perfect consent to this being, are contrary, opposed options. The will does not have degrees; neither is it a mosaic of fragments, a collection of diverse components. It is defined and judged in light of its form, not its matter. For this reason there are materially good actions that still stem from a bad will and others that are inadmissible according to content, to their matter, and are nevertheless morally good. To make a donation is to do a "good deed" and yet impure factors can be mixed in with it and bad preoccupations can motivate it. Inversely, doing evil to another, physically or emotionally wounding him are materially bad actions, but we cannot reject surgical procedures (for example) that inflict pain with the healing of the patient in view. . . In fact, the life of society, the regulation of commerce and traffic and even education are based on the processes of constraint where violence, repugnant in itself, is exercised starting from a good intention. Teachers can severely punish disorderliness, laziness, or more simply the insufficient work of students, yet this is for the sake of treating young people with the future of society in mind. The intervention of police can be feared but these public servants are supposed have the good in mind. Ultimately, in many cases, self-defense and defense of a neighbor can lead to violence of one's aggressors and even their death, but it is nevertheless "legitimate," acceptable, approvable, in short, just.

Beside these benign, normal and clear applications located at the very foundation of the social and moral life of humanity, beside all these acts with "materially" repugnant but useful, even necessary content, formalism also registers morbid excrescences, bears morbid fruit. When it is rigorously, implacably exercised, when it rejects any attenuating circumstances and exceptions, it can lead to consequences that, in their absurdity and severity are sure to shock the mind and heart, provoking accusations of legalism and Pharisaism. But beyond the inherent excesses in its very exercise, formalism can also lead to doctrines and theses that often appear paradoxical. Moralities of intention teach that the will—more precisely, the willing condition of a person—qualifies and decides on the meaning and price of moral action. Consequently strong (or rather, good) ones rather than weak ones are required. The powerful logic of tradition's judgment is clear: "the corruption of the best is the worst" and of exclaiming, disillusioned: "The malicious soul inflicts a great wound" (*Antigone* 651)! Daily life is peppered with instances, with confusing and distressing examples of this intuition, but it is ultimately in the religious domain that the paradox, an abyssal one, seems to be most powerfully manifest. Simone Weil remarked: "When the supernatural enters into a being that does not have enough love to receive it, it becomes evil."[9] Apparently this warning is related only to the traps and pitfalls encountered by souls on the spiritual, mystical path. In reality it conceptually reformulates prophetic cries in Holy Scripture: "Right are the paths of the LORD; the just walk on them, but the faithless stumble" (Hos 14:10). For the wicked "the Day of the LORD will be darkness, not light" (Amos 5:18). And we all know the Augustinian theologoumenon on the virtues of the pagans as splendid vices and Calvinist sermons on the prayers of the impious as an abomination before God...

Will and Practical Knowledge

The aggravation of the moral weight of an action by virtue of the moral condition of the agent, or more generally speaking, the dependence and determination of the meaning and value of volitions in terms of the ethical or religious status of the willing subject are located within the logic of moral formalism, which is a logic of the will. The homogeneity, the indivisibility, the integrality of the will constitute the metaphysical backdrop to formalism. Moral formalism has always been accused of deadening abstraction. It seems deprived of any possibility of true articulation; the concrete actions of "real" mean cannot be found in this empty desert. In reality formalism is no less apt to explain the infinite multiplicity of actions and behaviors of individuals than the existentialist opponents of essence. More simply, the intentional object of the moral will is not the particular manifestation of a material essence but an end to choose or reject. And formalism finds its true meaning only through the Kantian interpretation of the will as practical reason.

Since Aristotle philosophy has taught that beside and before the speculative, theoretical reason we possess a practical reason governing the domain of moral, juridical and political action. Yet practical reason reaches its complete form only in Kantianism where it will be purged of all technical and pragmatic connotation. Subsequently, it is only related to the moral domain as moral, and this purification of content will have a purification of form as its counterpart: it admits that to a content of the purely moral condition there corresponds a perfectly homogenous form. But it must be insisted that the homogeneity of the will is not only of a material simplicity. In a certain way homogeneity signifies the surpassing of any quidditative consideration in order to reach another order, the metaphysical. If the will is truly practical reason this is

---

9. Weil, *Cahiers. Oeuvres Complètes* VI, 3, 300.

because practical reason and theoretical reason are not opposed according to their respective content, but by their way of relating to this content. The essential moment of a properly metaphysical vision of practical reason occurs when it is understood that it does not have concepts, practical essences, different from concepts as intentional objects but rather that it is related to concepts in a *practical* way.

It is an elementary truth that for there to be knowledge there must be contents to be known, but does the practical reason have contents proper to it? Theoretical reason possesses specific contents according to the respective domains where it is exercised and, above all, it has categories, general principles that it applies to description, to analysis, to the structuration of its contents of every order. But does this mean that the practical reason would not also have a particular sphere for it to think through concepts proper to this sphere? Practical reason is related to the universe of moral will, of love and hate, compassion and transgression, of the permitted and the forbidden, of the commanded and tolerated—can we not, should we not collect and establish a set of moral essences? The casuistry of the moralists of the Counter-Reformation, or, more simply, the penal or civil codes of States seem to be examples of this kind of set of essences. But the fact that it relates to a domain where the will acts, where the work of vice and virtue is exercised and unfolded, does not yet render a truly practical rule. Prudence counsels means that allow us to obey moral or juridical prescriptions, but these means can very well translate only into pragmatic or technical precepts. A donation or courageous aid to someone in danger can be (as we have seen) material goods, and which do not belong to the moral universe properly so-called. Even more, a powerful theoretical intelligence is quite capable of manipulating precepts and moral commandments in order to convert them into criminal designs. Shylock only repeats the teaching of generations of spiritual authors and theologians: "the devil can cite Scripture for his purpose."[10] Finally, it is easy to recall that Theology can discourse on the existence and attributes of God, the generous author of all things, principle of all good, though most of its concepts still belong to the register of theoretical reason.

Contrary to theoretical reason, practical reason does not have its own contents of the material order and its discourse cannot be analyzed in terms of noematic structures. Poets and philosophers—and not only they—are happy to bring up the Voice of Conscience. At first glance the expression lacks rigor, it seems to belong more to the order of the *Weltanschauung* than to philosophy. In reality it is a term with authentic philosophical bearing. The conscience has a voice; it speaks, and, as such, it has apriority over what it says. Yet the irreducibility of this saying to its statements and recitations, to all objectification and structuration, its condition of being "without noematic correlate"[11] still does not mean the absence of any intentional object. Instead it wants to make appear the specific situation of the discourse of the will that is determined and characterized by the act of willing where the intentional object is repeated,

---

10. Shakespeare, *Merchant of Venice* I, iii, 93.
11. Levinas, *Autrement qu'être ou au-delà de l'essence*, 184.

rethought, or rather transubstantiated in terms of the intention. The bracketing, the refusal of material articulation in favor of the primacy of the will doubtlessly does not come down to a kind of facile apophaticism, a misrepresentation in feeling if not instinct, the "reasons of the heart" of Pascal. Aristotle and numerous thinkers after him have admitted and taught the least exactitude of practical reasoning, a domain where one could be content with verisimilitude instead of the truth. But since Kant it is understood that the expressions of practical reason have a regularity as strict as those of geometry: "They say. . .it is necessary to ascribe three angles to a triangle but it is also necessary to keep a promise!"[12] But how should we conceive this necessity of integral intelligibility in a universe that has always thought characterized and dominated by relativism, subjectivism, the passions, in short, by the irrational?

Practical intelligibility can be understood only once one breaks with every attempt at logical demonstration or conceptual deduction. The heart has *its* reasons and its reasons are of another order than *theoria*. Practical reason ignores the delights as well as the pitfalls of representation. If Scripture commanded: you must not make graven images, this is because "you cannot say the absolute good."[13] A minimum of casuistry is doubtlessly needed in choice of action, in the appreciation of the value of a moral act. It is fittingly known however that ultimately the meaning and the truth of volitions are not a function of their condition of being subsumable under a particular precept but dependent on their conformity to the Moral Law, to the obedience of their subject to the will of God. If in certain exceptionally grave situations the people are consulted through a referendum, this means that in these supreme moments the political cannot be reduced to a kind of technique, to the decisions and operations of those supposedly most competent citizens who *represent* the rest of the community. The refusal of representation flows from the will that is indivisible, indissoluble and unfit to be divided up. Yet if the will, the practical reason is not exercised according to a plurality of quidditative contents, it is nevertheless deployed in terms of noetic, normative principles. Essentially, one could enumerate two kinds. One belongs, so to speak, to the order of the singular, the other represents a regime of criteria. The face, cipher of the other is one of these superior principles; legality, conformity to the law is the other.

The emblematic category of Levinasian philosophy, the face is this originary reality that serves as principle and strict, non-relativizable criterion of all moral action. The simple appearance of the face of the other suffices to tell us, "thou shalt not kill." But the appearance of the face is not of the material, physical (hence, theoretical) order. The face cannot be reduced to a system of contents, to a node of meanings. More precisely, it does not impose itself in my sight in terms of its elements or traits. "In itself" the face is naked, empty of meaning; it *appears* only when I admit that it

---

12. Kant, *Akad.* XIX, 98.

13. Horkheimer, *Théorie critique: Essais*, 361.(*Critical Theory: Selected Essays*, trans. Matthew J. O'Connell et al. [New York: Continuum, 2002] 285).

expresses or is expressed without "objective" meaning. Ultimately it is through charity that we discover the face of the other, or rather, that it appears *as* a face. The gospel parable tells of a priest and Levite who passed by a man lying half dead on the side of the road while a Samaritan stopped. The unconscious man, divested of his clothes, lying in his own blood, had no human figure. Only the vision, the "attention" of the Samaritan gave him back his "humanity."[14] In itself the face, every face, not only the bloody one that the Samaritan saw, presents only an anatomical instance, a descriptive specimen of body parts. Even in its entire physiognomic expressivity a face has no practical impact. This practical impact is received only by virtue of an attentive gaze that contemplates it, that waits for human traits to appear and to be discerned in their own reality. The Face becomes the cipher of the Other only starting from the attentive and affectionate gaze of another, animated by a practical intention. The face is neither a universal nor an individual but rather a singular, even a unique intentional object of willing that is by nature homogenous, indivisible and integral and which is singular and unique only as willed by this will.

The gaze of the will submits the face to a practical reduction at the end of which it becomes one of these words by which the will "speaks."[15] Faces are, so to speak, organs of the will, or rather are like a true glossary of the will, a dictionary of love. Yet the will, as practical reason, still has another register of principles, less immediate, less concrete. This second series of principles of the eidetic order, eidetic in the most general sense comes from the "formalist" nucleus of the moral will. It is not here a matter of a plurality of precepts, but rather of synonyms in order to express a single law, one that is not a super-precept or even the matrix or common essence of all precepts, the quintessence of all commandments, but the regularity, the legality, the duty. Just as someone is not a sinner for having failed to actualize certain potentialities, for having transgressed certain commandments, but for having refused to found his life, his will on God. One is good or bad, a will is good or bad by virtue of a general attitude of approval or disapproval of the Law. The correlate of practical reason, of the will, its general correlate is what can be called legality. Legality is a general, foundational principle that makes a prescription, a rule the object of an acceptance, an approval. It is the root of practical rules as practical, the node of principles as they are the objects of the will. In short, it is not a Sovereign Rule of which all rules would be partial and particular instances but the single form that makes descriptive criteria into prescriptive principles. Ultimately, thanks to it the law moves me to obey it, thanks to it the law becomes the power of love.

---

14. Weil, "Formes de l'amour implicite de Dieu," in *Oeuvres complètes* IV 1, 293.

15. Rousseau, *Discours sur l'origine et les fondements de l'inégalité* parmi les hommes, in *Oeuvres complètes* 3, 141.

BOOK TWO—EIDETICS

Practical Feeling

The generality and formality of the Law prohibits the practical reason, the will from having a plurality of precepts as object, but does this amount to an exclusion of all articulation of practical intentionality? Rousseau wrote that "the first of the laws is to respect the laws," that respect for the law constitutes the universal "supplement" of particular laws.[16] But since Kant we know that the teaching of the philosopher of Geneva is to be specified and rectified. Respect is not of the same metaphysical order of the law: respect is located in the world of the willing subject while the law for which it makes possible the adoption as object is in the realm of the willed. The superior, general *noesis* that is the practical reason as willed is a *saying* of which the *said*, speech, is the legality, whereas respect is situated near the saying. It constitutes the specific mediational moment allowing the affirmation of the principle, not according to its sense as simple thetic articulation but as approved and desired position. In fact respect has a key role in the comprehension of the practical reason as willed: at its highest level it represents and almost recapitulates this universe of feeling that constitutes the beginning, the preamble, the elementary form of the practical. Strictly speaking only the will is practical, that superior level of desire that is always of moral pertinence. Yet the moral will possesses a pre-history, a genesis, a "preformation"[17] in the sphere of feeling that alone makes possible the conception of the specificity of the practical intelligibility.

Common sense already attributes a moral inscription to emotions. Like the irregular procedures, the "disordered bonds" of the violent, the unjust (*Laws* 716a-b) different from the balanced, harmonious movement, the emotions of good men are not the same as those of the miscreant, the coward or the miser! The human emotions belong to the moral sensibility, they are distant but nevertheless authentic instances, signs and manifestations of vice and virtue. But the too psychological, even physiological, and in any case primitive, elementary reality, "emotion" settles down into *feeling* which is considered to be an important manifestation of the moral condition. Feeling emanates from the heart; without requiring the deployment of effort or a call to reasoning, it translates what we could call the moral quality of man. In fact, it is like the emanation of the will in a pre-rational register. Some philosophers, especially of the eighteenth century, wanted to erect feeling into an essential category of the practical world. Anticipating the great Kantian teaching of the intelligibility of the practical, they tried to develop a theory of moral feeling. We would have proper means, sui generis criteria different from the theoretical of knowledge in practical matters. Our mind would discern through feeling the value of a reality, the good or evil of an action, and this feeling would not be content to know and understand good and evil, but would constitute a power translating the discernment into an effective choice. Moral

---

16. Rousseau, *Discours sur l'économie politique*, in *Oeuvres complètes* 3, 249s.
17. Schelling, *Recherches philosophiques sur l'essence de la liberté humaine*, in *Oeuvres métaphysiques*, 161.

feeling not only causes the moral sense of an action to be read, it also gives energy for the discernment to be transposed into approval or disapproval and the approval into inclination and dis-inclination.

The immediate and infallible character of moral feeling, that effective and efficacious practical judgment, is always insisted on but reflection will end by finding within this apparent immediacy a structuration, a mediation. The first eidetic occurrences of the practical are pleasure and pain, first, elementary categories of practical "knowledge." But pleasure and pain are immediate feelings. Without prior reflection I experience the stinging feeling of a burn or the delicious taste of a sauce or a pastry. This pre-reflexive immediacy of feeling, notably pleasure, leads to classical speculation to criticize it. The moralists are so severe towards pleasure because they think it belongs to the universe of a brute and dangerous immediacy and therefore as strange, ultimately hostile to the judgment that through its mediacy constitutes the proper sphere of the rational, or at least the reasonable. Despite some reservations and qualifications, pleasure will remain a privileged target of metaphysical critique in moral matters and the rigorisms of all kinds think they can reassure themselves of the soundness of their condemnations based on the justification of the theoretical, metaphysical order, motivated by the conception of feeling as immediate, thus sub-rational. Meanwhile, Hegelianism will be the textbook case of the trial of the immediate, what is without mediation, as metaphysically null and morally pernicious. This judgment has its share of truth—I would say, it would have its share of truth if all feeling was effectively only impenitent immediacy. But without questioning the supposed immediacy of pleasure and pain—and yet here also the elements and historical, cultural components could only nuance, weaken the analysis of undivided immediacy—the domain of feeling includes realities that surpass the analytic condition of immediacy and open onto synthesis. Ancient philosophy already knew the category of the irascible, the apparent sub-rationality of which is accompanied by a phenomenon of surmounting and surpassing, different from the simplicity of the immediate and the Kantian sublime clearly illustrates the role of the a priori even within the *Gefühl*. Yet Pity and Respect are the realities that reveal the presence of the synthetic condition in the world of feeling.

Pity seems to be an immediate feeling, even a supreme specimen of immediate feelings. Pity arises in the heart without preparation. It is born at the sight of something unhappy or through hearing a sad story. In one way or another it expresses the fact of being "touched" by the face of another. It is not prepared or consciously brought about. It swoops down on us without emerging over time. Or rather, it gushes from our gut without advanced warning and takes possession of us in an invincible and irresistible manner. Pity is a "pure movement of Nature, prior to all reflection."[18] It does not present itself formally, explicitly; it neither compares nor argues; it does not try to justify the legitimacy of its choice. In reality, if there is a choice it consists instead

---

18. Rousseau, *Discours sur l'origine et les fondements de l'inégalité*, in *Oeuvres complètes* 3, 155.

in the fact of accepting to turn one's attention, one's regard towards the Face. Once this is done, compassion can no longer be avoided: this is why it is so much easier to kill someone from afar, or above, or behind. Exposed to the gaze of another, his face, one is disarmed... The Samaritan found a half-dead man on the road; when he saw him he did not weigh the pros and cons of his attitude towards him. He only cast his gaze over him and the rest was implied by the feeling that seized him, that rose up within him. Of course, he had to consider the best way to help him, but the technical, pragmatic modalities decorating his action were a direct function of the feeling of pity that immediately welled up within him when he saw the wounded man.

Compassion towards the neighbor is born, almost irresistibly imposes itself. Nevertheless, if the feeling is truly a single, homogeneous, undivided reality, it is still not of the analytic condition. Despite the instantaneity, the instinctive character of its emergence, pity is not a single and undividable reality. The mystery, the "enigma" of pity is found in the question: "how can a suffering that is not my own become a determining motive of my will?"[19] But if we cannot cut into temporal pieces or quidditative elements the event or rather advent of pity, of compassion towards another, the monochrome reality of this feeling nevertheless has a structure of differentiation. The mystery of pity is that another man imposes himself immediately and as unconditional end of my will. But the immediacy and unconditionality of my feeling reveals a synthetic structure. Most often I feel pity towards someone nature has not favored, who has physical or psychological wounds, social defects, even the hideous marks of transgression or vice. Yet the marvel, the miracle (if you like) of pity is that I overcome my native repugnance towards vileness, that I control the tumultuous movements of pride that push me to retreat, to flee from what nauseates, scares or shocks me. Even when the will-to-pity is not conscious, pity is a continuous victory over itself. Everything naturally tends to stay in its being and pity is a reality that goes against this perseverance: it ceaselessly inflicts little deaths on man, until it causes me to adopt attitudes and accomplish actions that can lead to greater and greater deaths, and ultimately, to Death.

Pity relates to the face, it makes the will speak in relation to the neighbor as neighbor; *it* is the "saying" of the practical reason of which the "saids" are its faces. But practical reason is not related merely to individuals, particulars: it equally discourses in a universal register. The saying of the will with regard to the universal is respect. Respect is an impersonal, even "a priori" feeling.[20] Its truth is not the emotion felt towards a given individual; it is not born from the shock of a contingent encounter. Its intentional, true object is the law, or rather morality: as Kant said, respect for the

---

19. Housset, *L'intelligence de la piété*, 51.

20. Kant, *Critique de la raison pratique*, in *Oeuvres* 2, 697. [Usually the author references the German Akademie edition of Kant's works. But, particularly in this chapter, he references the French editions when important to do so. –Trans.]

law is "morality itself, considered subjectively as an incentive."[21] Respect is the face or subjective counterpart of the law and as such, it has a pure universality, a majestic formalism. But this universality and formalism have a synthetic status. If respect is not articulated according to a plurality of objects, of intentional precepts it still registers a structure of differentiation. Respect is certainly a feeling; it is not completely foreign to the world of emotion, yet it is not a direct emanation, an actually overpowered impulse, in short a phenomenon of the immediate, of the instinctive, but a victory won over our interests, our pride. The counterpart of the feeling experienced towards another human is the consciousness of oneself as of lesser weight and value, a consciousness that entails or rather implies the possibility and most often the actuality of a reduction (or even bracketing) of the self. It is as if one is almost crushed by the respect provoked by certain human beings, and above all by the announcement and intuition of the law. In and through respect one understands, one approves and assumes his own inferiority, and if consent to this condition unfolds from the feeling of respect with force and efficaciousness, it is no less a victory to win and consequently a synthesis to effect at each moment and in each volition.

Respect and pity make up the nerve of the *noesis* of practical reason according to its highest meaning and its highest generality: they incarnate the energy of the effective action of the will for the good. They almost represent the transcendental aesthetic of practical reason, that which makes possible its saying, an articulate and rational saying. Respect and pity are the major moments of the dynamism of the will. They constitute the subjective side of the copula of its a priori syntheses. But can we content ourselves with the profession of their unilaterality? The a priori feeling is the means of conceiving a rational discourse of the will without it being cashed out into a plurality of noematic correlates. It shows and explains how the practical reason, the will can be related to anything and effectively to the Good. But is the practical reason only related to the Good? Can the will only be conformed to the law? Philosophy is certainly right to distrust its positions that lead to the metaphysical absurdity of Manichaeism. However, when it holds a conception where the a prioriness concerns only the predicate, but the very movement to that which reason is related, can it be confined within a moral-metaphysical monism? Practical reason is a movement, an acting towards. . . It is related to the good through an a priori inclination. But it is a fact, a metaphysical fact that it is not always related to the good: it is related to good or evil. Can we take account of this practical directedness by means of the ancient discourse on "privative" evil? Can we say that the aim of evil is only the absence of inclination to the good? In short can we say that the practical reason, the will has only a single correlate, the good?

---

21. Kant, *Critique de la raison pratique*, in *Oeuvres 2*, 702 (*Critique of Practical Reason*, trans. Werner Pluhar [Indianapolis: Hackett, 2002] 99).

Book Two — Eidetics
The Knowledge of Good and Evil

Pity and respect are major instances of the *noesis* of the practical; they relate to their respective correlates in a practical way. Pity is moved by the face; respect is moved by the law. But if these practical aims certainly appear only by virtue of the energy animating the noesis, they are always only saids dissociable from the saying, "willeds" numerically distinct from the willing that wants them. Pity and respect largely contribute to the founding of the discourse of the will but, ultimately, they are not enough. Discourse of the will cannot be content with contents that emerge because of practical energy. These contents must still be delineated in terms of and according to the homogeneity of the will. If the will is interpreted as practical reason, its said must not simply be a product of its saying, but rather its counterpart, its parallel face. The will is an intentionality, but one in which the intention and its object are inseparably tied or rather have their parallel and solidary genesis. In other words practical knowledge is a *noesis* that implies its *noema*. To know the truth of the discourse of the will it is necessary to understand that its saying is its said, or even that it is a unique saying that implies only its said. It cannot be repeated enough that practical knowledge is not knowledge of practical *contents* but *practical* knowledge of contents. The intentional correlates of practical reason are not material essences, eidē, but a single intentionality that envelops, penetrates and sublates these essences. Particular essences according to their quiddity are like theoretical materials that the practical gaze transfigures. Or rather, at the end of a practical reduction only the common metaphysical essence of the eidē remains. This common metaphysical essence, possessing a more complete universality than those of the Face or the Law, is declined according to the duality of Good and Evil.

Good and evil prove to be ultimate "contents" of practical knowledge, indissociable from the will that wants them. But this integral implication has a whole prehistory, an entire theory of partial and secularized ontological proofs that present frequently banal (but occasionally fascinating) occurrences of "metaphysical implication." Every knowledge, every judgment is doubtlessly an implication reaching its object, its proper end. Yet the modalities of the implication, the makeup and scope of the judgment are different. Theoretical judgment implies an assent to its end but has nothing to do with an adhesion by feeling and says nothing about a call to existence of the object, its end. But the practical judgment (ultimately only a synonym for the will), constitutes precisely an approval transposed into an adhesion in order thereafter to lead to a tendency for the effective position of the object. The eidetic nature of the practical judgment involves implying its object in such a way that its non-position would be inconceivable, illogical. "To think God is to think him as tied to the affirmation about him."[22] Faith is not a theoretical judgment; God is not a reality indifferent to being

---

22. Marcel, *Journal métaphysique*, 153.

and non-being. The ontological proof is right: God cannot not exist. Said differently: a God that one could conceive as non-existent cannot be God!

The impossibility of the non-existence of God is not simply an implication of his concept as theoretical category. God—the God of faith and love—is not such a supreme *noema*, or if he is, he is a practical *noema*, a constitutive moment indissociable from the act of faith. "God" adds nothing to faith as the beloved adds nothing to love. After the Resurrection Christ says to the Apostles: "Blessed are those who have not seen, yet believe" (John 20:29). He does not specify in what, in whom. . .they believe. The acts of faith and love, of those theological virtues organically tied together, are practical noeses for which the object is indissociable from the intention. In other words, the intention in its truth is unconceivable without its object; it implies its correlate with all the force of the practical synthesis.

This necessary inclusion of the intentional object in the *noesis* of the will is expanded by the implication of attributes that are concomitants and consequences of it. First of all, each judgment of value implies a creative activity: the position assumed in relation to the predicate is part of the concept of the predicate or rather, it underlies the predication, connects the copula. Contemporary thought arduously and perspicaciously discerns the truth of the practical judgment where assent to the predicate entails adhesion to, engagement with its consequences that are so to speak its attributes. Political theology says: "The *praxis* of Imitation constitutively belongs to Christology. . .Christ must always be thought in such a way that he is not only thought."[23] A parallel intuition emerges in Simone Weil's *Cahiers*: "A recognition of the *I* in the starving is fictional, imaginary if it is not accompanied by an almost irresistible inclination to feed them."[24] And contemporary phenomenology puts the dot on the "i" summarizing these arguments when it raises "the impossibility of thinking the person without love."[25]

These examples of the implication of practical reason are authentic and meaningful illustrations and instances of the logic of the will, but they constitute only incomplete drafts of the essential idea that says that the intentional object of the will is given in and through its inclination and that this single inclination appears under a dual form. Analytic philosophers reject the conceptual status of the good: the good adds nothing to the predicate, it is, so to speak, only a "simple emotional sign" of our approval.[26] But approval is precisely something that aims for—and in a specific way—an intentional object. Knowledge of the good, practical knowledge, is not a *noesis* with a *noema* as its correlate. It is a *noesis* that is more than a theoretical judgment; it is this more that takes the place of intentional object. The immediacy and non-discursivity of practical knowledge here appear in their positive sense. Practical

23. Metz, *Glaube in Geschichte und Gesellschaft*, 64.
24. Weil, *Cahiers. Oeuvres Completes* VI, 2, 418.
25. Housset, *La vocation de la personne*, 452.
26. Hare, *Language of Morals*, 194ss.

judgment is immediate because it is given in and through the approval that precedes no evaluation or comparison. It is non-discursive, non-thetic because total, whole, integral. The good is that to which one is inclined: one does not incline to this or that, useful, agreeable, lovable things, but to the good. And the good is not aimed for as if located beyond the particular content of judgment. Instead, it precedes it, it is located before and ahead of it in the judgment as approval and adhesion. Practical knowledge is the judgment that conceives the good and adheres to it in and through the fact of conceiving it. The immediacy of practical knowledge does not mean that it has an atomic, punctual condition: practical knowledge is moved, directed to its object. If practical judgment rejects all reflexive movement, it still does not belong to the order of the simple. Common sense represents the will as stretching towards an end, and it is right to do so. But this tension that gives extension, so to speak, to the will is conformed to the homogeneity, the indivisibility and, consequently, the continuity of the will. However, the continuity of the will should not be understood in theoretical terms: the volition, practical judgment, is continuous not by lacking any interstice among its successive "sections," but by the fact that it is (and only is) an inclination.

Practical knowledge, the will, has the good as its proper intentional object—an eidos, a super-eidos if you like, that is different from theoretical eidē. Contrary to material essences and metaphysical eidē, the good cannot be understood as a neutral content, the object of an inference or a deduction without adhesion. The good is an object of desire; it is (and only is) desirable. As such, it motivates and moves adhesion. By its metaphysical nature, desire is the object of inclination—or rather of the inclination that is naturally related to the good that alone explains the advent of the inclination. The emergence of the energy excited by the desirable, the good, can be astonishing, inexplicable, but the existence of a structure, a mechanism proper to the arousal of the adhesion is implied by the practical judgment that is the will. The good as supreme eidos where the quiddity is inseparable, indissociable from the tension towards it, where the movement towards is precisely an essential eidetic moment, is the sui generis content of the will. The ancients and Scholastics already taught that the Good is the proper object of the Will. "The good is what all desire." But the movement towards of the desire is not the unique movement that shares the eidetic content of the will: there is also a movement away.

Beside the inclination to the good, practical reason possesses another primordial inclination—or rather, disinclination—that concerns evil. The will loathes evil. Its repugnance appears under diverse forms: fear and flight from pain, horror felt before the odious, disapproval of transgression and sin. Emotion is not only the joyous recognition of a positive reality; negative emotions equally exists, like disgust, repulsion, and terror. Beyond these elementary physiological-psychological instances of disinclination, there is an entire range of feelings and practical passions of repugnance of which hate is the highest manifestation. From physical pain to the terrible passion of hate, we are always dealing with instances of disinclination, of repugnance. The true intentional object of all these practical judgments is not a thing, an event, not even a particular person, but Evil. Evil is not deduced at the end of a chain of reasoning; it is discerned because it is felt immediately, without prior reflection. Like its metaphysical counterpart the good is what is intended in practical judgments of approval, evil is intended in practical judgments of disapproval. Evil is not an attribute attached to grievous, odious, or vicious entities. Rather, it is internal to them, it is what is within them making them evil. Ultimately (and firstly), evil is what makes instances in themselves of the theoretical order of knowledge ends of practical knowledge. Contents of punctual, simple condition are transubstantiated into movements of repugnance and thus into movements of the will, in short, into moments of the practical reason. Evil is also a super-eidos, the principle and root of disapproved, rejected contents as disapproved and rejected.

Good and evil are the two root-eidē of practical knowledge. They are not material essences or logical or epistemological categories, but they register a formal generality that excludes all quidditative dispersal (or structuration if you like). The will is homogeneous! On the other hand, and this is the essential, a movement of the will is a constitutive part of the metaphysical essence of these root-eidē. The knowledge pertaining to good and evil is of a different order than the knowledge pertaining to the things of nature, or generally speaking to all knowledge relative to events, to states of fact, and to qualities. Good and evil are not known in a neutral way; the subject's taking up a position is inseparable from this knowledge. Human history is initiated by a decision in relation to "the knowledge of good and evil" (Genesis 3:22). But this knowledge is not an "objective" analysis, a neutral reading of contents: the practical reason is essentially the faculty of "rejecting evil and choosing the good" (Isa 7:16). Since Aristotle, philosophy has spoken of "practical first principles," natural dispositions of the soul to desire the good and reject evil. The Scholastics talked about *synderesis*, that natural *habitus* that incites us to the good and makes us oppose evil. And later the moralists of the eighteenth century will transcribe into philosophical discourse the ancient and universal conviction about the presence in the soul of a moral sense, a sense of the just and unjust, of aversion towards the unjust and affection felt for the just.

The two super-eidē of practical reason are of equal value and bearing, enjoying a perfect symmetry. They represent two primordial movements of the mind, two movements in opposite directions. This vision of the primordiality of direction has important noetic consequences. The *aversio* to evil and the *conversio* to the good found an epistemological regime in two parts and a morality where good and bad are opposed without nuance and without compromise, and this for the good reason that adhesion to the good and repugnance of evil are of an irreducible metaphysical duality. Contrary to the universe of theoretical reason sharing a plurality of material essences and logical categories, the practical reason has only two "concepts," two fundamental "principles": "good and evil."[27] The eidē of the theoretical are *diversa*, each corresponding to a portion of the world of the understanding. They indicate multiple ways that theoretical reason is exercised. They are quiddities that divide up the universe of essences. They do not mutually exclude one another, but can be joined together, can make precise the details, complete the information of each other. The super-eidē of good and evil are *opposita*; they are mutually exclusive, incompatible. They are totalities of which the root, the metaphysical nerve is in the two opposed movements of practical reason, in the two primitive inclinations of the will. These two opposed inclinations determine the two great noetic registers of the will; they are equally at the origin of moral dualism. Adhesion to the good and repugnance of evil admit no halfway. A moral ontology could accommodate a gradual conception: as non-being is only the absence of being, evil could represent only the absence of the good. But this ultimately quantitative vision, reducible to portions of being, to calculable degrees of existence is excluded by the lofty intuition of Practical Reason as Will. The two spheres of the will do not occupy portions of the same space, but rather correspond to two movements in opposite directions. And one cannot influence the direction of a movement through a diminution, a weakening of its force. The sole true modification that it can be subject to is its turnaround, its reversal.

---

27. Kant, *Critique de la raison pratique*, in *Oeuvres* 2, 717 (*Critique of Practical Reason*, trans. Werner S. Pluhar [Indianapolis: Hackett, 2002] 99).

XII

The Reality and Scope of Evil

Evil as Metaphysical Category

The doctrine of the duality of the will, the teaching on the good and bad wills as two figures, two original, irreducible realities leads to the definitive foundation or rather completion of metaphysics. Metaphysics is not a doctrine of brute and undifferentiated being, an ontology, a discourse condemned to affirmation, therefore to being finally only the counterpart of a sterile apophaticism. Neither is it a scale of quiddities, a collection or register of the motley multiplicities of material essences, but a supreme articulation, that of the two super-eidē. From the auto-figuration of the Image, passing through the diverse levels of novelty, then through the discourse on the unique, we have not stopped deploying, exercising the work of the expansion of metaphysics. This expansion is inscribed in the real through the eidetics of space and time, but it is only in and through the will as practical reason distilled into the ultimate differentiation where the will is, so to say, torn apart that the expansion is perfected. The Expansion of Metaphysics is not the inclusion of qualities, moments, in short, essences: Metaphysics is not the Encyclopedia! It is nevertheless an integration of which the ultimate moment, the very point appears in the deduction of evil which is made possible thanks to the notion of the two principles of Practical Reason. The integration of evil unfolds in two stages. The first essentially amounts to a rupture with the various Neoplatonisms: evil is not non-being, absence, privation, weakness. By dint of venerating being, the classical ontologies were forced to refuse Evil a share in it. Speculation is reduced to subterfuge in order to deny being to what is opposed to the good and ends up "exterminating evil from existence."[1] This vision, this explanation of evil is prohibited to a philosophy that wants to be hermeneutically faithful to

---

1. Proclus, *De malorum subsistentiae* 4 (*Fragments That Remain of the Lost Writings of Proclus*, 79).

experience and presents the reasoned description of the existence of the creature in light of the doctrine of Kenosis. Kenosis is not a simple surmounting of non-existence, the filling of a hole, the dynamization of the inert. On the contrary, it is an incessant victory over evil accomplished within effective reality, through the trials inscribed within being. Only the grafting of evil into the tissue of being allows the enlargement of metaphysics to include within itself the opposite of the good, the enemy of meaning. But this essential rehabilitation of evil on the plane of being is conceivable only through considerations of meaning. Philosophy was able to interpret evil as non-being because it seemed to defy meaning. The extermination of evil from being only attests to the confusion of speculation placed in the presence of nonsense or anti-sense, the translation of the perplexity of reason before this supreme scandal. It is a reformulation on the ontological plane of the ancient Socratic intuition: evil is never voluntary! The thesis of the impossibility of consciously doing evil leads to the affirmation of its non-existence, which is evidently the avowal of a powerlessness to assign it a place. The great speculations of classical philosophy identified being and the good, and this identification can lead only to the negation of the existence of what is opposed to the good. But the truth of the idea that "evil is non-being" or even "evil is the form of non-being" (*Enneads* I, 8), is evidently the impossibility of attributing to it a meaning. If metaphysics rejects the Neoplatonic thesis and cuts short the absurd negation of the existence of what so intensely affects human life, this is because it intends to think evil, in other words to represent it, starting from, or rather in relation to the world of meaning. Metaphysics is neither ontodicy nor theodicy, namely an enterprise to justify the reality of evil starting from its "sense" or its supposed purposes. It doubtlessly neither wants to nor can silence the sorrowful investigation of the "why," but it will bracket that in order to undertake a conceptual investigation. Evil is not a material essence or a teleological category but it can be made the object of an eidetic analysis. Evil (like the good) is an eidos, rather, a super-eidos of the will, and, as such, without attempting to attribute to it a sense, we could draw it into the arena of metaphysics. Metaphysics is something more and other than ontology, and it is this through the intervention of the will which, alone, makes possible the paradigm of a supra-quidditative but articulated vision that buries reason neither into Indifference nor into the conception of Being as *das Strittige*. In sum, metaphysics is a *prima philosophia* articulated in and through an eidetics and finds its realization in the doctrine of good and evil.

The Positivity of Evil

Evil is not non-being, nothing, a solely negative or privative reality. Its acute positivity is corroborated by the most primitive experience as much as the most profound and it appears even as one of its fundamental eidetic moments. Whether located in the moral or physical domain, evil has a scorching *intensity*. The infinite range of physical and moral sufferings has nothing negative about it. From the sharp sting of a toothache to the agony of suffering caused by cancer, evil has a terrible intensity. And the anguish and terrors of the "psychic" domain are no less dull or weak. Hate is the highest demonstration of the radical positivity of evil, a powerful refutation of every Neoplatonic interpretation in terms of non-being. The interpretation of evil as negativity can doubtlessly receive suggestive illustrations in aging and the various maladies that carry phenomena of enervation in their wake. However, in reality the decay of intensity entailed by deterioration is only secondarily a privation of being. If the old and the sick seem to exist in a weakened, diminished way this is because the structural moments and elements of their organism suffer dysfunctions, ruptures, and inversions. The privation of being that seems legible through the phenomena of evil may come down to a loss of force, but this loss that makes manifest a diminution of the amount of being allotted to each creature is ultimately explained from the more or less gradual modification of the equilibrium of its structure. The evil that ravages us is manifest through sorrowful attitudes and events of enervation, but it still does not amount to a simple decrement of being. The great classical philosophies were capable of representing evil as a kind of crevice or hole, an empty place in being. However if being seems undermined from within by evil, this is because the lacerations it endures disrupts the equilibrium, the proportion between elements and therefore leads to the reversal of their reciprocal relations. Evil is never a simple absence intuitable through the image of an empty, closed space within a being. If you want to represent it in ontological terms it would be more fitting to speak of a goad that wounds, a shard that pierces. The void of negation is only "a local wound,"[2] whereas the evil that we suffer affects us in our entire being.

This being-affected-in-the-whole-of-its-being seems corroborated by the ontological conception of evil as a privation or general absence. In reality a void cannot be generalized unless it carries with it the entire entity that it is supposed to undermine. It is a simple, logical conclusion, a truism that a general and therefore unlimited void, no longer situated within an entity, becomes co-extensive with it and by this fact brings it toward its own condition of non-being. Ultimately the non-being of evil appears no longer as a moment or aspect, a component or adherent of the being it afflicts, but it ends up, so to speak, dragging it back into its tomb. The conception of evil as negativity leads therefore to the obliteration of the very being that it afflicts, wounds, negates. We therefore have to turn to the consideration of evil as internal to being, as its attribute, or rather, anti-attribute. Evil afflicts being, tormenting and lacerating it. But this passionate, active terminology only obscures its veritable fall back into the vision of evil as privation. The void and laceration, the absence as wound ultimately indicate a metaphysical assimilation of evil to non-being. We should subject it to the same criticisms. Evil as the emptiness of a given place, the laceration or amputation of a piece of Being, the wounding of an element in its structure always remains an ontological category subsumed under Being as one of its adherents or citizens. Men

2. Milton, *Paradise Lost* XII, 386.

consider life, which is the true synonym for being, as the supreme good: who does not want to live and to survive, who does not consider life the greatest value? The fear of death, of non-being brackets the quest of every other good and, inversely, the gift of one's life, one's being, remains the greatest of all sacrifices. Yet the elementary intuition of the supreme value of life, of the being that some medieval ontologies formalized by the definition *ens et bonum convertuntur* is not an ultimate and unconditional truth. Men have always existed who think honor is a good superior to being, and, inversely, who conceive certain conditions and moments of existence as worse evils than non-being. Coryphaeus told Oedipus: "better for you to want not to be at all than to be blind" (*Oedipus Rex* 1369). And Christ will say about Judas: "it would have been better for this man never to have been born" (Matt 26:25). Evil is not here a negation that weakens or diminishes being. Instead it is a reality that submerges, relativizes it. But if evil is not an internal hemorrhaging of being, neither is it Non-being conceived as counterpart of Being. If Christ thinks it would have been better for Judas Iscariot not to have been born, this means that non-being is not a zero being but rather an anti-being.

Instead of constituting phenomena, events interpreted in the negative, thrown into relief against the background of affirmations, diverse evils are themselves positive realities. Cold is not the pale absence of heat: it bites into my flesh. The hunger tormenting me is not merely the lack of food: it not only registers an emptiness but twists my limbs and makes me groan and shout. Vice is not the younger sister of virtue, or its shadow, or even a place left empty where it ought to bloom. Well to the contrary, avarice is a passion that leads to my subjecting myself and others to treatment and conduct that afflict, torment and wound. Lechery implies the contempt of one's own flesh and that of the other; it leads to miseries and troubles of all kinds. Evil means not merely the negation of love, richness, beauty but rather to powerful and vigorous affirmations of hate, extreme indigence, ugliness. The primordial passion of hate is not only a negative attitude: it implies desire for the realization of what has not value as the violent suppression of the good. If hate looks and moves downward, it is not simply because it is driven by a kind of natural heaviness: it comprehends and conceives the undignified, the petty, it lends "a positive regard (*Hinblicken*) to a possible negative value."[3] The bad will is not always realized by commission, omission is also a way, in truth a royal way, of transgression. It certainly appears under the pale, sickly colors of negligence, of non-action; it remains nevertheless essentially a positive reality. Omission is not an affair of mere laziness or fatigue, it does not express simply an inaptitude for choosing and deciding. Well to the contrary, it is like the twin sister—and as vicious—of the active transgression that unfolds in an abundance of cries, gestures and actions. Despite its modesty, its silence, its apparent passivity, omission is truly a conscious and knowledgeable consent to the advent of evil, to the victory that evil wins over the good: ultimately it is no longer a reality of the negative order.

---

3. Scheler, *Wesen und Formen der Sympathie*, 156.

Contrary to the non-active façade of omission, deformity is found so to speak halfway between the negative and the positive. We are hardly prepared to attribute to the phenomena of evil an eidetics properly speaking: if the moments of vice are certainly not only negations, privations of elements or of properties of virtue, we hesitate to assign them forms, proper qualities. We would rather be inclined to characterize the quidditativeness of the wicked in the register of *deformity*. The deformed is certainly lacking form but it is not simply the formless. It is an active opposition to form that leads to counterfeiting of form. Beside or in the margins of Form, the deformed makes figures congregate that in their savage multiplicity witness to the indeterminate plurality of what is different than what it should be. The name of the demon is "legion" (Luke 7:30) and effectively the cohorts of the deformed surround form, bypass it, scatter traps on its path and disturb its beautiful simplicity. The vision of the deformed resolutely leaves behind it variations of negativity, poor artifices wishing to explain the mysteries of evil by ontological abstractions, moments of negativity. Yet despite the vigorous alterations to which it submits form, deformity is still only a prehistory or prefiguration of the positive reality of evil. It is the twisting of form, of essence, its stricture or evaporation but not yet its surpassing. If evil is a positive reality, then positive amounts to a *position* and position is never the external, partial manipulation of a thing but a procedure that affects it in its entirety and modifies its situation, its order. The idea of deformity very well surpasses the themes of weakness, absence and non-being but ultimately it is still located on a quidditative plane. The deformed belongs to the world of essences: it is related to an essence that it bends, twists and assaults. Deformity is so to speak an offense perpetrated against an essence, it amounts to an interference with the eidetic vocation of a quality, a property, an entity. It is like an outrage perpetrated against the integrity of the form and, as such, it can elicit reactions of indignation, rejection, so many emotions and judgments in affinity with moral sense. However, despite its aptitude for engaging emotion, its "virtue" for provoking quasi-moral reactions, deformity still remains short of the true positivity proper to evil. The essential moment, "not to have to be" of the deformed is always located on the material plane. Deformity can represent a frontal attack on essence, it can lead to a deterioration that almost denatures it, yet its work is always confined in a world of the given, even if it is of the material, superior, eidetic given. But evil—and the good—are not realities of the material order, of the order of the given. If evil is positive, it takes a position, or rather it is a position, and precisely as this position it is incompatible with phenomena that are confined in a material, metaphysical register, in a register of simple entities, not tied together into a synthesis.

Originally position means simply the affirmation of the existence of something: "existence is positing,"[4] and only positing. Existence is not a predicate, it adds nothing to the content of the term of the judgment, of the intentional object. It does nothing

---

4. Kant, *L'unique fondement*, in *Oeuvres* 1, 327. (*Akad.* II, 73. "The Only Possible Argument in Support of a Demonstration of the Existence of God," in *Theoretical Philosophy, 1755–1770*, 119.)

but be, yet more or less intensely, which has hardly any metaphysical scope at all. In its literal truth position is doubtlessly only the attribution of existence but we know very well that there is no true conceptual difference between one hundred existing and non-existing thalers. However, there is a huge, infinite difference between one hundred counterfeit and one hundred legal thalers, and above all between stolen and given thalers. In its full, authentic sense position is not the assignment of existence to a content but a regime of predication where the synthesis that is judgment concerns the mutual relation of subject and predicate from which the order of moments and elements of the predicate unfolds. This position according to form has two levels: first, it concerns the configuration of eidetic moments from which consequences unfold concerning the conformity or non-conformity of a being to what we can call its native purpose. A second level exists: moral position, according to good and evil. Here also the conformity or not of an act or a being to its vocation is what is in question, but non-conformity is not simply a function of physico-metaphysical failures and malfunctions: non-conformity—like conformity—is the work of the will.

Position according to form always concerns the order of component moments of an eidos. It is realized according to formal causality that founds an entity and is naturally transposed into final causality. When the parts of a table are wood of good quality, capable of bearing a minimum of weight and are arranged together according to the order required for the constitution of its form, the position that presides over the fabrication of this object and its maintenance in existence is the principle of the conformity of this piece of furniture to its natural vocation. If the wood is badly chosen or poorly cut, if the legs are not solid, if its surface is not level, the table cannot fulfill its vocation and ends up causing dysfunction in the daily life of those who want to take a meal on it. However, simple non-conformity or absence of conformity do not yet represent a true occurrence of bad position according to form. The latter is less absence of conformity than explicit non-conformity. Bad position according to form signifies an inversion, a reversal of the action, of the function of an entity that never amounts to a simple deficiency: the entity that does not fulfill its vocation not only forfeits, it also slides into an action that is not its own, it assumes a role that does not belong to it. Here we are dealing with phenomena of what can be called an inverted world and of which countless poems and proverbs provide ample illustrations. Aristophanes' formula is, "the highest to the lowest" (*Lysistrata 772*). It is the paradigm of this treasury of popular wisdom noting the paradoxes and inversions that punctuate the course of things. Rivers flow uphill, the wolf and donkey wear wings and (as is said in the eighth of Virgil's *Eclogues*) the wolf flees before the sheep, the oak-tree bears apples. Surprising and shocking phenomena, observed with a mixture of fear and astonishment constitute, so to speak, the pre-formation, the non-ethical narthex of the lofty and somber metaphysico-moral category of perversion, the highest manifestation of bad position according to form. Here also it is a matter of the mutual relation of predicates determining the relation of an entity to its natural vocation. But the principle and criterion of this relation no longer comes from merely the metaphysics of essences; it is determined by the super-eidē of good and evil that constitute the logic of the moral law, of love.

Perversion is the (complete) reversal of order and if it is illustrated above all by occurrences in the domain of sexuality. This is because sexuality belongs to the world of intersubjectivity which, as such, is a universe of the will. There are natural prefigurations of perversion; diverse attitudes and behaviors exist that could be subsumed under the word "perverted," but strictly speaking perversion concerns only the world of the will because only the will exists according to a radical duality. The use, or more exactly, the abuse of realities for ends eidetically deviant from their proper ones is called "perverse." However we could also insist that in the proper sense only an attitude, a feeling, a motive of our will is perverse that is not merely deviant from these ends but is diametrically opposed to them. Deformity designates a denaturation of contents; it denotes an important modification of entities on the material plane; it can be manifest under the form of an unlimited diversity. But good and evil, good and bad go further: without necessarily modifying contents on the material plane, essences according to their quiddity, position according to good or evil realizes a radical inversion of the configuration of givens. In the strict sense of the term, attitudes are perverted where a structure, an articulation to virtuous, good purpose is reoriented according to a bad purpose. Alms, the gift of charity, is a supreme instrument of helping a neighbor. Inspired by selfish preoccupations, by hypocrisy, by depraved desire, it becomes an authentic manifestation of wickedness, malignancy. Sexuality in itself is a powerful instrument of the expression, the preservation, even the intensification of love, whereas rape, with completely unchanged eidetic contents, but animated by selfish motivations, manifests the true contrary of loving ends.

Kant calls "the propensity to evil…the perverted attitude of the mind."[5] Perversion less signals a singular occurrence of opposition against the law than a constant attitude, a permanent disposition to accomplish immoral acts. The permanence of the disposition makes possible the surpassing of fixation on acts with bad, perverted qualities: it makes us think less about given transgressions than transgression as such. A perverse man inspires a kind of fear; he terrifies; we are horrified by his inclination to invert things. The pervert goes "against nature"; his opposition to the law is almost systematic. One could say that he not only does bad things but that he does them for themselves, he does them because they are bad. And he enjoys doing them. The metaphysico-moral theme of perversion serves as a lofty illustration, even a striking confirmation of the formal essence of evil. True malice is not found in the pursuit of forbidden pleasures or in the empty accumulation of riches, but in the intention to follow, in our actions, in our diverse activities, a lecherous inspiration. Reflection on

---

5. Kant, *La religion dans les limites de la raison*, in *Oeuvres* 3, 65 (Akad. VI, 48. *Religion within the Bounds of Mere Reason*, trans. Allen Wood and George di Giovanni [New York: Cambridge University Press, 1998] 68).

perversion allows the discernment of the metaphysical truth of evil, a formal category that cannot consist in matter, in the given, but belongs to the world of the will, alone capable of this supreme form of position that is *opposition*, opposition to the law, to love.

The Spirituality of Evil

Since philosophy's beginnings the principle of evil has been sought in matter, the unfortunate and inferior counterpart to spirit. By its heaviness, gravity and corruptibility matter was the *malum metaphysicum*, principle and root of physical and moral evils. Matter is the necessary part of imperfection in the world, the origin of all weakness and ultimately of all deviation. Conceived in itself as pure inertia, through its particular manifestations in the human body, matter founds pleasure, the infinitely dangerous principle of manifold deviations from the law. Greek metaphysics resulted in a primitive dualism taken over by Christian moralisms in which the body is opposed to the spirit like good to evil. Yet, strictly speaking, this is not a true dualism because its two foundational categories, its original counterparts, are ultimately only two instances of the given. And evil is not of the given but a formal relation.

With more or less nuance or qualifications, directly or indirectly, classical philosophy and morals considered matter as the principle of evil. But matter is not in itself bad: according to true Judeo-Christian inspiration, it is rather a reality to accept and to celebrate. It represents the victory over primordial chaos; it constitutes this world taken by its Creator as "good" (Gen 1:31). The primitive beauty of matter is so to speak confirmed by the mysteries of the History of Salvation. The Incarnation of the Word divinizes the human body; Christ—and in his wake all men—is resurrected in the flesh and the materials of the earth will be used to construct the "walls of the heavenly Jerusalem."[6] Against the mistakes and excesses of various anti-materialisms, Christian theosophy even comes to understand "the human body as such" as belonging to "the spirit."[7] Some people criticize matter as the nucleus of sin, but "the chains do not make the criminal; they are the consequences and witnesses of the crime." In fact, matter constitutes a kind of wall against the rage of "pure" evil's fire and "softens the devouring flame" of the evil will. "Without it, bad men would become even worse; they would prove similar to the devil if animality did not give them a kind of benignity."[8] In reality, this (Christian) vision of a true teleology of matter, its protective role against the assaults of "pure" evil does not infringe on the thesis of the profound neutrality of matter, its indifference in relation to good and evil. The wicked are traditionally compared to savage beasts. People speak of their brutality but who would call the true brutes, the animals "brutal"? Vicious human beings are given the epithet

---

6. Teilhard de Chardin, *Écrits de temps de la guerre*, 54.
7. Oetinger, *Oeffentliches Denkmal der Lehrtafel...*, in *Sämmtliche Schriften* II, 1, 217s.
8. Baader, *Werke* I, 37.

"brutal"! Quotidian language serves to prove the attempt to express the baseness and perversion of a man by calling him a "total animal" (*de parfait animal*). But a human being—as Aristotle said—can be only "better or worse than an animal" (*Nicomachean Ethics* 1150a).

The animal's assimilation to evil is a synonym for the condemnation of the body, with all its potentialities for pleasure that the moralist always distrusts. The body is evidently the nucleus, the principle for every possible excess of sexuality and it is equally the location and source for transgressions of lesser luster like gluttony and greed, or even alcoholism. Yet as the cipher of matter the body presents it only according to a certain weakening or qualification. When matter is neutral, morally indifferent in its status of metaphysical abstraction, the human body, composition or synthesis of psychical, physiological, and cultural elements, does not have the same condition of indifference. The body does not predetermine us for good or evil but it does contain an original implication with regard to a voluntary position. It possesses a moral inclination even if most often it is a matter of *im*-morality. In a suggestive formula, Schelling characterizes the body as "a flower from which some draw honey, others draw poison."[9] Honey and poison are not here physical materials: without relation to joy and suffering, pleasure and pain, they register a native range for the movements of the will. We could even conjecture that behind every façade of anti-material dualism, the moralizing interpretation of the body is a preparation for the Christian and Kantian teaching of the spirituality of evil. When the Scriptures reiterate the great affirmative doctrine: "the creatures of the world are wholesome; there is in them no poison or death" (Wisdom 1:14), it founds not only the teaching on the non-original character of the occurrence of evil, but it leads also to the thesis of its spirituality. Creatures, as such, have a native goodness; they are components of the world, sharing in its primitive order, and, deprived of the will, they can neither negate nor betray it. Man, as a voluntary being, is capable of opposing order. But man is not only will: if his will is sovereign, it is nevertheless exercised within a material organism that filters and subdues it. Evil as such cannot characterize a being composed of spirit and matter. It is in the power of the human will to accomplish syntheses of opposition but it *is still not* such a synthesis.

The lofty Christian teaching on the devil, a fallen angel who *became* evil, powerfully illustrates the spirituality of evil. The bad spirit, the devil—as theosophy will say—is "a spiritualist."[10] With its severe anti-sensualism, Christian moral theology has not lost from view the essential spirituality of evil. It has been capable of castigating the pleasures of the flesh, the excesses of food and drink, and takes a resolutely condemnatory position against the concessions of weakness, against attempts to indulge the body. It nevertheless continues to confess that in its pure form, according to its premier paradigm, evil is not an affair of matter but the spirit, it comes not from

---

9. Schelling, *Conférences de Stuttgart*, in *Oeuvres métaphysiques*, 244.
10. Baader, *Werke* II, 416s.

the body but from the will. The active and efficacious archetype of evil is the devil who wants to extend his control over men, who wants to possess souls. Humans sell themselves to the devil for power, wealth, pleasure. The devil is only interested in their soul. He experiences no passion except the passion to do evil and to make evil done. Man pursues his goals through different transgressions where the bad intention is not willed for its own sake but only as it permits the satisfaction of desire. In fact, even the man wading in the mire of the grossest sin is ultimately inspired by spiritual passions, the three "idealist passions" of Kant: cupidity, ambition, the desire for domination. The man who transgresses against his neighbor, killing him, is certainly prepared to injure him and to deprive him of his pleasures and possessions. But behind transgressions against the neighbor, as violent and as material as they are, very often lies the passion to excel, to be known. Those careful observers who study human behavior and analyze human motivations know and teach that "the desire to be esteemed by others is a natural need as real as hunger. . .no appetite is more universal in human nature than that of honor." In short: one is moved by "a passion to be distinguished," by "a desire to be noted, considered, esteemed, praised, loved and admired by one's neighbors."[11]

The esteem and respect of others can certainly entail material profit, accumulation of wealth, attention and services and favors of various kinds. For the essential, one no less finds them when moved by an "idealist passion." The most puerile vanity, like the highest, pride, is hardly seeking an increase of possessions. What one seeks for so ardently are diverse figures of "greatness" that stand out against the background comparison and are thus situated on an immaterial plane. The immateriality proper to idealist passions is even found within the most primitive, vulgar vices. The excess constituting gluttony does not consist in the quantitative increase in food intake but in the passion with which one pursues particular dishes, in the concentration of attention on questions of secondary order and importance. Alcoholism certainly implies the consumption of a great quantity of brandy, wine or beer but the end it pursues is less tasting the drink itself than the strange freedom and enthusiasm produced by inebriation, which is therefore a contingent example, a kind of *ersatz* of spiritual realization.

The spiritual nature of evil is clearly seen through the figures under which it is habitually presented. Gluttony and the undue accumulation of possessions are authentic examples of vice and yet the perverted man, the miscreant, the traitor is hardly exhibited with the features of a fat man; the double chin does not suggest to us the author of dirty tricks; the paunchy guy is hardly perceived as the villain, the hypocrite, the pervert. Sadistic murderers are hardly ever imagined as overweight and Satan "the most unlimited" among the figures of evil is often represented with the features of a gaunt ascetic. A medieval story sees the demon as a person "without a back,"[12] in other words lacking thickness, without true substance. The essential immateriality,

---

11. Adams, *Discourses on Davila*, 28, 51, 26.
12. César de Heisterbach, *Miraculorum* 3, 6.

the spirituality of the devil shows through that eidetic intuition of substantiality. From a properly material point of view, the gauntness, the insubstantiality of the wicked is located in the proximity to weakness, to lack and therefore ultimately, to non-being. But—precisely—insubstantiality here goes together with intensity, gauntness and pallor goes with a dark acuity. If the demon has no back, if he is therefore reduced to a bi-dimensional condition, this does not affect his limitlessness but rather illustrates and manifests it.

The Impossibility of Evil

Spirituality as already the positivity of evil appears in a spectacular contrast with its primordial metaphysical truth: evil has no meaning; it is even a non-sense. It is tempting to say that in one way or another every non-sense is finally evil, but what matters is to understand and to affirm that evil as such is non-sense. The primordial essence—or un-essence—of evil is to be non-sense, and this absence or rather opposition to meaning governs and determines interrogations on its origin (in other words the efficient causality that it would have made happen) as well as on its role and teleological significance and therefore the final causality that would justify its existence. The great question emerging before the spectacle, or rather the attacks of evil—when you are subject to or see others subject to terrible sickness, accidents, cataclysms, or the hate and cruelty of other men—is *why*? Why does the playful little child waste away from cancer? Why does the young woman in the flower of youth die in a car accident? Or even more generally: why do the innocent suffer? Why is the good man persecuted? Why is the militant for a noble cause tortured? The why is an elementary cry rising up from our gut. It expresses revolt before the turns things take, an instinctive refusal against every occurrence and epiphany of evil. Eventually the why will be revealed as the true nerve of interrogations that lead to the necessary recognition of meaning, but on an elementary, empirical plane (as well as a phenomenological one). The why in face of evil amounts to the confession of the creature's radical confusion, to the expression of powerless revolt against the scandal of it all.

Philosophy tries to conceptualize the cry, to unfold its metaphysical implications. This leads to the double exclamation: evil cannot be and it cannot be willed. If the great classical systems strove to think evil as non-being, this is because they found it impossible to reconcile with being. "The extermination of evil from existence" is not a sophistication or ratiocination, a futile dialectical exercise. It is rather the necessary translation of the intuition of the impossibility of a phenomenon of anti-being. In fact, it is the realization of the positivity of evil that leads the vision of its impossibility to its logical consequences. As long as evil is read as lack, privation, weakness, it always remains conceived as having a role in the very universe where it is lack, privation, weakness. However, when its malignity is understood as radical positivity, the impossibility of the *malum* imposes itself on thought. Everything that is possible is so only according to the regime of being, within the arena of being. But, opposed to being, evil can be located only elsewhere, outside of being. It is thus necessarily impossible.

The paradoxical, if you like, excessive idea of the impossibility of evil has its counterpart in the Socratic aporia: evil is involuntary. Evil is profoundly irrational, belonging to non-sense, so how could it be consciously chosen? The proper, intentional object of the will is the good, so how could its contrary be willed? Since Socrates, rationalists of every stripe debated this problematic. It has myriads of transpositions onto the plane of moral conscience, even the domain of simple pragmatic explanation: one attempts to show that one had opted for evil without very well understanding it, that one was deceived, had been induced to err, or even that one was constrained, forced against one's will. We must admit the effective advent of evil, of evils, but we can quibble and justify ourselves, discuss the circumstances, plead ignorance and powerlessness. Since Aristotle human good sense has considered the arguments trying to prove the unconscious and involuntary character of human transgressions as absurd and fallacious. But men always venture into naïve and complicated or fastidious explanations that are also sometimes full of good sense for the sake of trying to unseat possible and actual accusations against their behavior and actions. When one cannot deny having done evil (and most of often this is the case), one tries to show that one has not consciously chosen it. The psalmist confesses to having sinned but rare are the transgressors who admit to having purely, integrally willed evil.

The thesis that "nobody does evil voluntarily" cannot be defended as such, but it is cashed out into an infinity of reflections on the degrees and levels of culpability. By ricochet it will also allow a better philosophical understanding of evil. The same thing goes for the paradox of the impossibility of evil which, all the while resolutely opposing Neoplatonic subterfuges, deepens the understanding of its para-ontological reality. When Platonism explains that evil has no idea, modern thought will define it as "a reality...that is not possible but only actual."[13] This conception of the actuality of sin as preceding—on the noetic, conceptual plane—its possibility will have immense repercussions in the interrogation on its coming into being. How to conceive the origin of evil? If God is, from where does evil come? If being is perfect, how does its perfection admit the advent of evils?

Theodicies are often absurd, ridiculous, even irritating and shocking. At their origin believing reason, or even reason, as such, is held at bay. Reason wants to affirm the perfection of God and Being, the integral domination of means and order in the world, but perfection is burdened with imperfection, meaning is overwhelmed by non-sense on all sides. Theodicy, the desperate attempt to "rehabilitate" the Ultimate, is born out of the unbearable test that the presence of evil imposes on reason. The intuition of the innate intelligibility of being, of the immaculate purity of the Most High violently slams into this sordid mixture of goods and evils that fills the world. We find both ferocious beasts and gentle, innocent beings, both tigers and lambs, and the tiger

---

13. Steffens, *Christliche Religionsphilosophie* II, 58ss.

makes us ask, "Did he who made the Lamb make thee?"[14] But our repulsion before the impure mixture of good and evil, and already of the sacred and profane, is far surpassed by the torment of intelligence before the pullulation of evils, the suffering of innocents, the victories that vice always has over virtue. We then leap into the arms of apologetics, attempting to show that evil is necessary for the world, even for the good itself. At the same time we try to minimize it. Evils doubtlessly exist, but not as many as is first thought and they are actually not so bad! The adventures of life are doubtlessly paired with defeats and tragedies, but, after all, "we do not erect the mountains without digging into abysses"![15] The universe is full of obscurity but the light can truly shine only within the darkness that enhances its clarity. Individuals certainly suffer but their suffering is bad only for themselves; it is useful, even necessary for the people who share in it, for the proper ordering of the whole world. Ultimately even moral evil seems to have its place: "Wickedness of souls has its place in the beauty of the universe; what is contrary to nature for them is for the universe conformed to nature" (*Enneads* III, ii, 17). The principal "argument" of theodicy is to recall the partial and subordinated position of the individual within the cosmos, the interpretation of what happens to a particular being from the perspective of the whole. But these comparative arguments that want to understand the individual starting from the Whole that contains and hangs over it are proven insufficient and in need of completion. One has then to insist on the relatively lesser place of evils in the world which leads to the statistical exercises of the Deist theologian who—to prove the immense superiority of goods over evils in this world—reports that of "6420 patients admitted to a hospital over a given period, 5476 were quickly healed and only 234 died. . ."[16] The telos of these attempts—and this in the face of sufferings and horrors of history—is to show and demonstrate "how slender is the entity of evil."[17]

These desperate attempts appear both ridiculous and shocking. And Leibniz's optimism (but not only his) can be excoriated as an obnoxious absurdity that amounts to "a bitter mockery of the unspeakable sufferings of mankind."[18] Philosophical and political optimism can demonstrate a lamentable superficiality and an unpardonable flippancy: is this a reason to slide into pessimism, to raise death and non-being as principles and ideals of existence? After all, pessimism is also only a primitive and unilateral doctrine: instead of a philosophical investigation of evil after formal considerations, it slides into a monist vision where the whole is subsumed by evil, a material essence! But beyond the deficiencies of theodicy *and* pessimism, another way is still to

14. Blake, "The Tyger," in *Songs of Innocence and Experience*, 148.

15. Chardin, *Écrits de temps de la guerre*, 77.

16 Thus W. Paley in Cherry, *Nature and Religious Imagination*, 98.

17. Leibniz, *Theodicée*, § 378 (*Theodicy*, ed. Austin Farrar, trans. E. M. Huggard [La Salle, IL: Open Court, 1951] 352).

18. Schopenhauer, *Le Monde comme volonté et comme représentation* IV, § 59, 614 (*The World as Will and Representation*, trans. E. F. J. Payne [New York: Dover, 1969] 326).

be explored in which religious inspiration, that of radical piety (instead of an intransigent fideism) leads rather to a renewal of the teaching on evil. One of the fundamental questions of theodicy was that addressed to the big yellow cat: "Did the same one who made the lamb make you?" The answer is given by the Bible: "the Lord causes to die and to live" (1 Sam 2:6), as well as by the Quran: "your Lord. . .is the one who makes live and makes die" (LIII 42–44). These passages ignore or rather reject theodicy; they start with the intuition of the all-powerful, of the unlimited efficaciousness of the Most High. However, the all-powerful is located here on an essentially ontological plane, that of being, not of the will. Death—physical death—is certainly an evil, in fact, the greatest of evils, but it should not be confused with moral evil. Moral evil is not supposed to have been called into existence by God. Theologico-philosophical speculations produce extraordinary distinctions in order to explain the dependence of every entity on God, creator and master of Providence, without having to attribute to him responsibility for moral evil. The great principle of the distinction between the ontological and the moral is the one between the material and formal. The material of each of our moral actions, the gesture making the fatal blow that deposits the poison or pulls the trigger, belongs to the ontological sphere. Its formal one—in other words, the intention animating its action—belongs to the arena of the will. The material of moral action, the matter that intention supports, is neutral, indifferent to the distinction between good and evil (as I have said). Each moral act possesses in this way the two levels of reality and the causality of its appearing. This duality can be tranquilly observed, it can present only peaceful parallelisms where God and the free creature, the ontological and the moral seem to get along well. But there are actions—and this is the case with every harmful, culpable, perverted action—where the necessary duality of being and intention (*facultas* and *voluntas*, willing power and moral intention in Augustinian terms) appear in a striking contrast, according to an unsupportable paradox. In order to dramatize the irreducible but also indissociable duality of the two causalities, Malebranche recalls the case of the murderer: "It is divine concurrence that makes the hand holding the sword "swing" down on the head of the victim and it is therefore the efficacious causality of the creator-conserver who is put in service of the criminal intention."[19] The same logic undergirds the sacrilege of illicit consecration and communion: God was obedientially bound to the gesture that transubstantiates the host and he maintains in existence the act by which a man mocks his holy abandonment in the Eucharist—blasphemy. To commune in a state of sin is "to cast God down to earth. . .while it is in my power. . .God cannot escape the sinful mouth that voluntarily drinks in its own damnation."[20] By the *voluntas*, an aspect of reality unhinges from being. And the bad will makes this duality appear as an opposition.

---

19. Malebranche, *Recueil de toutes les réponses à Monsieur Arnauld*, in Oeuvres VII, 561.
20. Greene, *Le Fond du problème: Rocher de Brighton*, trans. M. Sibon (Paris: Bouquins, 1981), 461, 322 in Hatem, *L'Écharde du Mal dans la Chair de Dieu*, 187s.

Radical Evil

Before the advent of the distinction between the material and formal in evil, but, in fact, even concomitant with it, philosophy was shown incapable of taking account of the radical originarity of evil. Perplexedly, reflection appealed to resources of linguistic neologisms. Augustine taught that if one wanted to attribute a cause to evil it could not be an efficient cause but only a causa *deficiens*.[21] Thomas will say that evil is not a cause that acts, a causa *agendo* but a causa *deagendo*.[22] The use of the prefix *de-* usually signals a negation. In this context it expresses the intuition of an act external to what is in progress in the world of being and thus a non-ontological causality. Sensing the insufficiency or rather inadequacy of the distinction between causing evil and simply admitting it, theologico-metaphysical speculation will frequently make recourse to metaphorical expressions. Some theologians talk about the "work of the left hand" of the Rabbis to explain that God created impure things like a person who "reluctantly throws something over his shoulder to his enemy. . .after having turned his back to him."[23] Reformed theologians up to Barth and Tillich spoke of the gift of existence made to evil by repression and rejection. These suggestive distinctions (albeit lacking in metaphysical rigor) will ultimately end up giving way to a philosophical theory founded on the radical autarky of the will in relation to being. Once the will is dissociated from being, it is removed from the competency of ontology and the causality of evil can be studied anew. It will finally appear in its complete autarky that manifests the vision of radical evil.

Evil is radical; it is not absolute. It enjoys an autarky—albeit an asymmetrical one. It does not depend on Being and does not find its origin in God. And yet it is still not a true counterpart of Being or an anti-God. The dualism taught by the philosophy of the will does not establish a double ontology. It professes the radical opposition between good and bad will that joins and divides the world of the will, independent of the world of being. The great metaphysical thesis on the will is that it is truly *from itself* and this auto-origination receives its elucidation starting with meditation on the bad will. In order to make clear interrogation on the origin of evil we do not need to ask with Boethius "where does evil come from" but "where does the bad will come from"? And the sole adequate response is: it comes from itself and only from itself. Leibniz wanted to rehabilitate the Socratic argument on the bad will. One doubtlessly wants evil, he argued, but one does not want it truly, or one wants it rather as if on did not. This is very clear and follows a good logic. One cannot want evil because in the face of a choice between good and evil only a bad person could choose evil. Consequently, in order to desire evil, one would already have to be evil. In other words "no

---

21. Augustine, *De Civitate Dei* XII, 7.
22. Thomas Aquinas, *De Malo* I, 1 ad. 8.
23. Schneur Zalman of Lyadi, *Likutei Amarim-Tanya*, 91.

one is himself voluntarily wicked, otherwise he would be it before having done it."[24] The argument aims for the refutation of the possibility of desiring evil consciously through the apparently totally absurd idea of a wickedness preceding any choice. But this wickedness is ultimately not at all absurd: supporting it is the observation of the innate and non-provoked malice of children and adults that develops into the doctrine of Original Sin and which is its ultimate range. The bad will, moral evil, is of a radical originarity. When I wish evil, it is I who wish it, not another, and when I try to "specify" the moment when I began to will evil, I find myself bound by inextricable difficulties. If per chance the interrogation to which I submit my memory amounts to determining the moment and act in and through which I engaged in evil, I will still not be able to understand *how* and *why* I have been able to make the "choice" of evil. Leibniz was right but despite himself: in order to choose evil, one must already be bad, in other words, have already willed the bad. Consequently, I have been already bad before every determinable decision; I will evil from the beginning.

This repetition of the Leibnizian argument does not have the purpose of prostrating man through an immemorial subjection to evil. It simply wants to show that evil, the bad will, is not come into the world from the fact of a force or an external or prior event, but that it has been able to appear only through and starting from itself. "Sin came into the world through sin!"[25] This definition seems to condemn reflection on the bad will to circle around and around, representing it then as constituting a circle—one that is certainly vicious. However, the circle of vice is almost perfect, impeccable; it amounts to imitating or rather aping the divine aseity. It is very difficult to conceive a causality that leads to evil, to assign to evil a cause. Yet if one gets there, this will be through a kind of tautological repetition. Evil is by virtue of evil, the bad will is by virtue of the bad will. This autistic, if you like, auto-constitutive condition of evil belongs to it thanks to the will of which it is, in its own way, a true realization. The will is indivisible, unrepresentable, homogenous. If it is at each moment to be understood as resuming and reaffirming itself, this repetition and reaffirmation has something puzzling about it. The puzzle of the mind before this mystery of the will when it is bad will joins astonishment to fright and perplexity to terror. The *hapax* of the bad will parades forth the contradictory, the mysterious, the shocking. The bad will does not have a true beginning in time, though it is still not eternal. You can understand how it might be the object of an option, or more precisely, how it could be chosen and yet come from itself. On the other hand, the life of the will is conceived only through the apparently insoluble opposition between its always intact power of recovering and altering its intention, even reversing its order. After all, if at a given moment the will wills—and it does so integrally and without mixture, without degree—good or evil,

---

24. Leibniz, *Confessio Philosophi*, 77.

25. Kierkegaard, *Le concept d'angoisse*, in *Oeuvres complètes* 7, 47 (*The Concept of Dread*, trans. Walter Lowrie [Princeton: Princeton University Press, 1957] 20; translation modified).

its truth as will implies that at each moment it is able to pass beyond its preceding determination in order to rush in the opposite direction.

The philosophy of the will cannot thus insist on the essential homogeneity of *voluntas*, on its condition of domination of integral self. The will is its own mistress at each moment, possessing a capacity to translate its incessantly active presence to self: the will wills and it does not, as a plant grows or a river flows. It is only action, not passivity, and the action that it is, it is at each moment. In other words the will is an action that takes place without interruption, an intention that is incessantly reaffirmed. However, this representation of its incessant action does not have to lead to a nominalism of the will. The will is not a succession of atom-volitions but rather a thread of intentions that, despite their authentic singularity of existence, constitute (according to a continuity of insertion and mutual agency) an extending line. This continuity and prolongation of self does not at all compromise the integral self-mastery at each moment. The permanence of the line is perfectly compatible with the consciousness of the weight of each fraction, each moment of time, of the vigorous intensity by which the will does not stop deploying and renewing its intention. An apparently insoluble contradiction opposes the essential thesis of the power of unlimited renewal of the will to any attachment in a constant, arrested figure. If the will is mistress of itself it cannot be subject to any fixation or coagulation. But every permanent structure seems to confiscate the autonomy of the intention, to deliver it over to the power of exteriority. Consequently the intention that endures almost without being called into question represents an authentic specimen of alienation from its self-mastery. The argument seems to operate through a paradox but it will nevertheless have a true metaphysical range if in its figures that remain the will effectively gives itself up to the exterior, abandoned to a power other than its own. But the moralists of every era strive to show that the will can, even must want to take a permanent shape and does not give itself over to the exterior, is not alienating itself. The analysis of moral character or even of vice and virtue illustrates with clarity the essential compatibility between the integral self-mastery of the will and its consolidation into a structure. In fact, it will end up leading to the conviction that this self-prolongation, this consolidation represents the highest form of the exercise of freedom, the supreme reality of the good and bad wills.

The intuition of the permanence of the moral will was represented under the form of a continuous line of intentions. But it would like better to surpass the vision of the will as line in favor of a structure with density and depth. The linear succession of similar intentions constitutes a less faithful image of the auto-repetition and auto-prolongation of the good or bad will than this incarnation of the permanence of moral will that is character. Its character has been called the moral nature of man but it has nothing to do with naturality. The character is certainly a reality of which the constancy and determination appear to be at the antipodes of a conception that would make the autarky, the effective freedom of the will depend on the possibility of an unlimited questioning of its choice. Character is certainly an internal, immanent determination, but one incompatible with the unconditional autonomy of the will. In reality, despite the whims of a superficial rationalism, constancy and permanence are not opposed to its freedom, but translate the vigor of its self-mastery. Our character is, so to speak, innate; we have had it almost as if from the beginning; we have possessed it since infancy. No one remembers having contracted his character, no one can say the moment that he chose it, when he had undertaken the course of action that led to its installation, its fixation, its reinforcement. We have not called forth our character; we have not "chosen" it;[26] yet we feel ourselves responsible for the volitions and actions that we accomplish starting from and in terms of it. Bad character is not something that falls on you from the outside. It is not something that is "in us without us" (Malebranche): it is not like a kidney stone or blood clot, not even like a pit "in" our psyche. We have certainly not chosen character, but we have assumed it.

The theme of character clearly illustrates the weight of the will, its inscription in existence and duration. Instead of representing the alienation of the will, character serves rather as guardrail before the temptations to confound freedom of the will with its dispersal in contingency. It allows reflection to distinguish the always-intact power of recommencing the will from the diverse driftings of the will into the accidental. In short, it shows that moral self-determination does not yet amount to alienation. However, the aporias of character are only the first paradoxes encountered by the investigation into the bad will. The reinterpretation of the idea allows the refutation of the accusation of an alienation that would take place unconsciously, in an immemorial past, outside of any trial and all choice. But what about the case of figures in which it is subject to a freely chosen determination, for which it will have opted knowingly? Theology calls the "servile will" the figure of the sinful will abandoned to transgression and which can no longer retrace its steps. The power of the will remains entire, but it is from now on at the service of a culpable intention. The mind is conscious of alienation, the heart can suffer the powerlessness of trying to tear itself from evil, but the will continues even despite itself to will and therefore accomplish the evil that offends and torments it. In this condition of subjection the will is incapable of enacting a reversal but it is still responsible and culpable. This enslavement is incomprehensible to logical reason; it shocks the conscience and defies good sense. How is the free will lost and lost so freely? And if it was freely lost, how could it not rediscover and return to itself in order to regain mastery over itself? The apparently paradoxical response is found at the end of a reinterpretation of the power of free will. A will engaged only in a conditional way, always capable of going back on its choice, of rediscovering a free disposition, would lack true seriousness, ultimate radicality. The ethical world, that of good and evil, is not a theatre; moral action is not a game. A game of course can be deeply serious, but ultimately it remains a game; it is an engagement that can be very passionate but which remains nevertheless temporary, conditional. Independently of the details of its theological interpretation, the servile will is a figure of the high

26. Schelling, *Conférences de Stuttgart*, in *Oeuvres métaphysiques*, 211.

radicality of the moral will. Instead of presenting *voluntas* as succumbing to a temptation from the outside, the theological notion of the enslaved will reveals its immanent efficaciousness, its ultimate autarky that makes possible its definitive engagement from which it can no longer return by its own powers. The subject of the servile will is like the man who commits suicide. He destroys his life by his own power, but he does not dispose of the power to bring it back from the death he gave to it. The sinner freely chooses evil, but he cannot be liberated from it by his own power. Instead of constituting an example of the limits of freedom to the degree that it can be forfeit, the servile will shows instead its unlimitedness. The free will is not content to have a hold over everything, it enjoys also and above all a hold over itself.

The servile will and Original Sin are figures of the radicality of the bad will, incapable of tearing itself away from the chains of transgression that it has imposed on itself. But these supreme illustrations of the ultimate seriousness of the bad will find a limit. If the servile will is not capable of freeing itself, it can be freed by divine pardon. If the subject of Original Sin cannot be redeemed by itself, it may partake of the work of Redemption thanks to the merits of Jesus Christ. In other words, by being gagged and bound, incapable of delivering itself from the evil that it has provoked, the will may be untied by an external force. Its alienation may be only partial, temporary. A figure of the bad will, its supreme figure, exists. In it the option for evil excludes any question of a choice. This supreme figure of the bad will is Hell.

Hell is a scandal to believing reason, in fact, to any reason, to, if you like, reason as such. The bad will leading to hell, or rather that *is* hell is non-sensical. It is evil in the strict sense and evil is non-sense. Hell is thus non-sense as such, non-sense in its "plenitude" and infinite efficaciousness! For believing reason the teaching on eternal damnation constitutes a veritable Stations of the Cross: how can an eternal privation and punishment be compatible with the Sovereign Goodness that is God? Despite its supreme pertinence this interrogation does not belong to metaphysics, in the occurrence of the philosophy of the will that wishes to bracket interrogation on the transcendent Judgment that confirms hell. Philosophy is content to envisage hell as the paroxysm and paradigm of the bad will, as the ultimate demonstration of the power and seriousness of the will. Hell illustrates the perfect immanence and infinite range of the will. In and through it the bad will reaches its end. This amounts to saying that it takes responsibility for itself and curves back into itself, becoming (infinitely) permanent. The eternity of hell witnesses to the ultimate seriousness that philosophy assigns to moral action. Transgressions, in fact, *the* transgression of which the weakest and most uncultivated is capable, demonstrate an infinite significance; it separates its agent from every relation of love with the other and excludes all communion with Love. And each will, the will of each man is then an entirely closed world, horribly sufficient to itself, enjoying an abyssal autarky. It has been written that hell is other people, but this is false. In the strict sense hell is oneself in separation from every other, a life lived in immanence, without hope of any unsealing from the outside.

Beyond the scattering into particular crimes localizable in time and space, beyond also the alienations (ultimately curable) of Original Sin and the servile will, hell represents the sui generis metaphysical universe of the bad will.

Evil for Evil's Sake

"Descriptions" of hell paint the torments and physical pains of the damned in horrific detail, but from a metaphysical point of view, hell is only a world of the will. Damnation is a result of accomplished misappropriation, of the definitive *aversio* of the free creature with regard to the Good, a misappropriation that is and only is the world of the will, of the will turned towards itself, curved back and fixed on itself. For Christian theosophy "only one's own will burns in hell,"[27] the will that is the essence of the life of rejection of the good, of installation in evil. Strictly speaking, damnation is an affair of the will; it illustrates and above all corroborates the teaching on the spirituality and radicality of evil. The bad will that is damned and ceaselessly reaffirms its damnation, its sinking into damnation, finalizes the metaphysical "purification" of the will. Reflection ultimately bracketed the material concomitants of transgression in order to reach the comprehension of the essentially spiritual nature of evil. However, the conception of the spirituality of evil is only the next-to-last stage of the formalization that alone allows the conception of the truth of evil. We still must negotiate this last stage, which leads to the realization of the proper disinterestedness of the bad will. Philosophical reflection clearly explains that riches and pleasures are only simple means for the bad intention of which the ultimate end would not belong to the moral order. One could almost say that pleasures and riches are only "pathological" accompaniments of the "practical" transgression, even as they are only lures and instruments that permit and foster the fragmentation and plunging of the will in evil. As paradoxical as this may appear, it is difficult to engulf in evil. It is difficult to desire evil for evil's sake, to remain constant, unwavering in the pursuit of iniquity when one is not aided and animated by the concrete and present recompense of a pleasure or possession. Following the philosophy of Duty, on the lookout for impure motives of his action, the man of "pure" bad will "should anxiously ask: have I done evil for evil's sake? Have I not acted with interest?"[28]

But very unfortunately, if the disinterested aspiration to evil is difficult it is nevertheless possible, even if this obstinacy, this callousness is only rarely found. Occurrences of bad will exist where evil is willed for evil's sake, purely, disinterestedly. The disinterestedness of the bad will is not something contingent or fortuitous: it takes place in knowledge of the cause, without the influence of lust or fear. Scotus defined pure sin as the condition of "the will that sins without sensible inclination and without

---

27. Weigel, *Vom Ort der Welt*, in *Sämtliche Schriften* I, 75s.
28. Sartre, *Saint Genêt, comédien et martyr*, 33.

error."[29] To sin without error signifies transgression with perfect knowledge; sinning without desire amounts to willing evil without attenuating circumstances, excuses of weakness or passion. A bad will so devoid of all reason, of all causality, of every heteronomous motivation that would relativize, blur, or mitigate its incandescent purity is properly diabolical. It does not tend towards evil with something else in view, beyond or outside of it; it wants evil for evil's sake. The diabolical condition of evil is seen in a particularly repulsive way in the figure of Eichmann. He sent millions of Jews to their death, but he reassured the tribunal—and there is no reason to doubt this—that he "had nothing against the Jews." Eichmann despised his colleagues who profited from their situation by extorting riches or favors from their victims; he himself sought no gratification, he only wanted to do his duty. . . Eichmann did not hate his victims and effectively, he was not led by lively or violent feelings of resentment, rejection or contempt. His bad will had nothing pathological about it, it was purely *practical*, a bad will that is only bad will, belonging to an evil that is only evil.

With the clarification of the necessarily disinterested essence of bad will the circle is closed. From now on evil shines with the light of a black star, it radiates with the anti-light of an energy that does not arouse any compromise with the heaviness of matter, the longings of the flesh, or even the vanities of the spirit. And its purity appears against the background of the rejection of all interestedness. But this discourse dealing in superlatives, this exalted liturgy chanted in the honor of moral evil, evil par excellence, the sole level of evil that is only evil seems, all the same, to leave outside of consideration phenomena that constitute the great portion of human experience of evil. The will is the principle and site of the highest manifestations of evil, but it is far from being the exclusive manifestation. The *malum metaphysicum* dear to the Leibnizians, in fact, to all classical philosophy, has doubtlessly hardly any meaning for a reflection where good and evil are interpreted starting from the life of the will. But who would refuse the appellation "evil" for certain harmful realities, terrible occurrences of material existence? Earthquakes and tidal waves, fires and epidemics or even car accidents, but also fractured or broken bones, cancers, or more simply the flu, insomnia, and bad digestion are each in their own way authentic specimens of evil, calamities that make a Calvary out of human existence when they do not quickly bring it to its end and leave it in a terrible condition. And on a different plane, but essentially in affinity or direct analogy with the evils of the body, one has only to recall the problems of depression, anguish, neurosis, and psychosis in order to cut short the too facile attempts to restrict Evil to the moral world, to keep it locked up exclusively in the register of the will. But despite the terrible reality of diverse physical evils in our world, only a resolutely voluntarist reading of evil seems to be able to do justice to its metaphysical truth; it alone can lead to a comprehension of evil proper to a universe of novelty and of free aspiration for the good. The integration of physical evil into the universe of moral evil is the unique discourse that can hold onto a philosophy

---

29. Scotus, *Ordinatio* II, d. 3. q. n. 2.

that is neither ontological nor theological, that is neither theodicy nor ontodicy, but tries to present a metaphysical interpretation of existence in its synthetic condition. Moral evil assumes physical evil: the will takes charge of the flesh. The body, the flesh is (as it were) plowed and penetrated by the will: it must be included in metaphysical considerations. If the body has an effective significance for the synthesis that I am, it must be affected by the will, subsumed under it, dominated by it. In other words, its phenomenological (or rather, metaphysical) bracketing is possible. Physical evil will be tacitly present well into the depths of spiritual evil, well into the extremities of pure evil. The inclusion, the integration of physical evil into moral evil unseals the circularity, opens the way for the surpassing of its strange self-absorption. Pure evil has been studied up to now according to its mechanism, its structure, its functioning. From now on a new question must be posed: what does this (pure, spiritual) evil affect? If the truth of evil is located in its autarky, its perfect immanence, by its very nature this immanence has a transcendental significance. Evil is not a thing, an entity, a given sphere of the real; it is a relation and it is evil precisely by means of this relation that it is. Evil is relation through what is external to it and through itself. In other words, it is evil for that which it is not and is also evil for itself.

The bad man is harmful to others and he wants to harm them. He makes them suffer in their flesh; he deprives them of their possessions, makes them undergo harsh treatment, submits them to torture. But these occurrences of physical evil inflicted on a neighbor are only secondary manifestations of the primary moral evil of hate for him. Hate is addressed to the other as other, as free will. The hateful opposition to the other is concerned with the spontaneity, the power of creativity proper to the other, and therefore also the "material" means that this spontaneity can take charge of, disseminate. If slavery is an absolutely immoral condition this is because it denies, attacks, even slowly obliterates the aspiration to exit the natural immanence that man shares with other creatures. The will acts by virtue of the spontaneity each free being has and is the nerve of his constant interior renewal. But this renewal can be carried out only through eidetic structures in which freedom is exercised. The eidetic structures of human freedom are essences and laws that allow it to become self aware, to identify and affirm itself. Freedom is certainly a pure eruption, but it emerges in a particular will, and this will needs points of reference and principles for its effective exercise. The reign of the law is a metaphysical condition for the exercise of individual freedom. It encourages the deployment of a spontaneity that in a world of non-law would remain latent but finally shrivels up into itself. Laws mark out the course of spontaneity and allow, even encourage, creative action in the world. The reign of the law (and of laws) returns to the world of essences as to its ultimate foundation. The norms of social existence have their ultimate source in the essences that define beings (Arendt). The Nazi regime was always transgressing laws that it did not even deem useful enough to abolish. The ultimate perversion, the true principle of all malignity was supposed to have been condensed into the Jewish race. But Hitler declared: I am the one who declares who is a Jew! The refusal to admit differentiated, normative essences also characterized the other great historical instance of totalitarianism, communist Russia. The Soviet regime first persecuted diverse social categories of the population. Then it proceeded to arrest and execute en masse persons of every social origin and political opinion. And in the archives of the secret police in Smolensk directives were discovered that prescribed the arrest of a certain percentage of the inhabitants of a given district, without any distinct criteria.

Treatment of human beings according to the simple quantitative criteria expresses a radical refusal to consider them according to what they are in themselves. Quantitative criteria are extrinsic; they bracket the essence, the proper content of beings. Henceforth deprived of any point of reference, men and women no longer know what they ought to do nor in what they should hope since they no longer know *what* they are. The will to enslave the other wants to reduce this other to our mercy. Deprived of any eidetic identity, a man no longer comes to act because he no longer comes to desire. The intentional object of the pure hate of another, of bad will toward him is ultimately his will. The malice that is the principle of my opposition to the other, of my negation of his freedom passes through diverse strategies in order to impoverish, to torment, in other words to elicit evils that strike him. But the truth of the bad will, its practical truth, is not to cause the enemy to suffer but to make him *bad*. The sadism of the torturer, his desire to do evil can ultimately be interpreted in psychological terms. The sadist enjoys the sufferings he inflicts on his victim. But the diabolical will does not cause the other pain; it would rather corrupt him. The devil is disinterested, the sole thing that matters to him is the soul, the will of the other. The bad person wants to become master of the will of his victim. But we do not possess wills like a toolbox or a drawer of clothes. Diabolical possession aims for the will as will; it does not pursue its immobilization: a will incapable of moving, of *willing*, cannot be possessed as a will. The strange dialectic of pure hate implies that the will continues to will, but wills as it ought not to will. The domination of my will by the pure practical hate of another's will implies the confirmation of the power of his will but by almost sublating it under *his* own bad will. The bad man desires that the one he hates also hates, that he wants evil for him and this bad will finds its completion when the other will become in his turn a bad will!

The apparent paradox of the pure bad will requiring that its intentional object, the will of another continues to be exercised but as bad will is dissolved once it is understood that pure evil, that is, moral evil is not merely opposition to another but also and above all opposition to oneself. The moral evil out which stems the entire spectrum of evils inflicted on its external victims is evil for itself. It harms—in fact it harms in the proper sense—the one whose will it is. The bad will that is ceaseless action is an intentionality; it appears as a radiation. In reality it is an enclosure in evil. The devils are confined in hell because the bad is locked in itself, plunged into evil. This enclosing is not a topological but metaphysico-moral idea. The man of bad will is condemned to evil; he can neither do good to another nor receive it from another. Electra cries out bitterly: "Those to whom too much evil has been done cannot keep from becoming bad" (*Electra* 307s). If suffering was only a physical trial it could be endured without embittering, making its subject spiteful and nasty, but when subjected to a bad will, hate, its animosity is transformed into a corrupting poison. The victim of hate is possessed by a spirit of vengeance; it wants to "render" evil to the one who has subjected it to hate. But corruption by suffering leads not only to the bad justice of making the other who hurt me pay his debts, but leads also to a gratuitous, unmotivated hate in regard to others who "have done nothing to me," to others in general. Ultimately the one who endures the hateful opposition of another can end up being possessed himself by the hate that he will then unleash on others. Man is a wolf for other men and the bad person is a bad person for other bad persons. Between wrongdoers there can only be temporary associations, forged in view of escaping punishment or accomplishing a misdeed. And theology perspicaciously teaches that among demons there can be no peace but only a kind of "concord" resulting "not from mutual friendship but from their common wickedness whereby they hate men and fight against God's justice."[30]

The bad person cannot will the evil of others but he can will his own good. The bad man can consider himself sly but in reality he is deeply mistaken because "those who do evil harm themselves" (Tob 12:10). Sinners are deceivers but above all deceived; they do not understand that they are harming themselves, that they are their own enemies. Moral predication with its pragmatic accents here overlaps with the lofty metaphysics of the bad will. The bad is bad for others and being so it is bad for itself. "Good moral sense" could be tempted to intervene by recalling that we are provided with an instinct to treasure ourselves, to find ourselves desirable above all, to love only ourselves. But we only love what we know to be loveable: "if evil sensed what it [truly] was it would not be able to love itself" (*Enneads* VI, vii, 8). The bad will wills evil for others as for itself. Evil is consequently evil for others as for oneself. The discussion on evil began with the Socratic thesis that no one can will evil. And it can also recall the other great teaching of Socrates: no evil can happen to the good man. But a Stoic counterpart to the Socratic teaching nearly provides the conclusion to the metaphysics of the (bad) will: "no one can do good to a bad man."[31]

From Evil to the Good

The two theses that "no evil can happen to the good man" and "no one can do good to the wicked" plant evil and good in a radical opposition unattenuatable by any transition. Evil is radically bad and good is integrally good. According to the parable of Lazarus and the rich man "a great abyss is fixed between the damned who suffer in Hades" and those "in Abraham's bosom" (Luke 16:26). But a substantial metaphysics

---

30. Thomas Aquinas, *Summa Theologiae* I, 109, a. 2 ad. 2 and 3.
31. Seneca, *Benef.* II, xxxv (*On Benefits*, 93).

of good and evil seems to lead to the conclusion that not only between their archetype, their paradigm, but between the least occurrences and examples of good and evil no bridge at all is possible. And this for the good reason that evil is not only the absence or privation of the good but its diametrical opposite. It follows that in good metaphysics the teaching on good and evil can be only that of an irreducible dualism and in morals the only consequential doctrine is that of an integral rigorism. Contrary to theologies penetrated by Hellenistic ontology that admit a third "place" between the two opposed worlds of Heaven and Hell, the intransigent refusal of a third way, proper to the Reformers, leads in Kant to the affirmation: "Purgatory is a logical impossibility."[32] The rigorous dualism professed by the metaphysics of the will begins with two conceptual theses in order to reject attempts to admit a third way. On the one hand, it rejects a gradualist vision, according degrees to evil and the good; on the other hand, it emphasizes the impossibility of any sort of neutrality in relation to good and evil.

The moral (and metaphysical) causalists of all kinds continue to establish scales for the occurrences and forms of evil, but evil is not a phenomenal reality bu,t so to speak, noumenal: its manifestations cannot be measured. Evil has no quantity; a number cannot be put to it. There are hardly any stable, objective scales to classify and hierarchize the occurrences and examples of malice, perversion, betrayal. It is certainly believed possible to observe outbursts of hate of various intensities, but hate in itself is a reality that is equal to itself, undivided. Big and little sins are certainly spoken about but on the metaphysical plane, that of the eidos, of the essence, little sin and big sin, venial and mortal, it is always *sin* and nothing but sin, an authentic reality of evil. The radical duality of good and evil amounts to their opposition and this opposition makes morally *impossible* (and therefore condemns) the supposed neutrality in relation to good and evil. In strict metaphysics a neutral position in relation to evil amounts to rejecting the good and espousing evil. In politics (but not solely) one is tempted to affirm: those who are not our enemies are our friends. In reality it is rather the contrary that is true. The one who does not experience a true friendship with another is his potential (and very easily, actual) adversary. To say that another does not love me hardly means attributing to him a kind of affective indifference. Rather, it is to observe, exasperated and pained, that he does not respond to my loving feelings but rejects them. The absence of faith is non-faith, the absence of virtue is vice. The great poet-theologian powerfully taught that indifference to evil or the absence of love for the good is evil. Those who have "neither virtue nor vice in their soul" are found in Hell (*Inferno,* canto 3, 39) and if good angels were "confirmed in the light," others are found eo ipso in a fixed "opposition" to God (*Paradiso,* canto 29, 50). The impossibility of neutrality stems from the nature of our intention to do good and evil. It is never a theoretical knowledge, a *noesis* that keeps its distance, but a practical knowledge that is an inclination. To know the good signifies willing it, to know evil

32. Kant, *Akad.* XVI, 240.

signifies rejecting it and a neutral knowledge in matters of evil is a non-rejection of evil. Who but the wicked could not reject evil? More precisely: not to recognize evil is already a bad volition. In his *Devotions*, John Donne recalls that our "worse sin is not to see our sin."[33] And absolute Idealism will translate into a concept the abhorrence of the intelligence before the terrifying ignorance of the principal practical truth: to will and to do evil is always culpable, but the most nefarious transgression is incapacity to distinguish "good and evil," mistaking them for each other.[34]

The non-distinction between good and bad signifies indifference to good and evil. We cannot deplore and condemn it enough, but above all we cannot understand it. Not to discern the difference between good and evil, between virtue and vice signifies that, very strangely, we seem not to conceive that good is good and evil is bad. Non-discernment does not register a bankruptcy of theoretical intelligence, the confusion of one empirical fact with another; it does not consist in taking one eidos for another. Good and evil are not material essences: inclination or disinclination towards are integral parts of their metaphysical content. The acuteness of the gaze of "the eye of the soul" is not yet enough for the discernment of the two Opposites; its "conversion" is required. But how to explain this conversion, how to make the gaze turn in one direction and not another? Knowledge, or more precisely, the recognition of good and evil, is a function of a mysterious positioning that takes the good for good and evil for bad. And it is this positioning that remains the primordial mystery. From an empirical, psychological point of view, the original positioning is quite simply that of a native egoism: I know because I recognize as good what pleases and profits me and evil what causes me pain and harms me. But—precisely—on a metaphysico-moral plane, this primitive position is transcended. Good and evil are no longer functions of pleasure and pain towards which the individual empirical subject experiences an inclination of the analytic order. Well to the contrary these are practical principles that alone can aim for and enfold a synthetic movement going beyond my own "natural" good and evil and even resolutely opposing it.

To know the good "practically" is to will it: it is an a priori synthesis where the inclination that is Love conquers the penchant for self-interest. This synthesis is a mystery: it comes down to surpassing and transcending our natural aspirations "without reason," without natural reason. But a second mystery of the will exists that ultimately is alone apt to take account of the positivity of evil. If the good implies a victory over nature, a going beyond the universe of immanence, of the entire sphere of analytic judgments, then evil according to its plenitude equally includes a combat against nature. The eidetic elements of spirituality, of the disinterestedness of malice, express the non-naturality, even the anti-naturality of evil. Writers and moralists have known how to emphasize the almost superhuman efforts contained in certain wicked

---

33. Donne, *Devotions upon Emergent Occasions*, 57, in Ellrodt, *Les poetes métaphysiques anglais* I, 19, n. 9.

34. Hegel, *Principes de la philosophie du droit*, § 170, 211.

behaviors, the combat that the bad man wages against diverse physical weaknesses, even against moral instincts of compassion and pity. Consent to the good is most often represented as valorous resistance to the attractions of concupiscence, a heroic effort of tearing oneself from false goods in order to go finally towards the true good. But the effort and the tearing away from false goods are not the exclusive appanage of virtuous action: vice can also demand the refusal of pleasure. As Malebranche said: "In order to demerit. . .it is necessary to run after false goods with more ardor, or to go farther than pleasure can invincibly take you."[35]

The two mysteries of desiring the good and desiring evil are "followed" by a third, of vaster and universally contemplated scope. It no longer concerns the possibility of willing what one "ought to" will and "ought not to" will but (as we have already seen in the explication of the idea of forgiveness) the question of passage, of transition from one will to another that, from the moral point of view, is opposed to it. Whether a matter of our total moral condition or even of habitus contrary to vice and virtue, or more simply of isolated volitions, the problem remains the same. Between good and evil the difference is not according to degree but nature; they are separated by a vast gulf. They are metaphysically opposed categories and from this fact appear condemned to remain without contact or relation. And, above all, it is difficult to understand how the will that they totally, integrally define can pass from one to the other and subsequently assume the opposite condition. Similar to the fundamental aporias of philosophy like the advent of being starting from non-being and the waking state starting from sleep, the movement from good to evil or evil to good remains inconceivable. But despite the apparent conceptual impossibility of explaining the change of the will, its passage from good will to bad will (or the reverse), such is a core matter of the central reality of morality and religion observable to all and imposed on each. Instead of resorting to subterfuges of dosage of opposed properties, of falling back into a vision representing evils as so many *Abschattungen* of the good, it is rather necessary, instead of condoning the bankruptcy of reason, to realize the effective reality of its situation where it can and must recognize the limits of its action. To take account of the passage of the will that is not simply creativity, but one leading to a complete reversal, philosophy must return with Kant to this "fact of reason" that is freedom or even to the other fact, Grace.

The analysis of a fact of reason signifies that one does not intend to give up on any philosophical consideration of the inexplicable leaps that punctuate the life of the will. But it is and remains clear that for a properly conceptual investigation there cannot be passage between good and evil. The highest fact of the will is thus condemned to remain a fact; the two fundamental principles of practical reason persist in an unmediated and unmediatable opposition. However this does not mean that any relation or reference between contraries is forbidden. If, on a properly metaphysical plane, the impasse is total, if good and evil, virtue and vice are frozen in an irreducible

35. Malebranche, *Traité de la nature et de la grâce*.

opposition, on the *transcendental* plane, the possibility of a relation, of a connection is offered. For classical ontology evil is understood as a privation, an accident, an excrescence of the good, but in either case it *is* by virtue of and starting from the good. But *this* conception of evil, desirous of deriving it starting from the good, remains inadequate because it attributes to evil (and the good) an ontological condition that encloses them in the register of being. However, a transcendental (non-ontological) reflection allows "a deduction" but in the inverse direction. Evil is not derived from the good but the idea of good is to be understood as derived from the idea of evil! One of the major stratagems of theodicy consisted in the demonstration of evil as useful, even necessary for the good. Evil is the shadow that allows the discernment of the light that is the good; suffering is the experience that aids an existential comprehension of the good; ultimately, sin itself, starting from the paradigmatic intuition of the *felix culpa*, is like a true condition for the advent of the Redemption. These variations of theodicy present dubious teleologies to the degree that they do not really respect the irreducible metaphysical difference between good and evil. However, a meditation exists that seeks a non-ontological, but practical and transcendental theodicy, capable of leading to a true deduction of the idea of the good in its goodness starting from the very horror we feel before evil.

Literature and philosophy abound with descriptions and definitions that imply a fecund return from a figure of evil towards that of the good. Analytic philosophy remarks that "the abnormal will throw light on the normal,"[36] and the novelist speaks of "the bitter proof of God."[37] These references are instances of referral to a notion starting from its contrary, and this referentiality means being distilled and generalized into the intuition of absurdity, even of the impossibility of evil which, in its turn, leads to the necessary position of the good. Human consciousness contains the idea, or rather, the "practical" feeling of the bad. This discernment, however much its instances and singular occurrences can vary, is universal and inherent. It accompanies a more or less acute feeling of revolt appearing under cover of an instinctive rejection of the very possibility of the shocking, the harmful, the repugnant. We each encounter in our life natural cataclysms and moral crimes, suffering caused by terrible illnesses and examples of abominable betrayals. These events and actions appear inadmissible and inconceivable; they are imposed on the mind like a brusque wave of irreducible nonsense before a universe that is supposed to be organized and dominated by Meaning.

The inconceivability and thus impossibility experienced by the moral sense before these events is clearly not of the physico-ontological but rather the metaphysico-moral order. It is translated by the question "why" that pins down the shocked and suffering consciousness. The why is hardly related to the physical causal process that led to events that distressed me. Instead it expresses the bewilderment, the stupor of

---

36. Austin, *Philosophical Papers*, 180.

37. Greene, *Le dixième homme*, 91, in Hatem, *L'écharde du mal dans la chair de Dieu*, 69 (*The Tenth Man* [New York: Washington Square, 1985] 109).

consciousness, incapable as it is of admitting a phenomenon contrary to the order of the world, opposed to the ends that govern it. The why manifests the perplexity of consciousness, its revolt before the turn of events, but it amounts to something more than the simple registering of a shock, the translation of a dissatisfaction. The why signifies not only that the consciousness rejects an event of the world, the quality of a thing, the moral property of a man. It is not only the powerless analysis of dissatisfaction, it also and above all translates the possibility of an alternative, a solution, a change. The why opens the area of interrogation, which destabilizes the factual world: the world is as it is, the why insinuates that it could be otherwise! The partial whys, those that wonder about a given event, a quality, a given property, refer to the possibility of a potential reality conceived as more advantageous, more appropriated than present reality, but which is only one among others and is above all not the symmetrical contrary, the opposed counterpart of the factuality that one wants to question. But things are different for the Why concerning Evil.

The why of Evil does not imply reference to one possible essence among others, but to an essence that is contrary, opposed and therefore unique. It marks the sad discernment of a reality that de facto is, but which *ought not* to be. But what ought not to be is referred to what ought to be, and this ought to be has variations of force, different modalities. These diverse possibilities, these *diversa* of the empirical world are a function of the intuition of a state of fact that could be altered, ameliorated, but of which the alteration, amelioration appears desirable only in a contingent, hypothetical way and is not necessitated as such. However, the rejection of evil is obligatory, necessary. Evil is and only is, by definition, what ought not to be, and the ought-not-to-be-ness is held in a relation of integral implication-opposition to ought-to-be-ness. The ought-not-to-be can be considered to have an analogous originarity to that of the ought-to-be. Nevertheless, as negation, it can only be referred to the affirmation of which it constitutes precisely the negation. From an empirical point of view, evil most often precedes the good. A congenital malady is evidently anterior to the treatment that will lead to its healing; the conditions of life in a society full of injustices and inequalities only slowly evolve into existence in a more just community that protects the interest of each of its citizens. And children—those doves, those cherubs—are born neither innocent, nor benevolent, nor altruistic. As a rabbinical text says in the context of the great rite for the confirmation undertaken by an adolescent at thirteen within the cultic and social order of Israel: "evil is thirteen years the elder of the good."[38] However, despite the dark obviousness of the history of every era and every society, of the entire spectrum of anthropological observations, from a metaphysical point of view, the good is prior to, not behind, evil.

Every man considers health an obvious condition; we are never conscious of it before it is damaged. The myth of the golden age, of an era of abundance and peace, is a collective archetype found among many peoples. For readers of the Bible, Adam

---

38. Strack-Billerbeck, *Kommentar zum Neuen Testament aus Talmud und Midrasch* IV, 1, 470.

and Eve were innocent before the Fall. Such examples of the anteriority of the good in relation to evil are located on the plane of conscience, not in material reality. They suggestively illustrate the principal anteriority (an anteriority of the transcendental order) of the good in relation to evil. They do not at all contradict the empirical precedence of evil over the good, but rather corroborate the ancient pre-philosophical and pre-theological intuition of the teleological role of the consciousness of evil in relation to the good. It is doubtlessly not a matter of a rehabilitation of innumerable attempts at theodicy to show the utility and even necessity of the deployment of evil as premise and condition for the advent of the good. No, these perverted apologetics have to be cut short, as inclined as they are to discover, in the cortege of evils that darken our existence, sui generis moments of the good; above all it is necessary to keep in mind the great injunction: "we must not do evil in trying to bring about good"! However, we can and must take account of the admirable lesson that the interrogation of and meditation on evil furnishes about the native orientation of conscience towards the good, the conscience that in its truth carries within it the indelible and original imprint of the idea of the good. There is certainly no middle way between Hell and Heaven and there is no transition, passage, commerce between good and evil. Yet human consciousness possesses, inscribed within, the power to discern evil that has as a native counterpart the comprehension of the good that is, eo ipso, aspiration for it.

XIII

The Good

Beyond Being, Beyond Essence

Transcendental theodicy leads to the deduction of the idea of the good, but the good is clearly not only an idea. The good is the foundational reality of metaphysics. It cannot be, or rather, cannot yet be, cannot completely be, but it appears as the form and end of all that can and should happen. It is not located in an ontological register. Its perfect formulation is given in the *Republic*: "the good is beyond being." The correct translation and interpretation of this famous "definition" remains uncertain: is the good beyond *being* or beyond *essence*? The difference is immense but the ambiguity of the expression seems ultimately invaluable and harbors a high teleology. The Good is deprived of being as well as essence. Or, more precisely, it surpasses both. It represents the highest manifestation of apophaticism, but of, if you like, a positive kind. Being is the strongest reality, the richest essence, but the good in its own way shows itself more powerful than being and richer than essence.

The good is "beyond being": what sense would it have if we add to it the affirmation of being? The good is good without regard for what effectively is or is not. Humans of every era have grasped this supra-ontological truth of goodness. We could always find ourselves in a situation where to continue to live implies cowardice, compromises, vice, and consequently conditions that make existence too unhappy and too dishonest, and thus too evil to hold onto it. One then chooses to hazard his life, even to sacrifice it. Life is doubtlessly dear to us; we attach ourselves to it with all our powers even when it is miserable and vicious. We can nevertheless extricate and break away from it and choose death. In this case we would no longer be living, we would no longer be, but it is better not to live than to live in evil, not to live at all than to live evilly! The possibility and actuality of choosing death—representing at least on the plane of feelings and intuitions non-being for us—illustrates the discernment of the meaning of the good in its distinction from being, which is conceived as an action, a combat. In other words, the non-being proper to the good is not an absence or even simple privation but a dis-appropriation and tearing away from oneself. Yet these renunciations and sacrifices, in spite of a profound kernel of intuition of the distinction, of the disassociation of the good and being, may include (and most often do) elements that are confused, ambivalent, and impure. The decision to renounce one's life can involve feelings of fear, fatigue, and disgust; the aspiration for honor is difficult to disassociate from vanity and pride, and even giving one's life for another can hide selfish aims. But a clear and pure, quasi-general and formal form of the disassociation of the good and being exists: the moral intuition. The great religions and moral philosophies have always commanded humans to obey precepts and laws, in other words, to "do" the good. But true conformity to the commandment does not depend on the actualization or effectuation of intention. Good and evil of the will belong to intention, not to execution. Execution can show itself more or less "faithful" to the aim of the intention. It is located in another area, a material area, not that of the formal act of the will.

The substantial and radical disassociation of the execution of intentions is the centerpiece, the basic kernel of a philosophical vision that rejects the thousand attempts to integrate completely the good (and evil) into the register of the philosophy of being. The profound telos of this separation is the demonstration of the non-ontological nature of the good, a rigorous and passionate bracketing of every relation and connection with being. A work of reduction is pursued that will yield the metaphysical essence of the practical, the moral. If intention in its purity—understand: its condition as freed from every reference and every reference to execution—spectacularly illustrates the truth of the good as located "beyond being," only the moral, the practical of Kantianism as such, is to separate, to dissociate from being. In other words, if you accept to abstract from the essential ontological dimension of the definition—the properly metaphysical meaning of the Platonic formula would emerge starting from the *Critique*. Consequently, we can and must say that the Good is beyond being because the intention has nothing to do with the execution. Its truth is of the formal order, not subject to incarnation in matter. Yet this interpretation or reinterpretation of the high intuition, the sublime vision of the *Republic* seems poor, sickly, in fact, insufficient and inadequate. It does not do justice either to the thematic of Kantian practice or to the metaphysical teaching of Plato. Intention is certainly not of the ontological order, it does not belong to the universe of being, but its condition as other-than-being has, all the same, an essential, if you like, unavoidable active and dynamic moment. Intention is not something that is elsewhere than being simply because it *was located* elsewhere. Intention is not just there, but it tends *towards*; it is not an essence but an aspiration. And the beyond being condition of the Good cannot be understood in terms of passivity, or even of a supreme passivity. If the moral, the practical is not of being, this is because it is otherwise than being, and this "otherwise" implies precisely a going beyond: namely, a surpassing that is a tearing away.

This logic of surpassing is also there when the good is interpreted as going beyond essence. The beyond essence signifies the condition of being exempt from, stripped of content. The Good brackets essences: like being—in fact, more properly than being—it cannot be considered a predicate. Even more: not only is it not a predicate in itself, but it cannot have any predicates. Predicates, essences construe possession, but the Good is "the Good because it has nothing."[1] (*Enneads* V, v, 13). The Good is foreign to all having and its condition of being exempt from predicates, unassimilatable to every material essence, receives a particularly suggestive translation in the traditional attempts to represent it under the form of poverty. If religions and philosophies recommend and even prescribe poverty to their adherents, this is not simply out of a "pragmatic" preoccupation with removing them from misbehavior, dependence on things, and attachments to beings. No, if poverty suits a good man for diverse reasons, it is not valuable for its consequences. It is adopted because of the fecund analogy with the Good that it displays. On the other hand, insistence on poverty is not something negative, the absence of a property, the assessment of powerlessness. The Good is not only of non-essence but it is *beyond* essence; it is not only deprived of every essence, but its truth is the surpassing of essences, victory over them. The renunciation that advocates the high moral philosophy of goodness is not synonymous with the indigence of the poor wretch, it does not amount to the fatalist acceptance of misery, it has nothing to do with the absence of imagination in the use of the fruits and products of the earth. The poverty that reflects the Good going beyond essence is not the privation suffered, inert and resigned, by the mediocre and lazy, by the embittered and anorexic. Instead, it is the self-dispossession of the rich, a combat carried out at each instant over one's possessions. Formulated even more generally: if the Good is poverty, it is such as an incessant struggle to vanquish not only its diverse possessions but oneself as possessor.

From Newness to Goodness

The exposition of the good in its condition of active dissociation with being completes the unfolding of the practical according to its extra- or rather supra-ontological truth. The Good appears as beyond being as well as beyond essence; it imposes itself as the truth of our philosophical journey; and it permits the rereading of the categories that punctuate its development. The good imposes itself as the moment of realization of the construction that articulates the expansion of metaphysics, the moment towards which all that precedes it has tended. The expansion of metaphysics has as its condition the emancipation of ontology, or rather the assignment of ontology to a merely

---

1. Plotinus, *Enneads*, trans. Stephen MacKenna.

"regional" position, which is in truth its proper place. Ontology can constitute the plinth of metaphysics, even the area where it is unfolded, but it is, so to speak, only the material of the form studied by metaphysics, the background from which its expansion is initiated. The keystone of the expansion is the necessity of detaching from being without succumbing to the temptation to conceive of this surpassing as simple becoming. Becoming only dynamizes, fluidifies being; it installs, or rather, reads potentiality within it. However, if the movements of the *dynamis* can don dazzling colors, can be declined with dramatic accents, potentiality remains the hidden face of being. It can, so to speak, shake being up, establishing movement within it, but it in no way amounts to a break with immanence where it is confined. Immanence doubtlessly does not interfere with the entire evolution where being as nature is elaborated and articulated. The primitive violence of nature is subjugated within, or rather, transposed into proportioned and harmonious structures: nature settles down into justice where immanence obtains an authentic articulation. Nature, with its hidden face or rather latent structure of justice makes explicit the proper potentialities of being and the beautiful clarity of immanence celebrates the high intelligibility of a structured, rational order. However, very unfortunately, these renewals of being with itself at the end of the sublime and serene procession of justice constitute only a process written in advance in all its elements and moments. By justice, being sounds its own depth, but this operation is only a kind of ontological anamnesis where, despite the wealth of details and the infinite diversity of events, nothing new happens. If subsequent events come in an unforeseeable way, if the moments of the process register an infinite variety, the *Geist* presiding over these happenings is always only the demon of Laplace. An ever more complex program establishes the formula of the process of things, but ultimately its disenchanted message remains that of the Qoheleth: "there is nothing new under the sun."

The newness cannot come by means of a fluidification of being, from the discovery of potentiality within it. It happens only through the freedom that unseals the compact integrity of being, through the freedom that interrupts the uncoiling of the series of phenomena of becoming through the insertion of spaces between them. These spaces are however not simply portions of space nor kinds of non-space. They are leaps. The being that has integrated becoming within itself through potentiality undergoes a shock that causes it so to speak to detach from itself in order to go forward or more simply elsewhere. Yet the shock that unfastens becoming from itself is not only the establishment of a spatial distance or even the rising up of an unprepared temporal moment, foreign to all immanent anamnesis. The essential of the leap that initiates freedom or rather that *is* freedom is the tearing away from self, the movement of breaking away from one's own system, in short the action of getting out of a process that unwinds with an immanent regularity. Freedom does not merely interrupt the series of phenomena reconstituted across distances and joined together at the end of the flow of a duration and which continue in the register of sameness. If freedom is authentically creative, the rupture that it creates cannot amount to a simple separation of phenomena previously tied together in an organic way: the realities successively separated by the leap must register a true metaphysical difference.

Freedom is the key to the advent of the truly new because the dissociation accomplished by the leap is integral and leads to the advent of a discontinuous metaphysical reality. But this discontinuity cannot be found among realities having nothing in common. Novelty doubtlessly brings about something not yet there, but the new must be related to the reality in relation to which it represents newness. The novelty establishes a rupture, a dis-relation, but the dis-relation is always only a case of relation. If the new was not tied in one way or another to the old, it would lack this other, this elder by relation to which alone it can impose itself as new. The conceptual and logical structure of novelty receives its formulation in the genial philosophical idea of the a priori synthesis. Contrary to the merely analytic articulation or organization of the realities of nature, of everything that populates the universe of immanence, the a priori synthesis marks the advent of a new conception of logical judgment. Notwithstanding all the apparent diversity and difference of one in relation to another, the things of immanence register a hidden identity. More precisely, they can and must be expressed by propositions where the subject and object are not radically different. The predicate only makes explicit the subject by unfolding its virtual possibilities: the course of nature and the discourse of justice are only so many examples of analytic judgment. Things are different for all that belongs to novelty, which in a strict sense is an affair of freedom. Freedom denotes the advent of realities that do not necessarily follow from their premises but nevertheless constitute a rational response to what the premises demand and require. A free act is the solution, the resolution of a situation that is not analytically implied by it. It is a novel response, but not in the elementary sense of a noetic given lying within a plurality of given but still unexploited possibilities. It is rather a lightning flash that imposes itself without any logical necessity but conforms to the deep essence of what proclaims it. To take account of the structure of freedom we must appeal to propositions where the subject does not contain—that is, pre-contain—the predicate and yet the predicate should agree with the intelligible truth of the subject. In other words, we have to make recourse to *synthetic* a priori propositions which are brought about by the new, namely, a predicate that does not result from the subject and yet corresponds to its intelligible structure.

The a priori synthesis expresses the creative power of rational subjectivity: the predicates they express impose themselves without binding necessity but with a full intelligibility. They are the fruits of the fecundity of spirit, of a fecundity in which the spirit draws its contents from its own interior depths—not as elements that it contains, given within it, but as fruits that ripen and come about with fidelity to what it is. The a priori synthesis presents the logical structure, the noetic framework of freedom and from this fact, a true general reformulation of temporal *protention*, it is the very nerve of the metaphysics of novelty. But if the a priori synthesis justifies freedom in a concept, is this concept enough to justify this novelty for which it is the condition and paradigm? Said differently: if freedom is the necessary condition for the possibility of novelty, can it also furnish a sufficient reason for its actuality? Freedom advocates for the possibility of an interruption that does not fall outside being in becoming, but which neither comes from its immanence as an analytic unfolding. It is the sui generis principle of the intelligibility of newness because by making possible within it the appearing in conformity to what is former, the given, it has creative fidelity as its own source and resource. But can freedom preside over the effective exercise of this creative fidelity? Freedom's highest metaphysical vocation is to prevent the leaps of novelty from being located on a merely ontological plane, for they are not only variants of the convulsions of becoming. It would be able to fulfill this role if it was more than a pure power, if it did not ultimately stand in the same ontological area as the nature that it would like to liberate from its servitude to analytical immanence. Freedom signals the surpassing of becoming through the unlocking of being, but does this unlocking suffice, or rather, does an unlocking exist that is simply unqualified, undetermined? Freedom appeared as the principle of true novelty, liberated from being wrapped up in being. But what is the proper metaphysical status of novelty-freedom?

Understood in its radical originality, freedom marks the advent of a new metaphysical region, the *practical*, which is no longer a sub-register of the ontological but its majestic counterpart. The practical that assumes a status of alterity in relation to being and brackets its contents, the material essences, appears effectively as a true counterpart to the ontological. If the world of the ontological is constituted by being, the universe of the practical *is* freedom. However, the symmetry that appears between these two metaphysical zones is misleading. Being and freedom seem to be counterparts: one is only the power of persevering in itself, the other is the force of unlocking; one is the principle of all continuities, the other is the source and artisan of ruptures. However, if sameness is imposed with a tranquil evidence in the world of being, could we permit some ruptures that are motivated and accomplished only by virtue of an analogous indifferentiation? Despite these hints of *dynamis*, of an intuition interpreting it as combative, as *das Strittige*, can being be represented ultimately as neutral? And can we conceive the practical as neutral? In its essence, the practical is only a superior synonym for the moral, it has always forever been determined, decided. For this reason freedom in itself does not yet work as the sufficient reason for the advent of the new. If novelty means rupture this is as a tearing away, and this tearing away amounts to the inversion of a tendency, a change in direction, and freedom, not being—or having—in itself any determination, cannot cause this other direction to arise. The tearing away must be the work of a reality that supports freedom by subsuming it under a determination. This reality in which freedom renounces its unlimitedness, its indeterminacy is *love*.

Love goes beyond justice and it is "naturally" against nature. It leads the a priori synthesis to its paroxysm, or rather to the realization, the ultimate actualization of its potentialities. The a priori synthesis is the logical nerve of judgments in which the subject shows its ultimate power, namely, the power of becoming less than itself, of thwarting its own aspirations, damaging its own interests, in short, opposing itself—and all this by virtue even of its own essence, in conformity to its concept. Love retains nothing and gives all, including itself. It requires nothing in exchange, not even fidelity and thus not even love! The circle is apparently closed: the tearing away that constitutes novelty has as its logico-metaphysical implication the victory over nature under its superior form of justice. With the non-requirement of fidelity, and thus the total gratuity of love, the very idea of exchange and thus all reciprocity is obliterated. The tearing away is a uni-directional and unilateral way, and this is ultimately its eidetic nature: it leaves itself, that is to say, it endeavors to move away from itself, to be disappropriated. But by its very nature is this self-exit condemned to an estrangement, a ceaseless distantiation without end, whether temporal or above all external, other than itself? Instead, does it not amount to an alterity that designates not only a movement starting from the self, but equally implies a reality other than the self, in short, another being? The supreme exigence of the non-exigence of fidelity is the mark of the heroic extremism of the tearing away from self. But in this last instance, through this complete rupture with the analytic, through this desire to denounce reciprocity, to reject all the residues and all the half-hidden traces of immanence, immanence seems to take its revenge. The tearing away can and must be integral and it must not allow any element of self-attachment to survive. However, all the while bracketing what is located on the plane of self-having, all the while resolving to stop its progress, to "suspend its flight," do we not fall back into this immanence that we have nevertheless ceaselessly rejected? The non-exigency of the fidelity of the beloved can sanction gratuity, the purity of the lover's love, and yet does it not smuggle immanence back into this supreme renunciation?

To palliate this supreme danger a simple remedy is applied, amounting to healing the shortcomings of the practical by a reintroduction of the ontological. If freedom's eidetic principle is the self-tearing away, for this tearing away to "succeed," the advent of another being, external and independent of the self is required. In other words, for the tearing away to be realized, freedom must be transposed into love. But even when it renounces the requirement of reciprocity, love possesses a determinate intentional object. The intentional object that alone perfects the aim of self-tearing away is the child deduced as unique. The child, the unique, exemplifies in an admirable way the metaphysical exigencies of love. In its authentic alterity, located essentially on the ontological plane, the child represents a goal of the self-tearing away that cannot be subsumed under the movement of the tearing away itself and thus restored to immanence. But to the degree that the ascending love of the child is weaker, less "natural" than the descending love of his or her procreator, the radical gratuity of the tearing away-love is strengthened. Put differently: the child enjoys an authentic autonomy, but its relation to the parent has nothing to do with a mechanism of exchange where symmetry, proportionality, would lead procreation back to being an event of immanence.

The deduction of the child as effectively existing other seems to rehabilitate the ontological as necessary for the accomplishment of the tearing away in love. Yet the other of the tearing away is not only another being: love procreates not only another that is, but another who *loves*. The ontological is recuperated, but it also registers limitations. It is only the foundation, the condition of the practical—necessary and not sufficient. The other that is the end of our tearing away in its realization, is its end not simply as an existing being but as a loving being, more precisely as a being capable of love. The unfaithful one who is the goal of my love does not love me at all or any more. This seems to be a fact, but he *could* love me. The child who does not respond to the love of his parents could, has the duty, to respond. . . The deduction of a being capable of love as the paradigmatic intentional object of the tearing away ought to make us rethink the proper *noesis* of love. Nature's slow ascension to the tearing away, from justice to love, is made through the transposition of the "faculty" at work within it. The prehistory of freedom is ultimately a natural history of becoming and relatively few efforts have been made to clarify the epistemologico-metaphysical vehicle. Justice has been shown to be a continuation of the politics of immanence by other means, but these means, despite a great diversity of structure, continue to correspond to analytic judgments. Put differently, the ontological region of love is governed by a logic of analysis. A radical mutation is effected with the appearing of freedom and its accomplishment in love: the work of the tearing away is understood according to the logic of the a priori synthesis. In reality, it is not enough to say that love lends itself to be displayed according to the a priori synthesis; we should rather say that love is the proper paradigm of diverse occurrences of this synthesis, that love is—and only is—an a priori synthesis "written in capital letters" (see *Republic* 368d). But to understand love as true archetype of the a priori synthesis permits a metaphysical deepening of great scope. The a priori synthesis was first given in order to take account of the relative propositions to the processes of nature; subsequently it was reformulated in the practical domain. However, the metaphysical investigation of love seems to assign to it the practical sphere as its original location, and this through the rereading of love in terms of the will.

The will appears to constitute a kind of apotheosis of undividedness, of homogeneity. In and through it the practical resolutely gets away from the theoretical; it is understood as sealed and locked in on itself. However, if as faculty the will effectively registers a homogeneity that strangely reflects the condition of immanence proper to nature (even if, in its truth, it is exercised only in and on itself) it could not be thought as confined in itself. In fact, it would rather have to be represented as attempting to purify itself from all that is not truly itself, of settling down, in short, as practicing a phenomenological reduction in good and due form. However the finality of the reduction possesses nothing of an autism or a solipsism. Well to the contrary if the will tries to exorcise all that does not belong to it in the strict sense this is in order to realize the work of the self-tearing away. The will can indulge, in general, repetitions of the exercise of its finality within itself, the true finality of its action will be always located outside and beyond itself. The will is ultimately love—or hate—but neither love nor hate has any relation with the bracketing of the other, another than the self. The will is the very realization of the a priori synthetic judgment. It realizes it in itself, but with its external realization as its supreme teleology. The will has itself as object, it wants only itself, but this reduction, however radical, is ultimately inverted in the pure desiring of another. This pure desire is the advent of the true novelty that is the hidden face of the good.

Kenosis as Will

The will is the nerve of reflection where the expansion of metaphysics takes shape. Kenosis has been offered as the paradigm of this going beyond self that is the truth of novelty, freedom, and love, but kenosis is set forth most appropriately in terms of the will—for philosophical reasons as much as theological. The will is the faculty that is not content to be or to be what it is. The will is an incessant action: it always wants. It either wants something new or wants the same thing, but in wanting the same thing, that is, itself, it wants, and thus is wanted in a renewed way. The will can only repeat itself; this repetition is truly a new action where it stops questioning itself. If Sartre is right, we are condemned to be free, but it is probably more precise and just to say that we are condemned to desire. This perennial renewal of the will seems to convey the incapacity to be satisfied with what we have, a gnawing disquiet that pushes us to recommence our action. In reality, however, it is not a matter of a heroic Promethianism, an obsession dissatisfied with the given that always recommences its action. The morality of duty is certainly a faithful expression of the metaphysical reality of the will: the will is always on the way to outrunning itself. In fact, this excess is its essence, its being. But what matters in the outrunning is not its appearing in a repetitive, incessant way. The ceaseless re-evaluation of the man of duty only divvies up the central work of freedom-love, namely the victory of self that is ultimately only an imperfect, shrunken synonym, even a kind of moralizing repercussion of the high metaphysical reality of kenosis.

Kenosis is the central mystery of the Incarnation: it expresses the Son's renunciation of his divine form in order to assume the form of a slave. This means that the perfect consents to become imperfect and consequently to pass into a condition rejected by its essence. This is an ontological contradiction, but what is contradictory in ontology can be resolved on a metaphysical plane. If the essence of God were his being, the Incarnation would effectively be impossible, even absurd. God is the absolute being, how could he "become" a finite being? We have to understand that the essence of God is not being, but "love" (1 John 4:8). And love—precisely—celebrates its completion in renunciation, self-gift, sacrifice. For a great Scholastic theologian the Christological is "verus metaphysicus."[2] The definition is just and appropriate. And it is appropriate to the degree that reflection on the Incarnation (read as kenosis) allows an essential recentering of metaphysics. Kenosis, the work and true activity of love, is revealed as the framework and nerve of freedom's ascension to the good. It translates the obedience of the Son, but obedience is an act and only an act of the will.

The obedience of the Son is the highest exercise of his will. It expresses the supreme realization of the will, which is victory over itself, and it is like the archetype of all particular victories that the will wins over itself. We speak of victory over oneself and kenosis and its ectypes seem effectively confined to the interiority of the will, unwinding within its internal spaces. This would be a true apotheosis of homogeneity, of that movement where "all circulates" within us. But the metaphysics of victory over self is only seemingly immanentist. The hymn of Philippians speaks of "the form of a servant" taken on by the Son (2:7). Yet before being the symbol of humility and poverty, the servant designates the subject, the agent of a service rendered. . . And from a properly philosophical point of view, if the victory over oneself takes place within the will, within the sole desire of the subject, can it not have some external purposes? On the eidetic plane the mystery of the will that overcomes itself has no need of an external referent; the will accomplishes its highest actions in itself, through and for itself. Yet what would be the meaning of a self-transcending that remains confined to itself, without rebounding onto the outside, onto others? What is a will that circles back onto itself without experiencing contact with other wills? Some theologians think the world was created to allow the Son to become flesh, but could the Idea of this Coming into the world be conceived in abstraction from the Redemption? Could the victories over self that punctuate the process of desire have meaning and significance without being referred to other desiring beings, other wills? Spiritual writers never stop insisting on abandonment of "one's own will": after all, it alone burns in Hell! But for the abandonment not to be an abstract mortification, a mechanical and morbid self-laceration, it must have, as it were by ricochet, a referent. The victory over self must draw its reasons and power from itself, but can it not refer to a purpose other than its own perfection?

The Good's Self-Diffusion

Kenosis is like an abridged version of the entire movement of nature towards the good, but it does not constitute a unique expression of it. Another theologoumenon, the *tztimtzum*, provides a second, perhaps even more fecund formulation of the metaphysical history of novelty. The two great conceptual metaphors are analogs on the metaphysical plane, but phenomenologically different essences. Kenosis is victory

---

2. Bonaventure, *Hex.* 1, 12–13.

The Good

over self, a self-surmounting. It is like the archetype of all tearing away from self and, its divine pedigree notwithstanding, it also presents on an analogous plane the intuition of the good as victory over its contrary, its opposite, evil. Yet while designating an act of retreat, diminution and constriction of God, the *tztimtzum* lacks any violent, constraining aspect. The Creator does not beat a retreat, but simply forsakes its periphery, relinquishes its maximum expansion, withdraws into itself. Besides, it is the softness and non-violence of the evacuation of spaces that allows the metaphysical reinterpretation of this retreat of the Most High. The theologoumenon of Kabbalistic speculation literally signifies diminution, retreat, shrinking, but it will nevertheless serve an account of the good as diffusion, as self-communication. Finally, if kenosis appears as the very truth of the will, the paradigmatic movement of all true desiring, the properly voluntary aspect is less marked in the *tzimtzum*, that moving witness to the sweet benevolence of the Creator, his infinite mercy.

The action of ceding place, of withdrawing into oneself is realized under the form of a shrinking, and the endpoint of the self-shrinking is obviously becoming nothing. To restrict ourselves to a spatial metaphor, the Abandonment could be represented as a state of zero extension. In his infinite mercy, the Good evacuates from all locations, abandons every place in order to reach the point of ultimate constriction, a place of no extension. However, the spatial metaphor is insufficient, even misleading since non-extension is the reflection or synonym of non-being. But the Abandonment practiced by, or rather, that the Good *is*, is not non-*being*. The abandonment of all space that one fills should not be read in ontological terms. The ultimate constriction that constitutes the life of the Good is realized in a zero condition, a non-being, a non-essence. However, the non-being of this non-essence does not designate an ontological nothingness. The Abandonment concerns the self, but the truth of self-abandonment is not the non-self, but movement away, distance from self. The great metaphysico-moral themes of weakness, humility, and ultimately poverty find their paradoxical completion in the self-diffusion that mystical philosophy has always understood as the sense and essence of the good. Weakness, humility and poverty suggest constriction, diminution and loss, in short, negative realities, while diffusion is precisely the most appropriate phenomenological essence to designate the active generosity, the charity in its positive reality.

Bonum est diffusivum sui, we read in great medieval texts, but self-diffusion not only connotes a movement, an operation of goodness and thus something that flows, that results from it, but goodness itself. In strictly conceptual discourse, we ought not to say that the Good diffuses this or that, or even that it self-diffuses, but that it itself is self-diffusion and nothing else. The good is weak, humble, poor and these sublime attributes are only pictorial expressions of the truth of Goodness. It can never be said enough that the Good is not simply non-being and non-essence. It is not a null-point, but a flow starting from this null-point. From a phenomenological point of view, the flow very faithfully expresses the truth of the good as self-diffusion. It expresses in its pictorial way the ultimate paradox that the Good retains nothing for itself, that it is only this non-retention, but that it is not, for all that, a simple flow into loss. The Good never stops self-diffusing but it does not disappear: it is precisely in diffusing, in flowing out that it is always—if I can say it—more itself, always more the Good. On the other hand, the flow retains and expresses the essential eidetic theme of the gentleness that proves to be also of metaphysical pertinence. Flow must express the diffusiveness while demarcating it from naturality and absence of meaning. The good is *diffusivum sui*, but this self-diffusion is not of a native superabundance. It is not necessary to represent the Good as full of riches that it would like to display and offer. The Good is not some superabundant inflated energy that ends up spilling over. Even if it is of a completely maternal mercy, we must avoid at all cost conceiving it as submitted to the necessity and servitudes of childbirth. The gentleness of the flow has nothing instinctive about it. Well to the contrary, it expresses the proper degree of infinite Love's inscription in the world, of Love without measure. If the Good retains nothing for itself, it gives all and if it gives itself completely, it can assign a rational articulation, a reasonable configuration to its self-diffusion. Some people talk about the ecstatic nature of love. Love is certainly ecstasy but in the sense of a self-disappropriation, a self-exit, but being-self-exit does not amount to being-outside-of-self. Self-diffusion is not alienation.

The non-ecstatic and non-instinctive character of self-diffusion, in the same way as its measured, rational action, shows the miracle of the good. It is an incessant *creatio ex nihilo*, without a shadow of the contingent, the arbitrary, of play, but it has nothing to do with a necessity imposed on oneself and one's other. The premise and preliminary of self-diffusion is freedom. Freedom is located on the narrow path between the Charybdis of contingency and the Scylla of necessity, but for the path to be effectively taken, freedom must be transubstantiated into love. The nerve of the self-diffusion is the freedom of love, which is never indigence, but rather a remarkable indulgence towards the weak, the small, even a fervent sympathy for what is not yet. This sympathy of an unlimited efficaciousness is not a natural inclination, it must not be suspected of profit-sharing in the unfolding of its action. Beyond the important quantity of rescue and support operations, of gifts offered with tact and courtesy, of all those after-sale services that diversely extend the Donation, the diffusion of the good is accomplished in the two principal variations of creation and procreation. The free self-diffusion without reason of the creation of the world, of the call to existence of beings, has as its counterpart, or rather, reflection, the procreation of children, those unique realities. According to its metaphysical truth, procreation should also be free, exempt from "reasons." Neither God nor man has to be perfected through the call into existence of another, created or procreated in his image, another capable of contributing something to him or preventing him from being denied something. The call must be free. For it to avoid the accusation of a weak, unreasonable gratuity, for it not to risk being taken for the unfolding of a kind of "spontaneity taking the form of entertainment,"[3] it must have some good, worthy, valid reasons for the sake of delivering the action and willing from the two pitfalls of contingency and necessity. These reasons boil down to the unique reason that is Love.

Love is the unique reason for self-diffusion, but love in itself is not a reason. In fact, it represents precisely a permanent offensive against sufficient reason that is the principal enemy of the supreme practical mystery that is Love. Love is certainly not irrational, but it still has no "reason." The common popular representation of the genesis of love strengthens the thesis of its quasi-eidetic absence-of-reason. We do not know how to explain why we love another and when we are asked how "this began" we end up speaking of a "lightning strike," a leap proper for designating practical realities. The moralist says, "Love begins from love":[4] once again we find ourselves before a great aporia that leaves reflection in despair and before which the sole escape is to make recourse with Kant to "a fact of Reason." At the level of finite freedom, reason certainly has no other choice than to rely on this "fact." However, it can be revitalized by a theological analogy. Creation is a supreme manifestation of the goodness of God, but it cannot be understood starting with a God who can only be god. If Christianity poses and develops the thesis of the Creator God, it is to the degree that God is Trinity, an eternal relation of love among its persons. This eternal relation of love in which the happiness of God consists is the pledge and guarantee that "the Word. . .did not produce things through a natural necessity," but by virtue "of a procession of love."[5] The reciprocal love of divine persons "liberates" the Creator from every need, from any indigence pressing him to call into existence another to bear his image, who could respond to him. God created through his free love the creature that did not yet exist; his action is a diffusion of love without any trace of a requirement of reciprocity. The love presiding over human procreation should obey the same logic of gratuity. If it is in fact tainted by moments of profit-sharing, if it obeys some external reasons foreign to love, on an eidetic plane, it is free diffusion of self. In short, it is Good only by virtue of this metaphysical affinity with the Divine Love.

The generous self-diffusion of the Good has its transcendental counterpart in the a priori synthetic judgment where the copula rushes forward to predicate X (*Critique* B 13) and above all in the *noesis* of the phenomenology that aims for its intentional object. Consciousness is always consciousness of something, something that it knows as not itself. It is therefore condemned in its self-exercise as intention to exit from itself. Things are different in the universe of the generous diffusion that not only aims for its end but also creates or procreates it. Some read in intentionality the essential condition of the consciousness of being oriented towards another than self, but intentionality can also mask the original rapacity of the self on the lookout for seizing and assimilating others. The generous self-diffusion has direction, a referral to another,

---

3. Sankara, *Commentary on the Brahmasutra* II, 1, 33, in Hulin, *Sankara et la non-dualité*, 99.
4. La Bruyère, *Les Caractères*, "Du Cœur," 9, in *Oeuvres complètes*, 153.
5. Aquinas, *Summa Theologiae* 1, 22 a. 1 ad. 3.

in common with intentionality, but the meaning of this reference is radically different. The aim of transcendental consciousness refers to the dis-covering of an essence that it makes its object through seizing and mastering it. The self-diffusion of love is production of being, a call to existence. Production of being in the proper sense is creation; in an analogous but very real sense it is procreation. Creation is gift of being, but this gift is not only the conferment of something, the presentation of a gift, or the communication of a thing. It is also, and above all, the communication of self. In its purely ontological sense creation is gift of being, but in the strict sense its being is being only the Creator, that is, in giving being, God, who "is not jealous" (*Timaeus* 29d), nearly gives something of himself, or rather gives himself. And considered on the eidetic plane human procreation also amounts to a gift of its own being, the "empirical" (though truly spectacular and sublime) translation of which is constituted by the diverse ways that the parent gives his flesh—his time, his health, his goods—to the child.

The creative-procreative self-diffusion is gift as communication of being, but it is equally gift as communication of love. Ultimately only a content, the communication of being can take place only once and for good. A true and thus definitive and irrevocable gift, the gift of being, must not be repeated. Once it has been communicated, the one who has rejected it will appropriate and possess it. Things are different for the communication of love. Love is not an entity, a thing, a content. It cannot be offered, transmitted, as a simple gift. Love is not a given, it cannot be communicated except in its sui generis reality of giving. The metaphysical truth of love, namely of a reality that is affirmed without limits and without end, emanates from its eidetic condition. Love is conceived as faithful, but, precisely, fidelity cannot be thought and desired as temporary, as provisional. It is, as such, the anthropologico-moral expression of a reality that *is* and *only* is as it is given and renewed perpetually. The creation-procreation that is the Good's self-diffusion can only be continuous creation-procreation. The phenomenological essence, "creation" receives its metaphysical deepening by the intuition of the continuity allowing the justification of its truth as the communication of love. Instead of fixating on the leap, the lightning flash aspect, the immediate accomplishment, the vision of generous self-diffusion permits the reinterpretation of creation, even ex nihilo, as a consent—a consent, namely, to the being of another. The consent cannot be reduced to an isolated, one-time act, to a kind of unique proclamation. It is something solid and durable, it refers to the permanence in the renewal—to the permanence of its own agent as the permanence of its end. However, permanence and solidity do not yet exclude vulnerability. Love is vulnerable; it is capable of receiving hurts and being wounded. It is not sheltered from infidelity; it can even encounter and suffer refusal, betrayal. But despite its poverty, its fragility, notwithstanding the absence of a response, even encountering hateful responses, it does not stop giving consent, which translates its autarky, the security of the deep self of Love that, if you like, spreads out, an autarky so powerful that the call to existence of another than it and above all another that can turn against it, cannot erode or undermine it. The self-diffusion that is the Good is a communication of love. It requires a self, principle, and source of flow, of diffusion, as well as other selves to receive and register its current.

Bibliography

Adams, John. *Discourses on Davila: A Series of Papers on Political History*. 1805. Reprint, New York: Da Capo, 1973.
Aquinas, Thomas. *Summa Theologiae*, Editio Leonina, t. IV-XII. Rome: Cerf, 1888-1906.
Ardrey, Robert. *The Territorial Imperative*. New York: Atheneum, 1966.
Augustine. *Confessions*. Translated by Henry Chadwick. New York: Oxford University Press, 1991.
Austin, J. L. *Philosophical Papers*. Edited by J. O. Urmson and G. J. Warnock. 2nd ed. Oxford: Clarendon, 1970.
Baader, Franz von. *Sämtliche Werke*. 16 vols. 1851-60. Reprint, Aalen: Scientia, 1963.
Bachelard, Gaston. *La poétique de l'espace*. 4th ed. Paris: Presses Universitaires de France, 1964.
Bacon, Francis. *Works*. Edited by James Spedding, Robert Leslie Ellis, and Douglas Denon Heath. New York: 1869–72.
Balthasar, Hans Urs von. *De l'intégration*. Translated by H. Bourboulon et al. 2nd ed. Paris: Desclée de Brouwer, 1983.
Balzac, Honoré de. *Béatrix*. In *La comédie humaine* II. Paris: Pléiade, 1935.
Benjamin, Walter. "Über den Begriff der Geschichte." In *Gesammelte Schriften* I/2, edited by Rolf Tiedemann and Hermann Schweppenhäuser, 691–704. Frankfurt am Main: Suhrkamp, 1991.
Benveniste, Emile. *Problèmes de linguistique générale*. Paris: Gallimard, 1966.
Bergson, Henri. *Oeuvres*. Paris: Centurion, 1959.
Bernet, Rudolf. *La vie du sujet*. Paris: Presses Universitaires de France, 1994.
Bérulle, Pierre de. *Oeuvres complètes*. Paris: Cerf, 1995–96.
Bissière, Roger. *T'en fais pas la Marie: Écrits sur la peinture 1945–1964*. Cognac: Le temps qu'il fait, 1994.
Blake, William. *Songs of Innocence and Experience: Shewing the Two Contrary States of the Human Soul 1789–1794*. New York: Oxford University Press, 1977.
Bloch, Ernst. *A Philosophy of the Future*. Translated by John Cumming. New York: Herder and Herder, 1970.
Boileau-Despréaux, Nicolas. *Oeuvres complètes*. Vol. 4. Paris: Garnier, 1870.
Bollnow, Otto Friedrich. *Mensch und Raum*. 3rd ed. Stuttgart: Kohlhammer, 1963.
Bonaventure, *Collationes in Hexaemeron, Opera omnia*, t. 6. Quaracchi: College of St. Bonaventure, 1882.
Bourdaloue, Louis. *Sermon sur la religion chrétienne. Oeuvres*. Paris: 1716.
Bulgakov, Sergei. *Du Verbe incarné*. Translated by Constantin Andronikof. Paris: Aubier, 1943.

Bibliography

Camus, Albert. *L'homme revolte*. In *Oeuvres complètes* II. Paris: Pléiade, 1965.
Casey, Edward S. *The Fate of Place: A Philosophical History*. Berkeley: University of California Press, 1998.
Caussade, Jean Pierre de. *L'Abandon à la Providence divine*. Paris: Desclée de Brouwer, 1966.
———. *Bossuet, maître d'oraison*. Paris: Bloud and Gay, 1931.
Chardin, Teilhard de, Pierre. *Écrits du temps de la guerre: 1916–1919*. Paris: Seuil, 1976.
Charpier, Jacques, and Pierre Seghers. *L'art de la peinture*. Paris: Séghers, 1970.
Cherry, Conrad. *Nature and Religious Imagination: From Edwards to Bushnell*. Philadelphia: Fortress, 1980.
Chrysippus, *Oeuvre philosophique*. Paris: Les Belles Lettres, 2002.
Claesges, Ulrich. *Edmund Husserls Theorie der Raumkonstitution*. The Hague: Nijhoff, 1964.
Claudel, Paul. *Le poète et la Bible I*. Paris: Gallimard, 1998.
———. *Théâtre I*. Paris: Pléiade, 1956.
Dalissier, Michel. *Anfractuosité et unification: La philosophie de Nishida Kitaro*. Geneva: Droz, 2009.
Derrida, Jacques. *Papier Machine*. Paris: Galilée, 2001.
———. *Sauf le nom*. Paris: Galilée, 1993.
Descartes, René. *Lettre à Clerselier*. In vol. 4 of *Oeuvres*. Edited by Charles Adam and Paul Tannery. Paris: Vrin, 1996.
Diderot, Denis. *Oeuvres esthétiques*. Paris: Garnier, 1968.
Donne, John. *Complete Poetry and Selected Prose*. Edited by John Hayward. London: Nonesuch Press, 1962.
———. *Devotions upon Emergent Occasions*. Edited by John Sparrow. Cambridge: The University Press, 1923.
Edwards, Jonathan. *Freedom of the Will*. Edited by Paul Ramsey. Works 1. New Haven: Yale University Press, 1957.
Ellrodt, Robert. *Les poètes métaphysiques anglais*. Vol. 1. 2nd ed. Paris: Corti, 1973.
Fénelon, Francois de Salignac de la Mothe-. *Correspondance*. Vol. 18. Geneva: Droz, 2007.
Fichte, Johann Gottlieb. *Gesamtausgabe*. Edited by Reinhard Lauth and Hans Jacob. 41 vols. Stuttgart-Bad Cannstatt: Frommann, 1962–2012.
Fuchs, Eric. *Fichte im Gespraech*. Band 6.1. Stuttgart-Bad Cannstatt: Frommann-Holzboog, 1992.
Gent, Werner. *Die Philosophie des Raumes und der Zeit*. Vol. 2. 2nd ed. Hildesheim: Olms, 1962.
Gilson, Etienne. *Peinture et réalité*. Paris: Vrin, 1963.
———. *Le thomisme*. 5th ed. Paris: Vrin, 1948.
Girard, René. *La violence et le sacré*. Paris: Grasset, 1972.
Greene, Graham. *Le dixième homme*. Translated by R. Louit. Paris: 1985.
Hare, R. M. *The Language of Morals*. Oxford: Clarendon, 1952.
Hatem, Jad. *L'écharde du mal dans la chair de Dieu*. 2nd ed. Paris: Cariscript, 1988.
Hegel, Georg Wilhelm Friedrich. *Cours d'esthétique*. Vol. 1. Translated by Jean-Pierre Lefebvre and Veronika von Schenck. Paris: Aubier, 1995.
———. *Encyclopédie des sciences philosophiques*. Translated by Bernard Bourgeois. 3 vols. Paris: Vrin, 1979–2004.
———. *Leçons sur l'histoire de la philosophie*. Translated by P. Garniron. Paris: Vrin, 1991.
———. *Phénoménologie de l'esprit*. Translated by Jean Hyppolite. 2 vols. Paris: Aubier, 1951.

Bibliography

———. *Principes de la philosophie du droit*. Translated by Jean-Louis Vieillard-Baron. Paris: Flammarion, 1999.

———. *Science de la Logique 2: La doctrine de l'Essence*. Translated by P.-J. Labarrière and G. Jarczyk. Paris: Aubier, 1976.

Heidegger, Martin. *Être et temps*. Translated by Emmanuel Martineau. Paris: Authentica, 1985.

———. *Schelling*. Translated by Jean-François Courtine. Paris: Gallimard, 1977.

Hobbes, Thomas. *The English Works of Thomas Hobbes of Malmesbury*. Edited by William Molesworth. Vol. 3. 1839. Reprint, Aalen: 1962.

Horkheimer, Max. *Théorie critique: Essais*. Translated by Collège de Philosophie. Paris: Payot, 1978.

Housset, Emmanuel. *L'intelligence de la piété*. Paris: Cerf, 2003.

———. *La vocation de la personne*. Paris: Presses Universitaires de France, 2007.

Hugo, Victor. *Les misérables*. Paris: Pléiade, 1951.

———. "La pente de la rêverie." In *Oeuvres poétiques* I. Paris: Pléiade, 1964.

———. *La Vision de Dante*. In *La légende des siècles*. Paris: Pléiade, 1950.

Hulin, Michel. *Sankara et la non-dualité*. Paris: Bayard, 2001.

Husserl, Edmund. *Die Bernauer Manuskripte über das Zeitbewusstsein (1917/1918)*. Edited by Rudolf Bernet and Dieter Lohmar. Husserliana 33. Dordrecht: Kluwer Academic, 2001.

———. *Leçons pur une phénoménologie de la conscience intime du temps*. Translated by H. Dussort. Paris: Presses universitaires de France, 1964.

———. *Méditations cartésiennes*. Translated by Gabrielle Peiffer and Emmanuel Levinas. Paris: Vrin, 1953.

———. "Notes pour la constitution de l'espace." Translated by Dominique Pradelle. In *La terre ne se meut pas*. Paris: Minuit, 1989.

Jacobi, Johann Georg. *Fliegende Blätter* 2. Werke VI. 1825. Reprint, Darmstadt: Wissenschafltliche Buchgesellschaft, 1968.

James, William. *The Principles of Psychology*. Vol. 1. Works of William James. Cambridge, MA: Harvard University Press, 1981.

Jankélévitch, Vladimir. *Traité des vertus* 2. Paris: Flammarion, 1986.

Jung, Carl. *Mysterium Coniunctionis*. Vol. 2. Zürich: Rascher, 1956.

Jüngel, Eberhard. *Gott als Geheimnis der Welt*. Tübingen: Mohr, 1982.

Kafka, Franz. *Am Dom. Kritische Ausgabe*. Frankfurt am Main: Fischer, 1990.

Kant, Immanuel. *Gesammelte Schriften/Akademie Ausgabe*. Reprint. Berlin: de Gruyter, 1968.

———. *Lectures on Ethics*. Edited by Peter Heath and J. B. Schneewind. Translated by Peter Heath. New York: Cambridge University Press, 1997.

———. Œuvres *philosophiques*. Edited by Ferdinand Alquié. Paris: Gallimard, 1980–86.

———. *Theoretical Philosophy, 1755–1770*. Translated and edited by David Walford, in collaboration with Ralf Meerbote. New York: Cambridge University Press, 2003.

———. *Theoretical Philosophy after 1781*. Edited by Henry Allison and Peter Heath. Translated by Gary Hatfield et al. New York: Cambridge University Press, 2004.

Kasher, Menahem. *Encyclopedia of Biblical Interpretation I*. New York: American Biblical Encyclopedia Society 1953.

Kierkegaard, Søren. *Oeuvres complètes*. Translated by P. H. Tisseau and E. M. Jacquet-Tisseau. Paris: Orante, 1966–86.

———. *Tagebücher: 1834–1835*. Edited by T. Haecker. 4th ed. Munich: Kösel, 1953.

Bibliography

La Bruyère, Jean de. *Oeuvres complètes*. Paris: Pléiade, 1941.

Lacoste, Jean-Yves, ed. *Dictionnaire critique de la théologie*. 3rd ed. Paris: Presses Universitaires de France, 2007.

———. *Expérience et absolu*. Paris: Presses Universitaires de France, 1994.

Lamartine, Alphonse de. "Harmonie: Le premier regret." *Oeuvres*. Bruxelles: Hauman et Compagnie, 1840.

Leibniz, Gottfried Wilhelm. *Confessio Philosophi*. Edited by Yvon Belaval. Paris: Vrin, 1970.

———. *New Essays on Human Understanding*. Translated and edited by Peter Remnant and Jonathan Bennett. New York: Cambridge University Press, 1996.

———. *Remarques sur la lettre de M. Arnauld*. In *Discours de Métaphysique et Correspondance avec Arnauld*, edited by Georges Le Roy. Paris: Vrin, 1970.

Levinas, Emmanuel. *Autrement qu'être ou au-delà de l'essence*. The Hague: Nijhoff, 1978.

———. *Totalité et infinité*. 3rd ed. The Hague: Nijhoff, 1968.

Lévi-Strauss, Claude. *La pensée sauvage*. Paris: Plon, 1962.

Locke, John. *An Essay Concerning Human Understanding*. Edited by Peter H. Nidditch. Oxford: Clarendon, 1975.

Malebranche, Nicholas. *Traité de la nature et de la grâce*. In *Oeuvres* III, 30. Paris: J. Vrin, 1958.

Marcel, Gabriel. *Homo Viator*. Paris: Aubier, 1944.

———. *Journal métaphysique*. Paris: Aubier, 1927.

———. *La métaphysique de Royce*. 2nd ed. Paris: L'Harmattan, 2005.

———. *Position et approches concrètes du mystère ontologique*. Louvain: Nauwelaerts, 1949.

Marion, Jean-Luc. *Au lieu de soi: L'approche de Saint Augustin*. Paris: Presses Universitaires de France, 2008.

———. *Le phénomène érotique*. Paris: Gallimard, 2003.

Marx, Karl. *Manuscrits de 1857–1858 ("Grundrisse")*. Translated by Jean-Pierre Lefebvre. 2 vols. Paris: Éditions Sociales, 1980.

Merleau-Ponty, Maurice. *Phénoménologie de la perception*. Paris: Gallimard, 1945.

———. *Signes*. Paris: Gallimard, 1960.

———. *Le visible et l'invisible*. Paris: Gallimard, 1964.

Metz, Johannes Baptist. *Glaube in Geschichte und Gesellschaft*. 5th ed. Mainz: Grünewald, 1992.

Montaigne, Michel de. *Essais*. Paris: Pléiade, 2007.

Nicole, Pierre. *Instructions théologiques et morales sur le symbole I*. Paris: G. Desprez, 1725.

Nishida, Kitaro. *Le lieu*. Translated by R. Kobayashi. Paris: Osiris, 2002.

Novalis. *Das allgemeine Brouillon*. In *Schriften 3*, edited by Richard Samuel. Darmstadt: Wissenschatfliche Buchgesellschaft, 1965.

Oetinger, Christoph. *Oeffentliches Denkmal der Lehrtafel einer weil Wirttembergischen Prinzessin Antonia*. In *Sämmtliche Schriften* II, 1. Reutlingen: Steinkopf, 1861.

Pascal, Blaise. *Oeuvres complètes*. Edited by Louis Lafuma. Paris: Seuil, 1963.

Pascal, Georges. *La pensée d'Alain*. 3rd ed. Paris: Bordas, 1957.

Philonenko, Alexis. *Jean-Jacques Rousseau et la pensée du malheur* II. Paris: Vrin, 1984.

Piles, Roger de. *Cours de peinture par principes*. Paris: Gallimard, 1989.

Poulet, Georges. *Études sur le temps humain I*. Reprint. Paris: Plon, 2006.

Proclus. *The Fragments That Remain of the Lost Writings of Proclus*. Translated by Thomas Taylor. London: Black, Young, and Young, 1825.

Robinet, André. *Malebranche et Leibniz: Relations personnelles*. Paris: Vrin, 1955.

Bibliography

Ronsard, Pierre de. *Oeuvres complètes*. 2 vols. Paris: Pléiade, 1938.
Rousseau, Jean-Jacques. *Oeuvres complètes*. 5 vols. Paris: Pléiade, 1959–96.
Sainte-Beuve, Charles Augustin. Oeuvres. Paris: Pléiade, 1950.
Sartre, Jean-Paul. *L'être et le néant*. Paris: Gallimard, 1943.
———. *Saint Genêt, comédien et martyr*. Paris: Gallimard, 1952.
Scarron, Paul. *Don Japhet d'Arménie*. Paris: Marcel Didier, 1967.
Seneca. *On Benefits*. Translated by Aubrey Stewart. London: Bell and Sons, 1887.
———. *On the Firmness of the Wise Man*. Translated by Aubrey Stewart. London: Bell and Sons, 1912.
Scheler, Max. *Wesen und Formen der Sympathie*. Edited by Manfred S. Frins. Bern: Francke, 1973.
Schelling, Friedrich Wilhelm Joseph von. *Introduction à la philosophie de la mythologie*. Translated by Jean-François Marquet. Paris: Gallimard, 1998.
———. *Oeuvres métaphysiques (1805–21)*. Translated by Jean-François Courtine and Emmanuel Martineau. Paris: Gallimard, 1980.
———. *Philosophie de l'Art*. Translated by C. Sulzer. Grenoble: Millon, 1999.
———. *Philosophie de la révélation*. Translated by Jean-François Marquet and Jean-François Courtine. 4 vols. Paris: Presses Universitaires de France, 1989–94.
———. *Werke*. Stuttgart-Augsburg: J. G. Cotta, 1856–61.
Schiller, Friedrich. *Sämtliche Werke* II. Munich: Hanser, 1962.
Schmidt, Alfred. "Verdinglichung; Vergegenständlichung." In *Historisches Wörterbuch der Philosophie* XI. Darmstadt: Wissenschaftlich Buchgesellschaft, 2001.
Schneur Zalman of Lyadi. *Likutei Amarim-Tanya*. Brooklyn: Kehot, 1981.
Scholem, Gershom. *Les grands courants de la mystique juive*. Translated by M.-M. Davy. Paris: Payot, 1960.
———. *Zur Kabbala und ihrer Symbolik*. Zürich: Rhein-Verlag, 1965.
Schönborn, Christoph von. *L'icône du Christ: Fondements théologiques*. 3rd ed. Paris: Flammarion, 1986.
Schopenhauer, Arthur. *Le Monde comme volonté et comme représentation*. Translated by C. Sommer. Paris: Folio, 2009.
Scotus, *Ordinatio* II, d. 44. In *Opera omnia* XIV. Citta del Vaticano, 2001.
Shakespeare, William. *Merchant of Venice* I, edited by Candace Ward. New York: Dover, 1995.
Shepard, Thomas. *Works* II. 1853. Reprint, New York: AMS, 1967.
Spengler, Oswald. *Der Untergang des Abendlandes*. Munich: Beck, 1998.
Staël, Germaine de. *De l'Allemagne* I-II. Paris: Flammarion, 1993.
Steffens, Henrich. *Christliche Religionsphilosophie*. 2 vols. Breslau: J. Max, 1839.
Strack, Hermann L., and Paul Billerbeck. *Kommentar zum Neuen Testament aus Talmud und Midrasch*. Vol. 4. Munich: Beck, 1928.
Strauss, Erwin. *Vom Sinn der Sinne*. Berlin: Springer, 1956.
Stroll, Avrum. *Twentieth-Century Analytic Philosophy*. New York: Columbia University Press, 2000.
Tengelyi, Laszlo. *L'histoire d'une vie et sa région sauvage*. Grenoble: Millon, 2005.
Valéry, Paul. *Monsieur Teste*. Paris: NRF, 1931.
Vető, Miklos. *De Kant à Schelling I-II*. Grenoble: Millon, 1998–2000.
———. *Le mal: Essais et études*. Paris: L'Harmattan, 2000.
———. *La métaphysique religieuse de Simone Weil*. 3rd ed. Paris, 2014.
———. *La naissance de la volonté*. Paris: L'Harmattan, 2002.

Bibliography

———. *Nouvelles études sur l'idéalisme allemand*. Paris: L'Harmattan, 2009.

———. "Le rôle de l'homme dans les mythes de mort chez le Bantou de l'Afrique orientale et du Congo." *Zaire* 15 (1961) 75–93.

Waehlens, Alphonse de. *La philosophie de Martin Heidegger*. Louvain: Institut supérieur de philosophie, 1948.

Weigel, Valentin. *Vom Ort der Welt*. In *Sämtliche Schriften* I. Stuttgart: F. Frommann, 1962.

Weil, Simone. *Oeuvres complètes*. Paris: Gallimard, 1988.

Whitehead, Alfred North. *Modes of Thought*. New York: Macmillan, 1938.

Wolff, Christian. *Philosophia prima sive ontologia*. In *Gesammelte Werke* II. Hildesheim: Olms, 1965.

Wolleb, Johannes. *The Abridgement of Christian Divinity*. Translated by Alexander Ross. 3rd ed. London, 1660.

Young, Edward. *Conjectures on Original Composition*. 1759. Reprint, Leeds: Scholars Press, 1966.

www.ingramcontent.com/pod-product-compliance
Lightning Source LLC
Chambersburg PA
CBHW060454300426
44113CB00016B/2584